Industrial Locomotives of Nottinghamshire

INDUSTRIAL LOCOMOTIVES of NOTTINGHAMSHIRE

Compiled by I. R. Bendall

Series Editor - R. K. Hateley

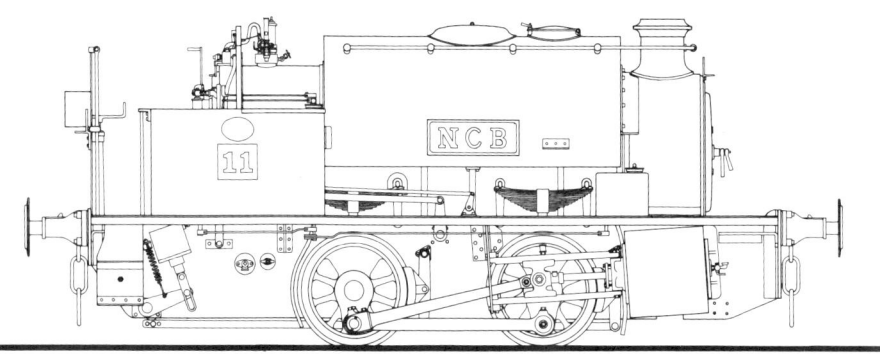

NCB 11 (HE 1493/1925), one of a fleet of low-height locomotives used at Pye Hill Colliery to work traffic under the GNR Pinxton branch. Drawing by Roger West.

INDUSTRIAL RAILWAY SOCIETY

Published by the INDUSTRIAL RAILWAY SOCIETY

at 47 Waverley Gardens, LONDON, NW10 7EE

© **INDUSTRIAL RAILWAY SOCIETY 1999**

ISBN 1 901556 11 5 (hardbound)

ISBN 0 901556 12 3 (softbound)

British Library Cataloguing-in-Publication Data
A catalogue record for this book is available from The British Library.

Printed by AB Printers Ltd, 33 Cannock St, Leicester, LE4 9HR

This book is copyright under the Berne Convention. Apart from any fair dealing for the purposes of private study, research, criticism, or review, as permitted under the Copyright Act, 1911, no portion may be reproduced by any process without the written permission of the publisher.

CONTENTS

Introduction	7
Maps	17
Industrial Locations	43
National Coal Board / British Coal	159
Locomotives of Contractors and Dealers	249
Preservation Sites	285
Non - Locomotive Systems	295
Indexes:	
Locomotives	331
Locomotive Names	369
Owners & Locations	373
Illustrations	385

INTRODUCTION

This book is a further volume in the series covering the industrial locomotives and railways of Great Britain and deals with the county of Nottinghamshire.

In this new volume the information previously published in the Pocket Book E has been greatly amplified. Many more sites are listed than were known about in the previous edition. It incorporates and describes not only the locomotives and their locations, but also includes non-locomotive, contractors' and preservation sites within the county. Appropriate maps have also been included.

In common with most of the Handbook series, this book describes a variety of industrial railways. Early industrial activity in the area was centred on the Erewash valley, particularly with the activities of the Butterley Company. The principal works was at Ripley in Derbyshire and this was served by a network of tramroads that extended to collieries in Nottinghamshire. Another early tramroad was the Mansfield and Pinxton Railway which served important mining operations in the Pinxton area. To the south a major iron works developed at Stanton, also in Derbyshire but with ramifications concerning Nottinghamshire. At Eastwood the coal mining operations of Barber, Walker resulted in a major industrial railway network in the area publicised by D.H. Lawrence. At Bennerley and Bestwood were sited the only ironworks included in Nottinghamshire. The Babbington and Wollaton districts contained some of the earliest pits in the county, initially served by tramroads to the Nottingham Canal and subsequently by another extensive network of industrial lines.

From the late Victorian era the workings for coal were extending to the east, to the area of Sherwood Forest east of Mansfield and to the north at Firbeck and Harworth. This extension concluded with the three collieries of Bevercotes, Calverton and Cotgrave, all primarily associated with the era of the National Coal Board and British Railways. Sherwood Forest became less rural with the development of numerous collieries and pit villages, but the remaining part of the county to the east and south has retained a more agricultural nature. However industries did develop in this area. Gypsum has been extracted from a belt from Newark to Loughborough and many quarries and mines, large and small, for this mineral are described herein. Narrow gauge railways have been used extensively for the extraction of gravel from the flood plain of the River Trent east of Nottingham.

The Trent Valley is well known as the location of many major coal-fired electricity generating stations and several of these fall within Nottinghamshire. All relied on rail transport although motive power has been predominantly supplied by main line railways and relatively few industrial locomotives are listed. The military have made use of areas within the county and rail operations are detailed at a number of these sites from Ranskill in the north to Ruddington in the south.

Thus we have a county where industrial railways have been dominated by colliery systems, but where a considerable variety could once be found.

The information is set out in five sections as follows:-

1. Locomotive worked systems at industrial premises.
2. Locations and locomotives operated by the National Coal Board / British Coal.
3. Known details of locomotives used on civil engineering contracts, including contracts involving the construction of many sections of public railway. Locomotives owned by dealers, hirers and manufacturers are also covered at the end of this section.
4. Preservation locations are included where the gauge exceeds 1ft 3in.
5. Known details of non-locomotive worked systems of sufficient length to be of interest.

Indexes are included for the ease of reference to locomotives and locations listed within the volume.

I am grateful for the help received over the years from many enthusiasts and correspondents who have answered questions or brought items to my attention and gladly given freely of their time and information. Much information has been gained from members of staff of the companies described in this book and of the locomotive builders. Thanks are also due to the members of the Industrial Railway Society, whose observations over the years form the basis of the Society's records. The journals and newsletters of like-minded societies such as the Industrial Locomotive Society and the Narrow Gauge Railway Society have also formed a reliable source of information. In particular the advertisement extracts published by the ILS have given many leads to follow. Likewise the Nottinghamshire Archives offices and various reference libraries have proved their worth and we thank their staff for their assistance.

My especial thanks to the following. All of them have given assistance over many years in different ways but some particular aspects are noted. A.C. Baker (WB and other locomotive builders data), A.J. Booth (illustrations), V.J. Bradley (proof reading and locomotive information), R. Carter (SLS Industrial records), M. Castledine (illustrations), M. Cook (locomotives of contractors), R.D. Darvill (coal industry and locomotive data), A.R. Etherington (system notes), C. Fisher (OK locomotives), S. Fountain (Eastwood and Watnall information), B. Gent (Lister locomotives), G.W. Green (company history and historical data), E. J. Hackett (recent movements), R. Hateley (production and maps), S. Hateley (indexing), F. Jones (illustrations), T.J. Lodge (Butterley Company data), B. Mettam (illustrations), A. Neale (illustrations), J.A. Peden (illustrations), K.P. Plant (RH and other locomotive builders data and company histories), P.D. Rowbotham (locomotive data and illustrations, ILS records), the late E.S. Tonks (locomotive records), R. Waywell (MR locomotives), R. Wear (AB and other locomotives, ILS records), R. West (cover drawing), J.K. Williams (historical data) and the late W.K. Williams (locomotive records).

Comments on and corrections to any information given in this book will be most welcome, as will all additional information. This should be sent to :

I R Bendall
Melton Mowbray
Leicestershire

EXPLANATORY NOTES

GAUGE

The gauge of the railway is given at the head of the list. If the gauge is uncertain, then this is stated. Metric measurements are used where the equipment was designed to these units.

GRID REFERENCE

An indexed six-figure grid reference is given in the text, where known, to indicate the location of salient features of the site.

NUMBER, NAME

A number or name formerly carried is shown in brackets ( ), if it is an unofficial name or number then inverted commas are used " "

TYPE

The Whyte system of wheel classification is used wherever possible, but when the driving wheels are not connected by outside rods but by chains or motors they are shown as 4w, 6w, 8w etc. For ex-BR diesel locomotives the usual development of the Continental system is used. The following abbreviations are employed:-

T	Side tank or similar. The tanks are invariably fastened to the frame.
tank	Tank locomotive where the type of tank fitted is not known.
CT	Crane Tank, a side tank locomotive equipped with load lifting apparatus.
ST	Saddle Tank, a round tank which covers the boiler top. This type includes the 'Box' and 'Ogee' versions popular amongst certain manufacturers during the nineteenth century.
WT	Well Tank, a tank located between the frames below the level of the boiler.
VB	Vertical boilered locomotive.
DM	Diesel locomotive; mechanical transmission.
DE	Diesel locomotive; electric transmission.
DH	Diesel locomotive; hydraulic transmission.
PM	Petrol or Paraffin locomotive; mechanical transmission.
R	Railcar, a vehicle primarily designed to carry passengers.
BE	Battery powered electric locomotive.
WE	Overhead wire powered electric locomotive.
F	Fireless steam locomotive.

CYLINDER POSITION

IC	Inside cylinders
OC	Outside cylinders
VC	Vertical cylinders
G	Geared transmission (used with IC, OC or VC)

FLAMEPROOF

Diesel or battery-electric locomotives that are flameproofed for use underground or in hazardous environments are shown with a suffix F to the type; e.g. 4wDMF.

ROAD/RAIL

Certain locomotives are capable of working on either rail or road (most are either Unilok or Unimog manufacture). These are indicated by R/R.

STEAM OUTLINE

Diesel or petrol locomotives with a steam locomotive appearance added are shown as S/O.

MAKERS

Abbreviations used to denote makers are listed on a later page.

MAKERS NUMBER AND DATE

The first column shows the works number, the second shows the date which appeared on the plate, or the date the loco was built if none appears on the plate.

It should be noted that the ex-works date given in the locomotive index may be in a later year than that recorded as the building date.

Rebuilding details are denoted by the abbreviation 'reb', usually recording significant alterations to the locomotive. It is difficult to draw a firm dividing line between rebuilding and overhaul and a few of the instances of 'reb' in this volume are better regarded as overhauls.

SOURCE OF LOCOMOTIVE

'New' indicates that a locomotive was delivered from the makers to a location. A bracketed letter indicates that a locomotive was transferred to this location or subject to temporary transfer away. Full details, including the date of arrival, where known, appear in the footnotes below.

DISPOSAL OF LOCOMOTIVE

A locomotive transferred to another location is shown by a bracketed number and footnote, the date of departure being given in the footnote if it is known. In other cases the following abbreviations are used:-

- OOU   Loco noted to be permanently out of use on the date shown.
- Dere   Loco noted to be derelict and no longer capable of being used.
- Dsm   Loco both OOU and incomplete on the date shown.
- Scr   Loco broken up for scrap on the date shown.
- s/s   Loco sold or scrapped; disposal unknown.

Many sales of locomotives have been effected through dealers and contractors and details are given where known. If the dealers name is followed by a location, e.g. Abelson, Sheldon, it is understood that the loco went to Sheldon depot before resale. If no location is given, the loco either went direct to it's new owner or else definite information on this point is lacking. If a direct transfer is known to have been effected by a dealer, the word 'per' is used.

GENERAL ABBREVIATIONS

- c   circa; i.e. about the time of the date quoted
- f or form formerly
- orig   originally
- reb   rebuilt
- RTC   rail traffic ceased

FOOTNOTE ABBREVIATIONS

In addition to the abbreviations listed below, the abbreviations used to denote the various locomotive builders are also used in footnotes where appropriate.

AMWD	- Air Ministry Works Department
APCM	- Associated Portland Cement Manufacturers Ltd
BEA	- British Electricity Authority
CEA	- Central Electricity Authority
CEGB	- Central Electricity Generating Board
contr	- Contractor
EMGB	- East Midlands Gas Board
HIW	- Holwell Iron Works, Asfordby Hill, Melton Mowbray, Leics
ICI	- Imperial Chemical Industries Ltd
MFP	- Ministry of Fuel & Power
MoD	- Ministry of Defence
MoDAD	- Ministry of Defence, Army Department
MoM	- Ministry of Munitions
MoS	- Ministry of Supply
MoW	- Ministry of Works
NCB	- National Coal Board
NCBOE	- National Coal Board, Opencast Executive
ROF	- Royal Ordnance Factory
USATC	- United States Army Transportation Corps
WD	- War Department
WDLR	- War Department Light Railways

MAIN LINE RAILWAY COMPANIES

The generally recognised abbreviations for main line railway companies have been used throughout, including the following :

BR	- British Rail
BRB	- British Railways Board
GCR	- Great Central Railway
GER	- Great Eastern Railway
GNR	- Great Northern Railway
GWR	- Great Western Railway
LMSR	- London Midland & Scottish Railway
LNER	- London & North Eastern Railway
LNWR	- London & North Western Railway
LSWR	- London & South Western Railway
M&GNJR	- Midland & Great Northern Joint Railway

DOUBTFUL INFORMATION

Information which is known to be of a doubtful nature is denoted as such by the wording chosen, or else printed in brackets with a question mark, e.g. (1910?).

ABBREVIATIONS USED FOR LOCOMOTIVE BUILDERS

AB	Andrew Barclay, Sons & Co Ltd, Caledonia Works, Kilmarnock, Strathclyde.
Adams	A.R.Adams & Son, Pill Bank Iron Works, Newport, Mon
AE	Avonside Engine Co Ltd, Avonside Engine Works, Fishponds, Bristol.
AEI	Associated Electrical Industries Ltd
Albert	
Atlas	Atlas Loco & Mfg Co Ltd, Cleveland, Ohio, USA

B	Barclays & Co, Riverbank Works, Kilmarnock, Ayrs.
Bg	E.E. Baguley Ltd, Burton-on-Trent.
BGB	Becorit (Mining) Ltd, Mansfield Woodhouse/Ilkeston.
BH	Black, Hawthorn & Co Ltd, Gateshead, Co. Durham.
Bilsthorpe	Stanton & Staveley Ltd, Bilsthorpe Brickworks, Notts
BLW	Baldwin Locomotive Works, Philadelphia, Pennsylvania, USA.
BP	Beyer, Peacock & Co Ltd, Gorton, Manchester.
BT	Brush Electrical Machines Ltd, Traction Division, Falcon Works, Loughborough.
Butterley	Butterley Co, Ripley, Derbys
Cafferata	Cafferata & Co, Newark, Notts.
CE	NEI Mining Equipment Ltd, Clayton Equipment, Hatton near Derby.
CF	Chapman & Furneaux Ltd, Gateshead, Co Durham (successors to BH)
Chaplin	Alexander Chaplin & Co Ltd, Cranstonhill Works, Glasgow.
Craven	J Craven, Walesby, Notts
Crossley	Crossley Bros Ltd (Manchester), Elstow Works, Bedford.
D&B	Du Croo & Brauns, Weesp, Netherlands.
Dar	Darlington Works (NER/LNER/BR).
DC	Drewry Car Co Ltd, London (suppliers only - see under RSH and Bg).
DC/Bg	Built by Bg for DC - works numbers identical
Derby	Derby Works (MR/LMSR/BR).
DK	Dick, Kerr & Co Ltd, Preston, Lancs.
EE	English Electric Co Ltd, Preston, Lancs.
EEV	English Electric Co Ltd, Vulcan Works, Newton-le-Willows, Lancs.
Elh	Eastleigh Works (LSWR/SR/BR).
FE	Falcon Engine & Car Works Ltd, Loughborough, Leics.
FH	F.C. Hibberd & Co Ltd, Park Royal, London.
FJ	Fletcher, Jennings & Co, Lowca Engine Works, Whitehaven.
FW	Fox, Walker & Co, Atlas Engine Works, Bristol.
Galloways	Galloways Ltd, Ardwick, Manchester
GB	Greenwood & Batley Ltd, Albion Ironworks, Leeds.
GECT	GEC Traction Ltd, Vulcan Works, Newton-le-Willows, Lancs.
Ghd	Gateshead Works (NER/LNER/BR).
Gibb	Easton Gibb & Son Ltd, contrs
GMT	Gyro Mining Transport Ltd, Rotherham, S.Yorks.
H	James & Fredk Howard Ltd, Britannia Ironworks, Bedford.
HB	Hudswell Badger Ltd, Hunslet, Leeds.
HC	Hudswell, Clarke & Co Ltd, Railway Foundry, Leeds.
HCR	Hudswell, Clarke & Rodgers, Railway Foundry, Leeds.
HE	Hunslet Engine Co Ltd, Hunslet, Leeds.
HG	Hopkins, Gilkes & Co, Teesside Engine Works, Middlesbrough, Yorks (NR) (successors to Gilkes, Wilson & Co)
HIW	Holwell Iron Works, Melton Mowbray, Leics
H(L)	Hawthorns & Co, Leith Engine Works, Leith, Edinburgh.
HL	R & W. Hawthorn, Leslie & Co Ltd, Forth Banks Works, Newcastle-upon-Tyne.
Hohen	Hohenzollern A.g., Dusseldorf, Germany.
Honeywill	Honeywill Bros, London (agents only)

Hor	Horwich Works (LYR / LMSR / BR)
House	B. House, Devizes, Wilts.
JF	John Fowler & Co (Leeds) Ltd, Hunslet, Leeds.
Johnson	H W Johnson & Co, Rainford, Lancs.
	(successors to E Borrows & Sons)
K	Kitson & Co Ltd, Airedale Foundry, Leeds.
KC	Kent Construction & Engineering Co Ltd, Ashford, Kent.
Kitching	W. & A. Kitching, Hope Town Foundry, Darlington.
KE	Kilmarnock Engineering Co Ltd, Kilmarnock, Ayrshire
KS	Kerr, Stuart & Co Ltd, California Works, Stoke-on-Trent, Staffs.
L	R.A. Lister & Co Ltd, Dursley, Glos.
LE	Lowca Engine Co Ltd, Lowca, Whitehaven.
Mkm	Markham & Co Ltd, Chesterfield, Derbys.
MR	Motor Rail Ltd, Simplex Works, Bedford, (formerly Motor Rail & Tramcar Co Ltd).
MV	Metropolitan Vickers Electrical Co Ltd, Trafford Park, Manchester.
MW	Manning, Wardle & Co Ltd, Boyne Engine Works, Hunslet, Leeds.
NB	North British Locomotive Co Ltd, Glasgow.
NBQ	North British Locomotive Co Ltd, Queen's Park Works, Glasgow.
Neasden	Metropolitan Railway, Neasden Works, London
NW	Nasmyth, Wilson & Co Ltd, Bridgewater Foundry, Patricroft, Manchester.
OK	Orenstein & Koppel AG, Berlin, Germany.
P	Peckett & Sons Ltd, Atlas Locomotive Works, Bristol.
P&K	Pearson & Knowles Coal & Iron Co Ltd, Dallam Forge, Warrington, Lancs.
R&R	Ransomes & Rapier Ltd, Riverside Works, Ipswich, Suffolk.
Reliance	[*possibly* Reliance Trucks Ltd, Vale Works, Heckmondwike, Yorks (WR) - this firm is not a known locomotive builder but produced road tractors easily modified for rail use. Alternatively the locomotive may have been built by FH with a radiator branded 'Reliance']
RH	Ruston & Hornsby Ltd, Lincoln.
RP	Ruston, Proctor & Co Ltd, Lincoln
RR	Rolls-Royce Ltd, Sentinel Works, Shrewsbury (successors to S).
RS	Robert Stephenson & Co Ltd, Forth St, Newcastle, and Darlington.
RSH	Robert Stephenson & Hawthorns Ltd.
RSHN	Robert Stephenson & Hawthorns Ltd, Forth Banks Works, Newcastle-upon-Tyne.
RWH	R & W Hawthorn & Co, Forth Banks Works, Newcastle-upon-Tyne.
S	Sentinel (Shrewsbury) Ltd, Battlefield, Shrewsbury
	(previously Sentinel Waggon Works Ltd).
Sdn	Swindon Works, Wilts (GWR/BR).
SMH	Simplex Mechanical Handling Ltd, Bedford.
SS	Sharp, Stewart & Co Ltd, Atlas Works, Manchester and Glasgow.
TH	Thomas Hill (Rotherham) Ltd, Vanguard Works, Kilnhurst, S. Yorks.
Thakeham	Thakeham Tiles Ltd, Storrington, Sussex.
TW	Thornewill & Warham, Burton-on-Trent, Staffs

VF	Vulcan Foundry Ltd, Newton-le-Willows, Lancs.
WB	W.G. Bagnall Ltd, Castle Engine Works, Stafford.
WCI	Wigan Coal & Iron Co Ltd, Kirklees, Lancs.
Wilson	A.J.Wilson, Carlton, Nottingham.
Wkm	D. Wickham & Co Ltd, Ware, Herts.
WR	Wingrove & Rogers Ltd, Kirkby, Liverpool.
YE	Yorkshire Engine Co Ltd, Meadow Hall Works, Sheffield.

LOCATION CODES

In the Industrial section each location entry is numbered in numerical sequence from 1. This number is prefixed by a letter indicating the key map on which the site appears. Similarly the locations in the other sections are each numbered from 1 and are prefixed by first the map letter and then also by N, C, D, P or H (for NCB, Contractor, Dealer, Preserved or 'Hand, Horse or Haulage' respectively. For example, EN25 denotes map E, and location 25 in the NCB section. The letter X as a prefix indicates an entry which, for whatever reason, is not indicated on any key map.

GENERAL REFERENCES

"The Canals of the East Midland", C.Hadfield, David & Charles, 1966
"Catalogue of Plans of Abandoned Mines, Vol III". HMSO, 1929
"Directory of Quarries, Clayworks, Sand & Gravel Pits", Quarry Managers Journal, vars edns
"Great Central Railway" (3 volumes), G Dow, LPC/Ian Allan, 1959/1962/1965
"List of Coal Mines in Notts 1896", Peak District Mines Historical Sociey, 1998
"History of Mining in the East Midlands, 1550-1947", A.R.Griffin, Frank Cass, 1971
"From Mills to Mines, Mansfield's Industrial History", D. Morley, Old Mansfield Society, 1996
"The Midland Railway, A Chronolgy", J. Gough, RCHS, 1989
"The Nottinghamshire Coalfield - A Century of Progress 1881-1981" A.R. Griffin, NUM, 1981
"The Railways of Newark on Trent", M.A. Vanns, Oakwood Press, 1999
"Newark, Aspects of the Past", T. Warner, Notts C.C., 1994
"Newark, The Magic of Malt", P. Stephens, Notts C.C., 1993
"Regional History of the Railways of Great Britain, Vol.9", R. Leleux, David & Charles, 1976
"Stone Blocks and Iron Rails", B. Baxter, David & Charles, 1966

Transactions : Institution of Mining Engineers
              National Association of Colliery Managers

Nottinghamshire Archives - collection of Trade Directories, Ordnance Survey Maps and certain Mining Records

MAPS

KEY MAPS

- A   Nottinghamshire
- B   North Nottinghamshire
- C   Worksop
- D   Retford
- E   Bevercotes
- F   East Nottinghamshire
- G   Edwinstowe
- H   Mansfield
- J   Teversal
- K   Pinxton
- L   Eastwood
- M   Awsworth & Bennerley
- N   Leen Valley
- P   Newark
- Q   Babbington
- R   Gedling
- S   Central Nottingham
- T   Colwick
- U   South-East Nottinghamshire
- V   South Nottinghamshire
- W   Gotham

Tramways in the Erewash Valley

DETAIL MAPS

- Pinxton
- Pye Hill
- Mapperley Brickworks

LEGEND FOR MAPS :

⎯⎯ Public railway (standard gauge)

⎯⎯ Industrial railway (standard gauge)

⎯⎯ Narrow gauge railway/tramway

⎯⎯ Canal or waterway

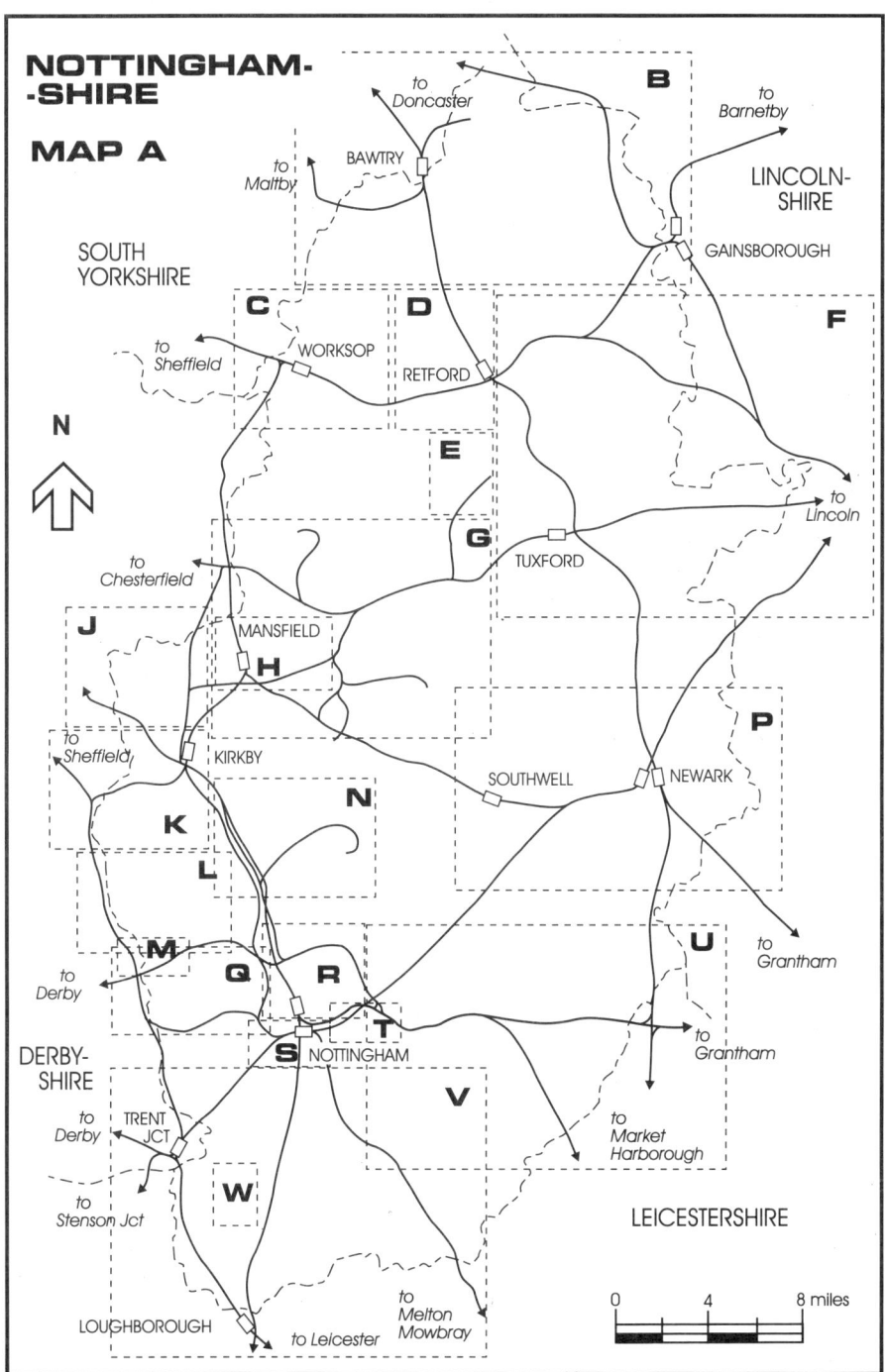

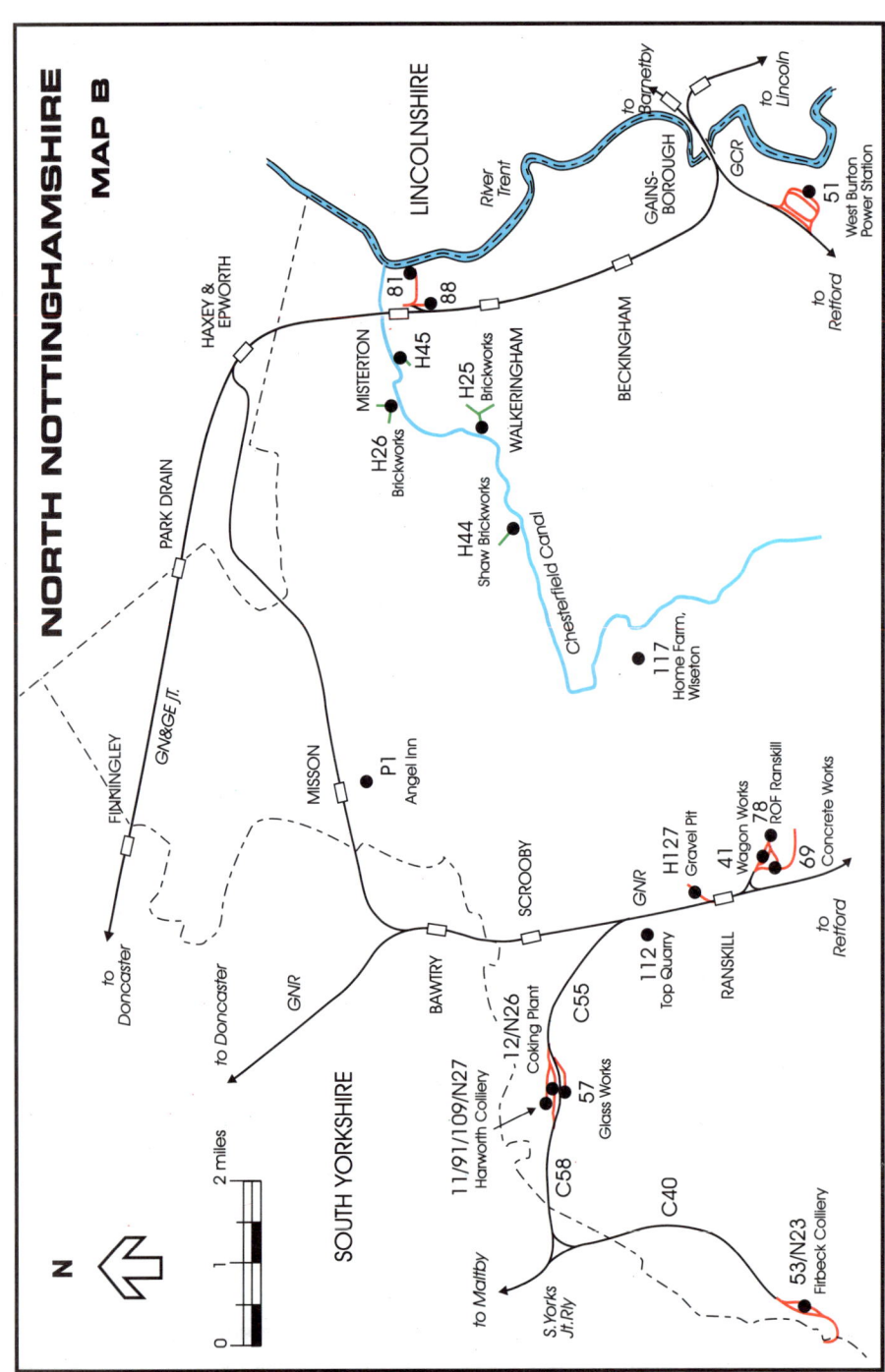

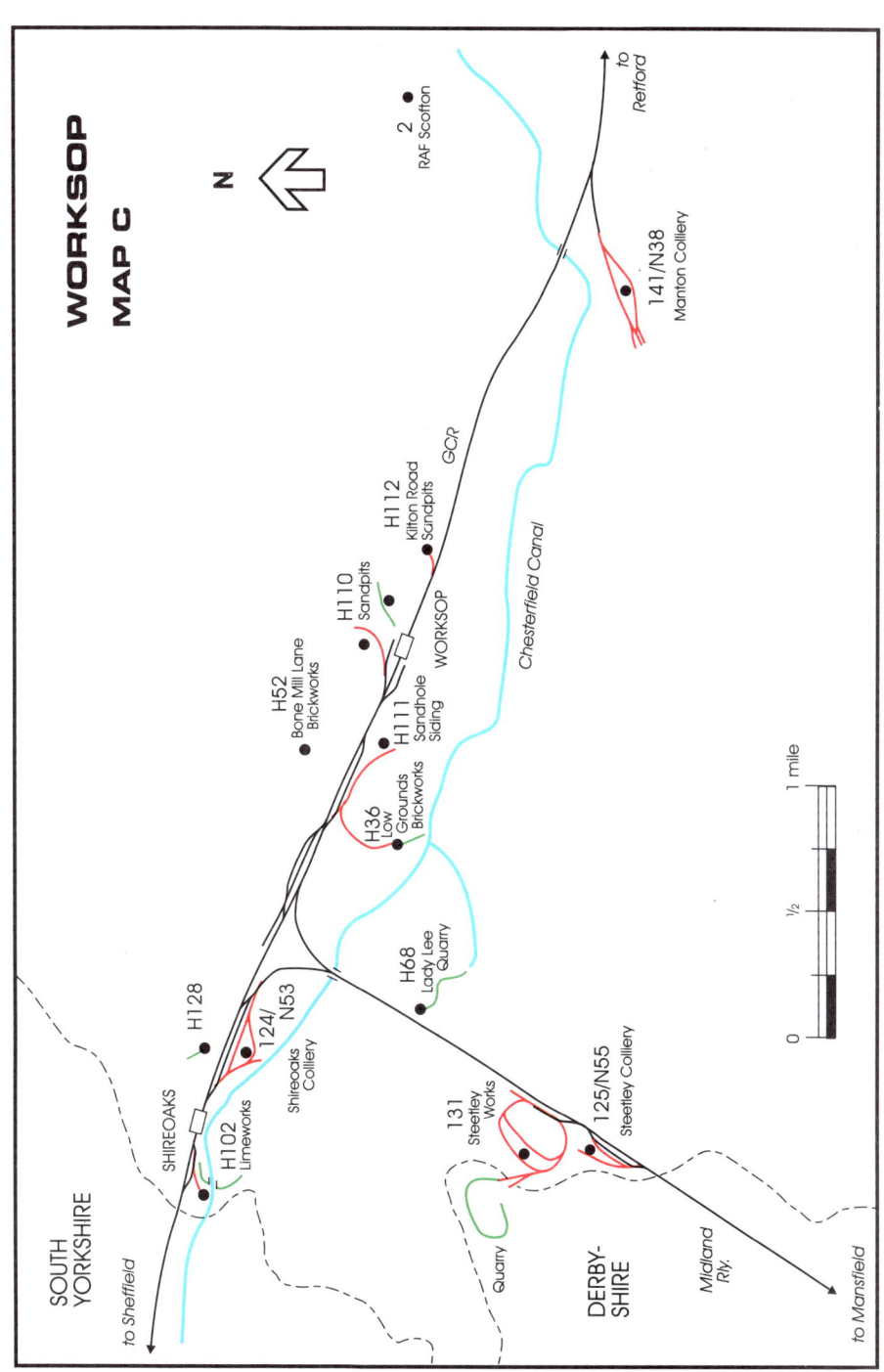

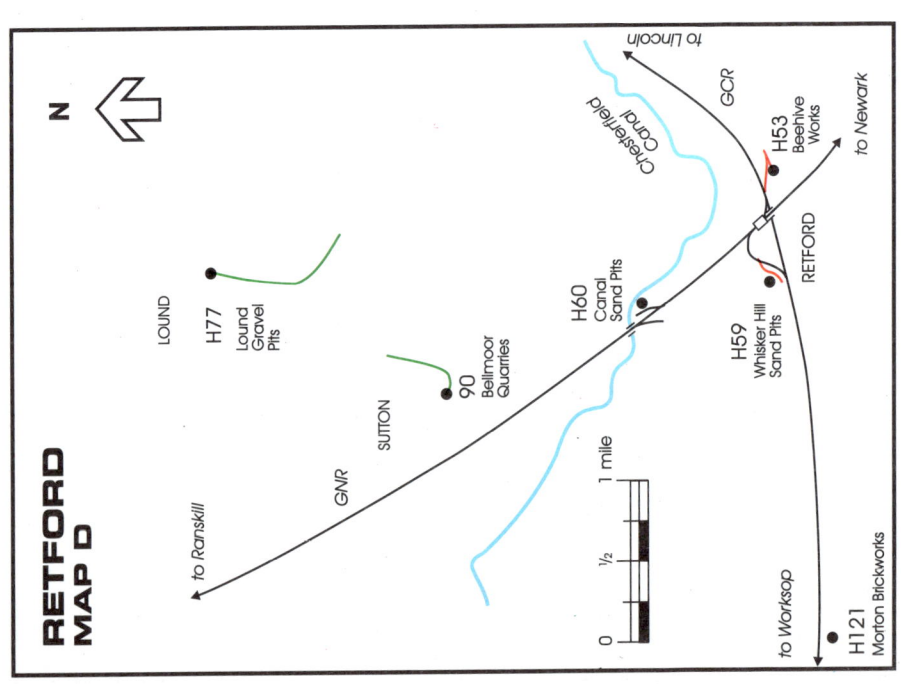

BEVERCOTES
MAP E

N ↑

A1(T)
ELKESLEY
D4 Nottingham Sleeper Co
A614(T)
N11
N10
Bevercotes Coll.
N36
N11 Lound Hall
TUXFORD
WALESBY
P4 John Craven
to Ollerton
to Ollerton

0 — 1 — 2 miles

RETFORD
MAP D

N ↑

to Ranskill
LOUND
H77 Lound Gravel Pits
SUTTON
90 Bellmoor Quarries
GNR
Chesterfield Canal
to Lincoln
H60 Canal Sand Pits
H53 Beehive Works
GCR
to Newark
H59 Whisker Hill Sand Pits
RETFORD
to Worksop
H121 Morton Brickworks

0 — ½ — 1 mile

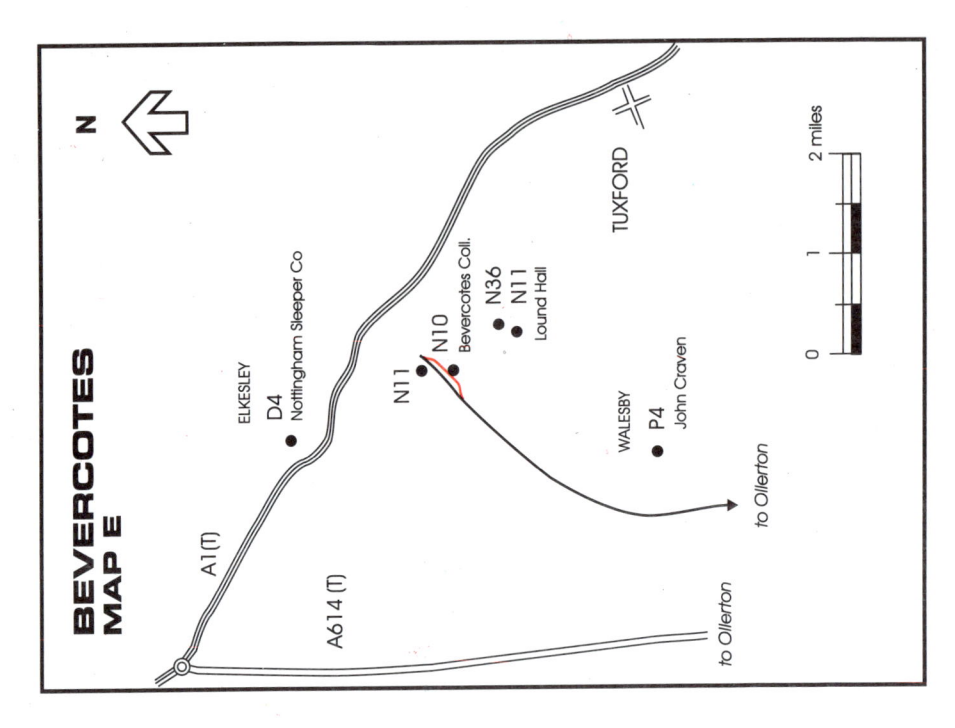

Nottinghamshire Handbook. Page 22

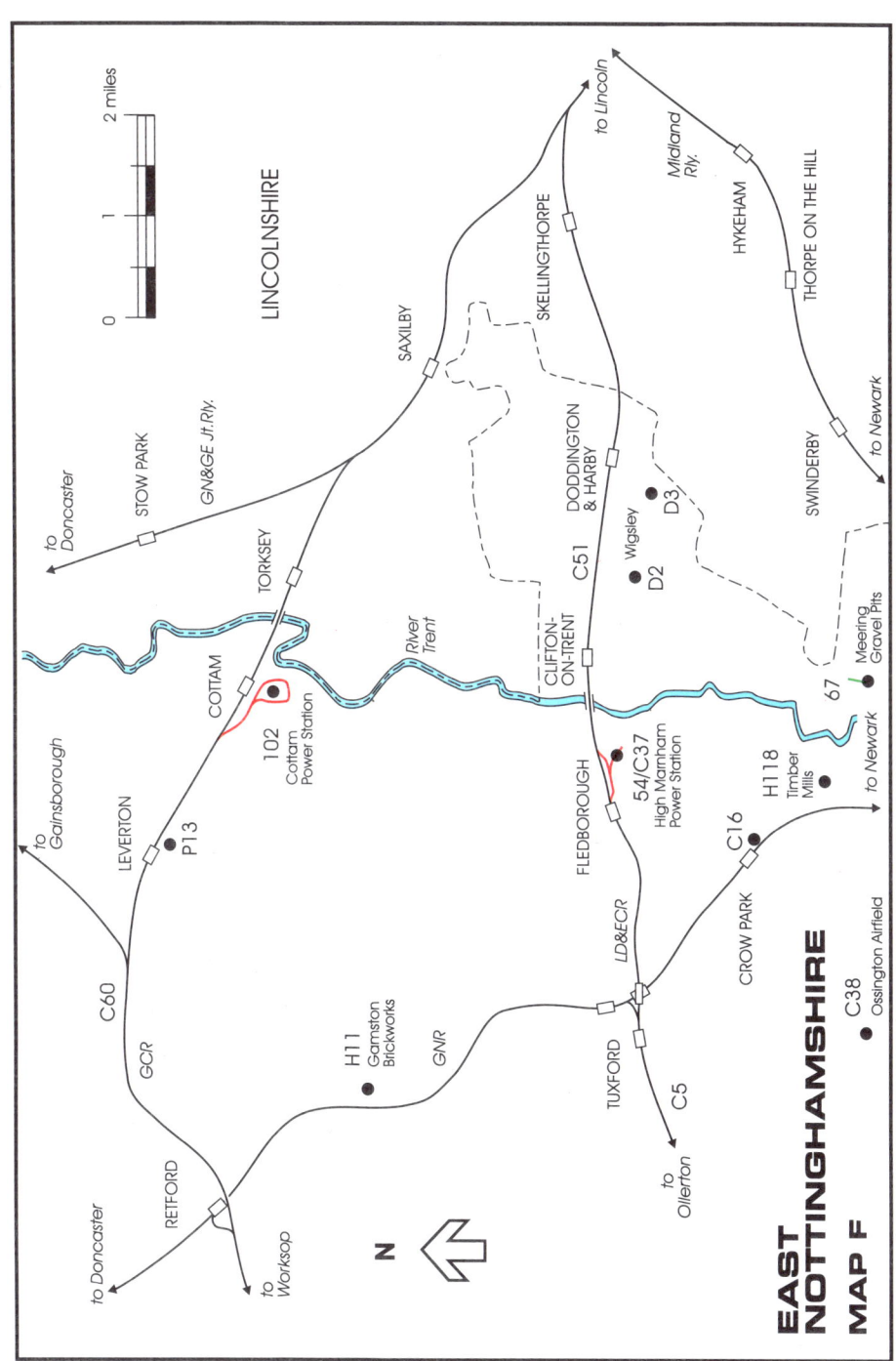

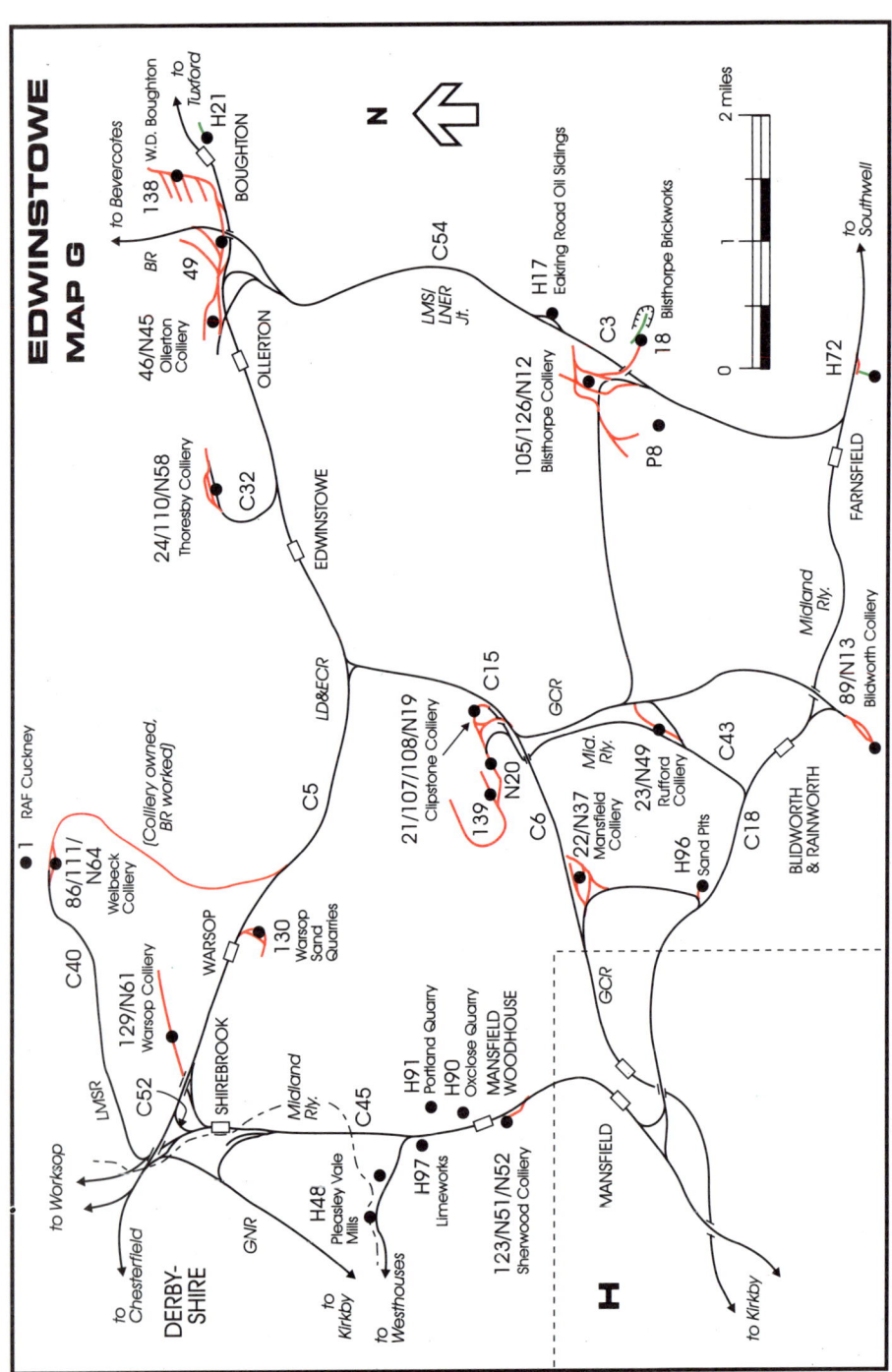

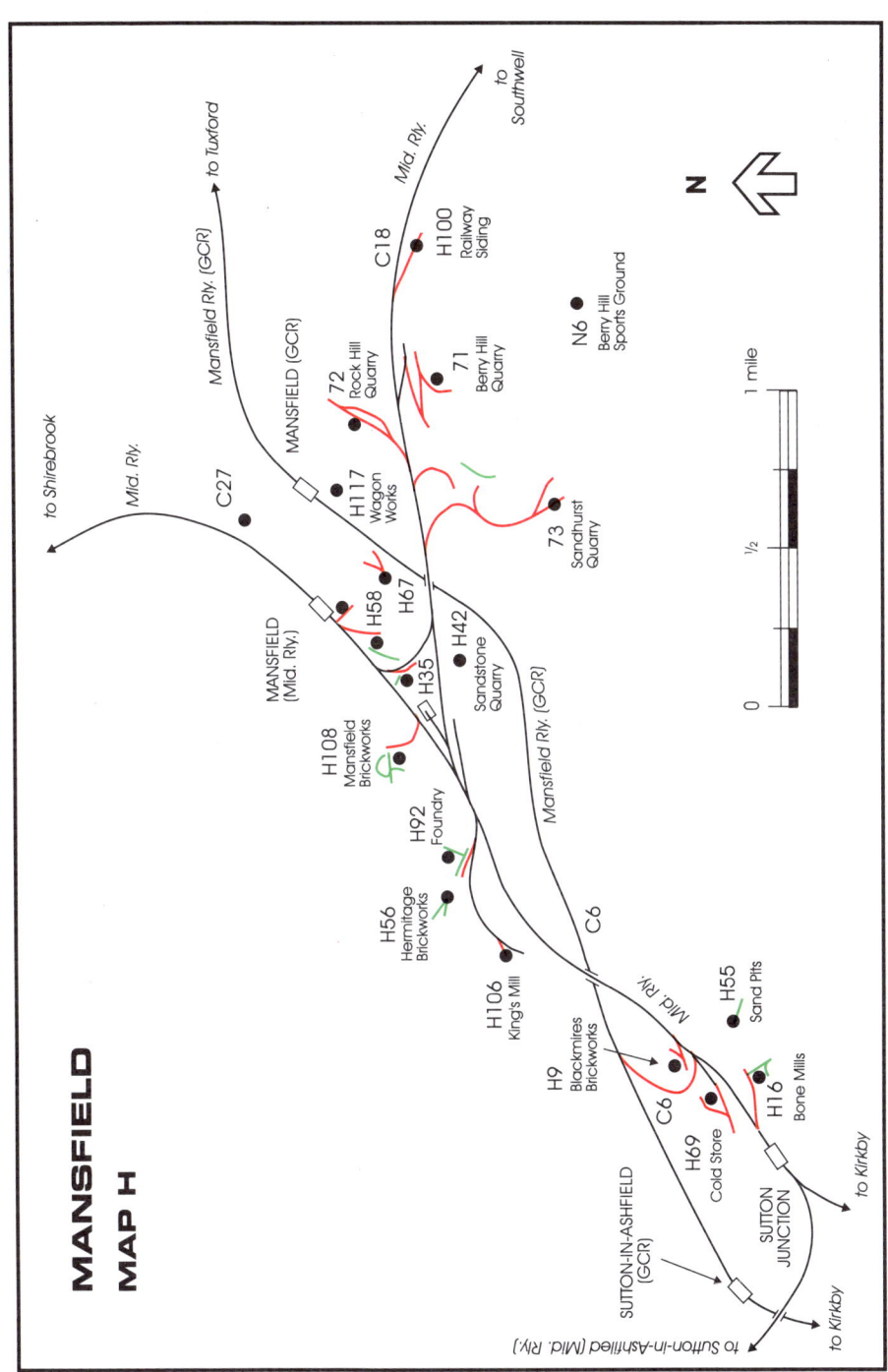

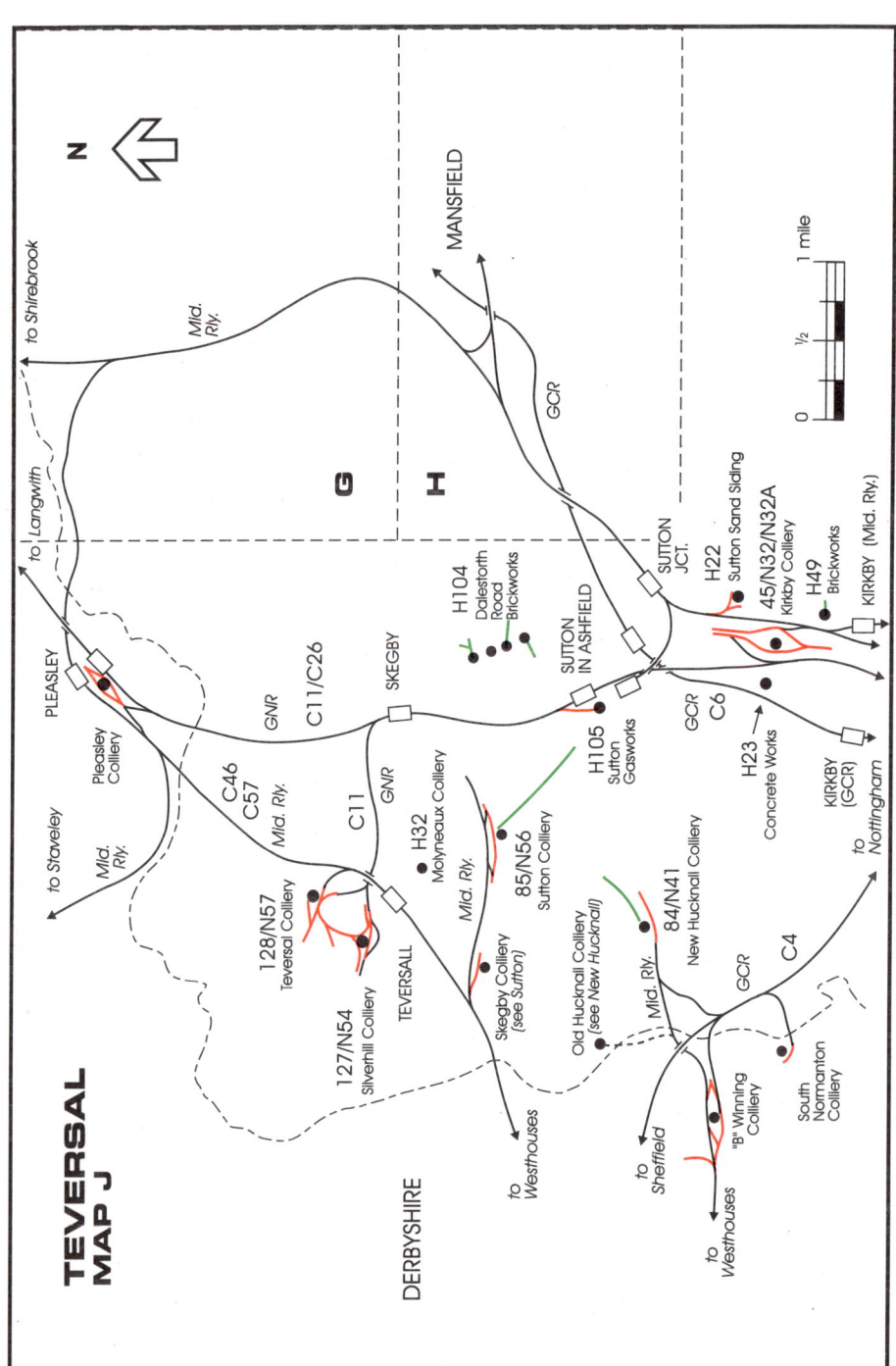

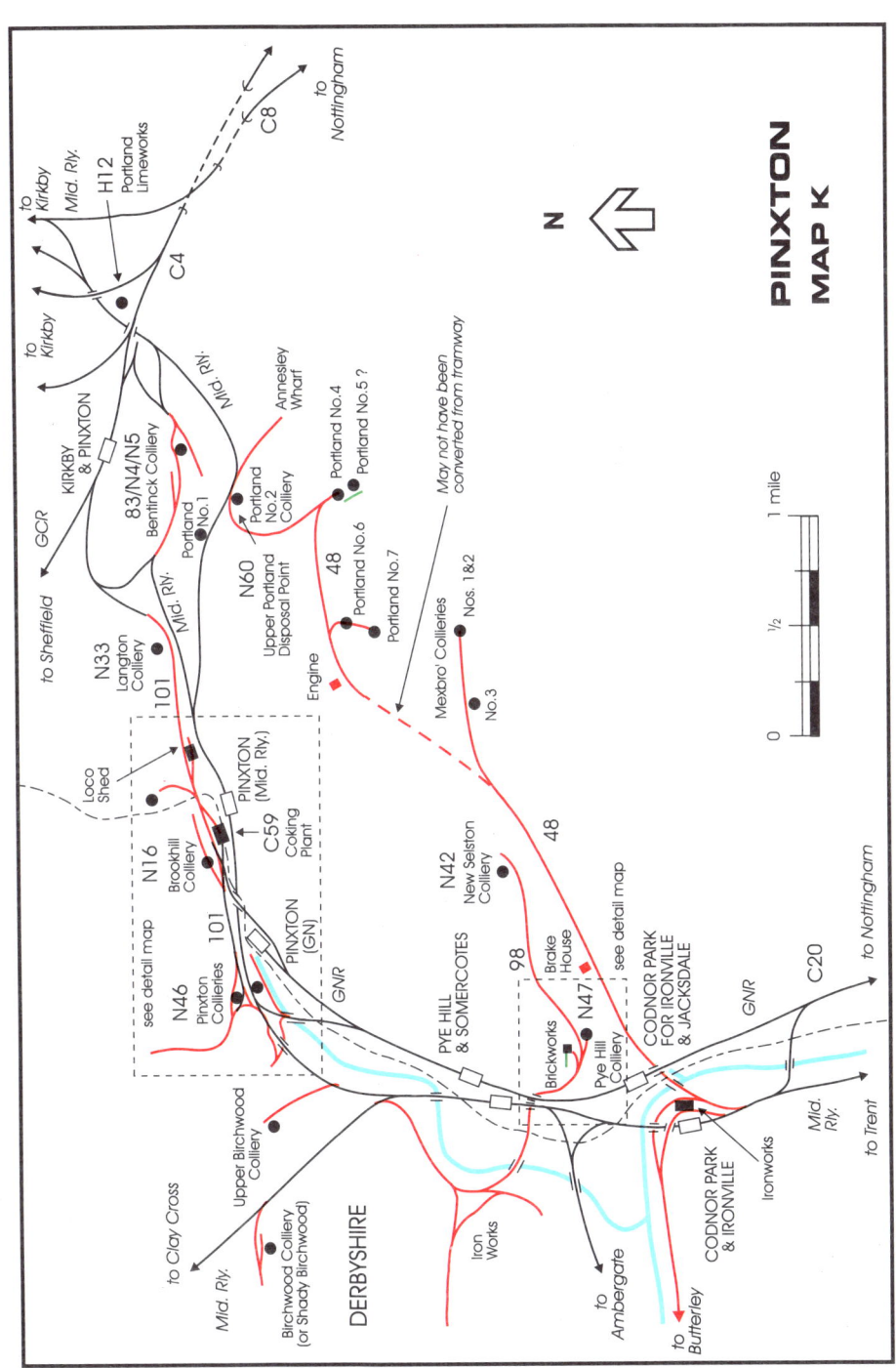

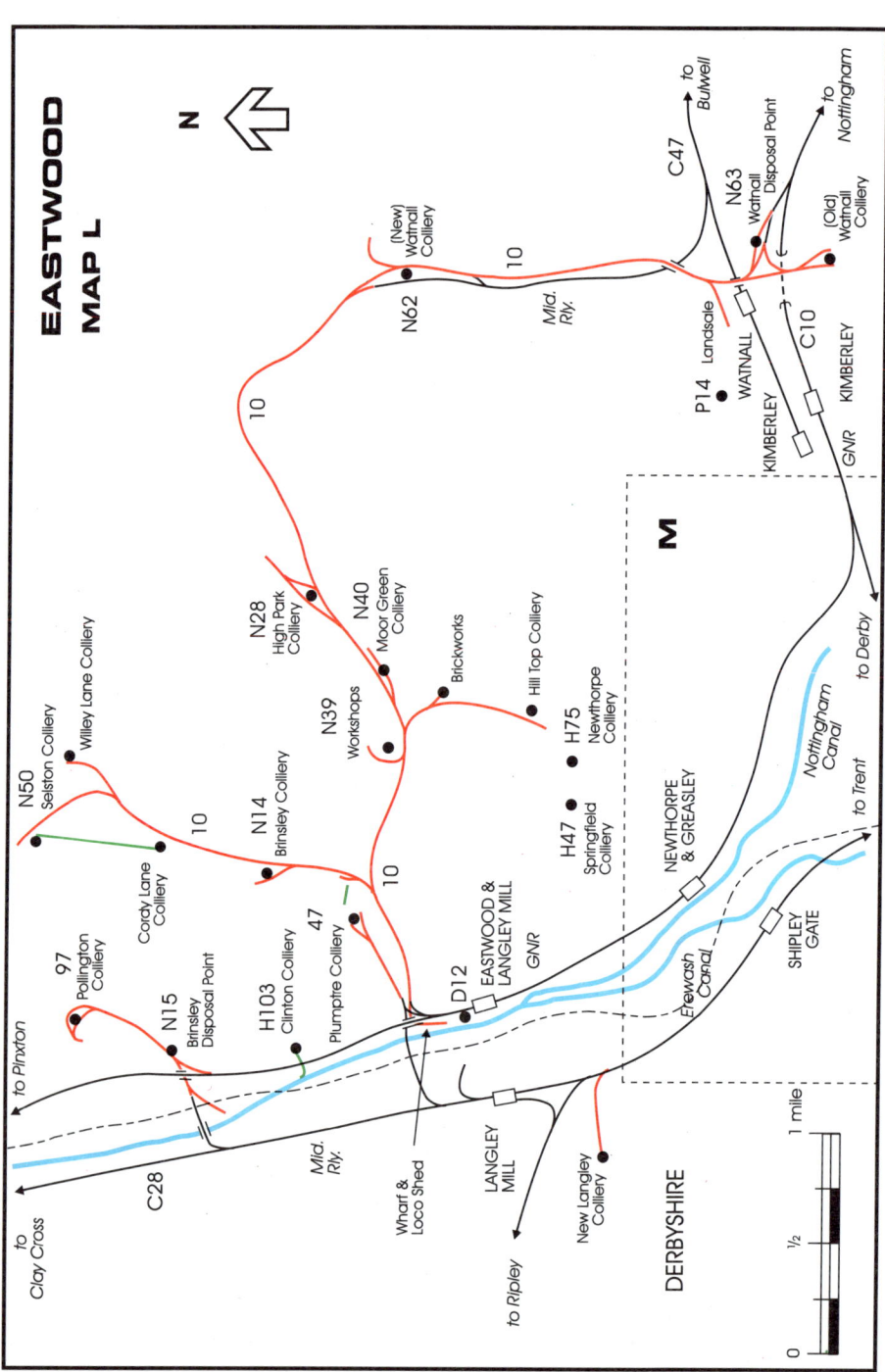

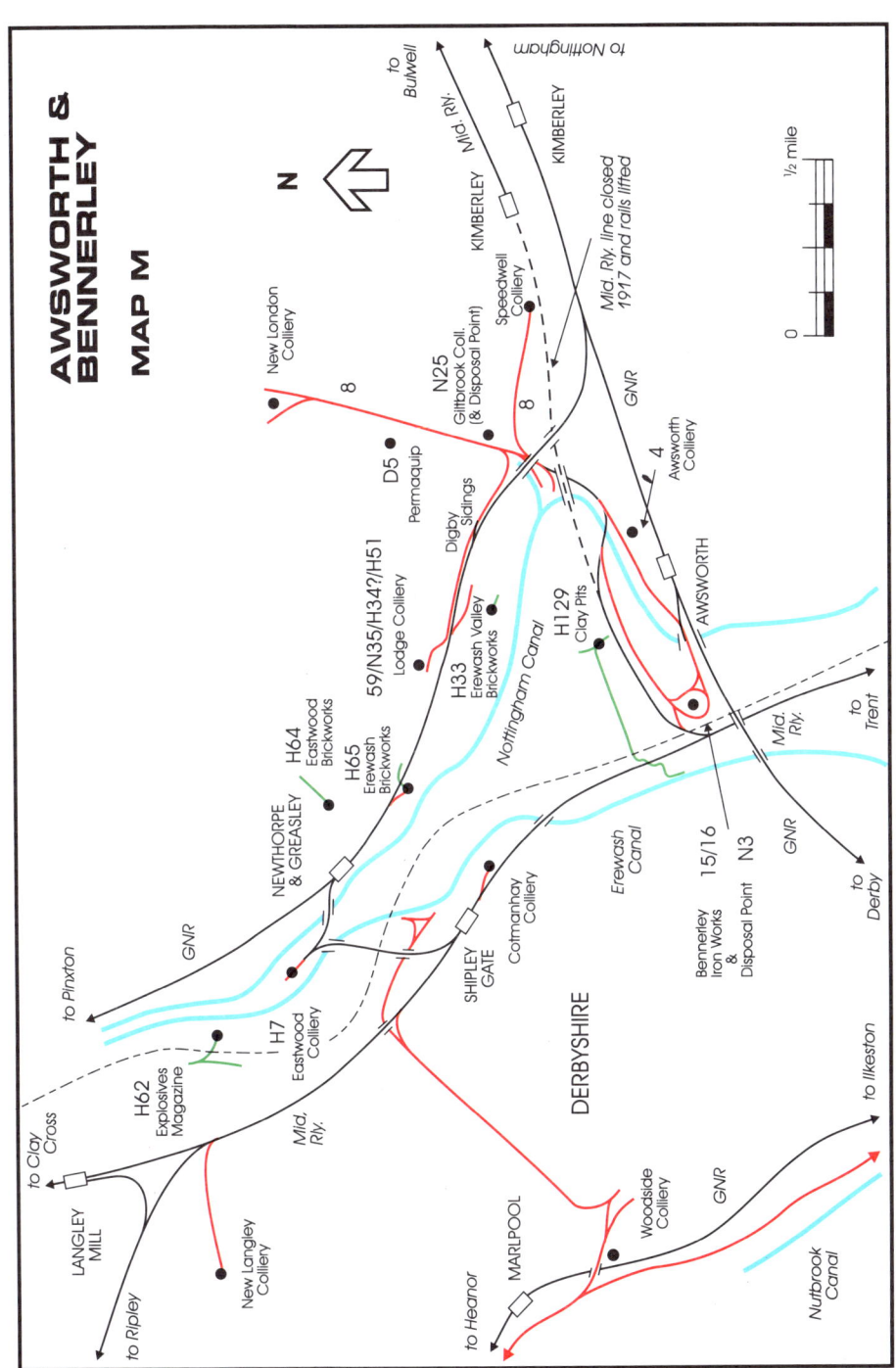

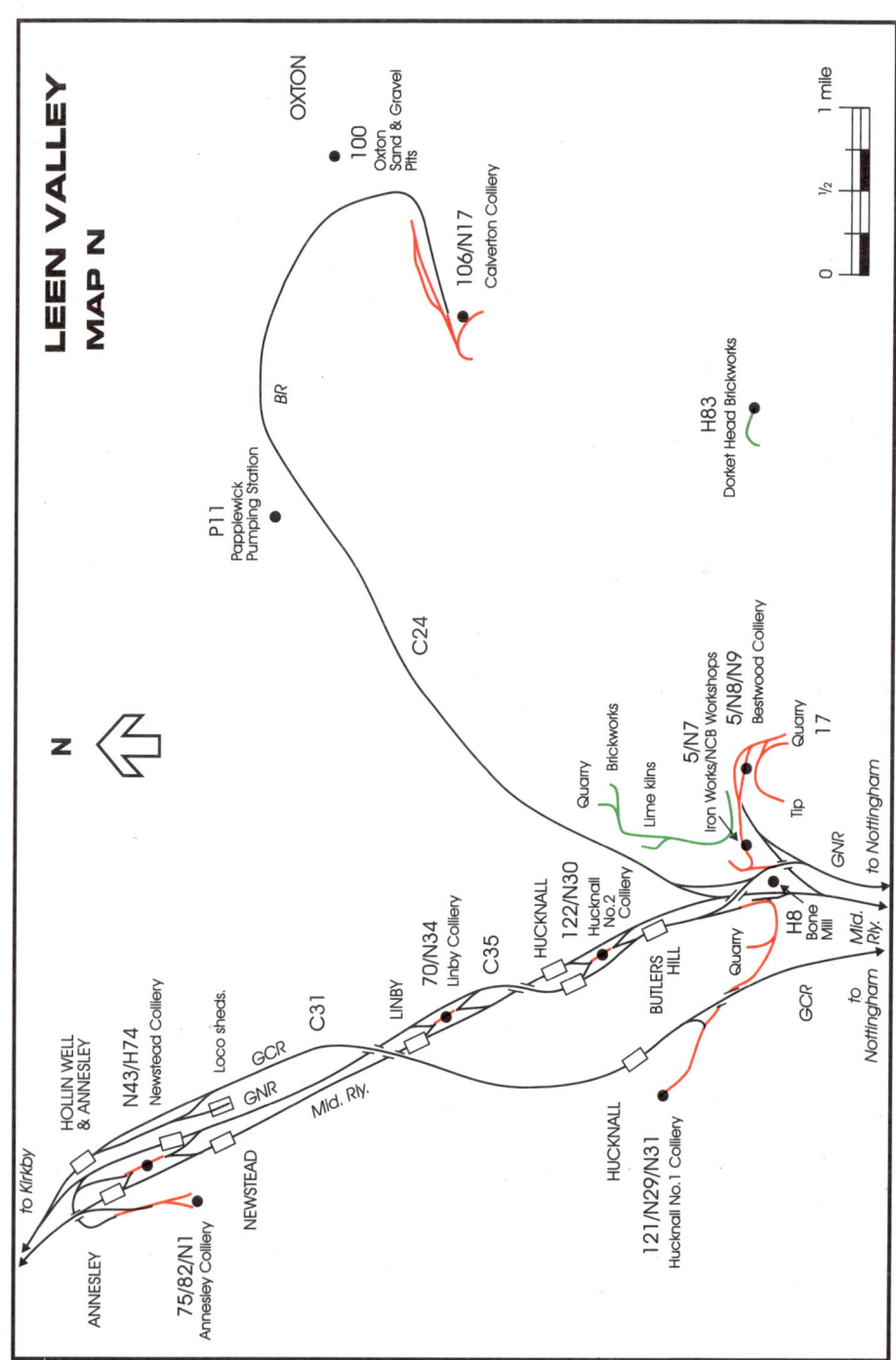

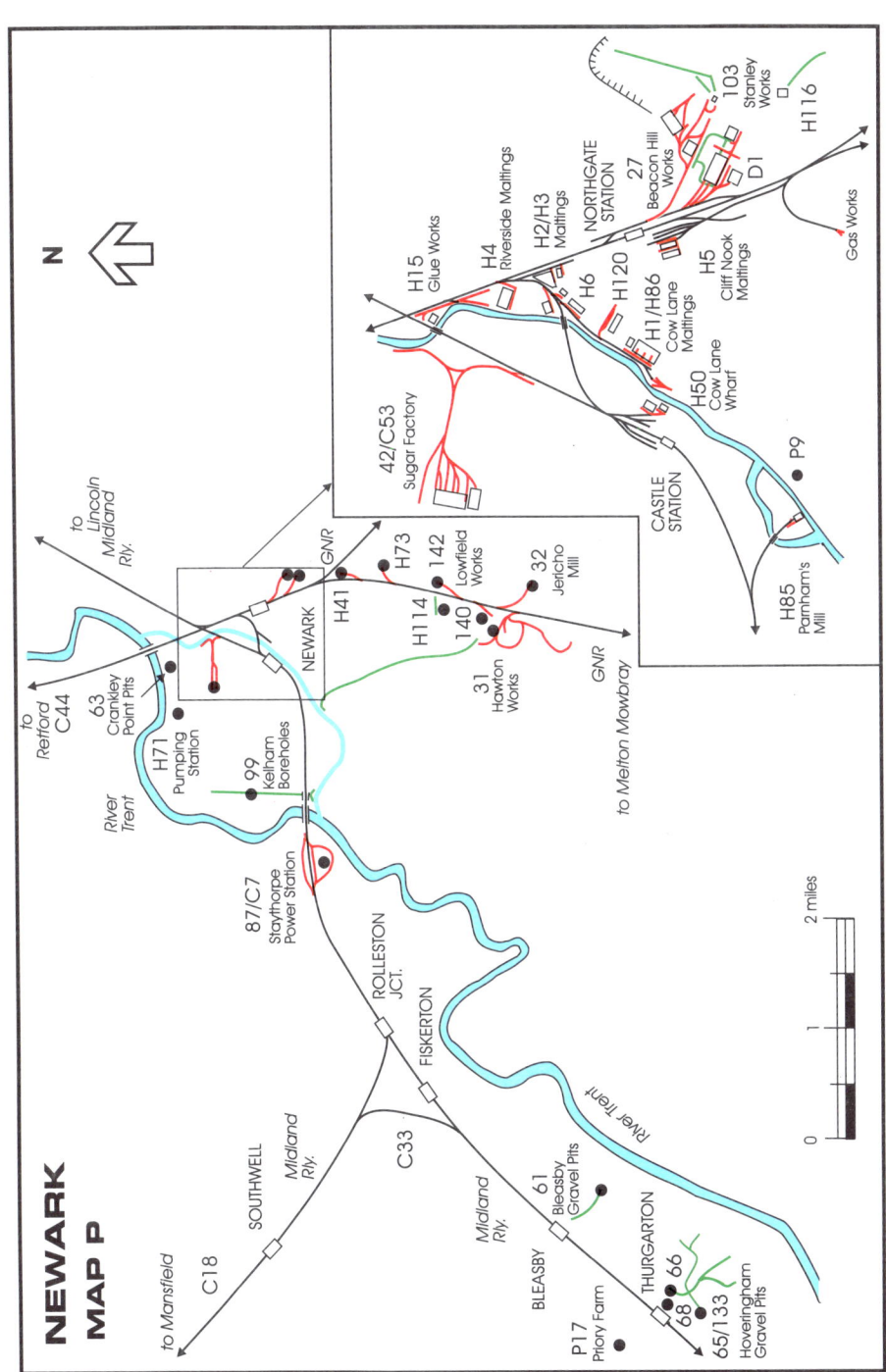

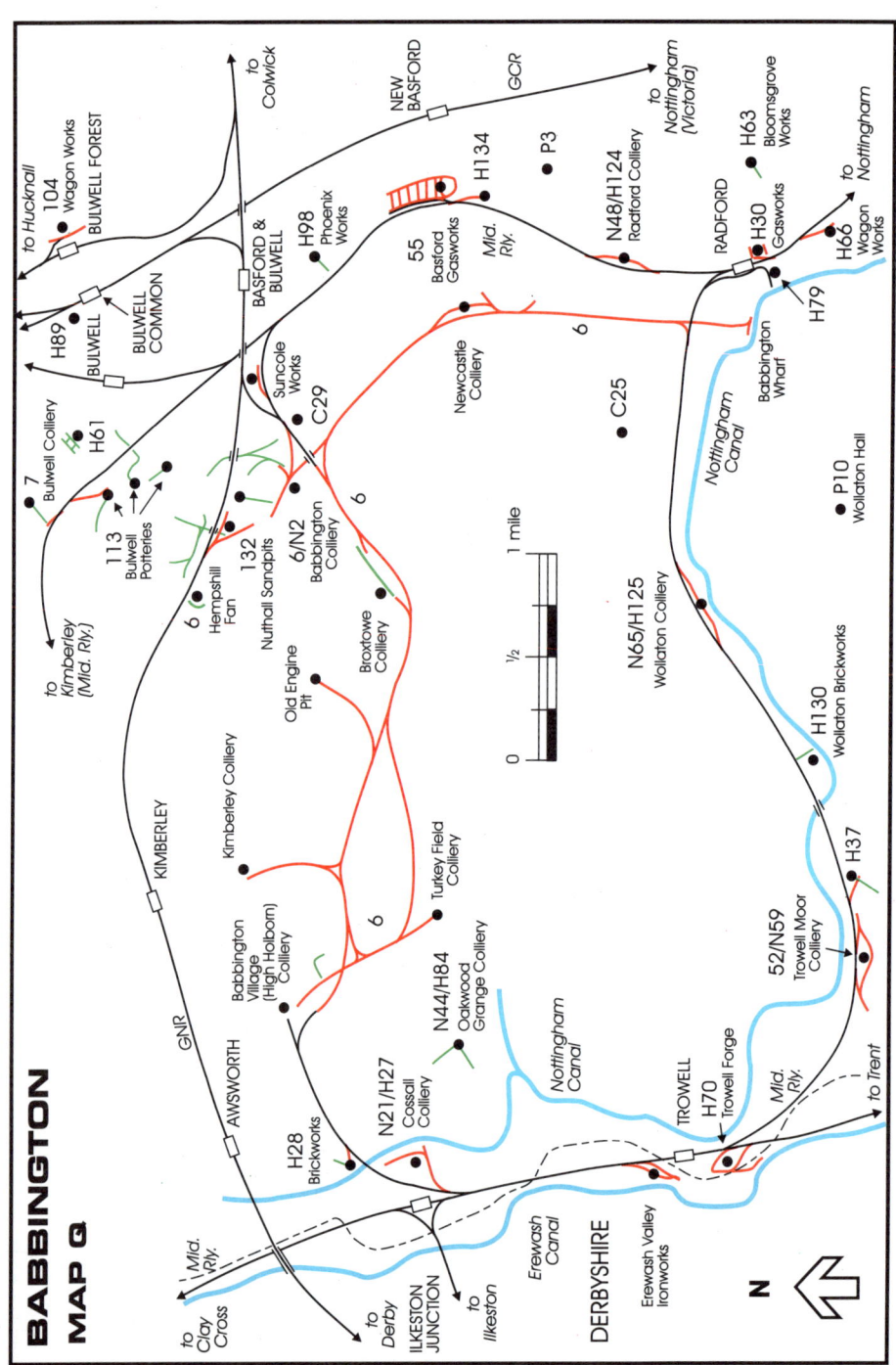

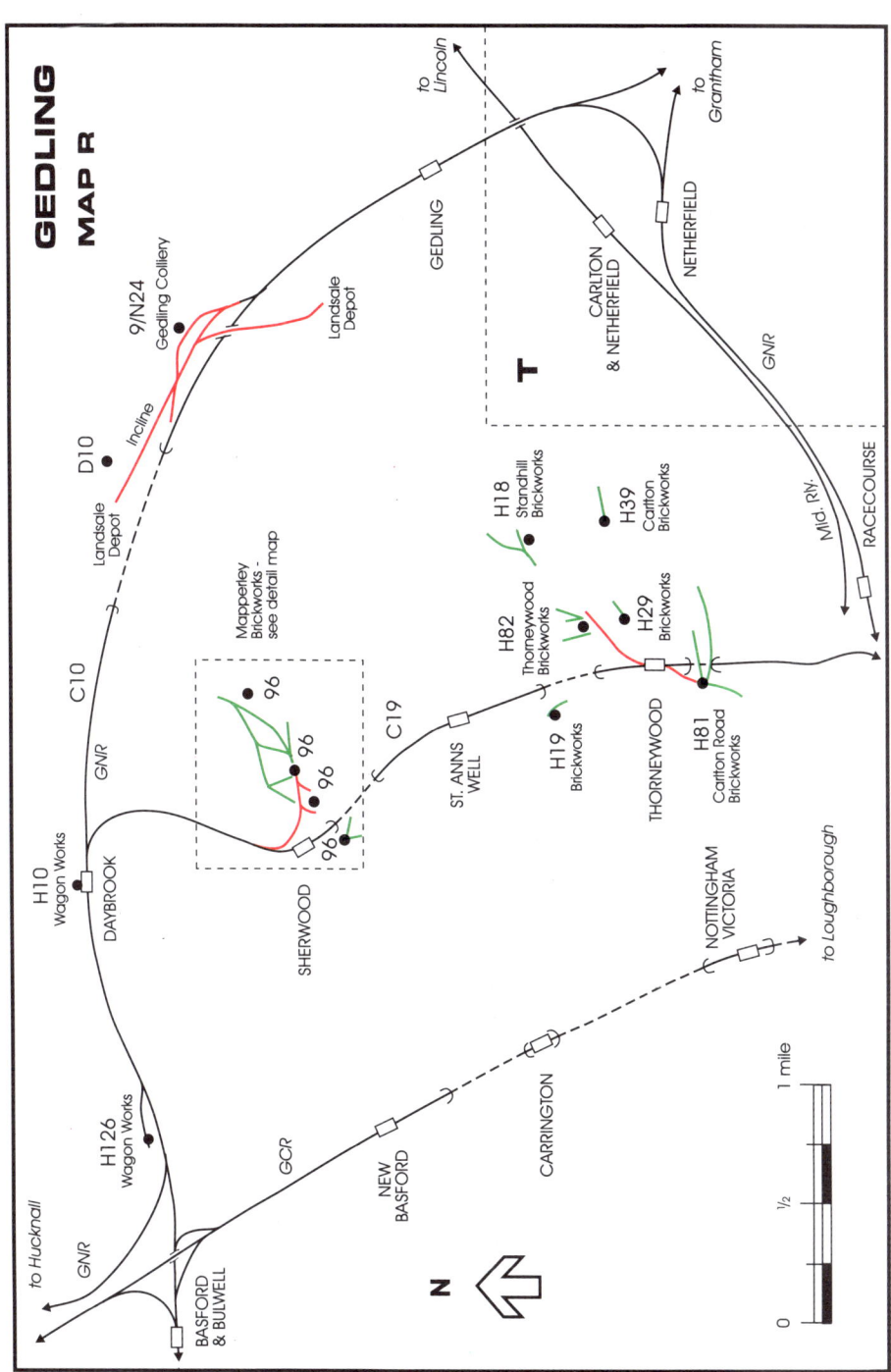

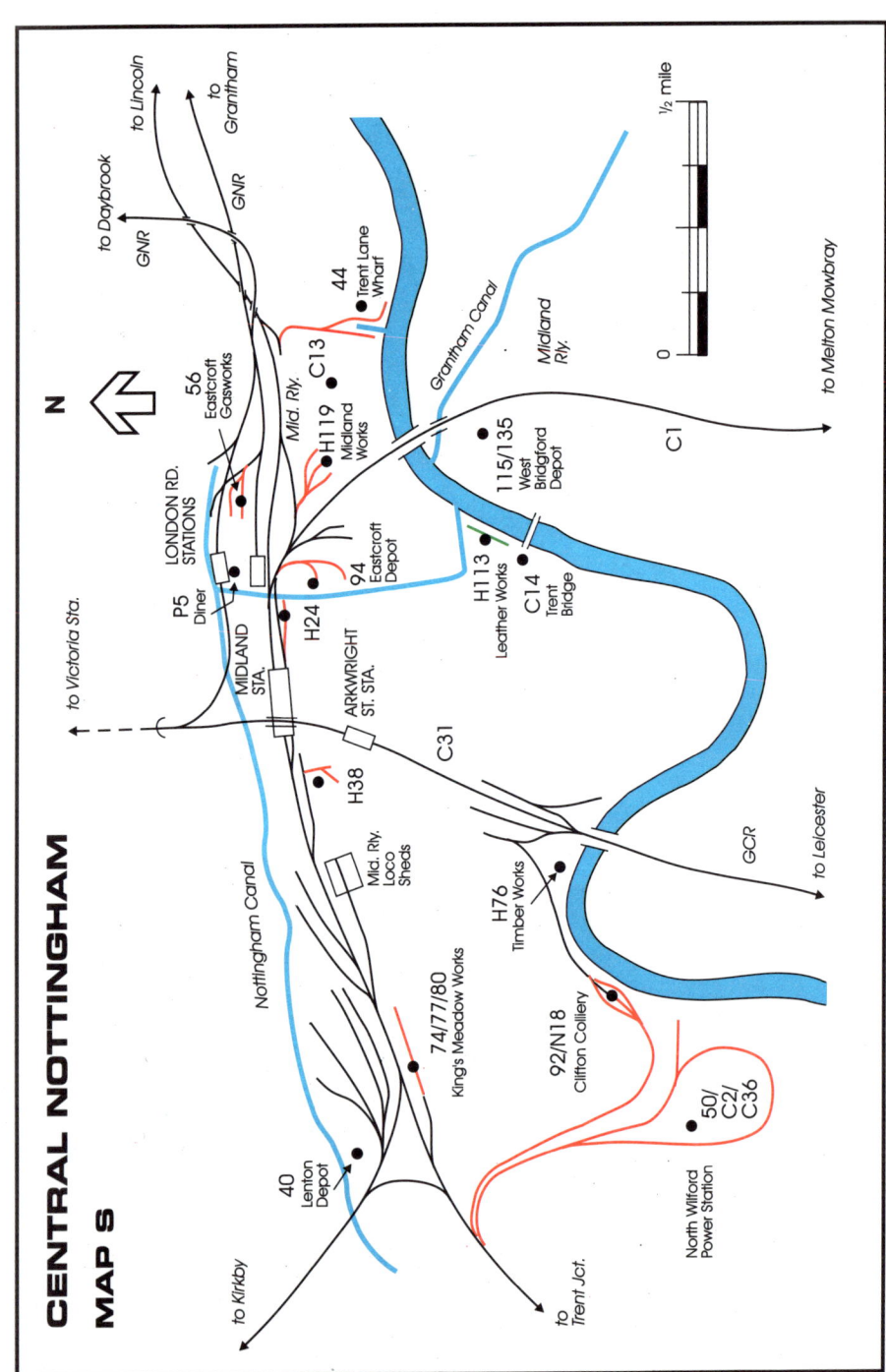

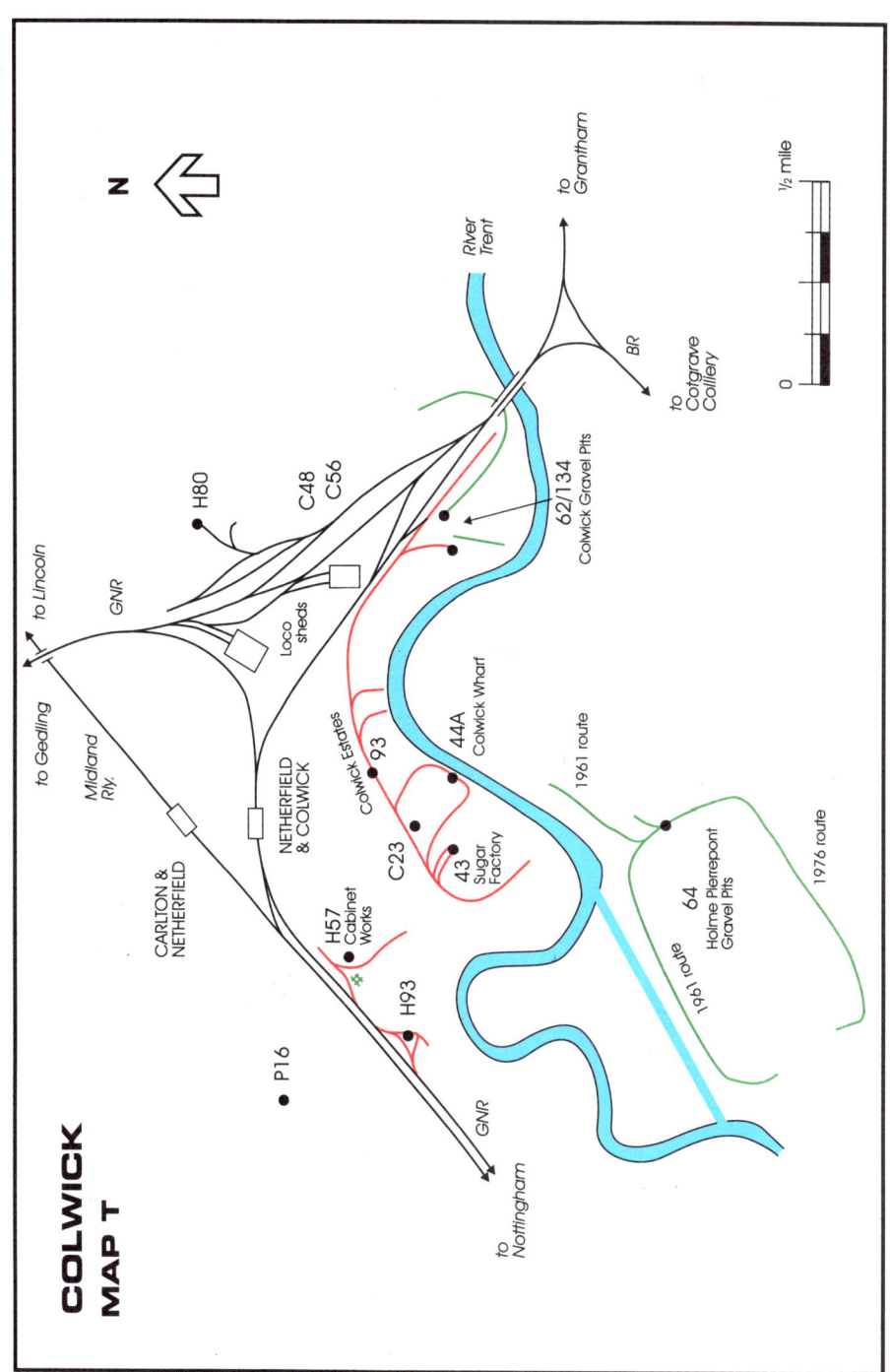

Nottinghamshire Handbook. Page 35

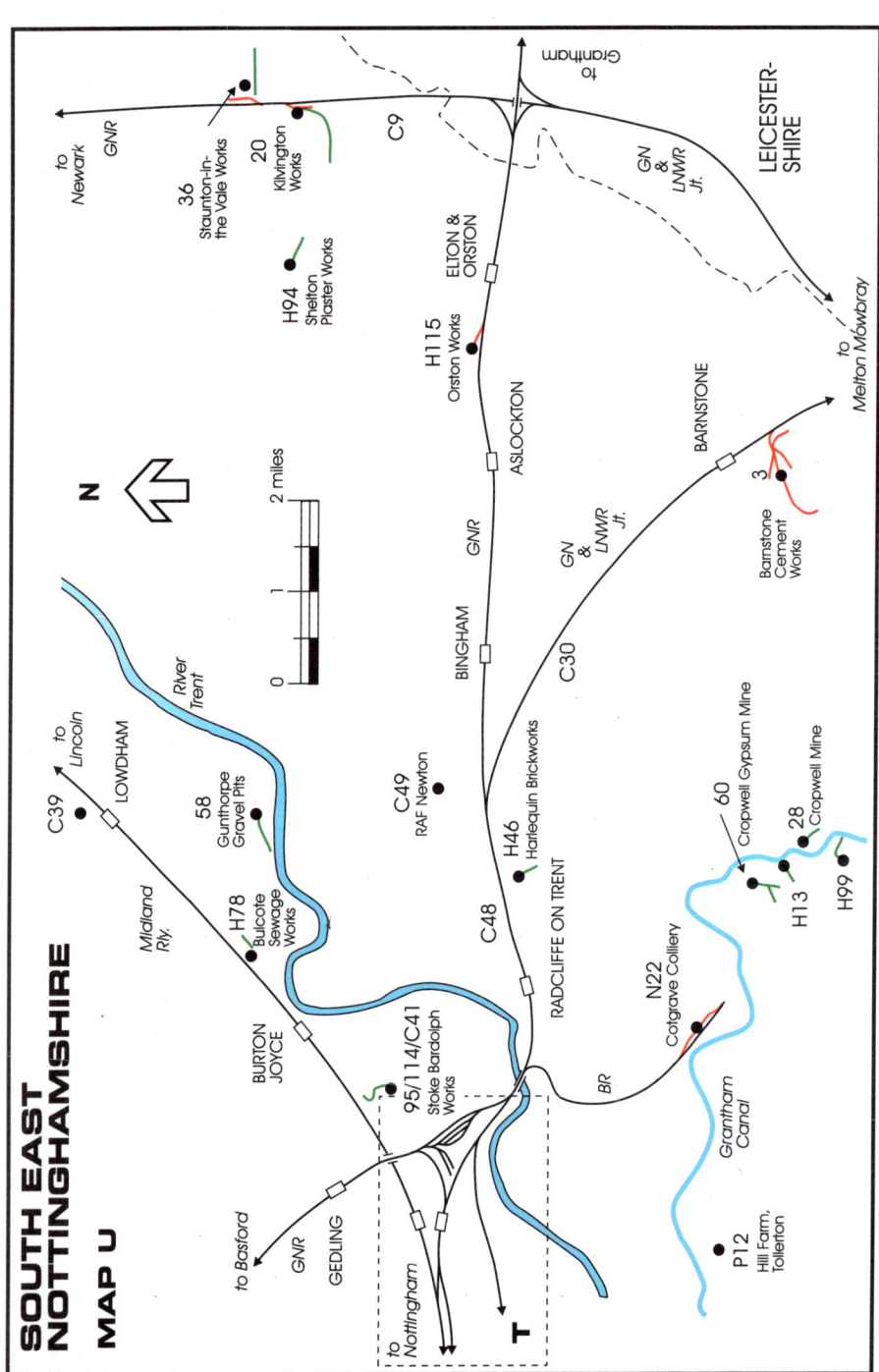

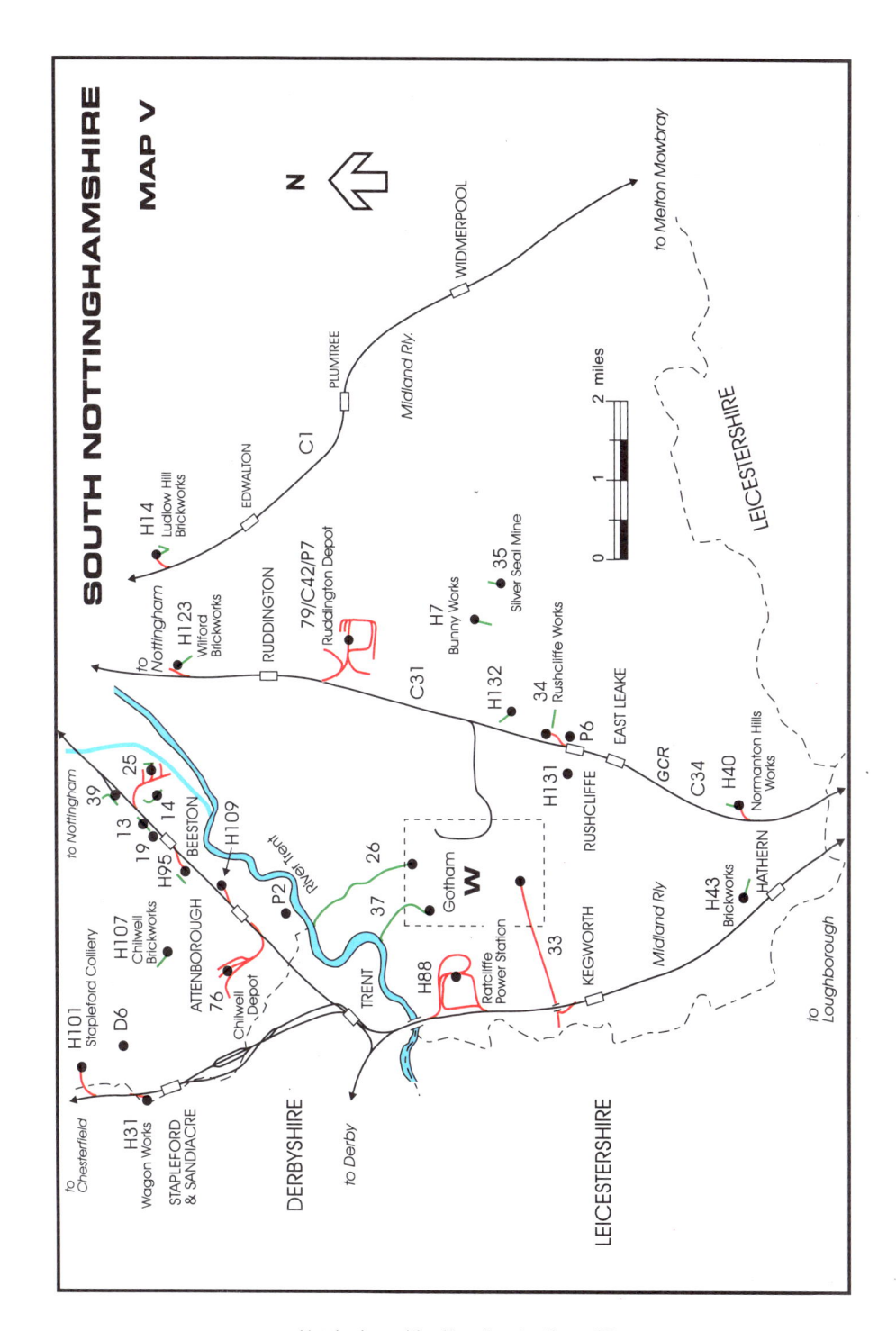

SOUTH NOTTINGHAMSHIRE
MAP V

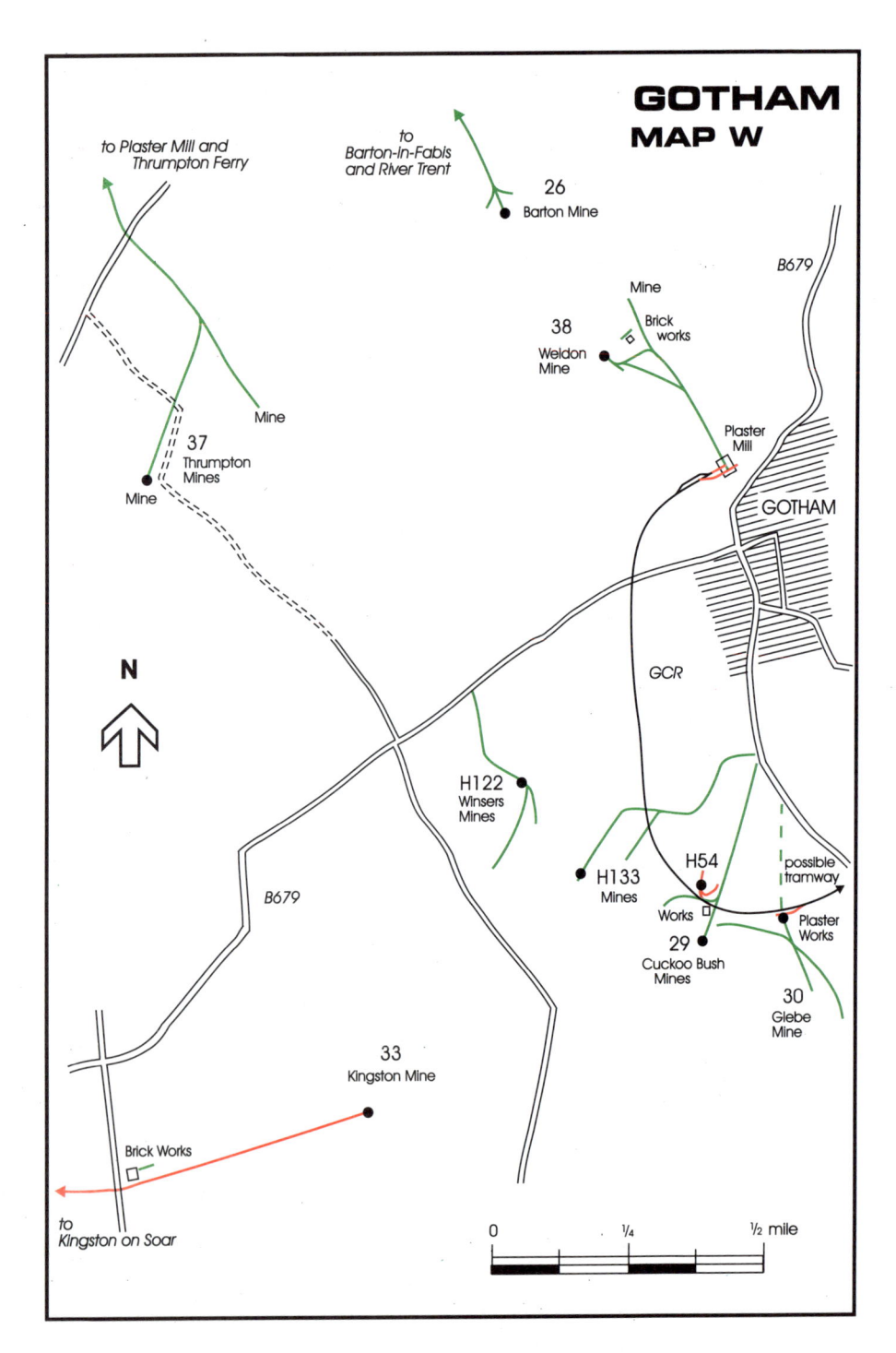

GOTHAM
MAP W

to Plaster Mill and Thrumpton Ferry

to Barton-in-Fabis and River Trent

26 Barton Mine

B679

Mine

Brick works

38 Weldon Mine

Mine

37 Thrumpton Mines

Mine

Plaster Mill

GOTHAM

GCR

N

H122 Winsers Mines

H54

possible tramway

H133 Mines

Works

Plaster Works

29 Cuckoo Bush Mines

30 Glebe Mine

B679

33 Kingston Mine

Brick Works

to Kingston on Soar

0   ¼   ½ mile

Nottinghamshire Handbook. Page 38

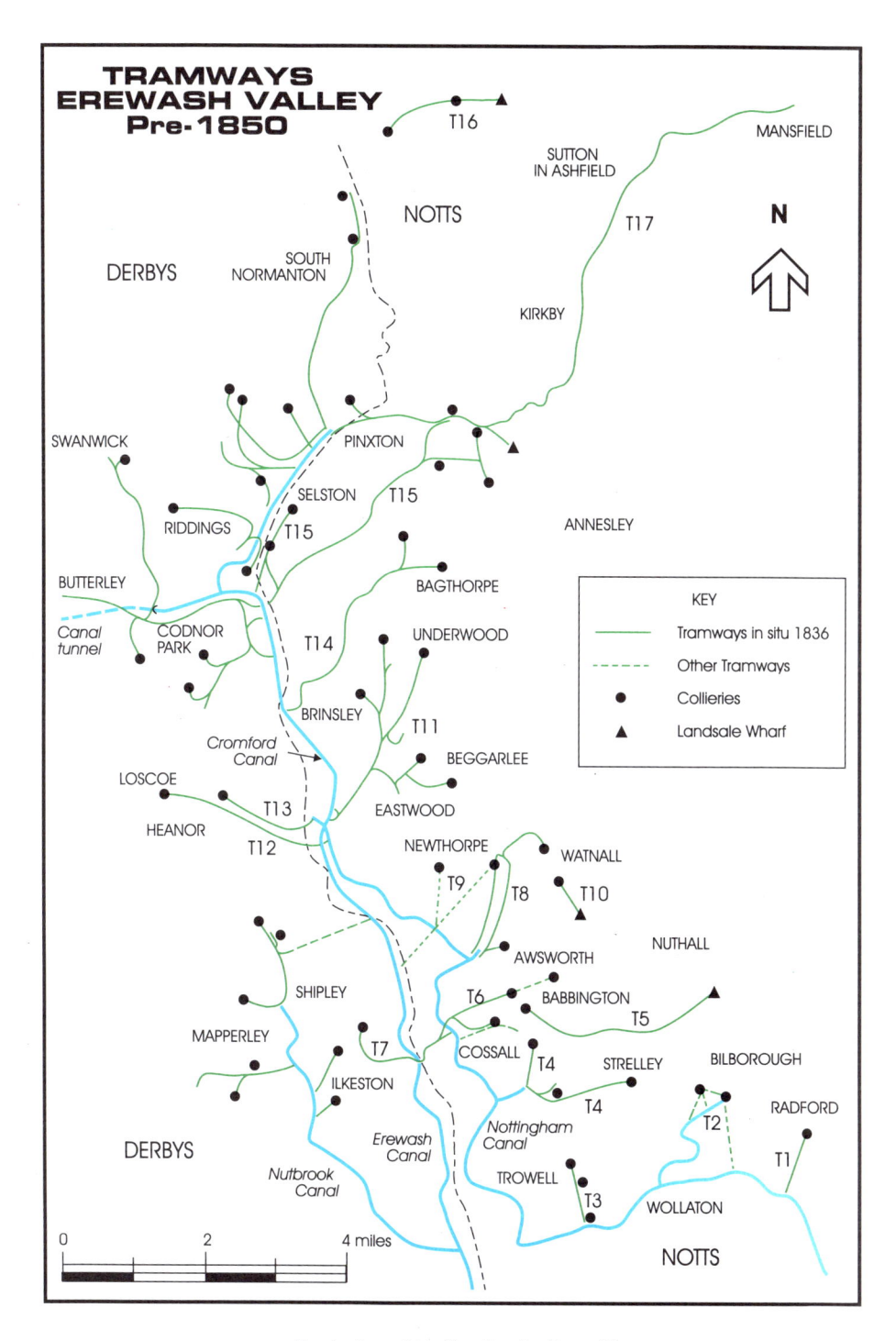

TRAMWAYS EREWASH VALLEY Pre-1850

KEY
- —— Tramways in situ 1836
- ---- Other Tramways
- ● Collieries
- ▲ Landsale Wharf

Nottinghamshire Handbook. Page 39

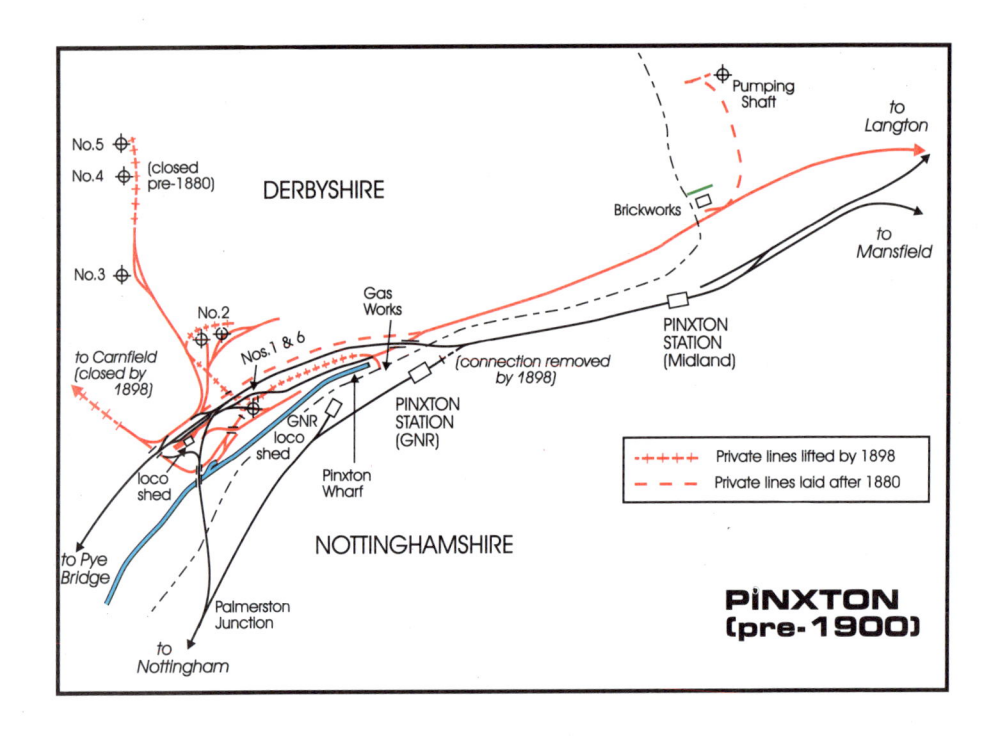

PINXTON (pre-1900)

- to Langton
- to Mansfield
- to Pye Bridge
- to Nottingham
- to Carnfield (closed by 1898)

Pumping Shaft
Brickworks
DERBYSHIRE
NOTTINGHAMSHIRE
No.5
No.4 (closed pre-1880)
No.3
No.2
Nos.1 & 6
Gas Works
(connection removed by 1898)
PINXTON STATION (Midland)
PINXTON STATION (GNR)
GNR loco shed
loco shed
Pinxton Wharf
Palmerston Junction

++++ Private lines lifted by 1898
---- Private lines laid after 1880

PINXTON (1914 onwards)

- to Langton
- to Mansfield
- to Pye Bridge
- to Nottingham

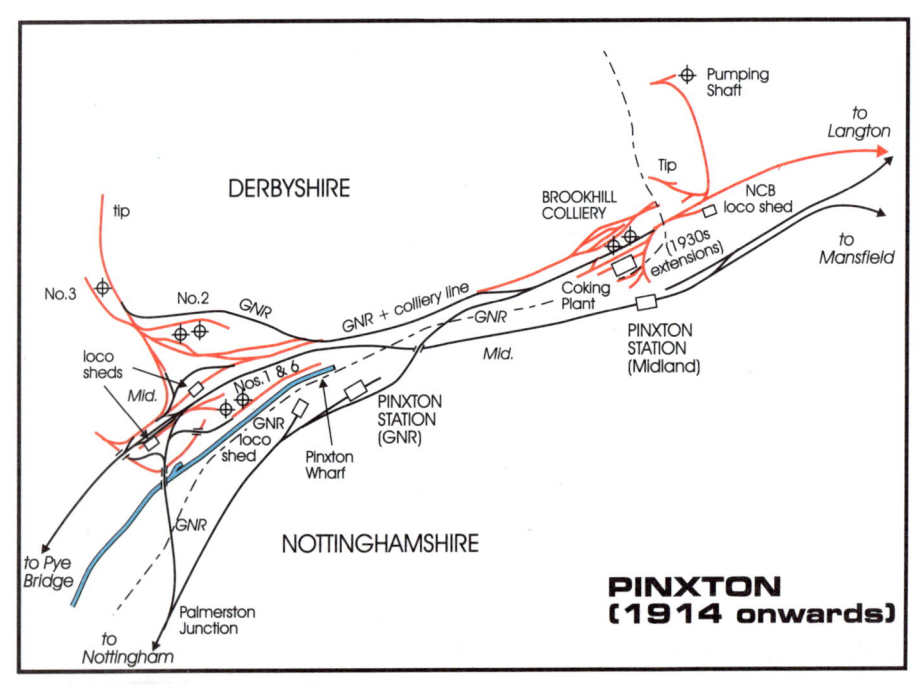

Pumping Shaft
Tip
BROOKHILL COLLIERY
NCB loco shed
(1930s extensions)
Coking Plant
DERBYSHIRE
NOTTINGHAMSHIRE
tip
No.3
No.2
GNR
GNR + colliery line
-GNR-
Mid.
loco sheds
Mid.
Nos.1 & 6
GNR loco shed
PINXTON STATION (Midland)
PINXTON STATION (GNR)
Pinxton Wharf
GNR
Palmerston Junction

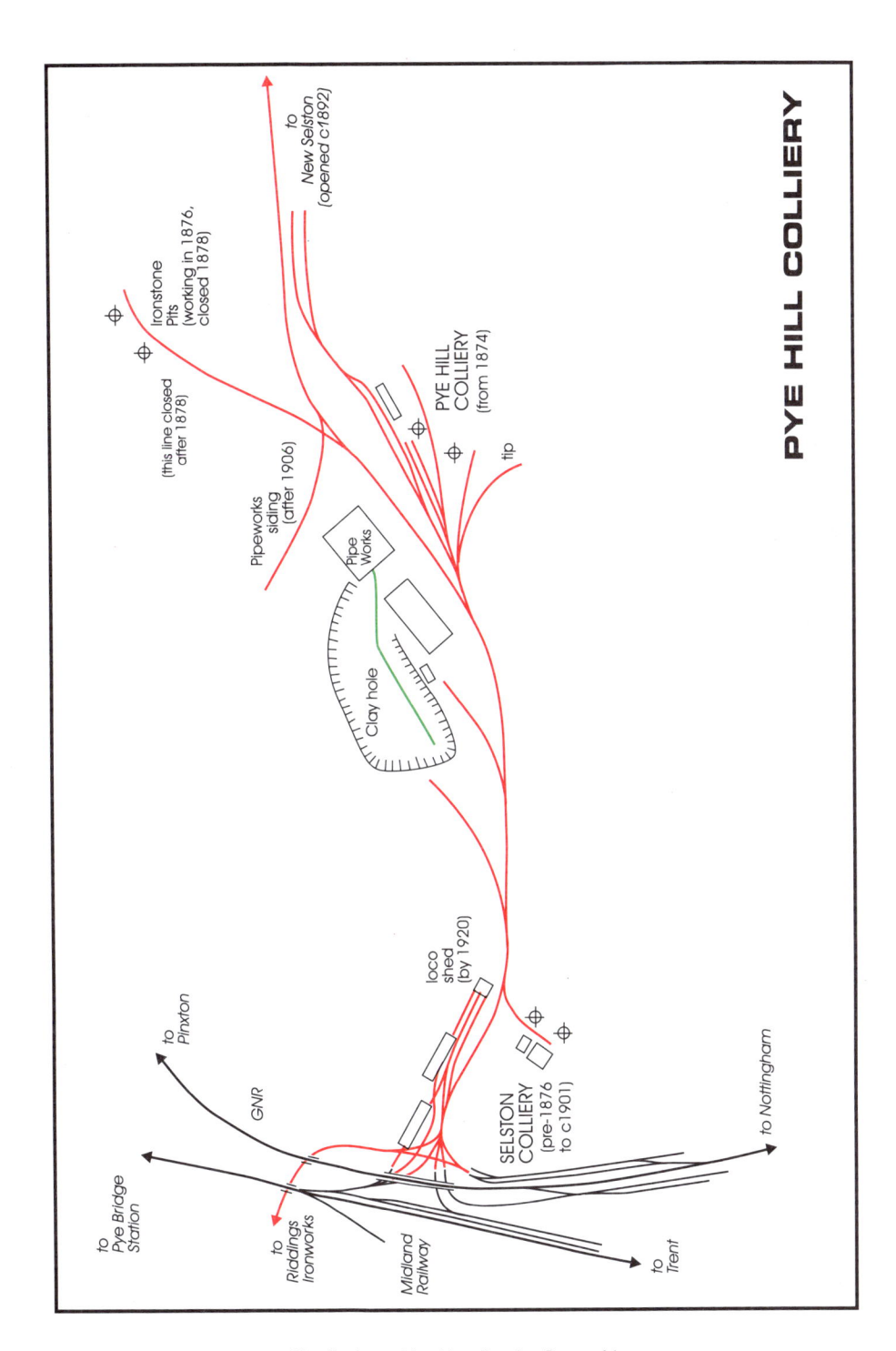

PYE HILL COLLIERY

- to New Selston (opened c1892)
- Ironstone Pits (working in 1876, closed 1878)
- (this line closed after 1878)
- PYE HILL COLLIERY (from 1874)
- tip
- Pipeworks siding (after 1906)
- Pipe Works
- Clay hole
- loco shed (by 1920)
- SELSTON COLLIERY (pre-1876 to c1901)
- to Pinxton
- GNR
- to Pye Bridge Station
- to Riddings Ironworks
- Midland Railway
- to Trent
- to Nottingham

Nottinghamshire Handbook. Page 41

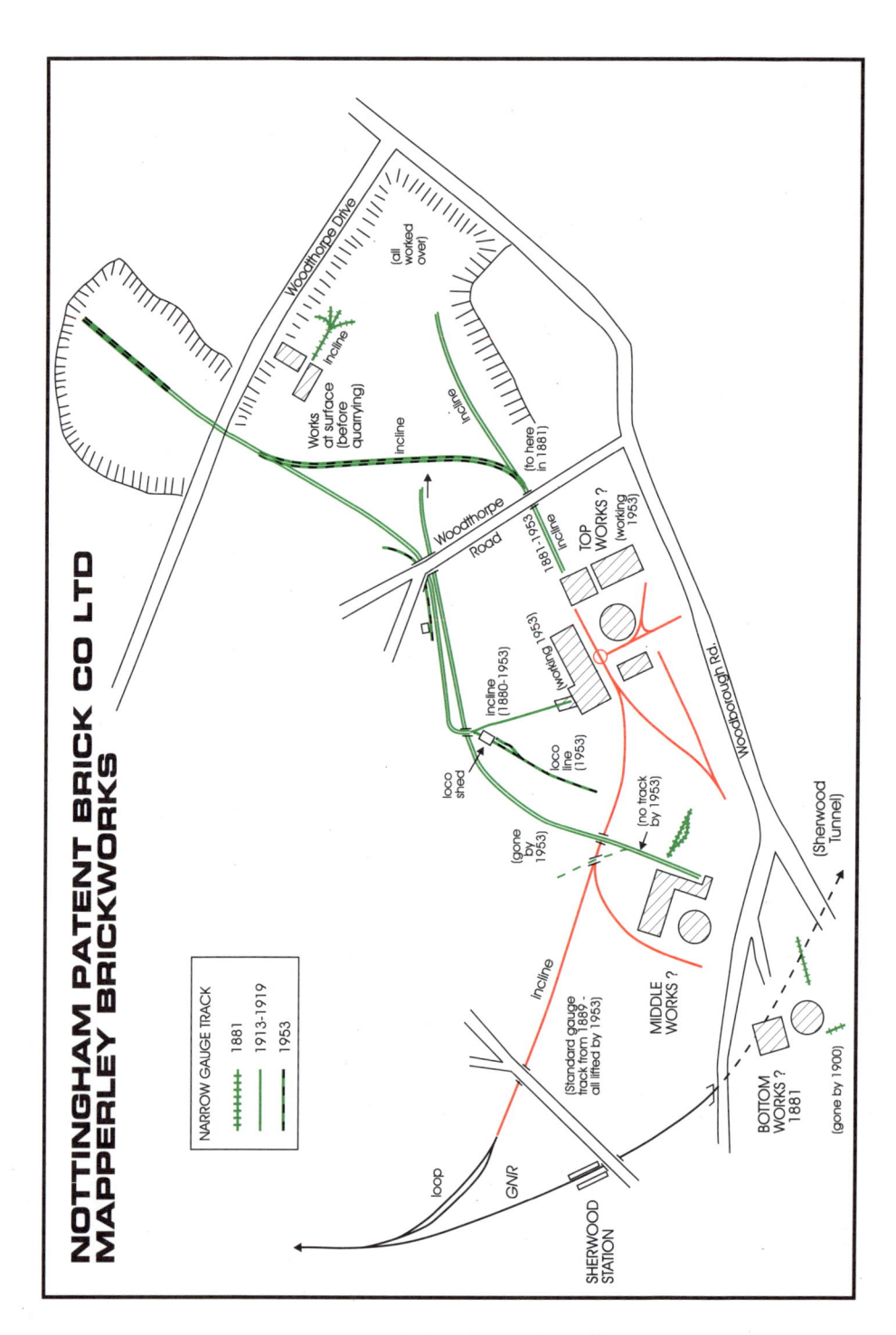

NOTTINGHAM PATENT BRICK CO LTD
MAPPERLEY BRICKWORKS

NARROW GAUGE TRACK
- +++++ 1881
- ——— 1913-1919
- ▬▬▬ 1953

Woodthorpe Drive

Works at surface (before quarrying)

incline

incline (all worked over)

incline (to here in 1881)

Woodthorpe Road

incline 1881-1953

TOP WORKS? (working 1953)

incline (1880-1953) (working 1953)

loco shed

loco line (1953)

(gone by 1953)

(no track by 1953)

Woodborough Rd.

MIDDLE WORKS?

incline

(Standard gauge track from 1889 - all lifted by 1953)

BOTTOM WORKS? 1881

(gone by 1900)

(Sherwood Tunnel)

loop

GNR

SHERWOOD STATION

Nottinghamshire Handbook. Page 42

SECTION 1

INDUSTRIAL LOCATIONS USING LOCOMOTIVES

AIR MINISTRY

ROYAL AIR FORCE STATION, CUCKNEY   G1
SK 57x70x

The natural camouflage of Sherwood Forest meant that during the Second World War the area was selected by the War Office for storage depots. Some were temporary and others continued to be used for the duration of the War. This site in Hatfield Plantation (about a mile south-east of Cuckney and immediately north of Welbeck Colliery) was established as a Maintenance Unit in 1939. The date of closure is unknown.

Gauge : 2ft 0in

AMW No.206	4wDM	RH	203016	1940	New	(1)
AMW No.229	4wDM	RH	203029	1940	(a)	(2)

(a)   ex RAF Rowthorn Depot, near Pleasley, Derbys, after 14/9/1944, by 12/11/1945.

(1)   to RAF Rowthorn Depot, near Pleasley, Derbys, after 10/8/1942, by 14/12/1942; returned after 14/12/1944, by 16/2/1945; to RAF Lakenheath, Suffolk, /1946 (by 17/1/1946).
(2)   to RAF Rowthorn Depot, by 26/11/1945.

ROYAL AIR FORCE STATION, SCOFTON, Ranby   C2
(also known as **RAF WORKSOP**)   SK 626813

This world war two airfield was located 3 miles north east of Worksop. Land was requisitioned in 7/1942. The airfield, constructed by George Wimpey & Co Ltd and A.M. Carmichael Ltd, opened on 7/11/1943. It ceased to be operational from 9/6/1958 and closed on 8/12/1960. The purpose to which the locomotives were put is unknown.

Gauge : 2ft 0in

AMW No.206	4wDM	RH	203016	1940	(a)	(1)
AMW No.229	4wDM	RH	203029	1940	(b)	(2)

(a)   ex RAF Rowthorn Depot, near Pleasley, Derbys, after 2/9/1943, by 4/1/1944.
(b)   ex RAF (depot unknown but possibly Fauld, Staffs.) by 19/1/1944.

(1)   to RAF Rowthorn Depot, after 3/3/1944, by 24/8/1944.
(2)   to RAF Rowthorn Depot, after 4/1/1944, by 14/9/1944.

ASSOCIATED PORTLAND CEMENT MANUFACTURERS LTD

On 1/6/1978 the company name was changed to Blue Circle Industries Ltd and the locations still operational on that date (Beeston Cement Terminal and Kilvington Cement Works) are listed under the new title.

BARNSTONE CEMENT WORKS U3

G. & T. Earle Ltd until c/1966. (Subsidiary of **APCM** from /1942)   SK 736351
Barnstone Cement Co Ltd until /1942;
Barnstone Blue Lias Lime & Cement Co Ltd until /1924
Barnstone Blue Lias Lime Co until /1896

A lime quarry and kilns opened in 1878 on a site south west of the GNR/LNWR Joint Saxondale Junction - Harby & Stathern line (opened 30/6/1879), ½ mile south east of Barnstone Station at SK 743353. A private line, which ran west for ½ mile to end at the lime works, is believed to date from 1880. The rail served quarry was located east of the works. Cement production dates from 1886 and the works was built on the site of the first quarry east of the original works. By 1900 there were two quarries, one south west of the exchange sidings and one at SK 736347, on the west side of the road to Barnstone Lodge. By 1950 a works extension with sidings was completed south of the lime works. The 2ft 0in gauge locomotives (i.e. more than the one we list) are said by Earle to have been employed to "reclaim topsoil" (overburden stripping?). Persistent rumours of narrow gauge locomotives abandoned in a flooded pit were not substantiated by divers. The works closed 29/11/1969.

Gauge : 4ft 8½in

	Name	Type	Cyl	Builder	No.	Date	Notes	Ref
	PHOENIX	0-6-0ST	IC	MW	44	1862 ?	(a)	(2)
	-	?	?	?			(b)	(1)
(? 19	DERBY ?)	0-4-0ST	OC	MW	584	1876	(c)	(3)
	HORWICH	0-4-0ST	OC	HCR	172	1877		
		reb		HC		1895	(d)	Scr c/1944
	BARNSTONE	0-4-0ST	OC	P	760	1899	New	(3)
	-	0-4-0T	OC	Elh		1910	(e)	(4)
	LANGAR	0-4-0ST	OC	P	1703	1926	New	(7)
No.6	BESCABY	0-4-0ST	OC	HL	3684	1929	(f)	(6)
	"GRANBY"	0-4-0ST	OC	P	1521	1918	(g)	(8)
	THE HERBERT TURNER	0-4-0DH		RH	513139	1967	New	(9)

Note that 4wPM MR 2033/1920 was owned by the Barnstone Cement Co. Although spares were ordered for it from the Barnstone address, it is believed to have worked only at Waltham-in-the-Wolds, Leicestershire.

(a)   ex unrecorded vendor, 3/1881. If indeed MW 44, then probably ex Midland Railway Co; earlier Unstone Coal & Coke Co, Unstone, Chesterfield, Derbys.
(b)   ex Walter Scott, contr, per A.T. Crow, auctioneer, 3/1882 (probably Rugby & Northampton Rly (LNWR) sale at Crick, 9-10/3/1882).
(c)   ex Benton & Woodiwiss, contr, 19, by direct purchase, 5/1884 (possibly last used by B&W on Thornton & Keighley Rly Extension contract and not sold at that A.T. Crow auction, 28/2/1884).
(d)   ex J.P. Edwards, contr, by direct purchase, /1899; to Arley Colliery Co Ltd, Warwicks, hire, /1903 (by 30/6/1903); returned (in /1903 ?).
(e)   ex Ministry of Munitions, Trumpington, Cambs, 10/1921; orig. LSWR (either 101 or 147, details unclear).

(f) ex Sir Lindsay Parkinson & Co Ltd, Chorley ROF (1937-1938) contract, Lancs; earlier Thos.W. Ward Ltd, Sheffield; orig Eston Sheet & Galvanizing Co Ltd, Cleveland.
(g) ex Air Ministry, Cranwell, Lincs, /1957.

(1) to a Mr Hall (or W. Hall), 10/1882.
(2) to Thos. W. Ward Ltd, for scrap, /1888.
(3) to ? , after 31/12/1898, by 31/12/1899; later with H.L. Bolton, contr.
(4) to George Cohen, Sons & Co Ltd, Stanningley, Leeds, (for scrap?), by 5/1939 or scrapped on site by /1939.
(5) derelict by 8/1950, scrapped, 6/1953.
(6) withdrawn /1964; scrapped, c5/1967.
(7) scrapped on site, by Speck of Bottesford, 9/1969.
(8) scrapped, after 9/1969, by 4/1970.
(9) to Melton Quarry, North Ferriby, Yorks (ER), /1970 (after 4/1970).

Gauge : 2ft 0in

-	4wDM	MR	7181	1937	New	s/s

possibly other internal combustion engine locomotives here

AWSWORTH COLLIERY CO LTD
(registered 2/12/1889)
AWSWORTH COLLIERY, Awsworth   M4
Awsworth Iron Co Ltd (from 1874 to c1887)   SK 479442
Heywood & Co in 1873
(possibly Lynch & Cadogan in 1876)

This colliery, opened between 1860 and 1869, was located east of the Midland Railway's Erewash Valley line (opened 1/7/1847) and south of its Bennerley Jct. - Bulwell Line (opened 1872), to which it was connected via the west end of the Digby Branch (purchased by the Midland in 1879). It was also connected to the GNR Awsworth Jct - Derby line (opened 1/1/1878) via its steeply graded Awsworth Colliery and Ironworks branch and a spur which ran north east from west of Awsworth Station. There may have been a wharf on the Nottingham Canal which passed immediately to the north of the colliery. A building at SK 477444, south of the Midland Railway branch, was probably the loco shed. In addition to coal, ironstone was worked until c1882 for the adjacent Awsworth Ironworks. This was located to the west and was then under the same ownership (see Bennerley Iron Co Ltd entry for details). It is probable that ironworks locomotives worked the colliery prior to the arrival of MW 204. The colliery closed shortly before 30/5/1899 when a sale was held, and the track was subsequently lifted.

Gauge : 4ft 8½in

-		0-6-0ST	IC	MW	204	1866	(a)	s/s
JACK		0-4-0ST	OC	P	580	1894	New	(1)

(a) earlier Exhall Colliery Co Ltd, Bedworth, Warwicks; here by 1/1887, when repaired by MW (and lettered "Awsworth Colliery Co").

(1) to E.P. Davis, Bennerley Ironworks, by 5/1901

B.A. COLLIERIES LTD

The company was registered on 31/3/1936 to acquire from 1/4/1936 the coal interests of the **Bestwood Coal & Iron Co Ltd** and the Nottinghamshire collieries of the **Babbington Coal Co Ltd**. The colliery businesses of the **Digby Colliery Co Ltd** and **Joseph Haigh Ltd** (of Morley, West Yorkshire) were acquired on 31/3/1937 and 25/6/1937 respectively.

BESTWOOD COLLIERY and IRONWORKS   N5

Bestwood Coal & Iron Co Ltd (registered 6/8/1872) until 1/4/1936   Colliery SK 557475
J. Lancaster & Co until 6/8/1872   Ironworks SK 552474

Sinking of the colliery commenced in 1873 and production started in 1876. An ironworks was built on an adjacent site to the west (SK552474) and was formally opened in 11/1881 and by 1886 there were two blast furnaces. In 1877 there was a narrow gauge tramway which ran north from the west side of the colliery to SK 553484 from where a short branch ran west to a lime kiln in a small quarry at SK 550485. The main line continued north and then east to a brick yard at SK 554487 and then north to end at a gravel pit at SK 554489 (1 mile). This line is presumed to have been horseworked and was shortlived. It may not have worked after 1881 when the ironworks was built across its route and in any event it had gone by 1893 together with the limestone quarry and gravel pit, neither of which attained any size. The brickyard had gone by 1905.

The colliery was first served by the Midland Railway's Bestwood Park branch (opened 17/1/1876) which ran north east from its line, 1¾ miles north of Bulwell station for ¾ mile to the empties sidings. The complex was also served, after the opening of the GNR Leen Valley line in 10/1881, by that company's Bestwood Colliery branch which ran north east from 1¼ miles north of Bulwell Forest station, to join the Midland branch at the colliery (agreement dated 16/1/1882). There was a separate GNR connection to the ironworks, adjacent to Bestwood Colliery station. Under an agreement dated 14/2/1908, a line was laid which ran east and then south from the GNR branch to terminate at SK 555467. Its purpose is unknown but some mineral must have been worked as the site became first a water filled hole and later an extension to the tip. In later years there was a loco shed at SK 553474.

In 1913 and 1950 a small quarry was being worked south west of the empty wagon headshunt and a short narrow gauge track ran into it. This is believed to be the sand pit listed as being worked by the colliery company in 1928. By 1948 a sand pit was being worked by the **Bestwood Sand Co Ltd**. Its location has not been positively identified but this site is the strongest possibility.

The ironworks closed for production and was demolished in the first half of 1936. The site was later used by the NCB for its Bestwood Central Workshops. In order to ventilate workings to the east of Bestwood, the sinking of the Calverton No.1 Shaft (SK 604503) began in June 1937 and was completed in 1939. It was also used for man riding and underground locomotives were employed there from 1943. By then the decision had been taken to develop **CALVERTON** as an independent colliery and the sinking of its No.2 Shaft commenced in January 1946. Both collieries were vested in the NCB, East Midlands Division, Area No.6, from 1/1/1947.

Gauge : 4ft 8½in

	-	0-4-0ST	OC	D&S				
			reb	HCR	197	1877	(a)	(1)
EARL FERRERS		0-6-0ST	IC	MW	561	1875	(b)	s/s after 8/1907
LANCASTER		0-4-0ST	OC	P	468	1888	New	(2)
ST.ALBANS		0-4-0ST	OC	Mkm	104	1891	New	(2)
BESTWOOD		0-4-0ST	OC	AB	1517	1919	New	(2)

(a) ex HCR, hire (to "Bestwood Coal & Iron Co Ltd, nr Nottingham"), from 31/1/1877.
(b) earlier J.Lancaster & Co, Heath End Colliery, Staunton Harold, Leics, EARL FERRERS, (probably the 6 wheels coupled tank loco for sale there, 31/5/1881; presumed not to have sold and transferred by Lancaster to Bestwood); here by c/1888.

(1) returned to HCR off hire, 28/3/1877.
(2) to NCB, East Midlands Division, Area No.6, with site, 1/1/1947.

The following locos were used underground, being delivered new to Calverton Shaft. The GB locomotives were to be used for coal haulage in the Top Hard seam to Bestwood main haulage.

Gauge : 2ft 0in

-	4wBEF	GB	1960	1943	New	(1)
-	4wBEF	GB	1961	1943	New	(1)
-	4wBEF	Atlas	2454	1945	New	(1)
-	4wBEF	Atlas	2466	1945	New	(1)

(1) to NCB, East Midlands Division, Area No.6, with site, 1/1/1947.

BABBINGTON and CINDERHILL COLLIERIES and RAILWAYS   Q6

Babbington Coal Co Ltd (incorporated 30/6/1925) until 1/4/1936
Babbington Coal Co until c/1927
Chas. Seely & Co until c/1873
Wright & Co until /1870
Thos. North until c/1868
Wakefield and North until 16/8/1847
Thos. North until c/1834

Comprising;
BABBINGTON (HIGH HOLBORN) COLLIERY (pre1836 - 1860)	SK491437
BABBINGTON WHARF, Radford (closed by 1934)	SK545400
BOBBERS MILL COLLIERY (pre 1854 - 1856)	not known
BROXTOWE COLLIERY (1869 - 1929)	SK524430
CINDERHILL (later **BABBINGTON**) **COLLIERY** (1843 - NCB)	SK534437
KIMBERLEY COLLIERY (c1840 - 1897)	SK502441
NEWCASTLE (WHITEMOOR) COLLIERY (1853 - 1928)	SK546423
TURKEY FIELD COLLIERY (c1840 - 1860)	SK498425

Thomas North was an innovative coal owner who sank a number of pits from 1830 onwards. One example of his foresight was his development of private railways from the 1830s, to link the pits with landsale yards convenient for the Nottingham trade. Unfortunately his efforts did not meet with financial success and on his death in 1868 his banker, J Wright, had to take over the business to try and recover some of the money that he was owed.

Babbington Colliery was first connected by a tramway to a wharf on the Nottingham Canal at SK 478429. This was probably laid before 1836, at which date North was building a tramway extending from Babbington Colliery, eastwards for 3 miles, to a landsale wharf south west of the Nottingham to Nuthall road at Cinderhill (SK 534436). This line was steeply graded but there is a contemporary account of an unknown locomotive being tried successfully there in 1838, though whether this led to regular working is not known. North sank his largest colliery, **CINDERHILL**, in 1841 - 1843 and had simultaneously been further developing his railways. Considering first the area west of Cinderhill, the gradients of the original line must have proved unsatisfactory as, perhaps as early as 1840, the west end of it was replaced by a revised route to the north, incorporating an inclined plane. From the old route south of Babbington village the new line climbed for ¾ mile to a summit at SK 503435 where the winding engine was located within a triangular junction. From here the line ran south east for 1 mile to join the old route east of Chilwell Dam Farm. Both **KIMBERLEY** and **TURKEY FIELD COLLIERIES** probably opened in the early 1840s and were connected by branch lines to the new route. The former by a line which ran north for half a mile from the triangular junction and the latter by one running south from the original route. The first main line railway connection was made by the Midland Railway Babbington Branch which opened in 5/1849. It left the Erewash Valley line (opened 1/7/1847) south of Ilkeston Junction Station and ran north east, close to the course of the old canal tramway, to **BABBINGTON COLLIERY**, where it joined North's line to CINDERHILL. A cut-off line to the south of BABBINGTON COLLIERY was later built and joined the inclined plane at SK 497432. This Midland Railway branch was leased to and worked by North. For some years a connection on the line of the original tramway to the wharf on the Erewash Canal remained in use. It crossed the Midland Railway Erewash Valley line on the level and a toll was charged by the Midland Railway. Plans dating from 1879-81 show this canal line closed and partly lifted. The line to TURKEY FIELD and the sidings at BABBINGTON Village had also been lifted together with the incline west from the summit. TURKEY FIELD and BABBINGTON COLLIERIES closed about 1860 but there was an ironstone mine at Babbington, operated in 1869 by **Crompton & Co**, which worked until 1875. The BABBINGTON (HIGH HOLBORN) shaft remained in use for many years as a pumping station. By 1917 it was dewatering the workings of the Cossall Coal Co Ltd. The 1879-81 plans also show, ¾ mile east of the summit, the earthworks of an abandoned route which had run east, and then north east, to an old shaft at Engine Wood (SK 517436). (Nothing else is known of this in the tramway era but see Broxtowe Colliery - below). On the branch which ran north to **KIMBERLEY COLLIERY**, there was a building on the east side which may have been a locoshed. Thus, by 1879, there were no collieries at work west of the triangular junction and that part of North's railway had been lifted. In 1913 work involving two short lengths of narrow gauge surface track was underway at a disused shaft, ¼ mile to the south west of Babbington village (SK495435). This work was shortlived. The Midland Railway Babbington line remained in situ in 1879 but there was no traffic at Babbington and by 1895 it had been cut back by several hundred yards. **BROXTOWE COLLIERY** had been opened in 1869 on the north west side of the railway to Cinderhill, but by 1879 was disused and marked as 'old coal pit'. KIMBERLEY COLLIERY closed in 1897 but, between 1889 and 1894, BROXTOWE had reopened. The screens were located some 300 yards north east of the colliery which was linked to them by a narrow gauge, double track, endless rope haulage. By 1906 the railway had been shortened back to a headshunt just west of BROXTOWE. From 1917, that colliery was linked in published statistics with a shaft known as NUTHALL WOOD. The latter has not been traced with certainty but is most likely to have been a continuing use of the one in Engine Wood at SK 517436, referred to earlier. Some time after BROXTOWE ceased to wind coal in 1929, the western section of North's railway was shortened back to a headshunt at Cinderhill. This was just long enough to give access to the south eastern line to **NEWCASTLE COLLIERY** and Radford.

North's line to Radford opened in 5/1844. It ran south east from the landsale wharf at Cinderhill, where it made end on connection with the western section and from where there was a connection north west into CINDERHILL COLLIERY. The Radford line ran south east, through North's Napoleon Square housing development, for 1½ miles before turning south for a further mile to end at **Babbington Wharf** on the Nottingham Canal, where there were extensive sidings. There was also a landsale yard east of the line just north of the wharf. By the time of the 1879 plan, this line had reached its maximum extent. NEWCASTLE COLLIERY had opened in 1853 on the east side of the line, together with a landsale yard. Earthworks which ran south east of the line south of Newcastle may have been evidence of a line to a BOBBERS MILL COLLIERY which was working in 1854 but had closed by 1857. The colliery site has not been identified but Bobbers Mill was at SK 550414. The earthworks could equally mark the intended start of a line proposed in 1845 to run to landsale yards in the city of Nottingham. If constructed, tunnelling and earthworks would have been very heavy. On 6/1/1875 the Midland Railway's Radford to Trowell line had opened and this crossed North's line on the level, ¼ mile north of Babbington Wharf. A north to west curve and sidings on the north side of the Midland Railway were put in for the exchange of traffic. NEWCASTLE COLLIERY closed in 5/1928 and was abandoned from 9/10/1929, but the landsale sidings remained. The line southwards from here, including the crossing and main line connection, had closed by 1934 and was converted into a road.

Turning now to the layout and history of the largest colliery, **CINDERHILL**, this was on the north side of the road separating it from the landsale yard and the early North's railways. A connection from them, running north west to the colliery, is likely to have been the original rail access. Cinderhill's main line connection dates from 1852 when a branch built and worked by North, under powers obtained by the Midland Railway, opened. This branch ran west from Basford Junction on the Midland Railway, ¾ mile north of Basford Station, for ¾ mile to the colliery and also bridged the Nuthall Road to reach North's original line at the landsale yard. The Midland Railway took over the working of the branch from 3/1877, by which time a connection had also been made from the GNR Nottingham - Derby line (which opened in 1875), ½ mile west of its Basford & Bulwell Station. It ran south east for ¼ mile to join the Midland Railway branch. In 1879 the colliery comprised screens and sidings with a gasworks to the south and a large brickworks to the east. The brickworks had an extensive narrow gauge system including an incline into clay workings to the north.

By 1879 there was an upcast shaft, known as the **HEMPSHILL FAN**, located south of the GNR line at SK 526445. It was used to ventilate part of the Cinderhill workings and also those of **BULWELL MAIN**. Hempshill was not rail connected but a semi-circular tub track from the shaft to the boiler house was in place until after 1913. The shaft had closed by vesting day (1/1/1947).

By 1913, the brickworks opencast workings extended north of the GNR line to SK 535444. The earlier workings were being filled using a second narrow gauge line at a higher level which ran from the screens. By the 1930s, this second tramway also extended north of the GNR, both passing under it at SK 535442. In 1934 the workings were producing clay, sand and limestone but by the end of the decade had almost reached their maximum extent. After 1937, B.A. Collieries participated in a venture to produce briquettes and oil from coal. A plant was erected at **CINDERHILL** to be operated by a separate company, **Suncole (Nottingham) Ltd** (registered 6/1937). Production commenced in 1938-9 but the process was unsuccessful and work ceased in 1940. Its sidings were located on the north side of the LMSR branch line between SK 542439 and SK 538438. Ground frames were provided at each end. There was no direct connection to the LNER and it is not known if colliery locomotives were allowed to work there. A further shaft, **CINDERHILL No.6**, was sunk during World War Two, located north of the colliery at SK 533442. A double track narrow gauge endless haulage was put in to link this shaft with the screens. The narrow gauge steam locomotives are recorded as having been used in connection with the sinking of a new shaft. Although No.6 would be the obvious contender, it is stated in annual returns to have been completed in 1943, before the arrival of the locomotives. From some time between 1894 and 1905, that part of Cinderhill Colliery working from Nos 1 & 2 shafts was being referred to in official reports as BABBINGTON (CINDERHILL No.1) COLLIERY, a confusing re-use of the old name. The remainder of the colliery was referred to as CINDERHILL No.4 until the new shaft opened in 1943 when it became CINDERHILL No.6. These were nominally independent units of about equal size, but with some common surface facilities and management. These two collieries, together with North's railway as far south as NEWCASTLE Landsale Yard, passed to the NCB, East Midlands Division, Area No.6, from 1/1/1947. The brickworks remained in the private sector as the **Babbington Brick Co Ltd**.

Reference : "Journal of Railway & Canal Historical Society", Peter Stevenson, 7/1969.

Gauge : 4ft 8½in

	NAPOLEON	0-6-0ST	OC	TW		1850	(a)	Scr /1945
	-	0-4-0tank		TW		1852	New	s/s
	-	2-4-0tank		TW		1857	New	s/s
	-	2-4-0tank		TW		1864	New	s/s
	GENERAL	0-4-0ST	OC	HE	67	1871	New	(1)
	COLONEL	0-6-0ST	OC	HE	577	1892	New	(2)
	ADMIRAL	0-6-0ST	OC	P	874	1900	New	(2)
	MICHAEL	0-6-0ST	OC	RSHN	7285	1945	New	(2)
75194		0-6-0ST	IC	RSHN	7144	1944	(b)	(2)

Notes :
(i) One of the TW locos is believed to have been named JOSEPHINE.
(ii) On 12/7/1873 the company advertised "wish to hire a 4-wheel or 6-wheel loco with 10in or 12in cylinders".
(iii) One 6-wheel 12in x 20in and one 4-wheel 9in tank locos for sale, 31/8/1877 (and a 13in, 4 wheel tank loco wanted). The 9in loco for sale was probably the tank loco by RP, 9in cyls, advertised in C.D.Phillips' register from 6/1878 to 7/1879 or later, the advertiser being noted as "Babbington".
(iv) A 4-wheel tank 9in x15in by RP of 1868 was advertised in "Machinery Market", 7/1878-12/1879, advertiser not stated but possibly the same Babbington locomotive.

(a) ex ? , contr. (Mansfield ?), /1855; rebuilt by colliery from 2-4-0tank.
(b) ex Ministry of Fuel & Power, Heanor Disposal Point, Derbys, 12/1946.

(1) may also have been at Tibshelf Colliery, Derbys; with John Whitehouse (engineers & dealers), Midland Engineering Works, Ilkeston, Derbys. (possibly being overhauled for Babbington Coal Co ?), after 3/1901, by 7/1903; to Oughterside Coal Co Ltd, Cumbs, by 10/1907.
(2) to NCB, East Midlands Division, Area No.6, with site, 1/1/1947.

Gauge : 3ft 0in

	DARLEY DALE	0-4-0WT	OC	D&B	42	1925	(a)	(1)
	KINDER	0-4-0WT	OC	OK	10903	1925	(a)	(1)

(a) ex Wm. Twigg, Matlock, Derbys. dealer, 4/1945; earlier Lehane, Mackenzie & Shand Ltd, contrs., Darley Dale, Derbys.
(1) out of use from after 4/1946; to NCB, East Midlands Division, Area No.6, with site, 1/1/1947.

BULWELL or BULWELL MAIN COLLIERY, Bulwell   Q7
Babbington Coal Co Ltd until 1/4/1936   SK 530459
Babbington Coal Co until c/1927
Chas. Seely & Co until c/1873
Wright & Co until /1870

This colliery, opened in 1869, was located ¼ mile north east of the Midland Railway Bennerley - Bulwell line which opened in 1877. Thereafter sidings were provided alongside this line 1¼ miles north west of Basford Junction. These were worked by the Midland

Railway and screens here were connected to the colliery by a narrow gauge tubway. This colliery is worthy of note in a railway context as, from or shortly after, the opening, one of North's old locomotives from the Babbington Railway was adapted to power an underground tub haulage. The locomotive, minus boiler, was inverted, fitted with a rope drum and mounted in an engine house at the pit top. From there ropes passed down the shaft and into the workings. The locomotive used cannot be identified. It is believed to have lasted until the abandonment of the colliery in 9/1945. One source states that it was named NORTH STAR as a loco.

Reference : "Mining in the East Midlands 1550-1947", A.R. Griffin, Cass, 1971.

Gauge : 4ft 8½in (stationary use)

-	?	OC	TW?	1850	(a)	(1)

(a) ex Babbington Collieries (either as rope haulage engine or as locomotive) after /1869

(1) rebuilt to haulage engine (minus boiler) and scrapped in this form c/1945.

DIGBY COLLIERIES Giltbrook M8
Digby Colliery Co Ltd until c30/4/1937
Digby Colliery Co until 25/8/1899
Digby Coal Co until c1889
Potter & Burns until ?
Nicholson & Hall in /1864

DIGBY (also known as **GILTBROOK COLLIERY** (1866-1928))	SK 485450
NEW LONDON COLLIERY (1876-1937)	SK 487462
NEWTHORPE COLLIERY (1863-1888)	SK 480457
SPEEDWELL COLLIERY (1870-1888)	SK 491448

In 1842 a shallow pit titled **NEW LONDON** was being worked at Greasley by Thomas North, and a plan of 1836 shows a horse tramway to that point - see Non-locomotive Section. There were also shafts and tramways in the vicinity of what became Digby Colliery. A colliery there, titled **GILTBROOK**, was operated in 1854 by 'a company of colliers', in 1855-9 by F. Shipley Jnr. and in 1860 by Cockburn & Jordan. Turning now to the shafts of the railway era, **NEWTHORPE** was sunk in 1863, **DIGBY** in 1866, **SPEEDWELL** in 1870 and **NEW LONDON** in 1876-8. With the exception of Newthorpe, which was never rail served, these collieries were connected to the Midland Railway's Erewash Valley line (opened 1/7/1847), at what was to become Bennerley Junction. From here a private line ran north east and then north to DIGBY COLLIERY (1 mile) and NEW LONDON COLLIERY (1¾ miles). The first ¾ mile was purchased by the Midland Railway in 1879 to enable its Bennerley - Bulwell line and the Digby Colliery branch to make use of its route. Thereafter the colliery railway made end on connection with the Midland Railway line just north of the point where it was crossed by its Bulwell line. A second connection to Digby Colliery was made after 1875 by means of the GNR Digby Colliery Branch which curved south east and then north from its Pinxton line, north west of Awsworth viaduct.

By 1879 the colliery railway consisted of a line which ran north from the Midland Railway to DIGBY COLLIERY (¼ mile), where the loco shed was located, and on to NEW LONDON COLLIERY (1 mile). There was a connection on the west of this line, at the Midland Railway junction, to the Giltbrook Chemical Works of Nottingham Corporation, and a branch from the same place ran east for ½ mile to **SPEEDWELL COLLIERY** and a small brickworks. The GNR spur met the colliery line at Digby Colliery where the workshops of the company and a large brickworks were located. South west of this colliery was a rail served wharf on an arm of the Nottingham Canal. The underground workings at Speedwell and the non rail served Newthorpe Collieries were abandoned on 9/10/1888, though both shafts were retained for ventilation. By 1913, both remaining collieries had been reconstructed with more extensive sidings. The brickworks at Digby was shown as disused, although still intact, with narrow gauge lines running into a clay hole to the east. The line to Speedwell remained, possibly for boiler fuel, the small brickworks having gone. By 1938 this line had been shortened back to west of Awsworth Lane. The connection to the chemical works remained. Digby Colliery ceased producing coal in 9/1928 and its underground workings were abandoned in 1/1930. New London and the remaining surface installations closed in 11/1937 to allow B.A. Collieries Ltd to use its production quota elsewhere. Part of the site at Digby Colliery became the **GILTBROOK DISPOSAL POINT** of the Ministry of Fuel & Power c1944 (see NCB Section)

Reference : "The Colliery Guardian", 7/9/1894

Gauge : 4ft 8½in

LITTLE JOHN	0-4-0ST	OC	HCR	97	1869	New	s/s by 1894
ANNIE	0-6-0ST	OC	FW	385	1878	New	(1)
HAROLD	0-6-0ST	OC	HC	247	1883	New	(3)
MURIEL	0-6-0ST	OC	HL	2081	1888	New	(2)

(1) to Ibstock Collieries Ltd, Leics, ANNIE, 11/1940.
(2) to Stewarts & Lloyds Ltd, Corby Works, Northants, 30 MURIEL, via Thos.W. Ward Ltd, /1940.
(3) to George Cohen, Sons & Co Ltd; later to Mersey Docks & Harbour Board, Liverpool, No.18, 3/1946.

GEDLING COLLIERY R9
Digby Colliery Co Ltd until c30/4/1937 SK 613438

This colliery was sunk between 1900 and 1902 and the first coal was mined in 3/1903. It was served by sidings on the north side of the GNR Daybrook - Gedling line, ½ mile north-west of the former Gedling Station. Mapperley Landsale Wharf (SK 602463) was connected to the colliery by a ¾ mile long line which ran north west from the colliery. The final section was a 900yd long rope-worked incline, ascending at a gradient of 1 in 13. A locomotive, usually AB 1000, was hauled up and down this incline at the start and end of each week to shunt the depot. Another branch crossed the GNR to serve tips south east of that line and a landsale depot alongside Arnold Lane. Gedling was further developed in the last years before nationalisation. The colliery was vested in the NCB, East Midland Division, Area No.6, 1/1/1947.

Gauge : 4ft 8½in

No.1	CATHERINE	0-6-0ST	OC	AB	1000	1903	New	(2)
	AUDREY	0-6-0ST	OC	P	1253	1911	New	(2)
	-	0-4-0ST	OC	P	451	1886	(a)	(1)
	QUEEN	0-4-0ST	OC	AB	1784	1923	(b)	(2)

(a) with Joseph Pugsley, dealers, Bristol, from c/1901 until after 10/1907 (advertised 'at work near Nottingham' in this period); earlier Bristol Gas Co, Stapleton Road Gasworks, Bristol. Possibly at Gedling Colliery on hire during 1902-4 or later.
(b) ex Hough & Sons, Newtown Boiler Works, Wigan, Lancs, /1932; earlier Bromilow, Foster & Co Ltd, Ashton's Green Colliery, St. Helens, Lancs (where for sale 2/1932).

(1) later with Combustion Engineering Co Ltd, Derby.
(2) to NCB, East Midlands Division, Area No.6, with site, 1/1/1947.

BARBER, WALKER & CO LTD
Barber, Walker & Co until 2/4/1918

The Barber and Walker families claim their participation in the coal mining industry as going back to 1680. The formal partnership dates from 28/9/1787. By 1836, the company were working a number of collieries in the Eastwood, Underwood and Brinsley areas, all of which were connected to the Cromford Canal at Langley Mill by tramways ('gang roads' in local parlance). Other collieries at Strelley and Billborough were connected to the Nottingham Canal at Cossall or Wollaton by tramways and branch canals. Only the workings centred on Eastwood and Langley Mill continued into the railway age. After an unsuccessful boring near Thurgarton in 1898, the company's next venture was Bentley Colliery in south Yorkshire, followed by development of the moribund Harworth Colliery project from 1917. The collieries were vested in the NCB from 1/1/1947, and the company was formally wound up on 27/7/1954.

References : "The Colliery Guardian", 20/5/1892
"250 Years in Coal - The History of the Barber, Walker & Co Ltd", C.H. Whitelock, Barber, Walker, c1954

EASTWOOD COLLIERIES and RAILWAYS   L10
Comprising :
  BEGGARLEE COLLIERY & WORKSHOPS (Colliery 1838 - 1873)   SK 476478
  BRINSLEY COLLIERY   (pre 1855 - NCB)   SK 464488
  CORDY LANE COLLIERY (closed by 1880)   SK 467497
  HIGH PARK COLLIERY (1854 - NCB)   SK 487487
  HILL TOP COLLIERY   (purchased 1857, worked 1866 - 1872)   SK 477468
  LANGLEY MILL LOCOSHED (pre 1931)   SK 454477
  MOOR GREEN COLLIERY (1868 - NCB)   SK 479478
  SELSTON (orginally **UNDERWOOD**) **COLLIERY** (1852 - NCB) SK 467505
  (OLD) WATNALL (LARKFIELD) COLLIERY (c1854 - 1879)   SK 507448
  (NEW) WATNALL COLLIERY (1872 - NCB)   SK 508480
  WILLEY LANE COLLIERY   (1840 - 1876)   SK 473500

In 1836, the company had a network of tramways or 'gang roads' extending north west from wharves on the Cromford Canal at Langley Mill (SK 454475) and on the Nottingham Canal to the south at SK 456470 to a junction at SK 464480. From there, one line ran north to collieries at SK 464494 (**BRINSLEY**) and SK 465505 (**PLAINSPOT**?). Branches ran east to SK 473500 (**WILLEY LANE**) and SK467487 (purpose unknown). The other line ran east from the junction to collieries at SK 468482 (**CONEYGREY?**) and SK 467468, ending at a place marked Beverlee (**BEGGARLEE**) engine. Many of these lines later became railways. At the same time there was a short isolated tramway in Watnall from a colliery (SK 501457) to a landsale yard (SK 504453). This did not survive into the railway era. After the opening in 1847 of the Midland Railway's Erewash Valley railway, those 'gang roads' still serving working collieries were converted into conventional railways. The first 35 chains of a line which curved to the east from north of Langley Mill & Eastwood station, formed the Midland Railway Beggarlee Branch and opened about 1849. Most of Barber, Walker's railway, which continued east from there, is said to have been constructed between 1850 and 1860. The company history gives 1855 as the date of introduction of the first locomotive, which predates any locomotives listed below.

The earliest plan seen dates from 1880, by which time a connection had been made from the up side of the GNR Pinxton Branch (opened 23/8/1875) by a south to east curve and by sidings which joined the colliery line just east of the end of the Midland Railway branch.

There was another connection from the down side which passed beneath the GNR main line to reach the same point (SK 456487). There was also a trailing connection, again passing beneath the GNR line, to the canal wharf where the Barber, Walker locoshed was then located. To complete the complex layout at this point, a second south to east curve from the GNR and a spur from the Midland Railway were connected to the start of the Butterley Co's **PLUMPTRE COLLIERY** branch. The Barber, Walker line ran east for ½ mile to a junction at SK 463480. There was a signal box at this point and the line thus far was fully signalled. One line headed north from here to pass to the east of **BRINSLEY COLLIERY**. This old colliery had been deepened in 1855 but was never a large producer and its sidings were minimal. After a further 1½ miles the line ended at **UNDERWOOD** (known as **SELSTON** from c1887) **COLLIERY**. This had been sunk between 1852 and 1855 and was deepened in 1880, when its ventilation system was combined with that of BRINSLEY. A tramway, gauge unknown, ran south from Underwood for ½ mile to the closed **CORDY LANE COLLIERY**, which, in 1880, may still have been a service shaft for UNDERWOOD. There was also a short branch which ran north east from the Underwood line to **WILLEY LANE COLLIERY** which had opened in 1840. It closed in 2/1876, but, in 1880, the railway was still intact. Two early collieries which lasted into the railway era, but which have not been accurately located, are **BEAUVALE (COPPICE** and **WATERSPOUT)**. They are believed to have been close to the Underwood line, north of BRINSLEY COLLIERY, and to have closed 1863-4. Nothing else is known.

The line which ran east from the junction reached **BEGGARLEE Workshops** on its north side, after ¾ mile. There had been a colliery on this site from 1838 until 1873. A branch ran south from this point for half a mile to **HILL TOP COLLIERY**. This was purchased by Barber, Walker in 1857 from Fullard and Richardson, who had sunk it. It was not worked until 1866 and closed in 1872. The site thereafter became a rail served landsale yard. In 1880, this branch also served a small brickworks at SK 478476, on its east side, just south of the junction. It had closed by 1913. The main railway turned north east from Beggarlee almost immediately reaching **MOOR GREEN COLLIERY**, which had been sunk in 1868, with installation of sidings completed in 1872. After a further ¾ mile, **HIGH PARK COLLIERY** was located to the north west of the line. Sinking of this commenced in 8/1854 but difficulties with water delayed opening until 1861. Thereafter it was a very profitable pit, being the first of Barber, Walker's to mine 1000 tons per day. From High Park the railway curved south east to **(NEW) WATNALL COLLIERY**, which was sunk between 1872 and 1876. By 1880, a brickworks had been built to the east of it. From here the private line ran south for another 1½ miles to end at **(OLD) WATNALL COLLIERY**, located east of Kimberley village. This had been sunk in the 1850s and closed in 10/1879 (abandoned 26/1/1880). OLD WATNALL COLLIERY was 5¾ miles from Langley Mill along the private railway, making this the longest such line in Nottinghamshire. In 1892 it was reputed to have 11 miles of running lines and nearly 11 miles of sidings. It is not known at what date the line had been completed to Old Watnall. By 1880, both the GNR and Midland Railway had lines at Kimberley. The former company's line opened in 1875. It passed under the private line in a tunnel, north of Old Watnall Colliery and made a steep connection to a triangular junction from ½ mile east of the tunnel. This served both old and new collieries. The Midland Railway, in 12/1877, opened its New Watnall Colliery Branch which curved north from its line, 1 mile east of Kimberley station, and ran parallel with the private line to reach the colliery after 1¼ miles. The private railway served all Barber, Walker's Collieries at this period except two. These were **EASTWOOD COLLIERY** (SK 460460), details of which are in the Non-locomotive Section, and **COTMANHAY COLLIERY** (SK 465450) which was in Derbyshire.

The complex layout of Barber, Walker's lines altered little after 1880, most changes being negative. The closed Willey Lane, Cordy Lane and (Old) Watnall Collieries, and their railways, had been removed by 1895 but by the same date, a new landsale yard had been established at Watnall (SK 505454). This was served by sidings which ran west from the private line, north of the triangular junction with the GNR. This yard was mechanised in 1932, with wagon tippler, conveyors and bunkers. The screens at Selston were renewed in 1906 and again in 1914, after which 8 loading tracks were provided. The brickworks east of Watnall Colliery were disused by 1913 but a large modern plant was built to the south by 1925. At Beggarlee, the engineering activities of the company were centralised with the building of new stores in 1919 and workshops in 1922. A locoshed, to hold nine locomotives, was built in 1931, replacing that at Langley Mill. A washery was provided at Moor Green from 1924. By about 1930, coal winding had ceased at Brinsley and High Park, the coal being transferred underground to be wound at Selston and Moor Green, respectively, where surface facilities were better. The Butterley Co's Plumptre Colliery had closed in 1912 and for a short while, its branch was realigned to the west to serve a small quarry. By 1938, the site was being used by Barber, Walker as a tip. A siding for the discharge of standard gauge wagons had been put in, west of the Selston line, at SK 464481 and a tramway, gauge unknown, was dumping dirt on the tip. Passenger services for mine workers were operated from at least 1874, when four old coaches were purchased from the LNWR. Originally these operated over the whole system, including the Hill Top branch. In 1946, six trains per day, comprising two bogie coaches, were operated from Langley Mill (just short of the Ripley to Eastwood road crossing) to Old Watnall coal wharf. One train per day, comprising one bogie coach, was then being worked from Langley Mill to Selston.

At Vesting Day a scheme was in progress at Moor Green to install locomotives underground in conjunction with the development of the Low Main seam. To free capacity for this at Moor Green shafts, a surface drift was driven from High Park workings to Moor Green Colliery yard and a narrow gauge tub line, with a steam rope haulage engine, was installed there in 1945. At about the same time, The Ministry of Fuel and Power, Directorate of Opencast Coal Production, set up a rail served Disposal Point at Watnall, on the north side of the Watnall LNER connection (see NCB Section). The canal wharf at Langley Mill still saw some use after the remainder of the Cromford Canal was abandoned in 1944. The Nottingham Canal had been abandoned in 1937. BRINSLEY, HIGH PARK, MOOR GREEN, SELSTON and WATNALL Collieries, together with BEGGARLEE WORKSHOPS and WATNALL BRICKWORKS (which had from, at the latest, 1925 been operated by a subsidiary company, **Watnall Brick & Tile Co Ltd**), were vested in the NCB, East Midlands Division, Area No.5, from 1/1/1947.

Reference : "The Industrial Locomotive", Nos. 87 and 88, Industrial locomotive Society, 1998

Gauge : 4ft 8½in

1	0-6-0T	IC	SS	1321	1862	New	(2)
4	0-6-0T	IC	MW	141	1865	New	(1)
6	0-6-0ST	IC	K	1856	1873	New	(4)
5	0-6-0ST	IC	K	1996	1874	New	(6)
7	0-6-0T	IC	RS	(? 634)	1851	(a)	(3)
8	0-6-0ST	IC	RWH	1947	1883	New	(6)
4	0-6-0T	IC	K	3501	1891	New	(6)
3	0-6-0T	IC	K	3520	1893	New	
	reb		AB		1920		(6)
7	0-6-0T	IC	K	3918	1900	New	(6)
No.9	0-6-0T	OC	AB	1649	1919	New	(5)
9	0-6-0WT	OC	Hohen	3283	1914	(b)	(4)

Note that Kitson locomotives returned to K for overhaul in the period up to 1905. [Return dates from K were 17/7/1902 (K 1856); 10/12/1897, 17/11/1903, 27/10/1905 (K 3501) and 7/9/00, 22/8/1904 (K3520).] K 1996 and 3918 were both eventually fitted with Belpaire boilers, possibly in 5/1945 and c9/1942 respectively.

(a)   ex LNWR 1801, 3/1875.
(b)   ex Harworth Colliery or MoM, Chilwell, /1919.

(1) replaced /1901, disposal unknown.
(2) s/s by /1892 or by /1919.
(3) s/s after /1892, by /1900.
(4) to Harworth Colliery, after 12/1919.
(5) to Harworth Colliery, after 2/1920, by 11/1922.
(6) to NCB, East Midlands Division, Area No.5, with site, 1/1/1947.

Gauge : 3ft 6in   (Used underground, in the Low Main Seam)

PIONEER	0-6-0DMF	HC	DM634	1946	New	(1)
VANGUARD	0-6-0DMF	HC	DM635	1946	New	(1)

(1) to NCB, East Midlands Division, Area No.5, with site, 1/1/1947.

HARWORTH COLLIERY, Harworth   B11
Harworth Main Colliery Co Ltd until 18/5/1922   SK 627913

This company was registered 2/7/1917 to take over from H.M. Government the works confiscated from the Northern Union Mining Co Ltd (which see). The original shaft was filled in and the sinking of the first new one commenced 4/6/1919. Coal was reached on 2/11/1923 and sinking was completed on 5/12/1923. The colliery was served by sidings at the west end of an LNER branch (built 6/1922 - 10/1923 by H. Symington & Sons Ltd, which see) which ran west from a junction at Scrooby, 1½ miles north of Ranskill station. This branch replaced a temporary overland line completed in 3/1914 for colliery construction purposes and left in situ until the permanent line was built. In 1929 a branch of the South Yorks Joint Railway (LMSR & LNER) was opened (built Mitchell Bros, Sons & Co Ltd, which see). This ran for 3½ miles, from Tickhill, south and then east, to the colliery where connection was made with the LNER line. From 1936, the locomotives also worked traffic at the adjacent coke works.

The colliery was vested in the NCB, East Midlands Division, Area No.3, 1/1/1947.

Gauge : 4ft 8½in

No.1		0-6-0WT	OC	Hohen	3283	1914	(a)	(1)
	HARWORTH No.2	0-4-0ST	OC	HC	1397	1919	New	(1)
3		0-6-0T	OC	AB	1649	1919	(b)	(1)
4	(HARWORTH)	0-4-0ST	OC	HC	476	1897		
		reb	HC			1905	(c)	(1)

(a) (possibly ex MoM, Chilwell, /1919; to Moor Green Colliery, /1919) ; ex Moor Green Colliery, after 12/1919.
(b) ex Moor Green Colliery, c/1921.
(c) ex Bentley Colliery, Doncaster, Yorks (WR), by /1943.

(1) to NCB, East Midlands Division, Area No.3, with site, 1/1/1947.

Gauge : 2ft 6in (Underground)

-	4wBEF	MV		1934	New	(1)
-	4wBEF	MV		1934	New	(1)
-	4wBEF	MV		1934	New	(1)

(1) to NCB, East Midlands Division, Area No.3, with site, 1/1/1947,

BAWTRY COKE OVENS & BY PRODUCTS PLANT, Harworth   B12
(also known as HARWORTH COKING PLANT, Bircotes)

This plant, opened in 1936, lay immediately to the south of Harworth Colliery and occupied a 20 acre site. The plant shared siding facilities with the colliery, and traffic was worked by the colliery locos. The loco hauled the coke car between the discharge side of the ovens and the quenching tower.

Gauge : 4ft 8½in

-		0-4-0WE	GB	1364	1935	New	(1)

(1) to NCB, East Midlands Division, Coking Plants, with site, 1/1/1947.

BEESTON BOILER CO LTD
BEESTON WORKS, Beeston, Nottingham.   V13
Beeston Foundry Co Ltd (registered 4/1893) until c/1934   SK 537367
Beeston Foundry Co from ?

The company was founded in 1880 and moved to this site in 1897. The works occupied 28 acres and, by 1904, was served by sidings on the north side of the BR Nottingham - Beeston line, 500yds east of Beeston Station. The standard gauge sidings were shunted by main line locomotives. Rail traffic ceased by 1975 and the works later closed.

(Note : a 4wBE of standard gauge was reported here 4/1968, said to be by GB. It was later deleted from the records having been declared to be a self propelled transfer car. Nothing further is known.)

Gauge : 2ft 1in

5	LITTLE GEORGE	0-4-0BE		WR	1298	1938	New	(1)

(1) Brockham Museum Association, Dorking, Surrey, 24/10/1975, via Alan Keef Ltd, Bampton, Oxon.

BEESTON & STAPLEFORD URBAN DISTRICT COUNCIL
BEESTON SEWAGE WORKS, Lilac Grove, Beeston   V14
(orig. Beeston Urban District Council)   SK 542366

Located south east of Beeston station but with no standard gauge connection, this site was served by an internal tramway which ran from the works at SK 542366 onto open land to the south east at SK 543361. The plant and locomotive are believed to have been transferred from the predecessors of the Boots Co Ltd, (which see) prior to 1937. Rail traffic was replaced by road transport in 1967. The Water Act 1973 transferred the responsibility for water reclamation to the newly created water authorities and Severn Trent Water Authority took over the works, without rail traffic, from 1/4/1974.

Gauge : 2ft 0in

-		4wPM	L	3681	1931	(a)	Scr /1959
-		4wPM	L	11435	1937	New	Scr /1959
-		4wDM	LB	44052	1959	New	(1)

(a)   ex Boots Pure Drug Co Ltd, Beeston.

(1)   to Wilsthorpe Light Rly., West Park, Long Eaton, Derbys, 30/11/1968.

BENNERLEY IRON CO LTD
BENNERLEY IRONWORKS, Awsworth M15
E.P.Davis until 7/1924 SK 472440
Awsworth Iron Co until wound up 3/1888

Located east of the Midland Railway Erewash Valley line at Bennerley Junction, this site comprised in 1879 the small **AWSWORTH IRONWORKS**, the closed (possibly as early as 1867) **BENNERLEY COLLIERY** and a brickworks. All of these were connected to the Midland's Digby Branch by a short spur on the west side, near to its junction with the Bennerley and Bulwell line. There was a short narrow gauge incline from the brick works into a clay hole to the east. In 1881 the ironworks was reconstructed with three blast furnaces and on change of ownership in 1888 became known as the **BENNERLEY IRONWORKS**. By 1899, and probably from 1881, the ironworks occupied the whole site, including the former colliery and brickworks. From some time after 1878, there was a GNR connection known as the Awsworth Colliery & Ironworks branch which ran from west of its Awsworth Station to the works. Prior to 1888 the Awsworth Colliery, located ½ mile to the north east, (see Awsworth Colliery Co Ltd entry) was in the same ownership and probably worked by an ironworks locomotive. The furnaces were dismantled by Thos.W. Ward Ltd in 1934 and in 7/1935, Ward's subsidiary, Bennerley Slag and Tarmacadam Co, was removing the tip. Part of the site later became the Bennerley Opencast Disposal Point (see NCB Section).

Gauge : 4ft 8½in

1		0-4-0ST	OC	HE	190	1878	New	(2)
3		0-4-0ST	OC	HE	264	1882	New	(1)
2		0-4-0ST	OC	AE	1340	1889	New	s/s
		0-4-0ST	OC	P	470	1888	(a)	s/s
3	BENNERLEY	0-4-0ST	OC	P	580	1894	(b)	s/s
	DEWSBURY	0-6-0ST	IC	HE	196	1878	(c)	(3)
4		0-4-0ST	OC	P	547	1892	(d)	s/s
No.5		0-4-0ST	OC	P	1479	1917	New	(4)

(a)   ex Erewash Valley Ironworks, Derbys, by 5/1901.
(b)   ex Awsworth Colliery Co Ltd, by 5/1901.
(c)   ex J.P. Edwards, contractor, by 10/1907.
(d)   ex Upper Forest & Worcester Steel & Tinplate Works Ltd, Morriston, Glam, per J.F. Wake, dealer, Darlington, after repairs at Peckett, Bristol, 5/1909 to 9/1909.

(1)   to Blackwell Colliery Co Ltd, Alfreton Colliery, via Markham & Co, Chesterfield, (repairs) 9/1886.
(2)   later with T. Naylor, contractor, Buxton; then at S. Taylor, Holderness Limeworks, Peak Dale, Derbys, by 10/1897.
(3)   to Erewash Valley Ironworks, Derbys, c/1919 (after 12/9/1919).
(4)   s/s after 11/1928.

BENNERLEY SLAG & TARMACADAM CO
BENNERLEY IRONWORKS SITE, Awsworth M16
SK 472440

The site and tips of the closed Bennerley Ironworks (see preceding entry) were being worked by this concern, the proprietor of which was Thos.W. Ward Ltd, by 5/1935. The sidings were brought back into use and locomotives employed until c1940.

Gauge : 4ft 8½in

No.2		0-4-0ST	OC	AE	1500	1906	(a)	s/s
No.4		0-4-0ST	OC	AE	1470	1905	(b)	s/s
	ASHBURY	0-4-0ST	OC	AE	1610	1911	(c)	(1)

(a) earlier Denby Iron & Coal Co Ltd, Denby Ironworks, Derbys; purchased by Thos.W. Ward Ltd, with works, /1930; at Bennerley by 5/1935.
(b) earlier Denby Iron & Coal Co Ltd, Denby Ironworks, Derbys; purchased by Thos.W. Ward Ltd, with works, /1930; at Bennerley by 7/1935.
(c) ex Thos.W. Ward Ltd, Grays Works, Essex, by 5/1935; orig Metropolitan Amalgamated Carriage & Wagon Co Ltd, Ashbury Works, Manchester.

(1) to Thos.W. Ward Ltd, Templeborough Works, Sheffield, c5/1940 (purchased 2/5/1940). Used as hire loco until sold to Ketton Portland Cement Co Ltd, Ketton, Rutland, No.5, 4/1946

BESTWOOD SAND LTD
BESTWOOD SAND PITS N17
? SK 560470

This site first appears under the above title in a quarries directory for 1948 (not listed in 1943) and is probably the same sand quarry listed, in 1928 only, as operated by Bestwood Coal & Iron Co Ltd. It has not been positively located but a small quarry, with narrow gauge track, shown on Ordnance Survey plans of 1913 and 1950, is a strong possibility. This was located south-east of Bestwood Colliery, adjacent to the headshunt of the colliery empties siding. (See also NCB Section.)

Gauge : 2ft 0in

-	4wDM	RH	177607	1937	(a)	(1)

(a) Spares, ordered 12/11/1943 by former owner, Wansford Quarries Ltd, Wansford, Cambs (where rail operations ceased c/1943), were to be sent to W.J. Simms, Sons & Cooke Ltd, Spring Close Works, Lenton, Nottingham, from whom Bestwood may have purchased the locomotive.

(1) to Thos.W. Ward Ltd, Templeborough, Sheffield, 24/6/1948; resold, after repairs, to London & Scandinavian Metallurgical Co Ltd, for shipment from Liverpool, 25/6/1949

BILSTHORPE BRICK CO LTD
BILSTHORPE BRICKWORKS   G18
(Innes Lee Industries)   SK 658607
British Steel Corporation, Stanton & Staveley Group until 29/3/1970
Stanton & Staveley Ltd until 29/7/1967
Stanton Ironworks Co Ltd until 1/6/1962.

The brickworks was opened in the 1920s, initially to provide materials for the sinking of Bilsthorpe Colliery and the erection of colliery housing. It was located south east of Bilsthorpe Colliery to which it was connected by a standard gauge siding worked by the colliery locomotives. For some time from 1931 lines extended into the housing estates. A narrow gauge system operated from the works eastwards, into the clay hole. This tramway was originally 2ft 0in gauge, but was relaid to 3ft 0in gauge c1960 to suit an available locomotive. It was altered again to 2ft 8½in for the same reason after 8/1964 but reverted to 3ft 0in in 1968 when a new locomotive was purchased.

Standard gauge rail traffic ceased in the 1960s and the narrow gauge system was replaced by mobile plant in 1978.

Gauge : 3ft 0in

| | | 4wDM | RH | 186340 | 1937 | (a) | (1) |
| | | 4wDM | MR | 40S323 | 1968 | New | (2) |

(a)   ex Stewarts & Lloyds Minerals Ltd, Nuthall Sandpits, c/1960.

(1)   scrapped on site by Ilkeston Metal & Waste Co Ltd, Ilkeston, Derbys, /1967.
(2)   to M.E. Engineering Ltd, Cricklewood, Greater London, 28/2/1980.

Gauge : 2ft 8½in

| 8418/18 | 4wDM | RH | 170205 | 1934 | (a) | (1) |
| 8418/19 | 4wDM | RH | 174140 | 1935 | (a) | s/s /1969 |

(a)   ex Stewarts & Lloyds Minerals Ltd, South Witham Ironstone Mine, Lincs, 8/1964.

(1)   to Stanton Ironworks, Ilkeston, Derbys, /1967.

Gauge : 2ft 4in (served tunnel kilns and brick dryers*)

| | | 4wBE | Bilsthorpe | | c1950 | New | (1) |
| (3720/36) | | 2w-2.BE | Bilsthorpe | | c1966 | New | (2) |

*   these are believed not to have been locomotives in the accepted sense but transfer cars carrying brick cars.

(1)   scrapped on site by Ilkeston Metal & Waste Co Ltd, Ilkeston, Derbys. /1967.
(2)   to M.E. Engineering Ltd, Cricklewood, Greater London, 28/2/1980.

Gauge : 2ft 0in

| | | 4wDM | MR | 8621 | 1941 | (a) | (1) |
| | | 4wDM | MR | | | (b) | (2) |

(a) ex MR, c/1953; earlier WD, reconditioned by MR, 12/1950.
(b) ex MR (hire), c/1959.

(1) to Stanton Ironworks, Ilkeston, Derbys, c/1959; sold to Gaunt(?), Kirkby-in-Ashfield, for scrap.
(2) returned to MR, c/1960.

BLUE CIRCLE INDUSTRIES plc
Blue Circle Industries Ltd until 8/10/1981
Associated Portland Cement Manufacturers Ltd until 31/5/1978

BEESTON CEMENT TERMINAL   V19
SK 535364

Standard gauge sidings served this cement terminal (opened after 1956), which occupied the former BR goods yard on the north side of the Beeston - Nottingham line, immediately east of Beeston station. Shunting was carried out by a road tractor with buffer beams fitted fore and aft (In the late 1980s, a County 1450 tractor, registration FRC 14V, was used). The terminal had closed by 1/1997.

Gauge : 4ft 8½in

(D2865)		0-4-0DH	YE	2848	1961	(a) (1)

(a) ex Kilvington Gypsum Works, for storage, /1984 (after 4/1984) (not used at Beeston).

(1) to Vic Berry Ltd, scrap merchants, Leicester, by 10/12/1984; scrapped 5/1985

KILVINGTON GYPSUM WORKS   U20
Associated Portland Cement Manufacturers Ltd until 31/5/1978   SK 797435
Nottinghamshire Gypsum Products Ltd until after 3/1961, by 1969

A gypsum works and quarries, opened about 1950, were served by a siding, which was in place by 1949, on the west side of the BR Newark - Bottesford West Jct. line, 2½ miles south of the former Cotham Station. Shunting was by BR until c1965. Thereafter a locomotive, stabled in the open at SK 798435, was used. Standard gauge rail traffic ceased c8/1982. The narrow gauge line ran between the works and quarries to the south. Quarrying ceased 23/12/1983, but the line was retained to remove stockpiles until the works closed on 30/3/1984.

Gauge : 4ft 8½in

-	4wDM	RH	305308	1952	(a)	Scr /1971
(D2865)	0-4-0DH	YE	2848	1961	(b)	(1)

(a) ex William Rigley & Sons (Nottingham) Ltd, Bulwell Forest Wagon Works, Bulwell, Nottingham, c/1965.
(b) ex British Railways, Goole, D2865; left Goole after 10/5/1970, by 7/1970 when reported standing at Newark goods yard; arrived. Kilvington, 9/1970.

(1) to Beeston Cement Terminal, /1984 (by 4/1984).

Gauge : 3ft 0in

No.	Name	Type	Builder	Works No.	Date	Origin	Fate
No.1	(f. 21)	0-6-0DM	RH	281291	1949	(a)	(4)
	THE CUB	4wDM	JF	3900015	1948	(b)	(1)
		4wVBT VCG	S	6896	1927	(c)	Scr 4/1954
(2)		0-6-0DM	RH	281290	1949	(d)	(5)
No.1		2-4-0DM	JF	20684	1935	(e)	(3)
No.2		2-4-0DM	JF	20685	1935	(e)	(2)
	-	4wDH	MR	102T007	1974	New	(6)
	-	4wDH	SMH	102T016	1976	New	(6)

(a) ex APCM Ltd, Ufton Works, Warwicks, /1952 (by 17/3/1953).
(b) ex G.& T. Earle Ltd, Humber Works, Hull, (loan), 3/1954.
(c) ex G.& T. Earle Ltd, Humber Works, Hull, 3/1954.
(d) ex G.& T. Earle Ltd, Humber Works, Hull, /1959 (by 10/11/1959).
(e) ex APCM Ltd, Harbury Works, Warwicks, 11/1970.

(1) returned to Humber Works, Hull, Yorks (ER), 6/1954.
(2) to Midland Rly. Co Ltd, Butterley, Derbys, 5/10/1974.
(3) to Midland Rly. Co Ltd, Butterley, Derbys, for spares, 5/10/1974.
(4) scrapped on site, weekend of 17/2/1984.
(5) to Northampton Loco Group, Irchester, Northants, 15/12/1984.
(6) to The Lord O'Neill, Shanes Castle, Randalstown, Antrim, Ulster, c12/1984, per Alan Keef Ltd.

BOLSOVER COLLIERY CO LTD

This company was registered on 20/1/1890 and sank the Derbyshire colliery of that name in 1890-1. Their first venture in Nottinghamshire was Mansfield Colliery, sunk in 1904-5, followed by three others. It became one of the largest colliery companies in the country.

CLIPSTONE COLLIERY   G21
SK 594632

Sinking of this colliery commenced in 1912 but was suspended from 1914 to 1920 due to the First World War. Coal was produced in 1922. The first rail connection was by a branch from the Mansfield Railway near Rufford Junction, 4 miles east of its later Mansfield Station. This was authorised by that company's act of 1914 and was opened on 13/6/1916, together with the connection to the War Department's **Clipstone Camp Military Railway** (which see). This was partly located on the colliery site. After the removal of the camp, c1919, its branch was incorporated into the developing colliery rail system which then ran north from the Mansfield Railway before diverging west to the empties and east to the fulls sidings. The opening on 29/12/1928 of the LMSR branch which ran north from Rufford Colliery to end at Clipstone, in separate empties and loaded branches, gave the colliery an alternative rail access. Dirt was originally tipped to the south east, using the standard gauge railway, but this was superseded by an aerial ropeway. There was also a briquetting plant which, together with the colliery, was vested in the NCB, East Midlands Division, Area No.3, from 1/1/1947.

Gauge : 4ft 8½in

CLIPSTONE No.1	0-4-0ST	OC	HL	3137	1915	New (a)	(1)
CLIPSTONE No.2	0-4-0ST	OC	HL	3630	1925	New	(1)

Note that HL 3389 and MW 1774 were here on loan from Rufford Colliery at unspecified dates.

(a) ordered new for Clipstone but probably used first at another colliery until rail connection was established.

(1) to NCB, East Midlands Division, Area No.3, with site, 1/1/1947.

Gauge : 2ft 4in (Underground)

-	0-4-0DMF		HE	3299	1945	New	(1)
-	0-4-0DMF		HE	3300	1945	New	(1)

(1) to NCB, East Midlands Division, Area No.3, with site, 1/1/1947.

MANSFIELD COLLIERY, Forest Town, Mansfield   G22
(also known originally as CROWN FARM COLLIERY)   SK 570616

Colliery sunk in 1904-5 and served by sidings at the end of the Midland Railway's Mansfield Colliery Branch (built by Hemingway & Co, no known locos; opened week ending 11/1/1905) which ran north for 1¼ miles from the Mansfield - Southwell line, 2 miles north west of Rainworth station. From 6/6/1913, the colliery was also served by sidings on the south side of the Mansfield Railway (GCR) which passed immediately to the north (see Baldry, Yerburgh & Hutchinson). These sidings were 2 miles east of Mansfield Central station. In 1914 the west side of the colliery was being used as a contractor's depot for the Mansfield Railway construction westwards to Mansfield. Some dirt tipping by standard gauge railway took place on the east side but later an aerial ropeway ran to a tip south of the colliery

The colliery was vested in NCB, East Midlands Division, Area No.3, 1/1/1947.

Gauge : 4ft 8½in

SIR HENRY	0-4-0ST	OC	YE	948	1908	New	(1)
MANSFIELD No.2	0-4-0ST	OC	HL	3052	1914	New	(2)
THORESBY No.1	0-4-0ST	OC	HL	3591	1925	(a)	(3)
DIANA	0-4-0ST	OC	HL	3912	1937	(b)	(3)

(a) ex Thoresby Colliery, by 11/1938.
(b) ex Thoresby Colliery, /1937.

(1) to Rufford Colliery, c/1936; returned, c/1936; scrapped, /1937.
(2) to Bolsover Colliery, Bolsover, Derbys, by 3/12/1943.
(3) to NCB, East Midlands Division, Area No.3, with site, 1/1/1947.

Gauge : 3ft 0in (Underground)

-	0-6-0DMF		HE	3328	1946	New	(2)
-	0-6-0DMF		HE	3329	1946	New	(2)
-	0-4-0DMF		HE	3332	1945	New	(1)

(1) to Bolsover Colliery, Bolsover, Derbys, by 1/1/1947.
(2) to NCB, East Midlands Division, Area No.3, with site, 1/1/1947.

RUFFORD COLLIERY

G23
SK 597604

This colliery, sunk between 1911 and 1913, first produced coal in 1915. It was originally at the north end of the Midland Railway Rufford Colliery branch which opened 20/6/1912 (see Naylor Brothers). This ran north east for 1 mile from ¾ mile north west of Rainworth Station. This line was later extended by the LMSR to Clipstone (opened 29/12/1928). Rufford Colliery was also served by connections from a GCR branch (opened 8/7/1918) which ran south from Clipstone and which was later extended to Blidworth Colliery (see Baldry, Yerburgh & Hutchinson). Dirt tipping by narrow and standard gauge railways and by an aerial ropeway was practised at different times.

The colliery was vested in NCB, East Midlands Division, Area No.3, 1/1/1947.

Gauge : 4ft 8½in

RUFFORD No.1	0-4-0ST	OC	MW	1774	1912	New	(2)
RUFFORD No.2	0-4-0ST	OC	HL	3389	1919	New	(3)
SIR HENRY	0-4-0ST	OC	YE	948	1908	(a)	(1)

(a) ex Mansfield Colliery, c/1936.

(1) to Mansfield Colliery, c/1936.
(2) to Bolsover Colliery, /1934; returned, c/1940; to NCB, East Midlands Division, Area No.3, with site, 1/1/1947.
(3) to NCB, East Midlands Division, Area No.3, with site, 1/1/1947.

THORESBY COLLIERY, Edwinstowe

G24
SK 636676

Sinking of this colliery commenced in 1925, coal being reached on 5/5/1928 with production commencing in that year. The colliery was served by sidings which ran east from the end of an LNER branch running north for ¾ mile from its Edwinstowe - Ollerton line, 1 mile west of Ollerton Station.

The colliery was vested in NCB, East Midlands Division, Area No.3, 1/1/1947.

Gauge : 4ft 8½in

THORESBY No.1	0-4-0ST	OC	HL	3591	1925	New	(1)
TOPHARD	0-4-0ST	OC	P	1791	1932	New	(3)
DIANA	0-4-0ST	OC	HL	3912	1937	New	(2)
JOHN	0-4-0ST	OC	P	1976	1939	New	(3)

Note that HL 3137 and MW 1774 were here on loan, from Clipstone and Rufford Collieries respectively, at unspecified dates.

(1) to Mansfield Colliery by 11/1938.
(2) to Mansfield Colliery, /1937.
(3) to NCB, East Midlands Division, Area No.3, with site, 1/1/1947.

THE BOOTS CO LTD
BEESTON WORKS
Boots Pure Drug Co Ltd until /1970
Boot & Co Ltd (registered 7/1883) until 7/11/1888.

V25
SK 545363

This company of manufacturing chemists was founded in Nottingham in 1888 by Jesse Boot. A factory was opened in 1892 in Island Street, north of Eastcroft Gasworks, Nottingham. A rail loading dock adjacent to the gasworks, connected to the GNR, was installed. About 1925, and for a short period thereafter, a private siding west of the LMSR Carrington Street Goods Depot was also being used. Boots established the first part of what was to become a large works on the 340 acre Beeston site with a soap factory in 1928 followed by other developments in 1930. The works was served by sidings which connected with the south east side of the LMSR Nottingham - Beeston line, 700 yards east of Beeston Station. A narrow gauge line was located on the south-east corner of the works and in 1955 ran south for 300 yards from SK 546366. This is believed to have been the 1ft 8in gauge line. The 2ft 0in gauge line was located west of the works at an effluent treatment plant. This was transferred to Beeston Urban District Council (which see) by 1937. Standard gauge rail traffic ceased in 5/1981 and the remaining track was donated to the Midland Railway Trust, Butterley, Derbys, and lifted during 1990.

Gauge : 4ft 8½in

No.1		0-4-0F	OC	AB	1984	1930	New	(3)
No.2	PNB292	0-4-0F	OC	AB	2008	1935	New	(4)
3		0-4-0ST	OC	AB	2166	1944	New	(1)
4		0-4-0DM		JF	4210037	1950	New	(2)
	B7211	0-4-0DE		RH	384139	1955	New	(4)

A Sentinel 4wVBT VCG loco was demonstrated here in 1953 or early 1954. Possible identities are S 9398/1950, S 9538/1952 or S 9561/1953.

(1) to United Glass Bottle Manufacturers Ltd, St.Helens, Lancs, 12/1956.
(2) to Whatlings Ltd, operators of NCBOE, Kelty Disposal Point, Fife, /1958.
(3) to Foxfield Light Railway, Dilhorne, Staffs, 5/6/1972.
(4) to The Midland Railway Trust Ltd, Ripley, Derbys, 12/1/1982.

Gauge : 2ft 0in

	-	4wPM	L	3681	1931	New	(1)

(1) to Beeston & Stapleford U.D.C., Beeston Sewage Works, Lilac Grove, Beeston.

Gauge : 1ft 8in

	-	4wDM	FH	2747	1943	(a)	s/s
	-	4wDM	FH	2742	1943	(b)	s/s

(a) ex FH 5/3/1947; originally Ministry of Supply; reconditioned and regauged by FH and consigned to Boots' shopfitting department, c/o engineers stores, Beeston.
(b) ex FH 11/3/1947; originally Ministry of Supply; reconditioned and regauged by FH and consigned to Boots' shopfitting department, c/o engineers stores, Beeston.

BRITISH GYPSUM LTD

This company was formed by the amalgamation from 1/4/1964 of all the gypsum interests of **British Plaster Board Industries Ltd** and which thereafter traded under the new company name. These companies had immediately prior to that date traded under the following titles;

    GYPROC LTD (incorporating from 1/4/1962,
        Cafferata & Co Ltd, Gypsum Mines Ltd and others outside Notts.)

    BRITISH PLASTER & BOARDS LTD (Incorporating from 30/10/1961,
        The Gotham Co Ltd, Marblaegis Ltd, J.W.Sheppard Ltd and others outside Notts.)

Prior to the above reorganisation, the five companies mentioned above had all been constituents of **The British Plaster Board Ltd** (registered 26/4/1917). The constituent companies, however, continued to trade under their old names from their date of joining BPB until the reorganisations of 1961 and 1962.

Brief historical notes are given below on each of the constituent companies which were active users of rail transport in Nottinghamshire, together with **Bell Rock Gypsum Industries Ltd** which was not acquired until 1967.

For convenience, all locomotive using locations operated by firms which subsequently became owned by British Gypsum Ltd are listed under the British Gypsum heading in this publication. A number of other gypsum mines and quarries which used tramways but had no known locomotives will be found in the Non-locomotive Section under the titles of their last operator.

ANDERSONS GYPSUM PRODUCTS LTD

The business was founded as D. Anderson & Son in 1849 and became D. Anderson & Son Ltd in 1879. It was based in Stretford, Manchester. Subsidiary company Andersons Gypsum Products Ltd operated its only rail served site, the Silver Seal Mine at Bunny, which had opened in 1938. Both companies became British Plaster Board subsidiaries in 1939, after which the works closed and the mine was operated by another BPB subsidiary, **Marblaegis Ltd**, until 30/10/1961. By that time, the rail system had long gone.

BELL ROCK GYPSUM INDUSTRIES LTD

This company was founded in 1947 to produce plaster panelled board at a plant in Chertsey, Surrey. By 1956, land with substantial underlying gypsum deposits was acquired at Staunton in the Vale and shortly afterwards, a quarry and plasterboard plant were established there. The company was absorbed by British Gypsum Ltd. in 1967

CAFFERATA & CO LTD

This company was founded in 1858 by William Cafferata, a Liverpool stockbroker. In 1862 he acquired the Beacon Hill site in Newark which included a boiler works, plaster mill, gypsum quarries and a brickworks. He continued producing boilers until 1868, both for his own use and for sale, the last Cafferata boiler being scrapped in 1920 in the Old Mill at Cafferata's Newark Plant.

In 1881, William's third son, Redmond Parker Cafferata, took over as director of the business, which became a limited company. As Beacon Hill Quarry was nearing exhaustion, a lease was taken on an existing quarry, 3 miles to the south at Hawton. This 158 acre site gave scope for future quarry extension. and a mill was later built there. The Barton Quarry, together with its wharf on the River Trent, was purchased in 1902. Land comprising Jericho Farm, east of Hawton, was bought in 1935 and a brickworks, quarry and later a plasterworks were opened there. In 12/1935 Cafferata and Co Ltd. became a subsidiary of the British Plaster Board, but continued to trade under its original name until 1/4/1962, when the title changed to Gyproc Ltd. The defunct site of the Belvoir and Newark Plaster Co Ltd, north of Hawton works, was purchased from later owners, Thos.W. Ward Ltd, in the early 1950s

THE GOTHAM CO LTD

The company was founded in December 1897 by Job Nightingale Derbyshire, when he acquired the Victoria Mineral & Plaster Company of Nottingham, which had operated a mine at Gotham. The mine was closed in 1899 but reopened in 1903 and later became known as Glebe Mine. In 1913 the company bought the mine, mill and business of the Cropwell Gypsum Mines Ltd, at Cropwell Bishop. In 1918 the company acquired the mill and mine at Thrumpton, where, after intermittent working, operations ceased in 1940. One other rail using activity, the Carlton Hill Brick Co Ltd, Nottingham, was acquired in 3/1919 and is mentioned in the Non-locomotive Section. The plaster mill adjacent to the Glebe Mine at Gotham was greatly enlarged over the years. In 2/1935 the company joined the British Plaster Board but retained its trading name until 30/10/1961 when it became part of British Plaster & Boards Ltd..

THE GYPSUM MINES LTD

This company was formed on 4/2/1903 by the amalgamation of the Kingston Gypsum Co Ltd, and the Sub-Wealden Gypsum Company Ltd, of Mountfield in Sussex. The former site remained the only one to operate in Nottinghamshire. The company joined the British Plaster Board in 7/1935 but continued to trade under its old name until 1/4/1962 when the title became Gyproc Ltd..

MARBLAEGIS LTD

This company was formed in 1914 to acquire the mine and mill at East Leake of the Brothers Patent Plaster Co Ltd. It became part of the British Plaster Board in 8/1935 and operation of Anderson's Silver Seal Mine was taken over from the 1939-45 period. The Marblaegis Mine at Rushcliffe, East Leake became the site of a large new plant built around 1950. The Marblaegis name was used until 30/10/1961 when the title became British Plaster & Boards Ltd.

J.W.SHEPPARD LTD

The Sheppard family were farmers in the Gotham district for many generations and their involvement in the gypsum industry dates back to the first half of the 19th century, when William Sheppard established a small gypsum mine on his farm at Redhill-on-Soar. In the early days rock was taken by horse and cart from the mine to the banks of the River Trent, where it was burnt and then broken up by hand. It was bagged and then sent down river by barge to the canal at Wilford, where it was sold.

William Sheppard moved his operation to Gotham, where he worked land leased from Lord Howe. In the 1870s Sheppard contracted to operate a mine at Gotham, and he transported the extracted mineral to a water-mill at Kegworth, some 3 or 4 miles away. The mine is believed to have been 'Winsers' (see Non-locomotive Section), of which his son, John Withers Sheppard is known to have been manager. The firm of J.W. Sheppard was formed in 1875 and, in 1903, they took over a mine in Gotham, which had been operated by James Ward of Nottingham. This mine had been sunk in Cuckoo Bush Hill, and became known as "Sheppards No.1 Mine (Cuckoo Bush)". In 1906 a mill was added. In 1909 Weldon Mine, which for a period was known as 'Sheppards No.2 Mine (Gotham Hill)', was acquired, with its own mill, from G.Stocker & Co Ltd. This mine had been operating since the 1860s . J.W. Sheppard traded as such, without becoming a limited company, until 30/3/1936. This was after the founder's death and at the time of becoming a British Plaster Board subsidiary. The company ceased trading at about the time of the reorganisation of 30/10/1961 which saw its remnants become part of British Plaster and Boards Ltd

References : "The History of BPB Industries", D. Jenkins, BPBI Ltd, 1973.
"The Railways of Newark on Trent", M.A. Vanns, Oakwood Press, 1999.

BRITISH GYPSUM LTD: locations using locomotives

BARTON GYPSUM MINES, Barton in Fabis. V26
Cafferata & Co Ltd until closure SK 527313
Exors. of Henry Green in /1895 and until 1902
H Green & Co in /1886
Green & Baker in /1885

The mine, which was a level, was opened shortly after 1877 on the north side of Gotham Hill and, by about 1880, had been connected by a tramway which ran north-west for 1½ miles to a wharf on the south bank of the River Trent, west of the village of Barton in Fabis. There were no subsequent changes in layout except for additional short sidings on to a tip north of the mine. Horses are presumed to have been used prior to the locomotives, both underground and on the surface tramway. A CLIFTON Gypsum mine was first listed in 1936. Its location is not known but manpower was common with Barton. It was still listed, without manpower, in 1945. BARTON mine was reported closed and all locomotives gone by 28/3/1955.

Much of the gypsum produced was processed at Newark, having been transported as far as Nottingham by barge and transhipped there to rail. In the opposite direction, materials including locomotive spares were, until 1945, consigned by rail to the LMSR Nottingham Canal sidings and then taken by the barge to Barton Plaster Wharf. The tramway between the river and the mine is believed to have closed about 1945. Thereafter gypsum and the spares went between Barton and Nottingham by lorry.

Gauge : 2ft 0in

-	4wPM	Dtz	709	1909	New (a)	(1)
-	4wPM	MR	1843	1919	New	s/s
-	4wDM	MR	5605	1931	New	(6)
-	4wDM	RH	166027	1932	(c)	(5)
-	4wDM	RH	172335	1935	New	(4)
-	4wDM	RH	192864	1939	(d)	(2)
-	4wDM	RH	198278	1939	(e)	(3)
-	4wDM	RH	175417	1936	(f)	(7)

NOTE that an "Otto" petrol loco was for sale at Barton Quarry, c/1920; this may well have referred to Dtz 709, although the actual disposal of the latter was much later.

(a) Exhibition loco displayed at Mining Exhibition, Manchester, 21/4/1911 and then sold to Cafferata & Co Ltd, Barton Mines.
(b) either ex MR, /1931, following rebuild, or ex Hawton Mine, c/1939.
(c) ex RH, Lincoln, where rebuilt from 1ft 8in gauge, after 17/10/1938, by 31/10/1939; earlier at Hawton Mine, Newark.
(d) ex Baldry, Yerburgh & Hutchinson Ltd, contrs., Lyness, Orkney, after 30/6/1943, by 18/11/1943.
(e) ex Hawton Works, Newark, after 4/5/1946, by 24/1/1947.
(f) ex Cropwell Bishop Mine, after c9/1949, by 3/1955.

(1) to Rhos Slate Quarry Co (Capel Curig) Ltd, Rhos Slate Quarry, Caerns, /1935
(2) to Long Meg Plaster & Mineral Co Ltd, Lazonby, Cumberland, after 28/7/1944, by 8/12/1948.
(3) to Cropwell Bishop Mine, after 18/2/1948, by 2/9/1949.
(4) to Gotham Co Ltd, Cropwell Bishop Mine after 2/10/1948, by 26/4/1950
(5) sold or scrapped after 15/11/1948, by 3/1955.
(6) to Long Meg Plaster & Mineral Co Ltd, Lazonby, Cumberland, 7/1949.
(7) to Cropwell Bishop Mine, by 3/1955.

BEACON HILL PLASTER WORKS, Beacon Hill, Newark   P27
(also known as the GREAT NORTHERN PLASTER WORKS)   SK 809541
Gyproc Ltd until 1/4/1964
Cafferata & Co Ltd until 31/3/1962
Newark Plaster Co until /1858

In 1853 both Robert Lineker and Brown & Rastrick were listed as Plaster merchants at Beacon Hill. By 1858 the Newark Plaster Co had either acquired one of these or built its own works there. This works was then known as the Great Northern Works and was located east of the GNR (which opened 7/1852), south of Newark Northgate station. It was connected to the main line by a siding (agreement dated 1/2/1875) which ran south east. By 1883, the sidings had been extended and a loco shed built. The Ordnance Survey plan of that year shows extensive workings to the east of the works at SK 813541 linked to it by a 400 yard narrow gauge tramway. There is evidence of inclines into the hole and although no track is shown, tramways employing steam rope haulage engines are known to have been used. By 1900 these workings appear disused and future quarrying was to the north. Maps from 1914 onwards show two short lines at SK 811543, An aerial photograph of 26/8/1933 shows that one of these extended into the quarry and also what appears to be a steam hauled train. In 1934 a steam road wagon was rebuilt as a narrow gauge locomotive. It worked until 1941 when the track was lifted and the loco abandoned in its shed. Gypsum was, in 1934, being worked from a hole titled CLAY PIT which may have been the work site for the locomotive. Further details are lacking. It is possible that one or more of the narrow gauge locomotives shown under the HAWTON entry as delivered to 'Cafferata Newark' may have also worked here. The standard gauge railway does not appear to have been used for quarrying at Beacon Hill. Rail traffic ceased in 1965, but the siding agreement was not terminated until 1/7/1975. The works continued in production, and was renamed "Cafferata Works" from 27/6/1974.

Gauge : 4ft 8½in

1		0-4-0T	OC	FJ	188	1882	New
		reb		Cafferata		1904	(2)
	ST.MONANS	0-4-0ST	OC	AB	279	1885	(a) (1)
	-	0-4-0ST	OC	HC	1611	1928	(b) (3)
No.4		0-4-0ST	OC	P	1963	1938	New (d) (4)

		4wDM	RH	218045	1942	(c)	(5)
-		4wDM	RH	236364	1946	(e)	(6)

(a) ex Thos.W. Ward Ltd, Sheffield 2/1926 (earlier with WD, Heytesbury Camp, Wilts).
(b) ex G.E. Simm (Machinery) Ltd, dealers, Skewen, West Glam, 26/4/1954; earlier Wirksworth Quarries Ltd, Derbys.
(c) ex Abelson & Co (Engineers) Ltd, Sheldon, Birmingham, on hire, 10/1962.
(d) to Jericho Mill, after 11/1962, by 17/4/1963; returned after 13/7/1963, by 1/11/1963.
(e) ex Rushcliffe Works, East Leake, c/1963 (by 13/7/1963); to Hawton Works, by 1/11/1963; returned.

(1) to Jericho Mill, by /1944
(2) to Hawton Works, after 24/8/1952, by 26/9/1953
(3) to Hawton Works, c/1960 (by 29/5/1960)
(4) to Hawton Works, c6/1964.
(5) returned to Abelson & Co (Engineers) Ltd, Sheldon, Birmingham, c6/1963.
(6) to Rushcliffe Works, East Leake, c/1965.

Gauge : 3ft 0in

-	4wTG	Cafferata	1934	(a)	(1)

(a) rebuilt from a 1907 built Leyland steam lorry, registration No. B2114 (builders number may be LH69292), /1934.

(1) scrapped on site by Lee, Grantham (presumably J Lee & Son (Grantham) Ltd), c4/1960.

CROPWELL BISHOP MINE U28
British Plaster & Boards Ltd until 1/4/1964 SK 680349
The Gotham Co Ltd until 30/10/1961
Cropwell Gypsum Mines Ltd from 5/10/1907 until 1913
Snaith Plaster & Cement Co Ltd in 1907
J.D.Snaith in 1900 and 1904
Cropwell Plaster Cement and Brick Co in 1885

There was, by 1885, a small works here on the east bank of the Grantham Canal, which was used to remove the product until 1923. In 1891 it was marked as a plaster and cement works. By 1921 a tramway ran south east into a quarry at SK 681347, where there was a drift mine which had opened between 1886 and 1913. This mine was still shown on a map dated 1950. Locomotives were used, presumably in the mine, from 1936 until about 1960. We have no information as to why two different track gauges were used. By 3/1961 the only track remaining was one short rope haulage. The works remained in production until at least 1973.

Gauge : 2ft 0in

-	4wDM	RH	198278	1939	(a)	(1)
-	4wDM	RH	172335	1935	(b)	(2)
-	4wDM	RH	175417	1936	(c)	(2)

(a) ex Cafferata & Co Ltd, Barton Mines, after 18/2/1948, by 2/9/1949
(b) ex Cafferata & Co Ltd, Barton Mines, after 21/10/1948, by 26/4/1950.
(c) regauged from 2ft 3in, c9/1949; to Barton Mines; returned by 3/1955.

(1) to Long Meg Plaster & Mineral Co Ltd, Lazonby, Cumberland, after 22/5/1955, by 30/9/1957.
(2) to Glebe Mine, Gotham, /1959.

Gauge : 2ft 3in

-	4wDM	RH	175417	1936	New (1)

(1) regauged to 2ft 0in, c9/1949 (after 2/9/1949).

CUCKOO BUSH MINE, Gotham   W29
Formerly known as **SHEPPARDS No.1 (or TOP END) MINE**   SK 534293
British Plaster & Boards Ltd until 1/4/1964
J.W. Sheppard Ltd until 31/10/1961
J.W. Sheppard until 30/3/1936
James Ward until 1903

Located ½ mile south of Gotham village, the first mine on this site was at SK 534292 and was probably the ALBERT Mine being operated in 1874 by **Neep & Ward**. It had closed by 1880 and was replaced by a new mine at SK 533293. The early owners and title of this are not known but by 1880 it was linked by a tramway, which ran north for.600 yards, to a wharf alongside Leake Road. A map dated 1901 shows this tramway severed by the construction of the GCR Gotham branch (which opened 2/5/1900). The mine may not then have been working as it is said to have been closed at the time of the Sheppard purchase. By 1904 there was a siding connection to the mine on the south side of the Gotham Branch, west of that to Glebe Mine, and the tramway north to the road had been lifted. In 1906 a plaster mill had been erected north of and adjacent to the mine and at this time there was a surface tramway connection to GLEBE MINE, then in The Gotham Co. ownership. This connection was shortlived and by 1920 had gone. Locomotives were used in the drift mine from 1933 until 1963 when an underground link with the Glebe Mine was made. Two of the locomotives listed below were abandoned underground until sold in 1973. The locomotives listed below are those believed to have been at Cuckoo Bush but Sheppard's spares orders as recorded by RH do not differentiate between this mine and Weldon. Hence there were probably unrecorded movements between them. The changes of gauge are as recorded in RH spares records, but why they were carried out is not known.

Gauge : 2ft 1½in (Underground)

-	4wDM	RH	166045	1933	New (a) (4)
-	4wDM	RH	182145	1936	New (b) (1)
-	4wDM	RH	192868	1938	(c) (2)
-	4wDM	RH	200766	1942	New (d) (3)
-	4wDM	RH	247178	1947	New (e) (4)

(a) delivered new as 2ft 1in gauge.
(b) ex RH, on hire 26/2/1937; purchased 11/6/1937; 2ft 0in gauge when new.
(c) ex Marblaegis Ltd, Silver Seal Mine, after 22/10/1938, by 6/9/1943 (possibly by 23/1/1941).
(d) delivered new as 2ft 1½in gauge; altered to 2ft 0in, c11/1947.
(e) delivered new as 2ft 2in gauge.

(1) to RH, for repair, 2/1939 (by 6/2/1939); repurchased by RH by 9/3/1939; to Borough of Slough, Slough, Bucks, on hire, after gauge altered to 2ft 0in, 5/6/1939.
(2) to Weldon Mine by 11/1954.
(3) to Glebe Mine, Gotham, c/1963.
(4) to Mr & Mrs C.Lawson, Tring, Herts, for preservation, 10/1973.

GLEBE MINE, Gotham W30
British Plaster & Boards Ltd until 1/4/1964　　　SK 537290 & 537292
The Gotham Co Ltd until 31/10/1961
Victoria Mineral & Plaster Co Ltd until /1897

Glebe mine was located ½ mile south of Gotham village. In the 1886 mines list, two Glebe Mines are shown, one which opened prior to 1874 was worked by **Thomlinson & Salkeld** and one, which opened after that date, by **Richard Carver**. We do not know which of these was the mine we are concerned with. In 1880 this mine had a short tramway linking it with a rough track which led north to Leake Road, Gotham. This rough track on a low embankment is still extant in 1999 and appears originally to have been a tramway. If so it was not shown as such on the 1880 Ordnance Survey map. The mine had closed in 1899 but reopened in 1903, together with a plaster works and a siding connection to the south side of the newly opened GCR Gotham Branch (agreement dated 27/4/1903). The mine tramway was extended to the siding and works. In 1905-6, for some unexplained reason, this line extended east to the adjacent Cuckoo Bush Works of J.W.Sheppard. By 1920 a new level had opened, east of the original mine and this was linked to the existing tramway. The works was greatly extended in the 1930s. Locomotives were used underground in the level from 1933 until the early 1970s when rails were replaced by conveyors and rubber tyred plant.

Gauge : 2ft 2in (Underground)

-	4wDM	RH	168790	1933	(a)	(4)
ELLEN	4wDM	RH	200069	1940	New	(3)
-	4wDM	RH	244559	1946	New	(3)
-	4wDM	RH	371547	1954	(b)	(2)
-	4wDM	RH	200766	1942	(c)	(1)

(a) ex Thrumpton Mine, after 14/6/1939, by 28/6/1939.
(b) ex J W Sheppard Ltd, Weldon Mine
(c) ex Cuckoo Bush Mine c/1963.

(1) to Alan M. Keef, Cote Farm, Bampton, Oxon, 10/1972.
(2) to P.R. Welsh, Tolgus Tin Museum, Redruth, Cornwall, c10/1972.
(3) to Mr & Mrs C. Lawson, Tring, Herts, for preservation, 11/10/1973.
(4) abandoned underground, by 6/1/1974; then sold for scrap, c/1975 (after 2/1974).

Gauge : 2ft 0in

-	4wDM	RH	172335	1936	(a)	(1)
-	4wDM	RH	175417	1936	(a)	(2)

(a) ex Cropwell Bishop Mine, /1959; a plan to regauge them to 2ft 2in was not implemented on 172335 and probably not on 175417.

(1) dismantled for spares, /1960 and remains scrapped.
(2) dismantled underground for spares by 3/1961 and remains sold for scrap after 2/1974.

HAWTON GYPSUM WORKS, near Newark P31
Gyproc Ltd until 1/4/1964 SK 802506
Cafferata & Co Ltd until 31/3/1962
Wilson & Robinson until /1881

The Wilson & Robinson partnership dated from pre-1840, with premises at Hawton. They constructed the 3ft 0in gauge **HAWTON TRAMWAY** from their works northwards for 1¼ miles to Spring House Wharf on the River Trent, possibly as early as 1848 when a lease mentioned a tramway, but definitely by 1867. This line was then horse worked. 3ft 0in gauge locomotives were introduced about 1882 and the Ordnance Survey of 1883-6 shows a works at SK 802507, with a quarry to the south of it, and two other works at SK 800510 and 795509. All were connected to the wharf at Newark (SK 790533) by the tramway which ran north west for 1½ miles. A Private Siding Agreement dated 3/11/1884 related to a siding on the west side of the GNR Newark - Cotham line, 2¼ miles south of Newark Northgate Station. This, and a ¼ mile connection which ran west to the works, was laid to dual gauge and the standard gauge traffic was worked by 3ft 0in gauge locos until the first standard gauge locomotive arrived (by 1924). From about 1899 the works was concentrated around SK 802507 and the other early works had gone. The quarry to the south was extending and by 1915 had reached SK 796500. It was rail served by a line then about ¾ mile long, curving round to form almost a circle and the ends were later linked up. Most of the railway remained 3ft 0in gauge until standard gauge locos arrived. From 1940 all remaining lines were standard gauge. The last narrow gauge section is believed to have been the Hawton Tramway to the river and to have closed c1940, without being converted. The Hawton Gypsum mine operated from c1931 until c1939 and at least one locomotive was used underground. The location of the mine is unknown. Subsequent changes saw the quarry grow ever larger and in 1958 it had reached SK 796492. From c1953, Hawton locomotives were registered by the Railway Executive to enable them to shunt at the nearby Jericho Mill (which see) until rail traffic ceased there c1963. Rail traffic at Hawton ended in 1975 (agreement terminated 31/7/1975) but its use in the quarry had ceased in the 1960s in favour of rubber tyred plant. Production at the works and at the, by now greatly enlarged, quarry continues.

Gauge : 4ft 8½in

	-	0-6-0ST	IC	MW	975	1886	(a)	s/s after 1/1929
10	HILDA	0-6-0ST	IC	MW	1048	1888	(b)	(1)
	-	4wVBT	VCG	S	8207	1930	New	(6)
	-	4wVBT	VCG	S	R5/8749	1936	(c)	(3)
	ST.MONANS	0-4-0ST	OC	AB	279	1885	(d)	(2)
No.6	ST.MONANS	4wVBT	VCG	S	9373	1947	New	(8)
1		0-4-0T	OC	FJ	188	1882		
			reb	Cafferata		1904	(e)	Scr c6/1955
	-	0-4-0ST	OC	HC	1611	1928	(f)	(4)
	FRANCIS	0-4-0ST	OC	P	1704	1927	(g)	(7)
	-	4wDM		RH	236364	1946	(h)	(5)
	HILDA	0-4-0ST	OC	P	1963	1938	(i)	(9)
	-	0-4-0ST	OC	P	2112	1949	(j)	Scr /1970
	-	0-4-0DH		RH	418793	1957	(k)	(10)

(a) earlier Walter Scott & Middleton Ltd, Redbourn Steelworks (1916-1920) contract, Scunthorpe, Lincs; here by 6/1925.
(b) earlier Holloway Bros. (London) Ltd, Sidcup - Farningham road construction (1921-1924), Kent; here by 5/1928 (possibly by 6/1925)
(c) rebuilt from steam lorry, /1936; to Jericho Mill, /1954; returned, /1955.
(d) ex Jericho Mill, c/1946.

(e) ex Beacon Hill Works, after 24/8/1952, by 26/9/1953, for repairs that were never completed.
(f) ex Beacon Hill Works, c/1960 (by 29/5/1960).
(g) ex M.& W.Grazebrook Ltd, Netherton, Staffs, 3/1961; to Jericho Mill, by 3/1963; returned after 7/1963, by 11/1963.
(h) ex Beacon Hill Works, after 7/1963, by 1/11/1963.
(i) ex Beacon Hill Works, after 3/1964, by 8/1964.
(j) ex Tutbury Works, Staffs, 4/1969.
(k) ex Kingston-on-Soar Gypsum Mines, 5/1971.

(1) scrapped after 4/1929, by 9/1947.
(2) derelict by 8/1952, scrapped on site 10/1954.
(3) out of use by 3/1961, scrapped after 5/1961.
(4) scrapped /1963 (after 1/11/1963).
(5) to Beacon Hill Works after 1/11/63, by c1965
(6) scrapped on site, after 5/1964, by 8/1964.
(7) scrapped on site by T. Price, Newark, 2/1968.
(8) to Main Line Steam Trust, Loughborough, Leics, 2/7/1973.
(9) to Main Line Steam Trust, Loughborough, Leics, 20/5/1973.
(10) to Steetley Co Ltd, Dowlow Works, Dowlow, Buxton, Derbys, per J. Lee & Son (Grantham) Ltd, c/1976 (after 8/10/1975)

Gauge : 3ft 0in

		(2-4-0T?)	OC	JF	4186	1882	New	(a)	(1)
	-	0-4-0ST	OC	RP	21232	1898	New	(a)	(2)
	-	? T	OC	JF	4503	1883	New	(a)	s/s
No.4		0-4-0ST	OC	MW	1528	1901	New		(3)
No.5	SWANSEA	0-4-0ST	OC	P	959	1902		(b)	(4)

(a) locomotives delivered new to 'Cafferata, Newark'. Whilst Hawton is a likely destination, it is possible that one or more went to a quarry line at Beacon Hill Works. The gauge of JF 4186 and 4503 is subject to confirmation.
(b) ex H. Arnold & Son Ltd, Doncaster, by 4/1919; earlier High Dyke branch (GNR) contract (1915-1919), Lincs; possibly to Hawton via Doncaster Plant Depot.

(1) returned to JF, Leeds, and resold to an unknown customer in Calcutta, India.
(2) advertised for sale in "The Engineer", 13/10/1911.
(3) out of use from /1940, scrapped on site /1947.
(4) out of use from /1940, scrapped on site 9/1947.

Gauge : 2ft 0in (locomotive here for repairs only)

	4wDM	RH	198278	1939	(a)	(1)

(a) ex Baldry, Yerburgh & Hutchinson Ltd, contractors, 'as lying at Woodhouse Mill' Yorks (WR), per Thos.W. Ward Ltd. c4/1946 (by 4/5/1946).

(1) to Barton Mines by 24/1/1947.

Gauge : 1ft 8in (underground at Hawton Mine)

      -              4wDM   RH   166027   1932   New   (1)

(1)   to RH, after 13/8/1938, by 12/9/1938; rebuilt to 2ft 0in gauge and thence to Barton Mines, after 17/10/1938, by 31/10/1939.

JERICHO BRICKWORKS & PLASTER MILL, New Balderton   P32
Gyproc Ltd until 1/4/1964   SK 805504
Cafferata & Co Ltd until 31/3/1962

The site was developed by Cafferata in 1935 and the first operations were a quarry and a brickworks. To this was added a plaster works in 1946 using equipment salvaged from the works at Bunny. The works were served by sidings (agreement dated 13/7/1935) on the east side of the LNER Newark - Cotham line, 2¼ miles south of Newark Northgate Station. The first quarry was north of the works, extending as far as SK 807509. It was short lived and may not have been rail served. By the 1950s rail traffic was light and, from 1953, Hawton locomotives were registered by the Railway Executive to enable them to cross the BR line and carry out shunting at Jericho Mill. Thereafter the resident diesel locomotive was little used and the Peckett locos were here only for storage or repairs. Traffic ceased in 1963, although the agreement was not terminated until 31/8/1972. The works continued in production and was later expanded considerably.

Gauge : 4ft 8½in

      ST.MONANS   0-4-0ST   OC   AB   279   1885   (a)   (1)
      -                         4wDM   RH   183060   1937   (b)   (3)
      -                       4wVBT VCG S   R5/8749 1936   (c)   (2)
      -                       0-4-0ST   OC   P   1963   1938   (d)   (4)
      FRANCIS   0-4-0ST   OC   P   1704   1927   (e)   (5)

(a)   ex Beacon Hill Works, by /1944.
(b)   ex J.C. Staton & Co Ltd, Tutbury, Staffs, 1/1953.
(c)   ex Hawton Works, /1954. *(Note; this transfer may not have occurred and the locomotive may have merely been observed here working from Hawton)*
(d)   ex Beacon Hill Works, c/1962.
(e)   ex Hawton Works, by 3/1963.

(1)   to Hawton Works, c/1946.
(2)   to Hawton Works, /1955.
(3)   to F. Watkins (Engineers) Ltd, Sling Plant Depot, Milkwall, Glos, /1963 (by 7/1963); resold to British Lely Ltd, Wootton Basset, Wilts, after 20/3/1965.
(4)   to Beacon Hill Works, /1963 (by 5/1963).
(5)   to Hawton Works, after 7/1963, by 11/1963.

KINGSTON-ON-SOAR GYPSUM MINE   V33
Gyproc Ltd until 1/4/1964   SK525287
The Gypsum Mines Ltd until 31/3/1962
Kingston Gypsum Co Ltd until 4/2/1903
  (or **Kingston on Soar Gypsum Co Ltd** ?)
Lord Belper until after 1886

The mines at Kingston were located on the west side of the extensive gypsum deposits of Gotham. The first shaft (SK 523287) was sunk in 1880 by the second Baron Belper and was known in 1886 as **WEST LEAKE MINE**. The rock was originally transported by the River Soar, to Zouch or Barrow-on-Soar, for grinding. By 1890, a mill had been built at the mine. The railway was laid in 1883, (original motive power unknown) and ran west from the mine for two miles, passing under the Midland Railway main line to reach a wharf on the River Soar at SK 495278. As traffic became heavier, a locomotive was purchased in 1885 and, at some time before 1895, a rail connection was made with the west side of the Midland Railway, north of Kegworth Station. This line ran north, alongside but at a lower level than the main line, to make a junction with the original route west of the Midland Railway bridge. A small brickworks was being operated by the company by 1895, north of the railway at SK 517286 with a very short incline into a clay hole to the east. This works closed soon after 1900, having worked very little ground, and does not seen to have had a standard gauge siding. It remained derelict for many years. Locomotive sheds were located west of the mine at SK 522286 and at the wharf, north of the exchange sidings. Kingston was a shaft mine, unlike most in the area which were drifts or levels. Locomotives were introduced underground in 1942 and worked until the early 1960s, by which time a surface drift had been driven allowing rubber tyred plant to be used. The mine and railway closed 5/1971.

Gauge : 4ft 8½in

LADY MARGARET	0-4-0ST	OC	FE	81	1885	New	Scr c/1945
MARGUERITE	0-6-0ST	IC	HE	15	1867	(a)	s/s
LADY ANGELA	0-4-0ST	OC	P	1690	1926	New	(2)
-	0-4-0ST	OC	WB	1575	1899	(b)	(1)
-	0-4-0DH		RH	418793	1957	(c)	(3)

(a)   ex Nailstone Colliery Co Ltd, Leics, /1911. (An unconfirmed note in IRS records suggests that this locomotive may have come from Ellistown Collieries Ltd, Leics., in 1911. There is also a suggestion that it was by H Hughes and thus not HE 15 at all).
(b)   ex Marblaegis Ltd, East Leake, /1950 (by 8/1950).
(c)   ex RH, Lincoln, 8/1/1963; earlier a demonstration loco.

(1)   to G.E. Baker (Metals) Ltd, Derby, for scrap, 5/1963 (noted 2/5/1963 at BR Derby locomotive shed in transit).
(2)   to Midland Railway Society, Shackerstone Station, Leics, 22/5/1971.
(3)   to Hawton Gypsum Works, 5/1971.

Gauge : 2ft 0in (Underground)

No.1	4wDM	RH	209430	1942	New	(3)
No.2	4wDM	RH	224308	1944	New	(4)
No.3	4wDM	RH	221593	1946	(a)	(1)
No.4	4wDM	RH	408427	1957	New	(2)

(a)   ex Marblaegis Ltd, Silver Seal Mine, Bunny, /1949 (by 25/5/1949).

(1) to Madoc Jones, dealer, St.Asaph, Flints, c/1961 (after 17/9/1958); resold to Halkyn District United Mines Ltd, Rhydymwyn, Flints, for spares, 20/7/1966.
(2) to Fauld Mine, Staffs, c/1965.
(3) to Long Eaton Railway Society, West Park Pleasure Rly., Long Eaton, Derbys, /1966.
(4) stored underground by 2/1968; to A.M.Keef, Cote Farm, Bampton, Oxon, 10/1972.

RUSHCLIFFE WORKS, East Leake V34
British Plaster & Boards Ltd until 1/4/1964 SK 553278 and SK 554280
Marblaegis Ltd until 31/10/1961
Brothers Patent Plaster Co Ltd until 1/4/1914 (in receivership by 1913)
Barnstone Blue Lias Lime & Cement Co Ltd until 1/1/1910

There was a mine, which probably worked limestone, and a small works on this site from around the time of the opening, in 7/1898, of the GCR London extension which passed immediately to the west of it at Rushcliffe Halt. By agreement dated 19/9/1899, the company had a private siding on the east side of the line known as Hotchley Hill siding where a small works was situated (SK 553278). In 1906 short narrow gauge lines ran east into a level at SK 555278 and north from the works. This level is believed to be the mine listed from 1913 to 1938 as **Hotchley Mills** (error for Hills?). A major expansion scheme between 1946 and 1950 was undertaken with new plasterboard works built to the north at SK 554280 and a remodelled standard gauge system requiring a locomotive. Further expansion occurred until by 1964 this was the country's biggest plasterboard plant. Locomotives were used underground for a period from c1943 until conveyors were installed in 1952. One locomotive (RH 221602) was retained to deal with waste material until after 3/1961. When this work ceased it was bricked up in a disused section of the mine until removed and sold in 1976. The use to which the petrol locomotive was put is unknown. Standard gauge rail traffic ceased from between 1980 and 1988 until 1998 when rail deliveries of gypsum commenced, using EWS locomotives. The rail system, including a locomotive, was retained throughout.

Gauge : 4ft 8½in

	0-4-0ST	OC	WB	1575	1899	(a)	(1)
-	4wDM		RH	236364	1946	New (b)	
-	4wDM		RH	398616	1956	New	(2)

(a) ex Gypsum Mines Ltd, Mountfield, Sussex, /1949.
(b) to Beacon Hill Works, Newark, c/1963 (by 13/7/1963); returned, c/1965.

(1) to Gypsum Mines Ltd, Kingston-on-Soar, /1950.
(2) to Trackwork Ltd, Long Sandall, Doncaster, S Yorks, 13/4/1994

Gauge : 2ft 0in

-	4wPM	MR			(a)	s/s
-	4wDM	RH	243393	1946	New	(1)
-	4wDM	RH	221602	1943	New	(2)

(a) origin unknown

(1) to J.W. Sheppard Ltd, Weldon Mine, Gotham, c/1954.
(2) abandoned underground after 3/1961; recovered, /1976; to GECT, Vulcan Works, Newton le Willows, Lancs, /1977; resold to Nobels Explosives Co Ltd, Ardeer, Strathclyde.

SILVER SEAL MINE, Bunny   V35
British Plaster & Boards Ltd until 1/4/1964   SK 586287
Marblaegis Ltd until 31/10/1961
Anderson Gypsum Products Ltd until c1939-45

The Silver Seal Mine and a plaster mill were opened at Bunny in 1938, the mill output going initially to Anderson's plasterboard plant, Park Road Works, Stretford, Manchester. The plaster mill was short lived, closing soon after the take over by The British Plaster Board Ltd in 1939. The machines were removed to Jericho Works at Newark for re-erection there. The mine continued in production, at first under the Marblaegis Ltd name. The locomotives were used underground in the drift mine but this mine was one of the first to remove the rails entirely and rely on conveyors and rubber tyred plant.

Gauge : 2ft 0in

		4wDM	RH	192868	1938	New	(a)	(1)
		4wDM	RH	221593	1946	New		(2)

(a) delivered before the mine was ready; commissioned on site by RH, 22/10/1938.

(1) to J.W.Sheppard Ltd, Weldon Mine, Gotham, by 6/9/1943 (possibly by 23/1/1941).
(2) to Gypsum Mines Ltd, Kingston-on-Soar, /1949 (by 25/5/1949).

STAUNTON-in-the-VALE GYPSUM QUARRY   U36
Bellrock Gypsum Industries Ltd. until 1967   SK 799443

By 1956, a works and quarry had been established with a standard gauge siding on the east side of the BR Newark line, two miles north of Bottesford Junction. The quarry was connected by a narrow gauge tramway which ran westwards to the plasterboard factory. The tramway closed and the remaining locos were offered for sale in February 1969.

Gauge : 2ft 0in

		4wPM	MR	5007	1929	(a)	(1)
1		4wDM	RH	187045	1937	(b)	(6)
	-	4wPM	MR			(c)	s/s c/1965
	-	4wDM	FH	-		(d)	(1)
63		4wPM	OK	5928	1935	(e)	(1)
3		4wDM	RH	183428	1937	(f)	
	By 3/1961, incorporated parts of	RH	168870			(5)
	-	4wDM	RH			(g)	(3)
	-	4wDM	RH	168870	1932	(h)	(2)
	-	4wDM	RH	168792	1933	(i)	(4)
6		4wDM	MR	9416	1949	(j)	(6)
7		4wDM	MR	9417	1949	(k)	(6)
5		4wDM	RH	339209	1952	(l)	(6)

(a) ex Wills & Alexander, contrs.
(b) ex Lehane, MacKenzie & Shand Ltd, contrs, PY 181, 8/1955, via George Cohen, Sons & Co Ltd.
(c) ex ?; here by 8/1955
(d) ex ? ; here by 8/1955 ("Planet Simplex" type loco)
(e) ex ? ; here by 8/1955 (reb with Ford Y8 engine).
(f) ex Lehane, Mackenzie & Shand Ltd, contrs., c/1957 (after 12/1/1949)

(g) ex Lehane, Mackenzie & Shand Ltd, contrs., c/1957.
(h) ex Richard Sankey & Son Ltd, Bulwell, c/1957 (after 14/12/1949).
(i) ex Richard Sankey & Son Ltd, Bulwell, c/1957 (after 23/11/1951, by 28/4/1958).
(j) ex MR, c/1965; earlier Holloway Bros, contrs.
(k) ex MR, 6/1965; earlier Holloway Bros, contrs.
(l) ex Mitchell Bros. Ltd, contrs., 10/1966.

(1) derelict by 9/1955; scrapped c/1957.
(2) dismantled by 3/1961; parts having been used to repair RH 183428; s/s by 10/1966
(3) s/s ? (after 3/1961 or after 10/1966?).
(4) s/s after 17/12/1962.
(5) to Abco Petroleum Ltd, Rye Harbour, Sussex, /1969.
(6) to A.M. Keef, Cote Farm, Bampton, Oxon, 12/1971.

THRUMPTON MINE V37
The Gotham Co Ltd until closure. SK 521307 and 518305
Wood Bros. by 1912, until 1917
Trent Mining Co from 1877 until between 1908 and 1912
Gregory & Robey in 1874

These mines were first listed in 1874. A sale notice of an auction by J.M. Pott on 23/5/1877 related to the Thrumpton Plaster works, including locomotive steam engines and a tramway from the mine to the River Trent. The earliest plan seen, dating from 1882, shows the mine then in use to be on the north west side of Gotham Hill at SK 518305. A former mine at SK 521307 had by then closed and its tramway had been lifted. The tramway ran north west from the mines, crossing a main road en route, to end at a mill and wharf on the River Trent at Thrumpton Ferry (1 mile) (SK 512316). In the 1886 mines list, owners are recorded as Robey & Co, though they may well have been the proprietors of the Trent Mining Co. The mine was on care and maintenance by 1923 but was working again from 1933 until discontinued in 5/1940. A separate Thrumpton Gypsum Quarry is listed for 1937 only, but nothing is known of this. The mine was still listed in 1945 but not working. It is not known how long the first period of locomotive haulage lasted or what if any means were employed thereafter until the arrival of the diesel locomotive. RH records indicate that only the one locomotive was on site in 1939 and the mine stood on occasions when it was out of order.

Gauge : 2ft 2in

Locomotives were in use by 1877.

-          4wDM   RH 168790 1933   (a)   (1)

(a) ex Chellaston Mine, Derbys, after 5/6/1937, by 15/7/1937.

(1) to Glebe Mine, Gotham, after 14/6/1939, by 28/6/1939.

WELDON MINE, Gotham W38

Formerly known as **SHEPPARDS No.2 (or GOTHAM HILL) MINE**   SK 532308
British Plaster & Boards Ltd until 1/4/1964
J.W. Sheppard Ltd until 31/10/1961
J.W. Sheppard until 30/3/1936
G. Stocker & Co Ltd until /1909
Stocker and Odames by 1856, until after 1874

George Stocker, trading as Stocker & Odames, had commenced his activities on Gotham Hill to the north of the village by 1856, working a Weldon mine (but not necessarily the later mine of that name). By 1880 a mill had been built in the village at SK 535305 and this was served by a 600 yard narrow gauge tramway which ran south from the mine then in use, at SK 532308, and one by then closed at SK 533310. A brickyard was located between the two mines and is thought to be the one operated by the **Yeomans** family from at least 1864. It had a short tramway into a clay hole to the north by 1899, when the owner was **Silas Bowley**. It closed not long afterwards. Stocker's mill became the terminus of the GCR Gotham branch which opened in 1900 and two sidings were provided. By 1938 the tramway route had been straightened somewhat and the brickworks removed. The surface tramway had closed by 1959. Locomotives were used underground from 1939. By 18/3/1961, Weldon Mine was not in production and the locomotives were in store in a shed on the surface. The works closed c1963. The remarks made under the Cuckoo Bush entry relating to movements between these sites and to changes of gauge, apply equally here.

Gauge : 2ft 1½in (Underground)

-	4wDM	RH	166045	1936	(a)	(1)	
-	4wDM	RH	192868	1938	(b)	(3)	
-	4wDM	RH	195843	1939	New (d)	(3)	
-	4wDM	RH	243393	1947	(c)	(3)	
-	4wDM	RH	371547	1954	New	(2)	

(a) ex Cuckoo Bush Mine, 1/1954.
(b) ex Cuckoo Bush Mine by 11/1954; wheelsets for 2ft 0in gauge were ordered from RH, for this locomotive, 3/12/1954.
(c) ex Marblaegis Ltd, Rushcliffe Mine, East Leake, c/1954.
(d) built as 2ft $0^{5/8}$in gauge.

(1) to Cuckoo Bush Mine by 3/1961.
(2) to Glebe Mine, Gotham by 3/1961.
(3) sold or scrapped after 3/1961 by /1963.

BRITISH RAILWAYS
BEESTON CREOSOTING DEPOT   V39
London Midland & Scottish Railway until 31/12/1947   SK 539369
Midland Railway until 31/12/1923

This sleeper depot and creosote works was served by sidings on the north side of the Beeston - Nottingham line, ¾ miles east of Beeston Station. The standard gauge sidings were normally worked by Engineers Department locomotives numbered in the 'ED' series but at times LMSR and BR capital stock was used. The 3ft 0in gauge was confined to an internal system serving the pressure impregnation cylinder. The depot was operating by 1886 and closed in 1965. A Freightliner depot then occupied the site.

Gauge : 4ft 8½in

	DANBY LODGE	0-6-0ST	IC	MW	1595	1903	(a)	(1)
ED1	(2 until 4/1949)	0-4-0DM		JF	21048	1935	New (b)	(2)
ED5		0-4-0DM		JF	4200044	1949	New (c)	(3)
ED6		0-4-0DM		JF	4200045	1949	(d)	(4)
ED2		0-4-0DM		JF	4200041	1949	(e)	(5)

(a) ex Cheadle Deviation (LMSR) construction, Staffs, after 12/1933, by 5/1936.
(b) here in 8/1936 but loaned elsewhere at times; noted at Stockport as "ROF No.5", 13/7/1940; was noted at Derby Works in 10/1943 and had returned to Beeston by 3/1946; to West India Dock Coal Depot, London, 14/9/1951; at Castleton Permanent Way Depot in 1955; returned to Beeston from Patricroft Locomotive shed (Manchester) after 1/1960.
(c) to Castleton Permanent Way Depot, Lancs, by 4/11/1950; returned here after 30/1/1954 (by 1955).
(d) ex Castleton Permanent Way Depot, Lancs, c12/1949 (after 15/10/1949, by 4/11/1950); returned to Castleton by 8/6/1952; returned to here after 10/12/1953, by 30/1/1954.
(e) ex ?; by 4/11/1950; to Derby Works, by 24/4/1952; ex Ditton Creosote Works, Lancs, by 30/1/1954.

(1) to George Cohen, Sons & Co Ltd, after c/1948; s/s.
(2) to BR Hellifield, Yorks. (for storage), via Derby Works, 7/1961; returned to Derby Works by 1/1962 and scrapped there 7/1962.
(3) to Derby Works, after 21/11/1954, by 15/1/1955; returned by 20/4/1958; to Castleton Permanent Way Depot by 1960.
(4) returned to Castleton Permanent Way Depot, Lancs, c/1955.
(5) returned to Ditton Creosote Works, after 30/1/1954, by /1955.

Gauge : 3ft 0in

		4wPM		MR	1902	1919	New	s/s
10	BATLEY	0-4-0ST	OC	WB	2233	1924	(a)	(1)
No.1		0-4-0ST	OC	WB	1889	1911	(b)	(2)
ED 10		4wDM		RH	411322	1958	New	(3)

(a) ex Wm.Twigg, dealer, Matlock, Derbys, /1945 (by 11/8/1945), via BR Derby Works; earlier Lehane, Mackenzie & Shand Ltd, contrs., Darley Dale, Derbys.
(b) ex M.E. Engineering Ltd, London, (hired at first), 6/1956; earlier Judkins Ltd, Tuttle Hill Quarries, Nuneaton, Warwicks (until after 5/1956); to BR Nottingham locomotive shed (repairs) by 11/2/1961; returned to Beeston by 7/10/1961.

(1) withdrawn, 10/1955; to Derby Works, after 21/11/1955, by 20/12/1955, and scrapped there.
(2) to S.A. Burgess, Haddenham, Ely, Cambs, 10/1962, via March locomotive shed (arriving c/1963)
(3) to Thos.W. Ward Ltd, Sheffield., 2/1965; resold to Cleveland Bridge & Engineering Co Ltd, for the Tinsley Viaduct motorway contract, Yorks (WR), 5/1966.

CENTRAL MATERIALS DEPOT, Lenton, Nottingham. S40
SK 560388

This Permanent Way yard (opening date unknown) was served by sidings on the east side of the Mansfield Jct. - Radford line, immediately north of Mansfield Jct. The sidings also ran parallel to the Beeston - Nottingham line. BR capital stock locomotives worked the traffic when the locomotive below was not present. Closed and the site redeveloped as a retail park.

Gauge : 4ft 8½in

ED 3   0-4-0DM   JF 4200042 1949   New (a) (1)

(a) to Castleton Permanent Way Depot, Lancs, by 4/11/1950; returned here, after 30/1/1954, by /1955.

(1) to Derby Works, c/1960 (by 16/10/1961) and then to Bedford locomotive shed, 1/1964.

RANSKILL WAGON WORKS, Ranskill B41
SK 672868

This works was opened by the LNER, c1945-7, on the south west side of the Ranskill Royal Ordnance Factory branch which ran south east from a triangular junction south of Ranskill Station. Buildings vacated by the Royal Ordnance Factory were used for wagon repairs. From 3/2/1948 a permanent locomotive allocation was made and in 1952 the locomotives were renumbered in departmental stock. The works closed c1959 and the track was removed by 1967.

Gauge : 4ft 8½in

| 4 | (68132) (8132) | 4wVBT | VCG S | 6517 | 1926 | (a) | (1) |
| 3 | (68181) | 4wVBT | VCG S | 8478 | 1931 | (b) | (2) |

(a) ex storage at Doncaster Works paint shop, Yorks (WR), 3/2/1948.
(b) ex Tyne Dock Locomotive Shed, Co.Durham, 3/9/1951.

(1) Withdrawn from service 6/1959; later scrapped (at Doncaster Works?).
(2) Withdrawn from service 11/1959; later scrapped (at Doncaster Works?).

BRITISH SUGAR CORPORATION LTD

NEWARK FACTORY, Newark   P42
(known as **KELHAM FACTORY** until 1974)
Home Grown Sugar Ltd (registered 13/2/1921) until 12/6/1936   SK 793554
British Sugar Beet Growers Society Ltd (registered in 1915)

The above Society owned 4½ square miles of land on the Kelham estate, from 1915, on which sugar beet could be grown. To process this beet, the factory was built in 1920-1921, possibly by Walter Scott & Middleton Ltd (which see) and appears to have opened in 11/1921. Home Grown Sugar Ltd was a government initiative to help establish a British sugar industry. The factory was served by sidings (agreement dated 10/12/1920) which ran west from the Midland Railway, Newark Castle - Lincoln St. Marks line, ½ mile north of Newark Castle Station. A line ran north from near the junction to a wharf on the River Trent at SK 800555. This had gone by 1969. The factory was expanded and modernised in 1974. Rail traffic ceased 4/1981.

Gauge : 4ft 8½in

	(CYPRUS)	0-6-0ST	IC	MW	596	1876		
			reb	MW		1900	(a)	Scr c/1933
	MARELL	0-6-0ST	IC	HE	876	1906	(b)	(2)
	Y.I.C.No.7	0-4-0ST	OC	P	1057	1905	(c)	(1)
(54	JULIA)	0-6-0ST	IC	HC	1682	1937	(d)	(3)
	SIR ALFRED WOOD	0-6-0DM		RH	319294	1953	New	(4)

(a)   ex Walter Scott & Middleton Ltd, contrs, (Newark ?), c/1922.
(b)   ex Walter Scott & Middleton Ltd, contrs, Newark, after 10/1921, by 7/1923.
(c)   ex Yorkshire Iron & Coal Co Ltd, after 9/1921 (probably after the closure of East Ardsley Ironworks, Yorks (WR) in /1929), by 10/1931.
(d)   ex Sir Lindsay Parkinson & Co Ltd, contrs, Temple Newsam Plant Depot, Leeds, c/1947 (by 6/1947), per (or via?). Thos.W. Ward Ltd, Sheffield.

(1)   withdrawn 1946; derelict by 8/1950; scrapped 6/1951.
(2)   withdrawn by 9/1954; offered for sale by 9/1955; s/s after 9/1956, by 5/1957.
(3)   to Newark District Council, Millgate Folk Museum, Newark, 17/4/1981.
(4)   to Woodston Factory, Peterborough, Cambs, c7/1983 (after 17/7/1982, by 4/8/1983).

NOTTINGHAM FACTORY, Mile End Road, Colwick, Nottingham   T43
(formerly known as **Colwick Factory**)   SK 617400
Second Anglo-Scottish Beet Sugar Corporation Ltd until 12/6/1936

Building of the works commenced in 1924 and it was opened in time for the 1925 campaign. It was served by sidings south of the Colwick Estate Light Railway (worked by the LNER and BR), at the west end of this line. Rail traffic ceased 1981 (by 7/1981), and the works was closed completely on 25/3/1982.

Gauge : 4ft 8½in

No.3		0-6-0ST	IC	HC	765	1907	(a)	s/s
No.1		0-4-0ST	OC	P	1439	1916	(b)	Scr 8/1963
	KING GEORGE	0-4-0ST	OC	HL	2839	1910	(c)	(1)
	-	0-4-0ST	OC	P	1649	1924	(d)	(2)
	-	0-6-0ST	OC	P	2000	1942	New	(3)
No.5		0-4-0ST	OC	P	1725	1927	(e)	Scr 7/1954

No.1	(FRED)	0-4-0DM	RH	319292	1953	New	(4)
No.2		0-4-0DM	RH	375718	1955	(f)	(5)
	-	0-4-0DE	RH	423657	1958	(g)	(6)

Note that a diesel loco was reported here, 6/1948 (on trials ?).

(a) ex Cox & Danks, Queenborough Shipbreaking Yard, Kent, /1925.
(b) ex WD Barnbow, near Leeds, by 2/1926; to Felstead Factory, Essex, c6/1953; returned, c/1954 (by 18/4/1954).
(c) ex Thos.W. Ward Ltd, Charlton Works, Sheffield, hire, 7/12/1933 (assumed to have come to Colwick rather than the company's other factory at Cupar, Fife).
(d) ex Thos.W. Ward Ltd, Charlton Works, Sheffield, hire, (for 4 weeks from) 29/11/1934
(e) ex Felstead Factory, Essex, 9/1951.
(f) ex Woodston Factory, Hunts, /1959.
(g) ex RH, Lincoln, loan 25/9/1960 (at NCB Harworth Colliery until 11/8/1960).

(1) returned to Thos.W. Ward Ltd, Charlton Works, Sheffield, off hire, c8/1/1934.
(2) returned to Thos.W. Ward Ltd, Charlton Works, Sheffield, off hire, c26/12/1934.
(3) to P for repairs, 4/1955, then to Ipswich Factory, Suffolk, 10/1955.
(4) to Spalding Factory, Lincs, c8/1981 (after 11/7/1981).
(5) to Spalding Factory, Lincs, 9/1981.
(6) returned to RH Lincoln, 26/10/1960 (thence to Associated Electrical Industries (Rugby) Ltd, Rugby, Warwicks, 19/12/1960).

BRITISH TRANSPORT COMMISSION
DOCKS & INLAND WATERWAYS EXECUTIVE

TRENT LANE WHARF, Trent Lane, Nottingham   S44
Trent Navigation Co Ltd until 1/1/1948   SK 589389

This wharf, constructed after 1925, was served by a ¾ mile line which opened in 3/1933 and ran south from Sneinton Junction on the LMSR Nottingham Midland - Carlton & Netherfield line, ¾ mile east of Nottingham Midland Station. The loco also worked at Riverside Wharf, Colwick, at SK 621400 (see below) for a period and travelled over the LMSR line between the two locations. The exchange sidings also served the private siding of the Midland Co-operative Laundries Association. Use of the locomotive had ceased by 1955 but the siding remained listed until some time between 1962 and 1976. The wharf passed to the British Waterways Board on 1/1/1963.

COLWICK RIVERSIDE WHARF   T44A
Trent Navigation Co Ltd until 1/1/1948   SK 621400

The opening date of this wharf is not known but no rail connection is shown in amendments to the "Handbook of Stations" until sometime between 1941 and 1949. Its sidings were connected to the south west end of the Nottingham Colwick Estates Light Railway. The use of the locomotive here was shortlived. Rail traffic to the wharf ceased some time after 1962.

Gauge : 4ft 8½in (both locations)

-		0-4-0DM	HC	D603	1936	(a)	(1)

(a) ex Ministry of Supply; earlier Tarmac Ltd, TARMAC No.1.
(1) scrapped /1955 (after 8/1955).

BUTTERLEY CO LTD
The Butterley Company until 18/4/1888

In 1790 Benjamin Outram, William Jessop, John Wright and Francis Beresford established an ironworks near Ripley, Derbyshire and exploited coal workings on the nearby Butterley Hall Estate. On 10/12/1792 the four men entered into a formal partnership agreement. This continued until Wright bought out Beresford in 1806. The business expanded by opening a forge at Codnor Park, Derbyshire and progressively opened collieries and brickworks together with a network of horse tramways on both the Derbyshire and Nottinghamshire sides of the Erewash Valley. Many of these were later converted to standard gauge mineral railways and the company eventually built 29 locomotives, all except two being for its own use. On Vesting Day, 1/1/1947, seven collieries (two of which were in Nottinghamshire), each with modern equipment and healthy finances, producing a total of 3 million tons of high quality coal per year, were handed over to the National Coal Board, along with more than 1000 wagons, 1800 houses, one brickworks and 2,500 acres of farm land. The Butterley Works, Codnor Park Forge and some of the brickworks remained in the company ownership.

References : "The Butterley Company 1790-1930", P. Riden, Author, 1973.
"Industrial Railway Record No 138". 'Butterley Locomotives',
Frank Jones & Trevor Lodge, IRS, Sept.1994.

KIRKBY COLLIERY, Kirkby in Ashfield J45
(also known as SUMMIT COLLIERY) SK 504572

The colliery was sunk in 1888-90 and was served by sidings on the west side of the Midland Railway, Mansfield - Kirkby line, ½ mile north of Kirkby Station. Both full and empties sidings were, from its opening in 1897, connected to the GNR Leen Valley Extension line which passed to the west of the colliery. By 1898 there was a brickworks in operation at the south end of the site which had a short narrow gauge incline into a clay hole. This had gone by 1939 and its site was covered by a tip. A new brick works at SK 505573, north east of the colliery, was built in 1921. The colliery was extensively modernised in 1913 - 1915 when the **LOWMOOR SHAFT** was sunk. Although on the Kirkby site, this was at first regarded as a separate colliery. The brickworks remained in Butterley Company ownership. The colliery was vested in the NCB, East Midlands Division, Area No.4, 1/1/1947.

Gauge : 4ft 8½in

B1C		0-4-0ST	OC	Butterley	1887	New?	(2)
B2C		0-4-0ST	OC	Butterley 1887 or 1889(a)			(1)
B7C		0-4-0ST	OC	Butterley			
				reb from 0-4-0 1903 or 1904			
			reb	Butterley	1914	(b)	Scr by /1947
B9C		0-4-0ST	OC	Butterley	1896		
			reb	Butterley 1916 or 1917(c)			(3)
B18C		0-6-0ST	IC	HC	591	1901 New	(3)
B19C		0-6-0ST	IC	HC	613	1902 New	(3)
B20C		0-6-0ST	OC	Butterley	1904	(d)	(3)
	BUTTERLEY No.30	0-6-0ST	OC	WB	2604	1939 New	(3)

Notes : per a boiler explosion report, in 1901 "B2C" was the only loco at Kirkby, where it had been since at least 1894.

ILS records list B10C 0-4-0ST OC Butterley 1896 as Butterley - Kirkby - Butterley (no dates). They also list an 0-6-0ST OC 12in at Kirkby, to Richard Thomas Ltd, Redbourne Hill Works, Scunthorpe, Lincs.

(a) possibly new here; to Butterley Works, Derbys, for repair, 20/11/1901; returned.
(b) ex Butterley Works, Derbys, 10/7/1928; returned ; ex Ollerton Colliery, c/1942.
(c) possibly new here; believed at Butterley works for repair prior to returning here 5/1946.
(d) ex Ripley Colliery, Derbys.

(1) at Codnor Park Works, Derbys, by 19/12/1901 when boiler exploded; to Brereton Collieries Ltd, Staffs.
(2) at Butterley Ironworks, Derbys 27/5/1927; returned to Kirkby; to Nottingham & Clifton Colliery Co Ltd, Clifton Colliery, Nottingham, c/1939.
(3) to NCB East Midlands Division, Area No.3, with site, 1/1/1947.

OLLERTON COLLIERY G46
SK 661677

Sinking commenced in 11/1923. Contractors, Francois Cementation Co Ltd. sank the shafts though the water-bearing strata, after which the sinking was completed by the Butterley Co. Coal was reached on 4/8/1925. The colliery was served by sidings on the north side of the LNER Mansfield - Tuxford line, 1 mile east of Ollerton Station and was later connected to the LMSR Mansfield - Southwell line, east of Farnsfield Station, by the Mid Nottinghamshire Joint line (LMSR and LNER) which opened in 1931. The surface railway was also used for dirt disposal to tips east of the colliery, north of the LNER exchange sidings, where a brickworks (see following entry) was also shunted by colliery locomotives. Vested in the NCB, East Midlands Division, Area No.3, 1/1/1947.

Gauge : 4ft 8½in

B7C		0-4-0ST	OC	Butterley				
				reb from 0-4-0 1903 or 1904				
				reb	Butterley	1914	(a)	(1)
B13C		0-6-0ST	OC	Butterley		1900		
				reb		1919	(b)	(3)
B17C		0-4-0ST	OC	HL	2466	1900	(c)	(2)
B21C		0-6-0ST	OC	Butterley	1906 or1907			
				reb		1919	(d)	(3)
22		0-4-0ST	OC	KS	3111	1918	(e)	(3)
	BUTTERLEY No.31	0-6-0ST	OC	WB	2605	1939	New	(3)
	BUTTERLEY No.51	0-4-0ST	OC	WB	2619	1940	New	(3)

(a) ex Butterley Ironworks, Derbys. c/1942.
(b) ex ?
(c) New to Butterley Co Ltd at unspecified location; here by ? .
(d) ex Bailey Brook Colliery, Derbys.
(e) ex MoM, Gainsborough, /1923.

(1) to Summit Colliery, c/1942.
(2) at Shell Refining & Marketing Co Ltd, (Stanlow, Cheshire?) by /1941; later with Cudworth & Johnson, dealers, Wrexham, c/1941 (by 3/1942). [If it was at the Stanlow site, it may then have been on hire from Cudworth & Johnson.]
(3) to NCB, East Midlands Division, Area No.3, with site, 1/1/1947.

PLUMPTRE COLLIERY, Eastwood   L47
(also known as **PLUMTRE** or **PLUMTREE COLLIERY**)   SK 462481

The colliery, sunk at some time between 1843 and 1854, was first connected by a private line to the end of the Midland Railway, Beggarlee Branch (opened 1849) adjacent to Messrs Barber, Walker's connection (SK 455477). The private line ran north east to the colliery (½ mile). A connection was made with the GNR Erewash Valley line, east of the Midland Railway junction, after the former opened in 1875. The siding accommodation at the colliery extended considerably between 1879 and 1898 but the colliery closed on 30th April 1912. The branch line remained until at least 1938, realigned to the north at the colliery end and apparently serving a quarry. Shortly afterwards it was lifted and both colliery and quarry sites were tipped on by Barber, Walker. We have no knowledge of how the colliery branch was worked but there were separate exchange sidings with both railway companies at Beggarlee. Possibilities are an outstationed Butterley locomotive, main line locomotives or an arrangement with Barber, Walker & Co Ltd.

PORTLAND and MEXBORO' COLLIERIES, Kirkby in Ashfield & Selston K48
Comprising :

PORTLAND No.1 COLLIERY	SK 480549
PORTLAND No.2 COLLIERY	SK 483544
PORTLAND No.3 COLLIERY	not known
PORTLAND No.4 COLLIERY	SK 485538
PORTLAND No.5 COLLIERY	SK 485536
PORTLAND No.6 & 7 COLLIERIES	SK 477538
MEXBORO' No.1 & 2 (HOLLY HILL) COLLIERIES	SK 473531
MEXBORO' No.3 (LOWER) COLLIERY	SK 469528

The earliest of these collieries, **PORTLAND No.1,** was sunk in 1821 on the north side of the Mansfield and Pinxton Railway, a horse worked line opened in 1819 (see Non-locomotive Section). About 1822 a direct tramway was made, partly horseworked and partly by inclines, from the Mansfield and Pinxton Railway, No.1 Colliery and some lime kilns west of there, to the Cromford Canal at Portland Basin, Codnor Park (SK 444514). **Nos.2 to 5 Pits** were all sunk between 1830 and 1843; indeed No.3 had already closed by 1843 and its location is not known to us. No.2 was located south of the Mansfield and Pinxton Railway, ½ mile east of No.1. No.4 (and a pit which was probably No.5) were located ½ mile south of No.2 and both these were linked by tramway branches to the line serving No.1 Colliery. **Nos.6 and 7,** which opened in 1843, shared the same site on the south side of the tramway to Codnor Park, ½ mile west of No.4 Pit. The Mansfield and Pinxton Railway was converted to a Midland Railway locomotive worked branch line and reopened in 1851. No.1 and 2 pits are presumed to have had connections from that time and the tramways linking Nos.4 to 7 Pits to the Midland Railway were converted to conventional railways, albeit retaining the rope worked incline which served Nos.6 and 7 Pits. The tramway to No.1 Pit and the lime kilns was not converted.

The **MEXBORO', MEXBRO'** or **MEXBOROUGH COLLIERIES** were sunk between 1843 and 1870, and by 1878 had been connected to the former tramway route at Dove Green (SK 462526) by a new railway which ran east to **MEXBORO' No.3** (also known as LOWER MEXBORO' or BOTTOM PIT) Colliery and terminated at **MEXBORO' Nos.1 and 2 (HOLLY HILL)** Colliery. Nos 1 and 2 were also known as North and South pits The old tramway west from Dove Green to Portland Wharf had been converted to a railway by 1878, retaining the self-acting incline. The section from Dove Green north to the incline serving PORTLAND Nos. 6 & 7 Pits had been lifted by 1878 and, if all Portland coal went out by the Midland Railway after 1851, then this may never have been converted to a railway.

One source gives PORTLAND No.1 Pit as having closed by 1843, but this is unlikely as the surface in 1878 was fully equipped for coal winding and the shafts were not abandoned until 1910. No.1 Colliery was served by sidings on the north side of the Midland Railway and presumably worked by them with the assistance of gravity and horses. The sidings at Portland No.2 Colliery, whilst not extensive, also formed the lower end of a three rail incline which came down from a small quarry, lime kiln and wharf (SK 490543) at Kirkby Woodhouse, shown on the plan as 'Annesley Wharf'. This was built as a tramway in 1826. Baxter (Stone Blocks and Iron Rails) claims it to have been in Mansfield & Pinxton ownership but if so it does not appear to have passed to the Midland Railway. When the quarry was working, the incline could have been self acting. A rope haulage engine would have been needed thereafter to get coal to the wharf. From No.2 Colliery, a line ran south to No.4. This was relatively level and probably where the locomotive B19C worked. A building, south of No.4 Pit at SK 486537, could well have been a loco shed. A shaft 200 yards south of No.4 Pit, with earthworks suggesting a tubway linking them, is believed to have been No.5 Pit. It was not in use in 1878 or 1914.

The line which ran west from between Portland Nos.2 and 4 Collieries was a rope incline for the first 1000 yards, probably a direct rope which would allow the short branch south to Nos.6 and 7 Collieries to be worked by the same engine, which was located at SK 473539.

The MEXBORO' line commenced as an incline, possibly self acting, which ran west from Nos.1 and 2 Colliery to No.3. From there a fairly level line ran west to Dove Green, and then south west to the top of a self acting incline at SK 452521. How this section was worked is not known. It is possible that a Butterley or Codnor Park locomotive came up the self acting incline which lowered coal to sidings at Portland Basin on the Cromford Canal, where the original tramway had ended. From here Butterley locomotives worked the traffic to its works or to the main line railways (see the forthcoming Derbyshire Handbook).

MEXBORO' No.3 Colliery was abandoned on 1/8/1885 and Nos.1 & 2 were abandoned on 16/11/1894. The line west of there had closed by 1895, except for the sidings at Portland Wharf which went before 1914. In the case of the PORTLAND Collieries, Nos.6 and 7,were last listed in statistics in 1878 and their incline was lifted between 1880 and 1895. The incline to Annesley Wharf had also been lifted by 1895. Portland No.1 Colliery closed in 1910 and No.4 Colliery was disused by 1914 when, in each case, the tracks were still in place. Abandonment plans for No.2 Colliery were deposited on 28/2/1921 and the sidings were lifted except for those immediately adjacent to the LMSR line which remained in 1939 as Upper Portland Sidings. At this time there was a small quarry to the south of these (SK 487544) with 200 yards of narrow gauge tramway. The site of No.2 Colliery became the **UPPER PORTLAND DISPOSAL POINT** of the Ministry of Fuel and Power c1945. (see NCB Section).

Gauge : 4ft 8½in

B19C	0-4-0VBT	1871	(a)	(1)

Note that it is probable that there were other Butterley locomotives here.

(a)   maker and origin unknown.

(1)   sold or scrapped, probably by /1902.

BUTTERLEY & BLABY BRICK COMPANIES LTD
OLLERTON BRICKWORKS G49
(Subsidiary of the **Butterley Co Ltd** from c1948) SK674673
earlier **Butterley Co Ltd**

This brickworks was built in 1924 and was located at the east end of the Ollerton Colliery complex. Shunting was by the colliery locomotives. The source of its clay is uncertain. It reopened in 1946 after a period of closure during World War II. It was not vested in the NCB. The tramway closed and was lifted c1957. The use to which the locomotive was put is not known.

Gauge : 2ft 0in

		4wDM	FH	2514	1941	(a)	(1)

(a) ex Waingroves Brickworks, Ripley, Derbys, c/1956 (after 8/1955).

(1) to Blaby Brickworks, Leics, c/1957.

CENTRAL ELECTRICITY GENERATING BOARD
Central Electricity Authority until 1/1/1958
British Electricity Authority until 1/4/1955

The electricity generation and supply industry was nationalised on 1/4/1948 when installations were vested in the British Electricity Authority (Central Electricity Authority from 1/4/1955). From 1/1/1958 generation and supply were segregated, power stations passing to the Central Electricity Generating Board. This was privatised from 31/3/1990 with power stations passing to **NATIONAL POWER plc** and **POWERGEN plc** (which see).

HIGH MARNHAM POWER STATION - see Eastern Electricity plc.

NORTH WILFORD POWER STATION, Nottingham S50
(also known as NOTTINGHAM POWER STATION) SK 563378
Nottingham Corporation Electricity Department until 1/4/1948

Construction of this station began on 17/9/1920. Locomotives were used by the contractors, **H. Arnold & Son Ltd**, and **Wilson Lovatt & Sons Ltd** (which see). It was officially opened on 17/9/1925. The station was served by sidings on the south side of the LMSR Nottingham - Beeston line, 1¼ miles west of Nottingham Midland Station, and also by a connection to the sidings of the Nottingham & Clifton Colliery Ltd (later NCB) to the north of the power station. During an extensive remodelling after World War II, part of the rail network was electrified with an overhead wire system. This was disused from c1959 as BR refused to work their locomotives under the wires. The power station closed in 1980; part of the site was demolished in 1985 but the remainder passed to the East Midlands Electricity Board as a distribution station.

Gauge : 4ft 8½in

No.7		0-6-0F	OC	AB	1487	1916	(a)	(5)
-		0-6-0ST	IC	HE	152	1876		
		reb		HE		1904	(b)	Scr /1934
	JOHN	0-4-0ST	OC	P	1608	1923	(c)	(4)
	MARY	0-4-0ST	OC	P	1906	1936	New	(3)
No.4		4wWE		Bg	3245	1949	New	(6)
No.5		4wWE		Bg	3330	1950	New	(6)
CASTLE DONINGTON No.2		0-4-0ST	OC	RSHN	7818	1954	(d)	(1)
WILLINGTON No.1		0-6-0DM		RSHN	7859	1956		
				DC	2573	1956	New	(2)
WILLINGTON No.2		0-6-0DM		RSHN	7860	1956		
				DC	2574	1956	New	(2)
No.1		0-4-0DE		RH	420140	1958	New	(8)
No.2		0-4-0DE		RH	420142	1958	New	(7)

(a) ex MoM Gretna, by 4/1925 (possibly in /1923).
(b) ex Wilson Lovatt & Sons Ltd, contractor on site, c/1926 (by 1/1927).
(c) ex Bradford Corporation Sewage Works, Esholt, Yorks (WR), via C. Jones, dealer, (Aldridge, Staffs ?), 7/1933.
(d) built for Castle Donington Power Station, Leics, but delivered new to Leicester Power Station (for storage) from whence it moved here, /1954.

(1) to Castle Donington Power Station, Leics, after 9/1955, by 1/1957.
(2) to Willington Power Station, Derbys, /1957 (after 1/6/1957).
(3) to South Yorkshire Chemical Works Ltd, Parkgate, Rotherham, 8/1959 (after 2/8/1959).
(4) sold or scrapped /1959 (after 2/8/1959).
(5) out of use from c/1958; scrapped after 3/1961.
(6) out of use from c/1959; to John Cashmore Ltd, Great Bridge, Staffs, for scrap, 7/1963.
(7) to Castle Donington Power Station, Leics, c3/1981 (after 26/9/1980, by 4/4/1982).
(8) to Tilsley & Lovatt Ltd, Blurton, Stoke on Trent, Staffs; resold to South Staffordshire Wagon Co Ltd, Tipton, W. Midlands, 10/1981.

STAYTHORPE POWER STATION - see National Power plc.

WEST BURTON POWER STATION, near Gainsborough   B51
SK 798858

Construction of this station began in 1958 and it was opened c1964. The station was served from its opening by BR 'Merry go round' trains, with the CEGB locomotive being used on internal traffic until 1979. The station continues in use and was taken into the ownership of National Power plc on 31/3/1990.

Note;: a blue 0-4-0D was noted here on 1/5/1960, during the construction period. This may have been a CEGB Project Group locomotive or one owned by a contractor.

Gauge : 4ft 8½in

WEST BURTON No.1	0-6-0DH	AB	486	1964	New	(1)

(1) to Meaford 'B' Power Station, Staffs, No.4, 26/7/1979.

COSSALL COLLIERY CO LTD
TROWELL MOOR COLLIERY, Stapleford Q52
Trowell Moor Colliery Co by 1895, until between 1900 and 1904. SK 495390
formerly **Dunn Bros**.
Lord Middleton pre 1870

Mining on Trowell Moor was carried out from about 1807 onwards, by Lord Middleton, at small pits along a tramway route from SK 504406 to a wharf on the Nottingham Canal at SK 508394. Lord Middleton is last recorded as working coal at Trowell in 1869. 'Old Engine' Pit of 1807 is believed to have been located to the east of the wharf at SK 510394. The tramway had been lifted and all the early collieries had been closed by the time of the Ordnance Survey of 1879. This shows a site at SK 507396 on the north side of the Midland Railway's Radford Junction - Trowell Junction line (which had opened 1/5/1875), with signs of a short siding by then already lifted. It could have been a coal loading point although this is conjecture.

This site of the later Trowell Moor Colliery was undeveloped at the time of the Ordnance Survey of 1878-79, although "The Mines List" records D.G. Dunn & Co. of Glasgow as working a Trowell Moor Colliery in 1879. It is possible that this was Old Engine Pit. The new colliery was sunk in 1881-2 and by 4/1883 there is known to have been a Trowell Moor Colliery signal box. This colliery was served by sidings, on the south side of the Midland Railway, Trowell Junction - Radford Junction line, 1 mile south east of Trowell Junction. Dunn Bros were listed as operating the mine in 1898 and hence were likely to have been the proprietors of the Trowell Moor Colliery Co. Production ceased on 29/9/1928 and the site subsequently became the **TROWELL MOOR DISPOSAL POINT** of the Ministry of Fuel & Power, Directorate of Opencast Coal Production from c/1943 to c/1947. The site passed to NCB, East Midlands Division, Area No.5 from 1/1/1947 as a pumping station and landsale depot, without rail traffic.

Gauge : 4ft 8½in

	0-4-0ST	OC	B				
-			reb	AB	210	1884	(a)	s/s

(a) ex AB, 24/12/1884; possibly earlier with Dunn Bros at another location.

NOTES : There is conflicting evidence regarding the above loco. A document in AB archives suggests that it was a rebuild of B 209/1874, but an AB spares order of 8/1905 and an overhaul record of 1908 both refer to a loco of Wm. Baird & Co Ltd, Cumnock, Ayrshire as being B 209/1874.
The 1884 invoice for AB 210 was in respect of "repair of an 8in loco for Dunn Bros., Stapleford". The "Colliery Guardian" of 18/11/1898, describing the Trowell Moor plant states; 'the colliery tank locomotive has 12½ inch cylinders and 4 wheels coupled'. Hence this is clearly not the locomotive repaired in 1884.

DONCASTER AMALGAMATED COLLIERIES LTD
FIRBECK MAIN COLLIERY, Langold B53
Firbeck Main Collieries Ltd until 1/7/1939 SK 583861

The Sheepbridge Company and the Doncaster Collieries Association combined to form Firbeck Main Collieries Ltd, which was registered on 13/12/1913. Firbeck Main Colliery was sunk in 1923-25. Coal was reached in 8/1925. The colliery was located at the end of the South Yorkshire Joint Railway (LMSR & LNER) Firbeck Colliery branch, which opened in 1926 (contractors - **Mitchell Bros, Sons & Co Ltd**, which see), 4 miles south of its junction with the

Harworth Colliery branch. However, in 1924, a temporary line had been laid alongside the proposed route, at a gradient of 1 in 20, to facilitate the construction of the colliery and Langold village. The locomotives were fitted from new with additional buffers to enable contractors type wagons to be used on the temporary line. The narrow gauge locomotive listed below is believed to have been used in connection with the colliery sinking and construction.

The colliery was vested in the NCB North Eastern Division, No.1 Area, 1/1/1947.

Gauge : 4ft 8½in

DAISY	0-6-0ST	OC	AE	1895	1923	New (a)	(1)
BILL	0-6-0ST	OC	AE	1920	1924	New	(1)

(a) locomotive delivered in parts to Worksop station, from where it was taken by road to the colliery for erection.

(1) to NCB, North Eastern Division, No.1 Area, with site, 1/1/1947.

Gauge : 2ft 2in

ALBERT EDWARD	0-4-0ST	OC	(MW	482	1873 ?)	
	reb	J.F.Wake			(a)	(1)

(a) ex Hickleton Main Colliery Co Ltd, Thurnscoe, Yorks (WR), c/1923-/1925.

(1) returned to Hickleton Main Colliery Co Ltd, c/1923-/1925.

EASTERN ELECTRICITY plc
HIGH MARNHAM POWER STATION, near Newton-on-Trent   F54
Eastern Group plc until 2/10/1996   SK 807712
PowerGen plc until 6/1996
Central Electricity Generating Board until 31/3/1990

Work on this station commenced 2/1956. Contractors were **Sir Alfred McAlpine & Son Ltd** (which see) and Taylor Woodrow Construction Ltd. Sidings were by Railway & General Engineering Ltd. Generating commenced in 1959 and it was fully operational by 1962. Extensive sidings were provided on the south side of the BR Tuxford (Dukeries Jct.) - Lincoln (Pyewipe Jct.) line, ¾ mile east of the former Fledborough station. Since 1969 the power station has been served entirely by 'Merry go Round' trains and the track layout has been rationalised. One loco has been retained for maintenance work.

Gauge : 4ft 8½in

1	0-4-0DH	AB	440	1958	New	(1)
2	0-4-0DH	AB	441	1959	New (a)	
3	0-4-0DH	AB	442	1959	New	(1)
4	0-4-0DH	AB	443	1959	New	(1)

(a) to Nechells Power Station, Birmingham, 10/1971; returned, 9/1/1972.

(1) to Meaford Power Station, Staffs, 11/1969. The three locomotives were transferred by rail; one developed overheated axle boxes and they were delayed en route. They eventually arrived on 17/12/1969.

EAST MIDLANDS GAS BOARD

In 1818 the Gas Light & Coke Co commenced gas production in Nottingham. During the 1840s and 1850s new plants were opened at Radford (which being laid out with capstans and wagon turntables, had no need of locomotives - see Non-locomotive Section), Basford and Eastcroft. They were bought by the Nottingham Corporation for £463,000 in 1874. On nationalisation of the gas industry, they were vested in the East Midlands Gas Board from 1/5/1949.

BASFORD GASWORKS, Radford Road, Nottingham   Q55
Nottingham Corporation Gas Department until 1/5/1949   SK 555423

Gasworks was served by sidings on the east side of the Midland Railway's Radford - Bulwell line (opened 2/10/1848), ½ mile south of the former Basford station. As it existed in 1881, the works was laid out for operation by wagon turntables and capstans. An extension to the south, completed around 1895, required the use of locomotives. Coal gas production and rail traffic ceased, c/1972.

Gauge : 4ft 8½in

			VICTORIA	0-4-0ST	IC	BP	3809	1895	New (a)	(1)
			IRENE	0-4-0ST	IC	BP	4164	1899	New (b)	(1)
No.3	VICTORIA		12631	4wDM		RH	305313	1951	New	(2)
No.2	IRENE No.394	12632		4wDM		RH	305318	1951	New	(2)
				0-4-0ST	OC	P	1879	1934	(c)	Scr 10/1967
		12630		4wDM		RH	305316	1951	(d)	(3)

(a) to Eastcroft Gasworks, Nottingham, and returned, /1946.
(b) to Eastcroft Gasworks, Nottingham, 1/1950; returned by /1952.
(c) ex Eastcroft Gasworks, Nottingham, 8/1965.
(d) ex Eastcroft Gasworks, Nottingham, /1970.

(1) scrapped on site by Thos.W. Ward Ltd, /1952 (by 6/1952).
(2) to A.W. Brown Ltd, scrap dealer, Long Eaton, Derbys, 6/1972.
(3) to A.W. Brown Ltd, scrap dealer, Long Eaton, Derbys, /1973.

EASTCROFT GASWORKS, London Road, Nottingham   S56
Nottingham Corporation Gas Department until 1/5/1949   SK 582384

This works was located on the north side of, and connected to, the GNR Goods Yard at its London Road (Low Level) station (siding agreement dated 25/3/1857). There was also a rail connected wharf on an arm of the Nottingham Canal which formed the northern boundary of the works. By 1904 Boots Pure Drug Co Ltd had a loading dock here to serve its nearby factory. It was a cramped layout made more difficult by the construction of the GNR line from Trent Lane Junction to Weekday Cross Junction (opened 15/3/1899) which spanned the works on a viaduct. Originally laid out with wagon turntables and capstans, remodelling under an agreement dated 16/5/1934, when new plant was installed, enabled a locomotive to be used. The works closed in 1970.

Gauge : 4ft 8½in

1				0-4-0ST	OC	P	1879	1934	New	(3)
	VICTORIA			0-4-0ST	IC	BP	3809	1895	(a)	(1)
	IRENE			0-4-0ST	IC	BP	4164	1899	(b)	(2)
1	(No.392)	12630		4wDM		RH	305316	1951	New	(4)

(a) ex Basford Gasworks, /1946.
(b) ex Basford Gasworks, 1/1950.

(1) to Basford Gasworks, /1946.
(2) to Basford Gasworks, by /1952.
(3) to Basford Gasworks, 8/1965.
(4) to Basford Gasworks, /1970.

G. B. GLASS LTD
HARWORTH WORKS B57
English Glass Ltd until c/1990 SK 624906
Glass Bulbs Ltd until /1989
  (Subsidiary of **AEI Ltd**)

This works was established c1949 immediately south of the NCB Harworth Coking Plant. It was served by sidings on the south side of the BR Tickhill - Mattesey line, 3½ miles east of Tickhill Jct. Rail traffic ceased 6/9/1991, but the works continues to operate (1999) under the title of Demaglass.

Gauge : 4ft 8½in

-		4wPM	Reliance *			(a)	s/s c/1951
-		4wDM	RH	299099	1950	New	(4)
-		4wDM	RH	210476	1941	(b)	(1)
-		4wDM	RH	299107	1950	(c)	(2)
-		4wDH	RH	513141	1966	New	(3)
161 301		4wDM	RH	458959	1961	(d)	(4)

* possibly built by FH using an engine and radiator by Reliance.

(a) ex British Thomson-Houston Ltd, Rugby, Warwicks.
(b) ex RH, Boultham Ironworks, Lincoln, hire, 2/11/1962.
(c) ex RH, Grantham Works, Lincs, 9/1964.
(d) ex Chesterfield Works, Derbys, after 9/4/1984, by 22/5/1986.

(1) to RH, Boultham Ironworks, Lincoln, off hire, 12/12/1962.
(2) to RH, 2/1966; resold to Lime Firms Ltd, Cil-yr-Ychen Limeworks, Pant-yr-odyn, Carms, 2/1966.
(3) to Telford Horshay Steam Trust, Horsehay, Salop, 23/3/1983.
(4) to Shropshire Locomotive Collection, Salop, 2/9/1992.

GUNTHORPE GRAVELS (TRENT) LTD
GUNTHORPE GRAVEL PITS U58
SK 679439

These pits were situated west of the A6057 road, on the north side of the River Trent. The tramway had gone by 7/1957. It has not been possible to locate a map showing the extent of the system but the pits were to the west of the location given which was the screens and loading point.

Gauge : 2ft 0in

		4wDM	MR	8762	1942	(a)	s/s
-		4wDM	(MR?)			(b)	(1)
-		4wDM	MR	8594	1940	(c)	(2)

(a) ex Petrol Loco Hirers (Ltd, Bedford?), earlier on hire (or New?).
(b) origin and details not known.
(c) ex Thos Cowman & Sons Ltd, Asfordby, Leics, by 19/8/1951.

(1) to Wreake Valley Gravel Co Ltd, Leics.
(2) to Wreake Valley Gravel Co Ltd, Leics, by 5/1955.

WILLIAM HALL
LODGE COLLIERY, Newthorpe M59
SK 474454

Sinking of this colliery was in progress in 1876 by William Hall, who had previously been manager at Digby Coal Co. **LODGE COLLIERY** opened in 1877 and was located on the north east side of the GNR Pinxton branch (opened 23/8/1875), ¾ mile south east of Newthorpe station and was served from the adjacent GNR Digby sidings. There was also, by 1880, a small brick kiln, later extended. A description of the plant in the Colliery Guardian dated 16/11/1894 refers to two locomotives being at the colliery where there was scarcely enough track to justify them. Two brickworks were then said to be working, one at the colliery and one 'some distance away' (site not identified). Part of the clay products were said to be "sent off by the Nottingham Canal". It is possible that the locos worked between Lodge Colliery and the canal wharf at Digby Colliery over the GNR mineral line which connected them. Hall died c1894-5 and the business was carried on for a while by his executors. The colliery closed in 1896 but the brickworks may have continued to operate until c1900. All was subsequently demolished. Lodge Colliery was reopened by **Manners Colliery Co** as a rail served colliery on the same site after 1913, by 1921. The new colliery made extensive use of rope haulage engines for shunting and had no known locomotives. More details can be found in the Non-locomotive Section under **Ilkeston Collieries Ltd** and in the NCB Section.

Gauge : 4ft 8½in

-	6wc tank	FW	(a)	s/s
-	6wc tank	GE	(b)	s/s

(a) origin unknown; 12in x 17in cylinders; here in /1894.
(b) origin unknown; 11in x 17in cylinders; here in /1894.

S. HEASELDEN & SON LTD
CROPWELL BISHOP GYPSUM MINES U60
Samuel Heaselden & Son until c1929 SK 674357
Samuel Heaselden until c1920

The first mine here was commenced in 1905. By 1915 a short tramway ran south-west from the works, on the south side of the road which runs west from Cropwell Bishop, to a mine at SK 675354. This mine had been closed by 1950 and replaced by another at SK 672354 to which the tramway then ran. The later mine had ceased production by 7/1957 and the tramway closed. Everything was still in place and the mine accessible in 1961 and for some time afterwards. By then the main business of the firm was road haulage. Horses are believed to have worked the tramway prior to the arrival of the locomotives.

Gauge : 1ft 10in

		4wDM	OK	4032	c1930	(a)	(2)
-		4wDM	OK	4156	c1930	(b)	(1)
-		4wDM	RH	177646	1936	(c)	(3)

(a) origin not known; carried plate 'J.B. Edwards 715'.
(b) origin not known.
(c) ex Derbyshire Gravel & Aggregates Ltd, Pinfold Works, Repton, Derbys, after 29/12/1939, by 25/7/1944.

(1) out of use by 7/1957; s/s c/1964, cab and bodywork remained on site c7/1967. .
(2) derelict by 7/1957; s/s c/1964.
(3) dismantled by 7/1957; scrapped on site 4/1965.

Gauge : 2ft 0in

727/71	4wDM	MR	5713	1936	(a)	(1)

(a) ex British Steel Corporation, Stanton Spun Pipe Plant, Ilkeston, Derbys, 5/8/1972; 2ft 0in gauge, stored here only.

(1) to Brockham Museum Association, Dorking, Surrey, 7/4/1975.

HOVERINGHAM GRAVELS (MIDLANDS) LTD
Hoveringham Gravels Ltd until c/1981;
Hoveringham Gravel Co Ltd until 16/5/1963.
(Subsidiary of **Harold Needler (Gravels) Ltd** from /1955)

This company opened its first pits at Hoveringham about 1939, and in the following years opened or took over others. The head office, which until after 1948 was in Doncaster and in 1953 was at Hull, had by 1959 been established at Hoveringham where workshops were also located. Gravel and sand were extracted from extensive workings along the valley of the River Trent. Not all had rail systems but details follow of those where locomotives are known to have been located. A quarries list of 1965 includes additional Hoveringham sites worthy of comment:-1. **East Retford Quarry**, Lound (probably a later use of the site we list in the Non-locomotive Section under North Notts Gravel Co Ltd). 2. **Balderton Quarry**, New Balderton (probably a later use of the site we list in the Non-locomotive Section under Newark Gravel & Concrete Co Ltd). 3. **Bestwood Quarry**, Northern Drive, Bestwood (probably a later use of the site we list in this section under Bestwood Sand Co Ltd). 4. **Girton Quarry**, Trentside, Girton (believed to be at SK 816673, opened after 1953, nothing else known).

At the sites listed below, rail traffic was gradually superseded by conveyor belt systems or, in the case of Holme Pierrepont Quarries, was replaced by mobile plant. About 1983 the Hoveringham company was acquired by the Tarmac Group, and the only extant locomotive, which at that time was standing out of use at Hoveringham Workshops, passed to the ownership of Tarmac Roadstone (Eastern) Ltd (which see).

Locomotives are known to have been on site at the following locations:-

BLEASBY GRAVEL PITS, Bleasby   P61
SK 715494

In 1948, gravel pits were listed at Bleasby being worked by both Hoveringham Gravel Co Ltd and Star Gravels Ltd. Another source says the pits passed from Star to Hoveringham at an unknown date. In any event the tramway here was installed c1948-50. In 1959 the line extended from pits at Bleasby village, where the loco shed was sited (SK 715494), to Gibsmere (SK 719489). The tramway closed c1960 and was removed. The pits had closed by 3/1961.

Gauge : 2ft 0in

-	4wDM	RH	192872	1938	(a)	(2)
L14	4wDM	RH	259770	1948	New	(1)
L15	4wDM	RH	279627	1949	New	(4)
-	4wDM	RH	210494	1941	(b)	(3)
L16	4wDM	RH	349081	1953	(c)	(7)
L12	4wDM	RH	279620	1949	(d)	(5)
L13	4wDM	RH	349080	1953	(d)	(6)
L8	4wDM	RH	259192	1948	(e)	(8)

(a)   ex Hainsworth (Brandesburton) Gravel Co Ltd, Driffield, Yorks (ER), after 13/8/1947.
(b)   ex Colwick Pits, /1955 (by 24/9/1955).
(c)   ex Hoveringham Pits, after 24/4/1955, by 24/9/1955.
(d)   ex Colwick Pits, c/1957 (after 6/1/1957).
(e)   ex Holme Pierrepont Pits, c/1957 (by 18/5/1957).

- (1) to Holme Pierrepont Pits, after 24/4/1955, by 24/9/1955.
- (2) out of use by 4/1955; to Hoveringham Pits by 24/9/1955.
- (3) to Robert Teal Ltd, Whisby, Lincs, 12/1957.
- (4) to Holme Pierrepont Pits, after 24/4/1955, by 24/9/1955; returned, c/1956 (by 18/5/1957); to Hoveringham Pits, c/1958.
- (5) to Holme Pierrepont Pits, c/1960 (by 18/3/1961).
- (6) to Crankley Point Pits, c/1960 (by 18/3/1961).
- (7) to Hoveringham Pits, c/1960 (by 18/3/1961).
- (8) to Colwick Pits, c/1960 (by 18/3/1961).

COLWICK PITS, Mile End Road, Colwick T62
(formerly **TRENT CONCRETE PITS**) SK 630401

In the mid 1950s, Hoveringham began working the Colwick Pits of Trent Concrete Ltd (which see). Both companies were by then subsidiaries of Harold Needler (Gravels) Ltd. The Trent works was at the east end of the Colwick Industrial Estate and, in 1956, was still connected to the standard gauge Colwick Estate Light Railway. The narrow gauge tramway used by Hoveringham ran to a pit on the north bank of the River Trent, south east of the BR Colwick Marshalling Yard. Its route was alongside the BR Grantham line, almost to Rectory Junction, from where it passed under the main line, turned north and, in 1952, ended at a pit at SK 635603. Use of the tramway ceased c1961. By 1976 the pits were worked out.

Gauge : 2ft 0in

-	4wDM	RH	210494	1941	(a)	(1)	
L12	4wDM	RH	279620	1949	(b)	(2)	
L13	4wDM	RH	349080	1953	(c)	(2)	
L8	4wDM	RH	259192	1948	(d)	s/s /1967	
L15	4wDM	RH	279627	1949	(e)	(3)	
L3	4wDM	RH	387889	1955	(e)	(3)	

- (a) ex Hoveringham Pits after 8/5/1952, by 3/1954.
- (b) ex Hoveringham Pits, /1954 (by 1/7/1954).
- (c) ex Hoveringham Pits after 24/4/1955, by 24/9/1955.
- (d) ex Bleasby Pits, c/1960 (by 18/3/1961).
- (e) ex Hoveringham Pits, c/1960 (by 18/3/1961).

- (1) to Bleasby Pits, /1955 (by 14/9/1955).
- (2) to Bleasby Pits, c/1957 (after 6/1/1957).
- (3) to Hoveringham Pits, c/1962.

CRANKLEY POINT PITS, Newark P63
(also known as **NEWARK QUARRY**) SK 792559

These extensive gravel pits, which opened after 1948, were situated on both sides of the River Trent between the BR East Coast Main Line and the Great North Road. The screens were located east of the road at SK 792559. It has not been possible to locate details of the track layout of the tramway employed for some years after 1960. Much of the area to the east had already been worked by 1958 when no tramway is shown.

Gauge : 2ft 0in

L14	4wDM	RH	259770	1948	(a)	(1)	
L13	4wDM	RH	349080	1953	(b)	(2)	
L9	4wDM	RH	375338	1954	(c)	(3)	

(a)   ex Hoveringham Pits, c/1960 (by 18/3/1961).
(b)   ex Bleasby Pits, c/1960 (by 18/3/1961).
(c)   ex Holme Pierrepont Pits, c/1960 (by 18/3/1961).

(1)   to Hoveringham Pits, /1962.
(2)   to Hoveringham Workshops, /1970.
(3)   to Holme Pierrepont Pits, /1967.

HOLME PIERREPONT GRAVEL PITS   T64
(also known as **NOTTINGHAM QUARRY**)   SK 619390
Star Gravels Ltd in 1948.

These workings, on the south bank of the River Trent, had opened by 1948, though the tramway may have been installed later. They were centred on screens and a loading point on the north side of Adbolton Lane, Holme Pierrepont. The rail system being used in 1961 comprised a short line which ran north and then east from the screens to a pit at SK 621394 and a longer line which ran west to pits at SK 610387. By 1976 considerable change had occurred. Adbolton Lane had been diverted to run north of the plant and the railway now ran south and south west for ¾ mile before turning north west to end near the road at SK 610383. The railway was replaced by mobile plant from 23/1/1976 until the pits were worked out in 1979. The site north of Adbolton Lane has since been redeveloped to form the National Water Sports Centre and County Park.

Gauge : 2ft 0in

L7	4wDM	RH	210493	1941	(a)	(1)
L5	4wDM	RH	370555	1953	New	(8)
L8	4wDM	RH	259192	1948	(b)	(2)
L11	4wDM	RH	387879	1955	New	s/s /1967
L10	4wDM	RH	387891	1955	New	(4)
L14	4wDM	RH	259770	1948	(c)	(5)
L15	4wDM	RH	279627	1949	(d)	s/s /1970
L9	4wDM	RH	375338	1954	(e)	s/s /1970
-	0-4-0DH	RH	443648	1960	New(f)	(3)
L12	4wDM	RH	279620	1949	(g)	(6)
L4	4wDM	RH	387878	1955	(h)	Scr /1968
L1	4wDM	RH	370566	1954	(i)	s/s /1972
L2	4wDM	RH	387890	1955	(j)	s/s c/1970
H481	4wDM	HE	6680	1970	New	(7)
H519	4wDM	HE	6681	1970	New	(7)
H595	4wDM	HE	6682	1970	New	(7)
H85	4wDM	HE	7178	1969	(k)	(7)

(a)   ex Hoveringham Pits after 15/6/1949, by 4/11/1952.
(b)   ex East Yorkshire Gravel Co Ltd, Brandesburton, Yorks (ER), c/1954 (by 2/4/1954).
(c)   ex Bleasby Pits, after 24/4/1955, by 24/9/1955; to Hoveringham Pits, c/1957; ex Hoveringham Pits, /1967.
(d)   ex Bleasby Pits, after 24/4/1955, by 24/9/1955; to Bleasby Pits, c/1956 (by 18/5/1957); ex Hoveringham Pits, /1967.
(e)   ex Hoveringham Pits after 24/4/1955, by 24/9/1955; to Crankley Point Pits, c/1960 (by 18/3/1961); returned, /1967.
(f)   ex RH, Boultham Works, Lincoln, on proving trials, 10/3/1960
(g)   ex Bleasby Pits, c/1960 (by 18/3/1961); to Hoveringham Pits, c/1962; returned, /1967.
(h)   ex Hoveringham Pits, c/1960 (by 18/3/1961).

(i) ex Hoveringham Pits after 18/3/1961.
(j) ex Hoveringham Pits, /1967.
(k) ex Walker & Partners, dealers, Staveley, Derbys, c7/1975.

(1) to Hoveringham Pits, after 12/12/1952, by 4/1955.
(2) to Bleasby Pits, c/1957 (by 18/5/1957).
(3) returned to RH, Ironworks, Lincoln, off trials, 22/10/1962 (rebuilt and renumbered 513850 and ultimately sold from English Electric Co Ltd, Vulcan Works, Newton le Willows, Lancs, to Ashanti Goldfields Ltd, Ghana, 2/1970).
(4) to Hoveringham Pits, c/1960 (by 18/3/1961); returned, /1966; to Hoveringham Pits, /1967.
(5) to Nottingham Scrap Metal Co Ltd, c/1968.
(6) to Hoveringham Works, for disposal, by /1973.
(7) to Hoveringham Works, after 19/11/1977, by 29/8/1978.
(8) to Hoveringham Pits, /1957; returned, /1967; to M.A.G.Jacob, Sawley, Derbys, for preservation, 29/5/1980.

HOVERINGHAM GRAVEL PITS, Hoveringham P65
(H. Arnold & Son Ltd until 1939) SK 702482

These were the first pits operated by the company from c1939. They were centred on screens and loading points east of the road from Thurgarton Station to Hoveringham village and were eventually to extend north-east as far as the Bleasby pits. By 1950 the narrow gauge tramway ran east to pits at SK 710482 and SK 710479, the area south-west from SK 712484 having already been worked. There was also a short branch to a pit north-east of the works at SK 703484. By 1958 the tramway route had changed completely. The pits formerly served were worked out and the line ran south-east from the works to pits south-west of Coneygre Farm at SK 705476 and SK 703475. Use of the tramway ceased c1966.

Gauge : 2ft 0in

	-	4wDM	FH	2193	1939	New	(4)
	-	4wDM	FH	2194	1939	New	s/s
		4wDM	MR			(a)	s/s
L7		4wDM	RH	210493	1941	New	(12)
	-	4wDM	RH	210494	1941	New	(1)
L12		4wDM	RH	279620	1949	New	(9)
L13		4wDM	RH	349080	1953	New	(2)
L16		4wDM	RH	349081	1953	New	(10)
L1		4wDM	RH	370566	1954	New	(7)
		0-4-0DM	RH	305327	1954	New	s/s /1967
L9		4wDM	RH	375338	1954	New	(3)
	-	4wDM	RH	192872	1938	(b)	(6)
L4		4wDM	RH	387878	1955	New	(5)
L3		4wDM	RH	387889	1955	New	(11)
L2		4wDM	RH	387890	1955	New	(8)
L14		4wDM	RH	259770	1948	(c)	(8)
L5		4wDM	RH	370555	1953	(d)	(8)
L15		4wDM	RH	279627	1949	(e)	(8)
L10		4wDM	RH	387891	1955	(f)	s/s /1972

Note : A visitor in 1955 was told that, prior to the coming of the RH locomotives, there were two by Simplex and four by Dorman, all later sent away except for the one converted to a pump. Since Simplex locos by FH had National engines and those by MR had Dorman engines, this is confusing. Perhaps two FH's and four MR's is what was meant ?

(a) origin and details not known but see note above.
(b) ex Bleasby Pits, after 24/4/1955, by 24/9/1955.
(c) ex Holme Pierrepont Pits, c/1957; to Crankley Point Pits, c/1960 (by 18/3/1961); returned, /1962.
(d) ex Holme Pierrepont Pits, /1957.
(e) ex Bleasby Pits, c/1958; to Colwick Pits, c/1960 (by 18/3/1961); returned, c/1962.
(f) ex Holme Pierrepont Pits, c/1960 (by 18/3/1961); returned there, /1966; returned here, /1967.

(1) to Colwick Pits, after 8/5/1952, by 3/1954.
(2) to Colwick Pits, after 24/4/1955, by 24/9/1955.
(3) to Holme Pierrepont Pits, after 24/4/1955, by 24/9/1955.
(4) dismantled; engine and frame used to build a pump; sold or scrapped after 24/9/1955.
(5) to Holme Pierrepont Pits, c/1960 (by 18/3/1961).
(6) out of use by 3/1961; s/s
(7) to Holme Pierrepont Pits (after 18/3/1961).
(8) to Holme Pierrepont Pits, /1967.
(9) to Colwick Pits, /1954 (by 1/7/1954); ex Holme Pierrepont Pits, c/1962; to Holme Pierrepont Pits, /1967.
(10) to Bleasby Pits, after 24/4/1955, by 24/9/1955; ex Bleasby Pits, c/1960 (by 18/3/1961); s/s /1967.
(11) to Colwick Pits, c/1960 (by 18/3/1961); returned, c/1962; s/s /1967.
(12) to Holme Pierrepont Pits after 15/6/1949, by 4/11/1952; returned after 12/12/1952, by 4/1955; to Scorton Quarry, Preston, Lancs, c5/1968; returned, 12/1968; s/s c/1970.

HOVERINGHAM WORKSHOPS, Hoveringham   P66
SK 701481

These workshops were located to the west of Hoveringham Pits and north of Hoveringham village. Road vehicles and mobile plant were repaired here and although no specific locomotives were reported under repair here, it is understood that such repairs were carried out. The locomotives listed below were stored here prior to disposal.

Gauge : 2ft 0in

L13	4wDM	RH	349080	1953	(a)	s/s
L12	4wDM	RH	279620	1949	(b)	Scr /1974
H481	4wDM	HE	6680	1970	(c)	(1)
H519	4wDM	HE	6681	1970	(c)	(1)
H595	4wDM	HE	6682	1970	(c)	(1)
H85	4wDM	HE	7178	1969	(c)	(2)

(a) ex Crankley Point Pits, /1970.
(b) ex Holme Pierrepont Pits, by /1973.
(c) ex Holme Pierrepont Pits, after 19/11/1977, by 29/8/1978.

(1) engines removed for use in other plant, remains scrapped after 20/9/1979, by 23/2/1980.
(2) to Tarmac Roadstone (Eastern) Ltd, c/1983 (after 28/2/1981, by 8/7/1984).

INNS & CO LTD
MEERING or BESTHORPE GRAVEL PITS, Besthorpe   F67
(C.A.E.C. Howard, Besthorpe Pits in 1943 ?): to Inns & Co by 1948   SK 814646

These pits, which opened c1937, were located between Besthorpe village and the River Trent. By 1951 the tramway extended north to a pit at SK 816654 and this pit was subsequently extended for a further half mile. By 1964 the tramway had been removed.

Gauge : 2ft 0in

		4wDM	MR	7456	1939	New	(4)
-		4wDM	RH	200481	1940	(a)	(1)
-		4wDM	MR	7358	1939	New (b)	(2)
-		4wDM	MR	4720	1937	(c)	(2)
-		4wDM	MR	5234	1930	(d)	(3)
-		4wDM	MR	7467	1940	(e)	(2)
-		4wDM	MR	5068	1930	(f)	(3)

(a) ex RH, (after overhaul), 24/7/1947. (previously Ministry of Supply, Largin Sawmills, Liskeard, Cornwall).
(b) ex Diesel Loco Hirers, hire until purchased 27/6/1951.
(c) ex MR (previously a hire locomotive until purchased 1/1952).
(d) origin unknown.
(e) ex Langridge Farm Pits, Nazeing, Essex, c/1959.
(f) ex Waterford Depot, Herts, c/1959; earlier Bradgate Granite Co Ltd, Leics.

(1) last known spares order 7/12/1953 (delivery to Charles Limb & Co, Saxilby, Lincs, who had previously ordered spares for Inns locos); assumed to be the unidentified RH which was scrapped c2/1961; frame still on site 3/1961.
(2) later at North Camp Gravel Pits, Hollybush Lane, Farnborough, Hants, /1963 (by 11/1963).
(3) to Waterford Depot, Herts, /1963.
(4) to Nazeing New Road Pits, Herts, c/1963.

INVICTA BRIDGE & ENGINEERING CO LTD
HOVERINGHAM WORKS, Hoveringham   P68
Hoveringham Engineering Co Ltd until c10/1965   SK701480?

This firm of structural engineers was established in buildings which were adjacent to, or had been part of, the workshops of Hoveringham Gravels Ltd. There was no standard gauge connection. From the name change of 1965, the company was a subsidiary of Aveling-Barford Ltd. The use to which the locomotive was put is not known.

Gauge : 2ft 0in

	4wDM	RH	200744	1940	(a)	(1)

(a) ex Bessacarr Gravel Co Ltd, Rossington Quarry, Bawtry Road, Doncaster, Yorks.(WR) after 29/4/1948.

(1) out of use by 10/1967; to Wilsthorpe Light Rly., West Park, Long Eaton, Derbys, 11/1972.

KINGSBURY CONCRETE CO LTD
RANSKILL WORKS B69
SK 668866

This site opened after World War II and was located within the Ranskill Royal Ordnance Factory complex, though outside the security area. It is believed to have been sited west of the exchange sidings where there were gravel workings. A siding shown on a Royal Ordnance Factory plan of 1967 at SK 671867 is noted as leased to the Kingsbury Concrete Co Ltd.

Gauge : 4ft 8½in

		4wDM	FH		(a)	(1)

(a) origin and details not known

(1) out of use by /1973; scrapped by 7/1974

LINBY COLLIERY CO LTD
LINBY COLLIERY, Linby N70
SK 535505

The company was registered on 26/8/1873 and the colliery, which was sunk between 1873 and 1875, was served by sidings on the east side of the Midland Railway's Nottingham - Mansfield line (opened 1848), south of Linby station. After the opening on 18/10/1881 of the GNR Leen Valley line, which passed to the east of the colliery sidings, additional connections were made to both fulls and empties sidings.

Vested in the NCB, East Midlands Division, Area No.6, 1/1/1947.

Gauge : 4ft 8½in

(LINBY COLLIERY No.1)								
POLLY	0-6-0ST	IC	HE	151	1876	New	(1)	
(LINBY COLLIERY No.2)	0-6-0ST	IC	HE	191	1877	New	Scr c/1942	
KING GEORGE	0-6-0ST	IC	HE	2409	1942	New	(1)	

(1) to NCB, East Midlands Division, Area No.6, with site, 1/1/1947.

MANSFIELD STANDARD SAND CO LTD
BERRY HILL SAND QUARRIES, Mansfield H71
SK 548603
Mansfield Sand Co Ltd until 7/1933.
Berry Hill & Stapleford Sand Co Ltd (registered 2/1926) until after 1928.
earlier Berry Hill Sand Co Ltd

Sidings to serve this quarry were in place, probably by 1895 and certainly by 1907. They were situated south of the Midland Railway Mansfield - Southwell line, ¾ mile east of of Mansfield East Junction. However very little ground had been worked by 1914. In 1950 the quarry had extended southwards and the rail system consisted of three sidings in the quarry, reached via a headshunt. This suggests a need for some form of motive power. The rail connection was still extant in 1982. By the 1970s this quarry had become extensive and was worked entirely by road plant.

Gauge : 4ft 8½in

SENTINEL		4wVBT	VCG	S	6935	1928	New	(1)
-		0-4-0ST	OC	MW	1427	1899		
			reb	MW		1916	(a)	(2)

(a)   ex Rock Hill Quarry, /1931.

(1)   to Sandhurst Quarry, following an off-site overhaul, /1944.
(2)   to Sandhurst Quarry, via HC, /1945.

ROCK HILL or STANDARD SAND QUARRIES, Fisher Lane, Mansfield   H72
Standard Sand Co Ltd (registered 1907) until 7/1933   SK 547605

This quarry opened in 1907 and was located on the north side of the Midland Railway Mansfield - Southwell line, ½ mile to the east of Mansfield East Junction. Sidings ran north-east to the quarry and the washery. The locoshed was at the extreme north end of the site (at SK 547607) by 1914, suggesting earlier locos. This quarry closed between 1934 and 1937 and the site beame a refuse tip.

Gauge : 4ft 8½in

-	0-4-0ST	OC	MW	1427	1899		
		reb	MW		1916	(a)	(1)

(a)   ex Worthington & Co Ltd, Burton-on-Trent, Staffs, No.5, /1926.

(1)   to Berry Hill Quarry, /1931.

SANDHURST QUARRIES, Mansfield   H73
Mansfield Sand Co Ltd (registered 7/1872) until 7/1933   SK 544596
(but **Carter, Barringer & Co Ltd** said to have been incorporated 1872 changed name 1877*).

In 1876 a quarry was being worked on the south side of the Midland Railway Mansfield - Southwell line adjacent to Berry Hill Road at SK 544602. There was a siding connection running south east from the Midland Railway line some 400 yards east of Mansfield East Junction. Horses provided the motive power prior to 1902. Between 1907 and 1911 these workings had moved west to what became Sandhurst Quarry in Bottle Lane (later Forest Road). A new connection to the Midland Railway at SK 540602, some 300 yards west of the earlier junction, was made in 1910 (by **H Ashley of Mansfield**). This eliminated the level crossing on the earlier line, and that closed by 1915. The new line ran south for ¼ mile to connect with existing lines at the quarry. The earlier line had closed by 1915. A branch to the east served the plant and further workings. There was also, in 1914, a short narrow gauge line here which may be where the later 2ft 0in gauge locomotives were employed. Sandhurst Quarry, which produced foundry sand, was worked out and closed c1961. The internal rail track was lifted by 2/1961 and the site has been re-used for housing.

*   see references :
       "From Mills to Mines", Don Morley, Old Mansfield Society, 1996.
       "Railways" Magazine, December 1946; February and April 1947.

Gauge : 4ft 8½in

EMPRESS		0-4-0ST	OC	HC	472	1896	(a)	
			reb			1941		(2)
SENTINEL		4wVBT	VCG	S	6935	1928		
			reb.			1944	(b)	(3)
-		0-4-0ST	OC	MW	1427	1899		
			reb	MW		1916		
			reb	HC		1945	(c)	(1)
-		4wVBT	VCG	S	9379	1947	New	(4)

(a) ex HC, 23/4/1902, earlier Pinxton Coal Co Ltd, PATSY.
(b) ex Berry Hill Quarry, /1944
(c) ex Berry Hill Quarry, via HC, Leeds, /1945

(1) to Gas Light & Coke Co, Beckton Gas Works, Essex, No.9, /1946.
(2) scrapped, after 8/1956, by 5/1958.
(3) out of use by 2/1961; sold or scrapped c/1962.
(4) out of use by 2/1961; scrapped c9/1963.

Gauge : 2ft 0in

-	4wDM	OK	5672	1934	(a)	(1)
-	4wDM	RH	189976	1938	(b)	(1)

(a) origin not known.
(b) ex Oxton Sand & Gravel Co, Oxton Pits, near Southwell (which see for further explanation), /1939, or by /1950.

(1) sold or scrapped after 1950, by 2/1960.

See also entry for Standard Sand Co Ltd in the Non-locomotive Section.

METROPOLITAN-CAMMELL CARRIAGE, WAGON & FINANCE CO LTD
KINGS MEADOW WORKS, Nottingham S74
Cammell Laird & Co Ltd until 31/12/1927 SK 560386

This railway rolling stock works was established in 1919 in the former Nottingham factory of the Ministry of Munitions (which see). This had previously been operated by Cammell Laird & Co Ltd on behalf of the Ministry. It was served by sidings on the south east side of the Midland Railway, Nottingham - Beeston line, 1¼ miles west of Nottingham Midland Station. The works closed in 3/1931 and was acquired by Thos.W. Ward Ltd c4/1935. It was taken over by the Ministry of Supply c/1937 for conversion to a Royal Ordnance Factory (see Ministry of Defence).

Gauge : 4ft 8½in

-	0-4-0WT	OC	KS	2489	1916	(a)	(1)
2	4wVBT	VCG	S	6516	1926	New	(2)

(a) ex Ministry of Munitions, with site, after /1918, by /1921.

(1) for sale by H. Stokes, dealer, Nottingham ("Machinery Market" 11/11/1927); then s/s
(2) to Saltley Works, Birmingham, /1930.

MIDLAND MINING plc
ANNESLEY COLLIERY, Newstead   N75
Coal Investments Ltd until 7/6/1996   SK 516534

This colliery was purchased from British Coal in 4/1995, together with the associated **Bentinck Colliery** where all coal from the combined mine was despatched using the 'Merry go Round' system. Production resumed on 30/5/1995. Bentinck is not listed here as industrial locomotives were not used after the British Coal period. See the entries in the NCB Section for fuller details of both the collieries. The combined colliery closed 4/1999.

Gauge : 2ft 1½in   (Underground locomotives)

It was believed that locomotives were taken over from British Coal but not used. Late information now shows that these locomotives were written off before the sale of the colliery (see NCB Section for details). This entry has been left in place to avoid confusion and also to avoid an unexplained gap in the location numbering sequence.

MINISTRY OF DEFENCE

On 1st April 1964 the Air Ministry (which see), the Admiralty, the Royal Ordnance Factories of the Ministry of Supply, and the War Department were reorganised under the control of this Ministry.

ARMY DEPARTMENT

CHILWELL CENTRAL ORDNANCE DEPOT   V76
War Department until 1/4/1964   SK 509349
orig. **Ministry of Munitions, National Filling Factory No.6**

This depot started life as a National Filling Factory. Work commenced on 13/19/1915, the contractors were Holland & Hannan and Cubitts Ltd. Production began in 3/1916. Part of the site became a RAOC Depot from some time between 1/1919 and 8/1919. In 1936-1940, Central Ordnance Depot (C O D), Chilwell, was established here. Its function was the supply of Motor Transport and other spares, and assemblies. From 1941, this work was also dealt with at CODs Bicester, Derby and Feltham although Chilwell remained the HQ. From 1946 it became a Central Ordnance & Vehicle Depot (COVD).

It was served by sidings (agreement dated 9/1915) which ran north from the Midland Railway Nottingham - Trent Jct. line, ½ mile west of Attenborough Station, and then passed under the main road to enter the depot. Most of the depot and all of the railway closed 31/3/1982. The site south of the main road has been redeveloped as a retail park and part of the main site has been used for housing.

Gauge : 4ft 8½in

-		0-6-0WT	OC	Hohen	3283	1914	(a)	(2)
-		0-6-0T	OC	DK		1915	(b)	(1)
-		0-4-0WT	OC	BP	20	1856	(c)	(3)

	ADAM		0-4-0ST	OC	P	1430	1916	New	(4)
	DARFIELD		0-6-0ST	IC	HE	162	1876	(d)	(5)
1	ROYAL ENGINEER		0-6-0T	OC	BLW	46489	1917	(e)	(6)
	DANBY LODGE		0-6-0ST	IC	MW	1595	1903	(f)	(7)
	AYNHO		0-6-0ST	IC	MW	1722	1908	(g)	(8)
74114	WD5 AVONSIDE		0-6-0ST	OC	AE	1742	1916	(h)	(9)
70226			0-4-0DM		HE	1858	1937	New	(10)
71498			0-6-0ST	IC	HC	1775	1944	New	(11)
70228	DAISY		0-6-0ST	OC	P	1204	1910		
				reb	Adams		1939	(i)	(12)
	EL 1		4wBE		EE	533	1922	(j)	(14)
70032			0-4-0DM		DC	2159	1941		
					EE	1190	1941	(k)	(18)
75076			0-6-0ST	IC	RSHN	7112	1943	(l)	(17)
75087			0-6-0ST	IC	HC	1746	1943	New	(15)
75180			0-6-0ST	IC	RSHN	7130	1944	(m)	(16)
71451			0-6-0ST	IC	HE	3215	1945	(n)	(13)
115	(75096)		0-6-0ST	IC	HC	1759	1944	(o)	(19)
116	(71437)		0-6-0ST	IC	HE	3201	1944	(p)	(20)
130	(75107)		0-6-0ST	IC	HE	3157	1944	(q)	(21)
131	(75111)		0-6-0ST	IC	HE	3161	1944	(r)	(22)
139	(75141)		0-6-0ST	IC	HE	3192	1944	(s)	(23)
158	(71444)		0-6-0ST	IC	HE	3208	1945	(t)	(24)
176	(75274)		0-6-0ST	IC	RSHN	7204	1945	(u)	(25)
184	(75285)		0-6-0ST	IC	VF	5275	1945	(v)	(26)
228			0-4-0DM		VF	5263	1945		
					DC	2182	1945	(w)	(27)
432	(8226)		0-6-0DH		RH	466623	1962	(x)	(28)
433	(8228)								
	THE CITY OF NOTTINGHAM		0-6-0DH		RH	468043	1963	New	(29)
434	(8229)		0-6-0DH		RH	468044	1963	New	(30)
435	(8230)		0-6-0DH		RH	468045	1963	(y)	(32)
248			0-4-0DM		AB	344	1941	(z)	(31)
212			0-4-0DM		VF	4861	1942		
					DC	2169	1942	(aa)	(33)

Notes: Three of the original locomotives were named ADAM (P 1430), EVE and JULIAN (loco identities unknown) after the children of Lord Chetwyn who organised the establishment of the Depot.

    SLS records refer to two battery locomotives (gauge not stated) at work at Chilwell in 1923.

(a)   ex Northern Union Mining Co Ltd, Harworth, 8/1914.
(b)   ex Dick, Kerr & Co Ltd, Littleton Reservoir contract, Middx, c4/1916
(c)   ex Air Ministry, Lenabo Aerodrome, Longside, Aberdeen, /1916; earlier Great North of Scotland Railway 14A.
(d)   ex Coventry Ordnance Works Ltd, Warwicks, here by 10/1916 (probably by 4/1916).
(e)   ex Shoeburyness Depot, Essex. ROD 660.
(f)   earlier Chas. Baker & Sons, contrs, Lockoford Sidings, Chesterfield, Derbys; for sale there 1/1916 and sold later (possibly but not necessarily direct to Chilwell).
(g)   earlier Walter Scott & Middleton Ltd, Chalk Farm (LNWR) widening contract (1913-1917), London
(h)   ex Brocton Camp Military Rly., Hednesford, Staffs, after 2/1922, by 1/1923.

(i)　　ex A.R. Adams & Son, dealer, Newport, Mon, DAISY, c/1939 (earlier United National Collieries Ltd, Risca Colliery, Mon).
(j)　　ex Bramley Depot, Hants.
(k)　　ex WD Kinnerley, Salop, c/1942.
(l)　　ex Kineton Depot, Warwicks, by 4/1944
(m)　ex West Hallam Depot, Derbys, /1944 (after 4/1944)
(n)　　ex Longmoor Military Railway, Hants, 21/7/1945
(o)　　ex Long Marston Depot, Warwicks, after 9/1944, by 11/1944.
(p)　　ex Kings Newton Depot, Derbys, 13/7/1945.
(q)　　ex Arncott Depot, Oxon, 8/1955.
(r)　　ex ? , by 1/1952; earlier Stirling Depot, Scotland, 5/1949.
(s)　　ex HE, 6/1956.
(t)　　ex Bicester Depot, Oxon, 3/1960.
(u)　　ex Bramley Depot, Hants, after 5/1949, by 10/1953.
(v)　　ex Bicester Depot, Oxon, 21/7/1945; to HE, Leeds, 5/1952: returned; to Shoeburyness Depot, Essex, by 1/1953; ex Bicester Depot, by 9/1959
(w)　　ex Leuchars Depot, Fife, 17/2/1972.
(x)　　ex Longtown Depot, Cumbria, 15/2/1963
(y)　　ex Ludgershall Depot, Wilts, 8/8/1973
(z)　　ex Branston Depot, Burton on Trent, Staffs, 10/3/1975
(aa)　ex ROF Kings Meadow, Nottingham, 15/11/1978

(1)　　to Stanton Ironworks Co Ltd, Ilkeston, Derbys, STANTON No.22, /1919.
(2)　　to Harworth Main Colliery Co Ltd, Harworth, /1919.
(3)　　to South Wales Primrose Coal Co Ltd, Gurnos, West Glam, JULIAN, /1919.
(4)　　for sale here ("Surplus" 16/6/1919); to Cleveland Bridge & Engineering Co Ltd, Darlington, by 12/1919.
(5)　　for sale here ("Surplus", 16/6/1919); to Skipton Rock Co Ltd, Yorks (WR), by 4/1920.
(6)　　to Thos.W. Ward Ltd, Sheffield, 10/1924; resold to Earl Fitzwilliams Collieries, New Stubbin Colliery, Yorks (WR), No.11, 1927.
(7)　　for sale here ("Surplus", 16/6/1919); to LNWR, /1919 and used on Standedge Tunnel widening work, Yorks (WR), c/1920.
(8)　　for sale here, ("Surplus", 16/6/1919); later Littleton Collieries Ltd, Conduit Colliery, Staffs, possiblly in 1920s; one unconfirmed report has it at the Park Royal, London, plant depot of Walter Scott & Middleton Ltd / Paulings & Co Ltd, in the late 1930s (1938?) (after use on a contract in Egypt); thence to Conduit Colliery by 7/1938.
(9)　　to Longmoor Military Rly., Hants, 8/1945.
(10)　to Royal Artillery Depot, Morfa Harlech, Merioneth, by 2/1943.
(11)　to Boughton Depot, 16/3/1945.
(12)　to Longmoor Military Rly., Hants, /1943.
(13)　to LNER, 8029, 7/1946.
(14)　to Ind Coope & Allsopp Ltd, Burton-on-Trent, Staffs, 11/1946.
(15)　to Stanton Ironworks, Derbys, for repairs, 3/1946; to Cumberland Coal Co, (Whitehaven) Ltd, Whitehaven, Cumberland, 28/4/1946
(16)　to West Hallam Depot, Derbys, 6/1947
(17)　to West Hallam Depot, Derbys, 12/2/1949
(18)　to Suez, Egypt, by 1/1952.
(19)　to HE, Leeds, 11/1953; ex Donnington Depot, Salop, 6/1962; to ? , c11/1963.
(20)　to Arncott Depot, Bicester, Oxon, 13/7/1956.
(21)　to Woodham Bros, Barry Dock, South Glam, 8/1963; Scr by 3/1965.
(22)　to Arncott Depot, Bicester, Oxon, by 10/1955.
(23)　to John Cashmore Ltd, Great Bridge, Staffs, 5/1963; then to HE, Leeds and rebuilt as HE 3888/1964

(24) to Arnott, Young Ltd, dealers, 11/1964; then to NCB, Yorkshire Division No.5 Area, Wharncliffe Woodmoor Colliery, 2/1965.
(25) to Bicester Depot, Oxon, 5/1960
(26) to HE, Leeds, 5/1963; scrapped by John Cashmore Ltd, Great Bridge, Staffs, by 1964.
(27) to R.E. Trem & Co Ltd, Finningley, Yorks (WR), for scrap, 17/1/1983.
(28) to Longtown Depot, Cumbs, 15/2/1972.
(29) to Bicester Depot, Oxon, 3/5/1973 & returned 13/12/1973; to Donnington Depot, Salop, 8/10/1981.
(30) to Bicester Depot, 9/8/1973, then to Donnington Depot, 16/1/1974.
(31) to East Riggs Depot, Dumfries, 30/7/1975
(32) to Bicester Depot, 20/3/1979.
(33) to R.E. Trem & Co Ltd, Finningley, Yorks (WR), for scrap, 17/1/1983.

Note: In 4/1916 (and 6/1916), spares were ordered from MW by an unknown customer for locos MW 1595, MW 1722 and DARFIELD, on the same order, suggesting that all three were at the same location (possibly Chilwell).

Gauge : 2ft 0in

LOD 758141	4wDM	RH	229633	1944	New	(2)
-	4wDM	HE	2670	1942	(a)	(1)
-	4wDM	HE	2937	1944	(b)	s/s
-	4wDM	HE	2515	1941	(b)	s/s
-	4wDM	HE	2722	1942	(c)	s/s

(a) ex Sir Alfred McAlpine & Son Ltd, Corsham contract, Wilts, by 2/1945.
(b) originally WD Long Marston, Warwicks; here by 2/1945
(c) originally Ministry of Buildings & Works, Corsham, Wilts.

(1) to No.13 Petrol Depot, Market Bosworth, Leics, by 7/1945.
(2) to Liphook Depot, Hants, by /1951.

NOTTINGHAM ROYAL ORDNANCE FACTORY
Kings Meadow, Wilford, Nottingham S77
Ministry of Supply until 1/4/1964 SK 560386

This factory was occupied by the Metro-Cammell Carriage, Wagon & Finance Co Ltd until 3/1931. It was taken over as an ROF (production commenced 1/1937) and served by sidings on the south side of the LMSR Nottingham - Beeston line, 1¼ miles west of Nottingham Midland Station. Rail traffic ceased c/1979.

Gauge : 4ft 8½in

No.1	GERT		0-4-0DM	HE	1847	1936	New	(2)
	(orig NOTTINGHAM)							
2	DAISY		0-4-0DM	HE	1898	1939	(a)	(2)
3	DAISY (f. 2)		0-4-0DM	HC	D622	1942	New	(1)
808			4wDM	RH	224347	1945	(c)	(5)
	ANNE		0-4-0DM	JF	22916	1940	(b)	(3)
102	(805)		4wDM	RH	224343	1944	(d)	(4)
212			0-4-0DM	VF	4861	1942		
				DC	2169	1942	(e)	(6)

(a) ex ROF Barnbow, Crossgates, Leeds by 12/1940
(b) MoDAD fleet; ex Bicester Depot, Oxon, 11/1964.
(c) ex ROF Woolwich, London, c/1966.
(d) MoDAD fleet; ex Asfordby Depot, Leics, between 9/1967 and 8/1969
(e) MoDAD fleet; ex Bicester Depot, Oxon, 1/5/1973

(1) out of use by 7/1963; to Thos. W. Ward Ltd, Templeborough Works, Sheffield, c/1963 (later used as a hire locomotive).
(2) to Bird's Commercial Motors Ltd, Long Marston, Warwicks, c12/1969.
(3) scrapped c/1973 (after 4/1971, by 6/1974).
(4) sold for scrap, c /1974 (after 9/1972, by 6/1974).
(5) to W.H. Davis & Sons Ltd, Langwith Jct., Derbys, 11/1977 (after 19/11/1977) (property of B.A. Mitchell, plant dealer, Shirebrook).
(6) to MoDAD, Chilwell Ordnance Depot, 15/11/1978.

RANSKILL ROYAL ORDNANCE FACTORY (ROF No.38)   B78
Ministry of Supply until 1/4/1964   SK 675866

This factory opened 10/1941 and was served by sidings which ran east from a triangular junction with the LNER Doncaster - Newark line, ½ mile south of Ranskill Station. After World War II, these exchange sidings also served the LNER Ranskill Wagon Works, which is believed to have been located in former ROF buildings. From here lines extended east and south into the secure areas of the depot. More of the factory closed c1966 and, by 1967, individual sidings were leased to the Kingsbury Concrete Co Ltd (which see) and one at SK 669867 to Cufflin Holdings for unspecified use. The remainder of the depot and one locomotive were retained on a care and maintenance basis by the Department of the Environment, Property Services Agency, until 1981. The remaining area was then offered for sale and the locomotive scrapped.

Gauge : 4ft 8½in

	OLYMPIA	0-4-0ST	OC	MW	1847	1914		
		reb		RSH		1941	(a)	(1)
	VICTORY	0-6-0ST	OC	MW	1286	1894	(b)	Scr 1/1958
	PARTINGTON	0-6-0ST	IC	VF	1236	1888	(c)	(2)
	ROF No.6 No.11	0-4-0DM		JF	22988	1942	(d)	(5)
No.4		0-4-0DM		HL	3949	1939	(e)	(4)
	MOW L1	0-4-0DM		JF	22943	1941	(f)	(4)
	-	0-4-0DM		AB	351	-1941	(g)	(3)

(a) ex Olympia Oil & Cake Co Ltd, Selby, Yorks (ER), OLYMPIA, via RSH, /1941.
(b) ex A.R.Adams & Son, dealers, Newport, Mon, CARINGTON, after 3/1941, by 10/1941; earlier Luffenham Stone & Asphalt Co Ltd, Luffenham, Rutland; to Maltby Factory, Yorks (WR), /1948, and returned.
(c) ex Rotherwas Factory, Herefords, /1943.
(d) ex Risley Factory, Lancs, /1943.
(e) earlier at Wrexham Factory (ROF No.34), Flints.
(f) ex United Kingdom Atomic Energy Authority, Capenhurst, Cheshire, /1955.
(g) ex Drigg Factory, Cumbs, /1956.

(1) to MoS Ruddington Factory.
(2) scrapped by Thos. W. Ward Ltd, 5/1951.
(3) to F.Watkins (Boilers) Ltd, Sling Plant Depot, Glos, 6/1959.
(4) to Arnott, Young & Co Ltd, Dudley Hill Station Depot, Bradford, for scrap, c/1966.
(5) scrapped c9/1981 (after 20/9/1979, by 27/11/1981).

Gauge : 2ft 6in

No.		Type	Builder	No.	Year		
No.1		4wDM	HE	2213	1942	New	(1)
No.2		4wDM	HE	2214	1942	New	(1)
No.3		4wDM	HE	2695	1942	New	(2)

(1) to Bishopston Factory, Renfrews, 12/1948.
(2) sold or scrapped after 5/1961.

RUDDINGTON ORDNANCE STORAGE & SUPPLY DEPOT   V79

War Department, until 1/4/1964   SK 575322
Ministry of Works, by 1948 and until after 1955
Ministry of Supply, until /?
orig. Royal Ordnance Factory No.14

This depot was built as **ROYAL ORDNANCE FACTORY No.14** for the manufacture of explosive materials for the Ministry of Supply. Construction commenced 1/12/1940 by John Mowlem & Sons Ltd (which see) and Wilson Lovatt & Sons Ltd, with production scheduled to start in 7/1941. Located west of the A60 road, it was served by sidings on the east side of the LNER (ex-GCR) Loughborough - Nottingham Victoria line, ½ mile south of Ruddington Station. Latterly, after closure as a through route, the northern terminal of this line was at this depot. By 1955, the function of the depot had changed. It became a surplus equipment storage and disposal site. Items handled, included vast numbers of road vehicles and a small number of locomotives. Sales were largely by auction but some were by tender. The railway was retained to handle incoming equipment. The depot closed in 1984. Much of the site has been redeveloped as a Country Park and some of the buildings have become the northern base of the Great Central (Nottingham) Ltd railway (see Preservation Section).

Gauge : 4ft 8½in

		Type		Builder	No.	Year		
	LANDORE	0-4-0ST	OC	AB	769	1896	(a)	Scr
	OLYMPIA	0-4-0ST	OC	MW	1847	1914		
		reb		RSH		1941	(b)	(1)
	ROF 14 No.1	0-4-0ST	OC	WB	2650	1942	New	(2)
	ROF 14 No.4	0-4-0ST	OC	AB	2124	1942	New	(3)
	ROF 14 No.14	0-4-0DM		JF	22979	1942	New	(4)
70210		0-6-0ST	IC	P	1691	1925	(c)	(5)
862	(CHELFORD No.1)	0-4-0DM		VF	4860	1942		
				DC	2168	1942	(d)	(6)
859		0-4-0DM		AB	357	1941	(e)	(9)
850		0-4-0DM		HE	2068	1940	(f)	(7)
842		0-4-0DM		AB	369	1945	(g)	(8)
8210		0-4-0DH		NBQ	27645	1958	(h)	(10)
249	(831)	0-4-0DM		VF	5258	1945		
				DC	2177	1945	(i)	(11)
250	(841)	0-4-0DM		AB	368	1945	(j)	(12)
	CHORLEY No.7	0-4-0DM		FH	2151	1940	(k)	(13)
229		0-4-0DM		VF	5264	1945		
				DC	2183	1945	(l)	(16)
400		0-4-0DH		NBQ	27421	1955	(m)	(15)
401	SALAMANDER	0-4-0DH		NBQ	27422	1955	(n)	(14)
408		0-4-0DH		NBQ	27429	1955	(o)	(15)

(a) ex Richard Thomas & Baldwins Ltd, Swansea Hematite Steelworks, Landore, West Glam, after repair at GWR Danygraig Works, Swansea, 8/1945.
(b) ex ROF Ranskill.
(c) ex MoS Kings Newton, Derbys, after 11/1950.
(d) ex MoS Kings Newton, Derbys, after /1957, by 9/1961.
(e) ex ROF Featherstone, Staffs, 14/6/1961
(f) ex Bicester Depot, Oxon, 25/4/1962
(g) ex ROF, Elstow, Beds, 22/10/1964
(h) ex Bicester Depot, Oxon, 1/7/1967
(i) ex Bicester Depot, Oxon, 24/7/1968.
(j) ex Bicester Depot, 20/1/1967.
(k) ex ROF Radway Green, Cheshire, 22/11/1967.
(l) ex Aldershot Depot, Hants, 17/6/1976.
(m) ex Bicester Depot, Oxon, 15/4/1975.
(n) ex Bicester Depot, Oxon, 20/3/1979.
(o) ex Yardley Chase Depot, Northants, 17/3/1981.

(1) sold to Steel Supply Co (Western) Ltd, Jersey Marine, Swansea, 10/4/1960; removed 5/1960; scrapped 4/1962.
(2) to ROF Elstow, Beds, after 2/1954, by 5/1956; returned; sold to Steel Supply Co (Western) Ltd, Jersey Marine, Swansea, 10/4/1960; removed 5/1960; scrapped /1961.
(3) out of use by 10/1962; to Thos.W. Ward Ltd, Langley Mill, Derbys, for scrap, /1963.
(4) to MoS Kings Newton, Derbys, by 4/1960
(5) never used here; scrapped by Donald Ward Ltd, Woodville, Derbys, 4/1960.
(6) to Bicester Depot, Oxon, 13/5/1964.
(7) to Branston Depot, Burton on Trent, Staffs, 2/12/1964
(8) to ROF, Bramshall, near Uttoxeter, Staffs, 20/1/1967
(9) to Sinfin Lane Depot, Derby, 3/8/1967
(10) to ROF, Yardley Chase, Piddington, Northants, 25/7/1968
(11) to Bicester Depot, Oxon, 17/6/1976.
(12) to Bicester Depot, Oxon, 17/4/1975.
(13) sold by auction 2/1968; to L.W. Vass Ltd, Ampthill, Beds, after 5/2/1968.
(14) to Track Supplies & Services Ltd, Wolverton, Bucks, 23/9/1981.
(15) to Ashchurch Depot, Glos, 26/10/1983.
(16) to Long Marston Depot, Warwicks, 18/11/1983.

Note : A BR movement order was seen for 0-4-0DM JF 22888/1939, originally at ROF Bridgend, Glamorgan. This locomotive was to go from Ruddington to ROF Sellafield, Cumberland, 1/1948 (later with JF, Leeds, /1950; to Colvilles Ltd, Clyde Ironworks, Lanarks, 3/1951). There is no evidence that it was used at Ruddington.
Another movement order relates to a locomotive LNER 7334 to move from MOS Lockoford Sidings, Chesterfield, Derbys, to MOS Ruddington on 17/2/1949. Since LNER 7334 was then still in capital stock as 68496, it is probable that 7334 is an error for 7344. The latter had become WD 88 in 5/1942 and IRS records show it sold by WD to Steel Breaking & Dismantling Co Ltd at Lockoford Sidings in 3/1947 and scrapped in 1949. In view of the movement order, the possibility has to be considered that it remained MOS or WD property whilst at Lockoford Sidings and moved to Ruddington for final disposal.

MINISTRY OF MUNITIONS
NATIONAL ORDNANCE FACTORY, Kings Meadow Road, Nottingham S80
National Projectile Factory until 1917   SK 560386
(built and operated by **Cammell Laird & Co Ltd**)

Construction of this factory commenced in 8/1915 and production started in 3/1916. It was served by sidings on the south east side of the Midland Railway Nottingham - Beeston line, 1¼ miles west of Nottingham (Midland) Station. After 1918, by 1921, the works passed to Cammell Laird & Co Ltd, becoming a railway carriage and wagon factory (see entries for Metropolitan-Cammell Carriage, Wagon & Finance Co Ltd and Ministry of Defence for later uses of the site).

Gauge : 4ft 8½in

-		0-4-0WT	OC	KS	2489	1916	New (1)
-		0-4-0ST	OC	?			(a) s/s
-		0-4-0ST	OC	AB?			(b) (2)
PUCK		0-4-0ST	OC	MW	1255	1893	(c) (3)

(a) ex AB, (9in x14in loco) 22/11/1915 (earlier Boyd & Forrest, possibly their AB 848/1899, although this was a 9x18in loco).
(b) origin unknown (12in x 20in loco "by Barclays")
(c) earlier Holme & King Ltd, Coventry Loop Line (LNWR) (1911-1914) contract; then via Marple & Gillott Ltd, dealers, Sheffield, after 8/1916 (possibly the 9in 4-wheels coupled loco they advertised 4-8/1916).

(1) to Cammell Laird & Co Ltd (with site), after /1918, by /1921.
(2) to Electric & Ordnance Accessories Co Ltd, Aston, Birmingham, per Thos.W. Ward Ltd, 25/7/1916.
(3) purchased from Cammell Laird & Co Ltd by Thos W. Ward Ltd, 28/11/1917; remained on site until sold to Ransomes & Marles Bearing Co Ltd, Stanley Works, Newark, 1/1/1918 (Ward's records have Newcastle-upon-Tyne, which is thought to be an error for Newark on Trent).

MORRIS, LITTLE & SON LTD
West Stockwith   B81
                                                                            SK 784942

A standard gauge tramway ran east, from a junction with the GNR & GER joint line at Misterton station, to a wharf and complex of chemical works at West Stockwith on the west bank of the River Trent. The line opened in the first quarter of 1881 (siding agreement dated 20/11/1878) and was ½ mile long. An old GNR carriage was used, presumably as a workmen's train. By 1884 the layout was substantially complete. The works had been established by 1864 when it was occupied by Morris Bros. & Geves. By 1895 the site was shared between three associated firms, Morris Bros. who made chemical manure, Morris Bros and Little, whose product was sheep dip and Morris & Co., copper precipitators. The last of these became Morris & Co (Stockwith) Ltd in 12/1922 but had ceased trading by the mid-1920s. Morris & Sons (Stockwith) Ltd, successors to Morris Bros, was wound up by resolution of 21/5/1928. This left Morris, Little & Sons Ltd to close down operations on the moribund site. The siding agreement was terminated from 20/4/1934 and, as part of the settlement, the land and track west of Stockwith Road passed to the LNER. They made no further use of it and the track was lifted in 8/1952. The last part of the works had been demolished by 1948.

Two locomotives were advertised for sale 15/2/1929, suggesting closure of the railway prior to that date.

References : "The Great Northern Railway", Vol.2, J. Wrottesley, Batsford, 1979.
"The Industrial Railway Record", No.128, p 406

Gauge : 4ft 8½in

NORTH STAR	0-4-0ST					(a)	(1)
PROGRESS	0-4-0ST	OC	HC	335	1889	New	
		reb	HC		1920		(1)

(a) origin and identity unknown.

(1) for sale 15/2/1929; s/s

N.H.& B. COLLIERIES LTD

This company was formed in 5/1944, by the merger of the **Blackwell Colliery Co Ltd** and the New Hucknall Colliery Co Ltd. The former, first registered on 20/3/1871 to work collieries in Derbyshire, had absorbed the ailing Sutton Colliery Co Ltd in (1901 or)1903. **New Hucknall Colliery Co Ltd,** first registered on 13/9/1874, had been a particularly successful undertaking, having sunk Bentinck and Welbeck Collieries largely with money earned at New Hucknall.

ANNESLEY COLLIERY, Annesley   N82
New Hucknall Colliery Co Ltd until 5/1944   SK 516534
Annesley Colliery Co Ltd until 12/1924
Annesley Colliery Co until 29/8/1904
W. Worswick until at least /1869.

Sinking of this colliery commenced in 1860 and was completed in 1867. It was originally worked by W. Worswick, as agent for the Duke of Newcastle. The colliery was served by a short branch which ran south from the Midland Railway's Nottingham - Mansfield line (opened 1848) at Annesley station for ¼ mile to the colliery. A GNR line, which opened 27/10/1881, left its Leen Valley line ½ mile north of Newstead & Annesley station and ran north and then west, to pass beneath the Midland Railway line and curve south to join the connection from the Midland Railway. A short narrow gauge line was used east of the colliery to serve a tip. There was a brickworks here in 1943 and at Vesting Day.

The colliery was vested in the NCB, East Midlands Division, Area No.4, 1/1/1947.

Gauge : 4ft 8½in

ANNESLEY COLLIERY No.1	0-6-0ST	IC	HE	31	1868	New	s/s after 8/1905
ANNESLEY COLLIERY No.2	0-6-0ST	IC	HE	11	1866	(a)	s/s after 9/1903
109A	2-4-0	IC	Derby		1867	(b)	(1)
ANNESLEY No.1	0-6-0ST	IC	HE	169	1876	(c)	(2)
No.3	0-6-0ST	OC	AB	1132	1907	New	
		reb	KE		1921		(3)
ANNESLEY No.1	0-6-0ST	OC	AB	1048	1905	New	
		reb	KE		1921		s/s
ANNESLEY No.2	0-6-0ST	OC	P	1924	1937	New	(3)

(a) ex Swannington Main Colliery, Swannington, Leics, c/1876-1879.
(b) ex Midland Railway,109A, on hire, 7/9/1885.
(c) ex Ingham's Thornhill Collieries Ltd, Dewsbury, Yorks (WR), 5/1900.

(1) returned to Midland Railway, after 24/9/1885.
(2) to Exors of E. Lister Kaye [presumed Denby Grange Colliery, Derbys], after 9/1/1902, by 16/1/1907.
(3) to NCB, East Midlands Division, No.4 Area, with site, 1/1/1947.

BENTINCK COLLIERY, Kirkby-in-Ashfield   K83
New Hucknall Colliery Co Ltd until 5/1944   SK 487549

The company acquired land in Kirkby in Ashfield in 1894, sinking began and coal production commenced in 1896 with coke ovens being built south of the colliery the same year. A brickworks was built on the north side, with a narrow gauge line into a clay hole to its north. Bentinck had two connections with the Midland Railway Mansfield - Pinxton line, which ran ¼ mile to the south. The empty wagon branch ran east from a point ¾ miles south west of Kirkby station, whilst the loaded branch was an eastward extension of the Langton Colliery branch (see Pinxton Collieries). The development of the colliery coincided with that of the MS&LR (GCR) lines. That from Beighton to Annesley opened 24/10/1892 and two connections were made from it. One for empties opened on 30/9/1901, ran east from Kirkby & Pinxton (later Kirkby Bentinck) station to a reversing point and then south west to join the Midland Railway empties line. The loaded branch opened in 12/1898 and curved to the south east from its Langton Colliery line to join the Midland Railway line west of the colliery. The coking plant is thought to have closed by 1924 and the brickworks closed between 1937 and 1943.

The colliery was vested in the NCB, East Midlands Division, Area No.4, 1/1/1947.

Gauge : 4ft 8½in

No.2		0-6-0ST	OC	AE	1349	1893	New	(3)
No.3	JUBILEE	0-6-0ST	OC	AE	1370	1897	(a)	(1)
	NEW HUCKNALL No.4	0-6-0ST	OC	AE	1490	1905	(b)	(2)
	HUTHWAITE 7	0-6-0ST	OC	HC	1305	1917	(c)	(4)
	BENTINCK No.3	0-6-0ST	OC	YE	2197	1928	New	(4)
	BENTINCK No.2	0-6-0ST	OC	YE	2307	1931	New	(4)

(a) ex Garratts Ltd, Cradley Heath, Staffs, by 5/1914 (probably by /1905 - but loco at AE, 7/1912).
(b) ex New Hucknall Colliery, after 7/1912, by 3/1922.
(c) ex New Hucknall Colliery, by 28/7/1946.

(1) sold or scrapped after 5/1914 (probably by /1928 when number reused)
(2) returned to New Hucknall Colliery, after 3/1922, by 11/1924.
(3) sold or scrapped after 2/1924 (probably by /1931 when number reused)
(4) to NCB, East Midland Division, No.4 Area, with site, 1/1/1947.

NEW HUCKNALL COLLIERY, Huthwaite   J84
(also known as **HUTHWAITE COLLIERY**)   SK 475585
New Hucknall Colliery Co Ltd until 5/1944
New Hucknall Colliery Co until 13/9/1879
William Muschamp until 1/1/1877

Sinking of this colliery commenced in 1876 to replace **OLD HUCKNALL COLLIERY** at SK 459591 which Muschamp had purchased from previous owners, John, William and Nathan Mellors. Abandonment plans indicate that Old Hucknall closed in 1868, but a Midland Railway branch from Blackwell, to replace an earlier horse tramway, was approved in 1873 and partly constructed. This indicates, if not continuity of output, at least an intention to reopen. **NEW HUCKNALL COLLIERY** reached coal in 1877 and was completed in 1879. By then the Midland Railway's extension of its Westhouses and Blackwell station to Blackwell 'B' Winning Colliery branch (all in Derbys) had been diverted to New Hucknall Colliery (1½ miles) and completed (opened 1/9/1879). The unfinished works towards Old Hucknall were abandoned. With the opening of the MS&LR line from Beighton to Annesley in 1893, that company made a branch, which opened the same year, running north east from a point 2½ miles south east of Tibshelf station to the colliery. In 1894 a coking plant of beehive ovens was in operation. The coal was fed from above using 'conical shaped wagons' adapted for the purpose and presumably narrow gauge. By 1895, a narrow gauge tramway incline climbed north east from the colliery for ½ mile to a landsale yard at Sutton Road (SK 478591). This tramway had closed by 1945, as had the coking plant. The colliery was vested, as **NEW HUCKNALL COLLIERY**, in the NCB, East Midlands Division, Area No.4, 1/1/1947.

Gauge : 4ft 8½in

PORTLAND No.1	0-6-0ST	OC	YE	325	1878	New	
		reb	AE		1905		(2)
NEW HUCKNALL No.4							
(PORTLAND No.4)	0-6-0ST	OC	AE	1490	1905	New (a)	(2)
HUTHWAITE 7	0-6-0ST	OC	HC	1305	1917	(b)	(1)

(a)   to Bentinck Colliery, after 7/1912, by 3/1922; returned by 11/1924.
(b)   ex Cudworth & Johnson, dealers, Wrexham, Denbighs, HENRY DAWSON, after 8/7/1939, by 9/1941; earlier Stancliffe Estates Co Ltd, Darley Dale, Derbys.

(1)   to Bentinck Colliery, by 28/7/1946.
(2)   to NCB, East Midlands Division, No.4 Area, with site, 1/1/1947.

SUTTON COLLIERY, Stanton Hill, Sutton-in-Ashfield   J85
(also known as **NEW SKEGBY, SKEGBY No.2** or **BRIERLEY HILL COLLIERY**)   SK 484603
Blackwell Colliery Co Ltd until 5/1944
(**Sutton Colliery Co Ltd** until c1901? or 1903)
New Skegby Colliery Co Ltd, registered 22/8/1882, until c1896?.
Skegby Colliery, Lime & Brick Co Ltd, registered 31/3/1862, until 1882

SUTTON COLLIERY was sunk in 1873-4 to replace **SKEGBY COLLIERY** (SK 466604) which dated from before 1847 and closed c1877. Skegby was originally owned by **John Dodsley** but c1858 it passed to a partnership styled **The Skegby Colliery, Lime & Brick Company**. It was located ¾ mile to the west of Sutton which was colloquially known as 'Brierley Hill', after the place of origin of the sinkers. From 1866, Skegby was served by the 17 chain Midland Railway Skegby branch which ran east from its Tibshelf - Pleasley line, 1 mile south west of Teversal station. This was extended east to Sutton Colliery in 1876 and the following year it was extended further to the Midland Railway's Stoneyford Lane siding. Both Skegby and Sutton had been small pits with no need of their own motive power. Sutton may have closed for a period after the Top Hard seam was abandoned from 17/2/1888. It was deepened after 1896 and generally modernised, probably leading to the need for a locomotive. A plan of 1914 shows extended sidings and coke ovens north of the colliery. There were also narrow gauge lines onto a tip and a double track narrow gauge incline which had been constructed prior to 1895 and which ran south east for 1 mile to a landsale yard in the centre of Sutton in Ashfield. This had closed by 1945.

The colliery was vested in the NCB, East Midlands Division, Area No.4, 1/1/1947.

Gauge : 4ft 8½in

	0-4-0ST	OC	HG	253	1868	(a)	s/s
RAVEN	0-4-0WT	OC	Johnson	56	1913	New	(2)
LUCERO	0-6-0T	IC	MW	1098	1888	(b)	(1)

(a) ex HC, Leeds, 2/3/1899; earlier Carnforth Hematite Iron Co Ltd, Carnforth, Lancs, FANNY.
(b) ex "A" Winning Colliery, Derbys, after 5/1928, by 9/1929.

(1) returned to "A" Winning Colliery, Derbys, after 1/1930, by 1/1931.
(2) to NCB, East Midlands Division, No.4 Area, with site, 1/1/1947.

WELBECK COLLIERY, Welbeck Colliery Village   G86
New Hucknall Colliery Co Ltd until 5/1944   SK 582704

The colliery was sunk between 1913 and 1915, opening in 1916. It was remote from existing railways and was first served by a 3 mile long mineral branch running north from the GCR Shirebrook - Tuxford line, 3 miles east of Shirebrook. This was made and owned by the colliery company from its opening on 19/4/1915, until purchased, 31/12/1927, by the LNER. Traffic, including mineworkers' passenger trains, was always worked by the mainline company. The LMSR did not propose a connection until 1925 and its branch line construction was authorised by Act of Parliament on 30/6/1926. The line (built by Mitchell Bros. Sons & Co Ltd, which see) ran for 3½ miles from the LMSR Mansfield - Worksop line, north of Shirebrook, to the colliery and opened for traffic 3/1/1928. There was a brickworks here by 1932 and probably from the construction period. Aerial ropeways were used for dirt disposal. In 1927 a plant was opened to produce motor spirit from cannel coal. This was known as 'Welbeck English Spirit' and for some years was retailed at each of the company's four collieries. In 1932 this plant was operated by the Fusion Corporation Ltd and from 2/1934 by Swallow Coal Distillation (Welbeck) Ltd. It closed after 1940.

The colliery and brickworks were vested in the NCB, East Midlands Division, Area No.3, 1/1/1947.

Gauge : 4ft 8½in

WELBECK No.5	0-6-0ST	OC	AE	1693	1914	New	(1)
WELBECK No.6	0-6-0ST	OC	AE	1831	1919	New	(1)

(1) to NCB, East Midlands Division, No.3 Area, with site, 1/1/1947.

NATIONAL POWER plc

This company, together with Powergen plc, was formed by the government, from 1/8/1989, in order to assume ownership from 31/3/1990, from the Central Electricity Generating Board, of those power stations in England and Wales which were to be privatised. The shares in both companies were later sold to the private sector. The electricity generation and supply industry had been nationalised on 1/4/1948 when installations were vested in the British Electricity Authority (Central Electricity Authority from 1/4/1955). From 1/1/1958 generation and supply were segregated, power stations passing to the Central Electricity Generating Board.

STAYTHORPE POWER STATION, Averham, Newark P87
Central Electricity Generating Board until 31/3/1990 SK768536, 766534
Central Electricity Authority until 1/1/1958;
British Electricity Authority until 1/4/1955
Derbyshire & Nottinghamshire Electric Power Company until 1/4/1948

Construction of what became the 'A' power station was commenced in 7/1946 on a site south of the LMSR, 2 miles west of Newark Castle station. Sidings and a coal discharge point were provided by Thos.W. Ward Ltd on the north side of the LMSR with a conveyor linking the sites. 'A' station was commissioned in 1950. Construction of 'B' station, located to the west of 'A', was commenced in 1957, by Balfour Beatty & Co Ltd (which see). In this case the sidings were on the south side of the BR line and the discharge point was adjacent to the station. The 'B' station was commissioned in 1962. Each station operated its rail system independently and had its own locomotive allocation and shed (SK 765539 & 767536). 'A' station closed c1980. Power generation at 'B' station ceased on 24/3/1994 and demolition was in progress during 9/1995. Construction of a gas fired power station on part of the site was proceeding during 1999.

Gauge : 4ft 8½in

#	No.1		4wDM		RH	224353	1945	(a)	(2)
	No.2	NANCY	4wDM		RH	263001	1949	New (b)	(5)
#	No.3		4wDM		RH	305314	1951	New	(3)
	-		4wVBT	VCG	S	(++)		(c)	(1)
	No.4		0-4-0DE		RH	312986	1952	New	(6)
	-		0-4-0DH		RH	418793	1957	(d)	(4)
	No.5A		0-4-0DE		RH	420137	1958	New	(9)
	No.1B		0-4-0DE		RH	421435	1958	New	(8)
	No.2B		0-4-0DE		RH	449754	1961	New	(7)

   #   operated from the mid 1950s by the Midlands Project Group of the CEGB.
  ++ either 100hp S 9398/1950 or 200hp S 9538/1952.

(a) ex Spondon Power Station, Derbys, c/1948 (by 26/10/1948); to Castle Donington Power Station, Leics, /1956 (by 1/11/1956); returned here, 10/1957.
(b) ordered for Carmarthen Bay Power Station, Burry Port, Carmarthens, but delivered new to Staythorpe
(c) ex S, for demonstrations, by 5/1952.
(d) ex RH, 11/9/1957 for trials; returned to RH by 26/11/1958; ex RH for further trials, 29/12/1958.

(1) returned to S, ex demonstration, 5/1952.
(2) to Drakelow Power Station, Derbys, c/1962 (after 11/3/1962).
(3) to Drakelow Power Station, Derbys, by /1963
(4) returned to RH, 3/10/1962; to British Gypsum Ltd, Kingston on Soar, 8/1/1963.

(5) to Market Bosworth Light Rly., Leics, 13/11/1983.
(6) to Marple & Gillott Ltd, Attercliffe, Sheffield, c9/1985 (by 30/10/1985); scrapped 11/1985
(7) to The Great Central (Nottingham) Ltd, Nottingham Heritage Centre, Ruddington, after 26/3/1994, by 1/5/1994
(8) to Ferrybridge Power Station, North Yorks, 16/6/1994
(9) to Grant Lyon Eagre Ltd, Scunthorpe Plant Depot, Humberside, after 10/7/1994, by 4/9/1994

NEWELL DUNFORD ENGINEERING LTD
MISTERTON WORKS, Misterton   B88
Ernest Newell & Co Ltd until /1968.   SK 777939

Ernest Newell & Co Ltd was registered in 1900; Newell was previously manager of Woods Patent Mills & Engineering Co Ltd which had opened after 1895, perhaps on this site. The business was the production of plant, steel castings and structural work mainly for the coal, steel and cement trade. Newell's works was served by sidings (agreement dated 24/9/1904) on the east side of, but at a lower level than, the GNR & GER joint line, immediately south of Misterton Station. These sidings, which also served Morris, Little's West Stockwith line and the gas works of the **Misterton & West Stockwith Gas Co Ltd**, are said to have been shunted by a horse originally. Newell's works was then quite small and a locomotive was probably not needed until after a further agreement dated 26/8/1925 for siding extensions. A GNR memorandum of 1912 refers to excessive shunting by them which the trader had no other means of carrying out. The company became a subsidiary of Hadfields Ltd of Sheffield. The siding agreement was terminated from 6/1/1969.

Gauge : 4ft 8½in

-	4wPM reb to 4wDM	KC	1926 c1947	New	(1)

(1) to W.H. Davis & Sons Ltd, Langwith Jct., Derbys, for storage and restoration, prior to preservation, /1972; but scrapped c/1974.

NEWSTEAD COLLIERY CO LTD

In 6/1872 the **Sheepbridge Coal & Iron Co Ltd** and the **Staveley Coal & Iron Co Ltd** jointly leased coal measures under the Newstead Abbey Estate. The Newstead Colliery Co was registered on 29/4/1878 as a joint subsidiary to sink NEWSTEAD COLLIERY (see Non-locomotive Section). The same company later developed BLIDWORTH COLLIERY.

BLIDWORTH COLLIERY, Blidworth   G89
(originally known as **NEWSTEAD No.2** Colliery)   SK 595567

This colliery was planned prior to 1919 and presumably postponed due to the war. Sinking commenced in 1924 and it opened in 1926 but there was a break in coal production between 8/1928 and 10/1929 whilst some reconstruction was carried out. The colliery was first served by a short LMSR branch which opened on 21/12/1925 and ran south from its Mansfield - Southwell line, ¼ mile east of Blidworth & Rainworth station. A second connection was made with the opening in 1931 of an LNER mineral line which had been authorised in 1919 and ran south from Rufford Colliery. The siding agreement was dated 9/3/1931. The internal colliery railway was also used for tipping dirt.

The colliery was vested in the NCB, East Midlands Division, Area No.3, 1/1/1947.

Gauge : 4ft 8½in

	(BLIDWORTH No.1)	0-6-0ST	OC	AE	1947	1924	New	(2)
	(BILLUM)	0-6-0ST	OC	AE	1952	1925	New	(2)
	ARTHUR	0-6-0ST	OC	AE	1892	1921	(a)	(1)

(a)   ex Yorkshire Main Colliery (1923) Ltd, Yorkshire Main Colliery, Yorks (WR), c/1925-26.

(1)   to Yorkshire Main Colliery (1923) Ltd, Yorkshire Main Colliery, Yorks (WR), c/1925-26.
(2)   to NCB, East Midlands Division, No.3 Area, with site, 1/1/1947.

Gauge : 2ft 0in   (Underground)

1	0-4-0DMF	HE	3356	1946	New	(1)

(1)   to NCB, East Midlands Division, No.3 Area, with site, 1/1/1947.

NORTH NOTTS GRAVEL CO LTD
BELLMOOR QUARRIES, Sutton, Retford   D90

SK 686834

This sand and gravel pit was located south east of Sutton village and north east of the Great North Road. In 1950 the narrow gauge tramway ran north from a tipping point at SK 686834, along the edge of the pit, to end at SK 690840. It was replaced by non-rail plant c1954.

Gauge : 2ft 0in

-	4wDM	RH	194783	1940	(a)	(1)

(a)   ex George W. Bungey Ltd, dealers, Hayes, Middx, c/1950; earlier Air Ministry, Fauld, Staffs,

(1)   to Chas. Limb & Co Ltd, (engineers or dealers), Saxilby, Lincs, c/1954.

LOUND QUARRIES, Lound

See Non-Locomotive Section for known details of this site.

NORTHERN UNION MINING CO LTD
HARWORTH COLLIERY, Harworth   B91
SK 627913

This Anglo-German syndicate was formed 1/8/1913 to develop the proposed colliery at Harworth. Sinking of the shaft was commenced, but was halted by the outbreak of World War 1. The assets were impounded by H.M.Government and the German employees were interned. The locomotive and workings were taken over 2/7/1917 by Harworth Main Colliery Co Ltd (later Barber, Walker & Co Ltd) (which see). A temporary rail connection from the GNR at Scrooby was authorised in 8/1912 and laid by the GNR c1914 for colliery construction purposes. The owners provided the sidings at the colliery.

Gauge : 4ft 8½in

| No.1 | | 0-6-0WT | OC | Hohen | 3283 | 1914 | New | (1) |

(1)   to Ministry of Munitions, Chilwell, 8/1914; later to Harworth Main Colliery Co Ltd.

NOTTINGHAM & CLIFTON COLLIERY LTD
CLIFTON COLLIERY, Nottingham   S92
Clifton Colliery Co Ltd until 11/1936   SK 565380
Saul Isaacs until 1/4/1876
Sir Robert Clifton until 5/1870

Coal measures here were proved in 1867 and sinking was commenced by Sir Robert Clifton with the first sod being cut on 19/6/1868. The colliery, opened 16/6/1870, was located on the north west bank of the River Trent. It was served by a ½ mile long private railway which ran south from the Midland Railway Nottingham - Beeston line, 1 mile west of Nottingham Midland Station, before curving north to the colliery. With the opening of its London extension, the GCR made a line which opened 25/7/1898, from the south end of its Queens Walk Goods Yard, south west for ¼ mile to the colliery. From c1923 a connection existed to the North Wilford Power Station of Nottingham Corporation Electricity Department, which was located south of the colliery and shared the Midland Railway exchange sidings.

The colliery was vested in the NCB, East Midlands Division, Area No.6, 1/1/1947.

Gauge : 4ft 8½in

	FRED	4-4-0T	IC	RS	1005	1855	(a)	Scr /1915
1	(CLIFTON)	0-6-0ST	OC	AB	886	1900	New	(1)
2		0-4-0ST	OC	P	1469	1917	New	(1)
	CLIFTON No.3	0-4-0ST	OC	AB	1706	1921	New	Scr /1945
B1C		0-4-0ST	OC	Butterley		1887	(b)	(1)

(a)   ex North London Rly., 25, /1869.
(b)   ex Butterley Co Ltd, (possibly at Kirkby Colliery), c/1939.

(1)   to NCB, East Midland Division, No.6 Area, with site, 1/1/1947.

NOTTINGHAM COLWICK ESTATES LIGHT RAILWAY CO
COLWICK ESTATES, Nottingham   T93
SK 630401

The Nottingham Colwick Estates Co developed a large trading estate from 1919, on the north bank of the River Trent, south west of the GNR Colwick Sidings. It was served by the standard gauge Nottingham Colwick Estates Light Railway, which was connected to the GNR/LNER line 1 mile south east of Netherfield and Colwick station at SK 630402. The light railway, which opened in 8/1919, ran south east from here to a headshunt at SK 634398 and northwest and west as far as Mile End Road, Colwick (SK 614400). The route length was 1½ miles and in 1938 it served 14 private sidings, all on the south side. The line was worked from the outset by the GNR and later by the LNER and BR. The use, if any, to which the narrow gauge locomotives were put is unknown. The light railway closed between 1981 and 1988.

Firms known to have used sidings served by the estates railway are listed below together with the dates of their first and last entry in the Handbook of Stations:-

    Anglo American Oil Co Ltd. (1938)
    Anglo Scottish Beet Sugar Co Ltd/ British Sugar Corporation Ltd. (1925-1976)*
    Armitage Bros. Ltd (1925-1956)
    Crittall-Luxfer Ltd /Luxfer Ltd. (1949-1956)
    Dominion Motor Spirit Co Ltd. (1938-1956)
    Foraky Ltd. (1949-1956)*
    Esso Petroleum Co Ltd. (1956-1976)
    Midland Coal Products Co Ltd. (1925-1956)
    Medway Oil & Storage Co Ltd. (1938-1956)
    National Benzole Co Ltd. (1925-1956)
    Peak Petroleum Co Ltd. (1941-1956)
    Petrofina Ltd (1976)
    Pilot Oils Ltd (1976)
    Power Petroleum Co Ltd. (1938)
    Pure Products Ltd. (1927-1956)
    Regent Oil Co Ltd. (1956)
    Russian Oil Products Ltd. (1938)
    Sealand Petroleum Co Ltd. (1938-1956)
    Shell Mex & B.P.Ltd. (1938-1956)
    Trent Concrete Co Ltd. (1925-1956)*
    Trent Navigation Co Ltd. / British Waterways. (1949-1956)*
    Shell Mex & B.P.Ltd. (1938-1956)

* firms using their own locomotives; see separate entries in this and Contractors Sections.

Gauge : 2ft 0in (probably used during construction of the railway)

-	4wPM	MR	863	1918	(a)	s/s
-	4wPM	MR	921	1918	(b)	s/s

(a)   ex MR, by 22/10/1920; earlier WDLR 2584.
(b)   ex MR, by 22/10/1920; earlier WDLR 2642.

NOTTINGHAM CORPORATION

CITY ENGINEERS DEPARTMENT
EASTCROFT DEPOT, Nottingham S94
formerly **Works & Ways Department** SK 580390

The Eastcroft site was in 1880 shown as a sanitary wharf located on the east bank of the Nottingham Canal and, despite its position south east of the Midland Railway Nottingham station complex, it had no rail connection. By 1895 Eastcroft Sanitary Siding had been installed which ran south from the Midland Railway, east of its station, to enter the depot. A second siding to the east served the Corporation's cattle market. The siding was shown in the Handbook of Stations for 1956 but use of locomotives had by then ceased. The purpose of the narrow gauge locomotives is unknown. It is likely that they were stored here between use on public works or housing contracts.

Gauge : 4ft 8½in

	4wPM	MR			(a)	(1)
reb to 4wDM						
	0-4-0DM	JF			(b)	Scr c/1952
	0-4-0VBT VCG	Chaplin	2368	1885	(c)	(2)

(a) origin and details not known, here by 3/1950
(b) origin and details not known,
(c) ex East Midlands Gas Board, Northampton Gasworks, 3/1966; stored here for Nottingham Industrial Museum.

(1) to ? , Nottingham, /1953.
(2) to Nottingham Industrial Museum, Wollaton Hall, Nottingham, 11/1977.

Gauge : 2ft 0in

1	4wPM	MR	1347	1918	(a)	(1)
2	4wPM	MR	1386	1918	(b)	s/s
3	4wPM	MR	5208	1930	New	(3)
4	4wPM	MR	5209	1930	New	(2)

(a) ex MR, 5/2/1926; earlier WDLR 3068.
(b) ex MR, 5/2/1926; earlier WDLR 3107.

(1) to Savidge Bros, 164 Queens Walk, Nottingham.
(2) to Sewage Disposal Department, Stoke Bardolph Sewage Works, 2/1939.
(3) sold or scrapped after 3/1953.

SEWAGE DISPOSAL DEPARTMENT
STOKE BARDOLPH SEWAGE WORKS U95
SK 633421

This works was opened c1930 on a large site used for the same purpose for many years previously (see Non-locomotive Section - sewage farm siding, Netherfield). The tramway was used to remove debris from screens to a tip. It was extended c1959 as part of a reconstruction project. The works was transferred to the Severn Trent Water Authority (which see) from 1/4/1974.

Gauge : 2ft 0in

		4wPM	L	4404	1932	New	(1)	
4		4wPM	MR	5209	1930	(a)		Scr 8/1961
3		4wDM	MR	9381	1948	(b)	(2)	

(a) ex Eastcroft Depot, 2/1939.
(b) ex City of Birmingham Water Department, Aqueduct contract, 16/8/1961.

(1) to Lanarkshire Moss Litter Co Ltd, Longriggend, Lanarks.
(2) to Severn Trent Water Authority, with site, 31/3/1974.

NOTTINGHAM PATENT BRICK CO LTD
MAPPERLEY BRICKWORKS, Nottingham   R96
Edward Gripper in 1864   SK 586431

This company, registered on 24/8/1867, operated a number of brickworks east and north of Nottingham. Those at Thorneywood and Dorket Head are dealt with in the Non-locomotive Section.

The complex at Mapperley consisted of four separate works and, although only one of these used a locomotive, it is convenient to deal with all of them here. All were in place by 1881 when all had tramways.

Two of the works were shortlived. One was located on the south west side of Scout Lane (now Woodthorpe Drive) at SK 587434. In 1881 this had a short tramway running into a hole to the east from where tracks radiated into the workings. This works had gone by 1899 and its site was later worked opencast for clay. The second (Bottom Works?) was on the north west side of Woodborough Road, west of the GNR Sherwood tunnel, at SK 581427. In 1881 this had two short lines running south and east from separate clay mills. This works had very limited clay reserves and had gone by 1899. A factory was later built on the site.

The two works which survived longest were on the north west side of Woodborough Road at SK 583430 (Middle Works?) and SK 588431 (Top Works?). Originally separate, they were later merged. In 1881 the former had only a short tramway incline running east whilst the latter had two double track rope haulages which, with many re-alignments, were to remain until the 1950s. One of the lines ran north and then north east, tunnelling beneath Woodthorpe Road. By 1919, it had also tunnelled beneath Woodthorpe Drive, to end at a new quarry north east of it. The second line ran east, passing under Woodthorpe Road, and, by 1919, had almost reached the Woodborough Road / Woodthorpe Drive junction. The whole of the area between the works and these roads was subsequently worked from one or other of the lines.

By 1953 the northerly line had been cut back to the foot of its first incline and a loco worked line, with a loco shed at SK 584432, ran south from there. Wagons had to be shunted through the shed to reach the incline. The rope worked line which ran east had by then turned north to reach the hole beyond Woodthorpe Drive. No tracks by then ran to the westernmost (Bottom?) works. There was one other line, an isolated 300 yard stretch north of the works with a building (SK 586432) which may have been a loco shed. The purpose is unknown but may have been overburden stripping.

After the opening in 1889 of the GNR Nottingham Suburban Railway, a connection was made to it in the form of a rope worked incline which ran south east for ¼ mile from north of Sherwood Station to the works. Kilns and stocking grounds at both works were served. The standard gauge tracks had all gone by 1953. The works are believed to have closed in the late 1960s and the site has largely been re-used for housing.

Gauge : 2ft 0in

| | | 4wDM | RH | 235715 | 1945 | (a) | (1) |

(a) ex Joseph Place & Sons Ltd, Hoddlesden, Lancs, by 26/9/1947

(1) out of use and off the rails 2/1968; sold or scrapped c/1968

JAMES OAKES & CO (RIDDINGS COLLIERIES) LTD
James Oakes & Company until 16/1/1925

The origins of this company lie with the Alfreton (later Riddings) Ironworks on the Derbyshire side of the Erewash Valley. At some time after 1836 the company began to mine coal and ironstone on the Nottinghamshire side, in the area north of what was to become Pye Hill Colliery. These workings were connected to the ironworks by a private railway, details of which will appear in the Derbyshire Handbook. Oakes' had three sites in Nottinghamshire at Pye Hill, New Selston and Pollington. The first two were connected and collectively known as Riddings Collieries. Cotes Park Colliery in Derbyshire was also owned. The Ironworks were sold to Stanton Ironworks Co Ltd, from 1/1/1920. This left the collieries and clay products works in Oakes' hands, as indeed the latter remained after the collieries were vested in the NCB. The clay works eventually passed to the Hepworth Group but by that time rail traffic had ceased.

POLLINGTON COLLIERY, Brinsley   L97
(also known as NEW BRINSLEY COLLIERY)   SK 454498

This colliery, sunk about 1875 and opened in 1876, was served by a line which ran east from the Midland Railway Erewash Valley line 1½ miles north of Langley Mill Station. The first 16 chains of this were Midland Railway owned and known as its Brinsley Branch. The line passed beneath the GNR Pinxton Branch, which had opened in 1875 and to which a trailing connection was made on the south side, then turned north east to the colliery (¾ mile). An early line had run south west from the colliery branch, between the two main lines, to a wharf on the Nottingham Canal. This was on the site of an early tramway and had been lifted by 1880. Abandonment plans for the colliery were deposited in April 1920 and the Midland Railway connection had been removed by 1921. The site of the GNR exchange sidings was later used by the Ministry of Fuel and Power, Directorate of Opencast Coal Production for its **BRINSLEY DISPOSAL POINT** (see NCB Section).

Gauge : 4ft 8½in

	VIXEN	0-6-0ST	OC				(a)	(1)
No.7	MARGARET	0-4-0ST	OC	HE	159	1877	New	Scr after 8/1917
No.8		0-4-0ST	OC	HE	223	1879	New	(2)

(a) origin and details not known

(1) to HE, /1895 (possibly in part payment for HE 637)
(2) to Northfleet Coal & Ballast Co Ltd, West Thurrock, Essex, after 19/4/1920, by 18/10/1920.

PYE HILL COLLIERY, BRICK AND PIPEWORKS, Riddings   K98

Pye Hill Colliery   SK 447523
Selston Colliery (later loco shed)   SK 443522

Prior to the sinking of **PYE HILL COLLIERY** in 1874, Oakes' private railway extended to its earlier **SELSTON COLLIERY** and ironstone mines east of the Midland Railway Erewash Valley line to which it was connected south of Pye Bridge station. This line was extended east for ¼ mile to the new Pye Hill Colliery. By 1880 it served a small brickyard to the north and had served an ironstone mine to the north east which is said to have closed in 1878. The brickyard had a short narrow gauge line in a clay hole. In 1875 the GNR had opened its Pinxton branch, which at this point ran along the east side of the Midland Railway, and a connection between this and Oakes' railway was made. **NEW SELSTON COLLIERY** was opened in 1892 at SK 676504, some ¾ mile east of Pye Hill, and the railway was extended to it. The earlier SELSTON Colliery probably ceased production in 1901, whilst **TUNNEL COLLIERY**, also located within this site but probably adjacent to one of the other collieries, had opened by 1874 and closed after 1905, by 1913. At some time between 1906 and 1914, extensive brick and pipe works were built north of Pye Hill Colliery, replacing the earlier small works. Locomotive stock is believed to have been pooled with the ironworks prior to 1/1/1920 (see list in forthcoming Derbyshire Handbook). It is equally possible that Pye Hill had a separate allocation from within the ironworks list prior to that date.

A constraint on locomotives that could be used was imposed as early as 1875 when the GNR line was built. The limited height of its bridges over the colliery sidings required cut down locomotives thereafter. There were short narrow gauge tramways into clay workings to the north east and south west of the brick and pipe works by 1914.

The colliery was vested in the NCB, East Midlands Division, Area No.5, 1/1/1947

Gauge : 4ft 8½in

No.9	0-4-0ST	OC	HE	637	1895	(a)	(3)
No.10	0-4-0ST	OC	AB	905	1901	(a)	(2)
No.11	0-4-0ST	OC	P	852	1901	(a)	(1)
No.12	0-4-0ST	OC	AB	1010	1905	(a)	(3)
1	0-4-0ST	OC	HE	1493	1925	New	(3)

NOTE that locomotives were supplied from the Alfreton Iron Works stock (see Derbyshire Handbook) until c/1920-1922.

(a)   ex James Oakes & Company, Alfreton Ironworks, Derbys, on separation of collieries and iron works 1/1/1920 (note that some could have been kept at Pye Hill from new).

(1)   to Cotes Park Colliery, Derbys, /1903 (may have gone to Cotes Park direct from the Iron Works without ever being at Pye Hill)
(2)   to Cotes Park Colliery, Derbys.
(3)   to NCB, East Midland Division, No.5 Area, with site, 1/1/1947.

OILFIELDS OF ENGLAND LTD
KELHAM BOREHOLES, near Newark   P99

SK 775544

Oil was discovered in 1908 when borings to prove coal measures were being made. This company was registered on 18/7/1918 and, after receiving approval from the Petroleum Executive, began drilling in 9/1920 on land leased at Kelham. A report in the 'Iron & Coal Trades Review' for 2/1/1920 stated that a railway had been laid from the main road to the drilling site east of the River Trent about two miles west of Newark. In 1922 the company turned its activities to Spain and ceased operations entirely in 6/1923. A Receiver was appointed 23/9/1923 and all work at Kelham ceased in 12/1923. The course of the railway which ran from SK 777553 to a possible drilling site at SK 775544 remains as a farm track. An agreement was made on 20/1/1920, with the Midland Railway, for a tramway worked by a motor tractor to pass beneath its bridge at SK 774538. The plan shows a junction south of the bridge and two wells are known to have been sunk, but there is no indication as to how much further south either line ran.

Gauge : 2ft 6in

     -     0-4-0PM   Bg   763   1919   New (a) s/s

(a)   New, 20/11/1919, to this company, but confirmation is required that it worked here.

OXTON SAND & GRAVEL COMPANY
OXTON PITS, Oxton, Southwell   **N100**

SK 614516?

This was a trading name used by Mansfield Standard Sand Co Ltd. for some sand and gravel workings of that company at Oxton. These were listed in directories of 1943 and 1948 and are believed to have been the flooded pits shown on later maps at Oxton Bogs. The pits were said to have been less productive than expected. These are located 1 mile north east of .Calverton Colliery, north of the B6386 road. There is no evidence of a tramway on a map revised in 1950. It is therefore uncertain if the locomotive was used at Oxton. Spares orders placed with RH between 1941 and 1948, under the Oxton trading name, stipulated delivery to the parent company at Sandhurst Quarry, Mansfield, where the locomotive had been put to use by 2/1950.

Gauge : 2ft 0in

     -     4wDM   RH   189976   1938   (a)   (1)

(a)   ex RH, 11/8/1939; earlier hired by RH from new to Bodenham Sand & Gravel Co Ltd, Bodenham, Herefords, until 6/1939

(1)   to Mansfield Standard Sand Co Ltd, Sandhurst Quarry, Mansfield, by 2/1950

PINXTON COLLIERIES LTD
PINXTON AND BROOKHILL COLLIERY RAILWAY, Pinxton   K101
Pinxton Coal Co Ltd (registered on 25/5/1899) until 8/1/1906
Pinxton Coal Company, until 25/5/1899
John Coke until 1847

Comprising:
BROOKHILL COLLIERY (Sunk between 1908 and 1913)	SK 462547
PINXTON No.1 & 6 COLLIERY (opened by 1842)	SK 450542
PINXTON No.2 COLLIERY (opened by 1836)	SK 448545
PINXTON No.3 COLLIERY (opened by 1842)	SK 446546
PINXTON No.4 COLLIERY (opened after 1842)	SK 446551
PINXTON No.5 COLLIERY (opened after 1842)	SK 446546
PINXTON LOCOSHEDS	SK 449543 & SK 450544
LANGTON No.7, 8 & 9 COLLIERY (sunk 1841-4)	SK 474551
COKING PLANT (Notts & Derby Coke & By-Product Co Ltd)	SK 463548

The complex of collieries and railways operated by Pinxton Collieries Ltd and its predecessors were located on both sides of the Nottinghamshire - Derbyshire border and their history can only be succesfully studied by disregarding the county boundary. The Pinxton Coal Company was a partnership dating from 1847 but throughout its existence was often referred to as Coke & Company since that family retained control.

The first mines, collectively known as **PINXTON OLD COLLIERY** worked from 1780 and eventually had nine shafts in the Pinxton Green area; all had closed by 1844. By 1836 there was a network of tramways centred on the end of the Pinxton arm of the Cromford Canal at SK 448541. Two of these tramways are important as their routes formed part of the later rail system. One ran south east from **PINXTON No.2 and PINXTON No.3 COLLIERIES** to reach the canal just south of **PINXTON No.1 & 6 COLLIERY**. The second line ran south east from **CARNFIELD COLLIERY** to the west end of the Pinxton line's wharf. These tramways were entirely in Derbyshire. From the opening of the Mansfield and Pinxton railway on 13/4/1819, some of the collieries were also connected to it. A mines list of 1842 includes, in addition to the Carnfield Collieries, Pinxton No.1, (Old) Pinxton No.9 (at SK 460551), **SLEIGHTS No.2** and **SLEIGHTS No.3**. The last two of these later became Pinxton No.2 and No.3. **PINXTON No.4 and No.5** (originally **SLEIGHTS No.4 and No.5**) **COLLIERIES** were sunk after 1842. Further confusion is caused by references in later records to No.2, 4 and 5 as **PLYMOUTH No.2, 4 and 5 COLLIERIES**, in the first case until the 1940s.

LANGTON COLLIERY, the first of this company to be located in Nottinghamshire, was sunk between 1841 and 1844 and eventually comprised three shafts, **Nos. 7, 8 & 9**, all on the one site, which was 1 mile east of the canal end and linked to it by a horse tramway. After the conversion of the Mansfield and Pinxton Railway to a Midland Railway locomotive line was completed in 1849, the Langton line was also converted and connected to the Midland Railway at SK 455544.

The earliest plan seen showing railways is an Ordnance Survey of 1877, by which time the Langton line also served a small brickworks at SK 464548 and continued west from the canal end, where there was a rail connected gasworks, to end at **No.1 & 6 COLLIERY**. This was located on the south side of, and connected to, the Midland Railway line at Sleights sidings, 1 mile west of Pinxton Station. At No.1 COLLIERY, the line from Langton was at a lower level than the other sidings which it tunnelled beneath, as did the line on the old tramway alignment from No.2 and No.3 COLLIERIES to the canal wharf at SK 448541. The first GNR connection was from Palmerston Junction, half a mile southwest of Pinxton station (opened 23/8/1875) and ran north to No.1 COLLIERY. The collieries north of the Midland Railway were not then directly linked to the GNR but were served by a connection from the Midland

Railway at SK 447543 which ran north to **No 3 COLLIERY**, which had screens and sidings, and to **No 2 COLLIERY** which was not then equipped for coal turning. This line had formerly continued to **No.4 and No.5 COLLIERIES** which, by 1877, had closed and been demolished. The old tramway from **CARNFIELD COLLIERY** had also been converted to a railway, with a connection to the Midland Railway at Sleights sidings, before passing beneath it to reach the canal. This line was in situ in 1877 but Carnfield Collieries are listed as closed in 1875.

By 1898, the GNR had gained access to the colliery line to Langton Colliery by a north eastern extension of its line along the north side of the canal from No.1 Colliery. This connected with the existing colliery line near the gasworks and then followed the earlier route beneath the Midland lines to a junction beyond. The connection from the northern collieries that tunnelled beneath No.1 Colliery sidings to reach the canal had been replaced by one using the south east end of the Carnfield line. This gave the GNR access to the northern collieries, albeit by way of a very short headshunt en route. The line northwards to Carnfield had been lifted. North of the Midland's Sleights sidings, No.2 COLLIERY was now equipped for coal turning and an independent track had been provided to join the Langton Line near its original Midland Railway connection. Along the Langton line there was now a siding which ran to **OLD PINXTON No.1** shaft at Pinxton Green (SK 464552), which was one of the original Pinxton shafts. This siding ran north from just east of the brickworks. LANGTON COLLIERY had, by 1898, an independent Midland Railway connection from its line east of Pinxton station, which also continued to BENTINCK Colliery (see N.H.& B.Collieries Ltd). This replaced its original Langton Junction at SK 456544. From 22/11/1892, Langton was also served by a MS&LR branch which approached from its Kirkby and Pinxton station to the east.

By 1914, major changes had taken place east of the Pinxton collieries. First was the building in 1905-06 of the Pinxton Coke Works of the **Notts & Derby Coke & By-Product Co Ltd**. This comprised 50 ovens by Coppee Co, located to the south of the private line to Langton. Second was the the sinking of the **BROOKHILL COLLIERY** to the north of it. The Midland Railway serviced these via the existing route from Sleights Sidings but the GNR had realigned its connection in 1905 to run north east from Pinxton Station, crossing the Midland Railway by an overbridge to join the earlier colliery company line, part of which was taken over. From there it provided its own connections east and west to Brookhill and Pinxton No.2 collieries repectively. No.1 Colliery south of Sleights Sidings had, by 1914, ceased winding coal, but perhaps not dirt. Rail access was maintained and some tipping was taking place east of the colliery. A locoshed there remained in use for repairs until after vesting day. North of Sleights Sidings, the supposed No.4 Colliery had ceased coal winding and No.2 Colliery was the only one working. This had by 1908 been redeveloped for a larger output with extensive sidings served by the GNR from the east as well as by the Midland from the west. A locoshed was built to the south at SK 449543. The line north from No.2 Colliery empties sidings towards the closed No.4 and No.5 Collieries had been temporarily reinstated to serve a tip. The brickworks north of the Langton line had closed and its site was being tipped on. The canal had closed north of Pye Bridge by 1921.

In 1927-8 the original coke ovens were replaced by 20 Coppee regenerative ovens and plant extensions to the south were made. Tipping was taking place by 1938 along the Langton branch on both sides.

The collieries and the railway were vested in the NCB, East Midlands Division, Area No.4 from 1/1/1947. However, the coking plant remained in the private sector. It was purchased by **Stanton Ironworks Co Ltd** in 1949 and used by them to carbonise Durham coal, pending completion of a plant at Stanton, Derbys, c1954. The company title became the **Pinxton Coking Co Ltd** in 1953 but the plant was sold by auction in 6/1955 and subsequently demolished by **Thos. W Ward Ltd** (see Contractors Section).

Reference : LNER Appendix to the working timetables dated 1/11/1947 (extracts in the Industrial Railway Record, Volume 3, page 384 and Volume 4, page 41).

Gauge : 4ft 8½in

Name	Type			Works No.	Date		Ref
MARY	0-4-0ST	OC	HCR	172	1877	New	(1)
BILLY	0-4-0ST	OC	HCR	215	1879	New	(5)
(FRANK ?)	0-6-0ST	IC	MW	205	1866	(a)	(4)
ASTLEY	0-4-0ST	OC	HCR	136	1873	(b)	(2)
MARY	0-4-0ST	OC	HC	254	1885	New	(6)
-	0-6-0ST	IC	EBW	522	1856	(c)	(3)
FRANK	0-4-0ST	OC	HC	308	1888	New	(7)
BILLY	0-4-0ST	OC	HC	350	1889	New	(8)
HARRY (by 11/1901)							
(ISABEL)	0-4-0ST	OC	HC	471	1896	New (d)	(11)
PATSY	0-4-0ST	OC	HC	472	1896	New (d)	(10)
FANNY	0-4-0ST	OC	HG		1866	(e)	(9)
DICK	0-4-0ST	OC	HC	603	1902	New (f)	(12)
TOM	0-4-0ST	OC	HC	604	1902	New (f)	(13)
PINXTON	0-4-0ST	OC	LE	246	1907	New	(14)
LANGTON	0-4-0ST	OC	LE	247	1907	New	(14)
LONGWOOD	0-4-0ST	OC	LE	248	1907	New	(14)
	0-4-0ST	OC	P	1273	1912	New	(14)
PECKETT No.2	0-4-0ST	OC	P	1975	1939	New	(14)

(a) here by c/1888 (and probably c/1880); earlier Thos. Oliver, Mansfield contract, FRANK, from 12/11/1870.
(b) ex HC, hire, 14/4/1885; earlier T. & R. Bower Ltd, Yorks (WR).
(c) ex HC, hire, 8/3/1887; earlier J. & J. Charlesworth (Rothwell Haigh ?), Yorks (WR).
(d) ex HC, on long term hire, 20/10/1896.
(e) ex HC, hire, 27/9/1901 (earlier Carnforth Hematite Iron Co, Carnforth, Lancs).
(f) ex HC, term hire, 10/2/1902.

(1) possibly replaced c/1885; later Barnstone Blue Lias Lime Co, Barnstone Cement Works, c/1889.
(2) returned to HC, off hire, 22/6/1885; then it remained a hire loco until sold to J.F. Wake, Middlesboro', for Tees Union Shipping Co , 2/1888.
(3) returned to HC, off hire, 9/4/1887; later sold to Wm. Rigby, contr., Driffield, Yorks (ER).
(4) possibly to Thos Riley, Preston - Kirkham (LYR) (1888-9) contract, Lancs, PRESTON and then to Fairhaven Estate Co Ltd, Fairhaven, Lancs; later L.P.Nott, Llanelly North Dock contract, Carms, PRESTON, from c/1898.
(5) to HC, 3/1/1890; then a HC hire loco until resold to Chas.Baker & Sons, contrs., Dudley Hill (Bradford), 5/10/1891.
(6) to HC, 25/11/1896; hired by HC to T.Bills, Felixstowe, Suffolk, 1/1897-3/1898; then to Thos. Docwra & Son, West Molesey Reservoir contract (1897-1903), Surrey, 13/4/1898.
(7) to HC, c12/1896; then to Holloway Bros, New Naval Barracks contract, Chatham Dockyard, Kent, 10/9/1897.
(8) to HC, c11-12/1896; then to J.J.Cordes & Co Ltd, Dos Works, Newport, Mon, 28/3/1898.
(9) returned to HC, off hire, 27/12/1901 then it remained a hire loco until sold to McCormick & Sons, contrs., Mountnessing, Essex, 26/7/1904.
(10) to HC, c2/1902; sold to Mansfield Standard Sand Co Ltd, Mansfield, EMPRESS, 23/4/1902.
(11) to HC, after 4/1903; later Admiralty, Upnor Depot, Sharnal Street, Kent, 14/4/1904.
(12) to HC, off hire 7/1907; resold to George Armitage & Sons Ltd, Thorpe Brickworks, Yorks (WR), 31/7/1907.

(13) to HC, off hire, 7/1907; resold to William Jones, dealer, London, but sent direct to Thos. Docwra & Son, Alexandra Dock contract, Newport, Mon, 17/11/1910.
(14) to NCB, East Midlands Division, Area No.4, with site, 1/1/1947.

POWERGEN plc

This company, together with National Power plc, was formed by the government, from 1/8/1989, in order to assume ownership from 31/3/1990, from the Central Electricity Generating Board, of those power stations in England and Wales which were to be privatised. The shares in both companies were later sold to the private sector. Previous ownership is shown for each individual station. The electricity generation and supply industry had been nationalised on 1/4/1948 when installations were vested in the British Electricity Authority (Central Electricity Authority from 1/4/1955). From 1/1/1958 generation and supply were segregated, power stations passing to the Central Electricity Generating Board.

COTTAM POWER STATION, Cottam   F102
Central Electricity Generating Board until 1/3/1990   SK 816797

This coal fired power station was built in the mid 1960s and from commissioning in 1969 was served by merry-go-round rail sidings which form the terminus of the truncated Clarborough Jct - Sykes Jct railway. Operated entirely by BR locomotives, but one preserved locomotive was here for a time as an exhibit at special events and open days.

Gauge : 4ft 8½in

No.1   CASTLE DONINGTON POWER STATION
       0-4-0ST   OC   RSHN   7817   1954   (a)   (1)

(a)   ex Castle Donington Power Station, Leics, 19/7/1992

(1)   to Midland Railway Centre, Butterley, Derbys (on loan), 7/5/1995

HIGH MARNHAM POWER STATION   see EASTERN ELECTRICITY plc

WEST BURTON POWER STATION
    see CENTRAL ELECTRICITY GENERATING BOARD

RANSOME HOFFMAN POLLARD LTD
STANLEY WORKS, Newark   P103
Ransome & Marles Bearing Co Ltd, registered 17/1/1917, until 1/1/1970   SK 807542
A. Ransome & Co Ltd until ceased trading 1931

This works, the main product of which was then woodworking machinery, was opened in 1900, the firm having relocated from London. It was served by sidings (agreement dated 15/6/1899) which ran south east from the GNR line, immediately south of Newark Northgate Station. By 1914 a 2ft 0in gauge system was used within the works to link various workshops; it crossed standard gauge lines at several places. In 1906 part of the works was let to the Underfeed Stoker Co Ltd, which had its own siding from then until the firm moved to Derby in 10/1924. Ransome & Marles Bearing Co Ltd opened c1917 in a northward extension of the works, with additional sidings. Locomotive use may date from then. In 1931 A. Ransome & Co Ltd ceased trading and the bearing company took over the entire works. Rail traffic ceased c4/1977 and the siding agreements were terminated from 24/11/1977.

Gauge : 4ft 8½in

	PUCK	0-4-0ST	OC	MW	1255	1893	(a)	s/s
	-	0-4-0ST	OC	P	981	1904	(b)	Scr /1949
	-	4wDM		RH	275881	1949	New	(1)
	-	4wDM		RH	305302	1951	(c)	(2)

(a) ex Cammell Laird & Co.Ltd, National Ordnance Factory, Nottingham, per Thos.W. Ward Ltd, 1/1/1918. (Wards show this loco as going to Newcastle on Tyne, probably an error for **Newark on Trent**.)
(b) ex Samuel Fox & Co Ltd, Stocksbridge, Yorks (WR).
(c) ex Annfield Plain Works, Durham, 3/1971 (may also have been at Newark c/1951).

(1) to Annfield Plain Works, Durham, 3/1971.
(2) to Market Overton Industrial Rly. Assoc., Rutland, Leics, 17/3/1979.

WILLIAM RIGLEY & SONS (NOTTINGHAM) LTD
FOREST WAGON WORKS, Bulwell, Nottingham　　　　　　　　　　Q104
Willam Rigley & Sons Ltd until after 1940　　　　　　　　　　　　SK 552453
William Rigley Ltd until 28/9/1922

This company of railway wagon builders & mining machinery manufacturers was formed in 1896 by William Rigley, a mining engineer. His first works was a small shed built on land he leased from the GNR at Bulwell Forest station, (agreement dated 1/3/1896). In 1906 he expanded to the east, onto 20 acres of land acquired from the Duke of St.Albans. The works was served by sidings on the east side of the GNR Leen Valley line, at Bulwell Forest Station. The works closed on 31/12/1964 and lay derelict. The steel framework of the main wagon workshop building was acquired by the Midland Railway Trust, dismantled during 1981 and taken to Butterley for re-erection. The site was later occupied by a super-store.

Gauge : 4ft 8½in

		STANLOW	0-4-0ST	OC	MW	1017	1887		
				reb			1922	(a)	Scr 17/11/1952
		RIGLEY No.2	0-4-0ST	OC	KS	4012	1919	(b)	(1)
		-	4wPM		Crossley			(c)	Scr /1952
1		(RIGLEY No.3)	4wDM		RH	305308	1952	New	(2)
2		-	4wDM		RH	294265	1950	(d)	(3)

(a) earlier C.J. Wills & Sons Ltd, Barking (Rippleway road contract (1920-1924)?), Essex; here by /1927.
(b) ex R.C.A. Palmer-Morewood, Swanwick Colliery, Derbys. /1939.
(c) ex Beswick's Limeworks, Hindlow, Derbys (possibly via a quarry at Wirksworth, Derbys, but this is unconfirmed).
(d) ex Francis T. Wright Ltd, Finedon, Northants, c/1960.

(1) boiler used for cleaning tank wagons, c/1953; scrapped, c/1956 (after 9/1956).
(2) to Nottingham Gypsum Products Ltd, Kilvington Gypsum Works, c/1965.
(3) to Albert Looms (Spondon) Ltd, scrap dealer, Spondon, Derbys, c10/1965.

RJB MINING (UK) LTD

This company was formed by Richard J.Budge, a director of the failed mining and civil engineering company A.F.Budge Ltd of Retford. Its first venture which involved rail served sites was the leasing from British Coal of two closed collieries, Calverton, on 23/5/1994, and Rossington, South Yorkshire, on 24/1/1994. In the latter part of 1994, HM Government issued the prospectus for the sale of the producing mines of British Coal to the private sector. RJB Mining (UK) Ltd was a successful bidder and acquired the remaining working mines and most opencast sites in England on 30/12/1994.

For earlier history and details of the collieries listed below see the relevant entry in the NCB Section of this book.

BILSTHORPE COLLIERY, Bilsthorpe   G105
British Coal until 30/12/1994   SK 653617

Coal was dispatched by rail using 'Merry go Round' trains with BR haulage throughout. Locomotives were used underground. Closed 26/3/1997.

Gauge : 2ft 4in (Underground locos)

No.1	BB2 70330	4w-4wBEF	CE	B3224A	1985	(a)	(2)
	-	4wBEF	CE	B3092A	1984	(a)	
	-	4wBEF	CE	B3092B	1984	(a)	
	-	4wBEF	CE	B3093A	1984	(a)	(3)
	-	4wBEF	CE	B3093B	1984	(a)	
	-	4wBEF	CE	B3328	1987	(a)	
	-	4wBEF	CE	B3364A	1987	(a)	(1)
	-	4wBEF	CE	B3364B	1987	(a)	

(a)   ex British Coal, with site, 30/12/1994.

(1)   to Prince of Wales Colliery, West Yorks, /1997.
(2)   to CE, 13/1/1998.
(3)   to Harworth Park Stores and thence to CE for use as a source of spares, 4/2/1999.

CALVERTON COLLIERY, Calverton   N106
British Coal until 23/5/1994   SK 603505

Coal was dispatched by rail using 'Merry go Round' trains with BR haulage throughout. Locomotives were used underground. Colliery closed 16/4/1999.

Gauge : 2ft 0in (Underground locos)

No.5	164/150	0-6-0DMF	HC	DM1310	1963	(a)	(5)
No.2	164/200	4wDHF	HE	8909	1979	(a)	(1)
No.7	164/312	4wDHF	HE	8911	1979	(a)	(3)
No.3		4wDHF	HE	8980	1980	(a)	(2)
No.4	164/323	4wDHF	HE	8984	1981	(a)	(3)
No.5	164/346	4wDHF	HE	9055	1982	(a)	(5)
No.6		4wDHF	HE	9056	1982	(a)	(4)
1B	164/373	4wBEF	CE	B3100B	1984	(a)	(6)
2B	164/374	4wBEF	CE	B3100A	1984	(a)	
3B	164/375	4wBEF	CE	B3155B	1984	(a)	

No.3	87127		4wBEF	CE	B0427	1975		
			reb	CE	B2926	1982	(a)	
No.14	820/11859	No.9	4wDHF	HE	7519	1977	(a)	(1)
No.21	820/18612	No.9	4wDHF	HE	9048	1981	(a)	(5)
No.1	20651		4w-4wBEF	CE	B3335	1987	(a)	
No.4	1357		4wBEF	CE	B2239A	1980	(a)	
No.1	138876		4wBEF	HE	9155	1991	(a)	(7)
No.2	138877		4wBEF	HE	9156	1991	(a)	(5)

(a) ex British Coal, with site, 23/5/1994.
(1) to Red Rose Steam Society, Tyldesley, Greater Manchester, 16/4/1997.
(2) to Red Rose Steam Society, Tyldesley, Greater Manchester, 19/7/1997.
(3) to Midland Railway Centre, Butterley, Derbys, after 7/6/1997, by 26/9/1997.
(4) to Moseley Industrial Tramway & Museum, Greater Manchester, 13/9/1997.
(5) abandoned underground on closure of the colliery, 4/1999.
(5) to surface, then s/s by 4/1999.
(6) to FMB Engineering, Oakhanger, Hants, 14/9/1999.

Gauge : 400mm (Underground: Becorit "Roadrailer" Trapped Rail System)

No.1	No.11	2adDHF	BGB	DRL50/400/414	1979	(a)	(1)
No.7	No.17	2adDHF	BGB	DRL50/400/418	1980		
		reb	BGB	DRL50/400/446	1986/	(a)	(1)
No.3	No.13	2adDHF	BGB	DRL50/400/438	1983	(a)	(1)
No.2	No.12	2adDHF	BGB	DRL50/400/439	1983	(a)	(1)
No.5	No.15	2adDHF	BGB	DRL50/400/440	198x	(a)	(1)
No.4	No.14	2adDHF	BGB	DRL50/400/442	1985	(a)	(1)
No.6	No.16	2adDHF	BGB	DRL50/400/443	1985	(a)	(1)

(a) ex British Coal, with site, 23/5/1994.

(1) abandoned underground on closure of the colliery, 4/1999.

CLIPSTONE COLLIERY, Clipstone
G107
SK 594632

Coal is dispatched by rail using 'Merry go Round' trains with BR haulage throughout. Locomotives are used underground.

Gauge : 400mm (Underground; Becorit Trapped Rail System)

	22714	1adBEF	BGB	25/400/001	1986	(a)
		1adBEF	BGB	25/400/002	1987	(a)
	22719	1adBEF	BGB	25/400/003	1987	(a)
	22677	1adDHF	BGB	30/400/003	1983	(a)
		2adBEF	BGB	50/400/001	1989	(a)
No.2	24982	2adDHF	BGB	50/400/407	1978	(a)
No.1	24981	2adDHF	BGB	50/400/408	1977	(a)
No.3	390/3	2adDHF	BGB	50/400/413	1978	(a)
No.3	24987	2adDHF	BGB	50/400/422	1980	
		reb	BGB	50/400/445	1985	(a)
No.4	24698	2adDHF	BGB	50/400/427	1980	
		reb	BGB	50/400/441	1985	(a)
No.5	24699	2adDHF	BGB	50/400/428	1980	(a)

No.6	22680	2adDHF	BGB 50/400/436	1982	(a)	
No.7	22658	2adDHF	BGB 50/400/437	1982	(a)	
	390/4	2adDHF	BGB 50/400/535	1978	(a)	
	22862	2adDHF	BGB100/400/002	1981	(a)	
No.3	164/353	2adDHF	BGB100/400/003	1982	(a)	
	22691	2adDHF	BGB100/400/004	1983	(a)	
No.5	164/364	2adDHF	BGB100/400/005	1983	(a)	
	22693	2adDHF	BGB100/400/006	1984	(a)	
	22776	2adDHF	BGB100/400/008	1984	(a)	
	22770	2adDHF	BGB100/400/009	1985	(a)	
	22779	2adDHF	BGB100/400/010	1986	(a)	
	22774	2adDHF	BGB100/400/012	1986	(a)	
	22784	2adDHF	BGB100/400/013	1987	(a)	

(a) ex British Coal, with site, 24/1/1994

CLIPSTONE EQUIPMENT HOLDING CENTRE, New Clipstone   G108
SK 593633

Underground locomotives stored here pending re-use.

Gauge : 3ft 0in

4		4wBEF		CE	B1575A 1978		
			reb	CE	B3575 1989	(a)	(1)
-		4wBEF		CE	B3563B 1989	(a)	(1)

(a) earlier Silverwood Colliery, South Yorks.
(1) to CE, after 18/4/1996, by 8/8/1996.

Gauge : 2ft 4in

No.27	06174	No.29	4wBEF		CE	B3044 1983	(a)	(1)
	-		4wBEF		CE	B3501 1990	(a)	
25			4wBEF		CE	B3043A 1983	(b)	(2)

(a) ex British Coal, with site, 24/1/1994.
(b) earlier Bevercotes Colliery.
(1) s/s by 18/4/1996.
(2) to CE, after 31/3/1998, by 30/6/1998; thence to Rossington Colliery, South Yorks, via Gascoigne Wood Colliery, North Yorks.

Gauge : 2ft 3in

-	4wBEF		CE	B2972A 1982		
		reb	CE	B3906/1 1992	(a)	
-	4wBEF		CE	B2972B 1982		
		reb	CE	B3906/2 1992	(a)	(1)

(a) earlier Ollerton Colliery.

(1) to CE, 3/1998; thence to Rossington Colliery, South Yorks, via Gascoigne Wood Colliery, North Yorks.

HARWORTH COLLIERY, Bircotes   B109
SK 627913

Coal is dispatched by rail using 'Merry go Round' trains with BR haulage throughout. Locomotives are used underground.

Gauge : 2ft 6in (Underground locomotives)

No.1	820/32099		0-6-0DMF	HC	DM724	1949	(a)	
No.2	820/32100		0-6-0DMF	HC	DM725	1949	(a)	
No.3	820/32101		0-6-0DMF	HC	DM726	1949	(a)	
No.6	820/34204		0-6-0DMF	HC	DM1309	1963	(a)	
No.4	820/32102	PHILLIP	0-6-0DMF	HC	DM727	1949	(a)	
No.5	820/32103		0-6-0DMF	HC	DM729	1949	(a)	
No.1			4wBEF	CE	B1831A	1979		
			reb	CE	B3290	1986	(a)	
No.2			4wBEF	CE	B1831B	1979	(a)	
	-		4wDHF	CE	B1530	1977	(a)	
			0-6-0DMF	HE	8848	1981		
				HC	DM1448	1981	(a)	
	-		0-6-0DMF	HE	8849	1982		
				HC	DM1449	1982	(a)	
	-		0-6-0DMF	HE	8850	1982		
				HC	DM1450	1982	(a)	
	-		4wBEF	CE	B3157A	1984		
			reb	CE	B3570	1989	(a)	
	-		4wBEF	CE	B3157B	1984		
			reb	CE	B3532	1988	(a)	
	-		4wBEF	CE	B3634A	1990	(a)	
	-		4wBEF	CE	B3634B	1990	(a)	
	-		4wBEF	CE	B3410	1988	(a)	
	-		4wBEF	CE	B3411	1988	(a)	
	-		4w-4wBEF	CE	B3689A	1991	(a)	(1)
	-		4w-4wBEF	CE	B3689B	1991	(a)	
	-		4w-4wBEF	CE	B3689C	1991	(a)	
	-		4w-4wBEF	CE	B3800A	1991	(a)	
	-		4w-4wBEF	CE	B3800B	1991	(a)	
	-		4w-4wBEF	CE	B3800C	1990	(a)	
15/20			4wBEF	EEV	3768	1966	(a)	
	-		4wBEF	CE	B3155A	1984	(a)	
10B	297/029		4w-4wBEF	CE	B3322B	1987	(a)	
11B	297/154		4w-4wBEF	CE	B3322A	1987	(a)	
12B			4w-4wBEF	CE	B3322C	1987	(a)	
14B	297/305		4w-4wBEF	CE	B3502A	1989	(a)	
15B	297/315		4w-4wBEF	CE	B3502B	1989	(a)	
PL1			4wBEF	CE			(a)	
PL2			4wBEF	CE			(a)	
	-		4wBEF	Bg	3435	1955		
				EE	2083	1955	(a)	
	-		4wBEF	Bg	3437	1956		
				EE	2301	1956	(a)	
	-		4wBEF	RSHN	7963	1957		
				EE	2521	1957	(a)	
	-		4wBEF	#	#	#	(a)	
	-		4wBEF	#	#	#	(a)	
No.10	820/54943		0-6-0DMF	HC	DM1286	1962	(a)	

(a) ex British Coal, with site, 30/12/1994.
(1) to Kellingley Colliery, West Yorks and thence to Gascoigne Wood Colliery, North Yorks, where arrived 16/1/1998.
 #   Locomotives not positively identified but are two of the following :
     EE 2086/Bg 3434/1955; EE 2300/Bg 3436/1956; EE 2522/RSHN 7964/1963.

THORESBY COLLIERY, Edwinstowe   G110
SK 636676

Coal is dispatched by rail using 'Merry go Round' trains with BR haulage throughout. Locomotives are used underground.

Gauge : 3ft 0in   (Underground locomotives)

A1	72920	4wBERF		TH	SE107	1979	(a)
A2	72427	4w-4wBEF		TH	SE117	1983	(a)
E2	74832	4wBEF		CE	B1504A	1977	
			reb	CE	B3156	1984	(a)
E3	74835	4wBEF		CE	B1504B	1977	
			reb	CE	B3239	1985	(a)
E1	74813	4wBEF		CE	B1504C	1977	
			reb	CE	B3102	1984	(a)
E5	74485	4wBEF		CE	B1843A	1979	(a)
E4	74427	4wBEF		CE	B1843B	1979	(a)
E6	73431	4wBEF		CE	B1850A	1979	(a)
E7	73433	4wBEF		CE	B1850B	1979	(a)
E10	76123	4wBEF		CE	B2273A	1981	(a)
E11	76138	4wBEF		CE	B2273B	1981	(a)
E9	76158	4wBEF		CE	B2274A	1981	(a)
E8	76159	4wBEF		CE	B2274B	1981	(a)
E12	71365	4wBEF		CE	B2986A	1982	(a)
E14	71364	4wBEF		CE	B2986B	1982	(a)
E16	72434	4wBEF		CE	B3045A	1982	(a)
E15	72430	4wBEF		CE	B3045B	1982	(a)
No.2	70331	4w-4wBEF		CE	B3224B	1985	(a)
No.3	70332	4w-4wBEF		CE	B3224C	1985	(a)
	-	4w-4wBEF		CE	B3352A	1987	
			reb	CE	B3478	1988	(a)
No.4	70724	4w-4wBEF		CE	B3352B	1987	
			reb	CE	B3565	1989	(a)
	-	4w-4wBEF		CE	B3477A	1988	(a)
	-	4w-4wBEF		CE	B3477B	1988	(a)
	-	4w-4wBEF		CE	B3591	1990	(a)

(a) ex British Coal, with site, 30/12/1994.

WELBECK COLLIERY   G111
SK 582784

Coal is dispatched by rail using 'Merry go Round' trains with BR haulage throughout. Locomotives are used underground.

Gauge : 2ft 4in   (Underground locomotives)

No.2	820/45106	0-4-0DMF	HC	DM771	1950	(a)
No.4	820/45105	0-4-0DMF	HC	DM772	1950	(a)

No.1	820/45104		0-4-0DMF	HC	DM773	1950	(a)	
No.6	820/24690		0-6-0DMF	HC	DM970	1956	(a)	
No.5	820/24691		0-6-0DMF	HC	DM971	1956	(a)	
No.3	820/24692		0-6-0DMF	HC	DM1011	1957	(a)	
No.8	820/55033	No.4	0-6-0DMF	HC	DM1287	1962	(a)	
No.9	820/55489	No.7	0-6-0DMF	HC	DM1332	1964	(a)	
No.2B	87830		4wBEF	CE	B2205A	1980	(a)	
No.3B	87829		4wBEF	CE	B2205B	1980	(a)	
	87828		4wBERF	TH	SE108	1979	(a)	(2)
No.4B	84800		4wBEF	CE	B3034A	1983	(a)	
No.5B	84801		4wBEF	CE	B3034B	1983	(a)	
	-		4wBEF	CE	B3161	1985	(a)	
	-		4wBEF	CE	B3234	1985	(a)	
	-		4wDHF	CE	B3270A	1986	(a)	
	-		4wDHF	CE	B3270B	1986	(a)	
	-		4wDHF	CE	B3270C	1986	(a)	
	-		4wDHF	CE	B3270D	1986	(a)	
	-		4wDHF	CE	B3270E	1986	(a)	
No.9			4w-4wBEF	CE	B3362B	1987		
			reb	CE	B3723	1991	(a)	(1)
No.10			4w-4wBEF	CE	B3363A	1987	(a)	
No.11			4w-4wBEF	CE	B3363B	1987	(a)	
	-		4w-4wBEF	CE	B3246	1986	(a)	
	-		4w-4wBEF	CE	B3445	1988	(a)	

(a) ex British Coal, with site, 30/12/1994.
(1) to CE, /1996; then to Maltby Colliery, South Yorks.
(2) to Thoresby Colliery for spares, /1997, and scrapped there.

ROTHERHAM SAND & GRAVEL CO LTD
TOP QUARRIES, Scrooby, Bawtry   **B112**
SK 652890

The quarry opened between 1937 and 1943 and was still listed in 1965. The grid reference given is the centre of the quarry. It has not been possible to locate a plan showing track layout or to determine the period during which the tramway worked.

Gauge : 2ft 0in

       -      4wDM   R&R   82   c1938   New   (1)

(1) to Clay Cross Co Ltd, Milltown Quarry, Ashover, Derbys, after 3/1950, by 9/1952.

RICHARD SANKEY & SON LTD (by 1898)
THE POTTERIES, Hempshill Lane, Bulwell, Nottingham   **Q113**
Sankey's Bulwell Brick & Tile Co Ltd in 1876 and 1885   SK 533452

A brickworks was established by 1876 at SK 537449, on the north east side of the Midland Railway Bennerley line, 1 mile north west of Bulwell Junction. It had no standard gauge connection, but a short narrow gauge line ran west, towards the Midland Railway and into a pit. By 1895 a pottery had been established on the south west side of the Midland Railway line at SK 533452, and by 1904 there was a siding which was worked by the Midland

Railway. In 1913 this works had a ¼ mile long narrow gauge incline running north west to a clay hole. A second pottery not connected to the main line railway had opened south of Hempshill Lane at SK 534446. This had a tramway incline into a hole to the north and had closed by 1938. It is not confirmed that this works was operated by Sankey's. By 1938 the original works had gone. A later narrow gauge line served workings to the west of the c1895 works and was locomotive worked with a loco shed located at SK 532451. This line was replaced by a conveyor system in the late 1950s. The works closed in the 1970s, the company continuing to manufacture plastic pots and horticultural goods from new premises on a nearby site.

Gauge : 2ft 0in

-	4wDM	OK			(a)	(1)
-	4wDM	RH	168870	1932	(b)	(2)
-	4wDM	RH	168792	1933	(c)	(3)

(a) origin unknown.
(b) ex L.J. Speight Ltd, Knowle Lock Contract, Grand Union Canal, Warwicks, after 27/3/1934, by 21/9/1934.
(c) ex Thos. Mosedale & Sons Ltd, Carrington Road Brickworks, Flixton, Lancs, after 16/10/1941, by 20/2/1948.

(1) "Machinery Market" dated 30/3/1934 lists for sale "10/12hp 'Montania' diesel loco". RH records, c1935, refer to an 11hp, 2 speed, 3 ton 'Montania' loco for sale here; s/s.
(2) to Bell Rock Gypsum Industries Ltd. Staunton in the Vale, after 14/12/1949, by /1957.
(3) to Bell Rock Gypsum Industries Ltd. Staunton in the Vale, after 23/11/1951, by 28/4/1958.

SEVERN TRENT WATER SERVICES LTD
Severn Trent Water plc until 1/9/1989.
Severn Trent Water Authority until 30/8/1989.

Severn Trent Water Authority was one of the ten regional water authorities created with the passing of the Water Act, 1973, which came into force on 1/4/1974, to be responsible for water resources, drainage and sewage treatment. From 1/9/1989 the Water Authorities were restructured and the responsibility for reservoirs, water empoundment, etc., passed to the National Rivers Authority. Water supply and effluent disposal became the responsibility of the regional water companies.

Locomotives have been used or kept at the following locations:-

SB	**Stoke Bardolph Water Reclamation Works**	SK 633421	**U114**

(Nottingham Corporation Water Works Dept., until 31/3/1974)
The narrow gauge railway was used between the screen house (SK 634420) and the tipping area at SK 633423. At the screen house end of the line was a siding to the locomotive garage. Rail traffic ceased c12/1993.

OR	**Orston Road East, West Bridgford, Nottingham.**	SK 585385	**S115**

Loco repairs & storage only.
(Trent River Board until 31/3/1974)

OF	**Owston Ferry Plant Depot,** (LINCOLNSHIRE)	SK 814994	**X116**

(Trent River Board until 31/3/1974)

HF	**Home Farm Wiseton**, temporary site	SK 712894	**B117**
GC	**Gringley Carr Pumping Station, Gringley on the Hill**		
	temporary site	SK 713949	**X118**
NW	**Newstead**, (STAFFORDSHIRE)	SJ 894404	**X119**

Gauge : 2ft 0in

No.13	U192		4wDM	RH	283507	1949	(a)	(3)
	OF							
No.14			4wDM	RH	283508	1949	(a)	(1)
	OF							
No.15	U190		4wDM	RH	283512	1949	(a)	(4)
	OF - OR							
No.16	U191		4wDM	RH	283513	1949	(a)	(5)
	OF - OR							
No.17	U195		4wDM	MR	22128	1962	(a)	(2)
	GC by 1/76 - OF - SB /1978 - OR 8/1980							
No.18	U197		4wDM	MR	22129	1962	(a)	(6)
	GC by 1/76 - OF - HF - SB 19/5/80 - OR 8/80 - SB c3/81 - OR /84							
No.19	U84 (f. U193)		4wDM	RH	7002/0567/6	1967	(a)	(9)
	GC by 1/76 - OR by 12/2/77 - HF by 14/3/81- NW by 3/82 - SB 31/1/84 - OR by 7/4/84							
No.20	U194		4wDM	RH	7002/0967/5	1967	(a)	(7)
	GC by 1/76 - OR by 12/2/77 - HF 14/3/81 - OF /81 - SB /82 - OR c6/84 (after 9/6/84)							
No.21	U477		4wDM	RH	7002/0967/6	1967	(a)	(6)
	GC by 1/76 - OF - SB c/82 (by 31/7/82) - OR c2/83 (by 10/4/83)							
	U196		4wDM	MR	9381	1948	(b)	(8)
	SB							
	U168		4wDM	SMH	40SD529	1984	New	(10)
	OR - SB 6/84 (by 9/6/84)							

(a) ex Trent River Authority, 1/4/1974.
(b) ex Nottingham Corporation Water Works Dept., Stoke Bardolph Sewage Works, 1/4/1974.

(1) scrapped after 14/4/1974, by 3/1975.
(2) to The Narrow Gauge Centre of North Wales, Gloddfa Ganol, Blaenau Ffestiniog, Gwynedd, /1981 (after 26/9/1980, by 27/8/1981).
(3) to Mill Lane Commercials, Sandiacre, Derbys, 13/7/1978; resold to West Lancs.Light Rly., Hesketh Bank, Lancs, 24/2/1979.
(4) to Mill Lane Commercials, Sandiacre, Derbys, 13/7/1978; resold to Bala Lake Rly., Gwynedd, 19/2/1979.
(5) to Mill Lane Commercials, Sandiacre, Derbys, 13/7/1978; resold to J.C. Jessett, Hadlow Down, West Sussex, 29/8/1978.
(6) to British Motor Auctions, Measham, Leics, for auction, 9/4/1984; sold to R.D. Geeson (Derby) Ltd, The Old Quarry, Pentrich, Ripley, Derbys, 12/4/1984.
(7) to British Motor Auctions, Measham, Leics, for auction, 22/6/1984; sold to R.D. Geeson (Derby) Ltd, Usher Lane, Ripley, Derbys, /1984.
(8) to R.D.Geeson Ltd, dealer, Pentrich, Derbys, /1981 (after 26/9/1980, by 10/7/1981); resold to Alford Valley Railway, Grampian, c11/1981.
(9) to Papplewick Pumping Station Trust, Longdale Lane, Ravenhead, by /1992 (after 6/5/1989, by 4/5/1992).
(10) to British Motor Auctions, Measham, Leics, for auction, /1994 (after 20/9/1993); sold to to R.D. Geeson (Derby) Ltd, Usher Lane, Ripley, Derbys, /1994; to Midland Railway Centre, Butterley, Derbys, 25/10/1994.

[Please note that location code number 120 is vacant]

SHERWOOD COLLIERY CO LTD

This company was registered on 29/1/1901 to sink the colliery of that name. It subsequently acquired the Hucknall Colliery Co Ltd between 1905 and 1913. Its collieries passed to the NCB on 1/1/1947.

HUCKNALL NO.1 COLLIERY, Watnall Road, Hucknall Torkard

Hucknall Colliery Co Ltd until after 1905, by 1913   N121
Hucknall Colliery Co until 5/7/1898   SK 527481
Ellis & Co until c1884

Sinking of this colliery was commenced in 1851, by J.E. Ellis, a Leicestershire Quaker. It was served by a branch which curved to the south west from the west side of the Midland Railway Nottingham - Mansfield line, 1¼ miles south of Hucknall Station, to run north-west for 1¼ miles to the colliery. From the opening of its Leen Valley line in 10/1881, the GNR made a branch which ran south from Butler's Hill station to join the colliery line west of the Midland Railway exchange sidings. The final connection was made in or after 1898, by a north to west curve from the GCR near the point where this crossed the colliery line. There was, from at least 1879 until after 1918, a short branch which ran north from the colliery line to a sand pit at SK 542474. Only a small area was worked, presumably for colliery consumption.

The colliery was vested in the NCB, East Midlands Division, Area No.6, 1/1/1947.

Gauge : 4ft 8½in

HUCKNALL COLLIERY No.1	0-6-0ST	IC	MW	110	1864	New	(2)
SHERWOOD No.2	0-6-0ST	IC	MW	147	1865	New	(4)
(HUCKNALL COLLIERY No.2)							
HUCKNALL COLLIERY No.3	0-6-0ST	IC	MW	388	1873	New	(1)
No.4	0-4-0ST	OC	MW	513	1874	New	s/s
No.4 (No.5)	0-6-0ST	OC	MW	1284	1894	New	(4)
(HUCKNALL TORKARD COLLIERIES)							
SHERWOOD No.6	0-6-0ST	OC	AB	1861	1925	New	(3)

(1)   for sale 3/1895; then to R.H. Longbotham, dealer, Wakefield, 7/1895, who resold to Chatterley-Whitfield Collieries Ltd, Staffs, ROGER, 1/1897.
(2)   for sale 18/5/1900; later Gates & Thomas, Kirkham-Blackpool (LYR/LNWR Jt) widening contract (1899-1903), Lancs.
(3)   to AB, for repair, /1945; then to Sherwood Colliery, 12/1946.
(4)   to NCB, East Midlands Division, No.6 Area, with site, 1/1/1947.

HUCKNALL NO.2 COLLIERY, Hucknall Torkard

Hucknall Colliery Co Ltd until after 1905, by 1913   N122
Hucknall Colliery Co until 5/7/1898   SK 540490
Ellis & Co until c1884

Sinking of this colliery commenced in 1866. It was served by sidings on the west side of the Midland Railway Nottingham - Mansfield line, south of Hucknall station. From 10/1881 the GNR Leen Valley line passed to the west of the colliery and connections were made from this to both fulls and empties sidings.

The colliery was vested in the NCB, East Midlands Division, Area No.6, 1/1/1947.

Gauge : 4ft 8½in

	Name	Type	Cyl	Builder	Works No	Date	Notes	Disposal
	ROCKET	0-6-0ST	IC	MW	871	1883	(a)	s/s
	-	4-4-0T	OC	BP	774	1868		
		reb		Neasden		1885 & 1890	(b)	Scr
	SHERWOOD No.3	0-6-0ST	IC	MW	1440	1899	(c)	(1)
No.5		0-4-0ST	OC	P	1584	1921	New	(1)

Note: it is probable that one or more of the locomotives shown as new to No.1 Colliery actually worked at No.2 Colliery. A loco named PIONEER may also have worked here.

(a) earlier Logan & Hemingway, Annesley - East Leake (MS&LR) (1894-1898) contract, ROCKET; here by early 1900s.
(b) ex Sherwood Colliery, c/1910; used as stationary boiler.
(c) ex Sherwood Colliery, c/1915.

(1) to NCB, East Midlands Division, No.6 Area, with site, 1/1/1947.

SHERWOOD COLLIERY, Mansfield Woodhouse   G123
SK 536625

This colliery was sunk in 1902 and 1903. It was served by sidings which were opened in 10/1903, on the west side of the Midland Railway Mansfield - Shirebrook line, ½ mile south of Mansfield Woodhouse Station. There was originally a lime kiln at the extreme north end of the colliery which was served by an extension of the colliery sidings. Its ownership is not known

The colliery was vested in the NCB, East Midlands Division, Area No.6, 1/1/1947.

Gauge : 4ft 8½in

No.	Name	Type	Cyl	Builder	Works No	Date	Notes	Disposal
No.3	BEATRICE	0-4-0ST	OC	P	442	1885	(a)	s/s after 10/1906
	SHERWOOD No.1	0-6-0ST	IC	MW	1597	1903	New	(3)
	SHERWOOD No.2	4-4-0T	OC	BP	774	1868		
		reb		Neasden		1885 & 1890	(b)	(1)
	SHERWOOD No.3	0-6-0ST	IC	MW	1440	1899	(c)	(2)
	SHERWOOD No.2	0-6-0ST	OC	P	1265	1912	New	(4)
	SHERWOOD No.1	0-6-0ST	OC	AB	1638	1922	New	(4)
		0-6-0ST	OC	P	1678	1927	New	(4)
	SHERWOOD No.6	0-6-0ST	OC	AB	1861	1925	(d)	(4)

(a) ex Baldry & Yerburgh, contr., No.3, BEATRICE, c8/1901.
(b) ex Metropolitan Rly., 28, /1905.
(c) ex John Ellis & Son Ltd, Kilby South Limeworks, Leics, FRANK, c/1906, by·/1908.
(d) ex AB, repairs, 2/1946; earlier Hucknall No.1 Colliery.

(1) to Hucknall No.2 Colliery, c/1910.
(2) to Hucknall No.2 Colliery, c/1915.
(3) to Thos. W. Ward Ltd, c/1923.
(4) to NCB, East Midlands Division, No.2 Area, with site, 1/1/1947.

Notes : "Colliery Guardian" dated 10/2/1928, advertised the sale by Sherwood Colliery Co Ltd of a MW loco with dimensions indicating an 'old I' class. Since none of known MW locos are of this type, PIONEER at Hucknall No 2 may have been the loco concerned.

SHIREOAKS COLLIERY CO LTD

This company was registered 31/12/1864 and later operated collieries in Derbyshire and Yorkshire (WR) in addition to those in Nottinghamshire listed below.

SHIREOAKS COLLIERY, Shireoaks   C124
Duke of Newcastle until 31/12/1864   SK 558809

Shaft sinking began in 3/1854 but it was not until 1/2/1859 that coal was reached. The colliery was served by sidings on the south side of the MS&LR Worksop - Woodhouse Jct. line (opened 16/7/1849) ¾ mile east of Shireoaks Station. From 1875 there was also access from the Midland Railway Shireoaks West curve to the east end of the colliery. There was a rail served wharf on the Chesterfield Canal, to the west of the colliery.

Locomotives from the Shireoaks allocation were supplied to **HARRY CROFTS** (or **SHIREOAKS No.3) COLLIERY** (worked 1928-9 only); Thorpe Salvin, Yorks (WR); and **SOUTHGATE COLLIERY** (opened ? ; closed 1936), Clowne, Derbys. DUDDON is believed to have worked at Harry Crofts and ALEXANDRA at Southgate.

The colliery was vested in NCB, North Eastern Division, Area No.1, 1/1/1947.

Gauge : 4ft 8½in

	NELLIE		0-4-0ST	OC	MW	538	1875	New	Scr c/1943
No.2	EDITH		0-4-0ST	OC	MW	849	1882	New	
			reb		MW		1908		(4)
	RUPERT		0-6-0ST	IC	MW	528	1875	(a)	(1)
	WINNIE		0-4-0ST	OC	MW	1423	1898	New	
			reb		MW		1907		(2)
	VICTORIA		0-4-0ST	OC	MW	1544	1902	New	Scr /1938
	ALEXANDRA		0-4-0ST	OC	MW	1580	1902	New	
			reb		MW		1920		(5)
	DUDDON		0-4-0ST	OC	HL	3261	1917	(b)	(5)
	MARS		0-4-0ST	OC	AB	1360	1913	(c)	(3)
	FEARLESS		0-4-0ST	OC	HL	3134	1915		
			reb		Adams		1932	(d)	(5)
ROF 5 No.8	RFF 55 No.8		0-4-0ST	OC	P	2018	1941	(e)	(5)

(a)   orig J. Bayliss, Settle & Carlisle Railway, Contract No.4 (1870-1876), Cumbs, RUPERT.
(b)   ex Ministry of Munitions, Queensferry, Flints, 14/5/1927, per George Cohen, Sons & Co Ltd.
(c)   ex Thos. W. Ward Ltd, Sheffield, hire, 26/2/1929.
(d)   ex Neath Abbey Fuel Co Ltd, West Glam, via Thos. W. Ward Ltd, /1938.
(e)   ex ROF Swynnerton, Staffs, 8/1946 (by 11/8/1946).

(1)   to Plumbley Colliery Co Ltd, Eckington, Derbys, RUPERT.
(2)   to Whitwell Colliery, Derbys.
(3)   returned to Thos. W. Ward Ltd, Sheffield, off hire, c22/8/1929.
(4)   scrapped after 11/8/1946.
(5)   to NCB, North East Division, No.1 Area, with site, 1/1/1947.

STEETLEY COLLIERY, Worksop   C125
SK 553786

Sinking of this colliery commenced in 5/1873 and it opened in 1876. It was served by sidings on the west side of the Midland Railway Worksop South Jct. - Whitwell line (opened 18/1/1875), 1½ miles south of Worksop South Junction. From the 1890s, it shared exchange sidings with the railway of the Steetley Lime and Basic Co Ltd whose premises were located to the north west. The sidings also served a brickworks on the north side of the colliery which, in 1899, had a narrow gauge incline which ran north east to a hole, passing under the lime company's line en route. Clay working had ceased by 1928.

The colliery was vested in the NCB, North Eastern Division, Area No.1, 1/1/1947.

Gauge : 4ft 8½in

JESSIE	0-4-0ST	OC	MW	1231	1891	New	
		reb	MW		1907		(1)
RFF 55 No.9 STEETLEY	0-4-0ST	OC	P	2043	1943	(a)	(1)

(a)   ex ROF Swynnerton, Staffs, 8/1946 (by 11/8/1946).

(1)   to NCB, North East Division, No.1 Area, with site, 1/1/1947.

STANTON IRONWORKS CO LTD
Stanton Ironworks Co until 24/12/1877

The company erected ironworks at Ilkeston, Derbyshire, in 1845. To supply these with raw materials the company developed coal mines, sand and ironstone quarries at locations throughout the East Midlands. Locations in Nottinghamshire which used rail transport are listed below.

BILSTHORPE BRICKWORKS   (see under **Bilsthorpe Brick Co Ltd**)

BILSTHORPE COLLIERY, Bilsthorpe.   G126
SK 653617

This colliery was sunk between 1925 and 10/1927. It was served by sidings (agreement dated 12/12/1929) at the end of an LNER branch which ran east from the Clipstone to Blidworth Colliery line, 1 mile south of Clipstone, for 3½ miles to the colliery and a brickworks to the east of it. This branch was first laid in 1924 as a temporary overland line for construction purposes and reconstructed as a proper railway by H. Arnold & Son Ltd (which see) in 1927-8. It was also connected to the LMSR and LNER Mid-Nottinghamshire Joint Line from its opening in 1931, at a point where this passed to the east of the colliery. The brick works was opened to supply materials for the sinking and construction of the colliery and for colliery housing. Under an agreement dated 19/3/1931, two temporary tracks were laid which ran south from the LNER at SK 647612 and crossed Mickle Dale Lane to reach the housing sites. A colliery loco is believed to have worked between the brickworks and sites. These sidings were out of use by vesting day but the connection was not removed until 1949. (see Bilsthorpe Brick Co Ltd for further details of the brickworks.)

The colliery was vested in the NCB, East Midlands Division, No.3 Area, 1/1/1947.

Reference : "Colliery Engineering", 11/1931
Gauge : 4ft 8½in

-	0-6-0ST	IC	P or MW			(a)	(1)
EMLYN	0-6-0ST	IC	HC	566	1900	(b)	(2)
ECCLES	0-4-0ST	OC	RP	13003	1888	(c)	(3)
BILSTHORPE No.1	0-6-0ST	OC	HL	3614	1925	New	(7)
CARNARVON	0-6-0ST	OC	AE	1423	1901	(d)	(4)
SILVERHILL	0-6-0ST	OC	AE	1341	1890	(e)	(5)
BILSTHORPE No.2	0-6-0ST	OC	AB	2077	1939	New	(7)
STANTON No.22	0-6-0T	OC	DK		1915	(f)	(6)
HARLAXTON	0-6-0T	OC	AB	2107	1941	(g)	(8)

(a) hired from Baldry, Yerburgh & Hutchinson Ltd, Clipstone.
(b) hired from Charles D. Phillips Ltd, Newport, Mon.
(c) ex Holwell Ironworks, Melton Mowbray, Leics.
(d) ex Teversal Colliery, by 11/1931.
(e) ex Teversal Colliery, /1936.
(f) ex Stanton Ironworks, Derbys.
(g) ex Harlaxton Ironstone Quarries, Lincs, (loan), 5/1946.

(1) returned to Baldry, Yerburgh & Hutchinson Ltd, (Clipstone?).
(2) returned to Charles D Phillips Ltd, Newport, Mon.
(3) to Holwell Ironworks, Melton Mowbray, Leics.
(4) returned to Teversal Colliery, by 11/1932.
(5) returned to Teversal Colliery, /1936.
(6) to Stanton Ironworks, Derbys.
(7) to NCB, East Midlands Division, Area No.3, with site, 1/1/1947.
(8) returned to Harlaxton Ironstone Quarries (ex loan), 3/1947.

SILVERHILL COLLIERY, Fackley.   J127
                                                                     SK 472617

The colliery was sunk in 1875. Its standard gauge rail system was connected to that of the older TEVERSAL Colliery, which see for details.

The colliery was vested in the NCB, East Midlands Division, Area No.2, 1/1/1947.

Gauge : 4ft 8½in

A locomotive was supplied by Teversal Colliery (which see) from those listed under that heading and kept at Silverhill. It was changed over as required. It is not now possible to confirm that the locomotive SILVERHILL (AE 1341), was used exclusively here, as claimed in the previous IRS publication 'Pocket Book E'.

TEVERSAL COLLIERY, Teversall.   J128
   (originally known as **BUTCHERWOOD COLLIERY**)   SK 475622

This colliery was sunk between 1862 and 1867. The first definite railway connection dates from 1/11/1869 when the Midland Railway Butcherwood Colliery branch opened. However, a Midland Railway branch from Tibshelf to Teversall Station had opened on 1/5/1866. It is probable that some temporary connection was made between station and colliery as the latter dispatched a large tonnage to London via the Midland Railway during 1869. The permanent Butcherwood Colliery branch ran north west from a point north of Teversall station (where its Pleasley extension would later commence) to the colliery (½ mile). With the opening of SILVERHILL COLLIERY in 1875, half a mile to the south west, a private line was made to it from Teversal. At Silverhill this line divided, one line running to empties sidings at the west end and the other to fulls sidings at the east. By 1895 a brickworks had been established on the south west side of Teversal Colliery and the area south east of the Silverhill connection was being worked for clay using narrow gauge inclines. By 1892 beehive type coke ovens had been erected on both sides of the connecting line. On 8/2/1897 the GNR opened its branch from north of Skegby Station to a junction at what became, in 1901, its Teversal Goods station. Here one GNR line continued west to Silverhill Colliery and a second turned north to Teversal Colliery. By 1914 the coke ovens north west of the connecting line had been enlarged and its two standard gauge sidings extended west to clay workings, the ones to the south of the Teversal Brickworks by now being exhausted. Both coke ovens and brickworks had gone by 1950 and are believed to have closed prior to vesting day (the clay workings were not listed in or after 1928). By Vesting Day, the ground had been tipped on using aerial ropeways. Passenger trains for the mineworkers were operated.

The colliery was vested in the NCB, East Midlands Division, No.2 Area, 1/1/1947.

Reference : "Colliery Guardian" 13/5/1892

Gauge : 4ft 8½in

	Name	Type	Cyl	Builder	Works No.	Year	Notes	Ref
	ROBIN HOOD No.3	0-6-0ST	IC	HCR	88	1870	New	(1)
	FRIAR TUCK	0-6-0ST	IC	HCR	102	1871	New	(1)
	-	0-6-0ST	IC	HCR	171	1875	(a)	s/s
	(SILVER HILL)	0-4-0ST	OC	AE	1341	1890	New (b)	(2)
	DEVONSHIRE	0-6-0ST	OC	AE	1419	1900	New	
		reb	HIW		Aug 1922			(2)
	CARNARVON	0-6-0ST	OC	AE	1423	1901	New (c)	(2)
No.2		0-4-0ST	OC	HC	576	1900	(d)	(2)
	CHURCHILL	0-6-0ST	OC	AB	2216	1946	New	(2)

A geared ($3^{1/3}$ to 1) loco, 6in x 12in cylinders, gauge not stated, was advertised for sale from here in "Colliery Guardian", dated 12/6/1891.- possibly a coke oven loco ?

(a) ex HCR, 5/11/1875; rebuilt from H&C 76/1866, earlier Earl of Durham, Lambton, Co.Durham.
(b) to Bilsthorpe Colliery and returned, /1936; to Pleasley Colliery, Derbys, c/1943; returned.
(c) may have been at Stanton Ironworks, Derbys, 3/1911 (spares ordered); if so, then returned by 1/1914; to Bilsthorpe Colliery, by 11/1931; returned, by 11/1932.
(d) ex Wellingborough Iron Co Ltd, Wellingborough Ironworks, Northants.

(1) to Stanton Ironworks, Ilkeston, Derbys.
(2) to NCB, East Midlands Division, No.2 Area, with site, 1/1/1947.

STAVELEY COAL & IRON CO LTD
WARSOP MAIN COLLIERY, Warsop Vale   G129
SK 548681

This company, whose operations were originally entirely in Derbyshire, was registered on 29/12/1863 although it had earlier origins

This colliery was sunk between 1893 and 1895. It was served by a private line which ran north east for ¾ mile to the colliery from the end of a ¼ mile Midland Railway line which opened in 3/1897 and ran north east from Shirebrook North station. The first connection to the colliery line was, however, a south curve from the LD&ECR line, 1 mile south east of Langwith Junction, which opened in 11/1896. At this time the colliery branch extended north eastwards for ¾ mile to a sand pit, west of Church Warsop village at SK 560660. By 1914 this line had been shortened back to empties sidings at SK 554683, where there was a small lime quarry which was worked intermittently from 1928 and remained until NCB days. Dirt tipping was to see the line extended east again in later years, although for a period from 1925 an aerial ropeway was used to dispose of the dirt. The Midland and later LMSR supplied one shunting locomotive to work here under an old agreement. This was usually a Midland Railway Class 1F 0-6-0T and was changed frequently.

The colliery was vested in the NCB, East Midlands Division, Area No.2, 1/1/1947.

Gauge : 4ft 8½in

DO WELL (BRISTOL)	0-4-0ST	OC	AE	1416	1901	(a)	(3)
ALBERT	0-6-0ST	IC	MW #	394	1872	(b)	(1)
DAVID	0-4-0ST	OC	AE	1999	1927	New	(2)
WARSOP	0-6-0ST	IC	HE	2408	1942	New	(4)

\# repaired by Thos.W. Ward Ltd, c1920 using parts, including the tank, of MW 902 of 1884.

(a)   ex Bonds Main Colliery, Derbys, after 1/1912, by 5/1912; returned by 12/1912; ex Bonds Main Colliery, after 3/1913, by 5/1914; to Staveley Works, Derbys, by 8/1914; returned here after 6/1915, by 1/1919; to Ireland Colliery, Derbys, by 2/1921; ex Hartington Colliery, Derbys, after 7/1932, by 12/1932.
(b)   ex Thos.W. Ward Ltd, Charlton Works, Sheffield, on hire, 27/10/1923.

(1)   returned to Thos.W. Ward Ltd, Charlton Works, Sheffield, 18/11/1924.
(2)   to Markham Colliery, Derbys, after 2/1932, by 8/1932.
(3)   to Ireland Colliery, Derbys, /1946.
(4)   to NCB, East Midlands Division, Area No.2, with site, 1/1/1947.

STAVELEY IRON & CHEMICAL CO LTD
WARSOP SAND QUARRIES   G130
                                  SK 565668

These workings were on the south side of the LNER line south east of Warsop Station. The quarry was served by standard gauge sidings connected to the LNER which ran right to the working face (¼ mile). The workings were in production by 1928. Horses are presumed to have been used prior to the arrival of the locomotive. Closure date is unknown.

Gauge : 4ft 8½in

		4wDM (f. PM)	H	950	1929	(a)	s/s c/1969

(a)   ex Park Gate Iron & Steel Co Ltd, Eaton Ironstone Quarries, Leics, c/1949.

STEETLEY REFRACTORIES LTD
STEETLEY LIMEWORKS, Rhodesia, Worksop   C131
Brickworks:- **Oughtibridge Silica Firebrick Co Ltd** until not later than 1970   SK 551788
Quarry:- **Steetley Dolomite (Quarries) Ltd** until not later than 1970
Steetley Co Ltd until 3/1951 (when it became the holding company)
Steetley Lime & Basic Co Ltd until 22/3/1944
Steetley Lime Co Ltd until 22/3/1930
Steetley Lime & Building Stone Company from 1/1/1885, until 7/1915

This dolomite quarry was in existence long before the railway era and had supplied stone for the Houses of Parliament. In 1888 plant was installed to produce doloma, used for furnace linings. The rail connection dates from the period 1884 to 1899 and by the latter date a standard gauge track ran north east from the Midland Railway Mansfield - Worksop line, immediately north of Steetley Colliery, to lime kilns in Steetley Wood (SK 552790) and on to quarry plant at SK 551792. From here short narrow gauge lines ran north and west into the quarry. By 1914 the narrow gauge lines, probably ropeworked, extended to the south west (SK 546789). A new quarry, also with narrow gauge track, had opened east of the limekilns in Steetley Wood. By 1951 the whole of the wood had been quarried, a standard gauge track was in place around its perimeter and a large new works had been built at SK 554792. This works was operated by subsidiary company, the **Oughtibridge Silica Firebrick Co Ltd** who from 1957 owned the working locomotive. With the end of rail traffic at the brickworks c1957, the locomotive was transferred to the quarries division until all rail traffic ceased (by 1980). The railway was connected to that of the adjacent Steetley Colliery and short term loans of locomotives between the two occurred. In early NCB days the colliery locomotives were washed out at the works by local arrangement. Note that the northern part of this works is in Derbyshire.

Gauge : 4ft 8½in

COXHOE No.1	0-4-0ST	OC	BH #	1038	1893	(a)	(1)
HEBE	0-4-0ST	OC	HL	3368	1919	New	Scr c6/1960
JUNE	0-4-0ST	OC	YE	2407	1942	New (b)	Scr c6/1960
MARGARET	0-4-0ST	OC	P	2044	1943	New	(2)
OUGHTIBRIDGE No.1	0-4-0DE		YE	2652	1957	New	Scr 4/1984

\# BH 1038 is recorded as overhauled by CF in 1901 and YE in 1923 and 1933.

(a) ex Coxhoe Works, Co.Durham, /1917.
(b) to Rainbow Bridge Quarries, Conisborough, Yorks (WR), /1948; returned; to Cadeby Quarries, Yorks (WR), /1950; returned.

(1) to Coxhoe Works, Co.Durham, by /1938.
(2) to NCB, East Midland Division, No.1 Area, Whitwell Colliery, Derbys, /1960. (by 9/4/1960).

Gauge : 2ft 5in (track lifted by 2/1961)

-	4wDM	RH	211682	1942	New	(1)

(1) scrapped c2/1961 (by 25/2/1961)

Gauge : 2ft 0in

-	4wPM	L	7040	1935	(a)	s/s
-	4wPM	L	10055	1938	New	s/s
-	4wPM	L	15613	1941	New	s/s

(a) ex L, 8/11/1935; earlier demonstration at Herts.& Essex Sand & Gravel Co Ltd, Church Lane, Wormley, Essex.

STEWARTS & LLOYDS MINERALS LTD
NUTHALL SANDPITS, Nuthall   Q132
Stanton Ironworks Co Ltd until 1/1/1950   SK 528442

The company had been quarrying sand since c1898 at this site, which was situated on the south side of the GNR Kimberley - Basford & Bulwell line, 1½ mile west of Basford & Bulwell Station. The sand was originally loaded directly into standard gauge wagons. In 1929 quarrying started on the north side of the line, and a 3ft 0in gauge tramway was laid in order to load wagons on the westbound track. The tramway passed over the LNER line on a steel bridge (agreement dated 15/2/1929) and up an inclined gantry, at the south end of which the wagons were tipped into standard gauge wagons. Haulage to the bridge was by locomotive and then by electrically operated main and tail rope haulage. Part of the standard gauge quarry line was retained to serve a clay pit where blast furnace pig bed sand was quarried. This was worked by an electric rope haulage.

Rail traffic ceased by 1963, and the site was used by the NCB to extend the spoil tip from the nearby Babbington Colliery.

Gauge : 3ft 0in

STANTON No.19	0-4-0ST	OC	MW	1038	1887		
	reb		HIW		1931	(a)	(1)
-	4wDM		RH	172888	1934	(b)	s/s
7660/31	4wDM		RH	186340	1937	(c)	(2)

Note : RH recorded, 4/11/1936, that one of two locos for sale by Stanton Ironworks Co Ltd was a '36 inch gauge 10 ton steamer' at Nuttall Sand Pits.

(a) ex Holwell Ironworks, Leics, 10/1931; earlier Harston Ironstone Quarries, Leics.
(b) ex Wellingborough Iron Co Ltd, Thingdon Mines, 6/1947; regauged from 2ft 4in.
(c) ex Church Mine, Islip, Northants, c/1950; regauged from 2ft 0in, at Buckminster Quarries, Lincs. (Note: spares were delivered to Stewarts and Lloyds, Mines Dept, Corby in 1945 and 1947 and to Bowne & Shaw Ltd, Wirksworth Quarry, Derbys on 16/8/1949. Whilst this casts doubt on the foregoing footnote, it may still be correct if the possibility of fitters from elsewhere maintaining locos at small sites is considered).

(1) sold to Thos. W. Ward Ltd, and scrapped on site /1948.
(2) to Stanton Ironworks Co Ltd, Bilsthorpe Brickworks, c/1961 (after 18/2/1961).

TARMAC ROADSTONE (EASTERN) LTD
HOVERINGHAM WORKSHOPS, Hoveringham. **P133**
SK 701481

In c1983 Hoveringham Gravels Ltd (which see) was acquired by the Tarmac Group. By this date rail traffic had ceased at the former Hoveringham quarries. The only locomotive extant, passing into Tarmac ownership, was at this time lying out of use at this site.

Gauge : 2ft 0in

H85	4wDM	HE	7178	1971	(a)	(1)

(a) ex Hoveringham Gravels (Midlands) Ltd, c/1983 (after 28/3/1981),

(1) to Tarmac Roadstone (Northern) Ltd, Central Workshops, Matlock, Derbys, c1/1984.

TRENT CONCRETE LTD
COLWICK WORKS, Nottingham **T134**
SK 630400

The works, which used the standard gauge locomotives from c1920 until some time in the 1930s, was served by sidings on the south side of the Nottingham Colwick Estates Light Railway. It is said to have been some distance to the west of the reference given above. At the latter there was a standard gauge siding, small works and narrow gauge loading point on the south west side of the estate railway, ½ mile south east of its junction with the LNER. The narrow gauge tramway ran south east from this plant, parallel to the LNER line before turning north east to pass beneath it and reach gravel pits to the north. This tramway and the pits were worked from the early 1950s by **Hoveringham Gravel Co Ltd** (which see) with its diesel locomotives whilst the petrol locomotives of the Trent Concrete Ltd remained derelict for some years.

Gauge : 4ft 8½in

-	4wPM					(a)	s/s c/1925
PATSY	0-4-0ST	OC	HCR	139	1874	(b)	Scr /1934
	reb	HC			1914		
JOHN	0-4-0ST	OC	AB	757	1895	(c)	s/s
NANCY	0-4-0ST	OC	P	1208	1909	(d)	(1)

(a) ex WD ?

(b) ex Crosse & Blackwell Ltd., Branston Works, Burton-on-Trent, Staffs, by /1925.
(c) ex Gas Light & Coke Co, Bromley-by-Bow Gas Works, London, after 12/1920, by 8/1925.
(d) ex Denton Colliery Co Ltd, Denton Colliery, Manchester, (for sale there, 9/1931; here by 5/1932).

(1) to Constables (Matlock Quarries) Ltd, Derbys, c/1936.

Gauge : 2ft 0in

-	0-4-0WT	OC	HC	(1142	1915 ?)	(a)	(1)
-	4wPM		MR	2093	1922	(b)	(3)
-	4wPM		MR	3858	1928	(c)	(3)
-	4wPM		MR	3975	1937	New	(3)
-	4wPM		MR	3997	1933	(d)	(2)
-	4wPM		MR	3988	1935	(e)	(3)
-	4wPM		MR	3981	1936	(f)	(3)
-	4wPM		MR	4713	1936	(g)	(3)
-	4wPM		MR	3992	1934	(h)	(3)

(a) if HC 1142, then earlier at WD, Slough, Bucks.
(b) ex McLachlan, contrs.
(c) ex Cleveland Bridge & Engineering Co Ltd.
(d) ex MR, 8/12/1933; reconditioning of MR 2292/1924.
(e) ex MR, 11/9/1935; reconditioned loco.
(f) ex MR, 8/6/1936; reconditioned loco.
(g) ex G.P. Trentham Ltd, contrs, after 3/11/1939.
(h) ex Star Gravels Ltd, Great Barr Gravel Pits, Staffs, c/1942.

(1) for sale 6/1921 and 8/1923; if indeed HC 1142, then to Oakeley Slate Quarries, Blaenau Ffestiniog, Merioneth, /1924 (who obtained their loco from "Nottingham").
(2) to Star Gravels Ltd, Great Barr, Staffs, 7/1939.
(3) derelict by 3/1954, scrapped /1958.

TRENT RIVER AUTHORITY
Trent River Board until 1/4/1974
River Trent Catchment Board until 1/4/1948

The following locomotives were used on river bank work as required, in the counties of Staffordshire, Nottinghamshire, Lincolnshire and Yorkshire. Between workings, they were stored at the following depots:-

Orston Road, West Bridgford	(SK 585385)	**S135**
Owston Ferry, LINCOLNSHIRE	(SK 814994)	**X136**

The Water Act of 1973 resulted in the Trent River Authority being reformed into the Severn Trent Water Authority (which see)

	-	4wPM	MR	5813	1934	New (a)	s/s
	-	4wPM	MR	5819	1935	New (b)	s/s
	-	4wPM	MR	5825	1936	New (c)	s/s
	-	4wPM	MR	5826	1936	New (d)	s/s
	-	4wPM	MR	5827	1936	New (e)	s/s
	-	4wPM	MR	5828	1936	New (f)	s/s
	-	4wPM	MR	5829	1936	New (g)	s/s
	-	4wPM	MR	5830	1937	New (h)	s/s
	-	4wDM	RH	247183	1947	New (i)	(1)
No.13		4wDM	RH	283507	1949	New (j)	(2)
No.14		4wDM	RH	283508	1949	New (j)	(2)
No.15		4wDM	RH	283512	1949	New	(2)
No.16		4wDM	RH	283513	1949	New	(2)
No.17		4wDM	MR	22128	1962	New	(2)
No.18		4wDM	MR	22129	1962	New	(2)
No.19		4wDM	RH	7002/0567/6	1967	New	(2)
No.20		4wDM	RH	7002/0967/5	1967	New	(2)
No.21		4wDM	RH	7002/0967/6	1967	New	(2)

(a) delivered new to Weston-upon-Trent, Derbys, 11/7/1934.
(b) delivered new to Hopwas Bridge, Tamworth, Staffs, 7/6/1935.
(c) delivered new to Hopwas Bridge, Tamworth, Staffs, 8/6/1936.
(d) delivered new to Keadby, Lincs, 8/10/1936.
(e) delivered new to Weston-upon-Trent, Derbys, 8/10/1936.
(f) delivered new to Elford Workshops, Tamworth, Staffs, 27/10/1936.
(g) delivered new to Elford Workshops, Tamworth, Staffs, 20/11/1936.
(h) delivered new to Osberton Hall, Worksop, 20/1/1937.
(i) delivered new to Gringley Carr Pumping Station, Gringley on the Hill, 23/9/1947.
(j) delivered new to Bawtry, Yorks (WR), 21/7/1949.

(1) sold or scrapped after 31/1/1951.
(2) to Severn Trent Water Authority, 1/4/1974.

WAR DEPARTMENT

No.17 PETROL DEPOT, BOTTESFORD   U137

Depot, location uncertain, operated by the Royal Army Service Corps. It would have been established during World War Two and closed shortly afterwards. These depots usually consisted of a network of narrow gauge tramways linking a railhead with dumps of petrol in jerricans in open storage, the dumps being spaced far enough apart to discourage the spread of fire.

Gauge : 2ft 0in

-	4wDM	RH	210955	1941	(a)	(1)
-	4wDM	RH	211655	1942	(b)	(2)
-	4wDM	RH	211614	1941	(c)	(3)
-	4wDM	RH	203006	1941	(c)	(5)
-	4wDM	RH	211605	1941	(d)	(4)

(a) orig MoS, location unknown; here by 23/10/1944.
(b) orig MoS, location unknown; here by 27/10/1947.
(c) orig MoS, location unknown; here by 30/10/1947.
(d) orig MoS, location unknown; here by 6/11/1947.

(1) left after 17/9/1947; later with W.O. Williams, dealer, Harlech, Merioneth, by 5/10/1949.
(2) left after 27/10/1947; s/s.
(3) left after 30/10/1947; later with George W. Bungey Ltd, dealers, Hayes, Middx, and to NCB, Horden Colliery, Co.Durham, by 25/6/1951.
(4) left after 6/11/1947; later with George W. Bungey Ltd, dealers, Hayes, Middx, and to Penrhyn Slate Quarries, Caernarvons, 9/1949.
(5) left after 16/1/1948; s/s.

BOUGHTON CENTRAL ORDNANCE SUB DEPOT, near Ollerton   G138
SK 682676

The depot, which opened in the early part of World War II, was served by extensive sidings on the north side of the LNER Ollerton - Tuxford line, ½ mile west of the former Boughton Station. The depot had closed by 2/1961 (probably c1959). After closure the site was redeveloped as an industrial estate.

Gauge : 4ft 8½in

	71440	0-6-0ST	IC	HE	3204	1945	New	(1)
	71441	0-6-0ST	IC	HE	3205	1945	New	(4)
	71498	0-6-0ST	IC	HC	1775	1944	(a)	(6)
821	(70031)	0-4-0DM		DC	2158	1941		
				EE	1189	1941	(b)	(2)
	70032	0-4-0DM		DC	2159	1941		
				EE	1190	1941	(c)	(3)
825	(70044)	0-4-0DM		AB	359	1941	(d)	(5)
	72221	0-4-0DM		VF	5257	1945		
				DC	2176	1945	(e)	(7)
851	(75521)	0-4-0DM		HE	2078	1940	(f)	(8)
123	(75048)	0-6-0ST	IC	HE	2897	1943	(g)	(9)
140	(75142)	0-6-0ST	IC	HE	3193	1944	(g)	(10)
184		0-6-0ST	IC	VF	5275	1945	(h)	(11)

(a) ex Chilwell Depot, 16/3/1945.
(b) ex Sinfin Depot, Derby, c/1951.
(c) ex Bicester Depot, Oxon, 6/1948.
(d) ex S, 10/10/1950 (earlier Old Dalby Depot, Leics, /1950).
(e) ex ? , /1946.
(f) ex Corsham Depot, Wilts, /1946 (this may have been the loco which went to Leeds 18/1/1948 (HE for repair?) and subsequently returned).
(g) ex Cairnryan Military Rly., Wigtown, 11/1953.
(h) ex Bicester Depot, Oxon, 9/7/1957

(1) to Sudbury Depot, Staffs, c/1946
(2) to Arncott Depot, Bicester, Oxon, 10/1953.
(3) to Suez, by 1/1952.
(4) to ? , 6/1946; then to Manchester Ship Canal Co, Manchester, 25/5/1948.

(5) to Arncott Depot, Bicester, Oxon, between 9/1953 and 12/1953.
(6) to LNER, 8025, 6/1946.
(7) to Wem Depot, Salop, by /1952.
(8) to Feltham Depot, Middx, by 12/1957.
(9) to Cairnryan Military Rly., Wigtown, 8/1957.
(10) to Bicester Depot, Oxon, 6/1958.
(11) to Bicester Depot, Oxon, /1959; then to Chilwell Depot, /1959 (by 9/1959)

CLIPSTONE MILITARY CAMP RAILWAY   G139

This camp was served by a ½ mile spur line which was constructed by the War Office and opened 13/6/1916. The line ran north and then north west from the GCR-worked Mansfield Railway, this section of which opened 6/6/1913, sharing the route of the proposed line to Clipstone Colliery (see Bolsover Colliery Co Ltd), which had been authorised in 1914, and opened the same day. A passenger station was constructed at SK 592630. From here the line crossed Clipstone Road to enter the camp proper which was located to the north thereof. There were two lines within the camp: one continued in a semi-circle to run east and terminated at SK 584635. The second line was a back shunt from north of the Clipstone Road crossing which ran alongside this road to end at SK 593633. The GCR took over its operation and maintenance from 17/12/1917; passenger trains were run to Mansfield. There are local recollections of the shunting loco travelling daily to and from the GCR Tuxford locomotive sheds and of the regular loco being named LIMERICK. The camp and railway closed c1919 after the end of hostilities. The rail connection and site south of the Clipstone Road became Clipstone Colliery with the empties sidings on the site of the passenger station. Much of the camp area was redeveloped by the colliery company as New Clipstone village.

Reference : "Clipstone Camp, An account of a military training camp of the First World War"; J.C. Fareham, Author, c1997

Gauge : 4ft 8½in

	HASTINGS	0-6-0ST	IC	HE	469	1888	(a)	(1)
	LIMERICK	0-6-0ST	IC	HE	457	1888	(b)	(2)
	-	0-6-0ST	IC	HE	187	1877	(c)	s/s
No 2	WD 97	?		*			(d)	(3)

* believed to be an 0-6-0tank, built or rebuilt by AE.

"Surplus" 1/5/1922 -1/7/1922 advertised for sale, at Tuxford Engine Sheds, two 0-6-0ST locos by Hunslet, W.D. Locos Nos.82 and 89. This could be consistent with HE 457 and 187, but there is no confirmation.

(a) earlier Price, Wills & Reeves, Immingham Docks (1906-1912) contract, Lincs; here by 10/1916.
(b) earlier Balfour, Beatty & Co Ltd, Ripon Camp construction contract, Ripon, Yorks (NR), 5/1915; known then to have been taken over by War Office, Camp Railways, Northern Command, by 9/1916 and spares to GCR Tuxford, for WD, 12/1916.
(c) earlier Wm Rigby, Margate West station (SECR) contract, Kent, SUTTON, 2/1914. (Not confirmed here; spares were ordered from War Office, Camp Railways, Northern Command, in 9/1916, but the loco could have been at any Northern Command site).
(d) spares ordered from AE for "No.2 WD 97" and sent to Military Camp Railways, Clipstone M.C. Rly, Notts.

(1) later Parkgate Iron & Steel Co Ltd, Parkgate, Rotherham, Yorks (WR), by 8/1918.

(2) later with Cohen & Armstong Disposals Corporation, /1923 ? (by 3/1925); then to Isaac J. Abdela & Mitchell Ltd, Queensferry Shipyard, Flints, by 7/1926.
(3) later at Belton Park Camp Military Railway, near Grantham, Lincs, where spares were ordered from AE for WD 97, 7/1919;

THOS. W. WARD LTD
LOWFIELD BRICKWORKS, Balderton   **P140**
Vale of Belvoir & Newark Plaster Co Ltd until 1927   SK 804506

The brickworks was established after 1884 to the south of the same company's plaster works and gypsum quarry (which see in Non-locomotive Section). It was served by a standard gauge siding, (agreement dated 21/11/1903) known to the GNR as Almond's Siding, after the owner of the company at that time. This was on the west side of the GNR Newark - Bottesford line, 2 miles south of Newark station. By 1915 a narrow gauge line ran north from the works to the gypsum quarry. The Belvoir & Newark Plaster Co Ltd was offered for sale as a whole in 1927 but only the brickworks was sold and the remainder closed at that time. The brickworks had closed by 1938 but subsequently re-opened. The siding was in situ until after 1956. by which time the closed works site had been sold to Cafferata & Co Ltd. A narrow gauge loco was used for an unknown purpose from 1940. A plan of 1950 shows the works still intact with the narrow gauge tramway in situ.

Gauge : 2ft 0in

    -                  4wDM   OK   (4571 #)   (a)   s/s

\# almost certainly OK 4571 which had been sold by Ward's to Capt. Lee, 23/3/1937, and which had identical dimensions.

(a)   ex Thos.W. Ward Ltd, Sheffield, 15/1/1940 (earlier Capt. Lee, 120, Whirlow Dale Road, Sheffield, but collected from Spinkhill Works, Renishaw, Derbys).

WIGAN COAL CORPORATION LTD
MANTON COLLIERY, Worksop   **C141**
Wigan Coal & Iron Co Ltd until 1/8/1930   SK 609783

The **Wigan Coal & Iron Co Ltd** was registered on 2/12/1865 and operated various collieries in Lancashire. Manton Colliery was the company's only venture outside that county. The **Wigan Coal Corporation Ltd** was an amalgamation of four Lancashire companies and acquired the colliery businesses of the Wigan Coal & Iron Co Ltd.

The colliery was sunk between 1898 and 1904 and produced coal from 1907. It was served by sidings, opened in 10/1900, which were a continuation of the short GCR Manton Wood Colliery branch and ran west for ¾ mile from the Worksop - Retford line, 2 miles east of Worksop Station. The narrow gauge surface locomotives were originally used for dirt disposal from No.4 shaft, the sinking of which was in progress at the time of nationalisation.

The colliery was vested in the NCB, North Eastern Division, Area No.1, 1/1/1947.

Gauge : 4ft 8½in

PRINCESS ROYAL	0-6-0ST	IC	*		(a)	(1)
MANTON	0-6-0ST	IC	WCI	1908	(b)	(4)
SHAH	0-6-0ST	IC	WCI	1874	(c)	(2)
LINDSAY	0-6-0ST	IC	WCI	1887	(c)	(2)
DAISY	0-6-0ST	IC	P&K	1910	(d)	(3)
SIEMENS	0-6-0ST	IC	WCI	1912	New	(4)

* builder not known; some resemblance to early Leeds built locos; tradition links it with the Crimean War where two EBW 0-6-0ST IC locos were sent in 1855

(a) ex Kirkless Ironworks, Wigan, Lancs, c/1898.
(b) ex Kirkless Ironworks, Wigan, Lancs. c/1910
(c) ex Kirkless Ironworks, Wigan, Lancs.
(d) ex Low Hall Colliery, Wigan, Lancs, /1943.

(1) to Kirkless Ironworks, Wigan, Lancs, /1916.
(2) to Kirkless Ironworks, Wigan, Lancs.
(3) to Low Hall Colliery, Wigan, Lancs, c/1943.
(4) to NCB, North Eastern Division, No.1 Area, with site, 1/1/1947.

Gauge : 3ft 0in

-		4wDM	RH	200483	1940	New	(1)
-		4wDM	RH	210489	1941	New	(1)
-		4wDM	RH	210490	1941	New	(1)

(1) to NCB, North Eastern Division, No.1 Area, with site, 1/1/1947.

WORTHINGTON - SIMPSON LTD
LOWFIELD ENGINEERING WORKS, New Balderton, Newark   P142
James Simpson & Co Ltd until 15/10/1917   SK 806512

The company was established at Pimlico, London in 1885 as hydraulics and general engineers. They relocated to this new works which was commenced in 1899 and was served by sidings (agreement dated 23/8/1900) on the east side of the GNR Newark - Cotham line, 2 miles south of Newark Northgate Station. By 1915 the track layout was extensive and some form of motive power would have been required. The reorganisation of 1917 saw control pass to an American company, the Worthington Pump & Machinery Corporation, whose UK assets were acquired. Rail traffic ceased 1969 and the siding agreement was terminated 31/7/1970.

Gauge : 4ft 8½in

-	4wDM	RH	224355	1945	New	(1)

(1) to John Lee & Son (Grantham) Ltd, Grantham, Lincs, 8/1969.

SECTION 2

NATIONAL COAL BOARD
BRITISH COAL CORPORATION

INCLUDING THE
OPENCAST COAL DISPOSAL POINTS
OF THE
MINISTRY OF FUEL & POWER
THROUGHOUT THEIR PERIOD OF OPERATION

BRITISH COAL CORPORATION - NATIONAL COAL BOARD
(Includes **Ministry of Fuel & Power, Directorate of Opencast Coal Production**)
British Coal Corporation from 5th March 1987.

On the nationalisation of the coal industry on 1st January 1947 ('Vesting Day'), the colliery related assets of the former companies were vested in the National Coal Board. Small mines with less than 30 men underground could be excluded and operate under NCB license. There were none of these in the Nottinghamshire Coalfield. Those companies nationalised had the option to include or exclude ancillary operations such as Brickworks. Those in Nottinghamshire were generally included. The title 'National Coal Board' remained in use until 1986 when the trading name 'British Coal' was adopted. The legal title became 'British Coal Corporation' from 5th March 1987.

DEEP MINES ORGANISATION

Collieries absorbed by the NCB on vesting day were placed in an organisation comprising eight Divisions, each of which was divided into a number of Areas. Each area was in turn sub-divided into Groups. However, Groups had little railway significance and reorganisations were frequent, hence these early Groups are disregarded in IRS publications.

Collieries in the county of Nottinghamshire were mostly included in the East Midlands Division where they initially formed part of Areas No.2, No.3, No.4 and No.5 and comprised the whole of Area No.6. The exception was that those collieries near Worksop were included in the North Eastern Division where they formed part of Area No.1.

The first of a number of subsequent reorganisations became effective from 1st July 1949, when East Midlands Division Area No.2 was abolished and its Nottinghamshire collieries were reallocated to Areas No.3 and No.4. The North Eastern Division was renamed Yorkshire Division c1965. The next change took effect from 26th March 1967 when a major national reorganisation replaced Divisions by eighteen 'New style' Areas. Surviving Nottinghamshire collieries comprised the whole of North Nottinghamshire and South Nottinghamshire Areas, with one colliery passing to North Derbyshire Area and three to South Yorkshire Area. From 1st August 1985 a new Nottinghamshire Area was formed by amalgamating the former North and South Areas. From 1st April 1987 North Derbyshire Area became part of Central Area but its one Nottingamshire colliery closed in 1989. The next reorganisation, effective from 1st April 1990, drastically reduced Area staff and much day to day control reverted to collieries. Areas became known as Groups but apart from this change the South Yorkshire and Nottinghamshire Areas remained unaltered.

From 1st September 1993, those collieries assessed to have a future in the Nottinghamshire Group merged with those in the Midlands and Wales Group to form a new Midlands Group. The others were transferred to a Closing Collieries Group.

WORKSHOPS ORGANISATION

Area Central Workshops were part of the deep mines organisation until June 1967, after which they passed to the direct control of National Headquarters.

COKING, TAR AND MANUFACTURED FUEL PLANTS

Administered by the Divisions of the Deep Mines organisation until 1st January 1963 when they were combined in a new Coal Products Division. By this time the one Coking plant (Harworth) and two briquetting plants (Cossall and Clipstone) in Nottinghamshire had closed. Cossall and Clipstone were operated as an integral part of the collieries of the same name and are not separately listed here.

BRICKWORKS

Administered by the Divisions of the Deep Mines organisation until 1st January 1962 when they were combined nationally, to form the Brickworks Executive. This operated through subsidiary companies, the one covering Nottinghamshire being known as the Midland Brick Co Ltd. These companies were sold to the private sector on 25th November 1973.

Some works on colliery premises were not vested. Those in the county which were vested comprised Annesley, Kirkby, Sherwood, Watnall and Welbeck. Since none of these made significant use of internal rail transport, they are not separately listed here. The Watnall works outlasted the adjacent colliery by many years but did not retain the rail connection.

OPENCAST WORKINGS

The first large scale opencast coal workings date from the war years and were operated by the Ministry of Fuel & Power through its Directorate of Opencast Coal Production who provided the management function, with Public Works contractors working the sites and disposal points. The NCB set up its Opencast Executive which took over these activities from 1st April 1952 and operated in exactly the same way. Hence it is convenient to cover the short pre-NCB history of these sites in this section. The Opencast Executive was sub divided into Regions. That covering Nottinghamshire was first designated North Midland then Central and finally Central East Region. Rail traction was not used on the working sites but confined to Disposal Points where coal was screened and loaded for sale. Locomotives were either the property of the NCB or of the contractor operating the Disposal Points. Nottinghamshire locomotives were a mixture of the two.

PRIVATISATION

During the 1990s, the industry continued to decline with several collieries being closed. Clipstone and Calverton passed to RJB Mining (UK) Ltd. The collieries and opencast operations throughout the UK that remained in production were offered for sale by H.M. Government. RJB Mining (UK) Ltd was the successful bidder for the collieries in England which passed into the new ownership on 30/12/1994. Exceptionally, two collieries (Annesley and Bentinck) which had ceased production before this date were subsequently purchased by Coal Investments Ltd in 4/1995 and reopened as a single unit.

LOCATION LISTINGS

Locations which have made any significant use of rail track, surface or underground, standard or narrow gauge, are listed below alphabetically, together with brief notes of the rail system and full details of locomotives where appropriate. The Grid References given are those of the locomotive shed where appropriate; this accounts for any small discrepancies with the references given in Section 1. The following abbreviations are used to save space when showing in which part of the organisation a location was placed at any given period:-

NE1	North Eastern Division, Area No.1.
EM2	East Midlands Division, Area No.2.
EM3	East Midlands Division, Area No.3.
EM4	East Midlands Division, Area No.4.
EM5	East Midlands Division, Area No.5.
EM6	East Midlands Division, Area No.6.
EM(C)	East Midlands Division, Coking Plants.
SYK	South Yorkshire Area.
NNT	North Nottinghamshire Area.
SNT	South Nottinghamshire Area.
NTS	Nottinghamshire Area.
SYG	South Yorkshire Group.
NTG	Nottinghamshire Group.
MG	Midlands Group.
CCG	Closing Collieries Group.
HQ	National Headquarters, Workshops Organisation.
CPD	Coal Products Division (later Group).
OE	Opencast Executive.
MFP	Ministry of Fuel & Power, Directorate of Opencast Coal Production.

ANNESLEY COLLIERY, Newstead   NN1
ex N.H.& B. Collieries Ltd   SK 516534

EM4 from 1/1/1947; SNT from 26/3/1967; Coal wound at BENTINCK COLLIERY from 29/2/1980 (or 23/8/1979?). BENTINCK COLLIERY became part of a combined ANNESLEY/BENTINCK COLLIERY in 3/1988 and continued to be the coal outlet; NTS from 1/1/1985; NTG from 1/4/1990; CCG from 1/9/1993; Production ceased 18/2/1994; Sold to **Coal Investments Ltd** in 4/1995 and subsequently reopened.

A BR branch ran south for ¼ mile from Annesley (ex LMSR) station to the colliery. There was also an ex LNER connection from its line, ½ mile north of Newstead Station, which curved west to pass beneath the ex LMSR main line and thence to the colliery. The ex LNER connection closed in 1968. Standard gauge rail traffic officially ceased 7/1/1984 although the last trains ran earlier (after 23/8/1979, by 29/2/1980). Locomotives were used underground during two separate periods between 1965 and 1994.

Gauge : 4ft 8½in.

	ANNESLEY No.2		0-6-0ST	OC	P		1924	1937	(a)	(3)
	No.3		0-6-0ST	OC	AB	1132	1907		
			reb	KE			1921	(b)	(1)
32	ANNESLEY No.1		0-6-0ST	OC	HC	1649	1931	(c)	(2)
EMFOUR.7	CHARLES BUCHAN		0-6-0DM		HC	D1018	1957	New	(6)
141C	STEPHEN / VANGUARD		0-6-0DH		TH	141C	1964		
			Incorporated frame of S					(d)	(4)
D16	ROBIN (D3618)		0-6-0DE		Dar		1958	(e)	(5)

(a) ex N.H. & B. Collieries Ltd, with site, 1/1/1947; to P, (repairs) after 5/1954, by 7/1954; returned, 7/1955.
(b) ex N.H. & B. Collieries Ltd, with site, 1/1/1947.
(c) ex HC, 4/1947; to Sutton Colliery /1948; returned, 10/1948; to Sutton Colliery after 10/1948, by 20/4/1949; returned by 4/1950.
(d) ex Linby Colliery after 4/1968, by 7/1968.
(e) ex Bestwood Colliery, 3/1970.

(1) to Sutton Colliery, /1947.
(2) to Kirkby Colliery, 9/1957.
(3) to Bentinck Colliery, after 11/1961, by 4/1962.
(4) to Linby Colliery, 5/1969.
(5) to Cotgrave Colliery, 24/7/1980.
(6) to Calverton Colliery, after 4/3/1980, by 4/1980.

Gauge : 2ft 1½in (Underground locomotives)

-	0-6-0DMF	HE	6607	1966	New	(1)
-	0-6-0DMF	HE	6608	1965	New	(1)
-	0-6-0DMF	HE	6609	1965	New	(1)
-	0-6-0DMF	HE	7418	1974	New	(1)
	4wBEF	CE	B0427	1975		
	reb	CE	B2926	1982	(a)	(2)
	4wBEF	CE	B3187	1985	(b)	(3)
-	4wBEF	CE	B3483	1988	New	(4)

(a) ex Sutton Colliery, (via CE), /1989.
(b) ex Sutton Colliery, (via CE), /1990.

(1) three locos abandoned underground, /1986-7, the fourth dismantled at surface for spares and the remains scrapped.
(2) to Calverton Colliery, 27/6/1990.
(3) to CE, c/1990; rebuilt as CE B3695, then to Asfordby Mine, Leics.
(4) to CE, /1989; then to Bentley Training Centre, S Yorks, c6/1989.

AWSWORTH DISPOSAL POINT

Alternative name for BENNERLEY DISPOSAL POINT (which see).

BABBINGTON and CINDERHILL COLLIERIES, Cinderhill   QN2
ex B.A. Collieries Ltd   SK 534437

EM6 from 1/1/1947; SNT from 26/3/1967; Rail traffic ceased c7/1983; NTS from 1/8/1985; Merged with HUCKNALL Colliery from 1/1986 and combined colliery CLOSED 10/1986.

At Vesting Day this site was shown as two separate collieries of approximately equal size, titled **CINDERHILL** and **BABBINGTON**. By 1952 they had, officially, become one, titled BABBINGTON, though the Cinderhill title remained in common use for many years afterwards. The railway sidings and screens were located near the CINDERHILL shafts. BABBINGTON coal was wound at No.6 Shaft, located to the north of the main Colliery at SK 533442. The use of the Babbington name should not be confused with the 19th century collieries at Babbington Village.

NCB sidings formed a continuation of a BR (ex LMSR) branch which ran west from ¾ mile north of Basford station to the colliery (¾ mile). An ex LNER line from Babbington Junction (½ mile west of Basford and Bulwell station) joined the ex LMSR line east of the colliery. A line ran south west from the junction of the NCB and BR lines, bridging the A610 road, to a reversing point at SK 532435, from where an NCB line ran south east, to the Newcastle Landsale Depot at Whitemoor (SK 546422) (1¾ miles). There was another landsale depot on this line just east of the reversing point. Use was made of the standard gauge railway for dirt tipping, initially north of the colliery. In the 1960s the old line was relaid south from the reversing point towards the closed Broxtowe Colliery, where a tip was established. The ex LNER connection had closed by 1966 and the NCB line to Newcastle also closed in that year. The line to the tip south of the A610 road closed in 1968.

2ft 0in gauge locomotives were used in the surface stockyard from 1958 to 1977 and underground throughout. There was, for some time after 1947, a surface double track endless rope haulage linking the No.6 shaft at SK 533442 with the screens to the south. The 3ft 0in gauge steam locomotives are believed to have been out of use use by Vesting Day. Locomotives were used underground from, at the latest 1957, until closure.

Gauge : 4ft 8½in.

	COLONEL		0-6-0ST	OC	HE	577	1892	(a)		(4)
	ADMIRAL		0-6-0ST	OC	P	874	1900	(b)		(2)
	MICHAEL		0-6-0ST	OC	RSHN	7285	1945	(b)		(6)
5194			0-6-0ST	IC	RSHN	7144	1944	(c)	#	(1)
(75005)	PHILIP	270/002	0-6-0ST	IC	HE	2854	1943	(d)		(11)
	PETER		0-6-0ST	IC	HE	2853	1943	(e)		(8)
5			0-4-0ST	OC	P	1584	1921	(f)		(3)
(No.5)			4wVBT	VCG	S	9576	1954	New		(12)

No.3			0-6-0DM		RSHN	7698	1954	New	(7)
6	VALERIE		0-6-0ST	OC	HL	3606	1924	(g)	(5)
No.3	FELIX		0-6-0ST	OC	AB	2344	1954	(h)	(9)
	PAUL	6/3214	0-6-0DM		RH	326671	1957	New	(16)
			0-4-0DE		YE	2682	1958	(i)	(10)
	JAYNE	164/160	4wDH		TH	137C	1964		
			Incorporated frame of S				New	(13)
	STEPHEN		0-6-0DH		TH	141C	1964		
			Incorporated frame of S				New	(14)
	ANDREW		0-6-0DH		TH	161V	1965	(j)	(15)

\# this locomotive may have been here to work a short lived and unconfirmed opencast coal disposal point at Broxtowe Colliery which was recorded in SLS records.

(a) ex B.A. Collieries Ltd, with site, 1/1/1947; to Clifton Colliery by 21/1/1948; returned by 4/2/1948; to Linby Colliery by 5/1950, returned by 3/1951.
(b) ex B.A. Collieries Ltd, with site, 1/1/1947; to WB, Stafford, repairs, 10/5/1956; returned 7/11/1956.
(c) ex B.A. Collieries Ltd, with site, 1/1/1947.
(d) ex Bestwood Colliery 10/1947: to Bestwood Central Workshops, after 18/2/1961, by 8/1961; returned after 8/1962, by 10/1962.
(e) ex Clifton Colliery, 11/1947; to Clifton Colliery 4/1948; ex Linby Colliery after 2/1957, by 4/1957.
(f) ex Hucknall No.2 Colliery by 3/1951.
(g) ex Bestwood Colliery after 12/1954, by 23/4/1955.
(h) ex Clifton Colliery, 6/1956; to Clifton Colliery, 17/7/1956; returned after 6/1/1957, by 4/1957.
(i) ex Whitwick Colliery, Coalville, Leics, demonstration by YE, 12/2/1958.
(j) ex Clifton Colliery, between /1966 and 3/1967; to BR Toton (tyre turning), 7/12/1974; returned, 14/12/1974.

(1) to Heanor Disposal Point, /1947.
(2) scrapped c/1948.
(3) to Hucknall No.2 Colliery by 9/1952.
(4) scrapped /1954.
(5) to Bestwood Colliery, after 4/1955, by 9/1955.
(6) to Clifton Colliery, after 7/11/1956, by 6/1/1957
(7) to Calverton Colliery, /1957 (by 10/1957).
(8) to Linby Colliery, after 4/1957, by 6/1957.
(9) to Clifton Colliery, after 4/1957, by 1/6/1957.
(10) to Grassmoor Colliery, Derbys, demonstration by YE, 17/2/1958.
(10) to Clifton Colliery, after 12/1963, by 9/1964.
(11) to Hucknall Colliery, after 12/1963, by 9/1964.
(12) to Clifton Colliery, after 12/1964, by 3/1967.
(13) to Linby Colliery, after 4/1967, by 4/1968.
(14) to Calverton Colliery, 5/9/1983.
(15) to Lansdowne International Ltd, Didcot, Oxon, 11/4/1985.

Gauge : 3ft 0in.

	0-4-0WT	OC	D&B	42	1925	(a)	(1)
DARLEY DALE	0-4-0WT	OC	D&B	42	1925	(a)	(1)
KINDER	0-4-0WT	OC	OK	10903	1925	(a)	(1)

(a) ex B.A. Collieries Ltd, with site, 1/1/1947.

(1) out of use by 1/1/1947; to Thos W. Ward Ltd, for scrap, 10/1947 (after 5/10/1947).

Gauge : 2ft 0in.

275/001	4wDM	RH	418780	1958	New	(1)
275/002	4wDM	RH	418781	1958	New (a)	(1)

(a) to Bestwood Central Workshops by 6/3/1965; returned after 6/3/1965.

(1) to GECT, Newton le Willows, Greater Manchester, for spares, after 3/1976, by 14/2/1978.

Gauge : 2ft 0in (Underground locomotives)

	-	4wBEF	?			(a)	(1)
	-	4wBEF	?			(a)	(1)
	-	4wBEF	?			(a)	(1)
No.1	6/4740	0-6-0DMF	HC	DM1116	1957	New (b)	(6)
No.2	6/4741	0-6-0DMF	HC	DM1117	1957	New (c)	(5)
No.3		4wDMF	RH	425795	1958	(d)	(2)
No.4		4wDMF	RH	441426	1961	New	(2)
		carried number		441427	in error		
No.5	164/150	0-6-0DMF	HC	DM1310	1963	New	(5)
	-	0-6-0DMF	HC	DM1348	1964	New	(3)
No.7	164/174	0-6-0DMF	HC	DM1380	1966	New	(5)
No.8	164/179	0-6-0DMF	HC	DM1393	1967	New	(4)
No.3	164/200	4wDHF	HE	8909	1979	(e)	(7)
	164/312	4wDHF	HE	8911	1980	(f)	(8)

(a) origins unknown.
(b) to HC, c/1966; returned, 9/1967.
(c) to HC, 7/3/1966; returned, 5/11/1966.
(d) ex Calverton Colliery, c/1977 (by 3/1978).
(e) ex Bentinck Training Centre, 10/1979.
(f) ex Bentinck Training Centre, c/1986 (after 11/6/1985).

(1) abandoned underground in No.5 Colliery workings by /1970
(2) to Sharlston Colliery, West Yorks, 3/1978.
(3) out of use on surface from c/1970, scrapped c/1980 (after 2/1980).
(4) to Calverton Colliery, 7/10/1985.
(5) to Calverton Colliery, c6/1986.
(6) abandoned underground after closure of colliery, 10/1986.
(7) to Calverton Colliery, 1/1988.
(8) to Calverton Colliery, 31/3/1989.

BENNERLEY DISPOSAL POINT, Awsworth MN3
SK 471441

Opened by MFP c1942; OE from 1/4/1952; Rail traffic ceased c1958; site retained on a care and maintenance basis until reopened 1971.

Located on the former **Bennerley Slag & Tarmacadam Co** (Bennerley Ironworks) site. Sidings ran north east from BR, 1 mile north of Ilkeston Junction station site. A locomotive was stored here 1968-9, during the closure period. Use of locomotives ceased with the introduction of rapid loading in 1984.

Gauge : 4ft 8½in.

15	MOMBASA	0-6-0ST	OC	WB	2167	1922	(a)	(3)
17	KILINDINI	0-6-0ST	OC	WB	2168	1922	(b)	(1)
	TRAFFORD PARK	0-6-0ST	OC	HE	1689	1931	(c)	(2)
75276		0-6-0ST	IC	RSHN	7206	1945	(d)	(4)
71494		0-6-0ST	IC	HC	1770	1944	(e)	(6)
75062		0-6-0ST	IC	RSHN	7098	1943	(f)	(5)
75166		0-6-0ST	IC	WB	2754	1944	(g)	(9)
75137		0-6-0ST	IC	HE	3188	1944	(h)	(8)
75194		0-6-0ST	IC	RSHN	7144	1944	(i)	(7)
71495		0-6-0ST	IC	HC	1771	1944	(j)	(10)
	-	0-4-0ST	OC	P	1749	1928	(k)	(11)
D2258		0-6-0DM		DC	2602	1957		
				RSHD	7879	1957	(l)	(13)
D2182	3/3	0-6-0DM		Sdn		1962	(m)	(12)
6678	4/33	0-4-0DH		HE	6678	1968	(n)	(13)

(a) ex Pauling & Co Ltd, earlier at ROF Featherstone contract, Staffs, c/1942-3 (by /1945).
(b) ex Pauling & Co Ltd, (earlier at Park Royal Plant Depot, London ?), c/1942-3
(c) ex John Mowlem & Co Ltd, Chingford, Essex, by 1/1945.
(d) ex Brinsley Disposal Point, by 3/1946.
(e) ex Shipley Collieries, Derbys, 2/1947; may also have been here in /1945 prior to going to Giltbrook Disposal Point.
(f) ex LMS, Derby Works (repairs), 2/1947; earlier Swannington Disposal Point, Leics, until after 5/1946, by 8/1946.
(g) ex YE, (repairs), after 11/1950, by 5/1953 (earlier at Pilsley Disposal Point, Derbys); to HE, after 14/4/1957 (repair No.58855 of 10/1958); returned c10/1958 and stored until 1961.
(h) ex Watnall Disposal Point after 1/1954, by 1/1955.
(i) ex Heanor Disposal Point, Derbys, by 9/1949; to Upper Portland Disposal Point 9/1949; ex Heanor Disposal Point after 3/1956, by 9/1956.
(j) ex Horton Grange Disposal Point, Northumberland, for storage, 6/1968.
(k) ex Tarmac Ltd, Matlock, Derbys, /1971 (stored pending preservation).
(l) ex BR. Derby, 1/1971; to BR, Toton (tyre turning) 12/1974; returned, c12/1974.
(m) ex Gatewen Disposal Point, Clwyd, after 3/1981, by 3/1982; to Wentworth Stores, South Yorks, 18/3/1982; returned, 6/5/1983.
(n) ex Widdrington Stores, Northumberland, 3/1982.

(1) returned to Pauling & Co Ltd, c/1942-3
(2) returned to John Mowlem & Co Ltd, after 4/1946
(3) returned to Pauling & Co Ltd, by 5/1947
(4) to Kelty Disposal Point, Fife, 10/1947.

(5) to Bluebell Inn Disposal Point, Northumberland, 4/1947.
(6) to Upper Portland Disposal Point, 9/1949.
(7) to Upper Portland Disposal Point, after 9/1956, by 1/1/1957.
(8) to Moor Green Central Workshops, after 9/1957, by 3/1958 (thence to Upper Portland Disposal Point).
(9) to Pilsley Disposal Point, Derbys, /1961.
(10) to West Hallam Disposal Point, Derbys, 5/5/1969.
(11) to B.W. Roberts, Tollerton, for preservation, /1972.
(12) to Coalfield Farm Disposal Point, Leics, 7/1983.
(13) to Wentworth Stores, South Yorks, 17/2/1984.

BENTINCK COLLIERY, Kirkby in Ashfield   KN4
ex N.H. & B. Collieries Ltd   SK 487549

EM4 from 1/1/1947; SNT from 26/3/1967; NTS from 1/8/1985: Merged with ANNESLEY COLLIERY from 3/1988. Surface remained open as coal outlet. NTG from 1/4/1990; CCG from 1/9/1993; production ceased c2/1994; ANNESLEY/BENTINCK COLLIERY sold to **Coal Investments Ltd** in 4/1995 and subsequently reopened, when rail traffic was again worked by BR.

In 1947 the colliery was served by two LMSR branches. The empty wagon branch ran west from 1 mile south west of Kirkby in Ashfield station to the colliery (¾ mile). The loaded wagon branch was a 1 mile extension of the Langton Colliery Branch (from east of Pinxton & Selston station). LNER connections were made to the empties sidings from a reversing point ½ mile east of Kirkby Bentinck station and to the loaded sidings by a circuitous 1 mile line which curved west, south and east from Kirkby Bentinck station. The ex LNER connections closed in the 1960s. The ex LMSR empties branch closed 8/1977 leaving their loaded branch with all traffic thereafter. Use of NCB surface locomotives ended with the introduction of BR trains loaded by rapid loading bunker from 3/1982.

Gauge : 4ft 8½in.

	-	0-6-0ST	OC	HC	1305	1917	(a)	(1)
	BENTINCK No.3	0-6-0ST	OC	YE	2197	1928	(a)	(6)
	BENTINCK No.2	0-6-0ST	OC	YE	2307	1931	(a)	(4)
(No.2)	BENTINCK No.1	0-4-0ST	OC	HC	576	1900	(b)	(2)
(68088)	LNER 985	0-4-0T	IC	Dar		1923	(c)	(5)
	EMFOUR.3	0-6-0T	OC	HC	1878	1954	New (d)	(9)
		0-4-0DE		YE	2682	1958	(e)	(3)
	ANNESLEY No.2	0-6-0ST	OC	P	1924	1937	(f)	(7)
	DAISY	0-4-0ST	OC	HL	2657	1906	(g)	(8)
	-	0-4-0DH		HE	6675	1966	New	(10)
	EMFOUR.9 LO59	0-6-0DM		HC	D1114	1958	(h)	(11)

(a) ex N.H. & B. Collieries Ltd, with site, 1/1/1947.
(b) ex Teversal Colliery, after 4/1950, by 7/1950.
(c) ex BR, Stratford Works, London, (DEPARTMENTAL No.34 ?), 12/1952.
(d) to Cotes Park Colliery, Derbys, after 1/1957, by 3/1957; returned after 5/1957, by 9/1957.
(e) ex YE, Sheffield, demonstration, 31/1/1958.
(e) ex Annesley Colliery, after 11/1961, by 4/1962.
(f) ex A Winning Colliery, Derbys, 11/1962.

(g)   ex Brookhill Locoshed, after 11/1968, by 3/1969.

(1)   to Clipstone Colliery, /1948.
(2)   to Sutton Colliery, after 3/1951, by 7/1951.
(3)   to Whitwick Colliery, Coalville, Leics, demonstration by YE, 12/2/1958.
(3)   scrapped on site, 9/1963.
(4)   to Y7 Preservation Group, Thurgarton, 8/1964
(5)   scrapped by Booth, Nottingham, 6/1966.
(6)   to Brookhill Locoshed, 1/1967.
(7)   scrapped after 12/1967, by 4/1968.
(8)   scrapped on site by Thos. W. Ward Ltd, 2/1971.
(9)   to Calverton Colliery, 20/7/1980.
(10) to Midland Railway Trust, Butterley, Derbys, 25/11/1983.

BENTINCK TRAINING CENTRE, Kirkby in Ashfield   KN5
SK 488553

Opened by SNT 1976; NTS from 1/8/1985; CLOSED c1988

A surface narrow gauge line for training underground locomotive drivers was located on the north side of BENTINCK Colliery.

Gauge : 2ft 0in.

	20726	0-6-0DMF	HC	DM812	1953	(a)	(5)
No.4	20725	0-6-0DMF	HC	DM836	1954	(b)	(5)
No.3	164/200	4wDHF	HE	8909	1979	New	(1)
	164/312	4wDHF	HE	8911	1980	New	(2)
	164/373	4wBEF	CE	B3100B	1984	(c)	(3)
	TRACEY	4w-4wBEF	GMT		1987	New	(4)

(a)   ex Bestwood Training Centre, 10/2/1977.
(b)   ex Bestwood Training Centre, 11/2/1977.
(c)   ex Gedling Colliery, 10/1984.

(1)   to Babbington Colliery, 10/1979.
(2)   to Babbington Colliery, c/1986 (after 11/6/1985).
(3)   to Gedling Colliery, c/1987 (after 11/6/1985).
(4)   to Markham Colliery, Derbys, c/1987 (by /1988).
(5)   to Blidworth Colliery, c/1988.

BERRY HILL MINERS WELFARE SPORTS GROUND, Mansfield HN6
SK 552594

Opened by Coal Industry Social Welfare Organisation, c1950.

A narrow gauge locomotive worked pleasure line was constructed c1957 and used infrequently thereafter.

Gauge : 2ft 0in.

		4wDM	RH	222068	1943	(a)	(1)

(a)   ex WD Liphook, Hants, 3/1957.

(1)   to Midland Railway Centre, Butterley, Derbys, 5/12/1995.

BESTWOOD CENTRAL WORKSHOPS, Bestwood NN7
SK 550474

Opened by EM6 1959; SNT from 26/3/1967; HQ from 6/1967; CLOSED.

Located on the west side of BESTWOOD Colliery (which see) and connected to its railway system. Locomotive repairs were carried out until about 1966.

Gauge : 4ft 8½in.

6	VALERIE	0-6-0ST	OC	HL	3606	1924	(a)	(2)
	BESTWOOD	0-4-0ST	OC	AB	1517	1919	(b)	(7)
	MICHAEL	0-6-0ST	OC	RSHN	7285	1945	(c)	(1)
	PHILIP	0-6-0ST	IC	HE	2854	1943	(d)	(3)
35		0-6-0ST	OC	RS	4156	1937	(e)	(8)
17	RUTH	0-6-0ST	OC	RS	4150	1937	(f)	(4)
	PETER	0-6-0ST	IC	HE	2853	1943	(g)	(5)
(No.4)		4wVBT	VCG	S	9578	1954	(h)	(6)

Note: see also locomotives marked * in Bestwood Colliery list which may have been at Central Workshops.

(a)   ex Calverton Colliery, after 6/1959, by 2/1961.
(b)   ex Bestwood Colliery, after 8/1959, by 2/1961; to Bestwood Colliery by 11/1961; returned after 3/1963, by 4/1963; to Bestwood Colliery by 6/1963; returned after 7/1964, by 9/1964.
(c)   ex Clifton Colliery, after 5/1960, by 2/1961.
(d)   ex Babbington Colliery, after 2/1961, by 8/1961.
(e)   ex Linby Colliery 17/8/1961; to Linby Colliery 4/1962; returned after 6/1964, by 3/1965.
(f)   ex Bestwood Colliery, after 4/1962, by 10/1962.
(g)   ex Linby Colliery, after 4/1962, by 10/1962.
(h)   ex Bestwood Colliery, after 8/1962, by 10/1962.

(1)   to Clifton Colliery, after 3/1961, by 10/1962.
(2)   to Bestwood Colliery, after 4/1962, by 10/1962.
(3)   to Babbington Colliery, after 8/1962, by 10/1962.

(4) to Bestwood Colliery, after 10/1962, by 3/1963.
(5) to Bestwood Colliery, after 11/1962, by 31/3/1963.
(6) to Bestwood Colliery, after 4/1963.
(7) to Bestwood Colliery, after 9/1964, by 3/1965.
(8) to Linby Colliery, after 3/1965, by 3/1966.

Gauge : 2ft 0in.

275/002   4wDM   RH 418781 1958   (a)   (1)

(a) ex Babbington Colliery by 6/3/1965 (after /1961).

(1) to Babbington Colliery after 6/3/1965 (by /1967).

BESTWOOD COLLIERY, Bestwood   NN8
ex B.A. Collieries Ltd   SK 553474
EM4 from 1/1/1947; SNT from 26/3/1967; Colliery CLOSED 7/1967; Washery CLOSED 3/1971.

Two parallel BR branches (ex LMSR and LNER) ran north east, from 1¾ miles north of Bulwell and 1¼ miles north of Bulwell Forest Stations respectively, to the colliery & adjacent CENTRAL WORKSHOPS. The ex LNER branch closed in the 1960s. The ex LMSR line was taken out of use in 10/1971. Locomotives were used underground throughout.

Gauge : 4ft 8½in.

	LANCASTER		0-4-0ST	OC	P	468 1888	(a)	(8)
	ST ALBANS	12/22	0-4-0ST	OC	Mkm	104 1891	(a)	(4)
	BESTWOOD		0-4-0ST	OC	AB	1517 1919	(b)	(9)
75156			0-6-0ST	IC	WB	2744 1944	(c)	(1)
75005			0-6-0ST	IC	HE	2854 1943	(d)	(2)
	SHERWOOD No.3		0-6-0ST	IC	MW	1440 1899	(e)	(3)
(6)	VALERIE	270/003	0-6-0ST	OC	HL	3606 1924	(f)	(10)
(No.4)			4wVBT	VCG	S	9578 1954	New (g)	(7)
	KING GEORGE		0-6-0ST	IC	HE	2409 1942	(h)*	(5)
17	RUTH		0-6-0ST	OC	RS	4150 1937	(i)	(9)
	PETER	270/004	0-6-0ST	IC	HE	2853 1943	(j)	(6)
No.3	FELIX		0-6-0ST	OC	AB	2344 1954	(k)	(17)
D14	DAVID (D3613)		0-6-0DE		Dar	1958	(l)	(16)
	ROBIN (D3618)		0-6-0DE		Dar	1958	(l)*	(11)
D15	SIMON (D3619)		0-6-0DE		Dar	1958	(m)	(14)
D2299			0-6-0DM		DC	2680 1960		
					RSHD	8158 1960	(n)*	(12)
	LESLEY (D2132)		0-6-0DM		Sdn	1960	(o)*	(15)
D2138			0-6-0DM		Sdn	1960	(o)*	(13)

Notes: It cannot be established if locomotives marked * were at Bestwood Central Workshops for part of the period covered. Some of Bestwood Colliery's long term allocation may have made unrecorded visits to the Central Workshops.

(a) ex B.A. Collieries Ltd, with site, 1/1/1947.
(b) ex B.A. Collieries Ltd, with site, 1/1/1947; to Calverton Colliery, 11/1952; returned, /1954; to Bestwood Central Workshops,after 8/1959, by 2/1961; returned by 5/11/1961; to Bestwood Central Workshops, 3/1963, returned by 6/1963; to Bestwood Central Workshops, after 7/1964, by 9/1964; returned after 9/1964, by 3/1965.
(c) ex WD after 1/1947.
(d) ex WD, 7/1947 (returned to UK ex store at Calais, 5/1947).
(e) ex Hucknall No.2 Colliery, /1951.
(f) ex Linby Colliery, after 6/1953, by 5/1954; to Babbington Colliery after 12/1954, by 4/1955; returned here after 4/1955, by 9/1955; to Calverton Colliery, by 1/6/1957; ex Bestwood Central Workshops after 8/1962, by 10/1962.
(g) to Bestwood Central Workshops after 8/1962, by 10/1962; returned here after 4/1963.
(h) ex Linby Colliery after 4/1959, by 6/1959.
(i) ex Appleby-Frodingham Steel Co Ltd, Scunthorpe, Lincs, 4/1961; to Bestwood Central Workshops after 4/1962, by 10/1962; returned here after 10/1962, by 3/1963.
(j) ex HE, after /1954, by 12/1955 (earlier at Clifton Colliery); to Linby Colliery by 2/1957; ex Bestwood Central Workshops after 11/1962, by 31/3/1963.
(k) ex Clifton Colliery after 3/1965, by 3/1966.
(l) ex BR, 8/1969.
(m) ex Gedling Colliery, 1/1970.
(n) ex BR, 19/7/1970.
(o) ex BR, 10/1970.

(1) to Pleasley Colliery, Derbys, 5/1947.
(2) to Babbington Colliery, 10/1947.
(3) to Hucknall No.2 Colliery, /1951.
(4) scrapped on site by T. (Spencer ?) Ltd, Nottingham, /1956 (by 29/3/1956).
(5) to Linby Colliery after 8/1959, by 1/1960.
(6) to Linby Colliery after 8/1963, by 5/1964.
(7) s/s after 8/1963, by 12/1963.
(8) scrapped on site by Ilkeston Metal & Waste Co Ltd, 10/1964.
(9) scrapped on site 7/1968.
(10) scrapped on site 10/1969.
(11) to Annesley Colliery, 3/1970.
(12) to Hucknall Colliery, 7/8/1970.
(13) to Pye Hill Colliery, 4/1971.
(14) to Linby Colliery, after 7/1971, by 8/1971.
(15) to New Hucknall Colliery, 7/1971.
(16) to Linby Colliery after 3/1971, by 9/1971.
(17) scrapped on site by Thos. W. Ward Ltd, after 7/1971.

Gauge : 2ft 0in (Underground locomotives)

	-	4wBEF	GB	1960	1943	(a)	(1)
	-	4wBEF	GB	1961	1943	(a)	(1)
No.1		4wBEF	Atlas	2454	1945	(a)	(2)
No.2		4wBEF	Atlas	2466	1945	(a)	(2)
	-	4wDMF	HE	4185	1950	New	(12)
	-	0-6-0DMF	HC	DM671	1948	(b)	(12)
	-	0-6-0DMF	HC	DM678	1952	New	(9)
No.3		0-6-0DMF	HC	DM679	1952	New	(3)
No.4		0-6-0DMF	HC	DM794	1953	(b)	(11)

No.6	-	0-6-0DMF	HC	DM879	1954	New	(3)
No.5	1/3043	4wDMF	HE	4755	1954	New	(6)
No.8	1/3042	4wDMF	HE	4756	1954	New	(4)
	-	4wDMF	HE	4757	1954	New	(12)
No.10	1/3044	4wDMF	HE	4758	1954	New	(5)
No.1		0-6-0DMF	HC	DM953	1956	New	(8)
No.12		0-6-0DMF	HC	DM954	1956	New	(11)
	-	0-6-0DMF	HC	DM1165	1959	New	(10)
No.1	275/101	4wDMF	HE	6042	1961	New	(7)
No.16	275/102	4wDMF	HE	6043	1961	New	(7)

(a) ex B.A. Collieries Ltd, with site, 1/1/1947.
(b) ex Calverton Colliery before /1977.

(1) to Calverton Colliery, via underground connection, as Calverton development proceeded, /1950s
(2) to Gedling Colliery, c/1955.
(3) to Calverton Colliery by 2/1968.
(4) to Linby Colliery, 6/1968.
(5) to Linby Colliery, 7/1968.
(6) to Linby Colliery, 8/1968.
(7) to Linby Colliery, c/1968.
(8) to Bestwood Training Centre, c/1968 (by 2/1969).
(9) to Linby Colliery, 30/12/1969.
(10) to Linby Colliery, c/1974.
(11) to Gedling Colliery by 2/1977 (c/1972?).
(12) s/s after closure of the colliery c/1972 (before 7/1978).

BESTWOOD TRAINING CENTRE, Bestwood

NN9
SK 553475

Opened by SNT c1968; CLOSED c1976.

A surface narrow gauge line for training underground locomotive drivers was located at the east end of BESTWOOD COLLIERY.

Gauge : 2ft 0in.

No.2	HEATHER 184/137	4wDMF	RH	425798	1958	(a)	(3)
No.3		4wDMF	RH	441427	1961	(a)	(4)
No.1		0-6-0DMF	HC	DM953	1956	(b)	(6)
R1		4wDMF	RH	441428	1961	(c)	(5)
	20726	0-6-0DMF	HC	DM812	1953	(d)	(1)
No.4	20725	0-6-0DMF	HC	DM836	1954	(d)	(2)

(a) ex Hucknall Training Centre, c/1968 (after /1967, by 30/6/1968).
(b) ex Bestwood Colliery, c/1968 (by 2/1969).
(c) ex Cotgrave Colliery, c/1972; never used here and believed not to have been converted from 2ft 6in gauge.
(d) ex HE, 9/1974 (earlier Linby Colliery).

(1) left here by 10/1976; at Bentinck Training Centre, 10/2/1977.
(2) left here by 10/1976; at Bentinck Training Centre, 11/2/1977.
(3) to Brecon Mountain Railway, Powys, 29/5/1977.
(4) to Llanberis Lake Railway, Gwynedd, 15/7/1977.
(5) s/s after 1/1977.
(6) to Gedling Colliery between 10/1976 and 6/1978.

BEVERCOTES COLLIERY, Bothamsall   EN10
SK 694740

Sinking commenced by EM3 c/1954; Opened 1961; CLOSED for redevelopment 1/1962; Reopened c1965; NNT from 26/3/1967; NTS from 1/8/1985; NTG from 1/4/1990.

Production ceased 30/4/1993 and the colliery was placed on a care and maintenance basis, but never resumed production. Shaft filling and the demolition of surface buildings took place in the latter part of 1993.

Colliery served by sidings at the end of a BR branch which ran north from 1½ miles east of Ollerton station site to the colliery (5 miles). The first mile had formerly been the Boughton Branch. A standard gauge NCB locomotive was here in 1961-2 only, otherwise rapid loading of BR trains was the system used. A surface narrow gauge loco was used in the stockyard during the construction period only. Locomotives were used underground from 1965.

Gauge : 4ft 8½in.

R2		0-4-0DE	RH 431762	1959	(a)	(1)

(a) ex Rufford Colliery, 1/1961.

(1) returned to Rufford Colliery, 2/1962.

Gauge : 2ft 6in. (not used here).

No.5 No.6 164/197		4wDHF	HE 8835	1978	(a)	(1)

(a) ex Hucknall Colliery, c/1987.

(1) to Booth Roe Metals Ltd, Rotherham, S.Yorks,. 15/9/1988.

Gauge : 2ft 4in.

-		4wDM	RH 375347	1954	New	(1)

(1) to Rufford Colliery, 4/9/1960.

Gauge : 2ft 4in (Underground locomotives)

No.1	820/05881	0-4-0DMF	HC DM1360	1965	New	(6)
No.2	820/05882	0-4-0DMF	HC DM1361	1965	New	(2)
	820/05883	0-4-0DMF	HC DM1362	1965	New	(2)
	820/05944	0-6-0DMF	HC DM1408	1968	New	(2)
No.5	820/05979	0-4-0DMF	HB DM1420	1972	New	(1)
	820/06287	0-4-0DMF	HC DM1383	1966	(a)	(2)
No.6	820/06288	0-4-0DMF	HC DM1384	1966	(b)	(2)

No.16		0-4-0DMF	HE	3591	1949	(c)	(7)
No.8	820/24683	0-6-0DMF	HC	DM969	1956	(d)	(2)
No.9	820/24689	0-6-0DMF	HC	DM866	1955	(e)	(2)
No.10	820/54943	0-6-0DMF	HC	DM1286	1962	(f)	(5)
No.11	04510	4wDHF	HE	8989	1981	New	(8)
No.21	04274	4wDHF	CE	B2946A	1984	(g)	(9)
No.22	05002	4wDHF	CE	B2946B	1984	New	(9)
No.23	04484	4wDHF	CE	B2946C	1984	New	(11)
No.24	04485	4wDHF	CE	B2946D	1984	New	(9)
	04279	4wBEF	CE	B2299	1982	(h)	(9)
		power unit for 3 car GMT manriding set					
No.25	05651	4wBEF	CE	B3043A	1983	New	(10)
No 26	06173	4wBEF	CE	B3043B	1983	New	(10)
	820/24687	0-6-0DMF	HC	DM868	1955	(i)	(4)
No.6	4/4791 SEA EAGLE	0-6-0DMF	HC	DM1125	1957	(j)	(3)
27		4wBEF	CE	B3204A	1985	(k)	(12)
28		4wBEF	CE	B3204B	1985	(k)	(10)
No.30	06134	4w-4wBEF	CE	B3289A	1986	New	(13)
No.31	06135	4w-4wBEF	CE	B3289B	1986	New	(13)

(a) ex Deep Navigation Colliery, Glamorgan, /1972; to Clipstone Colliery, 29/4/1976; returned by /1979.
(b) ex Deep Navigation Colliery, Glamorgan, /1972
(c) ex Rufford Colliery, 23/10/1972.
(d) ex Clipstone Colliery, 4/1975.
(e) ex Clipstone Colliery, 4/1976.
(f) ex Rufford Colliery, 1/4/1977.
(g) ex Swadlincote Test Site, Derbys, 2/7/1983, after display at ABMEC Mining Exhibition.
(h) ex Bevercotes Training Centre 8/1984.
(i) ex Clipstone Colliery, 10/1985.
(j) ex Blidworth Colliery.
(k) ex Mansfield Colliery 23/1/1989.

(1) to Rufford Colliery, 16/6/1974; returned here, 24/11/1975; to Bevercotes Training Centre, by 11/1976.
(2) s/s between /1980 and /1986.
(3) to Booth Roe Metals Ltd, Rotherham, S Yorks, 9/1984.
(4) scrapped between 10/1985 and /1986.
(5) to Bevercotes Training Centre, 14/7/1986.
(6) to Bevercotes Training Centre, 1/2/1990.
(7) to Rufford Colliery, 6/1954; returned 10/1972; s/s after /1980, by /1986.
(8) to Bevercotes Training Centre, c5/1991.
(9) abandoned underground at closure, 4/1993.
(10) s/s c/1993.
(11) to surface and scrapped, 4/1994.
(12) to CE, Hatton, Derbys, by /1994.
(13) to CE, Hatton, Derbys, /1995 (after 26/1/1995, by 31/3/1995)

BEVERCOTES TRAINING CENTRE, Bothamsall   EN11
SK 696743

Opened by NNT c1976; NTS from 1/8/1985; NTG from 1/4/1990. Closed /1993

A surface narrow gauge line for training underground locomotive drivers was located north east of BEVERCOTES COLLIERY. From c1991 a further track was laid in surface training galleries at the nearby **LOUND HALL TRAINING CENTRE** (SK 700728). These had recently been vacated by the closed **LOUND HALL MINING MUSEUM** (which see for details of locomotives here pre-1991). Lound Hall and Bevercotes sites were cleared of railway equipment by 12/1994.

Gauge : 2ft 4in (Bevercotes)

No.5	820/05979	0-4-0DMF	HB	DM1420	1972	(a)	(1)
	04279	4wBEF	CE	B2299	1982	New	(2)
		power unit for 3 car GMT manriding train					
No.27	No.29 06174	4wBEF	CE	B3044	1983	New	(5)
No.10	820/54943	0-6-0DMF	HC	DM1286	1962	(b)	(3)
No.1	820/05881	0-4-0DMF	HC	DM1360	1965	(c)	(4)
No.11	04510	4wDHF	HE	8989	1981	(d)	(4)
	-	4wBEF	CE	B3501	1990	(e)	(6)

(a) ex Bevercotes Colliery, 11/1976.
(b) ex Bevercotes Colliery, 14/7/1986.
(c) ex Bevercotes Colliery, 1/2/1990.
(d) ex Bevercotes Colliery, c5/1991.
(e) ex CE (trials), /1990; returned to CE, /1991; ex CE, after 20/5/1992, by 1/9/1992.

(1) dismantled /1988 and frame used as dead load vehicle - remains scrapped /1989.
(2) to Bevercotes Colliery by 9/1984.
(3) to Lound Hall Training Centre, 2/1990.
(4) scrapped 4/1994.
(5) to Clipstone Equipment Store, c4/1994.
(6) to Clipstone Equipment Store, 5/1994.

Gauge : 2ft 6in. (Bevercotes). Repair and storage only.

3		4wDHF	HE	8910	1979	(a)	(1)
		4wDHF	HE	8912	1979	(a)	(2)
		4wDHF	HE	9049	1981	(a)	Scr 4/1994
7	No.4	4wDHF	HE	7449	1976	(b)	Scr 4/1994

(a) ex Cotgrave Colliery, /1990.
(b) ex Harworth Colliery, /1992.

(1) to Lound Hall Training Centre, 5/1991.
(2) to Booth Roe Metals Ltd, Rotherham, after 6/1/1993, by 22/1/1993.

Gauge : 2ft 6in (Lound Hall)

		4w-4wBEF	BGB	50/10/001	1985		
	-		WR	L5004F	1985	(a)	s/s c/1994
	3	4wDHF	HE	8910	1979	(b)	s/s c/1994
	8	4wDHF	HE	7385	1976	(c)	(1)
	5	4wBEF	CE			(d)	s/s c/1994

(a) ex BGB, Ilkeston, Derbys, 2/1991 (earlier Harworth Colliery).
(b) ex Bevercotes Training Centre, 5/1991.
(c) ex Harworth Colliery, c/1992 (by 6/1/1993).
(d) ex Cotgrave Colliery, c/1992 (by 6/1/1993).

(1) to Leics C.C., Snibston Discovery Park, Coalville, Leics, after 1/12/1994, by 13/5/1995

Gauge : 2ft 4in. (Lound Hall). Static Training only.

No.6	820/24690	0-6-0DMF	HC	DM970	1956	(b)	(3)
	-	4wDM	RH	375347	1954	(a)	(1)
No.10	820/54943	0-6-0DMF	HC	DM1286	1962	(c)	(4)
		0-4-0DMF	HC			(b)	(2)

(a) ex Rufford Colliery, between /1960 and /1976.
(b) ex Welbeck Colliery, 3/1987.
(c) ex Bevercotes Training Centre, 2/1990.

(1) to National Mining Museum, Lound Hall (same site) /1976.
(2) stripped for spares and scrapped between 21/5/1988 and 2/9/1988.
(3) to Welbeck Colliery, c2/1990 (by 11/2/1990).
(4) to Harworth colliery, for spares, 4/1994.

Gauge : 1ft 7in. (Lound Hall). (static training only).

No.2		4wBEF	CE	B1804A	1978	(a)	s/s c/1994
		4wBEF	CE	B2278	1980		
		reb	CE	B3494B	1988	(a)	s/s c/1994

(a) ex Sherwood Engineering Training Centre, 19/2/1992.

BILSTHORPE COLLIERY, Bilsthorpe   GN12
ex Stanton Ironworks Co Ltd   SK 653617

EM3 from 1/1/1947; NNT from 26/3/1967; NTS from 1/8/1985; NTG from 1/4/1990; MG from 1/9/1993; to **RJB Mining (UK) Ltd** from 30/12/1994

Sidings at the end of a BR (ex LNER) branch which ran east from the Clipstone to Blidworth Colliery line, 1 mile south of Clipstone, to the colliery (3½ miles). Also connected to the BR (ex LMSR/LNER Joint) Ollerton to Farnsfield branch where it ran east of the colliery, until the mid 1960s. A line worked by the NCB ran south east from the colliery to the Stanton Ironworks Co's brickworks (½ mile) for some years after 1947. Use of NCB surface locomotives ceased c1974, by which time rail traffic was entirely handled by BR merry-go-round trains. A locomotive was used underground from 1949 to 1954 and others from 1983.

Gauge : 4ft 8½in.

	BILSTHORPE No.1	0-6-0ST	OC	HL	3614	1925	(a)	(5)
	(BILSTHORPE No.2)	0-6-0ST	OC	AB	2077	1939	(a)	(4)
(71488)		0-6-0ST	IC	HC	1764	1944	(b)	(2)
	-	0-4-0ST	OC	AB	1979	1930	(c)	(1)
		4wDH		RR	10231	1965	(d)	(3)
D7	10332	0-4-0DH		S	10189	1964	(e)	(6)

(a) ex Stanton Ironworks Co Ltd, with site, 1/1/1947.
(b) ex WD, Swindon Depot, Wilts, 6/1947.
(c) ex Thos. W. Ward Ltd, Templeborough Works, Sheffield, after 1/1963, by 23/3/1963.
(d) ex RR, c4/1965 (demonstration).
(e) ex TH, 10/2/1965.

(1) returned to Thos. W. Ward Ltd, Sheffield, 2/1964.
(2) to HC, between 12/1964 and 6/1965 and scrapped there 1/1966.
(3) to Parkside Colliery, Lancs, 7/1965 (demonstration).
(4) scrapped after 10/1965, by 4/1966.
(5) scrapped after 8/1969, by 6/1970.
(6) to Welbeck Colliery, 6/1/1976.

Gauge : 2ft 4in (Underground locomotives).

		0-4-0DMF		HE	3591	1949	New	(1)
	84800	4wBEF		CE	B3034A	1983	New	(2)
	84801	4wBEF		CE	B3034B	1983	New	(2)
	-	4wBEF		CE	B3092A	1984	New	(3)
	-	4wBEF		CE	B3092B	1984	New	(3)
	-	4wBEF		CE	B3093A	1984	New	(3)
	-	4wBEF		CE	B3093B	1984	New	(3)
	-	4wBEF		CE	B3364A	1987		
			reb	CE	3854	1992	(a)	(3)
	-	4wBEF		CE	B3364B	1987	(a)	(3)
	F821/61145	4w-4wBEF		CE	B3252C	1986		
			reb	CE	B3855	1992	(b)	(3)
No.1	70330 BB2	4w-4wBEF		CE	B3224A	1985	(c)	(3)
	-	4wBEF		CE	B3328	1987	(d)	(3)

(a) ex Gedling Colliery, via CE, Hatton, Derbys, /1992.
(b) ex Sherwood Colliery, via CE, Hatton, Derbys, /1992.
(c) ex Thoresby Colliery, via CE, Hatton, Derbys, /1992.
(d) ex Gedling Colliery, via CE, Hatton, Derbys, /1992 (after 6/1992).

(1) to Rufford Colliery, 6/1954.
(2) to Welbeck Colliery, 10/1983 (not used at Bilsthorpe).
(3) to RJB Mining (UK) Ltd, with site, 30/12/1994.

BLIDWORTH COLLIERY, Blidworth GN13
ex Newstead Colliery Co Ltd SK 595567

EM3 from 1/1/1947; NNT from 26/3/1967; NTS from 1/8/1985; CLOSED 3/1989.

Served by sidings at the end of a BR branch which ran south from Clipstone to the colliery. There was a second connection with BR east of Blidworth and Rainworth Station site until the BR line closed c1965. The railway was used for dirt disposal to tips north of the colliery until at least, the 1960s. Use of NCB surface locomotives ceased from 3/1987. Locomotives were used underground throughout.

Gauge : 4ft 8½in.

			0-6-0ST	OC	AE	1947	1924	(a)	(1)
	(BILLUM)		0-6-0ST	OC	AE	1952	1925	(a)	(3)
No.2	NCB	14815	0-4-0ST	OC	RSHN	7644	1950	New	(4)
No.1	NCB		0-4-0ST	OC	RSHN	7642	1950	(b)	(2)
	WELBECK No.6		0-6-0ST	OC	AE	1831	1919	(c)	(3)
D13	14814		4wDH		TH	175V	1966	New	(6)
D22			4wDH		RR	10228	1965	(d)	(5)

(a) ex Newstead Colliery Co Ltd, with site, 1/1/1947.
(b) ex Rufford Colliery after 2/1961, by 4/1963.
(c) ex Welbeck Colliery, c3/1963 (by 10/3/1963).
(d) ex TH, Kilnhurst, South Yorks, 11/11/1971.

(1) scrapped by Thos. W. Ward Ltd, after 6/1964, by 12/1964.
(2) to Warsop Colliery between 12/1964 and 5/1966.
(3) s/s after 9/1967, by 6/1968.
(4) scrapped on site 3/1972.
(5) to C.F. Booth Ltd, Rotherham, South Yorks, 18/9/1984.
(6) to Clipstone Colliery, 5/1/1988.

Gauge : 2ft 0in (Underground locomotives).

No.1		0-4-0DMF	HE	3356	1946	(a)	(4)
No.2	820/15760	0-4-0DMF	HE	4123	1949	New	(8)
No.3		4wDMF	RH	268863	1949	(b)	(2)
	-	4wDMF	RH	268859	1949	(b)	(1)
No.4		4wDMF	RH	268875	1952	(b)	(2)
No.5		4wDMF	RH	268858	1949	(b)	(2)
No.6		0-4-0DMF	HE	6051	1961	New	(5)
No.7		0-4-0DMF	HE	6060	1961	New	(6)
No.10		0-6-0DMF	HC	DM949	1955	(d)	(5)
No.9		0-6-0DMF	HC	DM950	1955	(c)	(5)
No.8		0-6-0DMF	HC	DM951	1955	(c)	(5)
No.11	820/18788	0-4-0DMF	HE	6621	1972	New	(8)
No.12	820/18789	0-4-0DMF	HE	6622	1972	New	(8)
No.15	820/17915	4wDHF	HE	7390	1977	New	(8)
No.16		4wDHF	HE	7391	1977	New	(6)
No.17		4wDHF	HE	7518	1977	New	(6)
No.14	820/11859	4wDHF	HE	7519	1977	New	(9)
No.18		4wDHF	AB	619	1978		
			HE	8569	1978	New	(6)

No.19	820/17926	4wDHF	AB	620	1978			
			HE	8570	1978	New	(8)	
No.20	820/18596	4wDHF	HE	9047	1981	New	(9)	
No.21	820/18612	4wDHF	HE	9048	1981	New	(9)	
No.23	20726	0-6-0DM	HC	DM812	1953	(e)	(7)	
No.22	20725	0-6-0DMF	HC	DM836	1954	(f)	(8)	
	-	4wBEF	CE	B0985	1977	New		
		reb	CE	B2928	1981		(3)	
No.1	20651	4w-4wBEF	CE	B3335	1987	New	(9)	
No.2	KESTREL 4/766	0-6-0DMF	HC	DM647	1954	(g)	(10)	
No.6	SEA EAGLE 4/4791	0-6-0DMF	HC	DM1125	1957	(g)	(11)	

(a) ex Newstead Colliery Co Ltd, with site, 1/1/1947.
(b) ex Harworth Colliery, 23/11/1953.
(c) ex Warsop Colliery, 3/1/1966.
(d) ex Warsop Colliery, 15/9/1966.
(e) ex Bentinck Training Centre, c/1988.
(f) ex Bentinck Training Centre, /1988.
(g) ex Linby Colliery, 10/1988.

(1) to Rufford Colliery, 13/8/1954.
(2) written off and s/s by 7/1978.
(3) to CE, /1980; thence to Ollerton Colliery.
(4) to (? Yorkshire), /1981.
(5) abandoned underground 8/1983.
(6) scrapped /1987.
(7) scrapped /1989.
(8) abandoned underground 3/1989.
(9) to Calverton Colliery, 30/3/1989.
(10) to Welbeck Colliery, 8/1989.
(11) to Bevercotes Colliery.

BRINSLEY COLLIERY, Brinsley LN14
ex Barber, Walker & Co Ltd SK 465487

EM5 from 1/1/1947; Worked as part of SELSTON COLLIERY by 1952 and surface CLOSED by 1958.

Served by MOOR GREEN COLLIERY RAILWAYS (which see). Locomotives were not used underground.

BRINSLEY DISPOSAL POINT, Brinsley LN15
SK 451493

Opened by MFP c1945; CLOSED 1946.

This shortlived site may have been no more than a tipping dock to load rail wagons from lorries. It was located at the former Pollington Colliery, GNR exchange sidings, on the east side of the LNER line, 1½ miles north of Eastwood Station **(see James Oakes & Co (Riddings Collieries) Ltd)**.

Gauge : 4ft 8½in.

75276   0-6-0ST   IC   RSHN 7206   1945   New (a)   (1)

(a)   on loan from War Department from new, /1945.

(1)   to Bennerley Disposal Point, by 3/1946.

BROOKHILL COLLIERY & RAILWAY, Pinxton   KN16
ex Pinxton Collieries Ltd

Brookhill Colliery	SK 462547
Brookhill Locoshed	SK 466548
Pinxton Coking Plant	SK 463548
Pinxton (No.2) Colliery	SK 448545
Pinxton Locoshed	SK 450544
Pinxton Loco Workshops	SK 449543

EM4 from 1/1/1947; Pinxton (No.2) Colliery - CLOSED 3/1950; SNT from 26/3/1967; Brookhill Colliery merged with BENTINCK COLLIERY, rail traffic ceased 8/1968 and surface CLOSED.
The Coking Plant was shunted by the NCB but owned by the **Notts & Derbys Coke & By-Product Co Ltd (Pinxton Coking Co Ltd** from 1953). It CLOSED 1955 (see the **Thos. W. Ward Ltd** entry in Contractors Section).

The NCB's railways commenced at sidings on both sides of the BR (ex LMSR) line at Sleights Sidings (1 mile west of Pinxton North station). Those on the north side served the working **PINXTON** (formerly **PINXTON No.2) COLLIERY**, where there was a loco shed. Those on the south side served **PINXTON No. 1 & 6 COLLIERY**, which no longer wound coal but workshops, including one for locomotives, were located there. The two sites were connected by an NCB line which passed, via a reversing point, beneath the ex LMSR lines. There was a second connection to No.1 & 6 Colliery by means of an ex LNER branch which ran north for ½ mile from Palmerston Junction (south west of Pinxton South station). Another ex LNER line ran north east from Pinxton South station, crossing over the ex LMSR lines, to reach sidings north of the **COKING PLANT** (½ mile). From here it ran west, parallel to the ex LMSR lines, to reach the fulls and empties sidings of PINXTON (No.2) Colliery. **BROOKHILL COLLIERY** was located north of the sidings at the coking plant and was reached by a short NCB line from the west. An NCB line also ran east to **LANGTON COLLIERY** (1½ mile). Langton (which see) had an independent ex LMSR connection from east of Pinxton North Station. NCB locos had running powers over the ex LNER line between No.2 Colliery and the coking plant to enable them to access the latter, together with Brookhill and Langton Collieries. After the ex LNER Pinxton branch closed from 7/1/1963, the NCB took over this connection. The ex LNER line from Palmerston Junction to the NCB's No.1 & 6 site had been lifted by 1958. In 1953 a new loco shed was opened south of the Langton line, east of Brookhill Colliery. The shed at No.2 colliery had closed by 1955. but the workshops at No.1 & 6 Colliery remained in use until sometime after 1956. The Coking Plant closed in 1955 and thereafter only Brookhill Colliery traffic remained, all of which passed to and from BR via the link at Sleights Sidings. Some internal dirt traffic to tips on the old No.2 Colliery site and along the Langton line remained. Pinxton Colliery, loco shed, exchange sidings and Brookhill Colliery were all located in Derbyshire. Locomotives were not used underground at either of the collieries.

Gauge : 4ft 8½in.

(PINXTON)	0-4-0ST	OC	LE	246	1907	(a)	(5)
incorporated parts of LE 247 and 248 from 1950							
LANGTON	0-4-0ST	OC	LE	247	1907	(a)	(1)
(LONGWOOD)	0-4-0ST	OC	LE	248	1907	(a)	(1)
-	0-4-0ST	OC	P	1273	1912	(a)	(7)
PECKETT No.2	0-4-0ST	OC	P	1975	1939	(a)	(9)
(10)	0-4-0ST	OC	AB	905	1901	(b)	(7)
RAVEN	0-4-0WT	OC	Johnson	56	1913	(c)	(2)
No.1	0-6-0ST	OC	HC	736	1905	(d)	(3)
75	0-6-0ST	OC	HC	1365	1919	(e)	(8)
EMFOUR.2.	0-6-0T	OC	HC	1877	1954	New	(13)
EMFOUR.4.	0-6-0T	OC	HC	1879	1954	New	(6)
SWANWICK No.2	0-6-0T	IC	HC	1496	1924	(f)	(4)
EMFOUR.9.	0-6-0DM		HC	D1114	1958	New	(12)
(COTES PARK No.1)	0-4-0ST	OC	HC	1813	1948	(g)	(10)
(COTES PARK No.2)	0-6-0ST	IC	HE	3197	1944	(h)	(10)
ANNESLEY No.2	0-6-0ST	OC	P	1924	1937	(i)	(11)
270/004	0-6-0ST	OC	RS	4156	1937	(j)	(13)

(a) ex Pinxton Collieries Ltd, with site, 1/1/1947.
(b) ex Cotes Park Colliery, Derbys, /1949.
(c) ex Cotes Park Colliery, Derbys, after /1948, by 8/1949.
(d) ex Eccles Slag Co Ltd. Scunthorpe, Lincs, /1951.
(e) ex Appleby-Frodingham Steel Co Ltd, Scunthorpe, Lincs, 3/1954.
(f) ex Swanwick Colliery, Derbys, after 10/1953, by 9/1954.
(g) ex Cotes Park Colliery, Derbys, after 4/1963, by 5/1963.
(h) ex Cotes Park Colliery, Derbys, after 10/1963, by 12/1963.
(i) ex Bentinck Colliery, 1/1967.
(j) ex Linby Colliery, after 4/1967, by 8/1967.

(1) dismantled for spares by 3/1950. Remains scrapped on site, after 3/1950, by 8/1950.
(2) scrapped by Wm. Bush Ltd, Alfreton, Derbys, /1950 (by 3/1950).
(3) to New Hucknall Colliery, after 6/1953, by 9/1954.
(4) to Swanwick Colliery, Derbys, after 2/1955, by 3/1955.
(5) to Kirkby Colliery,after 15/5/1955, by 7/8/1955.
(6) to Kirkby Colliery, after 8/1959, by 5/1960.
(7) scrapped after 9/1965, by 5/1966.
(8) dismantled by 3/1956 and scrapped after 3/1965, by 5/1966.
(9) derelict by 9/1957; scrapped after 9/1965, by 5/1966.
(10) scrapped after 12/1967, by 4/1968.
(11) s/s after 12/1967, by 4/1968.
(12) to Bentinck Colliery, after 11/1968, by 3/1969.
(13) scrapped on site by Thos. W. Ward Ltd, 5/1969.

CALVERTON COLLIERY, Calverton
ex B. A. Collieries Ltd

NN17
SK 603501

SNT from 26/3/1967; NTS from 1/8/1985; NTG from 1/4/1990; CCG from 1/9/1993.
Production ceased by British Coal, 19/11/1993; to **RJB Mining (UK) Ltd**, 23/5/1994.

What had begun as an additional ventilation shaft for BESTWOOD COLLIERY had become, by Vesting Day, a project for a full scale new colliery. No.2 shaft sinking had commenced and was completed in 6/1952. Coal winding began in 3/1953 and the coal preparation plant was commissioned in early 1954. The sidings and BR branch line were constructed by **Holloway Brothers. (London) Ltd** (which see in Contractors Section).

The BR branch opened on 24/9/1952 and followed a circuitous course north, east and then south from 1 mile south of Hucknall Byron station to the colliery (7 miles). A rapid loading bunker was completed in 9/1968, allowing the introduction of BR "merry-go-round" trains for small coal. NCB locomotives were retained to handle other grades until 1993. A narrow gauge locomotive was used in the surface stockyard from 1952 until 1976. Locomotives were used underground before Vesting Day in the connection from Bestwood and more extensively after production commenced. From 1979 conventional locomotives underground were supplemented by a trapped rail locomotive system.

Gauge : 4ft 8½in.

	BESTWOOD	0-4-0ST	OC	AB	1517	1919	(a)	(2)
	-	4wVBT	VCG	S	(9538?	1951)	(b)	(1)
No.1	ALAN	0-6-0DM		RSHN	7696	1953	New	(5)
No.2	BERYL	0-6-0DM		RSHN	7697	1953	New	(6)
No.3	(JUDITH)	0-6-0DM		RSHN	7698	1954	(c)	
		reb to 0-6-0DH		YE		1965		(9)
6	VALERIE	0-6-0ST	OC	HL	3606	1924	(d)	(3)
	-	0-6-0DH		YE	2895	1962	(e)	(4)
	CHARLES	0-6-0DH		YE	2940	1965	New (f)	(12)
D2299		0-6-0DM		RSHD	8158	1960		
				DC	2680	1960	(g)	(7)
LO56	EMFOUR 7							
	CHARLES BUCHAN	0-6-0DM		HC	D1018	1957	(h)	(8)
	-	0-4-0DH		HE	6675	1966	(i)	(9)
	JUDITH (ANDREW)	0-6-0DH		TH	161V	1965	(j)	(9)
D8		0-6-0DH		S	10072	1961	(k)	(11)
	BRIERLEY	0-6-0DH		S	10157	1963	(l)	(10)
10160	FENELLA	0-6-0DH		S	10160	1963	(m)	(13)
	JULIAN	0-6-0DH		S	10161	1964	(m)	(13)

(a) ex Bestwood Colliery, 11/1952.
(b) ex TH or S, 11/1953 (demonstration - may have come direct from Trimsaran Colliery, Carmarthen.).
(c) ex Babbington Colliery, /1957 (by 10/1957); to YE, for rebuild, c/1965; returned, 13/4/1965.
(d) ex Bestwood Colliery, /1957.
(e) ex YE, demonstration, 19/1/1963.
(f) ex TH, 28/3/1966; to TH (repairs) 11/2/1969; returned by 3/5/1969.
(g) ex Hucknall Colliery, 5/1978.
(h) ex Annesley Colliery, after 4/3/1980, by 4/1980.
(i) ex Bentinck Colliery, 20/7/1980.

(j)   ex Babbington Colliery, 5/9/1983.
(k)   ex Linby Colliery, 21/7/1988.
(l)   ex Sutton Colliery between 9/1989 and 6/1990.
(m) ex Gedling Colliery, 12/1991.

(1)   to TH or S, /1953.
(2)   to Bestwood Colliery, /1954.
(3)   to Bestwood Central Workshops, after 6/1959, by 2/1961.
(4)   to Austin Motor Co Ltd, Longbridge, Birmingham, demonstration, c1/1963.
(5)   to Kirkby Colliery, after 4/1967, by 12/1967.
(6)   to Bardon Hill Quarries Ltd, Coalville, Leics, c3/1976 (by 3/1976)
(7)   to Hucknall Colliery, 23/8/1978.
(8)   scrapped between 1/1984 and 7/1984.
(9)   scrapped on site by A.B. & P.G. Kettle Ltd, 1/1989.
(10) to Shropshire Locomotive Collection, Salop, 15/2/1993.
(11) to Shropshire Locomotive Collection, Salop, 16/2/1993.
(12) to Shropshire Locomotive Collection, Salop, 17/2/1993.
(13) to Yorkshire Engine Co Ltd, private site, 23/3/1994.

Gauge : 2ft 0in.

		4wDMF	RH	268880	1958	(a)	(2)
		4wDM	RH	331263	1952	New	(1)

(a)   ex underground c/1969.

(1)   to Rossington Colliery, South Yorks, 11/1976.
(2)   to Gedling Colliery, after 9/1978, by 3/1979.

Gauge : 2ft 0in (Underground locomotives).

3/3327		4wBEF	GB	1960	1943	(a)	(1)
		4wBEF	GB	1961	1943	(a)	(1)
		0-6-0DMF	HC	DM645	1948	New	(9)
		0-6-0DMF	HC	DM671	1948	New	(2)
		0-4-0DMF	HC	DM688	1948	New	(9)
164/154 2/3733		0-6-0DMF	HC	DM792	1953	New	(17)
793		0-6-0DMF	HC	DM793	1953	New	(10)
No.4		0-6-0DMF	HC	DM794	1953	New	(8)
		4wDMF	HE	4428	1953	New	(9)
		4wDMF	HE	4429	1953	New	(9)
		4wDMF	HE	4430	1953	New	(9)
		4wDMF	HE	4523	1954	New	(9)
		0-6-0DMF	HC	DM863	1956	New	(7)
		4wDMF	RH	268880	1958	New	(11)
No.3		4wDMF	RH	425795	1958	New	(6)
		4wDMF	RH	425797	1958	New	(9)
No.1	HEATHER						
No.2	184/137	4wDMF	RH	425798	1958	New	(3)
		0-6-0DMF	HC	DM1166	1959	New	(5)
		4wDMF	HE	6044	1961	New	(9)
		4wDMF	HE	6045	1961	New	(4)
164/141 No.23 1/2848/1		0-6-0DMF	HC	DM1280	1962	New	(17)

164/146 No.24		0-6-0DMF	HC	DM1321	1963	New	(17)
164/166		4wDMF	HC	DM1367	1965	New	(17)
164/167		4wDHF	HC	DM1368	1965	New	(12)
164/180 No.27 108289		0-6-0DMF	HC	DM1395	1966	New	(14)
164/176		4wDMF	HE	6332	1967	New	(17)
No.3		0-6-0DMF	HC	DM679	1952	(b)	(9)
No.6 -		0-6-0DMF	HC	DM879	1954	(b)	(9)
164/192 7332		4wDHF	HE	7332	1974	New	(18)
No.3		4wDHF	HE	8980	1980	New	(19)
164/323 No.4		4wDHF	HE	8984	1981	New	(19)
164/346 No.5		4wDHF	HE	9055	1982	(c)	(19)
No.6		4wDHF	HE	9056	1982	(c)	(19)
164/179 No.8 OLD BOB No.26		0-6-0DMF	HC	DM1393	1967	(d)	(14)
164/150 No.5		0-6-0DMF	HC	DM1310	1963	(e)	(19)
164/174 No.7 LITTLE JOHN							
No.25		0-6-0DMF	HC	DM1380	1966	(e)	(14)
No.2 No.22 6/4741		0-6-0DMF	HC	DM1117	1957	(f)	(16)
No.7 4/4792		0-6-0DMF	HC	DM1124	1958	(g)	(13)
164/162 No.14 HADDON HALL							
No.28		0-6-0DMF	HC	DM1331	1964	(g)	(14)
164/200 No.3 No.2		4wDHF	HE	8909	1979	(h)	(19)
No.14 820/11859 No.9		4wDHF	HE	7519	1977	(i)	(19)
No.20 820/18596 No.1		4wDHF	HE	9047	1981	(k)	(15)
No.21 820/18612 No.9		4wDHF	HE	9048	1981	(l)	(19)
No.1 20651		4w-4wBEF	CE	B3335	1987		
		reb	CE	B3605	1989	(j)	(19)
No.7 164/200 164/312		4wDHF	HE	8911	1980	(m)	(19)
87127		4wBEF	CE	B0427	1975		
		reb	CE	B2926	1982		
		reb	CE	B3621	1989	(n)	(19)
No.4 1387		4wBEF	CE	B2239A	1980		
		reb	CE			(o)	(19)
No.1 138876		4wBEF	HE/GMT	9155	1991	New	(19)
No.2 138877		4wBEF	HE/GMT	9156	1991	New	(19)
164/374 2B		4wBEF	CE	B3100A	1984	(p)	(19)
164/373 1B		4wBEF	CE	B3100B	1984	(p)	(19)
164/375 3B		4wBEF	CE	B3155B	1984	(p)	(19)

(a) ex Bestwood Colliery, via underground connection, as Calverton development proceded, c/1953. (Locos had worked in a district of Bestwood workings which subsequently became part of Calverton).
(b) ex Bestwood Colliery by 2/1968 when noted on surface (said to be going to HC for repair and return).
(c) ex Gedling Colliery, 8/1982.
(d) ex Babbington Colliery, 7/10/1985.
(e) ex Babbington Colliery, c6/1986.
(f) ex Babbington Colliery, c6/1986; to Ashington Central Workshops, Northumberland, 2/4/1987; returned 3/1988.
(g) ex Linby Colliery, c8/1988.
(h) ex Babbington Colliery, 1/1988.
(i) ex Blidworth Colliery, 30/3/1989; to Ashington Central Workshops, Northumberland, 1/1990; returned here 4/1990.
(j) ex Blidworth Colliery, 30/3/1989; to CE, Hatton, Derbys, 4/1989; returned /1990.

(k) ex Blidworth colliery, 30/3/1989
(l) ex Blidworth Colliery, 30/3/1989; to Ashington Central Workshops, Northumberland, 1/1990; returned here 2/1990.
(m) ex Babbington Colliery, 31/3/1989.
(n) ex Annesley Colliery, 29/6/1990.
(o) ex Warsop Colliery, 29/6/1990.
(p) ex Gedling Colliery, c1/1992.

(1) to Gedling Colliery, by /1951.
(2) to Bestwood Colliery, by /1977
(3) to Hucknall Training Centre, c/1967.
(4) to Linby Colliery, c/1968.
(5) to Gedling Colliery, c/1976 (by 1/1977).
(6) to Babbington Colliery, c/1977 (by 3/1978).
(7) to Gedling Colliery, by 1/1977.
(8) to Bestwood Colliery, by /1977.
(9) written off by 7/1978.
(10) dismantled underground for spares by 7/1978
(11) to Gedling Colliery, after 9/1978, by 9/1979.
(12) to Leeds Industrial Museum, Armley Mills, West Yorks, c/1988.
(13) dismantled for spares and remains scrapped c/1989.
(14) to Askern Colliery, South Yorks, 8/1991.
(15) scrapped 6/1991.
(16) to Golden Valley Railway, Midland Railway Centre, Butterley, Derbys, 12/5/1992.
(17) written off by 11/1991; disposal unknown.
(18) to Ashington Central Workshops, Northumberland, 4/1/1990; thence to Tanfield Railway, Marley Hill, Tyne & Wear, 27/8/1993.
(19) to RJB Mining (UK) Ltd, with site, 23/5/1994.

Gauge : 400mm. (Roadrailer trapped rail system).

No.1	No.11		2adDHF	BGB	DRL50/400/414	1979	New	(3)
No.7	No.17		2adDHF	BGB	DRL50/400/418	1980	New (b)	
		reb		BGB	DRL50/400/446	1986		(3)
No.3	DM3	164/353	2adDHF	BGB	RL100/400/003	1982	New (c)	(1)
No.5	DM5	164/364	2adDHF	BGB	RL100/400/005	1983	(a)	(2)
No.3	No.13		2adDHF	BGB	DRL50/400/438	1983	New	(3)
No.2	No.12		2adDHF	BGB	DRL50/400/439	1983	New (d)	(3)
No.5	No.15		2adDHF	BGB	DRL50/400/440	198x	New (e)	(3)
No.4	No.14		2adDHF	BGB	DRL50/400/442	1985	New	(3)
No.6	No.16		2adDHF	BGB	DRL50/400/443	1986	New	(3)

(a) ex Swadlincote Test Site, Derbys, 7/1983.
(b) to BGB, Ilkeston, Derbys, c/1985; returned 6/1986.
(c) to BGB, c/1986; returned c/1987.
(d) to BGB, /1988; returned 5/1988.
(e) to BGB, /1988; returned 2/1988.

(1) to Clipstone Colliery by 6/1987.
(2) to Clipstone Colliery by 6/1988.
(3) to RJB Mining (UK) Ltd, with site, 23/5/1994

CINDERHILL COLLIERY - see BABBINGTON COLLIERY

CLIFTON COLLIERY, Nottingham SN18
ex Nottingham & Clifton Colliery Ltd SK 565380
EM6 from 1/1/1947: SNT from 26/3/1967. CLOSED 7/1968.

A branch ran south east from the BR (ex-LMSR) line, 1½ miles west of Nottingham Midland station to the colliery (½ mile). A second branch to the colliery ran south west for ¼ mile from Queens Walk (ex-LNER) goods station. This connection closed in 1962. Also connected, at the ex LMSR exchange sidings, to the CEGB Nottingham Power Station located south west of the colliery. Locomotives were not used underground.

Gauge : 4ft 8½in.

B1C		0-4-0ST	OC	Butterley	1887	(a)	(1)	
	-	0-6-0ST	OC	AB	886	1900	(a)	(4)
	-	0-4-0ST	OC	P	1469	1917	(a)	(3)
75004	PETER	0-6-0ST	IC	HE	2853	1943	(b)	(5)
	COLONEL	0-6-0ST	OC	HE	577	1892	(c)	(2)
No.3	FELIX	0-6-0ST	OC	AB	2344	1954	New (d)	(6)
	MICHAEL	0-6-0ST	OC	RSHN	7285	1945	(e)	(7)
	PHILIP	0-6-0ST	IC	HE	2854	1943	(f)	(10)
	JAYNE	4wDH		TH	137C	1964		
		Incorporated frame of		S			(g)	(9)
	ANDREW	0-6-0DH		TH	161V	1965	New	(8)

(a) ex Nottingham & Clifton Colliery Ltd, with site, 1/1/1947.
(b) ex WD, France (via Dover), 7/1947; to Babbington Colliery 11/1947; returned 4/1948.
(c) ex Babbington Colliery by 21/1/1948.
(d) to Babbington Colliery, 6/1956; returned, 17/7/1956; to Babbington Colliery after 6/1/1957, by 4/1957; returned, after 4/1957, by 1/6/1957
(e) ex Babbington Colliery, after 7/11/1956, by 6/1/1957; to Bestwood Central Workshops after 5/1960, by 2/1961; returned after 3/1961, by 10/1962.
(f) ex Babbington Colliery, after 12/1963, by 9/1964.
(g) ex Babbington Colliery, after 12/1964, by 3/1967.

(1) scrapped /1947.
(2) to Babbington Colliery, after 21/1/1948, by 4/2/1948.
(3) to Gedling Colliery, 12/1949.
(4) scrapped on site by Thos. W. Ward Ltd, 4/1954.
(5) to HE, 1/1955; thence to Bestwood Colliery, 12/1955
(6) to Bestwood Colliery, after 3/1965, by 3/1966.
(7) scrapped after 3/1965, by 3/1966.
(8) to Babbington Colliery, after /1966, by 3/1967.
(9) to Pye Hill Colliery, after 4/1968, by 9/1968.
(10) scrapped after 5/1969, by 11/1969.

CLIPSTONE COLLIERY, New Clipstone   GN19
ex Bolsover Colliery Co Ltd   SK 594632

EM3 from 1/1/1947; NNT from 26/3/1967; NTS from 1/8/1985; NTG from 1/4/1990; Production ceased 30/4/1993. Reopened by **RJB Mining (UK) Ltd,** 24/1/1994.

A BR (ex LNER) branch ran north west from the Mansfield line, 2 miles south west of Clipstone junctions to the colliery (½ mile). Also connected to the BR (ex LMSR) branch which ran north from Rainworth to the colliery. This line closed 2/1980.

Locomotives were used underground from pre-vesting day. By 1987 these had been replaced by a trapped rail system which made use of locomotives both underground and on the surface.

Gauge : 4ft 8½in.

CLIPSTONE No.1	0-4-0ST	OC	HL	3137	1915	(a)	(2)
No.3 NCB (CLIPSTONE No.2)	0-4-0ST	OC	HL	3630	1925		
	Incorporated parts of RSHN 7643 from 1962					(a)	(8)
-	0-6-0ST	OC	HC	1305	1917	(b)	(1)
No.3 NCB	0-4-0ST	OC	RSHN	7643	1950	New	(5)
No.4	0-4-0ST	OC	P	1114	1907	(c)	(3)
(RUFFORD No.2)	0-4-0ST	OC	HL	3389	1919	(d)	(4)
9	0-6-0ST	OC	YE	2521	1952	(e)	(9)
-	0-6-0DE		RH	448157	1962	(f)	(6)
No.4 NCB 46778	0-4-0ST	OC	RSHN	7675	1951	(g)	(7)
(D9)	4wDH		TH	169V	1966	New	(12)
D16	4wDH		TH	190V	1967	(h)	(10)
D19	4wDH		TH	215V	1970	(j)	(11)
(D14) 28533	4wDH		TH	178V	1967	(k)	(13)
D13 14814	4wDH		TH	175V	1966	(l)	(14)
-	4wDH		TH	172V	1966	(m)	(13)

(a) ex Bolsover Colliery Co Ltd, with site, 1/1/1947.
(b) ex Bentinck Colliery, /1948.
(c) ex John Cashmore Ltd., Great Bridge, Staffs, c6/1957 (hire).
(d) ex Rufford Colliery, /1958.
(e) ex Appleby Frodingham Steel Co Ltd, Scunthorpe, Lincs, /1961.
(f) ex RH, hire, 1/3/1963.
(g) ex Ollerton Colliery after 3/1964, by 28/6/1964; to Ollerton Colliery after 28/6/1964, by 7/1964; returned after 7/1964, by 11/1964.
(h) ex Thoresby Colliery, 24/3/1972.
(j) ex Sherwood Colliery, c1/1980 (after 9/1979, by 4/1980).
(k) ex Harworth Colliery, 19/4/1983.
(l) ex Blidworth Colliery, 5/1/1988.
(m) ex Mansfield Coal Preparation Plant, /1991 (by 16/7/1991).

(1) to Welbeck Colliery c/1949 (by 4/1950).
(2) dismantled and some parts scrapped c/1958 (after 8/1957), remainder scrapped after 28/6/1964.
(3) to John Cashmore Ltd, Great Bridge, Staffs, off hire, /1957 (after 18/8/1957).
(4) a rebuild of this loco using parts of HL 3137, and to become CLIPSTONE No.1, commenced c/1958 but was not completed and all parts were scrapped after 28/6/1964.

(5) dismantled for spares /1960 and remaining parts scrapped after 10/1965.
(6) to Coppice Colliery, Derbys, demonstration, 11/6/1963.
(7) scrapped on site by Wm. Bush Ltd, Alfreton, Derbys, 3/1967.
(8) scrapped after 6/1968, by 11/1968.
(9) to Lound Hall Mining Museum after 9/1972, by 9/1973.
(10) to Marple & Gillott Ltd, Sheffield, 24/2/1982.
(11) to Marple & Gillott Ltd, Sheffield, 25/2/1982.
(12) to Walter Heselwood Ltd, Sheffield, 27/2/1984.
(13) to Shropshire Locomotive Collection, Salop, 27/11/1992.
(14) to Shropshire Locomotive Collection, Salop, 30/11/1992

Gauge : 400mm. (Roadrailer trapped rail system). Used in surface stockyard...

	-	2adDHF	BGB	DRL50/400/444	1985	(a)	(1)
	-	1adBEF	BGB	BRL25/400/002	1986	New	(2)
22719		1adBEF	BGB	BRL25/400/003	1987	New	(2)
	-	2adBEF	BGB	BRL50/400/001	1988	New	(2)

(a) ex BGB, Ilkeston, Derbys, 9/1986, on loan.

(1) returned to BGB, Ilkeston, off loan, /1987; subsequently exported to Mexico.
(2) to RJB Mining (UK) Ltd, with site, 24/1/1994.

Gauge : 2ft 4in (Underground locomotives).

No.14		0-4-0DMF	HE	3299	1945	(a)	(1)
No.13		0-4-0DMF	HE	3300	1945	(a)	(1)
No.17		0-4-0DMF	HC	DM693	1948	New (b)	(8)
-		0-4-0DMF	HC	DM695	1948	New	(8)
No.12		0-4-0DMF	HC	DM694	1948	(c)	(2)
	820/24688	0-6-0DMF	HC	DM865	1953	(d)	(12)
No.9	820/24689	0-6-0DMF	HC	DM866	1955	New	(7)
	820/24686	0-6-0DMF	HC	DM867	1955	New	(13)
	820/24687	0-6-0DMF	HC	DM868	1955	New	(11)
No.8	820/24683	0-6-0DMF	HC	DM969	1956	(e)	(6)
No.6	820/24690	0-6-0DMF	HC	DM970	1956	New	(5)
No.5	820/24691	0-6-0DMF	HC	DM971	1957	New	(3)
No.3	820/24692	0-6-0DMF	HC	DM1011	1957	(f)	(4)
No.3	820/45103	0-4-0DMF	HC	DM791	1950	(g)	(12)
	06287	0-4-0DMF	HC	DM1383	1966	(h)	(9)
No.4	820/45105	0-4-0DMF	HC	DM772	1950	(i)	(10)

(a) ex Bolsover Colliery Co Ltd, with site, 1/1/1947.
(b) to Rufford Colliery 9/8/1954; returned, 13/11/1954.
(c) ex Rufford Colliery, 1/1/1952.
(d) ex Rufford Colliery, 1/2/1955.
(e) ex Rufford Colliery, 4/1975.
(f) ex Rufford Colliery, 26/6/1961.
(g) ex Welbeck Colliery, 11/3/1976.
(h) ex Bevercotes Colliery, 29/4/1976.
(i) ex Welbeck Colliery, 19/9/1977.

(1) to Rufford Colliery, 8/1954.
(2) to Rufford Colliery after 1/1952.
(3) to Welbeck Colliery, 6/1973.
(4) to Welbeck Colliery, 3/1974.
(5) to Welbeck Colliery, 3/1975.
(6) to Bevercotes Colliery, 4/1975.
(7) to Bevercotes Colliery, 4/1976.
(8) written off 7/1976.
(9) to Bevercotes Colliery after 4/1976, by /1979.
(10) to Welbeck Colliery, 8/9/1986.
(11) to Bevercotes Colliery, 10/1985.
(12) scrapped /1987 (after 3/3/1987).
(13) scrapped by 2/1987.

Gauge : 400mm. (Roadrailer trapped rail system).

No.2	820/24982	2adDHF	BGB	DRL50/400/407	1978	New (a)	(2)
No.1	820/24981	2adDHF	BGB	DRL50/400/408	1977	New (b)	(2)
No.3	24987	2adDHF	BGB	DRL50/400/422	1980		
		reb	BGB	DRL50/400/445	1985	New (c)	(2)
No.4	24698	2adDHF	BGB	DRL50/400/427	1980		
		reb	BGB	DRL50/400/441	1985	New (d)	(2)
No.5	24699	2adDHF	BGB	DRL50/400/428	1980	New (e)	(2)
No.6	22680	2adDHF	BGB	DRL50/400/436	1982	New	(2)
No.7	22658	2adDHF	BGB	DRL50/400/437	1982	New (f)	(2)
	22862	2adDHF	BGB	RL100/400/002	1981	(g)	(2)
	22691	2adDHF	BGB	RL100/400/004	1983	New (h)	(2)
	22693	2adDHF	BGB	RL100/400/006	1984	New (i)	(2)
	22776	2adDHF	BGB	RL100/400/008	1984	New (j)	(2)
	22677	1adCEHF	BGB	RT30/400/003	1983	(k)	(2)
	22770	2adDHF	BGB	RL100/400/009	1985	New	(2)
	22779	2adDHF	BGB	RL100/400/010	1986	New(l)	(2)
	22774	2adDHF	BGB	RL100/400/012	1986	New	(2)
	22784	2adDHF	BGB	RL100/400/013	1987	New	(2)
	22714	1mBEF	BGB	BRL25/400/001	1986	New	(2)
No.3	DM3 164/353	2adDHF	BGB	RL100/400/003	1982	(m)	(2)
		1adDHF	BGB	30/400/001	1981	(n)	(3)
		2adDHF	BGB	DRL50/400/446	1986	(o)	(1)
No.5	DM5 164/364	2adDHF	BGB	RL100/400/005	1983	(p)	(2)
No.3	390/3	2adDHF	BGB	DRL50/400/413	1978	(q)	(2)
	390/4	2adDHF	BGB	DRL50/400/535	1978	(q)	(2)

(a) to BGB, Ilkeston, Derbys, 4/1982; returned 8/12/1982.
(b) to BGB, 2/1982; returned 31/3/1982.
(c) to BGB, 19/9/1984; returned 17/12/1985.
(d) to BGB, 3/12/1984; returned 29/3/1985.
(e) to BGB, 4/1982; returned 2/12/1983.
(f) to BGB, 5/1983; returned 10/1984.
(g) ex BGB, 1981 (after exhibition in Germany); to BGB, 14/12/1982; returned 11/5/1983; to BGB, 4/4/1985; returned 21/3/1986.
(h) to BGB, 12/10/1984; returned19/3/1985.
(i) to BGB, 19/4/1984; returned 3/5/1984.
(j) to BGB, 7/1986; returned 12/12/1986.

(k)   ex BGB, 11/1983 (earlier Solsgirth Colliery, Fife); to BGB, 3/1984; returned /1984; to BGB, 2/1985; returned 3/1985.
(l)   to BGB, 23/5/1986; returned 3/7/1986.
(m)   ex Calverton Colliery by 6/1987.
(n)   ex BGB (earlier Treforest Colliery, Mid Glam); to BGB, 20/2/1985; returned 21/3/1985.
(o)   ex BGB. Ilkeston, Derbys, c/1986 (loan).
(p)   ex Calverton Colliery by 6/1988.
(q)   ex Betws Colliery, Dyfed, 1/1992.

(1)   to BGB. Ilkeston, Derbys, c/1987.
(2)   to RJB Mining (UK) Ltd, with site, 24/1/1994.
(3)   sold or scrapped at unknown date.

CLIPSTONE EQUIPMENT STORE, New Clipstone   GN20
SK 593633

Opened by NNT / ; NTS from 1/8/1985;   Taken over by **RJB Mining (UK) Ltd**, /1994.

Located on the north west side of **CLIPSTONE COLLIERY**. No standard gauge track; the locomotive was here for resale only in 1983.

Gauge : 4ft 8½in.

| D18 | 117014 | | 4wDH | TH | 192V | 1968 | (a) | (1) |

(a)   ex Sutton Colliery, after 10/1982, by 10/1983.

(1)   to Walter Heselwood Ltd, Sheffield, 27/2/1984.

Gauge : 2ft 6in

| HT2 | | 4wDH | HE | 7328 | 1973 | (a) | (1) |
| 5 | | 4wBEF | EE | | | (b) | (2) |

(a)   ex Cotgrave Colliery, c10/1992.
(b)   origin unknown.

(1)   to Golden Valley Railway, Midland Railway Centre, Butterley, Derbys, 5/1994.
(2)   to Leicestershire County Council, Snibston Discovery Park, Coalville, Leics, 6/1993.

Gauge : 2ft 4in

| | - | 4wBEF | CE | B3501 | 1990 | (a) | (1) |
| No.29 | 06174 | 4wBEF | CE | B3044 | 1983 | (b) | (1) |

(a)   ex Bevercotes Training Centre, 5/1994.
(b)   ex Bevercotes Training Centre, c4/1994.

(1)   to RJB Mining (UK) Ltd, with site, /1994.

COSSALL COLLIERY, Cossall

QN21

ex Cossall Colliery Co Ltd

SK 477426

EM5 from 1/1/1947; EM6 from 3/1966; CLOSED 11/1966.

Sidings ran east for ½ mile from BR at Ilkeston Junction station to the colliery. No known locomotives; believed to have been worked by BR. (See also **TROWELL MOOR DISPOSAL POINT**).

COTGRAVE COLLIERY, Cotgrave

UN22

SK 654363

Opened by EM6 c1962; SNT from 26/3/1967; NTS from 1/8/1985; NTG from 1/4/1990; CLOSED 30/4/1993.

Site preparation for this new colliery began in 3/1954. Shaft sinking began in 6/1956 and was completed by 6/1960. Coal production commenced 1/1964. The colliery was served by sidings at the end of a BR branch, which opened in 1962 and ran south east for 2½ miles from a junction ¾ mile west of Radcliffe on Trent station. Use of standard gauge locomotives ceased from 1985, after which all coal sold by rail was loaded from a rapid loading bunker to BR hauled trains.. Locomotives were used underground from 1961. There was also an experimental locomotive-worked suspended monorail system from c1970 to c1981.

Gauge : 4ft 8½in.

10160	FENELLA		0-6-0DH	S	10160	1963	New	(4)
	JULIAN		0-6-0DH	S	10161	1964	New	(2)
			0-4-0DH	S	10165	1964	(a)	(1)
D16	ROBIN	(D3618)	0-6-0DE	Dar		1958	(b)	(3)

(a) ex S, hire, by 2/1964.
(b) ex Annesley Colliery, 24/7/1980.

(1) to S, ex hire, by 7/1964.
(2) to BR Toton (tyre turning), by 15/3/1976; returned c3/1976; to Gedling Colliery, between 3/1976 and 3/1977.
(3) to Moor Green Colliery, 30/3/1981.
(4) to Pye Hill Colliery, 26/9/1984.

Gauge : 2ft 6in (Underground locomotives).

No.3		4wDMF	RH 441427	1961	New	(1)
-		4wDMF	RH 441428	1961	New	(2)
H1	164/148	0-6-0DMF	HC DM1304	1963	(a)	(9)
H2	164/163	0-6-0DMF	HC DM1329	1964	New	(9)
H3	164/165	0-6-0DMF	HC DM1330	1964	New	(9)
H4		0-6-0DMF	HC DM1327	1964	(c)	(9)
H5		0-6-0DMF	HC DM1315	1963	(b)	(9)
HT1	164/189	4wDHF	HE 7327	1973	New	(9)
HT2		4wDHF	HE 7328	1973	New	(5)
HT3		0-6-0DMF	HE 7372	1973	(d)	(9)
HT4		0-6-0DMF	HE 7479	1976	(e)	(9)

HT5			4wDHF		HE	8910	1979	New	(3)
HT6			4wDHF		HE	9049	1981	New	(3)
No.6	164/202	No.5	4wDHF		HE	8912	1978	(f)	(3)
No.7	164/203		4wDHF		HE	8913	1979	(f)	(9)
No.8	164/204		4wDHF		HE	8914	1979	(f)	(9)
			4wBEF		EE	2083	1955		
					Bg	3435	1955	(g)	(7)
			4wBEF		EE	2301	1956		
					Bg	3437	1956	(h)	(7)
			4wBEF		EE	2521	1957		
					RSHN	7963	1957	(i)	(7)
			4wBEF		EE	2086	1955		
					Bg	3434	1955	(j)	(7)
			4wBEF		EE	2300	1956		
					Bg	3436	1956	(k)	(7)
			4wBEF		EE	2522	1958		
					RSHN	7964	1958	(l)	(7)
			4wBEF		GECT	5424	1976	(m)	(7)
			4wBEF		CE			(n)	(8)
			4wBEF		CE			(o)	(8)
			4wBEF		CE	B2933	1981		
				reb	CE	B3393B	1987	(p)	(4)
			4wBEF		CE			(q)	(8)
			4wBEF		CE	B3383	1987	(r)	(8)
			4wBEF		EE	3402	1963		
					EES	8421	1963	(s)	(6)
			4wBEF		EE	3224	1962		
					RSHD	8345	1962	(s)	(6)

(a) ex Hucknall Colliery, 1963.
(b) ex Hucknall Colliery, 11/1970; to Ashington Central Workshops, Northumberland. 12/1979; returned 5/1981.
(c) ex Hucknall Colliery, 5/1971.
(d) ex Hucknall Colliery, 12/1976.
(e) ex Hucknall Colliery, 1/1977.
(f) ex Hucknall Colliery, 2/1987.
(g) ex Ashington National Workshops, Northumberland, 3/10/1988; (earlier Snowdown Colliery, Kent).
(h) ex Ashington National Workshops, 27/1/1989 (earlier Snowdown).
(i) ex Ashington National Workshops, 23/3/1989 (earlier Snowdown).
(j) ex Ashington National Workshops, 19/10/1989 (earlier Snowdown).
(k) ex Ashington National Workshops, 19/1/1990 (earlier Snowdown).
(l) ex Ashington National Workshops, 15/3/1990 (earlier Snowdown).
(m) ex Ashington National Workshops, 30/3/1990 (earlier Snowdown).
(n) ex Ashington National Workshops, 29/1/1991.
(o) ex Ashington National Workshops, 9/5/1990; orig from a Kent colliery.
(p) ex Betteshanger Colliery, Kent, /1989; to Ashington National Workshops, 12/1989; returned here, 22/12/1989.
(q) ex Ashington National Workshops, 14/5/1990.
(r) ex Ollerton Colliery by 11/1991.
(s) ex Lea Hall Colliery, Staffs, 5/8/1991.

(1) to Hucknall Training Centre, c/1967.
(2) to Bestwood Training Centre, c/1972.
(3) to Bevercotes Training Centre, /1990.
(4) to Asfordby Colliery, Leics, /1990.
(5) to Clipstone Equipment Store, c10/1992.
(6) never put into use; remained out of use on surface: scrapped 6/1993 by McIntyre Ltd of Nottingham.
(7) numbered BL1 to BL7; numbers BL6 and BL7 never carried and these two locos remained out of use on surface; then to Snibston Discovery Park, Coalville, Leics, c6/1993. BL1 to BL5 moved to Harworth Colliery, c9/1993, following completion of salvage operations after closure of the colliery.
(8) numbered PL1 to PL4; PL4 to Lound Hall, c/1992 (by 6/1/1993); PL3 to ? ; PL1 and PL2 to Harworth Colliery, c6/1993.
(9) out of use by /1989; abandoned underground on closure of the colliery, 4/1993.

Suspended monorail system.

DMR1		1adDHF	BGB	DML25/1/101	1967	(a)	(1)
DMR2		2adDHF	BGB	DML40/401/1	1974	New	(2)

(a) ex Central Engineering Establishment, Bretby, Derbys, c/1970.

(1) scrapped c/1981.
(2) scrapped c/1982.

FIRBECK COLLIERY, Langold   BN23
ex Doncaster Amalgamated Collieries Ltd   SK 583861
NE1 from 1/1/1947; SYK from 26/3/19; CLOSED 11/1968.

Sidings at the south end of the BR Firbeck Colliery branch, 4 miles south of its junction with the Harworth Colliery branch. Locomotives were used underground until c1960.

Gauge : 4ft 8½in.

DAISY	0-6-0ST	OC	AE	1895	1923	(a)	(3)
BILL	0-6-0ST	OC	AE	1920	1924	(b)	(2)
WAVERLEY	0-4-0ST	OC	AB	889	1901	(c)	(1)
FIRBECK	0-6-0DM		HC	D1133	1959	New	(4)

(a) ex Doncaster Amalgamated Collieries Ltd, with site, 1/1/1947; to Handsworth Coal Preparation Plant, Yorks (WR), after 8/1964, by 4/1965; returned after 4/1965, by 9/1966.
(b) ex Doncaster Amalgamated Collieries Ltd, with site, 1/1/1947.
(c) ex Nunnery Colliery, Sheffield, Yorks (WR), /1948.

(1) to Kiveton Park Colliery, Yorks (WR), by 24/9/1950.
(2) to Dinnington Colliery, Yorks (WR), after 8/1959, by 9/1960.
(3) sold or scrapped after 6/1969, by 5/1970.
(4) to Manton Colliery after 8/1970, by 11/1970.

Gauge : 2ft 0in (Underground locomotives).

0-4-0DMF	HE	3619	1948	New	(2)
0-4-0DMF	HE	3620	1948	New	(1)

(1) to Valleyfield Colliery, Fife, 8/1960
(2) to Blairhall Colliery, Fife, 9/1960.

GEDLING COLLIERY, Gedling　　　　　　　　　　　　　　　　RN24
ex B.A. Collieries Ltd　　　　　　　　　　　　　　　　　　　　SK 613438
EM6 from 1/1/1947; SNT from 26/3/1967; NTS from 1/8/1985; NTG from 1/4/1990; CLOSED 8/11/1991.

Sidings ran north east from BR, 1 mile north of Gedling Station to the colliery (½ mile). A direct rope incline ran north west from the colliery to Mapperley Plains landsale depot (SK 602444) (¾ mile) until 1985. Latterly, a locomotive was hauled up and down this incline daily to shunt the depot. In earlier times the depot loco was stabled there between washouts. Another branch crossed over the BR line and ran south for ½ mile to serve a landsale yard in Arnold Lane. Locomotives were used underground from c1949.

Gauge : 4ft 8½in.

	CATHERINE	0-6-0ST	OC	AB	1000 1903	(a)	(3)
	AUDREY	0-6-0ST	OC	P	1253 1911	(a)	(4)
	QUEEN	0-4-0ST	OC	AB	1784 1923	(a)	(3)
	-	0-4-0ST	OC	P	1469 1917	(b)	(2)
		0-4-0DE		RH	412716 1957	(c)	(1)
	KING GEORGE	0-6-0ST	IC	HE	2409 1942	(d)	(7)
39		0-6-0ST	OC	RSHD	6947 1938	(e)	(6)
812478		0-4-0DM		RH	375714 1955	(f)	(8)
	SUSAN LP59/096	4wDH		TH	176V 1966	New	(9)
	GILLIAN LP56/097	4wDH		TH	182V 1967	New	(9)
D3619	SIMON	0-6-0DE		Dar	1958	(g)	(5)
	JULIAN	0-6-0DH		S	10161 1964	(h)	(10)
10160	FENELLA	0-6-0DH		S	10160 1963	(i)	(10)

(a) ex B.A. Collieries Ltd, with site, 1/1/1947.
(b) ex Clifton Colliery,12/1949.
(c) ex (Tyne Improvement Commission ?), demonstration, c/1958.
(d) ex Linby Colliery, 2/1961.
(e) ex Appleby-Frodingham Steel Co Ltd, Scunthorpe, Lincs, 4/1961.
(f) ex Hucknall Colliery after 12/1963, by 7/1964.
(g) ex BR, Lincoln, 9/1969.
(h) ex Cotgrave Colliery after 3/1976, by 3/1977.
(i) ex Linby Colliery, 22/4/1988.

(1) to (APCM Johnsons Branch ?), Kent, 27/5/1958.
(2) out of use by 2/1961; scrapped on site by Ilkeston Metal & Waste Co Ltd, 8/1963.
(3) scrapped after 3/1965, by 3/1966.
(4) scrapped on site by Nottingham Scrap Metal Co Ltd, after 4/1967, by 3/1969.
(5) to Bestwood Colliery, 1/1970.
(6) to Foxfield Railway, Dilhorne, Staffs, 15/2/1970.
(7) to Titanic Steamship Co Ltd, Ellastone, Derbys, 26/8/1977.

(8) to C.F. Booth Ltd, Rotherham, South Yorks, 28/11/1984.
(9) to Booth Roe Metals Ltd, Rotherham, South Yorks, 8/1988.
(10) to Calverton Colliery, 12/1991.

Gauge : 3ft 6in (Underground locomotives).

		4wBEF	Atlas	2445	1945	(a)	(1)
		4wBEF	Atlas	2446	1945	(a)	(1)

(a) ex Wm. Neill Ltd, St Helens, Lancs, c/1949.

(1) scrapped c/1960.

Gauge : 3ft 0in (Underground locomotives).

No.1	164/348	4wWEF	CE	B1874A	1981	New	(1)
No.2	164/349	4wWEF	CE	B1874B	1981	New	(1)
No.3	164/350	4wWEF	CE	B1874C	1981	New	(1)
No.4	164/351	4wWEF	CE	B1874D	1981	New	(1)
No.5	164/352	4wWEF	CE	B1874E	1981	New	(1)
No.6	164/389	4wWEF	CE	B3147	1985	New	(1)

(1) to Harworth Colliery, c1/1992.

Gauge : 2ft 0in (Underground locomotives).

			4wBEF	Atlas		1945	(a)	(1)
			4wBEF	Atlas		1945	(a)	(1)
No.1			4wBEF	Atlas	2454	1945	(b)	(1)
No.2			4wBEF	Atlas	2466	1945	(b)	(1)
			0-6-0DMF	HC	DM811	1953	New	(17)
No.23	20726		0-6-0DMF	HC	DM812	1953	New	(3)
	CHARLES I		0-6-0DMF	HC	DM813	1953	New	(3)
GEDLING No.4	No.22	20725	0-6-0DMF	HC	DM836	1954	New	(3)
No.5			0-6-0DMF	HC	DM837	1954	New	(17)
No.6			0-6-0DMF	HC	DM838	1954	New	(17)
No.7			0-6-0DMF	HC	DM975	1955	New	(17)
No.8			0-6-0DMF	HC	DM1033	1957	New	(17)
No.9			0-6-0DMF	HC	DM1034	1957	New	(17)
1R			4wDMF	RH	425794	1958	New	(17)
			4wDMF	RH	425796	1958	New	(6)
				carried 441424		in error.		
3R			4wDMF	RH	425799	1958	New	(17)
4R	No.4		4wDMF	RH	441424	1960	New	(11)
5R			4wDMF	RH	441425	1960	New	(10)
	3/3327		4wBEF	GB	1960	1943	(c)	(1)
			4wBEF	GB	1961	1943	(c)	(1)
No.10			0-6-0DMF	HC	DM1277	1962	New	(17)
No.11			0-6-0DMF	HC	DM1278	1962	New	(17)
			0-6-0DMF	HC	DM1166	1959	(d)	(4)
			0-6-0DMF	HC	DM863	1956	(e)	(5)
No.12			0-6-0DMF	HC	DM954	1956	(f)	(17)
No.4			0-6-0DMF	HC	DM794	1953	(f)	(17)

No.1		0-6-0DMF	HC	DM953	1956	(g)	(7)
-		4wDMF	RH	268880	1958	(h)	(8)
-		4wDHF	HE	9055	1982	New	(9)
-		4wDHF	HE	9056	1982	New	(9)
164/374		4wBEF	CE	B3100A	1984	New	(12)
164/373		4wBEF	CE	B3100B	1984	New(i)	(12)
164/376	4B	4wBEF	CE	B3155A	1984	New	(19)
164/375		4wBEF	CE	B3155B	1984	New	(12)
297/154	11B	4w-4wBEF	CE	B3322A	1987	New(j)	(14)
297/029	10B	4w-4wBEF	CE	B3322B	1987	New	(15)
	12B	4w-4wBEF	CE	B3322C	1987	New	(13)
-		4wBEF	CE	B3364A	1987	New	(16)
-		4wBEF	CE	B3364B	1987	New	(16)
297/305	14B	4w-4wBEF	CE	B3502A	1989	New	(13)
297/315	15B	4w-4wBEF	CE	B3502B	1989	New	(13)
	5B	4wBEF	CE	B3328	1987	New	(18)

(a) ex Wm. Neill Ltd, St Helens, Lancs, /1949.
(b) ex Bestwood Colliery, c/1955.
(c) ex Calverton Colliery by 3/1958.
(d) ex Calverton Colliery, c/1976 (by 1/1977).
(e) ex Calverton Colliery by 1/1977.
(f) ex Bestwood Colliery c/1972 (by 2/1977).
(g) ex Bestwood Training Centre after 5/1976, by 6/1978.
(h) ex Calverton Colliery after 9/1978, by 9/1979 (never went underground).
(i) to Bentinck Training Centre, 10/1984; returned c/1987 (after 11/6/1985).
(j) to CE, c10/1987; returned c/1987.

(1) scrapped c/1960.
(2) scrapped 4/1973.
(3) to Pye Hill Colliery, c/1970.
(4) to Linby Colliery, c/1977.
(5) scrapped c/1977.
(6) to Llanberis Lake Railway, Llanberis, Gwynedd, 15/7/1977.
(7) scrapped c/1978.
(8) sold or scrapped 3/1979.
(9) to Calverton Colliery, 8/1982.
(10) abandoned underground, /1982.
(11) to Lound Hall Mining Museum, c/1987 (by 14/5/1988).
(12) to Calverton Colliery, c1/1992.
(13) to Harworth Colliery, c1/1992.
(14) to CE, Hatton, Derbys, /1992; then to Harworth Colliery, /1992.
(15) to CE, Hatton, Derbys, /1992; then to Harworth Colliery.
(16) to CE, Hatton, Derbys, c/1992; then to Bilsthorpe Colliery.
(17) abandoned underground on closure of the colliery, 8/11/1991.
(18) to CE, Hatton, Derbys, /1992; then to Bilsthorpe Colliery, /1992.
(19) to CE, Hatton, Derbys, /1992; then to Harworth Colliery, /1993

GILTBROOK DISPOSAL POINT, Giltbrook, Newthorpe   MN25
SK 485449

Opened by MFP c1943 (by 1/1944); CLOSED 1946.

This disposal point was located on part of the site of Digby Colliery. It is believed to have used the former connection to the LNER at Digby Sidings, west of Awsworth Viaduct (see entry for B. A. Collieries Ltd). The disposal point consisted only of a tipping dock enabling lorries to load railway wagons. The loco shed was located south west of the Nottingham to Eastwood road.

Gauge : 4ft 8½in.

5032	0-6-0ST	IC	HE	2881	1943	(a)	(1)
75194	0-6-0ST	IC	RSHN	7144	1944	(b)	(2)
71494	0-6-0ST	IC	HC	1770	1944	(c)	(3)

(a)   New, or ex ? , on loan from MOS, by 1/1944.
(b)   New, or ex WD, Donnington, Salop, /1944
(c)   ex WD, 71494, (at Barby, Northants ?), after 9/1944, by 1/1946 (when spares ordered by MFP).

(1)   to Port of London Authority Royal Docks, London, loan from MOS, by 2/1944.
(2)   to Heanor Disposal Point, Derbys, by 3/1946.
(3)   to Heanor Disposal Point, or Shipley Collieries, Derbys, by 10/1946.

HARWORTH COKING PLANT, Bircotes   BN26
ex Barber, Walker & Co Ltd   SK 627911

EM(C) from 1/1/1947; CLOSED c1962.

Located on the south side of HARWORTH COLLIERY (which see). Shunting locomotives were hired from c1952 until c1958. At other times, colliery locomotives are presumed to have been used.

Gauge : 4ft 8½in (Shunting locomotives).

		78050	0-6-0ST	IC	HC	1639	1929	(a)	(7)
No.11			0-4-0ST	OC	AE	1830	1919	(b)	(1)
		77651	0-6-0ST	IC	MW	2004	1921	(c)	(2)
	AJAX	91126	0-4-0ST	OC	HL	3319	1918	(d)	(3)
	I.C.L.36		0-4-0ST	OC	P	851	1901	(e)	(4)
	BRAMLEY No.6		0-6-0ST	OC	HE	1644	1929	(f)	(9)
6	SPEY		0-4-0ST	OC	HL	3652	1927	(g)	(5)
3	TAME		0-4-0T	OC	AB	1615	1918	(h)	(6)
			0-4-0DE		YE	2682	1958	(i)	(8)

(a)   ex Thos. W. Ward Ltd, Templeborough Works, Sheffield, c/1952; to Thos. W. Ward Ltd, Templeborough by 29/5/1953; returned after 7/1955 (by 21/4/1957)
(b)   ex Thos. W. Ward Ltd, Templeborough, /1953 (after 29/5/1953); to Thos. W. Ward Ltd, Templeborough, after 1/8/1954, by 17/10/1954, returned by 9/7/1955.
(d)   ex Thos. W. Ward Ltd, Templeborough, by 17/10/1954.
(c)   ex Thos. W. Ward Ltd, Templeborough, by 5/1955.
(e)   ex International Combustion Ltd, Derby, c1/1956.

(f) ex Thos. W. Ward Ltd, Grays, Essex, by 9/1958
(g) ex W. H. Arnott Young & Co Ltd, Bilston, Staffs, c1/1957.
(h) ex W. H. Arnott Young & Co Ltd, Bilston, Staffs, 11/1957.
(i) ex Whitwell Colliery, Derbys, demonstation by YE, 11/3/1958.

(1) to Thos. W. Ward Ltd, Templeborough, South Yorks, c8/1955.
(2) to Thos. W. Ward Ltd, Templeborough, South Yorks, c7/1955 (after 9/7/1955)
(3) to Thos. W. Ward Ltd, Templeborough, South Yorks, after 17/10/1954, by 9/7/1955.
(4) scrapped after 4/1956, by 4/1957.
(5) to W. H. Arnott Young & Co Ltd, Bilston, Staffs, 11/1957.
(6) to W. H. Arnott Young & Co Ltd, Bilston, Staffs, 9/1958.
(7) to Thos. W. Ward Ltd, Templeborough, South Yorks, c/1958 (after 18/5/1958).
(8) to S Taylor, Frith & Co Ltd, Dove Holes, Derbys, demonstration by YE, 17/3/1958.
(9) to Thos. W. Ward Ltd, after 9/1958

Gauge : 4ft 8½in (Coke Oven Locomotive).

| | | 0-4-0WE | GB | 1364 | 1935 | (a) | Scr c/1965 |

(a) ex Barber, Walker & Co Ltd, 1/1/1947.

HARWORTH COLLIERY, Bircotes   BN27
ex Barber, Walker & Co Ltd   SK 627913

EM3 from 1/1/1947; NNT from 26/3/1967; NTS from 1/8/1985; NTG from 1/4/1990; MG from 1/9/1993.; **to RJB Mining (UK) Ltd** from 30/12/1994.

Sidings ran for 1 mile on the north side of BR at the point where the branches from Ranskill and Tickhill met, 4 miles south east of Tickhill, to serve the colliery and adjacent coking plant. Use of standard gauge locomotives ceased in 1983. By this time the branch from Ranskill had closed. Locomotives were used underground throughout the NCB period. The planned installation of an OHW electric system in 1992 did not proceed.

Gauge : 4ft 8½in.

No.4		0-4-0ST	OC	HC	476	1897		
		reb	HC			1905	(a)	(2)
No.1		0-6-0WT	OC	Hohen	3283	1914	(a)	(4)
	HARWORTH No.2	0-4-0ST	OC	HC	1397	1919	(a)	(1)
(No.3)		0-6-0T	OC	AB	1649	1919	(a)	(6)
	HARWORTH No.2 (WELBECK No.8)	0-4-0ST	OC	P	2110	1950	(b)	(8)
	-	0-4-0DE		RH	423657	1958	(c)	(3)
10	HARWORTH No.1	0-6-0ST	OC	YE	2522	1952	(d)	(7)
	-	4wDM		RH	299107	1950	(e)	(5)
D14	28533	4wDH		TH	178V	1967	New	(9)
D12	70491	4wDH		TH	174V	1966	(f)	(10)

(a) ex Barber, Walker & Co Ltd, with site, 1/1/1947.
(b) ex Welbeck Colliery, after 18/5/1958, by 16/5/1959.
(c) ex RH, Lincoln, hire, 27/5/1960. (Earlier demonstrated at Staveley Iron & Chemical Co Ltd, Staveley, Derbys, during 1958).
(d) ex Appleby-Frodingham Steel Co Ltd, Scunthorpe, Lincs, /1961 (after 25/2/1961).

(e) ex RH, Grantham, Lincs, hire, 22/9/1964; returned (10/1964?); ex RH, Grantham, hire, 17/9/1965.
(f) ex Thoresby Colliery, 1/1972.

(1) dismantled by 4/1957, scrapped on site (by Leeds firm ?) after 5/1959, by 8/1959.
(2) scrapped on site (by Leeds firm ?) after 5/1959, by 8/1959.
(3) returned to RH, Lincoln, 11/8/1960 (later to British Sugar Corporation Ltd, Colwick, loan, 25/9/1960).
(4) scrapped on site by Thos. W. Ward Ltd, 12/1963.
(5) returned to RH, Grantham, Lincs, c11/1964.
(6) scrapped 10/1966.
(7) to Teversal Colliery, 10/1967.
(8) to Hon. John Gretton, Market Overton, Rutland, 4/1973.
(9) to Clipstone Colliery, 19/4/1983.
(10) to Sutton Colliery, between 3/1983 and 11/1983

Gauge : 4ft 8½in (locomotive stored here pending preservation).

69523		0-6-2T	IC	NBH	22600	1921	(a)	(1)

(a) ex BR 10/1963.

(1) to Keighley & Worth Valley Railway, Haworth, West Yorks, 3/1965.

Gauge : 2ft 0in. (pleasure line for 1987 colliery open day).

No.4		4wBEF	CE	B2933	1981		
		reb	CE	B3393B	1987	(a)	(1)

(a) ex CE, Hatton, Derbys, 3/1987 (earlier at Tilmanstone Colliery, Kent).

(1) to CE, Hatton, Derbys, 8/1987 (thence to Betteshanger Colliery, Kent).

Gauge : 3ft 0in (Underground locomotives).

No.1	164/348	4wWEF	CE	B1874A	1981	(a)	(1)
No.2	164/349	4wWEF	CE	B1874B	1981	(a)	(1)
No.3	164/350	4wWEF	CE	B1874C	1981	(a)	(1)
No.4	164/351	4wWEF	CE	B1874D	1981	(a)	(1)
No.5	164/352	4wWEF	CE	B1874E	1981	(a)	(1)
	164/389	4wWEF	CE	B3147	1985	(a)	(1)

(a) ex Gedling Colliery, c1/1992.

(1) to CE, Hatton, Derbys, 5/1992.

Gauge : 2ft 6in.

	-	4wBEF	MV		1934	(a)	(2)
	-	4wBEF	MV		1934	(a)	(2)
	-	4wBEF	MV		1934	(a)	(2)
No.1	820/32099	0-6-0DMF	HC	DM724	1949	New	(9)

No.2	820/32100		0-6-0DMF	HC DM725 1949	New	(9)
No.3	820/32101		0-6-0DMF	HC DM726 1949	New	(9)
	-		4wDMF	RH 268858 1949	(b)	(1)
	-		4wDMF	RH 268859 1949	(b)	(1)
	-		4wDMF	RH 268863 1949	(c)	(1)
No.4			4wDMF	RH 268875 1952	New	(1)
No.6	820/34204		0-6-0DMF	HC DM1309 1963	New	(9)
No.4	820/32102	PHILLIP	0-6-0DMF	HC DM727 1949	(d)	(9)
No.5	820/32103		0-6-0DMF	HC DM729 1949	(d)	(9)
8	820/32105		4wDHF	HE 7385 1976	New	(6)
No.7	820/32104		4wDHF	HE 7449 1976	New	(5)
	-		4wDHF	CE B1530 1977	(e)	(9)
No.1			4wBEF	CE B1831A 1979	New	
			reb	CE B3290 1986		(9)
No.2			4wBEF	CE B1831B 1979	New	(9)
	-		0-6-0DMF	HE 8848 1981		
				HC DM1448 1981	New	(9)
	-		0-6-0DMF	HE 8849 1982		
				HC DM1449 1982	New	(9)
	-		0-6-0DMF	HE 8850 1982		
				HC DM1450 1982	New	(9)
	-		4wBEF	WR L3032F 1984		
				BGB 18/4/001 1984	New	(3)
	-		4w-4wBEF	WR L5004F 1985		
				BGB 50/10/001 1985	New (f)	(4)
	-		4wBEF	CE B3157A 1984		
			reb	CE B3570 1989	New(g)	(9)
	-		4wBEF	CE B3157B 1984		
			reb	CE B3532 1988	New (h)	(9)
	-		4wBEF	CE B3634A 1990	New	(9)
	-		4wBEF	CE B3634B 1990	New	(9)
	-		4w-4wBEF	CE B3689A 1991	New	(9)
	-		4w-4wBEF	CE B3689B 1991	New (m)	(9)
	-		4w-4wBEF	CE B3689C 1991	New	(9)
	-		4wBEF	CE B3410 1988	New	(9)
	-		4wBEF	CE B3411 1988	New	(9)
	-		4w-4wBEF	CE B3800A 1991	New	(9)
	-		4w-4wBEF	CE B3800B 1991	New	(9)
	-		4w-4wBEF	CE B3800C 1991	New	(9)
	15/10		4wBEF	RSHD 8289 1961		
				EE 3147 1961	(j)	(7)
	15/20		4wBEF	EE 3768 1966	(j)	(9)
10B	297/029		4w-4wBEF	CE B3322B 1987		
			reb	CE B3840 1992	(k)	(9)
12B			4w-4wBEF	CE B3322C 1987	(l)	
			reb	CE B3859 1992		(9)
14B	297/305		4w-4wBEF	CE B3502A 1989	(l)	(9)
15B	297/315		4w-4wBEF	CE B3502B 1989	(l)	
			reb	CE B3861 1992		(9)
11B	297/154		4w-4wBEF	CE B3322A 1987		
			reb	CE B3853 1992	(k)	(9)
			4wBEF	CE B3155A 1984		
			reb	CE B3904 1992	(n)	(9)

PL1		4wBEF	CE		(o)	(9)
PL2		4wBEF	CE		(o)	(9)
-		0-6-0DMF	HC DM1286	1982	(p)	(9)
-		4wBEF	EE 2083	1955		
			Bg 3435	1955	(q)	(9)
-		4wBEF	EE 2301	1956		
			Bg 3437	1956	(q)	(9)
-		4wBEF	EE 2521	1957		
			RSHN 7963	1957	(q)	(9)
-		4wBEF	#		(q)	(9)
-		4wBEF	#		(q)	(9)
-		4wBEF	CE B3649A	1990	(r)	(8)
-		4wBEF	CE B3649B	1990	(r)	(8)

\# Locos are two of : EE 2086/Bg 3434/1955; EE 2300/Bg 3436/1956; EE 2522/RSHN 7964/1958.

(a) ex Barber, Walker & Co Ltd, with site, 1/1/1947 (if then still extant).
(b) ex Welbeck Colliery, /1949.
(c) ex Sherwood Colliery, /1949.
(d) ex Denby Hall Colliery, Derbys, c/1967.
(e) ex Swadlincote Test Site, Derbys, c/1979.
(f) ex Mining Exhibition at National Exhibition Centre, Birmingham, 6/1985.
(g) to CE, /1989; returned /1989.
(h) to CE, /1988; returned 11/1988.
(j) ex Lea Hall Colliery, Staffs. 2/8/1991.
(k) ex CE, /1992 (earlier at Gedling Colliery).
(l) ex Gedling Colliery, c1/1992.
(m) to CE, 10/1992; returned /1993.
(n) ex Gedling Colliery, via CE, /1993.
(o) ex Cotgrave Colliery, c6/1993.
(p) ex Lound Hall Training Centre (for spares), 4/1994.
(q) ex Cotgrave Colliery, c9/1993.
(r) ex Western Area, /1994.

(1) to Blidworth Colliery, 10/1953.
(2) sold or scrapped by 10/1978 (possibly before 1/1/1947).
(3) to Asfordby Colliery, Leics, c/1991.
(4) to BGB, Ilkeston, Derbys, /1990 (thence to Lound Hall Training Centre).
(5) to Bevercotes Training Centre, /1992.
(6) to Lound Hall Training Centre, c/1992 (by 6/1/1993).
(7) to Big Pit Mining Museum, Blaenavon, Gwent, /1994 (by 6/1994).
(8) to North Yorks Area, 7/1994.
(9) to RJB Mining (UK) Ltd, with site, 30/12/1994.

HIGH PARK COLLIERY, Moor Green   LN28
ex Barber, Walker & Co Ltd   SK 487486

EM5 from 1/1/1947; Coal wound at MOOR GREEN by /1947; merged with MOOR GREEN c1950 and rail raffic ceased.

See MOOR GREEN COLLIERY.

HUCKNALL No.1 COLLIERY, Hucknall   NN29
ex Sherwood Colliery Co Ltd   SK 527481

EM6 from 1/1/1947; Merged with No.2 and rail traffic ceased 1950. CLOSED 1958.

The colliery was served by a branch which curved to the south west from the west side of the ex LMS line, 1¼ miles south of Hucknall Byron station and then ran north west for 1½ miles. There were two ex LNE connections, one a north to west curve ½ mile south of Hucknall Central Station and the other a connection from Butlers Hill station to a point west of the LMS exchange sidings. All standard gauge track had been lifted by 8/1951. The colliery surface was used as a site for an NCB timber impregnation plant, for some years from the late 1950s, with limited narrow gauge track. Locomotives were not used underground. **Hucknall Training Centre** (which see) had a narrow gauge surface line on this site from 1967.

Gauge : 4ft 8½in.

SHERWOOD No.2	0-6-0ST	IC	MW	147	1865	(a)	(1)
HUCKNALL TORKARD COLLIERIES							
(SHERWOOD No.4)	0-6-0ST	OC	MW	1284	1894	(a)	(2)
SHERWOOD No.3	0-6-0ST	IC	MW	1440	1899	(b)	(3)

(a) ex Sherwood Colliery Co Ltd, with site, 1/1/1947.
(b) ex Hucknall No.2 Colliery, by /1950.

(1) to Hucknall No.2 Colliery, /1947.
(2) to Linby Colliery, /1950.
(3) to Hucknall No.2 Colliery, 11/1950.

HUCKNALL No.2 COLLIERY (later HUCKNALL COLLIERY), Hucknall   NN30
ex Sherwood Colliery Co Ltd   SK 540490

EM6 from 1/1/1947; SNT from 26/3/1967; NTS from 1/8/1985; CLOSED 31/10/1986.

Sidings between and connected to each of the ex LNER & LMSR lines, south of Hucknall Town and Byron stations served the colliery. Use of standard gauge locomotives ceased from 1984. Locomotives were used underground from 1961.

Gauge : 4ft 8½in.

	SHERWOOD No.3	0-6-0ST	IC	MW	1440	1899	(a)	(2)
	5	0-4-0ST	OC	P	1584	1921	(b)	(3)
	SHERWOOD No.2	0-6-0ST	IC	MW	147	1865	(c)	(1)
(No.8)		0-4-0ST	OC	HC	1797	1947	New	(d)	(5)
		0-4-0DM		RH	375714	1955	New		(4)
(No.5)		4wVBT	VCG	S	9576	1954	(e)		(6)
	CHARLES	4wDH		TH	147V	1964	New		(7)
D2299	DIANA	0-6-0DM		RSHD	8158	1960			
				DC	2680	1960	(f)		(8)
LO26	IVOR	0-4-0DH		HE	5623	1960	(g)		(9)

Note: S 10165 may have been here in 1964, see entry for Cotgrave Colliery.

(a) ex Sherwood Colliery Co Ltd, with site, 1/1/1947; to Hucknall No.1 Colliery by /1950; returned, 11/1950; to Bestwood Colliery, /1951; returned, /1951.
(b) ex Sherwood Colliery Co Ltd, with site, 1/1/1947; to Babbington Colliery by 3/1951; returned by 9/1952.
(c) ex Hucknall No.1 Colliery, /1947.
(d) ordered by B.A. Collieries Ltd for Bestwood Colliery, but delivered here, New, 4/1947.
(e) ex Babbington Colliery after 12/1963, by 9/1964.
(f) ex Bestwood Colliery, 7/8/1970; to Calverton Colliery after 3/1978, by 8/1978; returned 23/8/1978.
(g) ex Newstead Colliery, 30/1/1984.

(1) scrapped by 9/1952.
(2) to Linby Colliery after 7/6/1953, by 11/1953.
(3) scrapped after 12/7/1954, by 9/1955.
(4) to Gedling Colliery after 12/1963, by 7/1964.
(5) to Linby Colliery after 3/1965, by 3/1966.
(6) out of use by 2/1968; scrapped after 11/1969, by 3/1970.
(7) scrapped on site by Raynor Plant Ltd, after 1/10/1982, by 1/1984.
(8) to C. F. Booth Ltd., Rotherham, South Yorks, 2/1984.
(9) to C. F. Booth Ltd., Rotherham, South Yorks, 30/10/1986.

Gauge : 2ft 6in (Surface locomotives).

Note : two of the RH locos from the underground stock (changed frequently) were used on the surface from 1963 until c1967.

Gauge : 2ft 6in (Underground locomotives).

No.1		4wDMF	RH 480678	1961	New	(6)
No.2		4wDMF	RH 480679	1961	New	(11)
No.3		4wDMF	RH 480680	1963	New	(7)
No.4	275/106	4wDMF	RH 480681	1963	New	(8)
H1	164/148	0-6-0DMF	HC DM1304	1963	New	(1)
H5		0-6-0DMF	HC DM1315	1963	New	(2)
H4		0-6-0DMF	HC DM1327	1964	New	(3)
HT3		0-6-0DMF	HE 7372	1973	New	(4)
HT4		0-6-0DMF	HE 7479	1976	New	(5)
No.5	No.6 164/19	4wDHF	HE 8835	1978	New	(9)
No.6	No.5 164/202	4wDHF	HE 8912	1978	New	(10)
No.7	164/203	4wDHF	HE 8913	1979	New	(10)
No.8	164/204	4wDHF	HE 8914	1979	New	(10)

(1) to Cotgrave Colliery, /1963.
(2) to Cotgrave Colliery, 11/1970.
(3) to Cotgrave Colliery, 5/1971.
(4) to Cotgrave Colliery, 12/1976.
(5) to Cotgrave Colliery, 1/1977.
(6) to Midland Railway Trust, c/o Weighbridge Motors, Somercotes, Derbys, c/1986.
(7) to Midland Railway Trust, Butterley, Derbys, 20/12/1986.
(8) scrapped c/1986.
(9) to Bevercotes Colliery, /1987.
(10) to Cotgrave Colliery, 2/1987.
(11) to Lound Hall Mining Museum, /1987 (by 24/7/1987).

HUCKNALL TRAINING CENTRE, Hucknall

NN31
SK 528480

Opened by EM6 by 1967; CLOSED 1969.

Surface narrow gauge track on the site of HUCKNALL No.1 COLLIERY for training underground loco drivers.

Gauge : 2ft 0in.

-		4wDMF	RH 392147	1956	(a)	(2)
-		4wDMF	RH 441423	1960	(a)	(2)
No.1	HEATHER	4wDMF	RH 425798	1958	(b)	(1)

(a) ex Linby Colliery by 1/1967.
(b) ex Calverton Colliery, c/1967.

(1) to Bestwood Training Centre, between 4/2/1968 and 30/6/1968.
(2) dismantled by 2/1968; sold or scrapped by 6/1970.

Gauge : 2ft 6in.

No.3	4wDMF	RH 441427 1961	(a)	(1)

(a) ex Cotgrave Colliery, c/1967.

(1) to Bestwood Training Centre, c/1968 (after 2/1968).

KIRKBY COLLIERY, Kirkby in Ashfield
ex Butterley Co Ltd

JN32
SK 504572

EM4 from 1/1/1947; SNT from 26/3/1967; CLOSED 7/1968.

Sidings between the BR (ex LMSR) line, ¾ mile north of Kirkby in Ashfield station and the ex LNER line south of Sutton in Ashfield station, served the colliery. The ex LNER line closed shortly before the colliery and in 1972 the ex LMSR main line was re-aligned to pass through the colliery site and eliminate a level crossing on its former route. Locomotives were not used underground.

Gauge : 4ft 8½in.

B9C		0-4-0ST	OC	Butterley		1896	(a)	(3)
B18C		0-6-0ST	IC	HC	591	1901	(a)	(1)
B19C		0-6-0ST	IC	HC	613	1902	(a)	(1)
B20C		0-6-0ST	OC	Butterley		1904	(a)	(2)
30	BUTTERLEY No.30	0-6-0ST	OC	WB	2604	1939	(a)	(5)
31	(75172)	0-6-0ST	IC	WB	2760	1944	(b)	(11)
	-	4wVBT	VCG	S	9398	1950	(c)	(4)
	BONNIE DUNDEE	4wVBT	VCG	S	9397	1950	New	(8)
	PINXTON	0-4-0ST	OC	LE	246	1907	(d)	(7)
33 (SWANWICK COLLIERIES No.4)	0-6-0ST	OC	P		1902	1936	(e)	(11)
32	(ANNESLEY No.1)	0-6-0ST	OC	HC	1649	1931	(f)	(10)
	-	0-4-0DE		RH	412716	1957	(g)	(6)

	EMFOUR 4	0-6-0T	OC	HC	1879	1954	(h)	(9)
	WINDSOR CASTLE	4wVBT	VCG	S	9532	1952	(i)	(8)
	-	0-4-0ST	OC	P	1687	1926	(j)	(12)
No.1	ALAN	0-6-0DM		RSHN	7696	1953	(k)	(13)

(a) ex Butterley Co Ltd, with site, 1/1/1947.
(b) ex Langwith Colliery, Derbys, 8/1947.
(c) ex S or TH, demonstration, by 4/1950.
(d) ex Brookhill Locoshed after 15/5/1955, by 7/8/1955.
(e) ex Swanwick Colliery, Derbys, 9/1957.
(f) ex Annesley Colliery, 9/1957.
(g) ex Glapwell Colliery, Derbys, demonstration by RH, 4/9/1958.
(h) ex Brookhill Locoshed after 8/1959, by 5/1960.
(i) ex Newstead Colliery after 8/1962, by 3/1963.
(j) ex A Winning Colliery, Derbys, after 11/1964, by 3/1965.
(k) ex Calverton Colliery after 4/1967, by 12/1967.

(1) scrapped /1948.
(2) derelict by 4/1950; scrapped 11/1950.
(3) derelict by 4/1950; scrapped after 3/1951, by 8/1952.
(4) returned to S or TH, ex demonstration, after 4/1950.
(5) sold or scrapped after 11/5/1958, by 5/1959.
(6) to RH, Boultham Works, Lincoln, ex demonstration, 21/11/1958.
(7) to Swanwick Colliery, Derbys, /1958 (after 11/5/1958).
(8) scrapped after 9/1965, by 5/1966.
(9) scrapped after 5/1966, by 4/1967.
(10) scrapped on site 3/1967.
(11) scrapped on site after 8/1968, by 2/1969.
(12) scrapped after 2/1969, by 4/1969.
(13) scrapped on site 5/1970.

KIRKBY DISPOSAL POINT, Kirkby in Ashfield   JN32A

Opened by MFP by 1946; CLOSED 1947 or 1948.

Believed located at the south end of Kirkby Colliery sidings, though the recollections on which this belief is based cannot now be checked. It is equally possible that Kirkby was an alternative name for Upper Portland Disposal Point

Gauge : 4ft 8½in.

75168		0-6-0ST	IC	WB	2756	1944	(a)	(1)
75163		0-6-0ST	IC	WB	2751	1944	(b)	(2)

(a) ex WD, by 4/1946 (earlier on loan to Port of London Authority).
(b) ex WD, France /1947.

(1) to Upper Portland Disposal Point, /1947.
(2) to Langwith Colliery, Derbys, c/1948.

LANGTON COLLIERY, Pinxton   KN33
ex Pinxton Collieries Ltd   SK474551
EM4 from 1/1/1947; SNT from 26/3/1967; Merged with **KIRKBY COLLIERY**, 11/1967;

Sidings on the north side of the BR (ex LMSR) branch which ran from east of Pinxton & Selston station to BENTINCK COLLIERY. Also connected to BROOKHILL RAILWAYS (which see) by a line which ran west from Langton to Brookhill and, until 1963, to the LNER at Pinxton South station. A third outlet was provided by a BR (ex LNER) branch which ran west from north west of Kirkby Bentinck station to this and Bentinck collieries. All rail traffic ceased after 1967 merger with Kirkby. The date when NCB locomotives from Brookhill Railways ceased to work to Langton is not known. Locomotives were not used underground.

LINBY COLLIERY, Linby   NN34
ex Linby Colliery Co Ltd   SK 535505
EM6 from 1/1/1947; SNT from 26/3/1967; NTS from 1/1/1985; CLOSED 3/1988.

Served by sidings on the east side of the BR (ex LMSR) line south of Linby station and on the west side of the BR (ex LNER) Leen Valley line. The latter closed in 1968. Locomotives were used underground from 1950.

Gauge : 4ft 8½in.

No.	Name	Wheels	Cyl	Maker	No.	Year	Note	Ref
No.1	POLLY	0-6-0ST	IC	HE	151	1876	(a)	(1)
	KING GEORGE	0-6-0ST	IC	HE	2409	1942	(b)	(6)
	COLONEL	0-6-0ST	OC	HE	577	1892	(c)	(2)
HUCKNALL TORKARD COLLIERIES								
		0-6-0ST	OC	MW	1284	1894	(d)	(3)
	SHERWOOD No.3	0-6-0ST	IC	MW	1440	1899	(e)	(4)
6		0-6-0ST	OC	HL	3606	1924	(f)	(5)
	PETER	0-6-0ST	IC	HE	2853	1943	(g)	(10)
(35)	JACQUELINE 270/004	0-6-0ST	OC	RS	4156	1937	(h)	(7)
	-	0-4-0ST	OC	HC	1797	1947	(i)	(8)
141C	(STEPHEN)	0-6-0DH		TH	141C	1964		
	VANGUARD	built on frame of S					(j)	(14)
D14	DAVID (D3613)	0-6-0DE		Dar		1958	(k)	(9)
D15	SIMON (D3619)	0-6-0DE		Dar		1958	(l)	(11)
(D8)		0-6-0DH		S	10072	1961	(m)	(13)
10160	FENELLA	0-6-0DH		S	10160	1963	(n)	(12)

(a) ex Linby Colliery Co Ltd, with site, 1/1/1947.
(b) ex Linby Colliery Co Ltd, with site, 1/1/1947; to Bestwood Colliery, after 4/1959, by 6/1959; returned after 8/1959, by 1/1960.
(c) ex Babbington Colliery, after /1947, by 5/1950.
(d) ex Hucknall No.1 Colliery, /1950.
(e) ex Hucknall No.2 Colliery, after 7/6/1953, by 11/1953.
(f) ex Holloway Bros. (London) Ltd, Calverton Colliery Railway contract, after 19/7/1952, by 1/12/1952.
(g) ex Bestwood Colliery after 12/1955, by 2/1957; to Babbington Colliery by 4/1957; ex Babbington Colliery, after 4/1957, by 1/6/1957; to Bestwood Central Workshops after 4/1962, by 10/1962; ex Bestwood Colliery after 8/1963, by 5/1964.

(h) ex Appleby-Frodingham Steel Co Ltd, Scunthorpe, Lincs, 4/1961; to Bestwood Central Workshops, 17/8/1961; returned, 4/1962; to Bestwood Central Workshops, after 6/1964, by 3/1965; returned after 3/1965, by 3/1966.
(i) ex Hucknall Colliery, after 3/1965, by 3/1966.
(j) ex Babbington Colliery, after 4/1967, by 4/1968; to Annesley Colliery, after 4/1968, by 7/1968; returned, 5/1969.
(k) ex Bestwood Colliery, after 3/1971, by 9/1971.
(l) ex Bestwood Colliery, after 7/1971, by 8/1971.
(m) ex Moor Green Colliery, 24/11/1975; to BR Toton 19/5/1976; returned after 5/1976, by 6/1976.
(n) ex Pye Hill Colliery, 15/8/1985.

(1) sold /1948; may have remained derelict, ½ mile from the colliery until after 5/7/1952 (per unconfirmed observation).
(2) to Babbington Colliery, by 3/1951.
(3) to ?, for scrap, after 7/1952, by 9/1952.
(4) scrapped, after 11/1953, by 7/1954.
(5) to Bestwood Colliery, after 6/1953, by 5/1954.
(6) to Gedling Colliery, 2/1961.
(7) to Brookhill Locoshed, after 4/1967, by 8/1967.
(8) scrapped on site, after 1/1970, by 3/1970.
(9) to Moor Green Colliery, 11/1971.
(10) scrapped on site, 9/1972.
(11) to Moor Green Colliery, 11/1975.
(12) to Gedling Colliery, 22/4/1988.
(13) to Calverton Colliery, 21/7/1988.
(14) to Booth Roe Metals Ltd, Rotherham, South Yorks, 1/1989 (per A.B. & P.G. Kettle Ltd).

Gauge : 2ft 1in (Underground locomotives).

			4wDMF	HE	4184	1950	New		(7)
4/766		CHATSWORTH HOUSE							
No.2		KESTREL	0-6-0DMF	HC	DM647	1954	New		(14)
		-	0-6-0DMF	HC	DM657	1954	New		(2)
4/1495		COLWICK HALL No.4	0-6-0DMF	HC	DM952	1955	New		(16)
		-	4wDMF	RH	392147	1956	New		(1)
No.7		4/4792	0-6-0DMF	HC	DM1124	1957	New		(13)
No.6		4/4791 SEA EAGLE	0-6-0DMF	HC	DM1125	1958	New		(14)
		-	4wDMF	RH	441423	1960	New		(1)
No.9		164/155	4wDMF	HE	6046	1961	New		(6)
		-	4wDMF	HE	6047	1961	New		(2)
No.11		164/169	4wDMF	HE	6079	1963	New		(6)
No.12		164/152	0-6-0DMF	HC	DM1308	1963	New		(10)
No.12A		164/161	4wDMF	HC	DM1316	1963	New		(16)
No.14		HADDON HALL							
		164/162	0-6-0DMF	HC	DM1331	1964	New		(13)
		-	4wDMF	HC	DM1334	1964	New		(9)
No.15		164/168	4wDMF	HC	DM1335	1964	New		(16)
No.17		164/177	4wDMF	HE	6333	1967	New	(g)	(16)
No.18		164/178	4wDMF	HE	6334	1967	New		(16)
No.8		1/3042	4wDMF	HE	4756	1954	(a)		(11)
No.10		1/3044	4wDMF	HE	4758	1954	(b)		(11)
No.1		275/101	4wDMF	HE	6042	1961	(c)		(3)

No.16	275/102	4wDMF	HE	6043	1961	(c)	(6)
	-	4wDMF	HE	6045	1961	(d)	(3)
	-	0-6-0DMF	HC	DM678	1952	(e)	(8)
No.23	20726	0-6-0DMF	HC	DM812	1953	(f)	(4)
No.4	20775 No.22	0-6-0DMF	HC	DM836	1954	(f)	(4)
No.19	164/188	4wDHF	HE	7089	1973	New	(16)
No.20	164/193	4wDHF	HE	7331	1974	New	(16)
	-	0-6-0DMF	HC	DM1165	1959	(h)	(5)
	-	0-6-0DMF	HC	DM1166	1959	(i)	(7)
No.21		4wDHF	HE	8834	1978	New	(15)
No.23		4wDHF	HE	8915	1979	New	(12)
No.22		4wDHF	HE	8916	1979	New	(16)
No.24		4wDHF	HE	8917	1979	New	(12)
No.5	1/3043	4wDMF	HE	4755	1954	(j)	(16)

(a) ex Bestwood Colliery, 6/1968.
(b) ex Bestwood Colliery, 7/1968.
(c) ex Bestwood Colliery, c/1968.
(d) ex Calverton Colliery, c/1968.
(e) ex Bestwood Colliery, 30/12/1969.
(f) ex Pye Hill Colliery, c/1972.
(g) to Ashington Central Workshops, Northumberland, 3/1978; returned 1/1979.
(h) ex Bestwood Colliery, c/1974.
(i) ex Gedling Colliery, c/1977.
(j) ex Bestwood Colliery, 8/1988.

(1) to Hucknall Training Centre, c1/1967.
(2) sold or scrapped, c/1971.
(3) withdrawn for spares, c/1971 and remains later scrapped (after 22/6/1977).
(4) to HE, 1/7/1974; later at Bestwood Training Centre.
(5) dismantled for spares and remains scrapped, 3/1974.
(6) withdrawn for spares 4/1977 and remains later scrapped, (after 22/6/1977).
(7) scrapped, c/1977 (by 7/1978).
(8) sold or scrapped by /1978.
(9) scrapped, c/1981.
(10) scrapped, c/1987.
(11) to Moseley Industrial Railway Museum, Cheadle, Manchester, 14/6/1988.
(12) to Sutton Manor Colliery, Lancs, 8/1988.
(13) to Calverton Colliery, c8/1988.
(14) to Blidworth Colliery, 10/1988.
(15) to Bickershaw Colliery, Lancs, 2/1988.
(16) abandoned underground on closure of colliery, 3/1988.

LODGE COLLIERY, Eastwood   MN35
ex Ilkeston Collieries Ltd   SK 474454

EM5 from 1/1/1947; Merged with **MOOR GREEN COLLIERY** 1/1960 and surface CLOSED.

Sidings on the north east side of BR, ¾ mile south east of Newthorpe station site. Rope haulage engine used, no known locomotives.

LOUND HALL MINING MUSEUM, Bevercotes   EN36
SK 701731

Opened by NNT in 1968 as part of Lound Hall Area Training Centre and later designated the NCB's NATIONAL MINING MUSEUM; NTS from 1/8/1985; CLOSED 1989 and site used for an extension of the BEVERCOTES locomotive training centre (which see).

No standard gauge rail connection. Locomotives were static exhibits.

Gauge : 4ft 8½in.

THE WELSHMAN	0-6-0ST	IC	MW	1207	1890	(a)	(1)
9	0-6-0ST	OC	YE	2521	1952	(b)	(1)

(a)   ex Gresford Colliery, Denbighs, 16/7/1971.
(b)   ex Clipstone Colliery, after 9/1972, by 9/1973.

(1)   to Chatterley Whitfield Mining Museum, Tunstall, Staffs, c8/1989.

Gauge : 2ft 6in.

No.2	4wDMF	RH	480679	1961	(a)	(1)

(a)   ex Hucknall Colliery, /1987 (by 24/7/1987).

(1)   to Chatterley Whitfield Mining Museum, Tunstall, Staffs, c8/1989.

Gauge : 2ft 4in.

-	4wDM	RH	375347	1954	(a)	(1)

(a)   ex Bevercotes Training Centre, /1976.

(1)   to Chatterley Whitfield Mining Museum, Tunstall, Staffs, c8/1989.

Gauge : 2ft 0in.

4R No.4	4wDMF	RH	441424	1961	(a)	(1)

(a)   ex Gedling Colliery, c/1987 (by 14/5/1988).

(1)   to Chatterley Whitfield Mining Museum, Tunstall, Staffs, c8/1989.

MANSFIELD COLLIERY, Forest Town
ex Bolsover Colliery Co Ltd

GN37
SK 570616

EM3 from 1/1/1947; NNT from 26/3/1967; NTS from 1/1/1985; Colliery CLOSED 3/1988; NTG from 1/4/1990; Washery CLOSED 1990.

The colliery was served by sidings on a loop south of the BR (ex LNER) line 2 miles east of Mansfield Central station. Also served until 7/1967 by a BR (ex LMSR) branch which ran for 1 mile to the colliery from the Mansfield to Southwell line. Locomotives were used underground from before vesting day.

Reference :- "Transactions", Institute of Mining Engineers, 1948 (underground locomotives).

Gauge : 4ft 8½in.

	(THORESBY No.1)	0-4-0ST	OC	HL	3591	1925	(a)	(3)
	DIANA	0-4-0ST	OC	HL	3912	1937	(a)	(4)
	VICTORY	0-4-0ST	OC	P	2092	1947	New (b)	(2)
R1		0-4-0DE		RH	420143	1958	(c)	(1)
D11		4wDH		TH	172V	1966	New (d)	(7)
(D21)		4wDH		TH	113V	1961	(e)	(5)
D10		4wDH		TH	170V	1966	(f)	(6)

(a) ex Bolsover Colliery Co Ltd, with site, 1/1/1947.
(b) to Rufford Colliery, /1947; ex Rufford Colliery, 7/1952 (by 30/8/1952); to Sherwood Colliery 10/1954; returned after 10/1954, by 4/1955.
(c) ex Rufford Colliery, 10/1959
(d) to RFS Ltd, Kilnhurst, South Yorks, repairs, 14/2/1990; returned 9/5/1990.
(e) ex TH, 26/3/1970.
(f) ex Sherwood Colliery, 26/6/1980.

(1) to Rufford Colliery, after 1/1960, by 4/1960.
(2) scrapped, after 1/1967, by 4/1967.
(3) scrapped on site by Thos. W. Ward Ltd, 4/1969.
(4) scrapped on site, after 10/1975, by 3/1976.
(5) to Marple & Gillott Ltd, Sheffield, 1/3/1982.
(6) to Booth Roe Metals Ltd, Rotherham, South Yorks, 21/8/1990.
(7) to Clipstone Colliery, /1991 (by 16/7/1991).

Gauge : 3ft 0in (Underground locomotives).

		-	0-6-0DMF	HE	3328	1946	(a)	(4)
No.17	M2	38103	0-6-0DMF	HE	3329	1946	(a)	(3)
	M3	820/38104	0-6-0DMF	HE	3388	1947	New	(6)
		-	0-4-0DMF	HE	3429	1947	New	(1)
		-	0-6-0DMF	HE	3434	1948	(b)	(4)
	M7	820/38107	0-6-0DMF	HE	3435	1948	(b)	(6)
		-	0-6-0DMF	HE	3535	1948	New	(4)
		-	0-6-0DMF	HE	3521	1948	(c)	(5)
No.15	No.9		0-6-0DMF	HE	3522	1948	(c)	(3)
		-	0-4-0DMF	HE	3332	1945	(d)	(2)
	M10	820/38110	0-6-0DMF	HE	3389	1947	(d)	(6)
	M11	820/38111	0-6-0DMF	HE	3391	1947	(e)	(6)
	M4	820/39509	0-6-0DMF	HE	5629	1959	New	(6)
	M12	820/39510	0-6-0DMF	HE	5630	1959	New	(6)

		4wBEF	CE	B3204A	1985	New	(7)
		4wBEF	CE	B3204B	1985	New	(7)
		4w-4wBEF	CE	B3353A	1987	New	(6)
		4w-4wBEF	CE	B3353B	1987	New	(6)

(a) ex Bolsover Colliery Co Ltd, with site, 1/1/1947.
(b) ex Bolsover Colliery, Derbys, c11/1948.
(c) ex Sherwood Colliery, 10/1951.
(d) ex Bolsover Colliery, Derbys, c/1952.
(e) ex Thoresby Colliery, 7/1952.

(1) to Bolsover Colliery, Derbys, c/1949.
(2) to A.R.C. Motor Co Ltd, Nottingham, 5/1955.
(3) to Thoresby Colliery, 2/7/1969.
(4) abandoned underground by 7/1978.
(5) written off by 7/1978.
(6) abandoned underground after 3/1988.
(7) to Bevercotes Colliery, 23/1/1989.

MANTON COLLIERY, Worksop   CN38
ex Wigan Coal Corporation Ltd   SK 609783

NE1 from 1/1/1947; SYK from 26/3/1967; SYG from 1/4/1990; Production ceased 11/2/1994 and shafts placed on care and maintenance 1994.

Sidings ran west from BR, 2 miles east of Worksop Station, to the colliery (¾ mile). The 3ft 0in gauge surface locomotives were initially used during the sinking of No.4 shaft, hauling dirt in 4 ton capacity tipping wagons to a tip. This shaft was completed in 1948 and whatever use was made of these locomotives thereafter is unknown. Locomotives were used underground on the 2ft 6in gauge from c1960. The 2ft 0in gauge underground locomotives listed here are believed not to have been used and probably did not go underground.

Gauge : 4ft 8½in.

MT/M/20	MANTON	0-6-0ST	IC	WCI		1908	(a)	(4)
MT/M/21	SIEMENS	0-6-0ST	IC	WCI		1912	(a)	(4)
	SULTAN	0-6-0ST	IC	NW	656	1902	(b)	(1)
MT/M/22	ROTHERVALE No.2	0-6-0ST	OC	YE	2241	1929	(c)	(3)
	MANTON No.2	4wVBT	VCG	S	9395	1950	New	(2)
MT/M/23	MANTON No.2	4wVBT	VCG	S	9548	1952	New (d)	(5)
No.20	MANTON 521/71	0-6-0DM		HC	D1121	1958	New	(12)
	DINNINGTON No.3	4wVBT	VCG	S	9526	1951	(e)	(7)
	ROTHERVALE No.7	0-6-0ST	OC	YE	1021	1909	(f)	(6)
(D2327)	521/12	0-6-0DM		RSHD	8186	1961		
				DC	2708	1961	(g)	(8)
No.19	FIRBECK 521/111	0-6-0DM		HC	D1133	1959	(h)	(10)
No.23		0-6-0DM		HC	D1090	1958	(i)	(9)
D2300	No.30 521/62	0-6-0DM		RSHD	8159	1960		
				DC	2681	1960	(j)	(10)
DL4	No.4	0-6-0DM		HC	D1152	1959	(k)	(13)
D2229	No.5 521/52	0-6-0DM		VF	D278	1955		
				DC	2552	1955	(l)	(11)

(a) ex Wigan Coal Corporation Ltd, with site, 1/1/1947.
(b) ex Clockface Colliery, Lancs, /1947.
(c) ex Thurcroft Colliery, South Yorks, /1948.
(d) to Kiveton Park Colliery, South Yorks, after 10/1953, by 4/1954; returned after 4/1954, by 7/1955.
(e) ex Dinnington Colliery, South Yorks, 3/1959.
(f) ex Treeton Colliery, South Yorks, 4/1961.
(g) ex BR, Gateshead. /1969.
(h) ex Firbeck Colliery, after 8/1970, by 11/1970.
(i) ex Dinnington Colliery, South Yorks, 25/2/1978.
(j) ex Shireoaks Colliery, 18/10/1978.
(k) ex Brookhouse Colliery, South Yorks, 3/1983.
(l) ex Brookhouse Colliery, South Yorks, 28/3/1983.

(1) to Chisnall Hall Colliery, Lancs, 1/1948.
(2) to Shireoaks Colliery, by 30/6/1951.
(3) to Thos. W. Ward Ltd, Sheffield, c1/1957 (after 9/7/1956, by 4/1957).
(4) scrapped on site by Thos. W. Ward Ltd, 3/1959.
(5) to Treeton Colliery, South Yorks, 4/1959.
(6) to Maltby Colliery, South Yorks, after 9/1961, by 2/1963.
(7) scrapped after 4/1967, by 4/1968.
(8) to Dinnington Colliery, South Yorks, 9/8/1971.
(9) to Dinnington Colliery, South Yorks, after 2/1978, by 5/1979.
(10) out of use by 12/1983; sold to Hoyland Dismantling Co Ltd, South Yorks, 8/1986.
(11) to South Yorkshire Railway Preservation Society, Meadow Hall, Sheffield, 25/5/1990.
(12) to Midland Railway Centre, Butterley, Derbys, 16/12/1992.
(13) to Booth Roe Metals Ltd, Rotherham, S.Yorks, for scrap, w/e 1/5/1993.

Gauge : 3ft 0in.

		4wDM	RH	200483	1940	(a)	(1)
		4wDM	RH	210489	1941	(a)	(1)
		4wDM	RH	210490	1941	(a)	(1)
		4wDM	RH	248484	1947	New	(1)

(a) ex Wigan Coal Corporation Ltd, with site, 1/1/1947.

(1) scrapped c/1959 (by 2/1961).

Gauge : 2ft 0in (Underground locomotives) (see introductory text)

ML 13	FAITH	0-4-0DMF	HC	DM664	1952	(a)	(1)
15/4/1		4wBEF	GB	2862	1959	(b)	(2)
15/4/2		4wBEF	GB	2863	1959	(b)	(3)

(a) ex Kiveton Park Colliery, South Yorks, c/1953.
(b) ex Steetley Colliery, c/1960 (by /1962).

(1) to Shawcross Colliery, West Yorks, c/1955.
(2) to GB, to be regauged, c/1962 (thence to Church Gresley Colliery, Derbys).
(3) to GB, to be regauged, c/1962 (thence to Rawdon Colliery, Leics).

Gauge : 2ft 6in.

No.1	141/81	4wBEF		Bg	3558	1960		
				MV	1175	1960	New	(4)
No.2	141/82	4wBEF		Bg	3559	1960		
				MV	1176	1960	New	(5)
No.3	141/83	4wBEF		Bg	3560	1962		
				MV	1177	1962	New	(2)
No.4	141/84	4wBEF		Bg	3561	1962		
				AEI	1178	1962	New	(3)
No.5	141/85	4wBEF		Bg	3562	1962		
				AEI	1179	1962	New	(3)
No.6	141/86	4wBEF		CE	B1575A	1978	New	(7)
No.7	141/87	4wBEF		CE	B1575D	1978	New	(9)
No.8	141/88	4wBEF		CE	B1575F	1978	New	(6)
	141/143	4wBEF		CE	B0953.1	1979	New	(9)
	141/142	4wBEF		CE	B0953.2	1979	New (f)	(9)
	141/141	4wBEF		CE	B0953.3	1979	New (f)	(9)
	-	2w-2wBEF		TH	SE110	1980	New	(9)
	390/71	4wDHF		HE	8947	1980	New	(9)
	390/72	4wDHF		HE	8948	1980	New	(9)
	390/73	4wDHF		HE	8949	1980	New	(9)
	390/74	4wDHF		HE	8950	1980	New	(9)
No.35		4wDHF		HE	8951	1981	New	(1)
No.9	141/89	4wBEF		CE	B2959A	1982	New (a)	(9)
No.10	141/90	4wBEF		CE	B2959B	1982	New	(6)
No.36	390/75	4wDHF		HE	8507	1981	(b)	(9)
No.1	524/11	4wBEF		CE	B1574E	1978		
			reb	CE	B3851	1992	(c)	(9)
	524/22	4wBEF		CE	B1574H	1978		
			reb	CE	B3851	1992	(c)	(9)
	-	4w-4wBEF		CE	B3882	1992	New	(9)
	-	4wBEF		CE	B3135B	1984		
			reb	CE	B4005	1993	(d)	(8)
	-	4wBEF		CE	B3518	1988	(e)	(10)
	-	4wBEF		CE	B3615	1990	(e)	(8)

(a) to CE, 2/5/1982; returned, 17/5/1982.
(b) ex Manvers Training Centre, South Yorks, 1/1984.
(c) ex CE, /1992 (earlier Dinnington Colliery, South Yorks).
(d) ex CE, /1994 (earlier Shirebrook Colliery, Derbys).
(e) ex CE, /1993 (earlier Bolsover Colliery, Derbys).
(f) delivered, new, via Williamthorpe Machinery Stores, Derbys.

(1) to Maltby Colliery, South Yorks, 1/1982.
(2) scrapped c/1983.
(3) to E. Nortcliffe Ltd, Sheffield,. 6/6/1983.
(4) sold to J.F. Hatfield Ltd, Mexborough, South Yorks. 28/2/1984.
(5) sold to Walker & Partners, Staveley, Derbys, 12/3/1985.
(6) to CE, /1989 (thence to Brodsworth Colliery, South Yorks).
(7) to CE, /1989 (thence to Silverwood Colliery, South Yorks).
(8) to CE, c/1994.
(9) abandoned underground on closure, /1994.
(10) to CE, /1995 (by 17/6/1995).

MOOR GREEN CENTRAL WORKSHOPS, Eastwood   LN39
(Formerly known as BEGGARLEE or NEWTHORPE SHOPS)   SK476478
ex Barber, Walker & Co Ltd
EM5 from 1/1/1947; EM6 from 3/1966; SNT from 26/3/1967; HQ from 6/1967. CLOSED

The former **BEGGARLEE WORKSHOPS** of Barber, Walker & Co Ltd were developed as an Area Central Workshops by the NCB. See **MOOR GREEN COLLIERY** for details of rail connection. Locomotive repairs ceased c1966.

Gauge : 4ft 8½in.

33		0-6-0ST	IC	HE	3196	1944	(a)	(27)
9		0-4-0ST	OC	HE	637	1895	(b)	(1)
	BUTTERLEY No.35	0-6-0ST	OC	WB	2816	1946	(c)	(3)
25	(B3C)	0-6-0ST	OC	Butterley		1892	(d)	(7)
B14C		0-4-0ST	OC	Butterley		1903	(e)	(2)
16	(BUTTERLEY No.50)	0-4-0ST	OC	WB	2607	1939	(f)	(13)
(4)	21	0-6-0T	IC	K	3501	1891	(g)	(5)
6		0-6-0ST	IC	K	1856	1873	(h)	(4)
B16C		0-4-0ST	OC	P	702	1898	(i)	(6)
41	(DURBAR)	0-6-2ST	IC	BP	# 5623	1912	(j)	(16)
26	MARY	0-6-0ST	IC	HE	1450	1925	(k)	(22)
12		0-4-0ST	OC	AB	1010	1905	(l)	(10)
11		0-4-0ST	OC	HE	1493	1925	(m)	(24)
40	WOODSIDE	0-6-2ST	IC	BP	# 6728	1931	(n)	(8)
15	GEORGE	0-4-0ST	OC	BP	6390	1927	(o)	(9)
37		0-6-0ST	IC	VF	5279	1945	(p)	(11)
(8)	24	0-6-0ST	IC	RWH	1947	1883	(q)	(14)
27	ENTERPRISE	0-6-0ST	IC	HE	1708	1935	(r)	(12)
29		0-4-0ST	OC	P	2056	1944	(s)	(15)
	BEAUMONT	0-4-0ST	OC	AB	972	1904	(t)	(17)
14	GEORGE EDWARD	0-4-0ST	OC	AB	705	1891	(u)	(18)
75137		0-6-0ST	IC	HE	3188	1944	(v)	(19)
38		0-6-0ST	IC	HE	3824	1954	(w)	(20)
18		0-4-0ST	OC	P	2045	1943	(x)	(21)
No.19		0-4-0ST	OC	AB	2366	1955	(y)	(23)
31		0-6-0ST	OC	WB	2817	1946	(z)	(26)
36		0-6-0ST	IC	VF	5286	1945	(aa)	(25)

Notes : other locomotives from the Moor Green Colliery allocation are likely to have been repaired at these Central Workshops.
These locomotives had exchanged worksplates (and tanks) by 1953.

(a)   ex storage for MFP at Watnall, after 6/1947, by 27/7/1947 (see Moor Green Colliery); to 'B' Winning Colliery, Derbys, by 10/1947; ex Moor Green Colliery, after 12/1963, by 5/1964.
(b)   ex Pye Hill Colliery, 4/1949.
(c)   ex Bailey Brook Locoshed, Derbys, after 1/1950, by 25/5/1952.
(d)   ex Bailey Brook Locoshed, Derbys, /1950 (after 1/1950).
(e)   ex Denby Hall Colliery, Derbys, 10/1950.
(f)   ex Denby Hall Colliery, Derbys, after 1/1951, by 25/5/1952; returned after 5/7/1952, by 6/1953; ex Pye Hill Colliery, after 5/1954, by 8/1954.
(g)   ex Moor Green Colliery by 25/5/1952.

(h) ex Moor Green Colliery, after 25/5/1952, by 5/7/1952.
(i) ex Denby Hall Colliery, Derbys, after 25/5/1952.
(j) ex Coppice Colliery, Derbys, after 4/1953, by 6/1953; returned by 9/1953; ex Coppice Colliery, after 3/1956.
(k) ex Coppice Colliery, Derbys, after 4/1953, by 6/1953; to Stanley Colliery, Derbys, after 6/1953, by 5/1954; returned after 8/1960, by 1/1961.
(l) ex Pye Hill Colliery 5/6/1953.
(m) ex Pye Hill Colliery, after 6/1953, by 4/10/1953; to Pye Hill Colliery, by 8/1954; ex Pye Hill Colliery, 2/1961.
(n) ex Coppice Colliery, Derbys, after 6/1953, by 3/1954.
(o) ex Mapperley Colliery, Derbys, after 9/1953, by 8/1954.
(p) ex Moor Green Colliery, after 10/1954, by 9/1/1955.
(q) ex Moor Green Colliery, after 1/1955, by 15/5/1955.
(r) ex Coppice Colliery, Derbys, after 1/1955, by 5/1955.
(s) ex Bailey Brook Loco Shed, Derbys, 18/11/1955.
(t) ex Stanley Colliery, Derbys, 3/1957 or 4/1957.
(u) ex Stanley Colliery, Derbys, after 8/1957, by 2/1958.
(v) ex Bennerley Disposal Point, after 9/1957, by 3/1958.
(w) ex Moor Green Colliery, 2/1958 or 3/1958.
(x) ex Bailey Brook Loco Shed, Derbys, after 8/1959, by 3/11/1959.
(y) ex Pye Hill Colliery, after 8/1960, by 1/1961.
(z) ex Heanor Disposal Point, Derbys, after 2/1961, by 8/1961.
(aa) ex Moor Green Colliery, after 2/1961, by 8/1961; returned there after 8/1962; ex Moor Green Colliery, after 10/1963, by 9/1964.

(1) to Pye Hill Colliery, /1950.
(2) to Pye Hill Colliery, after 21/3/1951, by 9/1952.
(3) to Bailey Brook Locoshed, Derbys, after 5/7/1952, by 3/1953.
(4) cab used in rebuild of Butterley of 1892 loco, remainder scrapped on site, 8/1952.
(5) to Moor Green Colliery, after 5/7/1952, by 6/1953.
(6) to Pye Hill Colliery, after 9/1952, by 25/3/1953.
(7) to Bailey Brook Locoshed, Derbys, after 6/1953, by 12/1953 (fitted with cab of K 1856 and 'reb Beggarlee 1953' plate).
(8) to Coppice Colliery, Derbys, after 3/1954, by 8/1954.
(9) to Mapperley Colliery, Derbys, after 8/1954, by 10/1954.
(10) to Pye Hill Colliery, after 8/1954, by 4/1955.
(11) to Moor Green Colliery, after 9/1/1955, by 4/1955.
(12) to Coppice Colliery, Derbys, after 7/1955, by 8/1955.
(13) to Denby Hall Colliery, Derbys, after 7/8/1955, by 3/1956.
(14) to Moor Green Colliery, after 8/1955, by 3/1956.
(15) to Bailey Brook Loco Shed, Derbys, 14/2/1956.
(16) scrapped (on site ?), /1957.
(17) to Stanley Colliery, Derbys, after 4/1957, by 3/1958.
(18) to Pye Hill Colliery, 2/1958.
(19) to Upper Portland Disposal Point, after 3/1958, by 8/1959.
(20) to Moor Green Colliery, after 3/1958, by 5/1959.
(21) scrapped after 3/11/1959.
(22) to Coppice Colliery, Derbys, after 1/1961, by 2/1961.
(23) to Pye Hill Colliery, 1/1961 or 2/1961.
(24) to Pye Hill Colliery, after 2/1961, by 8/1961.
(25) to Moor Green Colliery, after 9/1964, by 2/1965.
(26) scrapped after 8/1963.
(27) to Ashington Central Workshops, Northumberland, 5/1965.

Gauge : 3ft 6in.

VANGUARD	0-6-0DMF	HC	DM635	1946	(a)	(1)

(a) ex Moor Green Colliery, by 2/1961.

(1) to Moor Green Colliery, c/1964 (after 10/1963).

MOOR GREEN COLLIERY, Eastwood   LN40
ex Barber, Walker & Co Ltd   SK 481480

EM5 from 1/1/1947; EM6 from 3/1966; SNT from 26/3/1967; CLOSED 7/1985.

A branch ran east from the BR (ex LMSR) line, north of Langley Mill station, and was joined by a spur from the BR (ex LNER) line, north of Eastwood station after ½ mile. The section west of this point was the BR Beggarlee branch but was worked by the NCB. The branch continued east to **MOOR GREEN COLLIERY** (2½ miles) where the loco shed and **BEGGARLEE** (later **MOOR GREEN) WORKSHOPS** were located. The NCB line continued east to **HIGH PARK COLLIERY** (3¼ miles), thence south to **WATNALL COLLIERY** (4¾ miles) where connection was made with a BR (ex LMSR) branch which ran north for 1½ miles from east of Watnall station site. The NCB line then ran parallel with this to a landsale depot and a link with the ex LNER line, 1 mile east of Kimberley station. There had also been a branch running south from Beggarlee to a Landsale depot at **HILL TOP** (SK477468) which may have survived until after Vesting Day. Sidings in the fork of the ex LMSR and LNER lines at Langley Mill had formerly served a canal wharf and a loco shed (which later became a wagon works) had been located there. A branch ran north from 1¼ miles east of Langley Mill to **BRINSLEY COLLIERY** (¼ mile) and **SELSTON COLLIERY** (1¼ miles). This branch CLOSED by 1958 except for a short section north of the junction which served a wagon tippler located there to handle rail hauled dirt which was tipped to the west on the site of **PLUMTREE COLLIERY**. The lines east of **MOOR GREEN COLLIERY** CLOSED by 1954, except those in the vicinity of the Watnall LNER exchange sidings which were used by **WATNALL DISPOSAL POINT** (which see). The NCB brick works at Watnall lost its rail connection when the colliery closed but remained in operation into the 1970s. The miners' passenger service being operated at Vesting Day continued for some time during NCB ownership. The Langley Mill to Moor Green line remained in use until c3/1984 when it was shortened back to the dirt tippler and the BR connection was abandoned. Dirt disposal by rail ceased c11/1984 and the remaining railway CLOSED. Locomotives were used underground from pre-vesting day until closure.

Gauge : 4ft 8½in.

6		0-6-0ST	IC	K	1856	1873	(a)	(2)
5		0-6-0ST	IC	K	1996	1874	(a)	(4)
(8)	24	0-6-0ST	IC	RWH	1947	1883	(b)	(11)
(4)	21	0-6-0T	IC	K	3501	1891	(c)	(9)
(3)	20	0-6-0T	IC	K	3520	1893		
			reb	AB		1920	(a)	(5)
(7)	23	0-6-0T	IC	K	3918	1900	(a)	(8)
(75145)	(9) 33	0-6-0ST	IC	HE	3196	1944	(d)	(14)
75045		0-6-0ST	IC	HE	2894	1943	(e)	(1)
-		4wVBT	VCG	S	+		(f)	(3)
36		0-6-0ST	IC	VF	5286	1945	(g)	(19)
37		0-6-0ST	IC	VF	5279	1945	(h)	(12)
38		0-6-0ST	IC	HE	3824	1954	New (i)	(11)

	-	0-6-0DE		BBT	3094	1955	(j)	(6)
	-	0-6-0DE		YE	2635	1957	(k)	(7)
39		0-6-0ST	IC	HE	2866	1943	(l)	(18)
(31) 34		0-6-0ST	IC	HE	2882	1943	(m)*	(10)
D8		0-6-0DH		S	10072	1961	(n)	(20)
D1		0-6-0DE		YE	2605	1955	(o)	(16)
	-	0-6-0DE		RH	448157	1962	(p)	(15)
9		4wDH		S	10141	1962	(q)	(17)
10		4wDH		S	10163	1963	New	(17)
DE6		0-6-0DE		BT	179	1960		
				HC	D1176	1960	(r)	(21)
D11		0-8-0DH		S	10169	1964	New (s)	(24)
D12		0-8-0DH		RR	10178	1964	New	(22)
D13		0-6-0DH		RR	10190	1964	New (t)	(23)
D14	DAVID (D3613)	0-6-0DE		Dar		1958	(u)	(24)
D15	SIMON (D3619)	0-6-0DE		Dar		1958	(v)	(24)
(D16)	ROBIN (D3618)	0-6-0DE		Dar		1958	(w)	(23)

Note: It cannot be established if the locomotive marked * was at Moor Green Central Workshops for part of the period covered. Also some of Moor Green Colliery's long term allocation may have made unrecorded visits to the Central Workshops.

+ Probably 9538 which was the 200 HP S demonstration loco at that time.

(a) ex Barber, Walker & Co Ltd, with site, 1/1/1947.
(b) ex Barber, Walker & Co Ltd, with site, 1/1/1947; to Moor Green Central Workshops after 1/1955, by 15/5/1955; returned after 8/1955, by 3/1956.
(c) ex Barber, Walker & Co Ltd, with site, 1/1/1947; to Moor Green Central Workshops by 25/5/1952; returned after 5/7/1952; to Denby Hall Colliery, Derbys, 6/1953 or 7/1953; returned by 1/1956.
(d) ex 'B' Winning Colliery, Blackwell, Derbys, 10/1947.
(e) ex WD, by 9/1949 (loan).
(f) ex S, (demonstration), c9/1952.
(g) ex Denby Hall Colliery, Derbys, after 8/1952, by 4/1953; to Moor Green Central Workshops, after 2/1961, by 8/1961; returned after 8/1962; to Moor Green Central Workshops, after 10/1963, by 9/1964; returned here after 9/1964, by 2/1965.
(h) ex Denby Hall Colliery, Derbys, after 8/1952, by 4/1953; to Moor Green Central Workshops after 10/1954, by 9/1/1955; returned after 1/1955, by 4/1955; to Coppice Colliery, Derbys, /1962; returned by 31/3/1965.
(i) to Moor Green Central Workshops, 2/1958 or 3/1958; returned after 3/1958, by 5/1959.
(j) ex BBT, Loughborough, Leics (demonstration), 18/7/1956.
(k) ex Baddesley Colliery, Warwicks, demonstration by YE, 29/4/1957.
(l) ex Heanor Disposal Point, Derbys, after 9/1959, by 1/1961.
(m) ex Coppice Colliery, Derbys, after 8/1962, by 10/1962.
(n) ex S or TH (demonstration), 28/2/1963; purchased, 18/3/1963; to BR, Toton, 24/9/1971; returned, 29/9/1971.
(o) ex Coppice Colliery, Derbys, after 3/1963, by 5/1963.
(p) ex Coppice Colliery, Derbys, demonstration by RH, 4/12/1963.
(q) ex TH, 29/7/1963. (or S ?)
(r) ex Coppice Colliery, Derbys, 12/1966; to BR Toton, 5/1970; returned after 28/6/1970.
(s) to BR, Toton (tyre turning), 9/1971; returned, /1971.
(t) to BR, Toton (tyre turning), c11/1977; returned, 4/8/1978.

(u) ex Linby Colliery, 11/1971.
(v) ex Linby Colliery, 11/1975.
(w) ex Cotgrave Colliery, 30/3/1981.

(1)   returned to WD, c/1949.
(2)   to Moor Green Central Workshops for scrap, after 25/5/1952, by 5/7/1952.
(3)   returned to S, after demonstrations, c9/1952.
(4)   scrapped after 6/1953, by 8/1954.
(5)   scrapped after 5/1955, by 8/1955.
(6)   to Coppice Colliery, Derbys, (demonstration), 7/1956.
(7)   to Stanton Ironworks Co Ltd, Ilkeston, Derbys, demonstration by YE, 2/5/1957.
(8)   out of use by 2/1958; scrapped after 3/1960, by 8/1960.
(9)   scrapped after 2/1961, by 8/1961.
(10) to Coppice Colliery, Derbys, after 2/1963, by 4/1963.
(11) to Ellis Metals Ltd, Spondon, Derbys, after 2/1963, by 3/1963.
(12) to Coppice Colliery, Derbys, after 31/3/1963, by 8/1963.
(13) to HE, after 10/1963, by 12/1963 (thence to Coppice Colliery, Derbys).
(14) to Moor Green Central Workshops, after 12/1963, by 5/1964.
(15) to RH, ex demonstration, 14/2/1964.
(16) to Coppice Colliery, Derbys, after 6/1964, by 11/1964.
(17) to Bailey Brook Locoshed, Derbys, after 3/1964, by 5/1964.
(18) to Pye Hill Colliery, after 2/10/1964, by 11/1964.
(19) to New Hucknall Colliery, 3/4/1969.
(20) to Linby Colliery, 24/11/1975.
(21) scrapped on site, after 10/7/1975, by 3/1976.
(22) scrapped on site, c9/1984.
(23) scrapped on site by Vic Berry Ltd, 26/3/1985.
(24) scrapped on site by Vic Berry Ltd, 4/1985.

Locomotives stored here for **MINISTRY OF SUPPLY**:

The following locomotives were brought to the **MOOR GREEN COLLIERY RAILWAY** in 1947 on return from service overseas pending allocation to NCB collieries. It is possible that they were all initially stored at Watnall Colliery and that as many as 17 locomotives were involved, c1946-1947.

Gauge : 4ft 8½in

75145	0-6-0ST	IC	HE	3196	1944	(a)	(1)
75177	0-6-0ST	IC	WB	2765	1944	(a)	(2)
75178	0-6-0ST	IC	WB	2766	1944	(a)	(3)
75120	0-6-0ST	IC	HE	3170	1944	(b)	(4)
75055	0-6-0ST	IC	RSHN	7091	1943	(c)	(6)
71518	0-6-0ST	IC	RSHN	7172	1944	(d)	(5)
75146	0-6-0ST	IC	HE	3197	1944	(e)	(7)

(a) ex WD, France, via Dover, 6/1947 (at Watnall Colliery).
(b) ex WD, France, via Dover, 5/1947 or 6/1947 (at Moor Green Colliery).
(c) ex WD, Belgium, via Harwich, 7/1947 (at Moor Green Colliery & Workshops).
(d) ex WD, France, via Dover, 5/1947 or 7/1947 (at Moor Green Colliery).
(e) ex WD, France, via Dover, 5/1947 (at Moor Green Colliery).

(1) to Moor Green Central Workshops, by 27/7/1947.
(2) to Aberpergwm Colliery, Glam, (or Gwaun Cae Gurwen Disposal Point, per movement order?) 7/1947.
(3) to Park Colliery, Treorchy, Glam, 7/1947.
(4) to Desford Colliery, Leics, (from Watnall), 8/1947.
(5) to Nailstone Colliery, Leics, (from Watnall), 9/1947.
(6) to Hartington Central Workshops, Derbys, 9/1947.
(7) to 'A' Winning Colliery, Blackwell, Derbys 7/1947.

Gauge : 3ft 6in (Underground locomotives).

	PIONEER	0-6-0DMF	HC	DM634	1946 (a)	(3)
	VANGUARD	0-6-0DMF	HC	DM635	1946 (b)	(1)
No.2	FESTIVAL OF BRITAIN	0-6-0DMF	HC	DM732	1950 New	(4)
No.3	FESTIVAL OF BRITAIN	0-6-0DMF	HC	DM733	1950 New	(2)

(a) ex Barber, Walker & Co Ltd, with site, 1/1/1947.
(b) ex Barber, Walker & Co Ltd, with site, 1/1/1947; to Moor Green Central Workshops, by 2/1961; returned c/1964 (after 10/1963).

(1) written off by 7/1978.
(2) to Leeds Industrial Museum, Armley Mills, West Yorks, 18/7/1984.
(3) to Leeds Industrial Museum, Armley Mills, West Yorks, 19/12/1984.
(4) abandoned underground 7/1985.

NEW HUCKNALL COLLIERY, Huthwaite JN41
Ex N.H. & B. Collieries Ltd SK 475585
EM4 from 1/1/1947; SNT from 26/3/1967; CLOSED 2/1982.

Sidings at the end of the BR (ex LMSR) Blackwell branch, which ran east from Westhouses & Blackwell station, to the colliery (4 miles). Also served by an ex LNER spur running north east from BR, 2¼ miles north west of Kirkby Bentinck station. After closure of the ex-LNER main line (after 1966), this spur was used by BR trains which reversed at the colliery to access a BR tip. Locomotives were not used underground. Use of surface locomotives ceased by 1980.

Gauge : 4ft 8½in.

No.1	PORTLAND	0-6-0ST	OC	YE	325	1878	(a)	(4)
	NEW HUCKNALL No.4	0-6-0ST	OC	AE	1490	1905	(a)	(1)
	CARNARVON	0-6-0ST	OC	AE	1423	1901	(b)	(5)
	STIRLING CASTLE	4wVBT	VCG	S	9530	1952	New	(2)
	DEVONSHIRE	0-6-0ST	OC	AE	1419	1900	(c)	(7)
No.1	-	0-6-0ST	OC	HC	736	1905	(d)	(3)
	-	0-6-0ST	OC	HC	796	1907	(e)	(8)
SWANWICK COLLIERIES No.5		0-6-0ST	OC	P	1972	1940	(f)	(9)
	-	4wDH		S	10086	1961	(g)	(6)
36		0-6-0ST	IC	VF	5286	1945	(h)	(10)
	LESLEY (D2132)	0-6-0DM		Sdn		1960	(i)	(11)

(a) ex N.H. & B. Collieries Ltd, with site, 1/1/1947.
(b) ex Teversal Colliery, 25/7/1949.
(c) ex Teversal Colliery, 1/1/1955.
(d) ex Brookhill Colliery Railway, after 6/1953, by 9/1954.
(e) ex 'A' Winning Colliery, Derbys, 4/9/1954.
(f) ex Swanwick Colliery, Derbys, /1961.
(g) ex TH or S (demonstration), 11/1961.
(h) ex Moor Green Colliery, 3/4/1969.
(i) ex Bestwood Colliery, 7/1971.

(1) sold or scrapped after 3/1953 (when noted dismantled), by 10/1953.
(2) to 'B' Winning Colliery, Derbys, 4/9/1954
(3) to HC, after 9/1954, and scrapped there.
(4) scrapped after 3/1956, by 5/1956.
(5) to A Winning Colliery, Derbys, 8/12/1949.
(6) to Haydock Collieries, Lancs, (demonstration) 11/1961.
(7) scrapped on site after 2/1961, by 3/1963.
(8) scrapped on site by Wm. Bush Ltd, 12/1969.
(9) to Nottingham Scrap Metal Co Ltd, Basford, 13/11/1972.
(10) to Nottingham Scrap Metal Co Ltd, Basford, after 26/10/1973, by 1/1975.
(11) to Pye Hill Colliery, after 7/1980, by 3/1982.

NEW SELSTON COLLIERY, Selston   KN42
ex James Oakes & Co.(Riddings Collieries) Ltd   SK 467505

EM5 from 1/1/1947; Merged with PYE HILL COLLIERY, 8/1956.

See PYE HILL COLLIERY.

NEWSTEAD COLLIERY, Newstead   NN43
ex Newstead Colliery Co Ltd   SK 521534

EM4 from 1/1/1947; SNT from 26/3/1967; NTS from 1/1/1985; CLOSED 3/1986.

Sidings between the BR (ex LMSR and ex LNER) lines, north of Newstead stations. Surface locomotives were used between 1952 and 1983 and rail traffic ceased 7/1/1984. A short narrow gauge tramway ran on to a tip to the east. Underground locomotives were used from 1966 until closure.

Gauge : 4ft 8½in.

GLAMIS CASTLE	4wVBT	VCG	S	9531	1952	New	(2)
WINDSOR CASTLE	4wVBT	VCG	S	9532	1952	New	(1)
-	0-4-0DH		HE	5623	1960	(a)	(3)

(a) ex HE, (hire at first, later purchased), after 26/2/1961, by 4/1962

(1) to Kirkby Colliery, after 8/1962, by 3/1963.
(2) scrapped 10/1966.
(3) to Hucknall Coliiery, 30/1/1984.

Gauge : 2ft 3in (Underground locomotives).

148583	0-6-0DMF	HE	6610	1965	New	(1)
147349	0-6-0DMF	HE	6653	1966	New	(1)
95432	0-4-0DMF	HE	4687	1956	(a)	(1)
89431	0-6-0DMF	HE	7370	1974	New	(1)

(a)　ex Sandhole Training Centre, Manchester, 14/8/1971.

(1)　sold or scrapped, after 3/1986.

OAKWOOD GRANGE COLLIERY, Cossall　　　　　　　　　　　　　QN44
ex Oakwood Grange Colliery Co Ltd　　　　　　　　　　　　　　　SK 487423

EM5 from 1/1/1947; Merged with COSSALL 1955.

No rail connection or known locomotives. A very short narrow gauge system was used at the pit top.

OLLERTON COLLIERY, Ollerton　　　　　　　　　　　　　　　　GN45
ex Butterley Co Ltd　　　　　　　　　　　　　　　　　　　　　SK 661677

EM3 from 1/1/1947; NNT from 26/3/1967; NTS from 1/1/1985; NTG from 1/4/1990; CCG from 1/9/1993. Production ceased 18/2/1994.

Sidings extended for 1 mile along the north side of the BR (ex LNER) line, 1 mile east of Ollerton station. Also connected to the northern end of the BR (ex LMSR / LNER Joint) branch from Farnsfield. Traffic via this route ceased from 19/1/1959 and the siding agreement was terminated from 1/7/1959. Extensive use of surface railways for the tipping of dirt east of the colliery was made until the 1960s. A siding at the east end of the site serving the Butterley Co's Brickworks was worked by a colliery locomotive. Use of surface locos ceased 1988. Locomotives were used underground from 1950 onwards.

Gauge : 4ft 8½in.

13		0-6-0ST	OC	Butterley		1900	(a)	(1)
B21C		0-6-0ST	OC	Butterley		1907	(a)	(2)
(B22C)		0-4-0ST	OC	KS	3111	1918	(a)	(3)
	BUTTERLEY No.31	0-6-0ST	OC	WB	2605	1939	(a)	(5)
	BUTTERLEY No.51	0-4-0ST	OC	WB	2619	1940	(a)	(7)
	OLLERTON No.5	0-6-0ST	OC	RSHN	7794	1954	New	(8)
D1	(OLLERTON No.6)	0-6-0DM		HC	D961	1956	New	(9)
No.4		0-4-0ST	OC	RSHN	7675	1951	(b)	(4)
	DAVID	0-4-0DM		JF	22887	1939	(c)	(6)
D8	P.I.42713	0-6-0DH		RR	10257	1966	New	(12)
D15	P/I 47262	0-6-0DH		RR	10262	1967	New	(10)
D21	P.I.47453	0-6-0DH		RR	10270	1967	(d)	(13)
D26		4wDH		RR	10193	1964	(e)	(11)

(a) ex Butterley Co Ltd, with site, 1/1/1947.
(b) ex RSHD, 6/1961; to Clipstone Colliery, after 3/1964, by 28/6/1964; returned after 6/1964, by 7/1964.
(c) ex Thos W. Ward Ltd, Templeborough, Sheffield, /1965.
(d) ex TH, 16/3/1970.
(e) ex TH, 28/7/1972.

(1) derelict by 9/1948: dismantled /1950, some parts used on B21C and remains taken away for scrap 4/1953, possibly by Thos. W. Ward Ltd.
(2) scrapped by Thos W. Ward Ltd, 1/1957.
(3) scrapped, 3/1963, by 23/3/1963.
(4) to Clipstone Colliery, after 7/1964, by 11/1964.
(5) scrapped, after 5/1966, by 3/1967.
(6) to Thos W. Ward Ltd, Templeborough, Sheffield, /1966.
(7) scrapped by Wm. Bush Ltd, Alfreton, Derbys, after 2/1968, by 6/1968.
(8) scrapped 10/1971.
(9) scrapped after 6/1972.
(10) to TH, 26/10/1983.
(11) to Walter Heselwood Ltd, Sheffield, South Yorks, 27/2/1984.
(12) to Booth Roe Metals Ltd, Rotherham, South Yorks, 18/6/1988.
(13) to Rutland Railway Museum, Cottesmore, Leics, 7/12/1991.

Gauge : 2ft 3in (Underground locomotives).

	-	0-4-0DMF		HC DM769	1950	New	(5)
	-	0-4-0DMF		HC DM770	1950	New	(5)
No.2	820/45106	0-4-0DMF		HC DM771	1950	New	(3)
No 4	820/45105	0-4-0DMF		HC DM772	1950	New	(4)
No.1	820/45104	0-4-0DMF		HC DM773	1950	New	(1)
No.3	820/45103	0-4-0DMF		HC DM791	1950	New	(2)
	-	4wBEF		CE B0970A	1977	New	
			reb	CE B3002	1982	(a)	(9)
	-	4wBEF		CE B0970B	1977		
			reb	CE B3056	1983	New	
			reb	CE B3507		(b)	(9)
	-	4wBEF		CE B1801	1978	New	(9)
	-	4wBEF		CE B0985	1977		
			reb	CE B2928	1981	(c)	(9)
	-	4wBEF		CE B3383A	1987	New	(9)
	-	4wBEF		CE B3383B	1987	New	(8)
	-	4w-4wBEF		CE B3762	1991	(d)	(9)
	-	4w-4wBEF		CE B3763	1991	New	(9)
E	821/61126	4wBEF		CE B3251	1986		
			reb	CE B3699	1990	(e)	
			reb	CE B3906/5	1993		(9)
	-	4wBEF		CE B1515	1977	New	
			reb	CE B3124	1985	(f)	(9)
H	821/61161	4w-4wBEF		CE B3252A	1986		
			reb	CE B3873A	1992	(g)	(7)
G	821/61153	4w-4wBEF		CE B3252B	1986		
			reb	CE B3873B	1992	(g)	(6)
A	820/58256	4wBEF		CE B2972A	1982		
			reb	CE B3906/1	1992	(g)	(9)

B	820/58259	4wBEF		CE	B2972B	1982	
			reb	CE	B3906/2	1992	(g)	(9)
C	821/58009	4wBEF		CE	B3111	1984	
			reb	CE	B3906/3	1993	(g)	(9)
D	821/61120	4wBEF		CE	B3250	1986	
			reb	CE	B3906/4	1993	(g)	(9)

(a) to CE, 4/1982; returned, /1982.
(b) to CE, 1/1983; returned, c7/1983; to CE and returned.
(c) ex CE, /1981. (earlier at Blidworth Colliery).
(d) ex CE (New) after display at Powergen plc, High Marnham Power Station, 7/7/1991.
(e) ex Sherwood Colliery, 30/1/1992; to CE, /1992; returned /1993.
(f) to CE, c1/1984; returned /1985.
(g) ex CE, 12/1992; earlier Sherwood Colliery.

(1) to HC, c/1970 (then to Welbeck Colliery).
(2) to HC, 25/3/1971 (then to Welbeck Colliery).
(3) to Welbeck Colliery, 3/1971.
(4) to HC, 4/7/1972 (then to Welbeck Colliery).
(5) written off by 7/1978.
(6) to CE, /1994; then to RJB Mining (UK) Ltd, Stillingfleet Colliery, North Yorks, c/1995.
(7) to CE, 5/1994 (by 19/5/1994); then to Riccall Colliery, North Yorks, 1994.
(8) to CE, /1994 (by 23/9/1994).
(9) abandoned underground on closure, 18/2/1994.

PINXTON COLLIERY, Pinxton (Derbys.) KN46
ex Pinxton Collieries Ltd SK 448545

EM4 from 1/1/1947; Colliery CLOSED 3/1950; Locoshed CLOSED c1953-1956.

See **BROOKHILL COLLIERY & RAILWAY**.

PYE HILL COLLIERY, Jacksdale KN47
ex James Oakes & Co (Riddings Collieries) Ltd SK 443522

EM5 from 1/1/1947; EM6 from 3/1966; SNT from 26/3/1967; CLOSED 9/8/1985.

An NCB branch ran east from the BR (ex LMSR) line, ¼ mile south of Pye Bridge station and, until 1963, from the BR (ex LNER) line, ¼ mile north of Jacksdale Station, to **PYE HILL COLLIERY** (¼ mile) and **NEW SELSTON COLLIERY** (1 mile). Until closure of the ex LNER line, a low bridge over the colliery lines required the use of cut down locomotives. This bridge was removed in 10/1964. The NEW SELSTON line and a branch which ran north west from PYE HILL Colliery to the Riddings Ironworks of Stanton & Staveley Ltd were both lifted after 1960. The latter had seen little traffic since Vesting Day. An earthenware pipe works, which had remained in Oakes hands and was sited north west of Pye Hill Colliery, was also shunted by the NCB locomotives. The underground locomotives deployed here c1970 are believed not to have been used.

Gauge : 4ft 8½in.

3	(9)	0-4-0ST	OC	HE	637	1895	(a)	(5)
No.12		0-4-0ST	OC	AB	1010	1905	(b)	(7)
11	(No.1)	0-4-0ST	OC	HE	1493	1925	(c)	(11)
	RAVEN	0-4-0WT	OC	Johnson	56	1913	(d)	(1)
B14C		0-4-0ST	OC	Butterley		1903	(e)	(2)
5	(B16C)	0-4-0ST	OC	P	702	1898	(f)	(6)
16		0-4-0ST	OC	WB	2607	1939	(g)	(3)
	BEAUMONT	0-4-0ST	OC	AB	972	1904	(h)	(4)
No.19		0-4-0ST	OC	AB	2366	1955	New (j)	(9)
14	GEORGE EDWARD	0-4-0ST	OC	AB	705	1891	(i)	(10)
39		0-6-0ST	IC	HE	2866	1943	(k)	(8)
D2	I'LL TRY	0-4-0DE		RH	395293	1956	(l)	(13)
	JAYNE 164/160	4wDH		TH	137C	1964		
		built on frame of		S			(m)	(16)
D2138		0-6-0DM		Sdn		1960	(n)	(14)
	LESLEY (D2132)	0-6-0DM		Sdn		1960	(o)	(12)
10160	FENELLA	0-6-0DH		S	10160	1963	(p)	(15)

(a) ex James Oakes & Co (Riddings Collieries) Ltd, with site, 1/1/1947; to Moor Green Central Workshops, 4/1949; returned /1950.
(b) ex James Oakes & Co (Riddings Collieries) Ltd, with site, 1/1/1947; to Moor Green Central Workshops, after 4/6/1953; returned, after 8/1954, by 4/1955.
(c) ex James Oakes & Co (Riddings Collieries) Ltd, with site, 1/1/1947; to Moor Green Central Workshops, after 6/1953, by 10/1953; returned, by 8/1954; to Moor Green Central Workshops, 2/1961; returned, after 2/1961, by 8/1961.
(d) ex Sutton Colliery, /1948.
(e) ex Moor Green Central Workshops, after 21/3/1951, by 9/1952.
(f) ex Moor Green Central Workshops, after 9/1952, by 25/3/1953.
(g) ex Denby Hall Colliery, Derbys, 6/1953 or 7/1953.
(h) ex Stanley Colliery, Derbys, after 9/1953, by 5/1954.
(i) ex Moor Green Central Workshops, after 8/1957, by 2/1958.
(j) to Moor Green Central Workshops, after 8/1960, by 1/1961; returned, 2/1961.
(k) ex Moor Green Colliery, after 2/10/1964, by 11/1964.
(l) ex Mapperley Colliery, Derbys, after 4/1965, by 4/1967.
(m) ex Clifton Colliery after 4/1968, by 9/1968.
(n) ex Bestwood Colliery, by 4/1971; to BR, Toton 6/1978; returned, /1978.
(o) ex New Hucknall Colliery, after 7/1980, by 22/3/1982.
(p) ex Cotgrave Colliery, 26/9/1984.

(1) to Cotes Park Colliery, Derbys, c/1948.
(2) scrapped on site by Wm. Bush Ltd, Alfreton, Derbys, 7/1953 (after 7/6/1953).
(3) to Moor Green Central Workshops, after 5/1954, by 8/1954.
(4) to Stanley Colliery, Derbys, after 8/1954, by 1/1955.
(5) scrapped on site by Wm. Bush Ltd, 5/1956.
(6) to Wm. Bush Ltd, Alfreton, Derbys, after 30/3/1956, by 8/1956.
(7) scrapped, after 2/1965, by 6/1965.
(8) to Ashington Central Workshops, Northumberland, 5/1965.
(9) scrapped on site, after 7/1967, by 12/1967.
(10) scrapped on site by Wm. Bush Ltd, 10/1968.
(11) to Midland Railway Society, Shackerstone, Leics, 8/5/1971.
(12) to C.F. Booth Ltd, Rotherham, South Yorks, 27/11/1984.
(13) scrapped on site by Wm. Bush Ltd, 3/1985.

(14) to Midland Railway Trust, Butterley, Derbys, 20/8/1985.
(15) to Linby Colliery, 15/8/1985.
(16) scrapped on site, 10/1985.

Gauge : 2ft 0in (Underground locomotives).

		0-6-0DMF	HC	DM812	1953	(a)	(1)
		0-6-0DMF	HC	DM813	1953	(a)	(2)
		0-6-0DMF	HC	DM836	1954	(a)	(1)

(a) ex Gedling Colliery, c/1970.

(1) to Linby Colliery, c/1972.
(2) to Shireoaks Colliery, c4/1977.

RADFORD COLLIERY, Nottingham   QN48
ex Wollaton Collieries Co Ltd   SK 549410

EM6 from 1/1/1947; CLOSED 4/1965.

Sidings on the east side of BR, ½ mile north of Radford station.

No known locomotives.

RUFFORD COLLIERY, Rainworth   GN49
ex Bolsover Colliery Co Ltd   SK 597604

EM3 from 1/1/1947; NNT from 26/3/1967; NTS from 1/8/1985; NTG from 1/4/1990; CCG from 1/9/1993. CLOSED 26/11/1993.

Sidings between the BR (ex LMS and ex LNER) mineral lines which ran between Clipstone Colliery and Rainworth, 1 mile north of Rufford Colliery Junction (Rainworth). Use of standard gauge locomotives ceased 1988. The 3ft 0in gauge surface locomotive was used in connection with a shaft sinking contract. The use of the 2ft 4in gauge surface locomotive is unknown but was probably in the stockyard. Locomotives were used underground from 1948.

Gauge : 4ft 8½in.

	(RUFFORD No.1)	0-4-0ST	OC	MW	1774	1912	(a)	(1)
	RUFFORD No.2	0-4-0ST	OC	HL	3389	1919	(b)	(5)
2979	(RUFFORD No.3)	0-4-0ST	OC	HE	2407	1941	(c)	(4)
	VICTORY	0-4-0ST	OC	P	2092	1947	New (d)	(2)
No.1	NCB	0-4-0ST	OC	RSHN	7642	1950	New	(6)
9		0-4-0DE		RH	412708	1957	New (e)	(3)
D2	(R1)	0-4-0DE		RH	420143	1958	New (f)	(7)
D3	(R3)	0-4-0DE		RH	425479	1959	New (g)	(8)
D4	(R2)	0-4-0DE		RH	431762	1959	New (h)	(9)
D23	70076	4wDH		RR	10194	1964	(i)	(10)
D24	PLANT No.72241	4wDH		RR	10241	1966		
		reb		TH	247V	1973	(i)	(11)

(a) ex Bolsover Colliery Co Ltd, with site, 1/1/1947.
(b) ex Bolsover Colliery Co Ltd, with site, 1/1/1947; to Thoresby Colliery by 8/1948; returned by 18/4/1949.
(c) purchased by Bolsover Colliery Co Ltd, from Ministry of Supply, ROF Burghfield, Berks, 12/1946; uncertain if loco delivered before 1/1/1947 (Vesting Day), but spares ordered by NCB in 1/1947.
(d) may have been delivered to Mansfield Colliery before coming to Rufford.
(e) ex RH, demonstration, 30/4/1957 (new loco en route to customer).
(f) to Mansfield Colliery, 10/1959; returned, after 1/1960, by 4/1960.
(g) to Shirebrook Colliery, Derbys, 7/1962; returned, after 6/1960, by 12/1964.
(h) to Bevercotes Colliery, 1/1961; returned 2/1962.
(i) ex Sherwood Colliery, after 7/1982, by 10/1983.

(1) to Thoresby Colliery, by 8/1948.
(2) to Mansfield Colliery, after 7/1952, by 31/8/1952.
(3) to Colvilles Ltd, Ravenscraig Steel Works, Motherwell, Lanarks, 9/5/1957.
(4) to Sherwood Colliery after 9/1957, by 8/1958.
(5) dismantled by 15/9/1957; to Clipstone Colliery, for spares, /1958.
(6) to Blidworth Colliery after 2/1961, by 4/1963.
(7) to Marple & Gillott Ltd, Sheffield, 24/2/1982.
(8) scrapped on site by A.B. & P.G. Kettle, 12/1983.
(9) scrapped on site by A.B. & P.G. Kettle, 8/1985.
(10) to British Salt Ltd, Middlewich, Cheshire (per Kettle), 12/1988.
(11) to Booth Roe Metals Ltd, Rotherham, South Yorks, 1/1989.

Gauge : 3ft 0in.

-	4wDM	FH	3468	1950	(a)	(1)
C&M 682	4wDM	FH	3472	1950	(a)	(1)

(a) ex Cementation Co Ltd, Bentley, South Yorks, by 12/1952.

(1) sold or scrapped by /1959.

Gauge : 2ft 4in.

-	4wDM	RH	375347	1954	(a)	(1)

(a) ex Bevercotes Colliery, 4/9/1960.

(1) to Bevercotes Training Centre, by /1976.

Gauge : 2ft 4in (Underground locomotives).

No.12		0-4-0DMF	HC	DM694	1948	New (a)	(7)
No.15		0-6-0DMF	HC	DM864	1953	New	(4)
	820/24688	0-6-0DMF	HC	DM865	1953	New	(11)
No.11		0-6-0DMF	HC	DM869	1955	New	(4)
No.16		0-4-0DMF	HE	3591	1949	(b)	(5)
No.14		0-4-0DMF	HE	3299	1945	(c)	(8)
No.13		0-4-0DMF	HE	3300	1945	(c)	(8)
	-	4wDMF	RH	268859	1949	(d)	(9)
No.17		0-4-0DMF	HC	DM693	1948	(e)	(1)
No.1		0-4-0DMF	RH	370554	1954	New	(10)

No.2		0-4-0DMF	RH	374447	1954	New		(10)
No.3		0-4-0DMF	RH	374448	1954	New		(6)
No.4		0-4-0DMF	RH	374454	1954	New		(10)
No.5		0-4-0DMF	RH	374455	1954	New		(10)
No.6		0-4-0DMF	RH	374458	1954	New		(10)
No.8	820/24683	0-6-0DMF	HC	DM969	1956	New		(3)
No.3	820/24692	0-6-0DMF	HC	DM1011	1957	New		(2)
No.10	820/54943	0-6-0DMF	HC	DM1286	1962	New		(13)
No.8	820/55033 No.4	0-6-0DMF	HC	DM1287	1962	New		(14)
No.7	820/55032	0-6-0DMF	HC	DM1288	1962	New		(15)
No.9	820/55489 No.7	0-6-0DMF	HC	DM1332	1964	New		(16)
No.17	820/55521	0-6-0DMF	HC	DM1333	1964	New		(16)
No.5	820/05979	0-4-0DMF	HB	DM1420	1972	(f)		(12)
No.2	821/50072	4wBEF	CE	B0949/1	1976	New		(19)
No.1	821/50533	4wBEF	CE	B0949/2	1976	New		(19)
No.3	821/50420	4wBEF	CE	B0949/3	1976	New		
		reb	CE	B3490	1988	(g)		(19)
No.4	821/49872	4wBEF	CE	B1842A	1979	New		
		reb	CE	B3369	1987	(h)		(19)
-		4wBEF	CE	B1842B	1979	New		(19)
No.6		4w-4wBEF	CE	B3246	1986	New		(17)
-		4w-4wBEF	CE	B3362A	1987	New		(19)
No.9		4w-4wBEF	CE	B3362B	1987	New		
		reb	CE	B3723	1991	(i)		(19)
No.10		4w-4wBEF	CE	B3363A	1987	New (j)		(17)
No.11		4w-4wBEF	CE	B3363B	1987	New		(17)
-		4w-4wBEF	CE	B3445	1988	New		(17)
-		4w-4wBEF	CE	B3732	1991	New		(15)

(a) to Clipstone Colliery, 1/1952; returned.
(b) ex Bilsthorpe Colliery, 6/1954.
(c) ex Welbeck Colliery, 6/8/1954.
(d) ex Blidworth Colliery, 13/8/1954.
(e) ex Clipstone Colliery, 9/8/1954.
(f) ex Bevercotes Colliery, 16/6/1974.
(g) to CE, /1988; returned, /1988.
(h) to CE, /1987; returned, 1987.
(i) to CE, c/1991; returned, /1991.
(j) to CE, c11/1988; returned, /1989.

(1) to Clipstone Colliery, 13/11/1954.
(2) to Clipstone Colliery, 26/6/1961.
(3) to Clipstone Colliery, by 4/1975.
(4) written off 15/1/1970 and later scrapped.
(5) to Bevercotes Colliery, 23/10/1972.
(6) written off, 15/1/1970; sold or scrapped c/1970.
(7) written off 13/4/1973.
(8) written off 29/10/1974.
(9) written off 29/10/1974, but remained dismantled until at least 14/2/1978.
(10) written off 29/10/1974 and scrapped c/1975.
(11) to Clipstone Colliery, 1/2/1985.
(12) to Bevercotes Colliery, 24/11/1976.
(13) to Bevercotes Colliery, 4/1977.

(14) to Welbeck Colliery, 1/4/1977.
(15) abandoned underground, /1977.
(16) to Welbeck Colliery, 5/1978.
(17) to Ashington National Workshops, Northumberland, 3/1994; then to Tursdale Workshops, Co Durham, 4/1994.
(18) to CE, /1995 (by 17/6/1995).
(19) abandoned underground on closure, 11/1993.

SELSTON COLLIERY, Underwood   LN50
ex Barber, Walker & Co Ltd   SK 467505

EM5 from 1/1/1947; EM6 from 3/1966; SNT from 26/3/1967; Part merged with **MOOR GREEN Colliery** and the remainder with **PYE HILL Colliery**, 3/1968. Rail traffic ceased by 1958.

For rail system see **MOOR GREEN COLLIERY**

SHERWOOD COLLIERY, Mansfield Woodhouse   GN51
ex Sherwood Colliery Co Ltd   SK 536625

EM2 from 1/1/1947; EM3 from 1/7/1949; NNT from 26/3/1967; NTS from 1/8/1985; NTG from 1/4/1990; CLOSED 31/1/1992.

Sidings on the west side of BR (ex LMSR) line, ½ mile south of Mansfield Woodhouse station. No standard gauge locomotives from 1983. The extent of use of underground locomotives c1948-50, is not known. They were more widely used underground from 1982 and in the surface stockyard from 1988 to 1990.

Gauge : 4ft 8½in.

	Name	Type						
	SHERWOOD No.2	0-6-0ST	OC	P	1265	1912	(a)	(1)
	SHERWOOD No.1	0-6-0ST	OC	AB	1638	1922	(a)	(6)
	(SHERWOOD) No.6	0-6-0ST	OC	AB	1861	1925	(a)	(7)
	SHERWOOD No.4	0-6-0ST	OC	P	1678	1927	(a)	(8)
	VICTORY	0-4-0ST	OC	P	2092	1947	(b)	(2)
	-	0-6-0ST	OC	AB	1038	1905	(c)	(3)
	WELBECK No.7	0-6-0ST	OC	HC	1305	1917	(d)	(4)
	(RUFFORD No.3)	0-4-0ST	OC	HE	2407	1941	(e)	(5)
D10		4wDH		TH	170V	1966	New	(10)
D19		4wDH		TH	215V	1970	New	(9)
D24	PLANT No.72241	4wDH		RR	10241	1966		
		reb		TH	247V	1973	(f)	(11)
D23	70076	4wDH		RR	10194	1964	(g)	(11)

(a) ex Sherwood Colliery Co Ltd, with site, 1/1/1947.
(b) ex Mansfield Colliery, 10/1954.
(c) ex Eccles Slag Co Ltd, Scunthorpe, Lincs, after 10/1954, by 4/1955.
(d) ex Welbeck Colliery, after 3/4/1957, by 16/5/1959.
(e) ex Rufford Colliery, after 9/1957, by 8/1958.
(f) ex Thoresby Colliery, 12/12/1978.
(g) ex Thoresby Colliery, 25/4/1979.

(1) to Sheepbridge Coal & Iron Co Ltd, Sheepbridge, Derbys, repairs, by 8/1948 (possibly via Warsop Colliery); returned via Shirebrook Colliery, Derbys, 9/1948; to Warsop Colliery c30/11/1948.
(2) to Mansfield Colliery, after 10/1954, by 4/1955.
(3) sold or scrapped, after 18/8/1957, by 16/5/1959.
(4) out of use by 16/5/1959, scrapped, after 3/1963, by 5/1963.
(5) never used here, scrapped, after 10/1963, by 11/1964.
(6) scrapped, after 5/1966, by 4/1967.
(7) scrapped on site, 5/1968.
(8) scrapped, after 8/1969, by 4/1970.
(9) to Clipstone Colliery, after 9/1979, by 4/1980.
(10) to Mansfield Colliery, 26/6/1980.
(11) to Rufford Colliery, after 7/1982, by 10/1983.

Gauge : 2ft 3in.

		4wBEF	CE	B3428	1988	New	(1)

(1) to Littleton Colliery, Staffs, /1990.

Underground locomotives.
Gauge : 3ft 0in.

		0-6-0DMF	HE	3521	1948	New	(1)
		0-6-0DMF	HE	3522	1948	New	(1)

(1) to Mansfield Colliery, 10/1951,

Gauge : 2ft 3in.

		4wDMF	RH	268863	1949	New	(1)
A	820/58256	4wBEF	CE	B2972A	1982	New	(3)
B	820/58259	4wBEF	CE	B2972B	1982	New	(3)
C	821/58009	4wBEF	CE	B3111	1985	New	(3)
D	821/61120	4wBEF	CE	B3250	1986	New	(3)
E	821/61126	4wBEF	CE	B3251	1986	New	
		reb	CE	B3699	1990	(a)	(2)
F	821/61161	4w-4wBEF	CE	B3252A	1986	New	(3)
G	821/61153	4w-4wBEF	CE	B3252B	1986	New	(3)
H	821/61145	4w-4wBEF	CE	B3252C	1986	New	(4)

(a) to CE, 6/1990; returned, /1991.

(1) to Harworth Colliery, /1949.
(2) to Ollerton Colliery, 31/1/1992.
(3) to CE, /1992; thence to Ollerton Colliery.
(4) to CE, /1992; thence to Bilsthorpe Colliery, /1992.

SHERWOOD ENGINEERING TRAINING CENTRE, Mansfield   GN52

Opened within **SHERWOOD COLLIERY** site at unknown date; NTG from 1/4/1990; CLOSED 1992

Gauge : 1ft 7in.

No.2	-	4wBEF		CE	B1804A	1978	(a)	(1)
	-	4wBEF		CE	B1804B	1978	(b)	(2)
	-	4wBEF		CE	B2278	1980		
			reb	CE	B3494B	1988	(b)	(1)

Note; one of CE B1804A and B1804B was repaired as CE B3494A/1988

(a)   ex Bagworth Colliery, Leics, 5/8/1991.
(b)   ex Bagworth Colliery, Leics, c11/1991.

(1)   to Bevercotes Training Centre, 19/2/1992.
(2)   dismantled for spares, 2/1992.

SHIREOAKS COLLIERY, Shireoaks   CN53
ex Shireoaks Colliery Co Ltd   SK558809

NE1 from 1/1/1947; SYK from 26/3/1967; SYG from 1/4/1990; CLOSED 5/1990.

The colliery was served by sidings on the south side of the BR (ex LNER) line, east of Shireoaks station. A second access was from the BR (ex LMSR) Shireoaks West Curve, east of the colliery. Use of standard gauge locomotives ceased by 8/1982. Locomotives were used underground from 1970 with one also used in the surface stockyard from 1982.

Gauge : 4ft 8½in.

	ALEXANDRA		0-4-0ST	OC	MW		1580	1902	
				reb	MW			1920	(a)	(2)
	FEARLESS		0-4-0ST	OC	HL		3134	1915	
				reb	Adams			1932	(a)	(7)
	DUDDON		0-4-0ST	OC	HL		3261	1917	(b)	(6)
ROF 5 No.8	RFF 55 No.8	0-4-0ST	OC	P		2018	1941	(a)	(9)
	JESSIE		0-4-0ST	OC	MW		1231	1891	(c)	(1)
(RFF 55 No.9)	(STEETLEY)	0-4-0ST	OC	P		2043	1943	(d)	(9)
	MANTON No.2		4wVBT	VCG	S		9395	1950	(e)	(8)
	DINNINGTON No.3	4wVBT	VCG	S		9526	1951	(f)	(3)
	MALTBY No.1		0-4-0ST	OC	HL		3771	1930	(g)	(4)
	BIRLEY No.5		0-4-0ST	OC	P		1454	1917	(h)	(10)
	VICTORY		0-4-0ST	OC	AB		1654	1920	(i)	(5)
No.26	521/61		0-4-0DH		HC	D1343	1965	New (j)	(13)
D2300	No.30 521/62	0-6-0DM		RSHD	8159	1960		
					DC		2681	1960	(k)	(11)
D2607	521/21		0-6-0DM		HE		5656	1960	(l)	(12)
(D2332)	LLOYD		0-6-0DM		RSHD	8191	1961		
					DC		2713	1961	(m)	(15)
No.31	DINNINGTON No.2	0-6-0DM		RSHD	8187	1961		
(D2328)					DC		2709	1961	(n)	(14)

(a) ex Shireoaks Colliery Co Ltd, with site, 1/1/1947.
(b) ex Shireoaks Colliery Co Ltd, with site, 1/1/1947; to Steetley Colliery, after 24/9/1950, by 30/6/1951; returned by 25/10/1953.
(c) ex Steetley Colliery, c/1948.
(d) ex Steetley Colliery by 30/6/1951; to Steetley Colliery, after 10/1951, by 8/1952; returned after 9/1957, by 4/1958.
(e) ex Manton Colliery by 30/6/1951; to Kiveton Park Colliery, South Yorks, after 7/1951, by 4/1952; ex Steetley Colliery after 4/1962, by 4/1963.
(f) ex Dinnington Colliery, South Yorks, after 8/1951, by 29/8/1952.
(g) ex Maltby Colliery, South Yorks, c7/1955.
(h) ex Waleswood Coking Plant, South Yorks, 1/1956.
(i) ex Kiveton Park Colliery, South Yorks, c/1957.
(j) to BR, Doncaster (tyre turning), 11/1980; returned, c11/1980.
(k) ex BR, Allerton, 25/6/1969; to Steetley Colliery 12/9/1974; returned, 18/11/1974.
(l) ex Steetley Colliery, 5/1971; to Steetley Colliery, 8/1971; returned 17/5/1975; to Steetley Colliery, 7/1975; returned, 26/8/1980.
(m) ex Thurcroft Colliery, South Yorks, 29/6/1981.
(n) ex Steetley Colliery, after 8/1981, by 13/4/1982.

(1) sold or scrapped, c/1948.
(2) derelict by 9/1950; scrapped /1951, probably by 30/6/1951.
(3) to Dinnington Colliery, South Yorks, after 4/1953, by 10/1953.
(4) to Nunnery Colliery, South Yorks, 13/4/1956.
(5) to Kiveton Park Colliery, South Yorks, after 4/1958, by 12/1958.
(6) scrapped on site by Marple & Gillott Ltd, 1/1959.
(7) scrapped on site by Marple & Gillott Ltd, /1959.
(8) to Steetley Colliery, after 9/1963, by 3/1964.
(9) scrapped, after 8/1964, by 3/1966.
(10) sold or scrapped, after 4/1967, by 8/1967.
(11) to Manton Colliery, 18/10/1978.
(12) to Steetley Colliery, 16/1/1981.
(13) scrapped on site, 12-15/3/1982.
(14) to Kiveton Park Colliery, South Yorks, 13/5/1982.
(15) to Thurcroft Colliery, South Yorks, 3/9/1982.

Gauge : 2ft 0½in.

	524/64	4wBEF	CE	B2970A	1982	New	(1)

(1) to (Markham Main?) Colliery, South Yorks, /1991.

Gauge : 2ft 0in (Underground locomotives).

No.13	390/12101		0-4-0DMF		HE 3557	1948	(a)	(8)
No.56	390/12778		0-4-0DMF		HE 5597	1961	(b)	(1)
	CHARLES I		0-6-0DMF		HC DM813	1953	(c)	(4)
No.2	524/62		4wBEF		CE B1574A	1978	New	(6)
No.1	524/61 No.4		4wBEF		CE B1574B	1978	New	
				reb	CE B3133	1985	(d)	(2)
No.3	524/63		4wBEF		CE B1574D	1978	New	(7)
No.4	524/65		4wBEF		CE B2970B	1982	New	(9)
No.14	390/12102		0-4-0DMF		HE 3558	1948	(e)	(8)
No.101	No.5 390/HA/M/0630		0-6-0DMF		HC DM630	1948	(f)	(5)

```
       No.6                  4wBEF         CE B3101A  1984  New   (7)
             164/373         4wBEF         CE B3101B  1984  New   (10)
             390/1           0-4-0DMF      HC DM663   1952  (g)   (3)
```

(a) ex Elsecar Colliery, South Yorks, c/1970.
(b) ex Elsecar Colliery, South Yorks, 5/8/1975.
(c) ex Pye Hill Colliery, c4/1977; to Ashington Central Workshops, Northumberland, c/1979; returned, /1980.
(d) to CE, 5/1979; returned, 11/1979.
(e) ex New Stubbin Colliery, South Yorks, 2/8/1979.
(f) ex Manvers Training Centre, South Yorks, c/1983 (after 12/3/1982).
(g) ex Kiveton Park Colliery, South Yorks, 11/1986.

(1) scrapped, /1979.
(2) to CE, 8/1984, (thence to Shirebrook Colliery, Derbys).
(3) to Kiveton Park Colliery, South Yorks, 2/1987.
(4) to E. Nortcliffe Ltd, Rotherham, South Yorks, 9/5/1987.
(5) scrapped on site, c10/1987 (after 29/7/1987).
(6) to CE, 2/1989. (thence to Hatfield Colliery, South Yorks).
(7) to CE, /1989. (thence to Hatfield Colliery, South Yorks).
(8) written off after 5/1990.
(9) to (Markham Main?) Colliery, South Yorks, /1991.
(10) to CE, c/1991. (thence to Maltby Colliery, South Yorks).

SILVERHILL COLLIERY, Teversal   JN54
ex Stanton Ironworks Co Ltd   SK 472617

EM2 from 1/1/1947; EM4 from 1/7/1949; NNT from 26/3/1967; NTS from 1/8/1985; NTG from 1/4/1990; Production ceased 10/1992; CLOSED 1993.

Details of the standard gauge system and locomotives used are set out under the TEVERSAL COLLIERY heading. Teversal usually supplied one locomotive from its stock which was kept in a shed at Silverhill and changed as required. One loco, AE 1976, was dumped out of use here from c1957 and may never have been at Teversal. The use of standard gauge locomotives ceased in 1981. The extent of use of the underground locomotive is not known.

Gauge : 2ft 0in (Underground locomotive).
```
       COCK O'THE NORTH   4wDMF       RH 256268  1947   New    (1)
```

(1) to RH, after 19/6/1956, by 19/7/1956; for repair prior to transfer to 'A' Winning Colliery, Derbys (after 9/1956, by 26/2/1967).

STEETLEY COLLIERY, Worksop   CN55
ex Shireoaks Colliery Co Ltd   SK 553786

NE1 from 1/1/1947; SYK from 26/3/1967; SYG from 1/4/1990; Merged with SHIREOAKS Colliery 3/1983 and surface CLOSED.

Sidings on the west side of the BR (ex LMSR) line, 2 miles north of Whitwell station. The exchange sidings were shared with Steetley Refractories Ltd. Its premises were north of the colliery and the NCB locos were washed out there for several years after Vesting Day under a former arrangement. The underground locomotives here in 1959 and 1978 were not used here and were in store until transferred away.

Gauge : 4ft 8½in.

	JESSIE	0-4-0ST	OC	MW	1231	1891	(a)	(1)
(RFF 55 No.9)	(STEETLEY)	0-4-0ST	OC	P	2043	1943	(b)	(3)
	DUDDON	0-4-0ST	OC	HL	3261	1917	(c)	(4)
	FEARLESS	0-4-0ST	OC	HL	3134	1915	(d)	(2)
	MANTON No.2	4wVBT	VCG	S	9395	1950	(e)	(6)
	MANTON No.2	4wVBT	VCG	S	9548	1952	(f)	(6)
	OUGHTIBRIDGE No.1	0-4-0DE		YE	2652	1957	(g)	(5)
	DINNINGTON No.2	0-4-0ST	OC	HC	862	1909		
	Latterly carried plates			HC	989	1912	(h)	(7)
	-	0-4-0ST	OC	P	2109	1950	(i)	(10)
D2607	521/21	0-6-0DM		HE	5656	1960	(j)	(12)
No.31	DINNINGTON No.2	0-6-0DM		RSHD	8187	1961		
(D2328)				DC	2709	1961	(k)	(11)
	-	0-4-0DH		YE	2805	1960	(l)	(8)
D2300	No.30 521/62	0-6-0DM		RSHD	8159	1960		
				DC	2681	1960	(m)	(9)

(a) ex Shireoaks Colliery Co Ltd, with site, 1/1/1947.
(b) ex Shireoaks Colliery Co Ltd, with site, 1/1/1947; to Shireoaks Colliery, by 30/6/1951; returned after 10/1951, by 8/1952.
(c) ex Shireoaks Colliery, after 24/9/1950, by 30/6/1951.
(d) ex Shireoaks Colliery, after 6/1951, by 8/1952.
(e) ex Kiveton Park Colliery, South Yorks, after 9/1955, by 4/1958; to Shireoaks Colliery, after 4/1962, by 4/1963; returned after 9/1963, by 3/1964.
(f) ex Orgreave Colliery, South Yorks, after 11/1959, by 25/2/1961.
(g) ex Oughtibridge Silica Firebrick Co Ltd, Steetley, by 4/1963 (hire).
(h) ex Dinnington Colliery, South Yorks, after 6/1965, by 3/1966.
(i) ex Thoresby Colliery, 1/1967.
(j) ex Dinnington Colliery, South Yorks, after 9/1968, by 11/1968; to Shireoaks Colliery, 5/1971; returned 8/1971; to Fence Central Workshops, South Yorks, 28/5/1974; returned 30/10/1974; to Shireoaks Colliery, 17/5/1975; returned 7/1975; to Treeton Colliery, South Yorks, 3/12/1975; returned, 12/1975; to BR, Doncaster, South Yorks, 8/1977; returned after 8/1977, by 11/1977; to Shireoaks Colliery, 26/8/1980; returned, 16/1/1981; to Treeton Colliery, South Yorks, for 4 months in /1981; returned.
(k) ex Dinnington Colliery, South Yorks, 4/1973; to BR, Doncaster (tyre turning), 2/2/1977; returned, 10/2/1977.
(l) ex TH, 2/1974 (hire).
(m) ex Shireoaks Colliery, 12/9/1974.

(1) to Shireoaks Colliery, c/1948.
(2) to Shireoaks Colliery, after 6/1951, by 8/1952.
(3) to Shireoaks Colliery, after 9/1957, by 4/1958.
(4) to Shireoaks Colliery, after 6/1951, by 25/10/1953.
(5) to Oughtibridge Silica Firebrick Co Ltd, Steetley, /1963.
(6) sold for scrap, after 4/1967, by 8/1967.
(7) scrapped, after 9/1967, by 4/1968.
(8) to TH, after 4/1974, by 1/1975.
(9) to Shireoaks Colliery, 18/11/1974.
(10) scrapped on site by Walter Heselwood Ltd, after 9/1974, by 7/1975.
(11) to Shireoaks Colliery after 8/1981, by 13/4/1982.
(12) out of use by 8/1983; to Coopers (Metals) Ltd, Sheffield, 12/6/1984.

Gauge : 2ft 0in (Underground locomotives - stored).

		4wBEF	GB	2862	1959	New	(1)
	-	4wBEF	GB	2863	1959	New	(1)
524/21		4wBEF	CE	B1574G	1978	New	(2)
524/22		4wBEF	CE	B1574H	1978	New	(3)

(1) to Manton Colliery, c/1960 (by /1962).
(2) to CE, c/1979 (thence to Swadlincote Test Site, Derbys).
(3) to Thurcroft Colliery, South Yorks, 3/1981.

SUTTON COLLIERY, Sutton in Ashfield JN56
ex N.H. & B. Collieries Ltd SK 584603

EM4 from 1/1/1947; NNT from 26/3/1967; NTS from 1/8/1985; CLOSED 25/8/1989.

Sidings at the end of the BR (ex LMSR) Skegby branch, which ran east from 1 mile south west of Teversal station site to Stoneyford Lane siding (1 mile), served the colliery. Locomotives were used underground from 1982.

Gauge : 4ft 8½in.

	RAVEN	0-4-0WT	OC	Johnson 56	1913	(a)	(1)
MILLER	(ANNESLEY) No.3	0-6-0ST	OC	AB 1132	1907		
		reb	KE*		1921	(b)	(11)
	ANNESLEY No.1	0-6-0ST	OC	HC 1649	1931	(c)	(2)
	-	0-4-0ST	OC	P 1687	1926	(d)	(3)
	CARNARVON	0-6-0ST	OC	AE 1423	1901	(e)	(4)
	DEVONSHIRE	0-6-0ST	OC	AE 1419	1900	(f)	(5)
	BENTINCK No.1	0-4-0ST	OC	HC 576	1900	(g)	(6)
	PROGRESS	0-4-0ST	OC	P 1080	1907	(h)	(7)
No.5		0-6-0ST	OC	AE 1360	1895	(i)	(9)
BC55		0-4-0ST	OC	P 2022	1942	(j)	(12)
	RNCF No.3	0-4-0ST	OC	AE 1976	1925	(k)	(8)
	LO/62/ML	0-4-0DH		HE 6262	1962	New	(13)
	BALMORAL CASTLE	4wVBT	VCG	S 9399	1950	(l)	(10)
D18	117014	4wDH		TH 192V	1968	(m)	(14)
(D28)		4wDH		S 10073	1961	(n)	(15)
D17	101082	4wDH		TH 191V	1968	(o)	(17)

```
        D12    70491              4wDH      TH   174V   1966   (p)      (16)
        103    BRIERLEY  109189   0-6-0DH   S    10157  1963   (q)      (18)
```

* also carried spurious plates 'reb John Nixon & Co, Sutton 1950'. Nixon was the colliery loco fitter.

(a) ex N.H. & B. Collieries Ltd, with site, 1/1/1947.
(b) ex Annesley Colliery, /1947.
(c) ex Annesley Colliery, /1948; to Annesley Colliery, 10/1948; returned by 20/9/1949.
(d) ex 'A' Winning Colliery, Derbys, c9/1948, by 20/9/1949.
(e) ex 'A' Winning Colliery, Derbys, 17/3/1950.
(f) ex Teversal Colliery, after 4/1950, by 12/1950.
(g) ex Bentinck Colliery, after 3/1951, by 7/1951.
(h) ex P.A. Mudd Ltd, Doncaster, South Yorks, after 8/1951, by 10/1952.
(i) ex Pleasley Colliery, Derbys, after 10/1952, by 5/1953.
(j) ex Wm. Bush Ltd, Alfreton, Derbys, after 1/1955, by 4/1955 (earlier Butterley Co Ltd, Derbys).
(k) ex Wm. Bush Ltd, Alfreton, Derbys, 6/1956 (earlier ROF Creekmoor, Dorset).
(l) ex Wingfield Manor Colliery, Derbys, after 10/1964, by 4/1965
(m) ex Teversal Colliery, after 3/1976, by 5/1976; to Teversal Colliery, after 9/1976, by 6/1977; ex Teversal Colliery, 20/10/1981.
(n) ex Teversal Colliery, 8/9/1980.
(o) ex Teversal Colliery, 25/2/1982.
(p) ex Harworth Colliery after 3/1983, by 11/1983.
(q) ex Philadelphia Central Workshops Co. Durham, 13/7/1987.

(1) to Pye Hill Colliery, Derbys, /1948.
(2) to Annesley Colliery, after 10/1948, by 4/1950.
(3) to 'A' Winning Colliery, Blackwell, Derbys, after 9/1949, by 8/1951.
(4) to Teversal Colliery, 3/1950.
(5) to Teversal Colliery after 12/1950, by 8/1951.
(6) to Teversal Colliery, after 8/1951, by 8/1952.
(7) scrapped on site by Wm. Bush Ltd, after 9/1954, by 4/1955.
(8) to Teversal Colliery, after 7/1956, by 18/8/1957.
(9) scrapped, after 7/1961, by 1/1963.
(10) to South Normanton Offices, Derbys, (as stationary boiler), after 4/1965, by 9/1965.
(11) scrapped on site by Thos. W. Ward Ltd, 3/1968.
(12) scrapped on site by Thos. W. Ward Ltd, 3/1970.
(13) sold to R.E. Trem Ltd, of Finningley, South Yorks, 2/1982.
(14) to Clipstone Machinery Stores, after 10/1982, by 10/1983.
(15) to TH, 25/10/1983.
(16) to Booth Roe Metals Ltd, Rotherham, South Yorks, 3/1989.
(17) scrapped on site by A.B. & P.G. Kettle Ltd, 1/1990.
(18) to Calverton Colliery, after 9/1989, by 6/1990.

Gauge : 1ft 10in (Underground locomotives).

```
87127             4wBEF         CE   B0427  1975
            reb   CE            B2926  1982   (a)   (1)
                  4wBEF         CE   B3187  1985   New   (2)
```

(a) ex CE, 3/1982 (earlier Welbeck Colliery).

(1) to CE, /1989 (thence to Annesley Colliery).
(2) to CE, /1990 (thence to Annesley Colliery).

TEVERSAL COLLIERY, Teversal   JN57
ex Stanton Ironworks Co Ltd   SK 475622
EM2 from 1/1/1947; EM4 from 1/7/1949; NNT from 26/3/1967; CLOSED 7/1980.

NCB lines ran north west to **TEVERSAL COLLIERY** (¼ mile) and south east to **SILVERHILL COLLIERY** (½ mile), from the end of the BR (ex LMSR) Butcherwood branch (which in reality was a group of sidings running north west from ¼ mile north of Teversal Station site). There was, until 1968, a second access to the collieries in the form of BR (ex LNER) branches which ran north to TEVERSAL and east to SILVERHILL from Teversal goods station. An NCB workmans train, consisting of an ex-LNWR bogie coach of 1903, ran between platforms at the two collieries until at least 1955. The main locomotive shed was at Teversal with a semi permanent allocation of one locomotive at Silverhill. Changes were, however, too frequent to record thoroughly, hence a combined list is given. Locomotives were not used underground.

Gauge : 4ft 8½in.

		-	0-4-0ST	OC	AE	1341	1890	(a)	(1)
		DEVONSHIRE	0-6-0ST	OC	AE	1419	1900	(b)	(3)
(No.2)		BENTINCK No.1	0-4-0ST	OC	HC	576	1900	(c)	(2)
		CARNARVON	0-6-0ST	OC	AE	1423	1901	(d)	(4)
		CHURCHILL	0-6-0ST	OC	AB	2216	1946	(a)	(9)
(75088)			0-6-0ST	IC	HC	1747	1943	(e)	(6)
75022			0-6-0ST	IC	HE	2871	1943	(e)	(8)
		(RNCF No.3)	0-4-0ST	OC	AE	1976	1925	(f)	(5)
		EMFOUR.1.	0-6-0T	OC	HC	1876	1954	New (g)	(7)
		EMFOUR.5.	0-6-0DM		HC	D1016	1957	(h)	(11)
D1		101082	4wDH		TH	191V	1968	New	(14)
D18		117014	4wDH		TH	192V	1968	New (i)	(13)
		HARWORTH No.1	0-6-0ST	OC	YE	2522	1952	(j)	(10)
(D28)			4wDH		S	10073	1961	(k)	(12)
D27	87451	18458	4wDH		TH	140V	1964	(l)	(15)
D25			4wDH		RR	10195	1964	(m)	(16)

(a) ex Stanton Ironworks Co Ltd, with site, 1/1/1947.
(b) ex Stanton Ironworks Co Ltd, with site, 1/1/1947. to Holwell Ironworks, Leics, for repair, 6/1947; returned after 15/11/1947; to Sutton Colliery after 4/1950, by 12/1950: returned after 12/1950, by 8/1951.
(c) ex Stanton Ironworks Co Ltd, with site, 1/1/1947; (boiler, or possibly the complete locomotive, was reported to be under repair at P.A. Mudd Ltd, Doncaster, on 18/3/1950); to Bentinck Colliery, after 4/1950, by 7/1950; ex Sutton Colliery, after 8/1951, by 25/8/1952.
(d) ex Stanton Ironworks Co Ltd, 1/1/1947; to New Hucknall Colliery, 25/7/1949; ex Sutton Colliery, 3/1950,
(e) ex WD, 5/1947.
(f) ex Sutton Colliery, after 7/1956, by 18/8/1957.
(g) to Pleasley Colliery, Derbys, c6/1957; returned, 8/1957.

(h) ex Swanwick Colliery, Derbys, by 18/8/1957.
(i) to Sutton Colliery, after 3/1976, by 5/1976; returned, after 9/1976, by 6/1977.
(j) ex Harworth Colliery 10/1967.
(k) ex TH, 23/8/1973.
(l) ex Welbeck Colliery, after 3/1976, by 5/1976.
(m) ex Thoresby Colliery, after 22/9/1978, by 8/1979.

(1) to Wm. Bush Ltd, Alfreton, Derbys, by 7/1948.
(2) scrapped by Wm. Bush Ltd, after 9/1954, by 4/1955.
(3) to New Hucknall Colliery, 1/1/1955.
(4) to Pleasley Colliery, Derbys, 9/1956.
(5) scrapped by Birch, 11/1964.
(6) sold for scrap, after 4/1967, by 8/1967.
(7) scrapped by (Booth?) of Rotherham, Yorks (WR), 4/1968
(8) scrapped on site by Booth, 5/1968.
(9) scrapped on site, 5/1972.
(10) scrapped on site, 8/1972.
(11) scrapped by Wm. Bush Ltd, Alfreton, Derbys, after 6/1977, by 6/1978.
(12) to Sutton Colliery, 8/9/1980.
(13) to Sutton Colliery, 20/10/1981.
(14) to Sutton Colliery, 25/2/1982.
(15) to Marple & Gillott Ltd, Attercliffe, Sheffield, 25/2/1982.
(16) to Marple & Gillott Ltd, Attercliffe, Sheffield, 26/2/1982.

THORESBY COLLIERY, Edwinstowe   GN58
ex Bolsover Colliery Co Ltd   SK 636676

EM4 from 1/1/1947; NNT from 26/3/1967; NTS from 1/8/1985; NTG from 1/4/1990; MG from 1/9/1993. **RJB Mining (UK) Ltd** from 30/12/1994.

A BR (ex LNER) branch ran north then east from ¾ mile east of Edwinstowe station, to the colliery (1 mile). There was a rail served smokeless fuel plant (Rexco Ltd) west of the colliery and a tip to the east. Use of standard gauge locomotives ceased by 8/1978. Locomotives were used underground from 1949, the gauge being changed from 2ft 4in to 3ft 0in at that time.

Gauge : 4ft 8½in.

	TOPHARD	0-4-0ST	OC	P	1791	1932	(a)	(4)
	JOHN	0-4-0ST	OC	P	1976	1939	(a)	(7)
	RUFFORD No.2	0-4-0ST	OC	HL	3389	1919	(b)	(1)
	(RUFFORD No.1)	0-4-0ST	OC	MW	1774	1912	(c)	(2)
	-	0-4-0ST	OC	P	2109	1950	New	(3)
D12	70491	4wDH		TH	174V	1966	New	(5)
D16		4wDH		TH	190V	1967	New	(6)
D23		4wDH		RR	10194	1964	(d)	(10)
D24	PLANT No.72241	4wDH		RR	10241	1966		
	Collision damage repaired			TH	247V	1973	(e)	(9)
D25		4wDH		RR	10195	1964	(f)	(8)

(a) ex Bolsover Colliery Co Ltd, with site, 1/1/1947.
(b) ex Rufford Colliery, /1948, after 9/1948

(c) ex Rufford Colliery, by 8/1948.
(d) ex TH, 17/12/1971.
(e) ex TH, 30/12/1971; to TH, 20/3/1973; returned, 23/5/1973.
(f) ex TH, 24/3/1972.

(1) to Rufford Colliery, after 8/1948, by 18/4/1949.
(2) out of use by 4/1950; scrapped, after 3/1951, by 4/1952
(3) to Steetley Colliery, 1/1967.
(4) scrapped on site, 2/1969.
(5) to Harworth Colliery, 1/1972.
(6) to Clipstone Colliery, 24/3/1972.
(7) to Hon. John Gretton, Market Overton, Leics, 12/1972.
(8) to Teversal Colliery, after 22/9/1978, by 8/1979.
(9) to Sherwood Colliery, 12/12/1978.
(10) to Sherwood Colliery, 25/4/1979.

Gauge : 3ft 0in (Underground locomotives).

No.	Works No.		Type	Builder	Works No.	Year	Status	Notes
No.1	71262		0-6-0DMF	HC	DM648	1949	New	(9)
No.2			0-6-0DMF	HC	DM649	1949	New (a)	(2)
No.3			0-6-0DMF	HC	DM650	1949	New	(3)
No.4			0-6-0DMF	HC	DM651	1949	New	(4)
No.5	71266		0-6-0DMF	HC	DM652	1949	New	(9)
No.6			0-6-0DMF	HC	DM653	1949	New	(4)
No.7	71268		0-6-0DMF	HC	DM654	1949	New (b)	(9)
No.9	71270		0-6-0DMF	HE	3390	1947	(c)	(8)
			0-6-0DMF	HE	3391	1947	(c)	(1)
No.8	71269		0-6-0DMF	HE	3392	1947	(c)	(9)
No.11	71878		0-6-0DMF	HC	DM1014	1956	New	(9)
No.10	71724		0-6-0DMF	HC	DM1035	1956	New	(9)
	-		0-4-0DMF	HE	4612	1954	(d)	(6)
No.12			0-6-0DMF	HC	DM1394	1967	New	(5)
No.16			0-6-0DMF	HC	DM1397	1967	New	(7)
No.14	71213		0-6-0DMF	HC	DM1404	1968	New	(9)
No.15	38109	No.9	0-6-0DMF	HE	3522	1948	(e)	(9)
No.17	38103	M2	0-6-0DMF	HE	3329	1946		
		reb	HE	7370	1972	(f)	(9)
No.4	71802		0-6-0DMF	HE	7373	1974	New	(9)
No.6	71803		0-6-0DMF	HE	7413	1974	New	(9)
No.2	71801		0-6-0DMF	HE	7414	1974	New	(9)
No.18	71810		0-6-0DMF	HE	7415	1974	New	(9)
E2	74832		4wBEF	CE	B1504A	1977	New (g)	
		reb	CE	B3156	1984		(11)
E3	74835		4wBEF	CE	B1504B	1977	New (h)	
		reb	CE	B3239	1985		(11)
E1	74813		4wBEF	CE	B1504C	1977	New (i)	
		reb	CE	B3102	1984		(11)
A1	72920		2w-2wBEF	TH	SE107	1979	New (j)	(11)
E5	74485		4wBEF	CE	B1843A	1979	New (k)	(11)
E4	74427		4wBEF	CE	B1843B	1979	New (k)	(11)
E6	73431		4wBEF	CE	B1850A	1979	New (k)	(11)
E7	73433		4wBEF	CE	B1850B	1979	New (k)	(11)
E10	76123		4wBEF	CE	B2273A	1981	New	(11)

E11	76138	4wBEF	CE	B2273B	1981	New	(11)
E9	76158	4wBEF	CE	B2274A	1981	New	(11)
E8	76159	4wBEF	CE	B2274B	1981	New	(11)
E12	71365	4wBEF	CE	B2986A	1982	New	(11)
E14	71364	4wBEF	CE	B2986B	1982	New	(11)
E16	72434	4wBEF	CE	B3045A	1983	New	(11)
E15	72430	4wBEF	CE	B3045B	1983	New	(11)
A2	72427	4w-4wBEF	TH	SE117	1983	(l)	(11)
No.1	70330	4w-4wBEF	CE	B3224A	1985	New (m)	
		reb	CE	B3827	1991		(10)
No.2	70331	4w-4wBEF	CE	B3224B	1985	New	(11)
No.3	70332	4w-4wBEF	CE	B3224C	1985	New	(11)
	-	4w-4wBEF	CE	B3352A	1987	New (n)	
		reb	CE	B3478	1988		(11)
No.4	70724	4w-4wBEF	CE	B3352B	1987	New (o)	
		reb	CE	B3565	1989		(11)
	-	4w-4wBEF	CE	B3477A	1989	New	(11)
	-	4w-4wBEF	CE	B3477B	1989	New	(11)
	-	4w-4wBEF	CE	B3591	1990	New	(11)

(a) to HC, c/1972; returned, c/1972.
(b) to HC, 6/1972; returned, 24/2/1973.
(c) ex Bolsover Colliery, Derbys, 2/1952.
(d) ex Llanharan Colliery, Mid Glam, by 8/1957.
(e) ex Mansfield Colliery, 2/7/1969.
(f) ex Mansfield Colliery, 2/7/1969; to HE, 2/1972; returned, 5/1972.
(g) to CE, 9/1979; returned, c/1980; to CE, c/1984; returned, 12/1984.
(h) to CE, 9/1979; returned, c/1980; to CE, 7/1985; returned, 11/1985.
(i) to CE, 5/1982; returned, 1/1984.
(j) to TH, 11/1979; returned, 12/1979.
(k) 2 of these 4 locos to CE, /1988; reb. as B3468A and B3468B and returned, /1988.
(l) ex TH, 25/3/1983 (earlier Kellingley Training Centre, North Yorks).
(m) to CE, /1989; returned, /1990; to CE, /1991; returned, /1991; to CE, 11/1991; returned, /1992.
(n) to CE, /1988; ex Bentley Training Centre, South Yorks, /1989.
(o) to CE, c/1989; returned, c/1989.
(p) ex Mansfield Colliery, /1988.

(1) to Mansfield Colliery, 7/1952.
(2) written off 4/1974.
(3) written off 5/1976.
(4) written off 6/1977.
(5) written off 9/1977.
(6) written off by 7/1978.
(7) scrapped 6/1979.
(8) scrapped 12/1984.
(9) abandoned underground in Top Hard Seam, late 1980s.
(10) to CE, 11/1991; then to Bilsthorpe Colliery, /1992.
(11) to RJB Mining (UK) Ltd, with site, 30/12/1994.

TROWELL MOOR DISPOSAL POINT. Stapleford   QN59
SK 493391

Operated by MFP c1943-47.

Sidings on the south side of the BR Radford line, 1 mile south east of Trowell station. This site was formerly the Trowell Moor Colliery of Cossall Coal Co Ltd. It was retained for pumping (initially by the colliery company but without rail traffic) for **COSSALL** and **OAKWOOD GRANGE COLLIERIES** until c1955. Part was also used as a landsale depot.

Gauge : 4ft 8½in.

5071		0-6-0ST	IC	RSHN 7107 1943	New (a)	(1)
75137		0-6-0ST	IC	HE 3188 1944	(b)	(2)

(a)   on loan from WD.
(b)   ex WD, Bicester, Oxon, by 3/1946.

(1)   to PLA, London, 1/1945.
(2)   to Pemberton Disposal Point, Lancs, 12/1947.

UPPER PORTLAND DISPOSAL POINT, Pinxton   KN60
SK 483544

Opened by MFP by 12/1945; OE from 1/4/1952; CLOSED 1964.
Operated by contractors, **Wilson Lovatt & Sons Ltd** from the mid-1950s

Sidings ran south from BR, 1 mile east of Pinxton & Selston station, on the site of the closed **PORTLAND No.2 COLLIERY** (see Butterley Co Ltd). The earliest reference to this site that we have traced is a spares order for an 'Austerity' 0-6-0ST in 12/1945.

Note : pre-1948 records refer to WB 2751 and 2756 as being at **MFP, Kirkby Screens**. This is believed to have been at Kirkby Colliery but it has also been suggested that it was an alternative name for Upper Portland Disposal Point.

Gauge : 4ft 8½in.

75061		0-6-0ST	IC	RSHN 7097 1943	(a)	(1)
75168		0-6-0ST	IC	WB 2756 1944	(b)	(7)
75163		0-6-0ST	IC	WB 2751 1944	(c)	(2)
	THIKA	0-6-0ST	OC	WB 2197 1922	(d)	(4)
75194		0-6-0ST	IC	RSHN 7144 1944	(e)	(10)
71494		0-6-0ST	IC	HC 1770 1944	(f)	(6)
	TRAFFORD PARK	0-6-0ST	OC	HE 1689 1931	(g)	(3)
75064		0-6-0ST	IC	RSHN 7100 1943	(h)	(5)
71510		0-6-0ST	IC	RSHN 7164 1944	(i)	(8)
L3	MOMBASA	0-6-0ST	OC	WB 2167 1921	(j)	(9)
15	LOVATT	0-4-0ST	OC	BP 6390 1927	(k)	(11)
75137		0-6-0ST	IC	HE 3188 1944	(l)	(12)

Note : An unidentified USATC 0-6-0T was reported here 10/1947.

(a) ex WD, 1/1946; earlier Melbourne Military Railway, Derbys; to Pilsley Disposal Point, Derbys, 1/1946; returned, 2/1946.
(b) ex Kirkby Disposal Point, /1947.
(c) ex Langwith Colliery, Derbys, after 6/1947.
(d) ex Pauling & Co Ltd, Crymlyn Burrows, Glam, after 3/1948, by 5/1948.
(e) ex Bennerley Disposal Point, 9/1949; to West Hallam Disposal Point, Derbys, 1/1950; ex Coton Park Disposal Point, Derbys, 6/1951; returned to there by 6/1953; ex Bennerley Disposal Point, by 1/1/1957.
(f) ex ?; to HC Leeds 27/1/1948; returned to ?; ex Bennerley Disposal Point, 9/1949; to HC, Leeds, 12/1949 (thence to Alma Disposal Point, Derbys); returned 11/1950.
(g) ex John Mowlem & Co Ltd, Welham Green, Herts, after 1/1949, by 7/1949.
(h) ex Watnall Disposal Point, after 9/1949, by 10/1950.
(i) ex Skiers Spring Disposal Point, South Yorks, 9/1950.
(j) ex Pauling & Co Ltd, Park Royal Plant Depot, London (hire), after 5/1953, by 10/1953.
(k) ex West Hallam Disposal Point, Derbys, after 4/1958, by 8/1959.
(l) ex Moor Green Central Workshops after 3/1958, by 8/1959; to Alma Disposal Point, Derbys, 9/1959; returned by 18/2/1961.

(1) to Bluebell Inn Disposal Point, Backworth, 9/1946.
(2) to Langwith Colliery Derbys, c/1948.
(3) to Alma Disposal Point, Derbys, 7/1949 (c8/7/1949).
(4) to Swannington Disposal Point, Leics (hire), /1949, by 8/1949.
(5) to Skiers Spring Disposal Point, South Yorks, 20/9/1950.
(6) to Alma Disposal Point, Derbys, c/1951 (after 11/1950).
(7) to Rankinston Disposal Point, Strathclyde, /1951.
(8) to Wath and Elsecar Disposal Point, South Yorks, 4/1952.
(9) to Swannington Disposal Point, Leics, after 2/1954, by 8/1954.
(10) to Coton Park Disposal Point, Derbys, 15/12/1958.
(11) to West Hallam Disposal Point, Derbys, /1960.
(12) to West Hallam Disposal Point, Derbys, after 6/1964, by 8/1966.

WARSOP COLLIERY, Warsop Vale GN61
ex Staveley Coal & Iron Co Ltd SK 548681

EM2 from 1/1/1947; EM3 from 1/7/1949; NDY from 26/3/1967; CEN from 1/4/1987; CLOSED 25/8/1989.

The colliery was located at the end of a branch which ran east for 1¼ miles from the BR (ex LMSR) Shirebrook North Station. The first ¼ mile was owned by BR, which worked the branch. There was also a south east to south west connection with the BR (ex LNER) Langwith Jct - Clipstone line where this line crossed the branch. The ex LMSR line was closed from 1962 until 1976. It then reopened and the ex LNER one closed. NCB locos were used to tip dirt east of the Colliery. Use of standard gauge locomotives ceased 1979. It is not known if the three underground locos delivered in 1957 were put to use but locomotives were used underground from c1983. From pre-vesting day until the mid 1960s, the LMSR (BR) supplied one shunting loco to work here under an old Agreement. This was usually an ex-Midland Railway Class 1F 0-6-0T and was changed frequently.

Gauge : 4ft 8½in.

	WARSOP	0-6-0ST	IC	HE	2408	1942	(a)	(2)
	SHERWOOD No.2	0-6-0ST	OC	P	1265	1912	(b)	(1)
4	BIRKLANDS	0-6-0ST	OC	HC	1654	1934	(c)	(2)

No.1			0-4-0ST	OC	RSHN	7642	1950	(d)	(2)
	SHIREBROOK No.3		0-6-0ST	OC	YE	1300	1916	(e)	(2)
No.1	DL24		4wDH		TH	114V	1962	(f)	(3)
(D4)	DL4		0-6-0DE		RH	425473	1958	(g)	(4)

(a) ex Staveley Coal & Iron Co Ltd, with site, 1/1/1947.
(b) (may have first come here from Sherwood Colliery 12/1947, en route for Sheepbridge Coal & Iron Co Ltd, Sheepbridge, Derbys, repairs); ex Shirebrook Colliery, Derbys, 8/1948; returned 9/1948; ex Shirebrook Colliery c30/11/1948.
(c) ex Appleby-Frodingham Steel Co Ltd, Scunthorpe, Lincs, 12/1954.
(d) ex Blidworth Colliery, after 12/1964, by 5/1966.
(e) ex Shirebrook Colliery, Derbys, after 11/1964, by 4/1966.
(f) ex Newman Industries Ltd, Yate, Glos, 3/1966.
(g) ex Ormonde Colliery, Derbys, after 9/1970, by 5/1972.

(1) scrapped by Thos W. Ward Ltd, 12/1956.
(2) scrapped by Wm. Bush Ltd, Alfreton, Derbys, after 5/1966, by 4/1967.
(3) to Shirebrook Colliery, Derbys, 3/1980.
(4) scrapped on site by Wm. Bush Ltd, 11/1980.

Gauge : 2ft 0in (Underground locomotives).

	-	0-6-0DMF	HC	DM949	1955	New	(2)
	-	0-6-0DMF	HC	DM950	1955	New	(1)
	-	0-6-0DMF	HC	DM951	1955	New	(1)
No.3	1387	4wBEF	CE	B2239A	1980	(a)	(3)
No.1	1618	4wBEF	CE	B3141A	1984	New	(4)
No.2	1619	4wBEF	CE	B3141B	1984	New	(5)
No.4	1176	4wBEF	CE	B1562	1977		
		reb	CE	B2974	1982	(b)	(6)
	-	4w-4wBEF	CE	B3248	1986	New	(7)
No.5	1231	4wBEF	CE	B1829	1978	(c)	(8)

(a) ex Westthorpe Colliery, Derbys, c/1983.
(b) ex Shirebrook Colliery, Derbys, c/1985.
(c) ex Whitwell Colliery, Derbys, 2/1988.

(1) to Blidworth Colliery, 3/1/1966.
(2) to Blidworth Colliery, 15/9/1966.
(3) to Calverton Colliery, 29/6/1990.
(4) to Markham Colliery, Derbys, via CE, /1990.
(5) to Ashington Central Workshops, Northumberland, c/1989; then to Tanfield Railway, Co Durham.
(6) to CE, c/1990.
(7) to CE, c/1990 (then to Markham Colliery, Derbys).
(8) sold or scrapped c/1990.

WATNALL COLLIERY, Watnall
ex Barber, Walker & Co Ltd
EM5 from 1/1/1947; CLOSED 12/1950.

LN62
SK 507480

See **MOOR GREEN COLLIERY** and **WATNALL DISPOSAL POINT**.

WATNALL DISPOSAL POINT, Watnall

LN63
SK 508452

Opened by MFP c1945; OE from 1/4/1952; USE OF LOCOS CEASED by 1960.
Operated from the mid 1950s by **Holloway Brothers (London) Ltd**.

This Disposal Point, comprising screens, sidings and a locomotive shed, was located at the exchange sidings between the LNER and Barber, Walker railways at Watnall, at the end of an LNER branch which ran west and to the north of their line, 1½ miles east of Kimberley station. The locomotive shed was west of the disposal point. Operations were intermittent with periods when the site was on care and maintenance. Rail traffic may not have worked after c1954 with all later locomotives being in store. The disposal point continued to operate using road transport until final closure in the 1980s.

Gauge : 4ft 8½in.

75017		0-6-0ST	IC	HE	2866	1943	(a)	(3)
75015		0-6-0ST	IC	HE	2864	1943	(b)	(1)
75064		0-6-0ST	IC	RSHN	7100	1943	(c)	(2)
75137		0-6-0ST	IC	HE	3188	1944	(d)	(4)
71507		0-6-0ST	IC	RSHN	7161	1944	(e)	(6)
8416		0-6-0T	IC	Ghd		1877	(f)	(5)
	LOCO 28	4wDM		FH	3700	1955	(g)	(7)

(a) ex WD, 3/1946.
(b) ex Moorthorpe Disposal Point, West Yorks, 4/1946.
(c) ex Alma Disposal Point, Derbys, 12/7/1949.
(d) ex Pemberton Disposal Point, Lancs, by 1/1954.
(e) ex British Oak Disposal Point, Yorks (WR), for storage,11/1954.
(f) ex Skiers Spring Disposal Point, Yorks (WR), for storage,19/12/1954.
(g) ex Holloway Bros. (London) Ltd, for storage, after 14/4/1957, by 6/1957.

(1) to Frickley Colliery, West Yorks, 7/1948.
(2) to Upper Portland Disposal Point, after 9/1949, by 10/1950.
(3) to Heanor Disposal Point, Derbys, after 6/1951, by 4/1952.
(4) to Bennerley Disposal Point, after 1/1954, by 1/1955.
(5) to Upper Blaenavon Disposal Point, Gwent, 4/1955.
(6) to Walkden Central Workshops, Greater Manchester, 21/12/1955.
(7) to Holloway Brothers (London) Ltd, c/1960, by 2/1961.

WELBECK COLLIERY, Welbeck Colliery Village (later Meden Vale)   GN64
ex N.H. & B. Collieries. Ltd   SK 582784

EM3 from 1/1/1947; NNT from 26/3/1967; NTS from 1/8/1985; NTG from 1/4/1990; MG from 1/9/1993; **RJB Mlning (UK) Ltd** from 30/12/1994.

Sidings serving the colliery were located at the end of an NCB owned but BR worked branch which ran north from the BR (ex LNER) line, 1 mile east of Warsop station, to the colliery (3 miles). The colliery was also served, until 11/1959, by a BR (ex LMSR) branch which ran east for 3 miles from ¾ mile south of Langwith station. Use of standard gauge locomotives ceased by 1981. Locomotives were used underground from 1990.

Gauge : 4ft 8½in.

	WELBECK No.5	0-6-0ST	OC	AE	1693	1914	(a)	(5)
	WELBECK No.6	0-6-0ST	OC	AE	1831	1919	(a)	(4)
	VIOLET	0-6-0ST	OC	Mkm	110	1895	(b)	(1)
	DOWELL	0-4-0ST	OC	AE	1416	1901	(b)	(1)
	WELBECK No.7	0-6-0ST	OC	HC	1305	1917	(c)	(2)
	WELBECK No.8	0-4-0ST	OC	P	2110	1950	New	(3)
No.2	D5 87420	0-6-0DM		HC	D1085	1958	New	(7)
No.3	87419	0-6-0DM		HC	D1111	1958	New	(7)
	87451 18458	4wDH		TH	140V	1964	(d)	(6)
D7	10332	0-4-0DH		S	10189	1964	(e)	(8)

(a) ex N.H. & B. Collieries Ltd, with site, 1/1/1947.
(b) ex Ireland Colliery, Derbys, /1947.
(c) ex Clipstone Colliery, c/1949 (by 4/1950).
(d) ex TH, Kilnhurst, South Yorks, after 6/1972, by 6/1974.
(e) ex Bilsthorpe Colliery, 6/1/1976.

(1) to Ireland Colliery, Derbys, /1947.
(2) to Sherwood Colliery, after 3/4/1957, by 16/5/1959.
(3) to Harworth Colliery, after 18/5/1958, by 16/5/1959.
(4) to Blidworth Colliery, c3/1963, by 10/3/1963.
(5) scrapped after 3/1963, by 10/1963.
(6) to Teversal Colliery, after 3/1976, by 5/1976.
(7) scrapped on site by NCB, after 4/1980, by 10/1983.
(8) to Ward Ferrous Metals Ltd, Tinsley, South Yorks, 10/1985.

Gauge : 2ft 4in (Underground locomotives).

	-	4wDMF	RH	268858	1949	New	(1)
	-	4wDMF	RH	268859	1949	New	(1)
No.1	820/45104	0-4-0DMF	HC	DM773	1950	(a)	(8)
No.2	820/45106	0-4-0DMF	HC	DM771	1950	(b)	(8)
No.3	820/45103	0-4-0DMF	HC	DM791	1950	(c)	(2)
No.4	820/45105	0-4-0DMF	HC	DM772	1950	(d)	(3)
No.5	820/24691	0-6-0DMF	HC	DM971	1957	(e)	(8)
No.3	820/24692	0-6-0DMF	HC	DM1011	1957	(f)	(8)
No.6	820/24690	0-6-0DMF	HC	DM970	1957	(g)	(5)
	87127	4wBEF	CE	B0427	1975	New	(4)
No.8	No.4 820/55033	0-6-0DMF	HC	DM1287	1962	(h)	(8)
No.9	No.7 820/55489	0-6-0DMF	HC	DM1332	1964	(i)	(8)

No.17	820/55521	0-6-0DMF	HC	DM1333	1964	(i)	(6)
No.2B	87830	4wBEF	CE	B2205A	1980	New	(8)
No.3B	87829	4wBEF	CE	B2205B	1980	New	(8)
	87828	2w-2wBEF	TH	SE108	1979	(j)	(8)
No.4B	84800	4wBEF	CE	B3034A	1983	(k)	(8)
No.5B	84801	4wBEF	CE	B3034B	1983	(k)	(8)
	-	4wBEF	CE	B3161	1985	New	(8)
	-	4wBEF	CE	B3234	1985	New	(8)
	-	4wDHF	CE	B3270A	1986	New	(8)
	-	4wDHF	CE	B3270B	1986	New	(8)
	-	4wDHF	CE	B3270C	1986	New	(8)
	-	4wDHF	CE	B3270D	1986	New	(8)
	-	4wDHF	CE	B3270E	1986	New	(8)
No.2	KESTREL	0-6-0DMF	HC	DM647	1954	(l)	(7)
	-	4w-4wBEF	CE	B3246	1986	(m)	(8)
No.9		4w-4wBEF	CE	B3362B	1987		
		reb	CE	B3723	1991	(n)	(8)
No.10		4w-4wBEF	CE	B3363A	1987	(o)	(8)
No.11		4w-4wBEF	CE	B3363B	1987	(o)	(8)
	-	4w-4wBEF	CE	B3445	1988	(n)	(8)

(a) ex HC, 2/1971 (earlier Ollerton Colliery).
(b) ex Ollerton Colliery, 3/1971.
(c) ex HC, 4/8/1971 (earlier Ollerton Colliery).
(d) ex HC, 13/9/1972 (earlier Ollerton Colliery); to Clipstone Colliery, 19/7/1977; returned here 8/9/1986.
(e) ex Clipstone Colliery, 6/1973.
(f) ex Clipstone Colliery, 3/1974.
(g) ex Clipstone Colliery, 3/1975.
(h) ex Rufford Colliery, 1/4/1977.
(i) ex Rufford Colliery, 5/1978.
(j) ex TH, 24/3/1983 (earlier Kellingley Training Centre, North Yorks).
(k) ex Bilsthorpe Colliery, c10/1983.
(l) ex Blidworth Colliery, 8/1985
(m) ex Tursdale Engineering, Tursdale Workshops, Tyne & Wear, /1994, earlier Rufford Colliery.
(n) ex Tursdale Engineering, Tursdale Workshops, Tyne & Wear, 7/1994, earlier Rufford Colliery.
(o) ex Tursdale Engineering, Tursdale Workshops, Tyne & Wear, 8/1994; earlier Rufford Colliery; to CE, c9/1994; returned here /1994.

(1) to Blidworth Colliery, 10/1953.
(2) to Clipstone Colliery, 11/3/1976.
(3) to Clipstone Colliery, 19/9/1977.
(4) to CE, /1980 (thence to Sutton Colliery).
(5) to Bevercotes Training Centre, 3/1987.
(6) scrapped 12/1984.
(7) to Midland Railway Centre, Butterley, Derbys, 9/1993.
(8) to RJB MIning (UK) Ltd, with site, 30/12/1994.

WOLLATON COLLIERY, Wollaton
ex Wollaton Collieries Co Ltd

QN65
SK 521404

EM6 from 1/1/1947; Merged with RADFORD COLLIERY, 12/1961.

Sidings on the south side of BR (ex LMS) line, 2 miles west of Radford station. No known locomotives.

SECTION 3

LOCOMOTIVES

of

CONTRACTORS,

PLANT DEALERS

and

LOCOMOTIVE MANUFACTURERS

LOCOMOTIVES OF CONTRACTORS

Note that entries for dealers, scrap merchants, etc. are located at the end of this section.

JOHN AIRD & SONS
NOTTINGHAM - MELTON MOWBRAY CONTRACT S/VC1

The Midland Railway Bill for the construction of this line was passed in Parliament in 11/1871 as the Nottingham - Rushden Line Act. Two contracts were made for its construction :
Contract No.1 : London Road Junction (Nottingham) to Willoughby (Notts / Leics boundary).
Contract No.2 : Willougby to Melton Junction.
John Aird, of Belvedere Rd, Lambeth, was awarded both contracts and work commenced at Melton Junction in 10/1874. The line opened for goods traffic on 1/11/1879. This firm was trading as John Aird & Sons at the time the contract was awarded but appears also to have adopted the title Lucas & Aird from 1875 so this may be applicable during the latter part of the construction. Lucas & Aird also built the associated Kettering & Manton line (1875-1880).

Locomotives listed below are believed to have been used on these contracts. A sale on 11/6/1880 at the contractor's yard, Old Dalby, offered seven locos by HE and MW, 4 and 6 coupled, with 10, 12 & 13in cylinders. A plant sale on 16/11/1880 included a 6-coupled MW, 12 x 17in, built 1876.

Gauge : 4ft 8½in

	FORTESCUE	0-6-0ST	IC	HE	3	1865	(a)	(1)
142	TIME	0-4-0ST	OC	MW	559	1875	New (b)	(2)
	MIDLAND	0-6-0ST	IC	MW	656	1877	(c)	(3)

Some sources indicate that VICTORIA, 0-6-0ST IC MW 589/1876 was used on this contract, but this may be confusion with RUSHTON, 0-6-0ST IC MW 588/1876; both were apparently new to Lucas & Aird, Victoria Dock contract, London, though the name RUSHTON suggests the Kettering & Manton line. MW 588 was later to Beadle Bros, Erith, apparently via MW, ex-works again, 20/12/1880. MW 589 was later with Holwell Iron Co. Holwell Ironworks, Leics, 'HOLWELL No.11', before /1901.

(a) orig W.& J. Pickering, Barnstaple - Taunton (Devon & Somerset Rly) (1865-1867) contract, Devon. Later recorded (undated) by HE as J. Aird & Sons, Nottingham - assumed this contract.
(b) New to Nottingham - assumed this contract.
(c) MW records show new either to Nottingham or to Bromley (Bromley North - Grove Park (SER) (1877-1878) contract; possibly here new or after Bromley.

(1) spares supplied for this loco to John Aird & Sons (location unrecorded), 4/1901; s/s
(2) later Chas. Murrell, (Refuse Contractor ?), London (possibly c/1913-/1918).
(3) later Baker & Firbank, Ruskington - Lincoln (GN/GE Joint) (1880-1883) contract, Lincs, MELTON (possibly renamed by Aird?).

H. ARNOLD & SON LTD

NORTH WILFORD CONTRACT   SC2

Work by this Doncaster based contractor at North Wilford Power Station for Nottingham Corporation, 1926 - 1928.

Gauge : 4ft 8½in

CLARA		MW	?	?	(a)	(1)

(a)   origin unknown.

(1)   to Bilsthorpe contract, c/1927.

BILSTHORPE CONTRACTS   GC3

Construction of Bilsthorpe Jct. to Bilsthorpe Colliery branch, 1927 - 1928 (contract with the LNER let on 21/10/1926), also Blidworth Jct - Blidworth Colliery branch (contract with the LNER let on 19/8/1926) and Rufford Colliery - Clipstone Colliery line for LMSR, 1928 - 1929.

Gauge : 4ft 8½in

3		0-6-0ST	IC	MW	1590	1903	(a)	(1)
	CLARA			MW	?	?	(b)	s/s
	-	0-6-0ST	OC	BH	889	1890	(c)	(2)
	FULWOOD	0-6-0ST	IC	HE	529	1891	(d)	(3)

A four-coupled MW saddle tank is also associated with these contracts; may be the same loco as CLARA.

(a)   earlier at Kirk Sandall (Pilkington Brothers Ltd Glass Works) contract, Doncaster, c/1920.
(b)   ex North Wilford Power Station contract, c/1927.
(c)   earlier at Belmont Sidings Plant Depot, Doncaster, 8/1919.
(d)   earlier at Knostrop Sewage Works (Leeds City Council) contract, Yorks (WR), 12/1923; said to have worked on the Bilsthorpe branch (1927-1928) contract.

(1)   later at Dinting Tunnel (LNER) contract, Cheshire, by 4/1931 (possibly via Belmont Sidings Plant Depot, Doncaster and/or Barking - Upminster widening (LMSR) contract, Essex).
(2)   later at Royal Bethlem Hospital (6/1928-1930) contract, Shirley, Surrey.
(3)   said to have been used at Royal Bethlem Hospital (6/1928-1930) contract, Shirley, Surrey, but spares sent to Blidworth & Rainworth station, LMS in 4/1929 (for Blidworth branch contract ?) so sequence of contracts is unclear; later to Shanks & McEwan Ltd, Ollerton contract, by 1/1930.

BALDRY & YERBURGH

ANNESLEY - STAVELEY CONTRACT   J/KC4

Construction of railway (10 miles), north from Annesley for MS&LR, 1890 - 1892, probably including the Langton Colliery and New Hucknall Colliery branches. This work had originally been let as part of **Logan & Hemingway's** Annesley - Beighton contract in 1/1890 but the contract was revised in 2/1890. The line, much of which was in Derbyshire, was opened for freight on 24/10/1892.

Gauge : 4ft 8½in

No.6	HESKETH	0-4-0ST	OC	MW	634	1877	(a)	(1)
10	GAVIN	0-6-0ST	OC	BH	471	1881	(a)	(2)
		0-6-0ST	IC	MW	92	1863	(b)	s/s
No.2 #	(SOLENT)	0-4-0ST	OC	MW	882	1883	(c)	(3)
	PARKESTON	0-4-0ST	OC	HC	220	1882	(d)	(4)
No.11		0-6-0ST	IC	MW	1236	1891	New	(5)
No.12		0-6-0ST	IC	HC	347	1892	New	(6)

\# carried by 3/1894

Note : Markham & Co Ltd, of Chesterfield, invoiced repairs to several of these locomotives for Baldry & Yerburgh in the period 1890 - 1896. Other locomotives mentioned include LLIW (or L&NW) (not identified) in 5/1891, FLORENCE (possibly MW 92) in 4/1895 and "No.8" in 10/1893 and 3/1896. The latter *might* be 0-4-0ST OC MW 900/1884, originally "Kirk & Parry No.8"; later Baldry & Yerburgh, Towcester- Olney (STMJR, later S&MJR) (1887-1891) contract, Northants/Beds, and subsequently Staveley Coal & Iron Co Ltd, near Chesterfield, ALICE (early 1900s). No Baldry & Yerburgh contracts are known in Derbys or near Chesterfield at this period, the nearest being the Annesley and Tuxford contracts in Notts; the locos described may therefore have been used on these contracts, but confirmation is required.

(a)   earlier believed to have been with Watson, Smith & Watson, East & West Junction Rly contract, Towcester, Northants; where for sale from 3/1886 until /1887; then with Baldry & Yerburgh, Towcester - Olney (STMJR, later S&MJR) (1887-1891) contract, Northants/Beds. The use of BH 471 on the Annesley contract is unconfirmed, but Markham repaired MW 634 for B&Y in 5/1894, suggesting use on the Annesley/Tuxford contracts.

(b)   earlier George Bush, (Harborne Rly construction, 1872-1874 ?), Birmingham; later Baldry & Yerburgh, Kirkby (MW records).

(c)   earlier S Pearson & Son, Southampton Dock (1886-1890) contract, SOLENT, probably until 8/1890; later Baldry & Yerburgh, Kirkby (MW records).

(d)   orig Thos D Ridley, Harwich - Parkeston Quay (GER) contract, Essex, probably until 9/1886. Repaired by Markham & Co Ltd for Baldry & Yerburgh, 3-5/1890 and 6-10/1893, suggesting use on the Annesley/Tuxford contracts.

(1)   probably to later Baldry & Yerburgh contracts; then to Sir J Jackson Ltd, Hudson Dock Extension (1900-1904) contract, Sunderland, Co.Durham.

(2)   later to Haigh-Crigglestone-Horbury (L&YR) (1899-1902) contract, Yorks (WR), where for sale 7/1902. (Mkm repaired No.10 (unidentified) for Baldry & Yerburgh, 2-6/1896; confirmation is required that this No.10 was BH 471).

(3)   repaired by Mkm for Baldry & Yerburgh, 7/1894 and 6-9/1897; apparently re-sold, whilst at Mkm, by 9/1897 to Godfrey & Liddelow, (where later named MORECAMBE), presumably for the Heysham branches (Midland Rly) (1896-1898) contract.

(4) later Heaton Lodge - Wortley (LNWR) (1896-1900) contract, Yorks (WR),
(5) probably later to Haigh-Crigglestone-Horbury (L&YR) (1899-1902) contract, Yorks (WR).
(6) possibly later to Haigh-Crigglestone-Horbury (L&YR) (1899-1902) contract, Yorks (WR); with Furness Shipbuilding Co Ltd, Haverton Hill, Co.Durham, by /1918.

WARSOP - TUXFORD CONTRACT   F/GC5

Construction of the Warsop - Tuxford railway for LD&ECR, 5/1893 - 11/1896. Locomotives were used on this contract - no details available but could well have included locomotives listed above.

BALDRY, YERBURGH & HUTCHINSON LTD
Registered 3/1910 as successor to Baldry & Yerburgh.
MANSFIELD CONTRACT   G/H/JC6

Construction of Mansfield Railway (Clipstone East Jct. - Mansfield - Kirkby South Jct). Contract let 7/1911 and work commenced 8-9/1911. Clipstone Jct to Mansfield Colliery opened 6/1913 and Mansfield Colliery Jct - Mansfield in 6/1914. Clipstone West Curve and the Rufford and Clipstone Colliery branches were authorised on 8/7/1914 and the contract for the former two lines was awarded to Baldry, Yerburgh & Hutchinson Ltd in 5/1915, but the commencement of World War I resulted in work being slowed. The Clipstone Colliery branch together with the **Clipstone Camp Military Railway** (built by the War Office; construction possibly also by BY&H) opened 13/6/1916. Mansfield to Kirkby South Jct opened 4/9/1916. Clipstone West Curve opened 18/3/1918 and the Rufford Colliery branch on 8/7/1918.

BY&H also built the **Welbeck Colliery branch, GCR**, opened 19/4/1915, possibly using locos.

Up to 20 locos reported to have worked on this construction, full details required. The two locomotives identified are listed below.

Gauge : 4ft 8½in

-	0-6-0ST	IC	P	528	1893	(a)	(1)
-	0-4-0ST	OC	HE	313	1883	(b)	s/s

(a) earlier Hutchinson & Co, Mirfield - Huddersfield (Midland Rly) (1908-1910) contract, Yorks (WR); here by 9/1913.
(b) earlier Christie's Wharf contract, Charlton, London until after 4/1914; here by 3/1917.

(1) used on other contracts until after 4/1927; then s/s.

BALFOUR, BEATTY & CO LTD
STAYTHORPE CONTRACT   PC7

Construction of Staythorpe Power Stations for the Derbyshire & Nottinghamshire Electric Power Co Ltd, 1945-1948 period ('A' Station) and again for the Central Electricity Authority c1957 ('B' Station). In addition to the locos listed below, the permanent loco stock at the Power Station was ordered and/or used by Balfour Beatty & Co Ltd (see under National Power plc). The 1957 contract was completed largely with the use of these locos.

Gauge : 4ft 8½in

No.64		0-6-0ST	IC	HC	1650	1932	(a)	(1)
	BARNSLEY	0-4-0ST	OC	HC	727	1905	(b)	(2)

(a) earlier Skipton Rock Co Ltd, Embsay Quarry, Yorks (WR) until 8/1945. HC then record Midland Rolling & Haulage Co Ltd, Birmingham (boiler repairers ?), 2/1946; C. Jones Ltd, Aldridge, Staffs and Abelson & Co Ltd, Birmingham; then Balfour Beatty & Co, Staythorpe, (by) 4/1948; possibly to other contracts after 10/1948 but returned here by 9/1954.
(b) ex HC (hire), /1953 (after 9/1953).

(1) s/s after 9/1954.
(2) returned to HC, off hire.

Gauge : 2ft 0in

		4wBE	WR	5670	1957	New	(1)

(1) to Raynesway Plant Depot, Derby.

BALFOUR BEATTY RAILWAY ENGINEERING LTD
NEWSTEAD CONTRACT   KC8

Contract with Railtrack plc for relaying track on the Robin Hood Line, from Newstead to Kirkby Lane End Junction, 1995.

Gauge : 4ft 8½in

Q166 BCH (423)	4wDM	R/R Unimog	(a)	(1)

(a) ex Coleford Road Plant Depot, Darnall, South Yorks, /1995.

(1) returned to Coleford Road Plant Depot, Tinsley, South Yorks, /1995.

BENTON & WOODIWISS

BOTTESFORD CONTRACT   UC9

Construction of the Bottesford - Melton Mowbray (Contract No.1, let 10/1875) and Melton Mowbray- Tilton (Contract No.2, let 10/1875) sections of the GN&LNWR Jt Railways. [Tilton - Market Harborough (Leics) (Contract No.3) and the Bingham Branch (Notts) (Contract No.4) were let to Logan & Hemingway, which see]. The Newark - Bottesford (GNR) line became Contract No.5, let to Benton & Woodiwiss, 8/1876. The line opened in sections during 1879. The locos listed below are largely associated with the Leicestershire contract but may well have worked also on the Nottinghamshire section of the construction.

Gauge : 4ft 8½in

	(JOE?)	0-4-0ST	OC	MW	401	1872	(a)	(1)
	TILTON	0-4-0ST	OC	YE	280	1875	New	(2)
No.18		0-6-0ST	IC	MW	562	1876	New	(3)
No.17		0-6-0ST	IC	MW	563	1876	New	(4)
No.22	TRENT	0-6-0ST	IC	MW	626	1876	New	(5)

Notes :
(i)   MW 562 and 626 were new to Bottesford; MW 563 was new to Melton Mowbray.
(ii) There was an agreement dated 9/12/1878 with the GNR for the hire of a GNR loco for 'ballasting on the Bottesford, Melton and Tilton Railways from 10/12/1878 to 14/1/1879.
(iii) There was an agreement dated 23/6/1879 with the GNR for the hire of a GNR loco for 'conveying ballast from Newark to the Melton and Tilton Railway' from 23/6/1879 to 12/7/1879.

(a)   earlier John Barnes, Ashby & Nuneaton Rly (Mid Rly/LNWR Jt) (1869-1873) contract, JOE; then to Baldry & Yerburgh, Melton Mowbray.

(1)   later J.D. Nowell, Reddish, Cheshire - presumably Manchester Central Station railway (MS&LR) (1889-1892) contract.
(2)   acquired by YE, Sheffield, after 26/9/1883 and used as a hire loco before 26/9/1898; thence to Sheffield Corporation, Blackburn Meadows Sewage Works, Yorks (WR), c12/1898.
(3)   later Leicester (Belgrave Rd) - Marefield Jct (GNR) (1880-1886) contract, Leics; later M.W. Walmsley, Bury, Lancs.
(4)   to Awsworth Jct - Derby (GNR) (1875-1878) contract, Derbys
(5)   later J.D. Nowell, Levenshulme, Manchester - presumably Manchester Central Station railway (MS&LR) (1889-1892) contract.

NOTTINGHAM CONTRACT   L/RC10

Construction of Colwick Jct - Kimberley - Awsworth Jct for the GNR, 1873-1878. This was Contract No.1 of the Derbyshire & North Staffs Extension Lines and appears to have included branches to Cinderhill/Babbington Colliery and to Watnall Colliery. Contract let 3/1873 and line opened 23/8/1875. Contract No.3 was also let to Benton & Woodiwiss in 6/1875 for the construction of the Awsworth Jct - Derby Friargate section of the line in Derbyshire.

No details of the locos used in Nottinghamshire are confirmed; see the forthcoming Derbyshire Handbook for locomotives associated with the Derby contract, which may also have been used in Nottinghamshire.

WALTER BINNS
LEEN VALLEY CONTRACT   JC11

This Bradford contractor obtained the GNR contract for 10½ miles of the Leen Valley Extension Railway construction, between Kirkby South Jct. - Sutton - Skegby and Pleasley, in 2/1895. Construction commenced in 6/1895 and by 9/1896 the line was open for coal traffic to Kirkby Colliery. A further section opened for coal traffic in 8/2/1897 from Kirkby South Jct to Skegby as well as the Teversal and Silverhill colliery branches. On 7/5/1897, because of Binns' financial diffficulties, the works were transferred to the Halifax Commercial Banking Co, who appointed W.H. Hutchinson as manager.

Hutchinson completed this contract by 4/1898 and also, on 3/12/1897, obtained the contract for the Pleasley to Langwith Jct line, opened from Pleasley to Shirebrook Colliery on 26/11/1900 and to Langwith from 29/5/1901.

Binns' failure leads to complications in existing records over ownership of locomotives listed after the transfer of work to Hutchinson.

Gauge : 4ft 8½in

No.5	SUTTON	0-6-0ST	IC	MW	1290	1895	(a)	(1)
No.6	KIRKBY	0-4-0ST	OC	MW	1303	1895	New	(1)
No.9	PLEASLEY	0-4-0ST	OC	MW	1304	1895	New	(1)
	SKEGBY	0-4-0ST	OC	MW	915	1883	(b)	(1)
	-	0-4-0ST	OC	MW	653	1877	(c)	(2)
	-	0-6-0ST	IC	P	455	1887	(d)	(3)
	(? TEVERSALL) #	0-4-0ST	OC	P	440	1885	(e)	(4)

\#   Spelling uncertain (TEVERSALL or TEVERSAL) in P lists; may even have been location rather than loco name. Also in 3/1896 MW fitter (or supplied ?) a new boiler, etc., for loco TEVERSALL (unidentified) for Walter Binns.

(a)   ex Wortley South Jct. - Holbeck (GNR) improvements contract, Leeds, c/1896.
(b)   earlier Wrenthorpe widening (GNR) (1891-1894) contract, Yorks (WR).
(c)   ex Keighley Corporation Gasworks, Keighley, Yorks (WR), for sale there, 5/1895.
(d)   earlier Oldham Corporation Waterworks, Delph, Lancs, until 6/1893; then probably Thos. W. Ward (advertised "at Delph") until 10/1895.
(e)   ex Wm. Lounds, Cannock Lodge Colliery, Bloxwich, Staffs, c/1896, per Buggins, dealer, Birmingham.

(1)   to W.H. Hutchinson, Shirebrook contract, /1897.
(2)   possibly to W.H. Hutchinson, Shirebrook contract, /1897; later Hugh Symington & Sons, contrs, Coatbridge, Lanarks, by early 1900s.
(3)   possibly to W.H. Hutchinson, Shirebrook contract, c/1897; later Price, Wills & Reeves, Immingham Dock (1906-1912) contract, Lincs, SHEFFIELD.
(4)   possibly to W.H. Hutchinson, Shirebrook contract, /1897; later Price & Wills, contrs, (location unknown).

SIR JESSE BOOT PROPERTY & INVESTMENT CO LTD
NOTTINGHAM CONTRACT   XC12

This private company was registered on 6/12/1906, the directors (Sir Jesse Boot and his wife) also being associated with **Boots Pure Drug Co Ltd** (which see). In 1921 Sir Jesse Boot gifted the Highfields estate at Nottingham to Nottingham Corporation's University College as the site for the later University of Nottingham. It is presumed that these locos were used on the development work at this site.

Gauge : 600mm

	0-6-0WT	OC	HC	1317	1918	(a)	(1)
	4wPM		MR	?	?	(b)	(2)

(a)   ex War Department, Porton Camp, Wilts, after 1/5/1923, by /1924.
(b)   origin unknown.

(1)   for sale at Highfields, Nottingham, 4/1924; with Wm. Moss & Sons Ltd, Loughborough, Leics, contrs, /1925.
(2)   for sale at Highfields, Nottingham, 4/1924; s/s.

C.V. BUCHAN LTD
NOTTINGHAM SEWER CONTRACT   SC13
SK 585391

Sewerage improvements for Severn Trent Water Authority, 1974. A temporary plant depot was situated at Meadow Lane, Nottingham, for the duration of this contract. The locomotives worked underground as required.

Gauge : 2ft 0in

S105	4wBE	CE	5792C	1970	(a)	(1)
S106	4wBE	CE	5792D	1970	(a)	(1)
(S130)	4wBE	CE	5882C	1971	(b)	(1)

(a)   ex Swynnerton Plant Depot, Staffs, after 25/3/1973, by 6/1/1974.
(b)   ex Swynnerton Plant Depot, Staffs, after 6/1/1974, by 2/6/1974.

(1)   to Swynnerton Plant Depot, Staffs, after 2/6/1974, by 12/1/1975.

CLEVELAND BRIDGE & ENGINEERING CO LTD
NOTTINGHAM CONTRACT   SC14

The following locomotive was delivered to London Road Station, Nottingham; further details of its use are unknown. Cleveland Bridge & Engineering Ltd are said to have done work on "Trent Bridge, Nottingham" around 1924.

Gauge : 2ft 0in

-	4wPM	MR	2260	1924	New	s/s

L. COURT & CO
CLIPSTONE CONTRACT GC15

A number of advertisements were carried for sales by L. Court & Co, contractors, of London EC4. These included "Contract Journal", 14/9/1927 and "Machinery Mart", 16/9/1927 : "For Sale, plant including 14 locos, 10 and 12inch, 4 and 6 wheeled, standard gauge". Subsequently : "Auction 22/11/1927 re L. Court & Co, at Concentration Sidings, Mansfield, including 14 4 and 6 wheel locos up to 14inch." Finally "Contract Journal", 30/11/1927 and "Colliery Guardian", 2/12/1927 : "Five 6 coupled steam locos, 12 and 13inch, lying at Clipstone, near Mansfield".

None of these locomotives has been identified and the contract is uncertain. It is possible that construction of Mansfield Concentration sidings (located between Clipstone Jcts and Rufford Jct.) was commenced in the period 1915-1917 by Baldry, Yerburgh & Hutchinson. Further details would be most welcome.

H. COXHEAD & CO LTD
SUTTON-ON-TRENT CONTRACT FC16
SK 792659

This Middlesbrough based public works contractor is known to have had involvement with road improvement works. This contract may have been for improvements to the A1 Great North Road including a bridge over the GNR main line at Crow Park Station, near Sutton on Trent, c1928-1929.

Gauge : 2ft 0in

-	0-4-0ST	OC	KS	4254	1922	(a)	(1)
-	0-4-0ST	OC	KS	4270	1922	(b)	(2)

(a) orig R.H. Neal & Co, Plant Dealers, Barkingside, Essex; hired to Aubrey Watson Ltd, contrs, unknown location; here by 8/1928.
(b) orig R.H. Neal & Co, Plant Dealers, Barkingside, Essex, 176; hired to Aubrey Watson Ltd, contrs, Orpington, Kent; here by 8/1928.

(1) to Midland Macadams Ltd, Oldbury, Worcs, No.2, possibly 1/1931.
(2) to Midland Macadams Ltd, Oldbury, Worcs, No.1, probably c/1931, certainly by 8/1935.

CUBITTS & PAULING
RETFORD CONTRACT DC17

Contract for the Government in the Retford area, details unknown, 1941.

Gauge : 2ft 0in

-	4wDM		RH	189947	1938	(a)	(1)

(a) ex Pauling & Co Ltd, Wrexham (ROF) contract, Denbighshire, after 26/2/1941, by 9/6/1941.
(1) sold or scrapped after 18/8/1941.

ECKERSLEY & BAYLISS
MANSFIELD CONTRACT   G/HC18

Construction of the Mansfield to Southwell line (9 miles) for the Midland Railway. Work commenced in 4/1869 and the line opened to traffic in 4/1871. This partnership also built the Sutton to Mansfield (Kings Mill) deviation line for the Midland Railway, 1869 - 1872.

One locomotive was in use at Rainworth on 2/11/1869, with three locos working by the end of the month, four in 1/1870 and two on 30/6/1870. The identities of these locomotives are not known.

J.P. EDWARDS
NOTTINGHAM CONTRACT   RC19

Construction of the Nottingham Suburban Railway Co line (worked by the GNR) from Trent Lane Junctions, Nottingham to Daybrook Junction. The contract was let to this Chester based contractor with work commencing 6/1887 and the line opening 2/12/1889.
During this 1886-1890 period Edwards was also building the Midland Railway Ripley and Heanor branches in Derbyshire and locomotives may have moved between these jobs.
Sales at the end of these contracts included :
Auction 3/4/1889 off Ripley & Heanor contract, three 6 wheel locos 12, 13 and 14in (later adverts changed to one 4 wheel and two 6 wheel locos).
In 6/1889, J.P.Edwards, Chester had for sale seven locos, 10in to 16in, all 6 wheel except for one 10inch, 4 wheel coupled. Mostly Leeds built, one nearly new.
"Engineer". 13/12/1889; For sale by J.P.Edwards, Chester, on completion of the Nottingham Suburban Railway, plant including five locos - three Leeds built 12in to 14½in; two LNWR built 14¼in and 16in; all 6 wheel tank engines.
"Engineer", etc, Auction 26/2/1890 re J.P.Edwards, completion of Nottingham Suburban Railway at yards Sneinton, St. Anns Well and Sherwood, including three tank locos:
COCKER, 14¼in by LNWR, overhauled last June; NOTTINGHAM, 14¼in by HE, rebuilt 1888; and LADY CORNWALL, 16in by LNWR.

Gauge : 4ft 8½in

-		0-4-0ST	OC	MW	715	1878	(a)	(1)
DEWSBURY		0-6-0ST	IC	HE	196	1878	(b)	(2)
NOTTINGHAM		0-6-0ST	IC	HE	1	1865		
		reb		HE		1888	(c)	(3)
COCKER		0-4-2ST	IC	Kitching		1846		
		reb		Crewe		1866		
		reb from 0-4-2		Crewe		1886	(d)	(4)
LADY CORNWALL #		6w.tank		LNWR		?	(e)	(5)
-		6w.tank		"Leeds built"			(f)	(6)

\# May have been named LADY CORNEWALL, after the wife of a local landowner involved in the Golden Valley Rly, built 1876-1881, from Pontrilas to Dorstone, Herefords, by Scott & Edwards. LADY CORNEWALL (unidentified) was in use on construction c7/1877 and was later hired from J.P.Edwards early 1888 (presumably the same loco, but wherabouts unknown 1877-1888. Some sources suggest a 2-2-2T (later Braddock, etc.)). However in 6/1885 J.P.Edwards, Edgbaston, Birmingham had for sale a 6wh, -

4-coupled 16x22in side tank, and in 4/1886 a 6-wh 16in loco by LNWR, probably the same loco ? and possibly LADY CORNEWALL.
LNWR 2-4-0T IC 16x22in SS (719/1852?) (orig S.Staffs Rly 15) was sold to Scott & Edwards, 8/1873 - for sale by them, 7/1875 - 1/1876, described as by SS & Co. This clearly could fit the 6/1885 loco and possibly therefore LADY CORNEWALL, but further evidence is required.

(a) orig Beckett & Bentley, Facit - Bacup (L&YR) (1878-1881) construction, TAM O'SHANTER; probably for sale there, 8/1883.
(b) orig Baker & Firbank, Dewsbury-Batley (GNR) (1877-1880) contract, Yorks (WR): probably then to their Ruskington-Lincoln (GN&GE Jt.) (1880-1883) contract, Lincs and possibly then Scott & Edwards, Soho, Handsworth & Perry Barr Jcn Rly (1885-1888) contract, Birmingham. (6-wh cpld 13in HE for sale 9/1887).
(c) earlier probably Baker & Firbank, Barton Moss - Patricroft - Cross Lane (LNWR) (1878-1883) contract, Lancs, PATRICROFT; possibly then Scott & Edwards, Soho, Handsworth & Perry Barr Jcn Rly (1885-1888) contract, Birmingham (6-wh cpld 14in HE for sale 9/1887); rebuilt by HE, /1888 and to here (again ?) 11/1888 or soon after (tried in steam 16/11/1888).
(d) originally Cockermouth & Workington Railway, COCKER; to LNWR /1866; (probably with J.P. Edwards, Edgbaston, Birmingham, by 6/1885). Rebuilt to ST at Crewe Works, 1/1886 for J.P.Edwards and possibly then hired to Henry Jackson, Brighton & Dyke Railway contract, Sussex, 1886-1887.
(e) earlier probably Soho & Monument Lane widening contract (LNWR) Birmingham, (16in LNWR tank loco for sale 11/1888); this loco was also recorded as 16in cyls.
(f) origin and details not known.

(1) possibly the 10in loco for sale 6/1889; to Chas. Brand & Son, Mawcarse-Bridge of Earn (NBR) (1887-1890) contract, Perthshire.
(2) probably in the 12/1889 sale; later with E.P. Davis, Bennerley Ironworks, by 10/1907.
(3) in auction, 26/2/1890; to Exors of T.A. Walker, Manchester Ship Canal contract, Lancs.
(4) in auction, 26/2/1890; to Chinley-Hathersage (Midland Railway) (1888-1894) contract, Derbys.
(5) in auction, 26/2/1890; (presumably same loco for sale 12/1889); possibly to Chas. Braddock, Wigan area contracts (1889-1892) - confirmation required.
(6) in auction, 26/2/1890; s/s.

Gauge : 3ft 0in

LIZZIE	0-4-0ST	OC	MW	1038	1887	New	(1)
EDALE	0-4-0ST	OC	MW	1110	1888	New	(2)
UNION JACK	0-6-0ST	OC	MW	1123	1889	New	(1)

(1) to Chinley-Hathersage (Midland Railway) (1888-1894) contract, Derbys.
(2) possibly to Chinley-Hathersage (Midland Railway) (1888-1894) contract, Derbys; later John H. Gartside & Co Ltd, Stalybridge, Cheshire, c/1893.

J. FIRBANK
PINXTON CONTRACT   KC20

Construction of the Kimberley/Awsworth Jct to Pinxton railway for GNR. This was Contract No.2 for the Derbys & North Staffs Extension Lines; let to Firbank 8/1873 and opened to freight traffic, 23/8/1875. Probably also construction of colliery branches including those to Digby Colliery, Barber Walker Collieries at Eastwood, connection to branch from Midland Rly to New Brinsley (or Pollington) Colliery, and to Pinxton Collieries.

Locomotives assumed to have been used, but as yet none identified.

FLETCHER & CO (CONTRACTORS) LTD
Forest Road, Mansfield

MANSFIELD CONTRACT ?   HC21

Contract, details uncertain, in the 1929-1931 period.

Gauge : 2ft 0in

                              0-4-0ST   OC   KS   4248   1922   (a)   (1)

(a)   orig R.H. Neal & Co, Plant Dealers, Barkingside, Essex, No.147; sold by Thos.W. Ward Ltd, /1924-1925 (possibly to Fletcher); with Fletcher (location unknown), by 6/1929; at Mansfield Plat Depot by 1/1931.

(1)   to Alne - Pilmoor (LNER) widening contract, Yorks (NR), 5-6/1931; still there 9/1932; possibly returned to Mansfield, s/s.

UNKNOWN CONTRACT(S)   XC22

This contractor has also owned the following locomotives.

Gauge : 4ft 8½in

              -                 0-6-0ST   IC   MW   1418   1898
                                                reb   HE   (1928?) (a)   (1)

(a)   earlier Walter Scott & Middleton Ltd, repurchased by MW by 7/1915; (possibly retained by them until closure in 1927; thence to HE, /1927-1928 ?) and rebuilt by HE (1928 or 1931; sources differ); to Fletcher, Mansfield Depot (by) 1-2/1931.

(1)   used by Fletcher & Co on the Soho & Winson Green Goods Depot (GWR) contract, Birmingham, by 7/1931 until after 2/1935; at New Spun Pipe Plant Works (Staveley Coal & Iron Co Ltd) contract, Derbys, in 1/1936; to Sir Lindsay Parkinson & Co Ltd, Chorley Royal Ordnance Factory contract, Lancs, by 3/1938.

Gauge : 2ft 0in

	4wDM	Jung	#	1930	(a)	s/s
-	4wPM	MR	1790	1918	(b)	(1)
-	4wPM	MR	5303	1931	(c)	(1)
-	4wDM	MR	5889	1935	New	s/s
-	4wDM	MR	7218	1938	New	s/s
-	4wDM	RH	191666	1938	(d)	(2)

\# Fletcher advertised in "Contract Journal", 20/3/1940 and 10/7/1940, for sale or hire, a Jung diesel loco (4¾tons). This weight implies a 20hp Type MsZ 130 loco, of which the only two delivered to England (to unrecorded purchasers) were works nos. 4960 and 4966, both of 1930.

(a) origin uncertain (see note above).
(b) ex MR, 10/2/1933; earlier WDLR 2511.
(c) ex Petrol Loco Hirers, 9/5/1935.
(d) ex RH, Lincoln, 10/12/1938 (earlier new (on hire ?) to Lincolnshire County Council).

(1) Two 20hp Simplex petrol locos, 2ft gauge, assumed these two, were advertised for sale or hire by Fletcher in "Contract Journal", 20/3/1940, 10/7/1940, and 20/10/1943. On 21/1/1960, "Thos Fletcher & Co, Nottingham" had one MR loco for sale; otherwise s/s.
(2) A 16/20hp RH loco, assumed this one, was advertised for sale or hire by Fletcher in "Contract Journal", 24/7/1940. On 21/1/1960, "Thos Fletcher & Co, Nottingham" had one RH loco for sale; otherwise s/s.

Note that this firm advertised in "Contract Journal" with locos for sale or hire as detailed above and also on 14/8/1940 - a 20hp Simplex *diesel* loco

FORAKY LTD
COLWICK PLANT DEPOT TC23
SK 619403

This company, registered 8/1942, engineers specialising in shaft sinking, etc., whose plant yard was situated on the Colwick Industrial Estate, has owned the following locomotives:-

Gauge : 2ft 0in

-	4wBE	WR	5537	1956	(a)	(1)
-	4wDM	RH	174139	1935	(b)	(2)
-	4wDM	RH	264252	1952	(b)	(2)

(a) ex Kinnear Moodie & Co Ltd, contrs, Lewisham.
(b) ex Oakeley Slate Quarries Co Ltd, Blaenau Ffestiniog, Merioneth, after 10/1971, by 7/1972.

(1) used on a contract at Nangiles Mine, Truro, Cornwall; purchased by Wheal Jane Ltd, Nangiles, by 9/1969.
(2) one loco used on a contract at Wookey Hole Caves, nr.Wells, Somerset, c6/1974. Both sold to A. Keef, Bampton, Oxon, 12/1975.

HOLLOWAY BROTHERS (LONDON) LTD.

CALVERTON CONTRACT   NC24
SK 605505

Construction of the Calverton Colliery Branch for BR and sidings for the National Coal Board, 1951 - 1953.

Gauge : 4ft 8½in

11257		0-4-0ST	OC	Hor	1111	1910	(a) (1)
No.6		0-6-0ST	OC	HL	3606	1924	(b) (2)

(a) orig L&YR 614; sold by LMSR, 11257, to Holloway Bros, 10/1937; at Littlebrook Power Station contract, Dartford, Kent, /1949; at Calverton by 12/1951.
(b) ex Appleby-Frodingham Steel Co Ltd, Scunthorpe, Lincs, No.6, 11/1951.

(1) to Plant Depot, Nottingham, /1952 (after 19/7/1952).
(2) to NCB, East Midlands Division, No.6 Area, Linby Colliery, 6 VALERIE, after 19/7/1952, by 1/12/1952.

NOTTINGHAM PLANT DEPOT   QC25
SK 536410

Locos were kept at this plant depot in Beechdale Road, Aspley, Nottingham.

Gauge : 4ft 8½in

(11257)		0-4-0ST	OC	Hor	1111	1910	(a) (1)
-		4wDM		FH	3700	1955 New	(b) (2)

(a) ex Calverton Colliery Sidings contract, after 19/7/1952.
(b) to Watnall Screens Disposal Point, after 4/1957, by 6/1957; returned here c/1960 (by 2/1961).

(1) scrapped on site by A. Smith Metals, Basford, Nottingham, 7/1955.
(2) to Geo Campbell, Airdrie, Lanarks, by 1/1962.

W.H. HUTCHINSON
SHIREBROOK CONTRACT   JC26

Completion, after the failure of Walter Binns (which see), of the 10½ miles of the Leen Valley Extension Railway (for the GNR) between Kirkby South Jct - Sutton - Skegby and Pleasley by 4/1898 and also the contract, let on 3/12/1897, for the Pleasley to Langwith Jct line, opened from Pleasley to Shirebrook Colliery on 26/11/1900 and to Langwith from 29/5/1901.

Preliminary adverts in 2/1898 for a forthcoming auction at Sutton in Ashfield for W.H. Hutchinson, on completion of the Leen Valley Extension, mentioned seven MW locos, 4 and 6 wheeled, 8 to 13inch cylinders. However later adverts for apparently the same auction (on 26/4/1898) make no mention of any locos so presumably they were retained by Hutchinson for the Langwith contract. It will be noted that the details do not exactly tally with the locos listed below.

"Contract Journal" and "Colliery Guardian" record a sale 4-5/6/1901 re W.H. Hutchinson, GNR Leen Valley Contract No.2 at Shirebrook and Langwith Jct including five 4 and 6 coupled locos by MW & HC, 8,9,10,11,12inch.

Three unidentified 10 to 13in MW locos were for sale in 9/1902 off Hutchinson's contracts for the Yorkshire Dales Railway (Embsay Jct. - Grassington), and extensions at Colne (Midland Rly / LYR) (1900 -1902); some or all were probably from those listed below.

Gauge : 4ft 8½in

No.	Name	Type	Cyl	Builder	No.	Year	Note	Ref
No.3		0-6-0ST	IC	MW	1290	1895	(a)	(1)
	KIRKBY	0-4-0ST	OC	MW	1303	1895	(a)	(2)
	PLEASLEY	0-4-0ST	OC	MW	1304	1895	(a)	(3)
	SKEGBY	0-4-0ST	OC	MW	915	1883	(a)	(4)
	-	0-4-0ST	OC	MW	653	1877	(b)	(5)
	-	0-6-0ST	IC	P	455	1887	(b)	(6)
	TEVERSALL #	0-4-0ST	OC	P	440	1885	(b)	(7)
No.5	MAINDEE	0-6-0ST	IC	MW	488	1874	(c)	(8)
	BRUNEL	0-6-0ST	IC	MW	557	1875	(d)	(9)
	PEGGY	0-6-0ST	IC	HC	540	1900	(e)	(10)

\# Name may have been TEVERSALL or TEVERSAL. (see note under Walter Binns).

(a) ex Walter Binns, with contract, /1897.
(b) possibly ex Walter Binns, with contract, /1897. However not confirmed as being with W.H. Hutchinson on this or any other of his contracts.
(c) earlier Logan & Hemingway, Annesley- East Leake (MS&LR) (1894-1898) contract; with W.H. Hutchinson by c/1901, but whether on this contract is not confirmed.
(d) earlier Lovatt & Shaw, Pentyrch (Barry Rly) (1886-1889) contract, Glam; then probably Sir John Jackson, Barry Dock (1890-1897) contract, Glam, where auctioned 21/12/1897. Then to W.H.Hutchinson by c/1901 but whether on this contract is not confirmed.
(e) New to David Shanks, Northallerton contract, Yorks (NR); reputedly with W.H. Hutchinson, Shirebrook, by c6/1901 but unconfirmed.

(1) later H. Lovatt, Salford Dock extension (Manchester Ship Canal) (1902-1905) contract, Lancs.
(2) later Flower & Everett Ltd, Rainham, Essex, early 1900s.
(3) later Harold Arnold & Son, Seacroft Hospital construction (1900-1904), Leeds.
(4) later R. Finnegan, Cromer - Mundesley (GER/M&GNR Jt) (1903-1906) contract, Norfolk.
(5) later Hugh Symington & Sons, contrs, Coatbridge, Lanarks, by early 1900s.
(6) later Price, Wills & Reeves, Immingham Dock (1906-1912) contract, Lincs, SHEFFIELD.
(7) later Price & Wills, contrs, (location unknown); later Bairds & Dalmellington Ltd, Buccleugh Brickworks, Sanquhar, Dumfriesshire.
(8) later R.H. Longbotham & Co Ltd, dealers, Wakefield, Yorks (WR), early 1900s; then to Buxton Lime Firms Co Ltd, Ladmanlow, Derbys, by c/1912.
(9) to John J. Lee, dealer, Manchester (possibly by /1903 until c/1911 or later); then to Leeds Sand & Gravel Co Ltd, Rothwell & Stourton Quarries, Yorks (WR), by c/1914.
(10) apparently with David Shanks, contr, Newcastle-upon-Tyne, by c/1904.

KIER CONSTRUCTION LTD
MANSFIELD CONTRACT

HC27
SK 540612

Construction of Mansfield Outfall Sewer, Toothill Lane, Mansfield, for Severn Trent Water Ltd.

Gauge : 2ft 0in

		4wDH	AK	40	1992	(a)	(1)
		4wDH	AK	47	1994	New (b)	(2)

(a) ex AK, Ross-on-Wye, Hereford & Worcs, hire, 1/12/1993.
(b) ex AK, Ross-on-Wye, hire, c2/1994.

(1) returned to AK, off hire, by 5/1994
(2) returned to AK, off hire, by 6/10/1994.

JOHN TOWLERTON LEATHER
EREWASH VALLEY CONTRACT

LC28

Construction of the Erewash Valley line for the Midland Railway, 1847-1850. The first section of this, from Long Eaton Jct to Codnor Park Ironworks, was opened on 6/9/1847. Subsequently an auction at Shipley Wharf on 1/5/1849 for Leather on completion of this contract included two locomotives. This contract was in fact entirely in Derbyshire but is included here as the line was important to the development of industry and mines on the Nottinghamshire side of the River Erewash.

Details of the locomotives were given as: Two six-wheeled locos.

One American built, OC, 12x20in, 2 driving wheels, 4ft 8in, 4 trailing wheels 2ft 6in, Boiler 8ft 3in long, 3ft 8in diam., 98 tubes 8ft 3in long...and tender.

One made by Nasmyth, Gaskell & Co, IC, 12½x20in, 2 driving wheels, 5ft, 4 trailing wheels 3ft 7in, Boiler 8ft 2in long, 3ft 8in diam., 102 tubes 8ft 3in long.

Some of this information seems suspect, e.g. the IC for the Nasmyth, Gaskell loco.

Probable identities seem to be two locomotives originally with the Birmingham & Gloucester Railway :

B&GR 6, VICTORIA 4-2-0 OC Norris /1839; to Midland Rly (277?), 2/1847; disposed of 1848.

B&GR 29, UPTON 4-2-0 OC Nasmyth Gaskell 23/1841; to Midland Rly (allocated 285?, 2/1847), but sold to T. Leather, 3/1847.

4/1851 Joy's diaries record on a tour of colllieries in the Nottingham area that on contractor's work was one of the Norris locos that had been imported to England for the B&GR. How this relates to the above is not known.

F.J.C. LILLEY LTD.
NOTTINGHAM CONTRACT QC29

SK 537437

Sewer renewal contract at Cinderhill, Nottingham, for Severn Trent Water Authority, 1987. Locos used underground.

Gauge : 1ft 6in

EL7	4wBE	CE	5373/1 1967	(a)	(1)
	4wBE	CE		(a)	(1)

(a) ex Haunchwood Plant Depot, Galley Common, Warwicks, 3/1987.

(1) to Haunchwood Plant Depot, Galley Common, Warwicks, /1987 (after 9/4/1987, by 30/7/1987).

LOGAN & HEMINGWAY

BINGHAM CONTRACT UC30

Contract No.4 for the construction of the Stathern Jct. to Saxondale Jct. (Bingham) branch of the GN & LNW Joint Rly, contract let 10/1875 and line opened 30/6/1879. Contracts Nos.1, 2 and 5 were let to Benton & Woodiwiss (which see) and Contract No.3 (in Leicestershire) for Tilton - Market Harborough & Medbourne was let to Logan & Hemingway. A sale at Medbourne on the latter 2-5/3/1880 included seven 6-coupled MW locos built 1876; these may have included ones from the Bingham contract.

Gauge : 4ft 8½in

No.9		0-6-0ST	IC	MW	598	1876	New	(1)
No.12		0-6-0ST	IC	MW	610	1876	New	(2)

(1) to McGregor & Badman, Manchester South District Railway (1877-1880) contract.
(2) to Braddock & Matthews, West Lancs Rly (1879-1883) contract, Southport, Lancs, LIZZIE.

NOTTINGHAM CONTRACT S/N/VC31

Contract No.1, signed 9/1894, of the London Extension of the MS&LR for the construction of the Annesley - East Leake section of railway (19¾ miles). Also included appear to have been curves at Bulwell Common and Bagthorpe Jct; Gotham Gypsum Works branch (authorised 6/7/1895, opened 2/5/1900) and the Clifton Colliery branch (authorised 29/6/1893, opened 25/7/1898).

There are reports of twenty locos being used on this section. Many are unidentified but were probably from the 20 MWs new for the Beighton - Chesterfield (MS&LR) contract (1890 - 1892) or six or so earlier MWs. Sales advertised were for six 12in 6 coupled MW locos at or near Nottingham in 3/1896, and eight 12 and 13in 6 coupled tanks by MW at Ruddington on 26/2/1901.

Gauge : 4ft 8½in

	MAINDEE	0-6-0ST	IC	MW	488	1874	(a)	(1)
13		0-6-0ST	IC	MW	1144	1890	(b)	(2)
14		0-6-0ST	IC	MW	1153	1890	(c)	(3)
17		0-6-0ST	IC	MW	1190	1890	(b)	(4)
20		0-6-0ST	IC	MW	1191	1890	(b)	(5)
22		0-6-0T	IC	MW	1196	1890	(b)	(6)
30		0-6-0ST	IC	MW	1210	1891	(c)	(7)
	ROCKET	0-6-0ST	IC	MW	871	1883	(d)	(8)
	MONITOR	0-6-0ST	IC	MW	1225	1891	(b)	(9)

(a) orig Logan & Hemingway, East Usk Branch contract (1874-5?), Mon, No.7.
(b) orig Beighton - Chesterfield contract, Derbys.
(c) orig Beighton - Chesterfield contract, Derbys; use on this contract not confirmed.
(d) orig Logan & Hemingway, Hill's Dry Dock & Engineering Co contract (1883), Cardiff. possibly then to Penarth - Cadoxton (TVR) (1886-1888) contract, Glam.

(1) to W.H. Hutchinson, assumed on Leen Valley Extension contracts.
(2) later Hemingway & Co's No.9 (in early 1900s ?); possibly to Thos Oliver & Son, Neasden - Northolt (GCR) (1901-1905) contract, London/Bucks and also possibly to MoM, Gretna, Dumfries; later South Metropolitan Gas Co, East Greenwich Works, London, 25, /1918,.
(3) to Thos. Oliver & Son, Rugby-Woodford Halse (MS&LR) (1894-1898) contract, Warwicks/Northants.
(4) later J.T. Firbank, Amesbury branch (LSWR) (1899-1902) contract, Wilts, AMESBURY; possibly after use on J.T. Firbank, St. Johns Wood - Marylebone (MS&LR) (1894-1899) contract.
(5) later altered to 15 (Hemingway & Co) in 1903; subsequently Watford (1922-1925) contract, Herts.
(6) to S. Pearson & Son, Wootton Bassett - Patchway (GWR) (1897-1903) contract, Wilts/Glos, CORSTON, by 6/1899.
(7) later Hemingway & Co's 10 (in early 1900s); possibly later Cranwell Light Railway contract (1916-1919), Lincs.
(8) later at Hucknall Colliery Co Ltd, Hucknall Torkard No.2 Colliery, Notts, by early 1900s.
(9) later Gowdall & Braithwell Railway contract (1911-1916), Yorks (WR); S. Pearson & Son, Gretna Factory (MoM) construction, Dumfries.

THORESBY CONTRACT   GC32

Construction of the Thoresby Colliery branch and sidings for the Bolsover Colliery Co, during the 1922 - 1928 period.

Gauge : 4ft 8½in

10	0-6-0ST	IC	MW	1210	1891	(a)	(1)

(a) possibly previously Cranwell Light Railway (1916-1919) contract, Lincs; earlier Nottingham contract; here by 1/1928.

(1) to Mottram - Godley (LNER) (1928-1930) widening contract, Cheshire, after 4/1928, by 7/1928.

LONDON, MIDLAND & SCOTTISH RAILWAY
ROLLESTON CONTRACT   PC33

The LMSR Chief Civil Engineer's Department undertook a number of projects with direct labour during the 1920s and 1930s including the construction of the Rolleston West Curve during 1928-1929. A LMSR departmental locomotive was used on this contract.

Gauge : 4ft 8½in

    DANBY LODGE   0-6-0ST IC MW 1595 1903 (a) (1)

(a)   here by 6/1928; earlier at Horbury contract, Yorks (WR); loco was obtained by LNWR from MoM, Chilwell.

(1)   to Mirfield widening contract, Yorks (WR), after 3/1929, by 12/1930; later to Beeston Sleeper Works.

HENRY LOVATT

EAST LEAKE CONTRACT   VC34

Contract No.2 of the London Extension of the MS&LR for the construction of 16½ miles of railway from East Leake to Aylestone (Leics). For details, see the forthcoming Leicestershire Handbook.

LEEN VALLEY CONTRACT   NC35

Construction of the Leen Valley branch (6 miles - authorised 6/8/1880), for the GNR, from Leen Valley Jct to Newstead & Annesley Colliery together with several colliery branches. Contract let 5/11/1880 and lines opened throughout 27/10/1881.

Gauge : 4ft 8½in

    -    0-6-0ST IC MW 458 1874 (a) (1)

(a)   earlier John Barnes/T.J. Waller, Hellifield - Chatburn (L&YR) (1877-1880) contract, Lancs.

(1)   later probably East Leake - Aylestone (MS&LR) (1894-1898) contract, Notts/Leics, No.3.

WILSON LOVATT & SONS LTD
NORTH WILFORD CONTRACT SC36

Construction of North Wilford Power Station for Nottingham Corporation Electricity Department, 1923 - 1925.

Gauge : 4ft 8½in

-		0-6-0ST	IC	HE	152	1876	(a)	(1)

(a) earlier New Margarine Factory contract, Bromborough, Cheshire, until after 1/1921; here by 7/1923.

(1) to Nottingham Corporation Electricity Department, North Wilford Power Station, c/1926 (by 1/1927).

SIR ALFRED McALPINE & SON LTD
HIGH MARNHAM CONTRACT FC37

Construction of High Marnham Power Station for CEGB, 1957 - 1958.

Gauge : 4ft 8½

No.200		0-6-0ST	IC	HC	1749	1946	(a)	(1)

(a) ex Great Stanney Plant Depot, Cheshire, /1957

(1) to Great Stanney Plant Depot, c/1958 (after 5/1958).

SIR ROBERT McALPINE & SONS LTD
OSSINGTON AIRFIELD CONTRACT FC38
SK 74x64x

Wartime airfield located about 2 miles south of Tuxford. Contract for runway construction for the Air Ministry, 1941 - 1942.

Gauge : 2ft 0in

PN.2930	4wPM	(MR/FH?)			(a)	s/s
PN.4116	4wDM	MR	5865	1934	(b)	(1)
PN.4363	4wPM	MR	(? 7034	1936)	(c)	s/s
PN.4366	4wPM	MR	(? 7038	1936)	(d)	s/s
PN.4447	4wPM	MR	7356	1938	(e)	(2)
PN.5027	4wDM	MR	8715	1941	New	(3)
PN.5028	4wDM	MR	8716	1941	New	(4)
PN.5031	4wDM	MR	8719	1941	New	(5)
-	4wDM	MR	8725	1941	New	(6)

(a) earlier Scunthorpe contract, Lincs, /1938 (20hp "Simplex" type loco, originally numbered PN.1504; purchased /1920 for £250 from unrecorded vendor).
(b) ex a previous contract (or McA Plant Depot), /1941 (by 31/10/1941); loco was new to Kendoon Reservoir contract, New Galloway.
(c) ex a previous contract (or McA Plant Depot), /1941 (by 31/10/1941); earlier Ebbw Vale contract, Mon, until 20/7/1938. This loco was one of a batch of four secondhand locos (MR 7034/6/7/8) purchased from MR, 3/12/1937 and by deduction PN.4363 is most probably MR 7034.
(d) ex a previous contract (or McA Plant Depot), /1941 (by 31/10/1941); earlier Ebbw Vale contract, Mon, until 20/7/1938. This loco was one of a batch of four secondhand locos (MR 7034/6/7/8) purchased from MR, 3/12/1937 and by deduction PN.4366 is most probably MR 7038.
(e) ex a previous contract (or McA Plant Depot), /1941 (by 31/10/1941).

(1) to a later contract (or McA Plant Depot), c/1942 (after 31/10/1941); at Hayes Plant Depot, Middx, 28/12/1949; later s/s.
(2) to a later contract (or McA Plant Depot), c/1942 (after 31/10/1941); at Hayes Plant Depot, Middx, 8/2/1951; not at Hayes, 3/8/1953; at Hayes, 8/10/1955; s/s.
(3) to a later contract (or McA Plant Depot), c/1942 (after 31/10/1941); later at Hams Hall Power Station contract, Warwicks; at Hayes Plant Depot, Middx, 8/2/1951; s/s.
(4) to a later contract (or McA Plant Depot), c/1942 (after 31/10/1941); later at Hams Hall Power Station contract, Warwicks; s/s.
(5) to a later contract (or McA Plant Depot), c/1942 (after 31/10/1941); not at Hayes, 8/2/1951 or 3/8/1953; at Hayes Depot, 8/10/1955; later at Peat Development Co Ltd, Douglas Water, Lanarks.
(6) to a later contract (or McA Plant Depot), c/1942 (after 31/10/1941); s/s.

LOWDHAM PLANT DEPOT UC39
SK 673461

The company has kept locomotives at this plant depot between contracts.

Gauge : 4ft 8½in

No.71		0-6-0ST	IC	HC	1667	1936	(a)	(1)
No.83		0-6-0ST	IC	HC	1675	1937	(b)	(2)
-		0-4-0DM		RH	252684	1948	(c)	(3)

(a) ex South Lynn contract, Norfolk, 23/1/1958.
(b) ex South Lynn contract, Norfolk, 5/3/1958
(c) ex Spencer Works contract, Llanwern, Mon, c/1966; earlier Steel Company of Wales, Margam Works, Port Talbot, West Glam, 603, until 4/1960.

(1) to Roe Bros & Co Ltd, Rotherham, Yorks (WR) for scrap, 25/1/1960.
(2) to Roe Bros & Co Ltd, Rotherham, Yorks (WR) for scrap, 18/1/1960.
(3) to P.W. Spencer Ltd, Grassington, N Yorks, 1/1967.

Gauge : 2ft 0in

	PN.3028	4wBE	HC	E294	1929	(a)	s/s
	-	4wDM	MR	8998	1946	(b)	(1)
	-	0-4-0BE	WR	6308	1961	(c)	(2)
	-	0-4-0BE	WR	6309	1961	(c)	(2)
	-	4wBE	WR	J7208	1969	New	(2)
	-	4wBE	WR	J7272	1969	New	(2)

(a) ex unknown contract by 2/1968; earlier at Hayes plant depot, Middx, 8/10/1955.
(b) ex Hayes plant depot, Middx, by 2/1968.
(c) new; 18in gauge until 26/7/1962.

(1) used on various contracts; to Sir W.H. McAlpine, Fawley Hall, Fawley Green, Henley-on-Thames, Bucks, /1970.
(2) used on various contracts; to Kettering Plant Depot, Northants.

MITCHELL BROS, SONS & CO LTD
FIRBECK, HARWORTH & WELBECK CONTRACTS B/GC40

This firm of contractors, established in Glasgow and registered 11/1918, had a plant depot at Tickhill (South Yorks) (just over the county boundary) in the 1970s, which was possibly established in the 1920s in connection with these contracts. More than one contract was involved but it is convenient to treat them as a unit since the allocation of known locos is uncertain.

1] Firbeck Jcts (near Tickhill) - Harworth Jct - Harworth & Firbeck Collieries (South Yorks Joint Lines Committee (LNER/LMSR)), 1923 - 1929. In late 1923 (tendered 9/1923) Mitchell was awarded the contract for Firbeck Jcts to Harworth Colliery, but work towards Harworth colliery was delayed due to difficulties with Barber, Walker, etc. (1923 - 1925).
Meanwhile a temporary line was planned to Firbeck Colliery in connection with sinking operations; a permanent branch was decided on early in 1924 and Mitchell won the contract for this later in 1924 (10/1924 ?). The temporary line opened in 1924 and the permanent Firbeck branch on 1/10/1926 (with maintenance by contractor until 1/10/1927). In 12/1924 five contractors locos were said to be in use; in 4/1926 eight locos.
In 10/1926 Mitchell apparently got a further contract for Harworth Jct to Harworth Colliery, plus the east curve at Harworth Jct., and the connecting line south of Harworth colliery to the ex-GNR branch, but it is unclear whether the 1923 contract to Harworth had been cancelled/amended. The Harworth branch was completed 1/3/1928 (with maintenance by the contractor for a further year) but was not opened until 22/4/1929.

2] Welbeck Colliery Branch (LMSR), (by) 1927 - 1929 - opened 1/1/1929.

Details of the Harworth construction contracts are complex; for further information see :
References : "Railways of the South Yorkshire Coalfield", Arthur L. Barnett, RCTS, 1984
"South Yorkshire Joint Railway", Oakwood Press

Gauge : 4ft 8½in

No.6	0-6-0ST	IC	MW	1499	1901	(a)	(1)
No.8	0-6-0ST	IC	MW	1568	1902	(b)	(2)
No.9	0-6-0ST	IC	MW	1569	1902		
		reb	MW		1925	(c)	(3)
No.10	0-6-0ST	IC	MW	1600	1904	(d)	(3)
No.11	0-6-0ST	IC	MW	1519	1901	(e)	(4)
No.12	0-6-0ST	IC	MW	2017	1925	New (f)	(5)
No.16	0-6-0T	OC	HC	1523	1925	New (g)	(6)

(a) orig Mitchell Bros, Potterhill - Barrhead (G&SWR) (1900-1902) contract, Lanarks; not confirmed on Firbeck contract but spares to Welbeck contract, 10/1927 -6/1928 and repaired by K for Mitchell, 10-12/1928.
(b) orig Mitchell Bros, Cairn Valley Light Railway (G&SWR) (1901-1905) contract, Dumfries; not confirmed on Firbeck contract but spares to Welbeck contract, 5/1929.
(c) orig Mitchell Bros, Shireoaks - Laughton (Sheffield & Midland Committee) (1902-1905) contract, S.Yorks; reputedly used on Firbeck contract and then spares to Welbeck contract, probably 2/1928 and certainly in 1/1929.
(d) orig Mitchell Bros, Cairn Valley Light Railway (G&SWR) (1901-1905) contract, Dumfries; not confirmed on Firbeck contract but spares to Welbeck contract, probably 2/1928 and certainly in 1/1929.
(e) earlier Cadbury Bros, Bournville, Birmingham / John Price & Sons (contractors), London, (early 1920s?; possibly used by Price on a contract for Cadbury's) and to MW; sold to Mitchell Bros, to Firbeck contract, 5-6/1925; spares to Harworth, 10/1927, 3/1928.
(f) New to Tickhill, after 12/1924; spares to Welbeck contract, 12/1927 and 8/1928.
(g) New to Firbeck contract, 12/1925.

(1) later Sir Lindsay Parkinson & Co Ltd, Chorley ROF construction, Lancs, c/1937 (by 2/1939).
(2) later Sir Lindsay Parkinson & Co Ltd, Chorley ROF construction, Lancs, c/1937 (by 3/1938).
(3) later Sir Lindsay Parkinson & Co Ltd, Grimsby Fish Dock contract (1930-1934), Lincs.
(4) Spares to Tickhill Plant Depot, 5/1930; later Sir Lindsay Parkinson & Co Ltd, Chorley ROF construction, Lancs, c/1937 (by 4/1939).
(5) later Whitehead Iron & Steel Co Ltd, Newport, Mon, by 4/1935.
(6) to Earl Fitzwilliam's Collieries Co, New Stubbin Colliery, Rawmarsh, Yorks (WR), 11/1929.

The locomotive listed below was delivered to this firm of contractors; details of use unknown.

Gauge : 600mm

-	4wPM	MR	3858	1928	New	(1)

(1) later with Trent Concrete Ltd, Nottingham.

WILLIAM MOSS & SONS LTD
Company, registered 5/1919, which specialised in work in re-inforced concrete. By 1924 it had a plant depot at Loughborough, Leics.

CARLTON CONTRACT UC41
SK 633421

Construction of new settling tanks at Stoke Bardolph Sewage Works, Stoke Ferry Lane, Carlton, Nottingham for Nottingham Corporation, 1931.

Gauge : 2ft 0in

-	4wPM	MR	5339	1931	New	(1)

(1) later with George W.Bungey Ltd, dealers, Hayes, Middx.

JOHN MOWLEM & SONS LTD
RUDDINGTON CONTRACT

VC42
SK 570324

Construction of ROF Ruddington for War Office. Work commenced 12/1940 for expected completion in 7/1941.

Gauge : 4ft 8½in

SWYNNERTON	0-6-0ST	OC	HC	1208	1916	(a)	(1)
HAYLE	0-6-0ST	IC	HC	1539	1924	(b)	(1)

Also possibly another 0-6-0ST, HC, unidentified.

(a) ex Swynnerton ROF construction contract, Staffs, /1940.
(b) ex Swynnerton ROF construction contract, Staffs, /1941.

(1) later at Hatfield Plant Depot, Herts, by 2/1943.

NAYLOR BROS
RUFFORD CONTRACT

GC43

Construction of the Rufford Colliery branch for Midland Railway, 1911-1912 (branch opened 20/6/1912). The locomotives detailed below were offered for sale at Rainworth, 6/6/1912.

Gauge : 4ft 8½in

(No.5 ?)	0-6-0ST	IC	MW			(a)	(1)
(No.6 ?)	0-6-0ST	IC	MW			(a)	(1)
TISSINGTON	0-4-0ST	OC	MW	1280	1894	(b)	(2)

(a) origin unknown (12in cyls).
(b) orig Parsley Hay - Ashbourne (LNWR) (1896-1899) contract, Derbys.

(1) to ?
(2) to Henry Leetham & Sons Ltd, York, c/1912.

ELISHA WRIGHT OLDHAM
NEWARK CONTRACTS

PC44

Construction, by this contractor of Poppleton, York, of the GNR main line, Hougham (near Grantham) - Newark and from River Trent - Retford, 1850-1852. Tenders invited 4/1850; work ceased 3/1852 because of the failure of Oldham. His trustees, Yorkshire Banking Co, took over his plant and J. Cubitt (Engineer to GNR) paid the men and work resumed. In 7/1852 Cubitt took over the contract as trustees had not paid the men. Line opened 7/1852.

On 2-3/8/1852 an auction at Newark of plant used on this contract included 'three locomotive engines' (not identified).

THOMAS OLIVER
MANSFIELD CONTRACT   GC45

Construction of the Mansfield - Shireoaks East Jct railway for Midland Rly, 1869 - 1875. Five engines (not necessarily all locomotives) were reported to have been at work in 1872; the only one yet identified is listed below. The line opened for goods traffic on 3/2/1875.

Gauge : 4ft 8½in

	FRANK	0-6-0ST	IC	MW	205	1866	(a)	(1)

(a)   earlier Brassey & Ballard, Bedford - Radlett (Midland Rly) (1865-1867) contract, Beds; here by 11/1870.

(1)   later Coke & Co, Pinxton Collieries, before c/1888 (possibly c/1877).

TEVERSAL CONTRACT   JC46

Construction of the Teversal - Pleasley extension line for the Midland Railway, 2/1875 - 3/1877.
Two locomotives were in use on this contract on 2/11/1875.

BULWELL CONTRACT   QC47

Construction of the Bennerley - Bulwell line and the Watnall New Colliery branch for the Midland Railway, 8/1875 - 7/1879.
One locomotive was employed on 31/8/1875. Six locomotives and portables were in use on 5/12/1876 and 31/7/1877. Twelve locomotives and six portables were here on 1/1/1878; continuing figures were six locos, seven portables (2/4/1878), eight locos, seven portables (8/6/1878 and 2/7/1878) and four "engines" in 1/1879. Identities not known.

W.R. PARKER & CO
COLWICK CONTRACT   TC48

This Cardiff based contractor undertook work to extend and improve access to Colwick Yard (contract let 13/4/1888) and also Radcliffe - Saxondale Jct widening for the GNR, 1888-8/1890.
The following locos, owned by W.R. Parker & Co at this period, are believed to have worked on this contract, but confirmation is required.

Gauge : 4ft 8½in

	RADCLIFFE	0-6-0ST	IC	HE	172	1872	(a)	(1)
	WOODSIDE	0-6-0ST	IC	HE	266	1881	(b)	(2)

(a) orig J. Firbank, Preston Park - Cliftonville, Brighton (LBSCR) (1876-1879) contract, Sussex.
(b) orig J. Firbank, Woodside & South Croydon Rly (1881-1885) contract, Surrey.

(1) presumed to Cardiff on completion of contract; purchased by Taff Vale Rly at Cardiff on bankruptcy of W.R. Parker, after 10/1892.
(2) possibly to Kirkgate Fork, Wakefield, (L&YR/GNR) (1892-1893) reconstruction contract, Yorks (WR); later S. Pearson & Son, Chesterfield contract, Derbys, 22.

SIR LINDSAY PARKINSON & CO LTD
EAST BRIDGFORD CONTRACT

UC49
SK 680410

Construction of new RAF station, Newton, East Bridgford, 1939-1940.

Gauge : 2ft 0in

		4wDM	HE			(a)	s/s
-		4wDM	MR	7386	1939	New	s/s
-		4wDM	MR	7391	1939	New	(1)

(a) ex Chorley ROF contract, Lancs (after repairs at HE, 12/1938 -c1/1939) (20hp loco).

(1) to Kottler & Heron Ltd, contrs, Northampton, by 17/2/1947; later at Slindon Gravels Ltd, Slindon, Sussex, by 2/2/1955.

A.H. PRICE & CO
NOTTINGHAM

XC50

Details unknown.

Gauge : 2ft 0in

-	0-4-0WT	OC	HC	1161	1915	(a)	(1)

(a) orig Harper Bros.& Co, Richmond Camp construction, Yorks; with Price, Nottingham, by /1931.

(1) later Harold Potter & Co, dealers, Nottingham, (by 12/1933?).

PRICE & WILLS

TUXFORD CONTRACT FC51

Tuxford - Lincoln (Pyewipe Jct.) construction for LD&ECR. Contract let 10/1894; line opened 16/11/1896.

Gauge : 4ft 8½in

STANLOW	0-4-0ST	OC	MW	1017	1887	(a)	(1)
TAWE	0-4-0ST	OC	MW	1020	1887	(a)	(2)
FRANCES	0-4-0ST	OC	HC	435	1895	New	(3)
EASTNEY	0-6-0ST	IC	HC	441	1895	(b)	(4)

(a) earlier T.A. Walker, Manchester Ship Canal construction (1887-1894), Lancs.
(b) orig J. Price, Portsmouth Dockyard contract, Hants.

(1) later C.J. Wills & Sons Ltd, Rippleway (London - Tilbury Road) (1920-1924) contract, Barking, Essex.
(2) later Price, Wills & Reeves, Immingham Dock (1906-1912) contract, Lincs.
(3) later C.J. Wills /Price, Wills & Reeves, Spurn Head Rly (WD) (c1915-1918) contract, Yorks (ER).
(4) probably to Barry Low Level Dock (1894-1899) contract, Glam.

WARSOP CONTRACT GC52

Construction of Warsop - Shirebrook curve (½ mile) for LD&ECR. Tender accepted 12/1897; line opened 9/1/1899.

Gauge : 4ft 8½in

RUNCORN	0-6-0T	IC	MW	1025	1887	(a)	(1)
BIRKENHEAD	0-6-0T	IC	MW	1100	1888	(a)	(1)
MORECAMBE	0-6-0ST	IC	MW	1393	1898	(b)	(2)

(a) earlier Barry Low Level Dock (1894-1899) contract, Glam, (use on Warsop contract not certain).
(b) New to Price & Wills at Arkwright Town, Derbys; (use on Warsop contract not certain).

(1) later Price, Wills & Reeves, Immingham Dock (1906-1912) contract, Lincs.
(2) later Heysham Harbour construction (1897-1904) contract, Lancs.

WALTER SCOTT & MIDDLETON LTD
KELHAM CONTRACT   PC53

Contract at Newark, c/1922. Almost certainly the construction of Kelham Sugar Beet Factory for Home Grown Sugar Ltd. However, Walter Scott & Middleton also had a contract for Muskham Bridge, Newark (near Kelham; possibly the crossing of the A1 road over the River Trent) by 3/1922.

Gauge : 4ft 8½in

MARELL	0-6-0ST	IC	HE	876	1906	(a)	(1)	
BRADFORD	0-6-0ST	IC	MW	899	1884	(b)	(2)	
CYPRUS	0-6-0ST	IC	MW	596	1896			
	reb		MW		1900	(c)	(1)	

(a) ex Scunthorpe contract, Lincs, after 6/1920, by 10/1920.
(b) ex Scunthorpe contract, Lincs, c/1920.
(c) ex Scunthorpe contract, Lincs, c/1920 (probably used on Kelham contract).

(1) to Home Grown Sugar Ltd, Kelham, /1922.
(2) later Stanmore Branch (Met. Rly.) (1930-1932) contract, Middx.

SHANKS & McEWAN LTD
OLLERTON CONTRACT   GC54

Construction of the Farnsfield - Ollerton railway (LNER & LMSR Joint). Work commenced 1929; line opened for goods traffic 30/11/1931 and New Ollerton Goods depot in 2/1932. On completion of the contract several locos were left abandoned for some years at Farnsfield until their final scrapping. This was noted in 1942, but may in fact have occurred earlier, possibly about 1940.

Gauge : 4ft 8½in

8		0-4-0ST	OC	AB	675	1891	(a)	Scr by /1942
1		0-4-0ST	OC	AB	267	1884	(b)	Scr by /1942
4	LIVERPOOL	0-6-0ST	OC	P	564	1897	(c)	Scr by /1942
	LAUCHOPE	0-6-0ST	IC	HE	619	1894		
		reb		Gibb		1911	(c)	(1)
30		0-6-0ST	IC	MW	996	1886	(d)	Scr by /1942
55	PETERHEAD	0-6-0ST	IC	MW	1378	1898	(e)	(2)
37	WOODHALL	0-6-0ST	IC	MW	1668	1905	(f)	(5)
	DON	0-6-0ST	IC	MW	1293	1895	(g)	(4)
	BIRKENHEAD	0-6-0ST	IC	MW	1530	1901	(g)	Scr by /1942
38	ROSEHALL	0-6-0ST	IC	HC	531	1899	(h)	(4)
82		0-4-0ST	OC	HC	638	1903	(h)	Scr by /1942
3		0-6-0ST	OC	BH	(? 167	1873)	(i)	(6)
49		0-6-0ST	IC	MW	1579	1902	(j)	Scr by /1942
31		0-4-0ST	OC	MW	793	1882	(k)	Scr by /1942
53		0-4-0ST	OC	AB	1027	1904	(l)	(4)
	FULWOOD	0-6-0ST	IC	HE	529	1891	(m)	(3)

(a) with Northumberland Quarries Ltd, Forestburngate, Rothbury, Northumberland, WINGATE until after 6/1921; here by 6/1930.
(b) earlier Clydebridge Steel Works contract, (1917-1919), Cambuslang, Lanarks; here by 6/1930.
(c) earlier Shieldhall Dock construction (Clyde Navigation Trust) (1924-1931), Glasgow.
(d) (possibly earlier Shieldhall Dock construction (Clyde Navigation Trust) (1924-1931), Glasgow); at Mossend, Lanarks, 11/1927; here by 3/1930.
(e) earlier Shieldhall Dock construction (Clyde Navigation Trust) (1924-1931), Glasgow until after 12/1927; here by 4/1930 (and in 8/1930).
(f) possibly earlier Shieldhall Dock construction (Clyde Navigation Trust) (1924-1931), Glasgow; at Mossend, Lanarks, 8/1929; here by 12/1929 (and in 3/1930, 1/1931).
(g) ex Sheffield Corporation Waterworks, Ewden Valley, /1929.
(h) earlier Edinburgh - Glasgow road construction contract (1925-1934)
(i) earlier Mossend Steelworks Extension (1914-1919) contract, Lanarks; identity not confirmed.
(j) earlier Topham, Jones & Railton Ltd, Johore Causeway contract, Singapore, 6/1921 and then to Crymlyn Burrows Depot, Swansea; here by 12/1929.
(k) earlier Dick, Kerr & Co Ltd, Surrey, 10/1908; here by 12/1930.
(l) earlier Hamilton, McCulloch & Co Ltd, Larkhall, Lanarks (for sale 6/1928?); here by 7/1930.
(m) earlier H. Arnold & Son Ltd, Blidworth contract (in 4/1929), here by 1/1930.

(1) also on Ambergate widening (LMSR) (1930-1932) contract, Derbys, before or after Ollerton; later Whitemoor Yard (LNER) (1931-1932) contract, Cambs, by 11/1931.
(2) also on Ambergate widening (LMSR) (1930-1932) contract, Derbys, probably after Ollerton, but order uncertain, later Bromsgrove to Stoke Works widening (LMSR) contract, Worcs, by 9/1932.
(3) to Whitemoor Yard (LNER) contract, March, Cambs, by 4/1931.
(4) to Corby Works Extension (S&L Ltd) contract, Northants, by /1935.
(5) also on Ambergate widening (LMSR) (1930-1932) contract, Derbys, probably after Ollerton, but order uncertain; later Corby Works Extension (S&L Ltd) contract, Northants.
(6) to Shanks & McEwan Ltd, Carnbroe Slag Hill, Lanarks, by 6/1935.

H. SYMINGTON & SONS
HARWORTH CONTRACT BC55

Construction of the Harworth Colliery branch (2½ miles) for the GNR from the GNR main line near Ranskill, 1922 - 10/1923. The line had originally been authorised about 1911 and a temporary line brought into use 3/1914, but work was then suspended during World War I.

Reference : "The Railway Engineer", May 1923.

Gauge : 4ft 8½in

| ORMISTON | 0-6-0ST | IC | HC | 531 | 1899 | (a) | (1) |

Note that in 11/1924 AB invoiced Symington for repairs to a 10in loco including carriage from Harworth and to Parkhead after repair; HC 531 was a 12in loco so this postulates a second loco on this contract.

(a) earlier Gretna Munitions Factory contract, Dumfriesshire.

(1) to Edinburgh - Glasgow road contract, c/1924.

J & G TOMLINSON

COLWICK CONTRACT   TC56

Colwick railway widening contract for GNR. Details of the contract are uncertain and the locomotive information is unconfirmed.

Gauge : 4ft 8½in

WILLIE	0-6-0ST	IC	MW	(a)	s/s
HARE	0-4-0ST	OC	HE	(a)	s/s

(a)   ex ? (both were 12in locos).

SKEGBY CONTRACTS   JC57

Construction of the Skegby branch extension for the Midland Railway, 3/1875 - 3/1877. A contractor's locomotive was working traffic on 5/9/1876.

Construction of the Pleasley branch extension (to Pleasley Jct) for the Midland Railway, 4/1880 -2/1882. A locomotive was in use, 2/11/1880, when there was a temporary line to carry stone from a quarry for the construction of the Meden Viaduct. Seven locomotives and portables were in use on 4/1/1881.

This contractor also built the Bestwood Park branch for the Midland Railway, 1874 -1/1876 - no locomotives known.

TRACKWORK ASSOCIATES LTD
HARWORTH CONTRACT   BC58

Contract, by this company based at Long Sandall, South Yorkshire, on the Harworth Colliery branch, for BR, 1987.

Gauge : 4ft 8½in

CHARLES	4wDM	RH	417889	1958	(a)	(1)

(a)   ex Thom Lane Plant Depot, Long Sandall, South Yorks, by 3/3/1987.

(1)   to Thom Lane Plant Depot, Long Sandall, South Yorks, /1987.

THOS. W. WARD LTD
PINXTON CONTRACT   KC59

Contract for the dismantling of the coke ovens at Pinxton of the Pinxton Coking Co Ltd in 1955. The locomotive was brought in to be included in an auction and was never used here.
Gauge : 4ft 8½in

                    -              0-4-0ST   OC   AB   973   1904   (a)   (1)

(a)   ex Burdale Quarries Ltd, Burdale Limestone Quarries, Yorks (ER), 11/1955 or 12/1955.

(1)   still here 7/1956 and 9/1957; s/s by 8/1961.

JOHN WARING & SONS
RETFORD CONTRACT   FC60

Construction of the Retford - Gainsborough railway for the MS&LR, 1847-1849. Contract let 2/1847 and line opened 16/7/1849. Because of unsatisfactory performance, the contract was taken out of Waring's hands and was completed by Peto, Betts & Giles, but this seems to have been at a late stage in the work, c6/1849.

An auction of plant 30/7/1849 -1/8/1849 at Clarbro and at Welham, near Retford for Waring & Sons included:
One 6-wheeled locomotive engine & tender, coupled on leading four wheels.
One 4-wheeled coupled locomotive and tender.
In 12/1850 plant advertised for sale at Welham included one 4-wheeled locomotive and tender - owner not stated (particulars from Joseph Wright, on the premises), but probably a Waring locomotive.
Neither loco has yet been identified, but LNWR Southern Division 82 (a Bury type 0-4-0 built by Maudslay, Sons & Field in 1838), sold to "Waring, East Lincolnshire" in 3/1847, and/or Monmouthshire Railway No.11, purchased from Waring in 9/1849, may be involved.

DEALERS YARDS & OTHER SITES

ABBOTT & CO (NEWARK) LTD
BEACON HILL WORKS, Newark **PD1**
SK 808541

The company was established by Thomas Abbot in 1874 but did not occupy this site until after 1884. The company was registered in 1898. The works, opened before 1895, was served by a siding which ran east from the GNR south of Newark (Northgate) Station and was located immediately south of Ransome & Marles Stanley Works. Whilst primarily a boiler maker and repairer, contract repairs to at least one industrial locomotive took place here. This was in 1942 when P 981 was repaired for Ransomes & Marles Bearing Co Ltd.

C & S COMMERCIAL SPARES LTD
WIGSLEY WOOD SCRAP YARD, Clifton Lane, Thorney. **FD2**
f. J.R. Clarke (Plant Dealers) SK 845708

Locomotives stored in the yard of this firm.

Gauge : 4ft 8½in

A1092	4wDM	RH	224354	1945	(a)	s/s
SF 364	4wDM	RH	338415	1953	(a)	s/s

(a) ex Clarke Chapman - John Thompson Ltd, Thompson Cochrane Division, Lincoln, c10/1977 (by 19/11/1977).

A. CLARKE
WIGSLEY PLANT DEPOT **FD3**
SK 861703

Locomotive stored for some years in the yard of this firm of plant dealers, located about six miles east of Tuxford.

Gauge : 4ft 8½in

-	4wDM	RH	215753	1942	(a)	(1)

(a) ex Ruston Bucyrus Ltd, Lincoln, c9/1971.

(1) scrapped c/1980 (after 7/10/1979).

NOTTINGHAM SLEEPER CO LTD
ALPINE INDUSTRIAL PARK, Elkesley

ED4
SK 682763

JF 4220021 is on static display together with an ex-BR coach on a short length of track. The remaining locomotives have been stored in this yard.

Gauge : 4ft 8½in

	THE TANK	4wDM	FH	2914	1944	(a)	
9135	KESTREL	0-4-0DH	JF	422021	1962	(b)	
502		0-4-0DE	BBT	3067	1954	(c)	(1)
508		0-4-0DE	BBT	3098	1956	(c)	(1)
510		0-4-0DE	BBT	3100	1956	(c)	(2)
18242		0-4-0DH	JF	4220022	1962	(d)	(3)
27876		0-4-0DH	NBQ	27876	1959	(e)	
	HEM HEATH 3D	0-6-0DM	WB	3119	1956	(e)	
No.13D		6wDH	TH	181V	1967	(e)	(4)
D2128		0-6-0DM	Sdn		1960	(f)	

(a) ex B. Roberts, Tollerton, 5/11/1988.
(b) ex National Power plc, Padiham Power Station, Burnley, Lancs, 3/2/1994; prev ROF Chorley, Lancs.
(c) ex British Steel plc, Port Talbot Works, West Glam, 7-21/6/1993.
(d) ex Royal Ordnance plc, Chorley Factory, Lancs, after 14/6/1994, by 14/9/1994.
(e) ex Chatterley Whitfield Mining Museum, Tunstall, Staffs, after 14/4/1994, by 14/6/1994.
(f) ex Peak Rail Ltd, Matlock, Derbyshire, 24/4/1996.

(1) to Coopers (Metals) Ltd, Sheffield, for scrap, c10/1993.
(2) scrapped on site by 12/8/1995.
(3) to Peak Rail Ltd, Matlock, Derbyshire, after 18/4/1996, by 19/5/1996.
(4) to Peak Rail Ltd, Matlock, Derbyshire, after 26/6/1996, by 31/7/1996.

THE PERMANENT WAY EQUIPMENT CO LTD
Giltway, Giltbrook, Nottingham

MD5

The company is engaged in the manufacture and repair of self-propelled vehicles and equipment for permanent way maintenance and construction. It moved to these premises (SK 484455) from Bulwell. The vehicles listed below have been used for hire and demonstration.

Gauge : 4ft 8½in

F511 LRR	4wDM	R/R	PQ	1989	New
G276 NAU	4wDM	R/R	PQ	1989	New
M491 PTV	4wDM	R/R	PQ	1994	New
N798 XRA	4wDM	R/R	PQ	1996	New
P161 FAU	4wDM	R/R	PQ	1997	New

PILLATT & CO LTD
STAPLEFORD IRONWORKS, Stapleford   VD6

This iron and brass foundry opened in 1903 (company registered 1/1904) but the location is unknown. There are references to this company in "Machinery Mart". The issue of 15/11/1918 refers to one D.M. Davies, a scrap merchant having supplied a locomotive from Llanmorlais Colliery, Glamorgan to Pillatt. That for 28/3/1919 refers to a works extension. The firm was still trading in 1954 when they were manufacturing boiler furnaces and incinerators. There is no evidence of any private siding, or of other dealing in locomotives.

HAROLD POTTER & CO LTD
Canal Street, Nottingham   SD7
Harold Potter & Co until 7/1937

Established by 1924 as Machinery & Metal Merchants, with offices in Nottingham. By 1940 the company was located in Canal St, Nottingham and by 1966 at Daleside Rd, Nottingham.

Gauge : 2ft 0in

		0-4-0WT	OC	HC	1161	1915	(a)	s/s

(a)   ex A.H. Price & Co, Nottingham (by 12/1933 ?).

SAVIDGE BROS.
164 Queens Walk, Nottingham   SD8

As this address is a private house, Savidge Bros. could have been agents or contractors.

Gauge : 2ft 0in

		4wPM	MR	1347	1918	(a)	s/s
		4wPM	MR	1379	1918	(b)	s/s

(a)   ex Nottingham Corporation, Works & Ways Dept., Eastcroft, Nottingham.
(b)   ex MR; earlier WDLR.

W.J.SIMMS, SONS & COOKE LTD
SPRING CLOSE WORKS, Lenton, Nottingham   QD9

A firm of building contractors; loco possibly here for repairs only, if at all.

Gauge : 2ft 0in

		4wDM	RH	177607	1937	(a)	(1)

(a)   spares ordered by previous owners, Wansford Quarries Ltd, Wansford, Hunts, on 12/11/1943, were to be delivered here (loco on site or not?).

(1)   subsequently at Bestwood Sand Ltd, Bestwood by 24/6/1948.

P. TUXFORD
MAPPERLEY PLANT DEPOT
RD10
SK 604444

Plant dealers yard, situated at Podder Lane, Mapperley, Nottingham.

Gauge : 2ft 6in

-	0-4-0DMF	HE	3411	1947	(a)	(1)

(a) ex Mill Lane Commercials, Sandiacre, Derbys, c/1976; earlier NCB, South Midlands Area, via Frank Berry Ltd., Leicester.
(1) to Leeds City Council, Leeds Industrial Museum, Armley Mills, Leeds, 28/10/1985.

WALKER, HILL & CO
Churchgate, Nottingham
XD11

An 0-4-0CT with 12in cylinders was offered for sale by this firm of engineers in 1920.

THOS. W. WARD LTD
EASTWOOD (GNR) GOODS YARD
LD12

Locomotives brought here for scrapping.

Gauge : 4ft 8½in

STANTON No.15	0-6-0ST	OC	AE	1456	1902	(a)	(1)
STANTON No.16	0-6-0ST	OC	AE	1617	1912	(a)	(1)
STANTON No.23	0-6-0ST	OC	AE	1882	1921	(a)	(1)

(a) ex Stanton & Staveley Ltd, Stanton Works, Ilkeston, Derbys, c6/1963.

(1) scrapped on site, 7/1963.

H. WIDDOWSON & SONS LTD
CARR STREET WORKS, Nottingham
XD13

Gauge : 4ft 8½in

| COLDSTREAM | 0-4-0ST | OC | MW | 1327 | 1896 | | |
| | | | reb | Galloways | 1922 | (a) | (1) |

(a) ex Galloways Ltd, Ardwick, Manchester, /1934.

(1) to Teesside Bridge & Engineering Works Ltd, Cargo Fleet, Middlesbrough, Yorks (NR).

SECTION 4

PRESERVATION SITES

ANGEL INN, Misson, near Bawtry BP1
SK 688947

The locomotive stood on display in the grounds of this public house.

Gauge : 4ft 8½in

       ANNIE   4wDM   RH   237924   1946 (a)   (1)

(a)   ex General Refractories Ltd, Bawtry Works, Austerfield, Yorks (WR), c/1973.

(1)   to Hallamshire Railway Society, Chapeltown, South Yorks, 8/1984.

T.H. BARTON
BARTON TRANSPORT, Barton Ferry VP2

Pleasure line operated in 1939 by T.H. Barton. The line ran for about 200 yards from the Tea Rooms to Ferry Farm House Station (SK 518336). The track is reputed to have come from the family quarry at Rigger Lane, Little Eaton, Duffield, Derbys.

Gauge : 2ft 0in

       ROCKET   4-2wPMR S/O   Albert   s/s by /1940

TOM BROOKS
BASFORD SCRAP YARD QP3
SK 554416

Locomotive kept for preservation for some years by this director of the Nottingham Scrap Metal Co Ltd.

Gauge : 4ft 8½in

       -                   0-4-0ST   OC   AB   1651   1919 (a)   (1)

(a)   ex Stanton & Staveley Ltd, Holwell Iron Works, Asfordby, Leics, 2/1973.

(1)   Scrapped on site, after 18/8/1978, by 7/10/1979.

J. CRAVEN
WALESBY LIGHT RAILWAY EP4
SK 684707

A private garden railway built at East View, Main Road, Walesby. John Craven purchased narrow gauge equipment from 1972, and commenced construction of this railway after moving to Walesby in 1975. The first locomotive was purchased and track laying to dual (2ft and 3ft) gauge started in 1978. As purchases of further stock continued, some was stored at other private locations nearby and in Lincolnshire. John died suddenly in 1995 and his widow supervised the dispersal of the equipment.

Reference : "The Narrow Gauge No.160", NGRS, Spring 1998.

Gauge : 3ft 0in

	(W6/11-4)		2-2wPMR	Wkm	9673	1964	(a)	(2)
	W6/11-2		2-2wPMR	Wkm	7441	1956	(a)	(1)
	W6/2-2		4wDM	RH	418770	1957	(c)	(3)
TR11	PWM 2187	A155W	2w-2PMR	Wkm	4164	1948	(d)	(4)
			2w-2PMR	Wkm	4092	1946	(e)	(4)

(a) ex British Aluminium Co Ltd, Lochaber Works, Inverness-shire, 30/8/1978.
(b) ex British Aluminium Co Ltd, Lochaber Works, Inverness-shire, 4/10/1978.
(c) ex British Aluminium Co Ltd, Lochaber Works, Inverness-shire, 7/11/1982.
(d) ex BR, Bangor, Gwynedd, 9/1986; regauged from 4ft 8½in.
(e) ex Moseley Industrial Tramway & Museum, Greater Manchester, after 9/4/1994, by 5/2/1995.

(1) to The Lord O'Neill, Shanes Castle, Co. Antrim, Northern Ireland, 15/4/1979.
(2) to Irish Narrow Gauge Trust, Co. Leitrim, Eire, 1/11/1996.
(3) to Alan Keef Ltd, Ross-on-Wye, Hereford & Worcs, after 15/9/1996, by 6/12/1996.
(4) to Mosley Industrial Tramway & Museum, Greater Manchester, 3/11/1996.

Gauge : 2ft 0in

FOXHANGER	4wDM	House	c1974	(a)	(2)	
-	4wDM	RH	441944	1960	(b)	
	Reb.to	4wPM	Craven		1981	(1)
-	4wDM	RH	421433	1959	(c)	(3)
-	4wDM	MR	9778	1953	(d)	(4)
-	4wDM	FH	2163	1938	(e)	(5)

(a) ex Waterways Recovery Group, Kennet & Avon Canal, Devizes, Wilts, 7/5/1979.
(b) ex Yorkshire Water Authority, Knostrop Works, Stourton, West Yorks, 10/4/1981.
(c) ex Anglian Water Authority, Lincolnshire Rivers Division, Southrey, Lincs, 1/5/1986.
(d) ex C.A.E.C. Howard Ltd, Bedford, 4/1987; earlier Yorkshire Handmade Brick Co Ltd, Alne, near Easingwold, North Yorks.
(e) ex Cleethorpes Coast Light Railway, Cleethorpes, Humberside, 5/1994.

(1) to C.& D. Lawson, Notts, 7/1983.
(2) to J.R. Rainbow, Gloucester, 3/7/1983.
(3) to T.W.F.Hall, North Ings Farm, Lincs, 27/7/1986.
(4) to T.W.F.Hall, North Ings Farm, Lincs, after 30/5/1987, by 20/5/1988.
(5) to Alan Keef Ltd, Ross-on-Wye, Hereford & Worcs, after 15/9/1996, by 6/12/1996.

SAM FAY'S BAR & RESTAURANT, London Road, Nottingham   SP5
Grand Central Diner until c7/1993   SK 580392

The locomotive stood on a plinth outside this restaurant, situated in the former London Road High Level Station building.

Gauge : 4ft 8½in

		0-4-0ST	OC	P	1555	1920	(a)	(1)

(a)   ex Riber Castle Wildlife Park, Matlock, Derbys, 14/10/1986.

(1)   to Mike Wood, 29/7/1998 and to Stratford & Broadway Railway Society, Long Marston, Worcs, 15/9/1998 after temporary storage at Church Gresley, South Derbys.

GREAT CENTRAL RAILWAY (NOTTINGHAM) LTD
G.C.R. NORTHERN DEVELOPMENT ASSOCIATION

RUSHCLIFFE HALT SITE, East Leake   VP6
SK 553277

Initial site used for storage from c1990 of stock associated with the northern extension of the preserved Great Central line. Subsequently (from late 1991) locomotives other than the one listed below moved to the Ruddington Heritage site.

Gauge : 4ft 8½in

		4wDM	MR	2026	1920	(a)

(a)   ex Davy Morris Ltd, North Road, Loughborough, Leics, after 2/8/1990, by 18/8/1990.

RUDDINGTON HERITAGE CENTRE   VP7
SK 577323

A museum and operating headquarters for the preservation of the northern section of the Loughborough - Nottingham (Great Central) railway was set up from 1991 using buildings and 11 acres of land formerly part of the Ministry of Defence Ruddington depot (which see). The remainder of this site became a Country Park and an operating line was laid through this with the intention of connecting with the ex-BR line to the site. Three miles of this line to Rushcliffe Halt is now owned by this group.

Gauge : 4ft 8½in

			0-6-0ST	IC	HC	1682	1937	(a)	
			4wDM		RH	512572	1965	(b)	(1)
			0-6-0DE		YE	2895	1964	(c)	(2)
	No.2	CASTLE DONINGTON							
		POWER STATION	0-4-0ST	OC	RSHN	7818	1954	(d)	
	56		0-6-0ST	IC	RSHN	7667	1950	(e)	
(68088)	No985		0-4-0T	IC	Dar		1923	(f)	
D2959			0-4-0DE		RH	449754	1961	(g)	

20094	(D8094)	Bo-Bo.DE		EE	3000	1961	
				RSHD	8252	1961	(h)
20135	(D8135)	Bo-Bo.DE		EE	3606	1966	
				VF	D1005	1966	(h)
08885	(D4115)	0-6-0DE		Hor		1962	(i)
63	CORBY	0-6-0ST	IC	RSHN	7761	1954	(j)
(52060)	977813	2-2w-2w-2DMR		Derby	C&W	1960	(k)
53926	977814	2-2w-2w-2DMR		Derby	C&W	1959	(k)
	-	0-4-0T	OC	HE	1684	1931	(l)
5379	(45379)	4-6-0	OC	AW	1434	1937	(m)
53645		2-2w-2w-2DMR		Derby	C&W	1958	(n)
(D9520)	45	0-6-0DH		Sdn		1964	(o)
13180		0-6-0DE		Derby		1955	(p)

(a) ex Newark & Sherwood District Council, Millgate Folk Museum, Newark, 6/1991.
(b) ex British Gypsum Ltd, Erith, London, 9/8/1991.
(c) ex Steetley Quarry Products Ltd, Chaddesden, Derby, 25/9/1992.
(d) ex Powergen plc, Castle Donington Power Station, Leics, 27/11/1992.
(e) ex North Woolwich Old Station Museum, Greater London, 28/1/1994.
(f) ex Great Central Railway (1976) Ltd, Loughborough, Leics, 11/3/1994.
(g) ex National Power plc, Staythorpe Power Station, after 26/3/1994, by 1/5/1994.
(h) ex BR., Toton, 8/6/1994 (after asbestos removal at MC Metals, Glasgow).
(i) ex BR, Doncaster, 15/6/1994.
(j) ex Keighley & Worth Valley Light Railway, Haworth, West Yorks, c6/1997 (after 3/5/1997).
(k) ex BR, 6/1997.
(l) ex Great Central Railway plc, Loughborough, Leics, c5/7/1997.
(m) ex Avon Valley Railway, Bitton, Avon, 20/11/1997.
(n) ex Bodmin & Wenford Railway plc, Bodmin, Cornwall, /1997.
(o) ex Rutland Railway Museum, Cottesmore, Leics, 6/3/1998.
(p) ex Great Central Railway plc, Loughborough, Leics, after 22/3/1997, by 28/3/1997.

(1) to Trackwork Ltd, Kirk Sandall, South Yorks, 3/1997.
(2) to Barnsley Metropolitan Borough Council, South Yorks, 14/3/1997.

A. B. & P. G. KETTLE
Bilsthorpe   GP8

Locomotive preserved on static display at a private address.

Gauge : 2ft 6in

P9261		0-4-0DM		HE	2254	1940	(a)	(1)

(a) ex W. Smith (dealer), Baughurst, Hants, 21/2/1990.

(1) to John Quentin, Hereford & Worcs, 14/10/1992.

NEWARK & SHERWOOD DISTRICT COUNCIL
MILLGATE FOLK MUSEUM, Newark PP9
SK 794538

Locomotive on static display at this location.

Gauge : 4ft 8½in

    -                0-6-0ST   IC   HC   1682   1937   (a)   (1)

(a)   ex British Sugar Corporation Ltd, Kelham Factory, Newark, 17/4/1981.

(1)   to Great Central (Nottingham) Ltd, Ruddington, c6/1991.

NOTTINGHAM INDUSTRIAL MUSEUM
WOLLATON HALL, Wollaton, Nottingham QP10
SK 530392

Locomotive on static display at this location.

Gauge : 4ft 8½in

                      0-4-0VBT   VCG   Chaplin 2368   1885   (a)   (1)

(a)   ex East Midlands Gas Board, Northampton Gasworks, 3/1966; stored at Nottingham Corporation, Eastcroft Depot, London Road, Nottingham, until 11/1977.
(1)   to Glasgow Museum of Transport, Glasgow, 2/11/1980.

PAPPLEWICK PUMPING STATION TRUST
PAPPLEWICK PUMPING STATION, Longdale Lane, Ravenshead NP11
SK 583521

This former Nottingham City Waterworks (later Severn Trent Water Authority) steam driven pumping station is now preserved and operates on several occasions during the year.

Gauge : 2ft 0in

    L8   L203N U84   4wDM   RH 7002/0567/6 1967   (a)   (1)

(a)   ex Severn Trent Water Authority, Orston Road East Plant Depot, West Bridgford, Nottingham, after 6/5/1989, by 4/5/1992.

(1)   to Midland Railway Centre, Butterley, Derbyshire, after 18/5/1996, by 18/10/1996.

BRIAN W. M. ROBERTS
HILL FARM, Tollerton

UP12
SK 614363 & SK 611363

Locomotives were kept at two sites at this farm. P 1749 was a static exhibit on a short length of track to the east side of the Gamston - Tollerton road, (SK 614363). Later a railway was established adjacent to the farm buildings, on the west side of the road, at grid ref. SK 611363. The locomotives and rolling stock were sold by auction 5/11/1988.

Gauge : 4ft 8½in

	FFIONA JANE	0-4-0ST	OC	P	1749	1928	(a)	(1)
	JAMES I (KESTREL)	0-4-0ST	OC	P	2129	1952	(b)	(3)
60130	KESTREL							
	(FOLESHILL No.1)	0-4-0ST	OC	P	2085	1948	(c)	(4)
	THE TANK	4wDM		FH	2914	1944	(d)	(2)

(a) ex Tarmac Roadstone Holdings Ltd, Cawdor Quarry, Matlock, Derbys, via storage at NCB Bennerley Opencast Disposal Point, /1972.
(b) ex Quainton Railway Society, Bucks, 27/3/1982.
(c) ex Yorkshire Dales Railway, Embsay, NorthYorks, 25/1/1986.
(d) ex Chasewater Light Railway Preservation Society, Norton Canes, Staffs, 4/1986.

(1) to P. Clarke, Fulstow, Lincs, 10/1977.
(2) to Nottingham Sleeper Co Ltd, Elkesley, 5/11/1988.
(3) to The Pallot Working Steam Museum, Trinity, Jersey, Channel Islands, 30/7/1989.
(4) to The Pallot Working Steam Museum, Trinity, Jersey, Channel Islands, c9/1989.

P. ROLLIN
South Leverton, near Retford

FP13
SK 783812

Locomotive moved to this private site for preservation and restoration.

Gauge : 4ft 8½in

| 76084 | 2-6-0 | OC | Hor | 1957 | (a) | (1) |

(a) ex Peak Rail Ltd, Buxton, Derbys, 14/1/1983.

(1) to Ian Storey Engineering Ltd, Hepscott, near Morpeth, Northumberland, 12/9/1997.

C.F. & T. STIRLAND
36 Trough Lane, Watnall
LP14
SK 499456

Locomotive preserved at this private location.

Gauge : 3ft 0in

NANCY	0-6-0T	OC	AE	1547	1908	(a)	(1)

(a) ex Staveley Minerals Ltd, Eastwell Ironstone Quarries, Leics, 10/1961.

(1) to The Lord O'Neill, Shanes Castle, Co.Antrim, 10/1972.

SUNDOWN ADVENTURELAND
Rampton, near Retford
DP15

Pleasure line (the "Rocky Mountain Railroad") operated from 1993 at this childrens' amusement park.

Gauge : 1ft 6in

2-4-0RE		SL	546.4.93	1993 New

A.J. WILSON
6 Trentdale Road, Bakersfield, Nottingham
TP16
SK 607408

Some of the following locomotives of this owner have been kept at this private house. WASP and RH 224337 were stored at a private site at Sibthorpe, near Retford.

Gauge : 2ft 0in

WASP	2w-2.PM	Wilson		c1969	New	(3)
-	4wPM	Thakeham		1950	(a)	(1)
-	4wDM	MR	22258	1965	(b)	(2)
06/22/6/2	4wDM	RH	224337	1945	(c)	(4)

(a) ex R.P. Morris, Longfield, Kent, c3/1971.
(b) ex Staveley Lime Products Ltd, Hindlow, Derbys, 3/1969.
(c) ex J.& K. Harris, Scrap Metal Merchants, March, Cambs, 14/6/1995.

(1) to Wey Valley Light Railway, Fareham, Surrey, 4/1971.
(2) to Corris Railway Society, Loughborough Store, Leics.
(3) to A.J. Wilson, 35, Holt Park Road, Leeds, West Yorks, 3/1997.
(4) to A.J. Wilson, 35, Holt Park Road, Leeds, West Yorks, 27/3/1997.

Y7 PRESERVATION GROUP
PRIORY FARM, Thurgarton

PP17
SK 696491

Locomotive restored for preservation at this private location.

Gauge : 4ft 8½in

0-4-0T	IC	Dar	1923	(a)	(1)

(a) ex NCB, East Midlands Division, No.4 Area, Bentinck Colliery, 8/1964; earlier BR 68088, orig. NER 985.

(1) to Main Line Steam Trust, Loughborough, Leics, 26/7/1975.

SECTION 5

NON - LOCOMOTIVE WORKED SYSTEMS

INTRODUCTION

It is difficult to define exactly which locations justify inclusion in this section. The following are the main criteria that have been used :

Included are :
   All sites known to have had narrow gauge lines including post 1850 shaft mines (ie those with cages).
   Those standard gauge systems which had something more than a single siding shunted by main line locomotives.

Excluded are :
   Sites mentioned elsewhere in this book.
   Mills, Maltings, Council Depots, Coal Yards etc. which have only one siding and no features of particular interest.
   Also industrial equipment which is moved on rails but which does not form a railway in the usual sense.

Note that brickworks are included only where there is definite evidence of tramways/inclines.
   Early Ordnance Survey maps are not totally reliable in depicting such features.
   There are many 'grey' areas, in particular with mills and maltings. For instance, the above criteria result in not all of the many maltings in Newark qualifying for inclusion.
A summary of pre-1850 horse tramways follows the main list.

ASSOCIATED BRITISH MALTSTERS LTD

COW LANE MALTINGS Newark   PH1
Gilstrap Earp & Co Ltd until 1928   SK 799545
J. Gilstrap & Sons until c1883

Located at Cow Lane wharf on the River Trent, these predate the railway. The maltings were served by sidings at the south end of the GN/Midland Railway Joint Newark Spur Line (which opened 1/12/1869). Three tracks ran east from wagon turntables into the maltings. Shunting by capstan or horse is assumed. The sidings closed after 1956, and in 1960 the company built a new headquarters building on the site of the maltings.

NORTH MALTINGS, Northgate, Newark   PH2
Gilstrap Earp & Co Ltd until 1928   SK 803549

Opened in 1884. Served by sidings on the west side of the GNR Doncaster line immediately south of the junction with the Newark Curve line. A wagon turntable gave access to two lines along the south side of the maltings. Closed after 1956.

BRANSTONS MALT KILNS, Maltkiln Lane, Newark   PH3
Ipswich Malting Co Ltd until c1960   SK 804548
J.W. & H. Branston until c1938-1956

Opened in 1863 and served by a siding on the west side of the GNR Doncaster line between Newark station and the junction with the Newark Curve line. A wagon turntable gave access to a line along the south side of the maltings. Closed after 1956.

RIVERSIDE MALT KILNS, Hatchets Lane, Newark   PH4
Ipswich Malting Co Ltd until c1960   SK 803551
J.W. & H. Branston until c1938-1956

Opened by 1872. Served by a siding (agreement dated 10/4/1872) on the west side of the GNR Newark to Doncaster Railway, north of its junction with, and connected to, the GNR/Midland Railway Joint Newark Curve line at its junction with the GNR. A wagon turntable accessed two sidings along the south side. Shunting believed to be by horse or capstan. Closed after 1956.

HUGH BAIRD & SONS LTD

CLIFFNOOK (or SYDNEY STREET) MALTINGS, Cliffnook Lane, Newark   PH5
Gilstrap Earp & Co Ltd until 1925-1928   SK 804544
Harvey & Earp until c1882

Located on the west side of Newark GNR goods yard, these maltings were constructed c1879 (before 1884). Wagon turntables were used to access sidings along the south and west sides of the buildings. Shunting by capstan or horse is assumed. Closed after 1956.

SPITAL MALTINGS, Maltkiln Lane, Newark   PH6
J Hole & Co until 1934   SK 803548

Opened between 1884 and 1890, these maltings were located east of the junction between the GNR/Midland Railway Newark Curve and its spur line, or Cow Lane Branch. They were served by 2 sidings (agreement of 12/8/1892) alongside the junction. The maltings closed in 1973 and were destroyed by fire in 1990.

H.J. BALDWIN & CO LTD
MIDLAND PRODUCT WORKS, Bunny   VH7
Albert Walker c1900 -1904   SK 582287
Thomas Walker c1876-1885

Located between Bunny village and Bunny Hill, a brickworks and clay hole were in place by 1899 but no tramway was shown. By 1919 they had closed but reopened by Baldwin c3/1936. In 1950 there was a tramway incline into a clay hole to the south west. By 1969 this was lifted but the considerably modified works survived until much later. In 1997 the area had become a landfill site. Baldwin had a private siding at the nearest station, East Leake, in 1956.

BARBER, WALKER & CO
EASTWOOD COLLIERY, Bridge Street, Eastwood   MH7
Dr Manson until 1838   SK 460460

This colliery, a large one for its time, was located between the Erewash and Nottingham Canals, 1 mile south east of Langley Mill. From about 1849 it was served by the Midland

Railway's Eastwood Branch which ran north from Shipley Gate station to the colliery (½ mile). From 1875 the GNR also served the colliery by means of a short branch running west from Newthorpe & Greasley station. Whilst shunting by main line locomotives is probable, the use of a locomotive from the Barber Walker list (see Industrial Locomotives Section) cannot be completely ruled out. The colliery was abandoned in 5/1881 but most of the Midland Railway branch was left in situ for many years afterwards.

BAYLES & WYLIE LTD
BONE MILL, Forge Mills, Bulwell   **NH8**
J. & T. Walker until c1930-1938   SK 547472

By 1881 a siding ran east from the Midland Railway line, 1½ miles south of Hucknall Station, to a wagon turntable. From there one line ran south into the bone mill and a second ran east to the adjacent corn mill of T.A. Loweth. Both sidings closed after 1956.

WM. BEELEY
BLACKMIRES BRICKWORKS, Sutton Forest   **HH9**
                                                                         SK 514590

This works, established by 1864, was located north west of the Midland Railway line ½ mile north east of Sutton Junction Station. By 1877 there was a siding connection (known as Dukes Siding?), including a line around the kilns. There were extensive workings to the north west but no tramway is shown. The siding was listed in 1895 but both it and the works had been removed by 1898. The site was later used as a construction depot for the building of the Mansfield Railway (see Contractors Section).

THOS. BELL & SON LTD
WAGON WORKS, Daybrook Notts.   **RH10**
                                                                         SK 578446

This small works, which opened in 1938, was located on the north side of the LNER Daybrook Station with sidings connected to the goods yard (agreement dated 28/1/1938). Closed after 1956.

BOLEHAM BRICK & TILE WORKS LTD
GAMSTON BRICKWORKS, Causey Lane, Gamston, Retford.   **DH11**
                                                                         SK 724769

Opened c1900. Served by sidings (agreement dated 22/1/1900) on the east side of the GNR line, 2 miles south of Retford station. Closed by 1912 ? No known narrow gauge tramway.

WM. BOOTH
PORTLAND LIMEWORKS, Kirkby in Ashfield KH12
SK 498553

Limeworks operated by Booth in 1877 although dating from earlier. Sidings serving the limekilns were connected to the east side of the Midland Railway line, ½ mile south of Kirkby in Ashfield Station. There is no evidence of internal tramways and the site had closed by 1890. The MS&LR extension to Annesley passed right through the kiln site.

Owner ? (THE BRICK & MINERAL CO LTD, c1900 ?)
BRICK & TILE WORKS, Cropwell Bishop UH13
(possibly **Vincent Parker** (of the nearby Canal Inn), c1885 SK 677354

Located on the west bank of the Grantham Canal, west of Cropwell Bishop village, this works was open by 1891 when it had a short incline into a clay hole to the west. The works was disused but intact in 1915, by which time the tramway was not shown.

BRIDGFORD ESTATES LTD
LUDLOW HILL BRICKWORKS, West Bridgford VH14
Bridgford Brick Co Ltd (by 1948) SK 588363
T. & J. Smart (in receivership by 3/1943)

Opened between 1885 and 1888, this works was served by a siding on the east side of the Midland Railway, ¾ mile north of Edwalton station. It closed between 1956 and 1967. Two short tramways ran south into a hole in 1899. By 1914 only the westernmost remained and this had gone by 1950. The works was owned by Bridgford Estates Ltd in 1956.

BRITISH GLUES & CHEMICALS LTD

CHEMICAL MANURE & GLUE WORKS, Newark PH15
Quibell Bros. Ltd by 1876, until 1920 SK 802554
Harvey & Quibell in 1869 and 1871.

Opened by 1869 and located on the west side of the GNR Doncaster to London line, south of its flat crossing with the Midland Railway, Nottingham to Lincoln line. The sidings (agreement dated 14/2/1871) serving the works were located on the west side of the GNR Doncaster line north of its junction with the Midland Railway/GNR Joint Newark Curve. Additional sidings south of the works, which had formerly served a GNR pit for gravel ballast, were taken over c1931. Some shunting was performed by the GNR but in addition a rope haulage engine and a capstan were used for internal movements. Narrow gauge tramways were used within the building on several floors, linked by lifts, as part of the process and there was a short line outside linking two buildings. The siding agreement was terminated from 17/3/1970 and the works closed in 1975 by which time it was owned by **Croda International Ltd,** who had built new premises nearby.

SUTTON FOREST BONE MILLS, Hamilton Road, Sutton in Ashfield **HH16**
Samuel Meggitt & Sons Ltd until between 1912 and 1922. SK 513586

The original works was located south east of Hamilton Road (then Blackmires Lane). The works existed by 1876 but then had no rail connection. By 1898 a new works had been built between the road and the parallel Midland Railway line to the north west. A siding connection had been installed, ¼ mile north east of Sutton Junction Station, and an internal railway of unknown gauge linked the various buildings, and included a level crossing of Hamilton Road to reach the original works. The mills closed by 1936 and much was demolished soon afterwards. By 1941 the remaining buildings alongside the main line had become the structural steel works of **Stokes, Taylor & Shaw Ltd** (registered 2/1937). The internal railway was removed but the BR connection remained until after 1956.

BRITISH PETROLEUM CO LTD
EAKRING ROAD OIL SIDINGS, Eakring **GH17**
Anglo Iranian Oil Co Ltd until 17/12/1954 SK 660619

This site was located east of the LMS/LNER Mid Notts Joint Line, 1 mile north of the connection to Bilsthorpe Colliery. It was used to load locally produced crude oil. It opened 12/8/1940 and closed 1/8/1966.

W. & J. BROUGHTON
STANDHILL BRICKWORKS, Standhill Road, Carlton **RH18**
Mrs. Ruth Buxton (in 1895-1900) SK 598417
Buxton & Walker (in 1885)

Opened by 1883 and expanded by 1899. A narrow gauge tramway ran east from the works into a clay hole. W. & J. Broughton were owners in 1904. By 1919 the tramways had gone and the works was disused.

BULWELL BRICK CO LTD

BRICKWORKS, The Wells Road, Carlton **RH19**
  SK 587414

This works, which was located south east of The Wells Road, had a short tramway which, in 1881 and 1913, ran east into a hole. This clay hole was worked out by 1930 but the works continued in production.

KETT STREET, BRICKWORKS, Bulwell **RH20**
  SK 536450

This brick works was established before 1876 to the north east of the Midland Railway's Bennerley line, 1 mile north west of Bulwell Junction. It had no standard gauge connection but in 1876, a narrow gauge tramway passed under the Midland's line to a clay hole at SK 533449. The hole was still worked in 1934 but both it and the works had closed by 1937.

BUTTERLEY & BLABY BRICK COMPANIES LTD
KIRTON BRICKWORKS, Boughton   **GH21**
SK 690679

A brickworks was constructed after 1950 on the south east side of BR adjacent to Boughton Station. In 1967 there was a short incline running north east from the works into a clay pit.

BUTTERLEY CO LTD
SUTTON SAND SIDING, Kirkby in Ashfield   **JH22**
SK 507575

This sand pit, located east of the Midland Railway line, ½ mile south of Sutton Junction station, was in place by 1877 and owned by the Butterley Co Ltd by 1895. The line included temporary tracks within the pit and would have needed motive power, albeit probably a horse. The siding had closed by 1922.

CHARCON TUNNELS LTD
PRE CAST CONCRETE WORKS, Southwell Lane Estate, Kirkby in Ashfield   **JH23**
SK 501571

This works, which produced concrete tunnel lining segments, had an isolated standard gauge track in the stockyard from which standard gauge rail cranes loaded road vehicles and put finished segments to stock. The rail operation had been replaced by road cranes by 1981 when 4wDC Smith 23929 was noted out of use. There had previously also been others which were diesel conversions of steam cranes.

FREDERICK CLEAVER
WAGON WORKS, FOUNDRY & SAWMILL, Queens Road, Nottingham   **SH24**
SK 577393

This works, established prior to 1864, was located south of the Midland Railway line east of Nottingham Midland Station. The workshops were accessed by traversers. It closed after 1885 and the works had been removed by 1899 (siding still listed in 1895).

COCKINGS (WALKERINGHAM) LTD
WALKERINGHAM BRICKWORKS, Carrhill Road, Walkeringham   **BH25**
Cocking & Son by 1885, until c1930   SK 753926.
Thos. Cocking by 1864

Located on the east side of the Chesterfield Canal, west of Walkeringham Village. The company was established by 1864. A tramway was used and in 1950 extended east, passing under Carrhill Road before diverging north and south to pits at SK 757928 and SK 756924.

GEORGE COOPER LTD

BRICKWORKS, Gringley Road, Misterton **BH26**
SK 761944

Located on the north side of the Chesterfield Canal, south west of Misterton Village. It was in situ by 1890 and in 1919 had short inclines running into pits to the north and west. The tramways had gone by 1948.

COSSALL COLLIERY CO LTD
(Registered 7/1877)

COSSALL COLLIERY, Cossall **QH27**
Lynch & Cadogan from 1873 SK 478427

In 1879 this consisted of two pits. The older one had been sunk before 1873 and was located at SK 475425, on the east side of Babbington Junction (south of Ilkeston Junction station), on the Midland Railway Erewash Valley line. It had a single siding. The newer Hewlett Pit was located 300 yards to the east and sinking had commenced in 2/1878. Coal production started in 1879 when screens were built. At the time of the 1879 Ordnance Survey, sidings had not been provided. They must have been installed in that year as the earlier pit was then abandoned. Its siding was later taken up. Hewlett Pit was on the west bank of the Nottingham Canal where there is believed to have been a wharf. A small Patent Fuel Plant had been put in by 1894 and this worked until at least 1940. The Ordnance Survey of 1899 shows sidings which ran east from the Midland Railway to Hewlett Pit and then turned north to a tip. How these sidings were worked is not known. By 1/1/1947, when the colliery was vested in the NCB, East Midlands Division, No.5 Area, narrow gauge lines extended for 200 yards onto a tip to the south.

BRICKWORKS, Newtons Lane, Cossall Marsh **QH28**
SK 478431

This works had been established by 1879 north of the Midland Railway Babbington branch where that line crossed the Nottingham Canal. There was then no rail connection or tramway shown. By 1899 there was a trailing connection from the Midland Railway branch, which by then was disused east of here. There was also a short incline to a pit north of the works; the latter is believed to have closed between 1937 and 1948.

JAS. CLAYTON
BRICKWORKS, Carlton Road, Carlton **RH29**
SK 594410

A brickworks, owned by Clayton in 1876 and 1885 at least, on the south east side of Carlton Road. In 1881, a short tramway ran north east from the works, parallel to the road, into a hole. The works had closed by 1899.

EAST MIDLANDS GAS BOARD
RADFORD GAS WORKS, Nottingham QH30
Nottingham Corporation Gas Department until 1/5/1949 SK 549400

Works opened c1850 on the east side of the Midland Railway line (opened 2/10/1848) south of Radford Station. Sidings which ran east from the Midland Railway were accessed by wagon turntables and are believed to have been worked by capstans.

EDWARD EASTWOOD
EREWASH VALLEY WAGON WORKS, Stapleford VH31
(**Steer & Barnes** were railway carriage builders at Stapleford in 1864) SK 483364

The works, owned by Eastwood from c1900, was served by railway sidings and traversers on the west side of the Midland Railway line north of Stapleford & Sandiacre station. It was open by 1879 but ownership prior to 1900 is uncertain. The works closed after 1938.

EASTWOOD & SWINGLER
MOLYNEAUX COLLIERY, Fackley JH32
J. & G. Buxton (or T. Buxton ?) c1856-1865 SK 478609

Located south west of the Fackley to Sutton road, this was an old and troubled colliery which, apart from the tub track underground and at the pit top in later years, probably made no use of tramways. It is included here only because, in spite of accidents and an inrush of water in 1869, it managed to survive as a landsale pit until 1879. Owned by Eastwood & Swingler by 1873, abandonment plans were deposited by them on 27/1/1881. Although only ¼ mile from the tramway to Skegby Old Wharf and to the Midland Railway Teversal branch, there is no evidence of a connection to either. Its buildings survived until after 1914.

EREWASH VALLEY BRICK PIPE AND POTTERY CO LTD
EREWASH VALLEY BRICKWORKS, Newthorpe Common MH33
SK 477451

This works had been established by 1899 on land south east of the GNR line, opposite the Digby exchange sidings, 1 mile south east of Newthorpe and Greasley Station. A short siding was provided north east of the works by agreement dated 29/12/1904, which was listed in 1912 only. A tramway ran east into a small clayhole and there was another in the works yard. The venture must have been shortlived as the works is shown as closed in 1913. The site, together with the railway siding, passed to the **Manners Brick Co Ltd** in 1916 but there is no record of any further use.

RICHARD EVANS
NEWTHORPE LODGE COLLIERY, Newthorpe.　　　　　　　　　　　　　　　　　　**MH34**

This colliery first appears in mines lists of 1875 and abandonment plans were deposited soon afterwards for its three parts; NEWTHORPE (5/2/1876), NEWTHORPE DAYHOLE (21/2/1877) and NEWTHORPE LODGE (19/1/1876). We have not identified the site of these with certainty but it is tempting to associate them with the site of LODGE COLLIERY which was sunk by William Hall in 1878 (see Industrial Locomotives Section). The term 'Dayhole' usually indicates a drift mine.

FISHER BROS
LIMEWORKS & QUARRY, Quarry Lane, Mansfield　　　　　　　　　　　　　**HH35**
Wm. Bingham & Son (in 1864)　　　　　　　　　　　　　　　　　　　　　　　　　SK 533604

Limeworks, opened prior to 1864 and owned by Fisher Bros in the 1876-1908 period, located within the triangle formed by the Midland Railway Worksop, Nottingham and Southwell lines south west of Mansfield Station. A map of 1877 shows no rail track but in 1898 there was a short length of presumed narrow gauge at the kilns. A Midland Railway siding along the north to east leg of the triangle could have served the works but was at a higher level and had gone by 1907. The whole site had closed by 1914.

GENERAL REFRACTORIES LTD

LOW GROUNDS BRICKWORKS, Shireoaks Road, Worksop　　　　　　　**CH36**
Worksop Brick Co Ltd (Registered 10/3/1900) until 14/6/1929　　　　　　SK 572799
T.N. Whitaker until 1904-8
Wm. Traunter until 1885-95.

An old established works which was located 300 yards south west of the MS&LR line south east of Shireoaks East Junction. The works was in situ by 1884 and in 1897 had two inclines into workings to the east. A standard gauge connection, made by agreement dated 19/10/1906, curved west and south from the GCR at SK 575803 to the works. There were several sidings at the works including one to serve the wood distillation works which had been established west of the brickworks in about 1912 by **Shirley, Aldred & Co Ltd** Shunting was largely by main line locomotives and the agreements were terminated from 31/12/1975.

BRICKWORKS & BRAMCOTE SAND PITS, Coventry Lane, New Stapleford　　**QH37**
　　　　　　　　　　　　　　　　　　　　　　　　　　　　　　　　　　　　　[34] SK 501392

The works was established about 1928. By 1938 it was served by sidings on the south side of the LMS Radford to Trowell Line, 1½ miles east of Trowell Junction. Sand pits to the south of the works were worked by **Coolee Ltd** and the **Bramcote Sand Co** who were joint occupiers of the General Refractories siding. By 1943 at the latest, Coolee Ltd was a General Refractories subsidiary company. On a map of 1955, a narrow gauge tramway, shown as disused, ran south west from the works to the sand pits. All had gone by 1971.

GODDARD, MASSEY & WARNER LTD
ENGINEERING WORKS, Traffic Street, Nottingham   **SH38**
Goddard & Massey (in 1881 & 1895) until before 1904   SK 572391

Works established by 1881 when it was served by a siding on the south side of the Midland Railway, west of its Nottingham station. In 1919 internal lines ran south from the siding, for about 100 yards, into the works which closed after a reciever was appointed on 1/4/1914.

GOTHAM CO LTD
CARLTON BRICKWORKS, Star Lane (later Dale Road), Carlton   **RH39**
Carlton Hill Brick Co (in 1904 & 1912)   SK 601411
Star Brick Co c1885-1888

Date of opening unknown. In 1919 a tramway ran east from the works for ¼ mile to a clay hole but the site was shown as disused. Whether tramways were used in the Gotham period is not known. The works, owned by the Gotham Co Ltd by 1922 and which may have been worked by Hallam in 1948, closed finally between 1956 and 1980.

H.M. GOVERNMENT EXPLOSIVES MAGAZINE
NORMANTON HILLS, Normanton on Soar   **VH40**
Barnstone Blue Lias Lime Co Ltd from 1896 to?   SK 537242
Henry Lovatt 1894 - 1896

These workings were located east of the GCR line 1¼ miles south of East Leake station. A limeworks and associated quarry was opened there c1894, and worked until about 1896, presumably utilising his locos, by **Henry Lovatt**, contractor for the construction of that section of the GCR. By agreement dated 16/12/1896, the site and kilns were given a permanent rail connection, ownership having passed to the Barnstone company. The plan relating to this agreement shows a narrow gauge line running north towards the quarry or mine. A plan of 1919 shows no narrow gauge track and the limeworks as disused. It is probable that the change to an explosives magazine had occurred by then. The siding was listed under that heading in 1925 and 1938. The final closure date is unknown.

(GREAT NORTHERN RAILWAY CO)?
GRAVEL PIT, Newark   **PH41**
    SK 809531

This pit was served by three sidings in 1884 and was on the east side of the GNR Bottesford Line, 1 mile south of Newark Station. At that time it had reached its maximum extent and had closed by 1899, being thereafter flooded and marked as a fishpond.

GREGORY'S SANDSTONE LTD
QUARRY and MASON'S YARD, Nottingham Road, Mansfield HH42
Robert Lindley 1861-c1900 SK 535599
Charles Lindley 1832-1861

This extensive quarry opened in 1832. It was located south of the Midland Railway line between Mansfield South and East Junctions, but had no rail connection. A standard gauge line within the quarry was used from before 1914 by a rail crane to move blocks of stone for sawing. By 1988 a diesel rebuild of a Smith steam crane was in use. The works closed in 1995 but the crane was still on site in 4/1997.

HATHERN WARE LTD
HATHERN STATION BRICKWORKS, Sutton Bonnington VH43
Hathern Station Brick & Terra Cotta Co Ltd by 1895, until c1928-31 SK 514242
Hathern Station Brick & Terra Cotta Co (in 1885)

Opened between 1869 and 1876 and served by a siding on the north east side of the Midland Railway, north west of Hathern station. A hole east of the works was served in 1919 by a tramway. The works is now a trading estate.

HILL BROS
SHAW BRICKWORKS, Gringley on the Hill BH44
Geo. Tomlinson until 1904 SK 738920

Located on the north side of the Chesterfield Canal, north of Gringley on the Hill village. Established between 1869 and 1881, a short tramway ran north west into the clay workings in 1948. The works had closed by 1961.

Owner? (HILL BROS)?
MISTERTON BRICKWORKS, Grove Wood Road, Misterton BH45
SK 768944

Located on the south side of the Chesterfield Canal, south of Misterton Village. It was in situ by 1890 and in 1919 had a very short line running south towards a pit. This tramway had gone by 1948. and the works had closed by 1951.

WILLIAM HILL
HARLEQUIN BRICKWORKS, Radcliffe on Trent UH46
Radcliffe Brick Co Ltd until c1900 SK 660394

Brickworks located on the south side of the Saxondale road, ¾ mile east of Radcliffe village. The works had opened by 1881 and in 1899 there was a short tramway running south from the works into a clay hole. The works, or at least the clay hole, closed after 1927, by 1943.

HILL TOP COLLIERY CO LTD
SPRINGFIELD COLLIERY, Nottingham Road, Eastwood   **LH47**
Eastwood Brick & Tile Works Ltd in 1912   SK 470466
Hill Top Colliery, Brick & Tile Co Ltd registered 9/6/1906
Springfield Colliery Co Ltd in 1904
Knighton & Smith until 1880

The opening date of this colliery, which was first listed in 1874, is unknown. A map of 1880 shows a very small colliery, having no connection to a main line railway, but with a few yards of narrow gauge track at the pit top. The colliery was abandoned 11/10/1880; reopened c1900-4 but closed again by 1913, together with a small brickworks on the same site. The Hill Top Colliery, Brick & Tile Co Ltd was registered 9/6/1906 to acquire, from T.W.S. Jones (proprietor of Springfield Colliery Co Ltd ?) collieries at Newthorpe (presumably Springfield). It worked again, in the ownership of the Hilltop Colliery Co Ltd, for a short period c1923 and then closed for good.

WILLIAM HOLLINS & CO LTD
PLEASLEY VALE MILLS, Mansfield Woodhouse   **GH48**
    SK 527647 & SK 517648.

These old established textile mills (1784) were located alongside the River Meden and, between 1886 and 1895, a rail served warehouse was erected on the north side of the Midland Railway Tibshelf to Pleasley Junction line (opened 8/1882), ½ mile north west of Pleasley Junction. Between 1925 and 1929 a second fan of sidings was put in ½ mile to the west to serve the company's Upper Mill. The sidings were still listed in 1956.

BENJAMIN HOLMES & SONS
BRICKWORKS, Lowmoor Road, East Kirkby   **JH49**
Benjamin Holmes until c1908   SK506566

Opened c1898 on the east side of Lowmoor Road, opposite the Midland Railway Kirkby locomotive shed. There was no main line connection but in 1914 there was an incline running east into a clay pit. The works closed after 1948. In 1950 it was shown as disused and the tramway had gone.

HOVERINGHAM GRAVEL CO LTD
COW LANE WHARF, Newark.   **PH50**
Trent Concrete Co Ltd until 1954.   SK 798546

This wharf was located on the south east side of the River Trent. A group of four sidings was installed following an agreement dated 16/10/1931. These were connected to the south end of the LMSR/LNER Joint Newark Spur line via the private siding of R. Bishop & Sons (see R. Peach & Co Ltd). Due to the radius of the curves on the wharf shunting was not by main line locomotive. (Rail cranes or tractors ?) The sidings closed after 1956.

ILKESTON COLLIERIES LTD
LODGE COLLIERY, Newthorpe Common   **MH51**
Manners Colliery Co Ltd until c3/1933.   SK 474453

Lodge colliery had closed in 1896 (see **Executors of Wm Hall**, Industrial Locomotive Section, for earlier details). It was reopened between 1913 and 1916 on the same site and the sidings north east of the GNR, connected to their Digby Sidings, were reinstated. Motive power within the colliery sidings was by a main and tail rope haulage engine and a number of return wheels and this time industrial locomotives were not used. The colliery was vested in the NCB, East Midlands Division, No.5 Area from 1/1/1947.

J & A JACKSON LTD
BONE MILL LANE BRICKWORKS, Worksop   **CH52**
                                                                                            SK 578804

A short 2ft 0in gauge hand worked line with Hudson wagons was in use in 1980. The business later became a builders merchants on the same site without a railway.

W.J. JENKINS & CO LTD
Beehive Works, Thrumpton, Retford   **DH53**
Charles Hopkinson until c1896   SK 708802

This engineering works was located on the south east side of the MS&LR locomotive shed, ¼ mile east of the Retford flat crossing. A siding was provided by agreement dated 28/1/1879 and assigned to Jenkins from 30/8/1896. An internal rail system was developed, linking the various workshops, including at least one wagon turntable. The agreement for the main line connection was terminated from 1/10/1970.

J A KING & CO
PLASTER SLAB WORKS, Hill Road, Gotham   **WH54**
                                                                              SK 535294

This company was registered 1/1925 and their new works was connected in that year to the north side of the LNER Gotham branch, (agreement dated 3/8/1927) ¾ mile south of Gotham Wharf. It appears also to have had a short internal narrow gauge line. Rail traffic had ceased by 1956.

Owners? (possibly WILLIAM JAMES KIRK ?)
SAND PIT, Sutton Forest   **HH55**
                                                                                SK 518586

This possible owner, resident at Priestcroft Cottage, Forest Street, Sutton in Ashfield, was trading in sand in 1869 and 1876. A complex of shallow sand pits dating back to the 1870s included one which has, on a map of 1898, a feature which may have been a short narrow gauge incline. Closed by 1914.

LANE BROS
HERMITAGE BRICKWORKS, Hermitage Lane, Mansfield   HH56
SK 523600

Opened about 1900-04, this works was located on the north side of, but not connected to, the Midland Railway Kings Mill Branch, 300 yards east of Kings Mill. Two narrow gauge tramways ran west into a pit in 1914 but the works was not thereafter listed.

WM. LAWRENCE & CO LTD
CABINET WORKS, Vale Road, Colwick   TH57
SK 614406

The company was established in 1875, but was not on this site until 1898. A siding (agreement dated 28/10/1898) on the south east side of the GNR line, ¼ mile south west of Netherfield and Colwick station, served the works. The siding was also used by Messrs Spray & Burgess Ltd for some time from 1914. A plan of 1950 shows what appears to be narrow gauge trackwork in a timber stockyard south west of the works. Standard gauge rail traffic ceased after 1956.

R. LINDLEY
LIMEWORKS & QUARRY, Station Street, Mansfield   HH58
SK 534605.

Established by 1864, the limekilns were located south east of, and served by a siding from, the Midland Railway Nottingham line, ¼ mile south west of Mansfield Station. In 1876 the quarry being worked was 200 yards south of the works and linked to the kilns by a tramway of unknown gauge. Lindley also had a second siding on the south east side of the Midland Railway Goods station, from which a line ran south east from a turntable to a stone saw mill on the opposite side of Station Street at SK 537607. The whole enterprise closed between 1907 and 1912, and by 1914 the limeworks site had been reused for Midland Railway sidings and the stone saw mill as a timber yard.

LONDON & NORTH EASTERN RAILWAY CO

WHISKER HILL SAND PIT, Biggins Lane (later Ordsall Rd), Retford   DH59
Great Northern Railway Co until 11/1/1923   SK 697802

A sand pit was opened by 1897 north of the MS&LR Whisker Hill Junction and served by a siding connection to the curve leading to the GNR station. It was still active in 1916 when three sidings entered the workings. The pit closed after 1937.

CANAL SAND PITS, West Retford   DH60
SK 693814

Sand pits were established between 1897 and 1916 on both sides of the GNR Doncaster line, 1 mile north west of Retford Station. They were served by sidings making trailing connections with both running lines. The pit closed after 1937.

M. McCARTHY & SONS LTD
LIME BURNERS & BRICKWORKS, Thames Street, Bulwell QH61
SK 535452

Opened by 1928 on an earlier limeworks site. Limestone quarries here and in nearby Bold Street and Catherine Street were worked intensively in the 1930s. The extent of rail use is unknown but a network of narrow gauge tracks in the Thames Street stockyard is shown on a map of 1953.

Owner ? (McDONALD & CO ?)
EXPLOSIVES MAGAZINE, Eastwood MH62
SK 458463

The possible owner, McDonald & Co, was recorded as trading in explosives at Eastwood in 1888. In 1880 a tramway ran north west from a wharf on the Erewash Canal to a magazine at SK 457464 and then south for 200 yards to a further one at SK 456462. All had gone by 1899.

MANLOVE, ALLIOTT & CO LTD
BLOOMSGROVE WORKS, Ilkeston Road, Nottingham QH63
SK 556403

This large engineering works was in situ by 1869. It had no standard gauge connection but a map of 1919 shows an internal track emerging from the south west corner of the works. This company built a steam tram in 1876, reputedly tried on Nottingham street tramways. They also acted as agents for the supply of at least two narrow gauge steam locomotives for use overseas. The works remained in operation by the same company until after 1956.

MANNERS BRICK CO LTD

EASTWOOD BRICKWORKS, New Eastwood MH64
Eastwood Brick & Tile Works Ltd (From c1904 until 1920) SK 467458
(see also **Erewash Valley Brick Pipe & Pottery Co Ltd** Erewash Valley Brickwoks entry)

Opened between 1880 and 1899, this works was located on the north east side of the GNR railway, adjacent to Newthorpe & Greasley station goods yard. In 1899 and 1913 there was a tramway incline into a small clay hole to the north. A standard gauge siding was put in by agreement dated 16/11/1905. There had previously been a loading dock on a parallel GNR siding. The new siding extended north west to serve the works of **Wilkins Wire Ropes Ltd** (later **British Ropes Ltd**) until after 1929. The works was shown on a map of 1960 without a tramway but with extensive areas having been worked to the east.

EREWASH BRICKWORKS New Eastwood MH65
Erewash Valley Brick Pipe & Pottery Co. Ltd until 1916-1920) SK 468456

This works was established between 1895 and 1900 on land to the south west of the GNR line ¼ mile south east of Newthorpe & Greasley station. It was originally linked to a loading dock at Newthorpe GNR station (agreement dated 24/3/1902). However, this was soon replaced under an agreement dated 29/12/1904 by sidings from the GNR line into the works. The clay workings were on the north east side of the main line and served by a narrow gauge tramway. The works remained in situ in 1960 but the tramway had gone.

J.T. MARSHALL & CO LTD
WAGON WORKS, Derby Road, Lenton QH66
Marshall Brothers until 18/7/1884. SK 552394

This works, located on the west side of the Midland Railway at Lenton station goods yard, was connected to the Midland Railway in 1881 by a wagon turntable serving what was known as Marshall's siding. At the time of registration in 1884, it was proposed to acquire the Sandiacre Wagon Works (in Derbys). It is not known if this occurred. The last reference to the wagon works was in 1900, by which date the firms other business of timber merchant was being conducted from this site. The rail access closed in the period 1941-1949.

MEADOW FOUNDRY CO LTD
Bath Street, Littleworth, Mansfield HH67
Bradshaw & Sansom from 1864 until 1868 SK 540606

Located north west of the Mansfield Railway, but never connected to it, ¼ mile south west of Mansfield Central Station. The foundry, opened by 1852, was owned by the Meadow Foundry Co Ltd from 23/11/1872 and by 1897 had an internal railway system consisting of about 150 yards of track, gauge unknown, linking the workshops. Motive power unknown, possibly cranes. The foundry was demolished in 1960.

J.& W. MOSLEY
LADY LEE QUARRY, Haggonfields, Worksop CH68
John Ellis in 1864 SK 561798
John Ellis and William Richard Knight in 1853

This was an old quarry located west of the end of a ½ mile arm of the Chesterfield Canal. It had been working in the 1850-60s when there were also lime kilns. It may then have closed as it was absent from trade directories until 1895 when Mosley is listed as the proprietor. No tramway is shown on a map of 1885, but in 1897 a line ran south east for 400 yards from the quarry to the canal (SK 564794). The quarry closed c1912-14 and, by the latter year, the track had been removed.

Owner ? (NATIONAL COLD STORES (MANAGEMENT) LTD ?)
DEPOT Sutton in Ashfield. HH69
SK 512588

These premises were built between 1914 and 1950 on the north west side of the LMSR line, ½ mile north east of Sutton Junction Station. There were sidings on each side of the buildings with a long headshunt curving to the west. The depot is believed to have been built c1940 as the Ministry of Food, Sutton Cold Store and had passed to National Cold Stores by 1956.

DAVID NEW & CO
TROWELL FORGE, Trowell QH70
SK 478402

Opened by 1877 (c1869-1877). In 1879 it was served by sidings on the west side of the Midland Railway line at Trowell Junction. One line ran round the northern perimeter of the works and thence south to a wharf on the Erewash Canal at SK 478398. The forge was shown as disused in 1899 and had been removed by 1913. The siding was not listed in 1904.

NEWARK CORPORATION WATER WORKS

PUMPING STATION, Muskham Bridge, Newark. PH71
SK 788561

No rail connection. Located south of the bridge carrying the Great North Road over the River Trent. A map of 1915/1938? shows the works as closed but with a 100 yard length of rail track on the south bank of the river. It had gone by 1950.

PUMPING STATION, Farnsfield GH72
SK 656568

In situ by 1895 when it was served by a siding on the south side of the Midland Railway line, 1 mile east of Farnsfield station. This siding closed by 1949. By 1920 a short narrow gauge tramway ran south from this siding to the pumping station.

NEWARK GRAVEL & CONCRETE CO LTD
BALDERTON GRAVEL PIT, Balderton, Newark. PH73
SK 809524

Located and served by sidings (agreement dated 29/11/1930) on the east side of the LNER Bottesford line, 1½ miles south of Newark station. Three sidings ran north east to a loading point. Motive power is unknown. Though main line locomotives were supposed to exchange traffic at LNER junction, they regularly entered the sidings. These were still listed in 1956.

NEWSTEAD COLLIERY CO LTD
NEWSTEAD COLLIERY, Newstead   **NH74**
Newstead Colliery Co until 29/4/1878   SK 521534

Sinking of this colliery commenced in 1873, coal being reached in 1875. The colliery was served by sidings on the east side of the Midland Railway line, north of Newstead Station. On 27/10/1881 the GNR Leen Valley line, which passed to the east of the colliery, opened and connections were made from that line. The empty wagon connection north of the colliery was made from the GNR Annesley Colliery branch. The colliery was vested in the NCB, East Midlands Division, Area No.4 on 1/1/1947.

NEWTHORPE COLLIERY (1931) LTD
NEWTHORPE COLLIERY, Nottingham Road, Eastwood   **LH75**
Nerwthorpe Colliery Ltd from 1913 to 1917   SK 473466

This colliery was listed only once in a directory of 1932 although marked on maps of 1913 and 1960. There was no standard gauge connection and details of surface track at this very small site are unknown. It is probable that the colliery was closed throughout the period 1917 to 1931 and that the second period of operation ended with final closure in 1932.

NIXON, KNOWLES & CO LTD
Longwall Avenue, Queen's Drive Industrial Estate, Nottingham   **SH76**

A narrow gauge line, noted in 1982, served a timber impregnation plant.

NORTH NOTTS GRAVEL CO LTD
GRAVEL PIT, Lound   **DH77**
  SK 698857

Opened by 1943, these pits were worked in the late 1950s by means of a tramway running south from lorry loading points and screens to a pit at SK 701844. Motive power is unknown but a locomotive has to be a possibility as a similar pit in the same ownership was so served (see Industrial Locomotives Section).

NOTTINGHAM CORPORATION

BULCOTE SEWAGE WORKS, Burton Joyce   **UH78**
  SK 655443

A short railway of 1ft 6in gauge, was in use in 1967.

REFUSE DESTRUCTOR, Triumph Road, Nottingham QH79
SK 548399.

A map of 1938 shows a very short tramway on the north side of this works, east of the canal. This may be the remains of a Midland Railway branch from Radford which served a Nottingham Corporation Sanitary and Works & Ways yard on this site in 1904 and 1929 but had closed by 1938.

SEWAGE FARM SIDING, Netherfield TH80
SK 632410

This siding ran north-east for ¼ mile from the eastern side of the GNR Colwick sidings. It probably opened at the time of a siding agreement dated 29/11/1890 and closed after c1956. The GNR end of this siding was relocated several times as their yard developed. There was a GNR rail served gravel ballast pit south east of the sewage works siding in the 1880s and, by 1899, a short spur ran south east from the latter to a pumping station (SK 632408). This had gone by 1914.

NOTTINGHAM BUILDER'S BRICK CO LTD
(Registered. 11/12/1881)
CARLTON ROAD BRICKWORKS, Carlton RH81
W. Terry until 1871 SK590406

This works was connected to the GNR at Thorneywood station, after its opening in 1889, by a line running south west from there for ¼ mile. This siding was shared with a number of oil companies after 1910. Tramways ran east and south from the works to clay holes up to ¼ mile away. The former crossed over the GNR line en route. The works closed between 1948 and the liquidation of the company on 21/2/1950.

NOTTINGHAM PATENT BRICK CO LTD
(Registered 1867)
THORNEYWOOD BRICKWORKS, Burgass Road, Carlton RH82
William Burgass in 1864 and until 1867 SK 594413

This works was open by 1864 and after 1889 was connected to the GNR at Thorneywood station by a line running north east from there for 600 yards and thence around the kilns. The standard gauge connection closed with the GNR line in 1951. In 1883 there were two short tramways into clay workings to the north which by 1919 were quite extensive. Tramways were still in use in 1951. The works had closed by 1980.

DORKET HEAD BRICKWORKS, Arnold NH83
Robinson & Sykes in 1885 SK 593474

This works was being operated in 1885 but may have closed for a period soon afterwards. Nottingham Patent were operating a works at Arnold, believed to have been this one, from 1904. A map of 1914 shows a tramway running west into a clay hole. The tramway had had gone by 1950 but the works was still in operation.

OAKWOOD GRANGE COLLIERY CO LTD
OAKWOOD GRANGE (originally GRANGE) COLLIERY, Cossall   QH84
Grange Colliery Co 1932-1936   SK 488425
A. Lomas, Grange Farm, Cossall, 1930

This drift mine opened in 1932 on the site of a small scale outcrop working which had been abandoned in 1930. It was located to the east of Cossall village and had no standard gauge connection. There were two short narrow gauge tramways on the colliery surface. It was vested in the NCB, East Midlands Division, No.5 Area from 1/1/1947.

THOS. PARNHAM & SONS
FLOUR MILL, Mill Gate, Newark   PH85
Thorpe & Son until 1886   SK 793537

This was a water mill located on the river at the west end of a Midland Railway branch, which opened c12/1853 from their line ½ mile east of Newark Midland Railway Station. There were a number of sidings at the mill. The rail connection was removed in 12/1942.

R. PEACH & CO LTD
R. Bishop & Son Ltd until 1937

COW LANE MALTINGS, Newark.   PH86
   SK 799544

These maltings were located south of the end of the GNR/Midland Railway Joint, Newark Spur line. They were in situ by 1884. By agreement dated 14/4/1891, a single siding for Bishops was provided. This did not enter the maltings and had formerly been used (by agreement of 30/11/1888) by the **Newark Urban Sanitary Authority**. From 1931 it was used to access a complex of sidings for Trent Concrete Co Ltd (see Hoveringham Gravel Co Ltd) Closed after 1956.

SPITAL MALTINGS, Newark.   PH87
   SK 802547

These maltings opened after 1884 and were served by a siding (agreement dated 28/2/1891) on the east side of the GNR/Midland Railway Joint, Newark Spur line, south of its junction with the Newark Curve. Two wagon turntables gave access to lines running east into the maltings. Horses or capstans are believed to have been the motive power. The maltings closed in 9/1980, but rail traffic ended by 14/10/1973 when the spur line was taken out of use.

POWERGEN plc
RATCLIFFE POWER STATION, Ratcliffe on Soar   VH88
Central Electricity Generating Board until 31/3/1990   SK 503500

This large power station is located east of the main railway line from Trent to Leicester. It has been worked on the MGR system, using main line locomotives, since its opening in 10/1967. It is unusual in that continuous reversing loops were provided to enable trains to arrive or leave in either direction whilst using the same discharge hoppers. This required the provision of two main line connections at 1¼ and 2½ miles south of the site of Trent Station. The south facing connection and tracks were taken out of use by 1997.

WILLIAM RIGLEY & SONS (NOTTINGHAM) LTD
BULWELL COMMON WAGON WORKS, Bulwell **RH89**
SK 550449

A small wagon repair shop, with sidings and a traverser, was located on the east side of the GCR at Bulwell Common goods yard (siding agreement dated 24/12/1919). Closure date unknown.

HARRY ROUSE

OXCLOSE LIMESTONE QUARRY, Oxclose Lane, Mansfield Woodhouse **GH90**
T. Eastwood by 1934 until 1937 SK 534633
A. Eastwood & Sons in 1928 and 1931

A small site, at the extreme north end of Mansfield Woodhouse Midland Railway goods yard, is shown on the 1876 and 1914 Ordnance Survey to have had several short narrow gauge tracks.

PORTLAND QUARRY, Common Lane, Mansfield Woodhouse **GH91**
SK 537636

This quarry and limeworks were operating by 1883. An undated photograph shows six narrow gauge tracks radiating from a turntable. No tracks are shown on the 1914 Ordnance Survey. The quarry probably closed between 1937 and 1943.

SANDERSON & ROBINSON LTD
IRON FOUNDRY, Sheepbridge Lane, Mansfield **HH92**
SK 526601

The company was registered in 3/1904 and the works is believed to date from then. It was served by a siding on the north side of the Midland Railway Kings Mill branch, 7 chains west of its junction with the Nottingham to Mansfield line. Internal tracks, possibly narrow gauge, linked the various workshops. The siding was still listed in 1956. The works closed c1980.

GEORGE SANDS & SON LTD
STRUCTURAL ENGINEERING WORKS, Vale Road, Colwick **TH93**
SK 612404

A siding (agreement dated 11/11/1904) on the south east side of the GNR line, ½ mile south west of Netherfield and Colwick station, served this structural engineering works and connected with an internal system linking the various workshops. Motive power was rail cranes. Rail traffic ceased after 1956.

SHELTON BRICK & PLASTER CO LTD
SHELTON BRICK, TILE, PIPE & PLASTER WORKS, Shelton   **UH94**
Vale of Belvoir and Newark Plaster Co Ltd until not later than 16/10/1873.   SK 774439
William Jacobs until 14/3/1867

Originally a very small works, owned by Shelton Brick & Plaster Co Ltd by 1881. The Ordnance Survey of 1883 shows a tramway running south east into a hole at SK 776437, but not one reputed to have run north from the works to the Shelton to Thoroton road. At that time the GNR were proposing a branch to link the works with Kilvington on the Newark to Bottesford line. This was not built and the works closed soon afterwards. It was not listed in 1885 and the site had been cleared by 1920.

JAMES SHIPSTONE & SONS LTD
BREWERY, Rylands Road, Beeston   **VH95**
Beeston Brewery Co Ltd from 11/1897 until 7/1922   SK 532361
New Beeston Brewery Co Ltd (registered 10/1896)
Beeston Brewery Co until 1896

Constructed before 1883, it then had sidings on the north west side of the Midland Railway, south east of Beeston station. A map of 1913 shows an isolated internal line, possibly narrow gauge, at the west end. The brewery had passed to J. Shipstone & Sons Ltd by 1925 and later became a maltings.

WM. SILLS

CROWN FARM JUNCTION SAND PIT, Ratcher Hill, Mansfield   **GH96**
    SK 570595

Opened between 1904 and 1907 and served by sidings on the east side of the Midland Railway Mansfield Colliery Branch immediately north of its junction with the Mansfield to Southwell line. One of the sidings entered the workings. The siding connection was deleted from the Handbook of Stations in 1963.

PLEASLEY JUNCTION LIME WORKS & QUARRY, Mansfield Woodhouse   **GH97**
Sykes? until not later than 1887   SK 533641

Opened in 1862, this site was served by sidings (originally known as Sykes' Sidings) on the west side of the Midland Railway Mansfield to Worksop line at Pleasley Junction. Narrow gauge lines were used within the quarry until after 1938, and the standard gauge connection was still listed in 1956.

RICHARD SIMON & SONS LTD
PHOENIX WORKS, Vernon Road, Basford   **QH98**
                                                                          SK 550435

Established between 1900 and 1904, the works of this weighing machine and drying plant manufacturer had no main line connection. A plan of 1950 shows an internal tramway, presumably narrow gauge, linking two of the large workshops.

G SMITH
LIME WORKS & QUARRY, Swabs Lane, Cropwell Bishop   **UH99**
                                                                          SK 678343

This small works, active by 1869, was owned by Smith by 1895. Very little ground had been worked by 1919, when a map showed a tramway running east from the kilns for 500 yards to a wharf on the Grantham Canal, perhaps to bring in coal. It may have been the Cropwell Bishop Works of the Barnstone Blue Lias Lime Co Ltd by 1904 (not confirmed). It was not listed in a directory of 1928 and had probably closed by then.

STANDARD SAND CO LTD
RAILWAY SIDING, Racecourse Lane, Mansfield   **HH100**
                                                                          SK 555603

A single siding on the south side of the Midland Railway Southwell line, 1¼ miles east of Mansfield East Junction, was located east of Racecourse Lane. It was put in between 1907 and 1912; its purpose is unknown as there was little evidence of sand workings and it had closed by 1930.

THE STAPLEFORD REAL ESTATE CO LTD
STAPLEFORD COLLIERY AND BRICKWORKS, Pasture Lane, Stapleford   **VH101**
John Piggin in 1895-00.   SK 488383
D. G. Dunn & Co 1877-8
Stapleford Colliery Co 1874-6
Stapleford Lime Co in 1873

The colliery, sunk prior to 1873, was served by a line which ran east for ¼ mile from the Midland Railway at Stanton Gate station. Working was suspended in 1875 and may not have resumed as abandonment plans were deposited on 1/11/1878. Dunn may have acquired the colliery to add its coal reserves to those of his nearby Trowell Moor Colliery (see Industrial Locomotive Section). By 1879 the railway had been removed and the site was then a brickyard. In 1899 a short length of narrow gauge tramway ran into a hole, east of the works, but by 1913 this had gone and the clay hole was flooded. The site was owned by The Stapleford Real Estate Co Ltd c1908 - 1912.

STEETLEY CO LTD
SHIREOAKS LIMEWORKS AND QUARRY, Shireoaks   CH102
Steetley Lime & Basic Co Ltd until 16/12/1930   SK 552813
Steetley Lime Co Ltd until c1916
J.B. Evans until 12/7/1887
Joseph Pickering until 18/10/1883
Pickering & Mumford until 13/1/1879

The lime works was served by a siding (agreement dated 21/12/1876) on the south side of the MS&LR line, west of Shireoaks station. A quarry south of the kilns and a wharf on the Chesterfield Canal were linked by tramway (gauge unknown). By agreement of 8/3/1894, a subway was made beneath the canal to enable the tramway to reach new workings to the south east. By 1914 this tramway was some 400 yards long, its maximum extent, and ended at SK 553810. The quarry and its tramway closed after 1937. The agreement for the standard gauge connection was terminated from 21/8/1952.

STONEY LANE BRICK CO
CLINTON COLLIERY, Stoney Lane, Brinsley   LH103
Peter Newton in 1902   SK 453485
John Beardsley in 1876 and 1886

This small colliery and brickworks was located some ¼ mile east of the Nottingham Canal, west of Brinsley village. A tramway ran between the two. The sinking date is unknown but it was working in 1876. The GNR Pinxton branch passed over the tramway and by agreement dated 15/7/1881, a siding, known as Stoney Lane Siding, and a loading wharf were installed on the east side, north of the bridge over the tramway. The latter was to be connected to the loading wharf. No tramways were shown on the Ordnance Survey of 1901, but the colliery, owned by Stoney Lane Brick Co in 1905, was not abandoned until 1909.

SUTTON IN ASHFIELD BRICK CO (1928) LTD (and Others)
DALESTORTH ROAD BRICKWORKS, Sutton in Ashfield   JH104

There was in 1877 a group of four brickworks located east of Forest Road Skegby, two north and two south of Dalestorth Road. None had a main line rail connection and none had internal tracks until after 1898. A map of 1914 however shows one works, styled the Dalestorth Brickworks (SK 503600), to have a short incline to the south east. Another, not named (SK 501603), had one running east. The other two works were disused by 1914 but the one at SK 503598 had an incline into a hole to the south west. The other at SK 502601 was not shown with any track. All had closed by the late 1930s. Ownership of specific works has not been established but George Boot, Aaron Barke and Henry Shaw were all proprietors in 1912. Later owners were Boot Bros (1928 & 1932), S.E.Carding & Co (1922 & 1925) and Sutton in Ashfield Brick Co (1928) Ltd. George Boot was still operating one works in 1948.

SUTTON IN ASHFIELD URBAN DISTRICT COUNCIL
SUTTON GASWORKS, Sutton in Ashfield JH105
SK 497592

This works was located west of Sutton in Ashfield GNR station. It probably dated from the installation of a rail connection made by agreement dated 1/7/1910, which ran south along the west side of the GNR goods yard before dividing and ending at two wagon turntables. These were linked to produce a triangular layout. A plan of 1914 shows what may be a network of narrow gauge lines on the south side of the works, connected by turnplates. The rail connection closed between 1938 and 1944. The works had closed by 1955.

J.A. TAYLOR LTD
KINGS MILL, Mansfield HH106
Charles & Edward Cauldwell by 1895; until c1925 SK 520599
Geo. Adlington in 1876 and 1888
Wm. Adlington in 1864 and 1869

This corn mill was served by a siding at the end of a Midland Railway branch which ran west from its Nottingham line, 1¼ miles south west of Mansfield Station. This branch was on the original course of the Mansfield and Pinxton Railway of 1819 and the mill was probably in existence by that time. The siding had closed by 1949.

WM. THOMPSON
CHILWELL BRICKWORKS, School Lane, Chilwell VH107
Henry Thompson until c1908 SK 513357
Wm. Roberts in 1864

This old established works was located on the west side of Chilwell and was without rail connection. In 1883 there were kilns on both sides of School Lane but no tramways were shown. By 1913 the works on the east side had gone, whilst that to the west had a short incline running north west into a clay hole and there was another line within the hole. By 1938 only the incline remained and this had gone by 1955. The clay hole was not listed in 1943 but the works was still operating in 1948. The site was later redeveloped for housing.

J. TOMLINSON
MANSFIELD STONE & BRICKWORKS, Victoria Terrace, Mansfield HH108
(VICTORIA STEAM BRICKWORKS in 1877)
Millott & Mettham c1876-1880 SK 530603
Mansfield Brick & Stone Co Ltd until c1885-1895.

Served by a siding which ran north west from the Midland Railway Nottingham line, ½ mile south west of Mansfield Station. By 1898 there were 200 yard long tramways to workings north and west of the works. By 1914 that to the west had extended and the other had gone. The quarry appears to have closed by 1928. The works and siding were removed between 1938 and 1956.

TRENT GRAVELS LTD
GRAVEL PITS, Long Lane, Attenborough   VH109
SK 522350

Installed between 1928 and 1932, there were sidings on the south east side of the LMS line, 1 mile south west of Beeston Station. There were extensive pits to the east. The pits were flooded and working was by floating dredgers, hence tramways are unlikely. The sidings remained in situ in 1961.

JAMES TURNER & SON LTD
James Turner & Son until c1908

SANDPITS, Carlton Road and Gateford Road, Worksop   CH110
SK 585799

These sandpits was served by sidings on the north side of the MS&LR, Worksop Station. The first siding agreement is dated 26/4/1893 for a single short siding. By 1901 this had been extended to a tipping dock, west of Carlton Road, which was crossed by a narrow gauge tramway. This tramway ran into a sand pit east of Carlton Road. By 1914 pit and tramway extended north east for some 200 yards to SK 587798. The pit was approaching maximum extent and closed by 1928. By agreement of 30/10/1908, a line from the original siding ran north into a quarry titled Gateford Road. In 1914 this line was some 250 yards long. Nothing is known of the motive power for any of these lines. **Shell Mex Ltd** had a third party agreement to use one siding and some bulk oil tanks from 1916 until 1932. The closure of Gateford Road Quarry after 1931 meant the end of the sand traffic and on 31/12/1933 the site and the remaining siding were disposed of to the **Worksop Corporation.**

SANDHOLE SIDINGS, Sandy Lane, Worksop   CH111
SK 579799

Main line sidings on the south side of the MS&LR line, west of Worksop station were in situ by 1884. These were known as Sandhole Sidings suggesting earlier workings. Turner's involvement is believed to date from an agreement of 5/12/1891 for a line from a junction with the MS&LR to serve a pit on the south side of Sandhole Sidings. At this time and from at least 1884, there was an acid works to the west of the sand pits at SK 576807. This was operated until 25/10/1895 by **Samuel Warburton and Sons** and thereafter by **C. H. Smith Esq.** This works had a short siding from the main line and was purchased by Turner on 6/3/1901, closing then, or soon afterwards. The siding was later extended to form the sand pit access and Turner's original rail connection vanished under more mainline sidings. By 1925, **Turners Glassworks Co Ltd** had opened a works partly on and to the south of the acid works site. A line from the west side of the sand pit sidings served this works which was sold to **CWS Ltd** on 5/7/1932. They retained rail access until at least 1956. Turners were the last users, latterly to load sand brought by road from other pits, their agreement was terminated on 31/5/1969 at about the time the business passed to **Alan S. Denniff Ltd.**

KILTON ROAD SAND PIT, Worksop   CH112
Worksop Sand Co Ltd until 30/8/1919   SK 591797

This sandpit was served by a siding opened, under an agreement of 26/2/1910, on the north side of the GCR line, ¼ mile south east of Worksop station. The pit had closed and the siding was disused from 4/1941 but the agreement was not terminated until 2/10/1947.

TURNEY BROS LTD
LEATHER WORKS, Trent Bridge, Nottingham   **SH113**
                                                                                                                    SK 581384

This works, established in 1861, was located on the south side of the Nottingham Canal, west of its connection to the River Trent. A short tramway of about 2ft gauge linked the ground floors of the various buildings and the yard. It was used to move hides around on flat 4-wheeled wagons. The works was still open in 1956.

VALE OF BELVOIR AND NEWARK PLASTER CO LTD.
(Registered 14/3/1867)
LOWFIELD PLASTER WORKS, Newark   **PH114**
(**BOW BRIDGE PLASTER WORKS** until c1900)
William Scott (or **Stocker**?) until 1868   SK 804510
Robert Lineker until 1855

Established in 1850, without a rail connection. A siding agreement of 21/6/1886 relates to sidings on the east side of the GNR Bottesford line, 2 miles south of Newark station. By 1915, narrow gauge tramways were in use in the gypsum quarry south of the works. Use of the standard gauge sidings had ceased by 3/5/1920 when they were reported unfit for traffic. The works closed between then and 1927. After an unsuccessful attempt to sell the business as a going concern the adjacent brickworks and this site were sold to **Thos. W. Ward Ltd.** The plaster works was demolished and its quarry linked up to that of the brickworks (see Industrial Locomotive Section under Thos. W. Ward Ltd).

ORSTON GYPSUM MINE, BRICK & PLASTER WORKS, Orston   **UH115**
Jacobs until 14/3/1867   SK 764402

Established by 14/3/1865 when an agreement was made for a siding on the north side of the GNR line, ½ mile west of Elton and Orston Station. The mine closed in 1895 and a map of 1915 shows the works as disused. It was later demolished but the siding was retained by the railway company.

BEACON HILL PLASTER AND BRICKWORKS, Newark   **PH116**
                                                                                                                               SK 812538

The works at Beacon Hill were established before 1869 and were never rail connected. Despite having extensive quarries to the south, no map showing tramways has come to light. Between 1900 and 1904, the brickworks is believed to have passed to Beacon Hill Brick Co (Newark) Ltd and the plaster works to have closed. The brick works is not listed in a directory of 1908 and assumed closed by then.

WAGON REPAIRS LTD
WAGON WORKS, Mansfield   **HH117**
orig **C. Clough & Co Ltd**   SK ??????

A small wagon repair shop, with sidings and traverser, was located on the east side of the Mansfield Railway (GCR), south of Mansfield Central station. The siding agreement dates from 12/4/1920 and the works, owned by Wagon Repairs Ltd by 1938, closed between then and 1956.

E. C. WALTON & CO LTD
TIMBER MILLS, Sutton-upon-Trent   FH118
                                          SK 792660(approx)

The works was located on the west side of the LNER line north of Crow Park station. By agreement dated 19/6/1925, a narrow (about 3ft) gauge tramway from the works ran on to a loading platform in the goods yard. The works internal tramway was still in existance in 1981.

THOS. W. WARD LTD
MIDLAND WORKS, Meadow Lane, Nottingham   SH119
Railway & General Engineering Co Ltd (until between 1976-1982)   SK 584391

The company was registered in 4/1900 and the works built by 1904. It was connected to Midland Railway goods lines in the fork of their Carlton and Edwalton lines, south east of Nottingham Midland Station. Extensive internal sidings served the various workshops and are believed to have been shunted by rail cranes. Rail traffic ceased between 1982 and 1986.

WARWICK & RICHARDSONS LTD
BREWERY, Northgate, Newark   PH120
Richard Warwick & Sons until 1889-90   SK 802543

Open by 1872, this brewery was located on the east side of the GNR/Midland Railway Joint Newark Spur line. Three sidings put in c1872, (agreement dated 28/9/1874), and accessed by a wagon turntable, ran along the north side of the brewery. Closed after 1956.

WIGAN COAL & IRON CO LTD
MORTON BRICKWORKS, Checker House.   CH121
                                          SK 658791

This brickworks was established on the south side of the GCR in the vicinity of Checker House station, to provide bricks for the sinking of Manton Colliery and its associated housing. The siding agreement dates from 10/1/1899 and the rails were removed 6/10/1917 by when the works is assumed to have closed. Whether a tramway was used to work the clay is unknown.

WINSER & CO
WINSER'S MINES, Kegworth Road, Gotham   WH122
                                          SK 529296

Located south west of Gotham village, these mines were in operation by 1874. In 1885, by which date they were operated by Winser & Co, three sites (shafts/drifts?) were linked to a works by short tramways and a 300 yard line ran north from there to Kegworth Road at SK 528299. Motive power is unknown and by 1900 the mines had closed, leaving the site derelict. The manager in 1885 was J.W. Sheppard (see British Gypsum entry in Industrial Locomotive Section).

WILFORD BRICK CO LTD
WILFORD BRICKWORKS, Ruddington Lane, Wilford   VH123
                                                                                                                                    SK 568358

Opened by 1900 this works was served by a siding on the east side of the GCR line, 2 miles south of Arkwright Street station. A plan of 1919 shows an incline running from the works into a hole to the south east. The standard gauge connection had closed between 1949 and 1956. The works later became a trading estate.

WOLLATON COLLIERIES LTD
(formed 1875)

RADFORD COLLIERY, Old Radford   QH124
                                                                  SK 549410

Sunk in 1900, this colliery was served by sidings on the east side of the Midland Railway, ½ mile north of Radford Station. Worked by main line loco and gravity. It was vested in the NCB, East Midlands Division, No.6 Area from 1/1/1947.

WOLLATON COLLIERY, Wollaton   QH125
                                                                  SK 521404

Sunk by 1875, this colliery was, from that date, served by sidings on the south side of the Midland Railway, Trowell line 2 miles west of Radford Station. It was also served by a wharf on the Nottingham canal which passed to the south of the colliery. The sidings were worked by main line locomotive and gravity. It was vested in the NCB, East Midlands Division, No.6 Area from 1/1/1947.

FRANCIS T. WRIGHT LTD
WAGON WORKS, Leen Valley Junction, Daybrook   RH126
                                                                         SK 563442

Wright operated from sidings north of the GNR line at Leen Valley Junction by agreement dated 19/4/1906. By 1921, a wagon works had been erected on the same site which eventually had extensive sidings and a traverser. (A report of it being owned after 1956 by W. H. Davis & Sons (Wagons) Ltd is unsubstantiated.)

Owner?
GRAVEL PIT, Ranskill   BH127
                                                                          SK 663880

Located on the east side of the GNR line, north of Ranskill station. A long siding and loop curved into the pits which were extant in 1884 and 1898. There is no evidence of ownership in Oliver & Airey's 1895 list of private sidings. 1904 and 1912 RCH lists show no such sidings. Since by 1918 the pits had closed at about their 1898 extent and track had been lifted, closure pre 1904 is credible.

Owner ?
? MINE, Shireoaks CH128
SK 559811

Two shafts about 80 yards apart were sunk between 1897 and 1914, on the site of a former brick works on the north east side of the GCR line, south east of Shireoaks station. Their purpose is unknown and by 1914 they were marked as old shafts, linked by a single track tubway. They may have been connected with Shireoaks Colliery which was on the other side of the GCR line.

Owner ?
CLAY WORKINGS, Awsworth MH129
SK 475444

In 1880 a tramway ran south west for almost half a mile from clay pits north of the Midland Railway Bennerley to Bulwell Line, passing under the Erewash Valley line to end at a wharf on the Erewash Canal at Cotmanhay, Derbys (SK 469440). The clay pits had closed by 1899 and the tramway had gone.

Owner ?
WOLLATON BRICK WORKS, Coventry Lane, Wollaton QH130
(possibly Jas. Clayton in 1885) . SK 509394

This works was opened prior to 1883 and was located on the south side of the Midland Railway Trowell to Radford line, 2 miles east of Trowell Junction. It had no rail connection but was originally served by a wharf on the north side of the Nottingham Canal at the point where the early horse tramroad from Trowell Moor Collieries ended. There were open clay workings on both sides of the Midland Railway line but no tramway is shown until a map of 1955. The works had gone by 1971.

Owner ?
GYPSUM PIT, Rushcliffe H131
SK 550280

A disused mine is shown on maps of 1880, 1899 and 1915 at this site south west of Leake Road. No track is shown but earthworks suggest there may have been a short tramway earlier.

Owner ?
GYPSUM PIT, Hotchley Hill, Rushcliffe VH132
SK 556285

In 1899 there was a small working pit some 200 yards north of Hotchley Farm with two very short tramways therein. This was marked as a plaster pit and closed soon afterwards. Either this or the previous entry may have been a site known to have been occupied in 1900 by Derbyshire & Co.

Owner ?
GYPSUM MINE, Gotham　　　　　　　　　　　　　　　　　　　　　　**WH133**
　　　　　　　　　　　　　　　　　　　　　　　　　　SK 531293 &534294

This site, located west of Leake Road, Gotham was in operation by 1887. Two mines were linked by a tramway which ran north east for 600 yards to a yard and weighbridge on Leake Road, located immediately north of that of CUCKOO BUSH MINE (see Industrial Locomotive Section). Construction of the GCR Gotham Branch (c1900) severed this tramway but the mine may then not have been working. By 1913 the tramway had been lifted and its course became Eyres Lane.

Owner ?
SIDING, New Basford　　　　　　　　　　　　　　　　　　　　　　　**QH134**
　　　　　　　　　　　　　　　　　　　　　　　　　　　　SK 554422

Between 1913 and 1919 a siding was put in on the east side of the Midland Railway south of Basford Gasworks in order to fill in a large pond and part of the site of the Scotholme Nursery. The siding was retained to serve the reclaimed site but its user and purpose are not known.

INCLINES AND HORSE TRAMWAYS up to c1850.

Since a number of these lines were later converted to, or influenced the route of, conventional industrial railways, a short summary is given of those lines which were in whole or in part located in Nottinghamshire. A two mile long wooden tramway from pits at Strelley to Wollaton, constructed c1603, is credited with being the first surface tramway in the country. It lasted less than 15 years. Further developments awaited the opening of the Erewash (1779), Cromford (1794) and Nottingham (1796) Canals. These inspired the construction of a number of tramways linked to collieries. The last phase started with the opening, in 1819, of the Mansfield and Pinxton line which, unlike its predecessors, was a public railway, had private industrial tramways connected to it, and was later to be converted to a branch of the Midland Railway.

The basis of this listing is those lines extant in 1836 and depicted on that year's first edition of the one inch Ordnance Survey map. Where known, information is added in respect of lines closed before or opened after that date. Baxter (Stone Blocks and Iron Rails - David & Charles 1966) has been used with some caution as there are discrepancies between this and other sources, notably the 1836 map.

NOTTINGHAM CANAL TO RADFORD COLLIERY (Barber Walker & Co)   T1

A tramway ran north from a canal wharf east of Radford Bridge (SK 545400) to the colliery at SK 548407 (½ mile). Only the wharf remained in 1880.

NOTTINGHAM CANAL TO BILBOROUGH (Barber Walker & Co)   T2

Three short lines were projected in 1802 north east, north and north west from the Bilborough canal arm (SK 525403) to collieries in Bilborough Woods. Construction is not confirmed. By 1836 there was a straight track which fell at a uniform gradient from a colliery at SK 532415 south east to the canal at SK 534405 which may have been a tramway. The collieries and any tramroads had closed by 1840. The disused canal arm closed with the construction of the Midland Railway (c1875).

NOTTINGHAM CANAL TO TROWELL MOOR COLLIERY (Lord Middleton?)   T3

A tramway ran north from a canal wharf at SK 509394, a site then known as Engine Pit, to a number of collieries on Trowell Moor, ending at SK 503406 (¾ mile). See Cossall Coal Co Ltd in Industrial Locomotives Section.

NOTTINGHAM CANAL (ROBINETTS ARM) TO STRELLEY COAL YARD   T4

Tramways, built after 1824, ran north from the east end of the Robinetts Arm (SK 492420) to 'old engine' (colliery or pump?) east of Cossall at SK 494426 (½ mile) and east, via pits near Catstone Hill, to Strelley Coal Yard at SK 515418 (1½ miles). All had gone by 1880.

BABBINGTON COLLIERY TRAMWAY (Thos. North)　　　　　　　　　　T5

This line was in place in 1836 from Babbington Colliery (SK 492436) to the Nottingham road at Cinderhill (SK 534436) (3 miles). See B.A. Collieries Ltd in Industrial Locomotives Section for full details.

NOTTINGHAM CANAL AT COSSALL MARSH TO COLLIERIES　　　　　T6

Two tramways ran north east from a wharf at Cossall Marsh (SK 478429). The northernmost was in 1836 a short line extending to SK 483433. A composite map of unspecified date shows it extending to North's Babbington Moor Colliery (1 mile). The other tramway ran south of this to a colliery at SK 486434 (½ mile). Prior to this a line from this point, used only for a short period, had run to the canal south of Cossall Marsh Aqueduct. The Midland Railway Babbington Branch (1849) later ran on an alignment between them and they are believed to have closed by then. Baxter refers to a line heading north east from Cossall Common to pits near Grasscroft Farm (SK 493440). This is not shown on the 1836 map and was probably an extension of the line mentioned above which ran to Babbington Moor.

NOTTINGHAM CANAL AT COSSALL MARSH TO ILKESTON　　　　　T7

This line ran south west from the canal opposite the end of the lines above (T6). It crossed into Derbyshire shortly before reaching the Erewash Canal at SK 472422 and continued to collieries near Cotmanhay (1½ miles). This line had gone by 1880.

NOTTINGHAM CANAL AT GILT BROOK TO WATNALL　　　　　　　T8

Two parallel tramways ran north east from near Giltbrook. One commenced at a wharf at SK 483446 and ran alongside the Gilt Brook. After 1¼ miles it joined the other line, which had commenced on the north side of the Greasley Arm at SK 484448, and ran via a landsale depot on the Eastwood to Nottingham Road, to end at Wood Pit. This was north west of Watnall Hall at SK 494463. The later Digby and New London Collieries railway (see B.A. Collieries in Industrial Locomotives Section) followed a route which was largely between the two tramways. A short branch tramway ran east from the wharf at SK 483446 to a pit at Gilt Briggs Farm (SK 487447). The Midland Railway Bennerley - Bulwell line (1879) later followed its course.

EREWASH & NOTTINGHAM CANALS TO NEWTHORPE COMMON & NEW LONDON　　　　　　　　　　　　　　　　　　　　　　　　　　　　T9

This tramway is described by Baxter as having run from near Botany Bay Wharf on the Erewash Canal (in Derbyshire), across River Erewash (into Nottinghamshire) and the Nottingham Canal, to Newthorpe Common Colliery (1 mile). A branch at Erewash Brickworks ran north east to an old pit east of Newthorpe (1 mile) and was in situ in 1817. This line is not shown on the 1836 map and is presumed to have closed by then. The wharf at Botany

Bay is presumed to have been that at SK 469440 later used by the clay tramway. The 1880 Ordnance Survey map shows a track running to cross the Nottingham Canal at Langley Bridge (SK 476450) where the track divides. The Erewash Valley Brickworks here was a much later erection. The colliery at Newthorpe Common has not been located. The old pit east of Newthorpe was almost certainly on the New London site (SK 486463). The route has not otherwise been fixed.

WATNALL COLLIERY TRAMWAY.   T10

A short tramway ran south east along the south west side of the Nottingham road at Watnall from a colliery at SK 501457 to a coal yard at SK 504453. It had gone by 1880.

CANALS AT LANGLEY MILL TO PITS AT BRINSLEY, UNDERWOOD & BEGGARLEE
(Barber Walker & Co)   T11

Tramways, from wharves on the Erewash Canal at SK 454473 and the Nottingham Canal at SK 456470, combined to run north east to a junction north of Eastwood Hall. From here one line ran north to Underwood and one east to Beggarlee. A further line diverged north east from the Underwood line to end at Willey Lane. These tramways, some of which later formed the route for Barber Walker's private railways, are discussed under that heading in Industrial Locomotives Section.

EREWASH CANAL AT LANGLEY MILL TO COLLIERIES AT LOSCOE   T12

A tramway ran west from a wharf at SK 456457, entering Derbyshire almost immediately and terminated at collieries at Loscoe (2½ miles). This tramway was still extant in 1880 by when there was a short eastward extension over the Erewash Canal to a wharf on the adjacent Nottingham Canal. All had gone by 1899.

EREWASH CANAL AT LANGLEY MILL TO BAILEY BROOK COLLIERY   T13

A tramway ran south west and then west from a wharf at Langley Mill Basin (SK 453472), entering Derbyshire almost immediately and then ran on the north side of tramway T12 before turning north west to end at Bailey Brook Colliery (1¼ miles). All had gone by 1880.

CROMFORD CANAL AT BRINSLEY WHARF TO NEW BRINSLEY AND BAGTHORPE
(Joseph Wilkes?)   T14

A tramway ran for three miles, north east from the canal at SK 449490 to collieries at New Brinsley and on to a junction north of Bagthorpe village. From here lines ran north to a colliery at what became Inkerman (SK 468524 approx.) and east to one at Middlebridge (SK 475578). By 1880 the southern part had been reused for the railway to Pollington Colliery (see James Oakes & Co in Industrial Locomotives Section) and the rest had gone.

CROMFORD CANAL AT CODNOR PARK TO PORTLAND COLLIERIES
(Butterley Co)   T15

A tramway ran north east from the canal at Portland Wharf (SK 444514) to the Portland Collieries and there made two connections with the Mansfield and Pinxton Railway (3 miles). This is discussed in the Butterley Co, Portland and Mexbro Collieries entry in Industrial Locomotives Section (which see). There was also a short tramway running north from Portland Wharf to collieries and ironstone mines south west of Selston (SK 446527). The colliery was later developed by James Oakes & Co and this part of the tramway had gone by 1880.

COLLIERIES WEST OF SKEGBY TO SKEGBY OLD WHARF (John Dodsley?)   T16

In 1836, a tramway ran east from pits in Spring Wood (SK 485606) for ½ mile to Skegby Old Wharf (SK 481607). This was alongside the Fackley to Sutton road. Evidence of earthworks on later maps suggests that the tramway was later extended west to serve other pits and ended at the later Skegby Colliery at SK 466604, 1 mile from the wharf (see N.H. & B. Collieries, Sutton Colliery in Industrial Locomotives Section). This was rail connected from 1866 by means of the Midland Railway Skegby branch. Whether the tramway survived at that time is not known. The track at the western end, if not all of it, had gone by 1877.

MANSFIELD AND PINXTON RAILWAY CO.   T17

This public railway was opened on 13/4/1819. It ran north east from the north end of the Pinxton branch of the Cromford Canal to the Portland Wharf at Mansfield, some 7¾ miles in length of which all but the Pinxton Wharf was in Nottinghamshire. The line climbed from each end to a summit at Kirkby in Ashfield which resulted in the colloquial name Summit being applied to the later Kirkby Colliery. The track was a form of edge rail laid to about 4ft 4in gauge. By 1836 there were a number of branch tramways. Some, entirely in Derbyshire, connected at Pinxton Wharf. Of those in Nottinghamshire there was, some half a mile east of Pinxton, a short line which ran north west over the county boundary to a pit at SK 460548. A connection with the Butterley Co tramway [ref. T15] was made at lime kilns (SK 473547) east of Portland No.1 Colliery and another, including a branch from No.3 & 4 pits, joined at Portland No 2 Colliery (SK 484546). This point also marked the start of an incline which ran south east for ¼ mile to Annesley Wharf at Kirkby Woodhouse (SK 490543). Here there was a quarry and limekilns. Baxter claims this to be a branch of the Mansfield & Pinxton Railway but, if so, it does not appear to have been sold with the remainder of the undertaking to the Midland Railway in 1848. It was still in place in 1880 as a standard gauge incline but the connection was via the colliery lines, suggesting Butterley Co ownership at that time. The Mansfield & Pinxton main line was reconstructed as a conventional railway by the Midland Railway. The Kirkby to Mansfield section reopened on 9/10/1849 and the remainder from 6/11/1851. The new line used most of the tramway route but at King's Mill, Mansfield, a later realignment to the south left the mill on a siding and by-passed a viaduct over the mill pond.

Reference : "Priestley's Navigable Rivers & Canal", David & Charles (reprint), 1966.

INDEXES

LOCOMOTIVE INDEX

INDEX OF LOCOMOTIVE NAMES

INDEX OF LOCATIONS AND OWNERS

LOCOMOTIVE INDEX

NOTES : Information normally relates to the locomotive as built.

Column 1 — Works Number (or original company running number for locomotives built in main line workshops without a works number).

Column 2 — Date ex-works where known - this may be a later year than the year of building or the year recorded on the worksplate.

Column 3 — Gauge.

Column 4 — Wheel arrangement.

	Steam Locomotives :	Diesel Locomotives :
Column 5	Cylinder position	Horse power
Column 6	Cylinder size	Engine type #
Column 7	Driving wheel diameter	Weight in working order
Column 8	Either weight in working order and/or Manufacturers type designation	Page references
Column 9	Page references	

 # Manufacturers of petrol and diesel engines :

Ailsa	- Ailsa Craig Ltd, Salfords, Redhill, Surrey
Beardmore	- William Beardmore & Co Ltd, Parkhead, Glasgow
Blackstone	- Blackstone & Co Ltd, Rutland Engineering Works, Stamford, Lincs
Caterpillar	- Caterpillar Tractor Co Ltd
Cummins	- Cummins Engine Co Ltd, Shotts, Lanarkshire
Dorman	- W.H.Dorman & Co Ltd, Tixall Rd, Stafford
EE	- English Electric Co Ltd
Ferguson	- Harry Ferguson Ltd, Coventry
Ford	- Ford Motor Co Ltd, Dearborn, Michigan, USA
Fowler	- John Fowler & Co (Leeds) Ltd, Hunslet, Leeds
Gardner	- L. Gardner & Sons Ltd, Barton Hall Engine Works, Patricroft, Manchester
JAP	- J.A.Prestwich Industries Ltd, Northumberland Park, Tottenham, London
Leyland	- Leyland Motors Ltd, Leyland, Lancashire
Lister	- R.A. Lister & Co Ltd, Dursley, Gloucestershire
MAN	- Maschinenfabrik Augsurg-Nürnburg AG, Germany
McLaren	- J. & H. McLaren Ltd, Midland Engineering Works, Leeds
National	- National Gas & Oil Engine Co Ltd, Ashton-under-Lyne, Lancashire
Paxman	- Davey, Paxman & Co Ltd, Colchester, Essex
Perkins	Perkins Engine Co Ltd, Peterborough, Northants
Petters	- Petters Ltd, Staines, Middx
R-R	- Rolls-Royce Ltd, Oil Engine Division, Shrewsbury
Ruston	- Ruston & Hornsby Ltd, Lincoln
Saurer	- Armstrong Saurer Ltd, Newcastle upon Tyne

ANDREW BARCLAY, SONS & CO LTD, CALEDONIA WORKS, Kilmarnock — AB

No.	Date	Gauge	Type		Cylinders	Wheels	Notes
267	11.4.1884	4ft 8½in	0-4-0ST	OC	13 x 20	3ft6in	277
279	2.11.1885	4ft 8½in	0-4-0ST	OC	11 x 18	3ft3in	70,74,76
294	23.6.1887	4ft 8½in	0-4-0ST	OC	12 x 20	3ft6in	
675	*17.2.1891	4ft 8½in	0-4-0ST	OC	12 x 20	3ft2in	277
705	30.11.1891	4ft 8½in	0-4-0ST	OC	14 x 22	3ft5in	215,225
757	*24.2.1896	4ft 8½in	0-4-0ST	OC	10 x 18	3ft0in	151
769	24.2.1896	4ft 8½in	0-4-0ST	OC	14 x 22	3ft6in	112
886	7.9.1900	4ft 8½in	0-6-0ST	OC	15 x 22	3ft5in	122,187
889	4.7.1901	4ft 8½in	0-4-0ST	OC	12 x 20	3ft2in	194
905	12.2.1901	4ft 8½in	0-4-0ST	OC	14 x 22	3ft5in	127,182
972	*13.9.1904	4ft 8½in	0-4-0ST	OC	14 x 22	3ft5in	215,225
973	21.7.1904	4ft 8½in	0-4-0ST	OC	14 x 22	3ft5in	280
1000	*29.12.1903	4ft 8½in	0-6-0ST	OC	12 x 20	3ft2in	53,195
1010	23.3.1905	4ft 8½in	0-4-0ST	OC	14 x 22	3ft5in	127,215,225
1027	28.10.1904	4ft 8½in	0-4-0ST	OC	13 x 20	3ft6in	277
1038	11.4.1905	4ft 8½in	0-6-0ST	OC	15 x 22	3ft5in	229
1048	26.6.1905	4ft 8½in	0-6-0ST	OC	14 x 22	3ft5in	115
1132	26.11.1907	4ft 8½in	0-6-0ST	OC	14 x 22	3ft5in	115,163,235
1360	17.12.1913	4ft 8½in	0-4-0ST	OC	14 x 22	3ft5in	144
1487	13.11.1916	4ft 8½in	0-6-0F	OC	17 x 18	3ft5in	91
1517	5.5.1919	4ft 8½in	0-4-0ST	OC	14 x 22	3ft5in	47,170,171,183
1615	9.11.1918	4ft 8½in	0-4-0T	OC	14 x 22	3ft5in	198
1638	17.4.1922	4ft 8½in	0-6-0ST	OC	14 x 22	3ft5in	143,229
1649	10.12.1919	4ft 8½in	0-6-0T	OC	16 x 24	3ft7in	56,57,199
1651	23.12.1919	4ft 8½in	0-4-0ST	OC	16 x 24	3ft7in	286
1654	2.2.1920	4ft 8½in	0-4-0ST	OC	14 x 22	3ft5in	231
1706	19.1.1921	4ft 8½in	0-4-0ST	OC	14 x 22	3ft5in	122
1784	25.1.1923	4ft 8½in	0-4-0ST	OC	14 x 22	3ft5in	53,195
1861	1.4.1926	4ft 8½in	0-6-0ST	OC	15 x 22	3ft5in	142,143,229
1979	8.1.1930	4ft 8½in	0-4-0ST	OC	14 x 22	3ft5in	178
1984	5.5.1930	4ft 8½in	0-4-0F	OC	15 x 18	3ft0in	66
2008	23.1.1935	4ft 8½in	0-4-0F	OC	15 x 18	3ft0in	66
2077	31.10.1939	4ft 8½in	0-6-0ST	OC	14 x 22	3ft5in	146,178
2107	31.3.1941	4ft 8½in	0-6-0T	OC	18 x 24	3ft9in	146
2124	29.4.1942	4ft 8½in	0-4-0ST	OC	14 x 22	3ft5in	112
2166	29.4.1944	4ft 8½in	0-4-0ST	OC	14 x 22	3ft5in	66
2216	26.6.1946	4ft 8½in	0-6-0ST	OC	14 x 22	3ft5in	147,237
2344	17.3.1954	4ft 8½in	0-6-0ST	OC	15 x 22	3ft5in	165,171,187
2366	7.2.1955	4ft 8½in	0-4-0ST	OC	14 x 22	3ft5in	215,225

* indicates invoice date (which may not be the exact despatch date)

No.	Date	Gauge	Type	Power	Engine	Trans.	Notes
344	21.1.1941	4ft 8½in	0-4-0DM	153hp	Gardner 6L3	21T	108
351	17.3.1941	4ft 8½in	0-4-0DM	80hp	Gardner 6LW	14½T	111
357	29.9.1941	4ft 8½in	0-4-0DM	153hp	Gardner 6L3	21T	112
359	13.12.1941	4ft 8½in	0-4-0DM	153hp	Gardner 6L3	21T	154
368	11.5.1945	4ft 8½in	0-4-0DM	153hp	Gardner 6L3	21T	112
369	11.5.1945	4ft 8½in	0-4-0DM	153hp	Gardner 6L3	21T	112
440	2.9.1958	4ft 8½in	0-4-0DH	302hp	R-R C8SFL		93
441	18.3.1959	4ft 8½in	0-4-0DH	302hp	R-R C8SFL		93
442	7.4.1959	4ft 8½in	0-4-0DH	302hp	R-R C8SFL		93
443	29.4.1959	4ft 8½in	0-4-0DH	302hp	R-R C8SFL		93

	486	24.3.1964	4ft 8½in	0-6-0DH	302hp	R-R C8SFL		91
#	621	16.12.1977	2ft 0in	4wDHF	90hp	Perkins 6/354 11.8T		179
#	622	29.12.1977	2ft 0in	4wDHF	90hp	Perkins 6/354 11.8T		180

619 / 620 were laid down as works numbers 621 / 622 but completed as 619 / 620 per official records. They are also allocated HE 8569 / 8570.

AVONSIDE ENGINE CO LTD, AVONSIDE ENGINE WORKS, Bristol   AE

	1340	1889	4ft 8½in	0-4-0ST	OC	14 x 20	3ft3in	SS	59
	1341	1890	4ft 8½in	0-4-0ST	OC	14 x 20	3ft3in	SS	146,147,237
	1349	1893	4ft 8½in	0-6-0ST	OC	14 x 20	3ft3in	B2	116
	1360	12.1895	4ft 8½in	0-6-0ST	OC	14 x 20	3ft6in	B2	235
	1370	22.10.1897	4ft 8½in	0-6-0ST	OC	14 x 20	3ft3in	B2	30T 116
	1416	1901	4ft 8½in	0-4-0ST	OC	14 x 20	3ft3in	SS	148,245
	1419	1900	4ft 8½in	0-6-0ST	OC	14 x 20	3ft3in	B2	147,220, 235,237
	1423	1901	4ft 8½in	0-6-0ST	OC	14 x 20	3ft3in	B2	146,147,220, 235,237
#	1456	.1902	4ft 8½in	0-6-0ST	OC	16 x 22	3ft6in		284
#	1470	.1905	4ft 8½in	0-4-0ST	OC	14 x 20	3ft6in		60
	1490	1905	4ft 8½in	0-6-0ST	OC	14 x 20	3ft3in	B2	116,117,220
#	1500	.1910	4ft 8½in	0-4-0ST	OC	14 x 20	3ft3in		60
	1547	1908	3ft 0in	0-6-0T	OC	10 x 18	2ft6½in		19T 292
#	1610	.1911	4ft 8½in	0-4-0ST	OC	14 x 20	3ft1in		60
#	1617	.1912	4ft 8½in	0-6-0ST	OC	16 x 22	3ft6in		284
	1693	1914	4ft 8½in	0-6-0ST	OC	14½x20	3ft6in	B4	118,245
	1742	1916	4ft 8½in	0-6-0ST	OC	14 x 20	3ft3in	B3	29T 108
	1830	15.7.1919	4ft 8½in	0-4-0ST	OC	14 x 20	3ft3in	SS3	28T 198
	1831	8.10.1919	4ft 8½in	0-6-0ST	OC	14½x20	3ft6in	B4	118,179,245
#	1882	1921	4ft 8½in	0-6-0ST	OC	16 x 24			284
#	1892	1921	4ft 8½in	0-6-0ST	OC	14½x20	3ft6in		121
	1895	29.11.1923	4ft 8½in	0-6-0ST	OC	14½x20	3ft6in	B5	33T 93,194
	1920	31.3.1924	4ft 8½in	0-6-0ST	OC	14½x20	3ft6in	B5	33T 93,194
	1947	3.9.1924	4ft 8½in	0-6-0ST	OC	15 x 20	3ft6in	B5	33T 121,179
	1952	4.5.1925	4ft 8½in	0-6-0ST	OC	14½x20	3ft6in	B5	33T 121,179
	1976	2.11.1925	4ft 8½in	0-4-0ST	OC	13 x 18	3ft0in		24T 235,237
	1999	16.5.1927	4ft 8½in	0-4-0ST	OC	14 x 20	3ft3in	SS	30T 148

ASSOCIATED ELECTRICAL INDUSTRIES LTD   AEI

1178	1962	2ft 6in	4wBEF	90hp	DBF12 [Bg 3561]	214
1179	1962	2ft 6in	4wBEF	90hp	DBF12 [Bg 3562]	214

ALAN KEEF LTD, Ross-on-Wye   AK

40	.1992	2ft0in	4wDH	40hp	Perkins 3.152 3½T Type K40	265
47	.1994	2ft0in	4wDH	40hp	Perkins 3.152 3½T Type K40	265

ALBERT CAR ENG.   Albert

		2ft 0in	4-2wPMR S/O			286

ATLAS LOCO & MANUFACTURING CO LTD, Cleveland, Ohio, USA — Atlas

2445	1945	3ft 6in.	4wBEF		10T	196
2446	1945	3ft 6in.	4wBEF		10T	196
2454	1945	2ft 0in	4wBEF		7T	48,172,196
2466	1945	2ft 0in	4wBEF		7T	48,172,196
	1945	2ft 0in	4wBEF		7T	196
	1945	2ft 0in	4wBEF		7T	196

SIR W.G.ARMSTRONG, WHITWORTH & CO (ENGINEERS) LTD — AW
Newcastle upon Tyne

1434	.1937	4ft 8½in	4-6-0	OC	18½x26 6ft0in	73½T	289

BARCLAYS & CO, RIVERBANK WORKS, Kilmarnock, Ayrshire — B

209	1874	4ft 8½in	0-4-0ST	OC	92

BRUSH BAGNALL TRACTION LTD, Loughborough & Stafford — BBT

L - Assembled at Loughborough
S - Assembled at Stafford

S	3067	21.1.1955	4ft8½in	0-4-0DE	300hp	National M4AAU6	43T	282
L	3094	.1955	4ft8½in	0-6-0DE	400hp	Mirrlees TL6		218
L	3098	.1956	4ft8½in	0-4-0DE	300hp	National M4AAU6	43T	282
L	3100	.1956	4ft8½in	0-4-0DE	300hp	National M4AAU6	43T	282

E. E. BAGULEY LTD, Burton on Trent — Bg

763	20.11.1919	2ft 0in	0-4-0PM	10hp				128
3245	1949	4ft 8½in	4wWE					91
3330	1950	4ft 8½in	4wWE					91
3434	1954	2ft 0in	4wBEF	EM2B1	64hp	[EE 2086]		193,202
3435	1954	2ft 0in	4wBEF	EM2B1	64hp	[EE 2083]		137,193,202
3436	1956	2ft 0in	4wBEF	EM2B1	64hp	[EE 2300]		193,202
3437	1956	2ft 0in	4wBEF	EM2B1	64hp	[EE 2301]		137,193,202
3558	1960	2ft 6in	4wBEF	DBF12	90hp	[MV 1175]		214
3559	1960	2ft 6in	4wBEF	DBF12	90hp	[MV 1176]		214
3560	1961	2ft 6in	4wBEF	DBF12	90hp	[MV 1177]		214
3561	1962	2ft 6in	4wBEF	DBF12	90hp	[AEI 1178]		214
3562	1962	2ft 6in	4wBEF	DBF12	90hp	[AEI 1179]		214

BECORIT (MINING) LTD, Ilkeston, Derbys — BGB

18/4/001	1984	2ft6in	4wBEF	18hp	3T	[WR L3032F]	201
DML25/1/101	1967	Monorail	1adDHF	25hp	Perkins 3.152		194
RT30/400/001	1984	400mm	1adCEHF	30hp			190
RT30/400/003	1983	400mm	1adCEHF	30hp			135,190
DML40/1/401	1974	Monorail	2adDHF	40hp			194

50/10/001	1985	2ft6in	4w-4wBEF	50hp	10T	[WR L5004F]	177,201
BRL25/400/001	1986	400mm	1adBEF	25hp			135,190
BRL25/400/002	16.4.1987	400mm	1adBEF	25hp			135,189
BRL25/400/003	1987	400mm	1adBEF	25hp			135,189
BRL50/400/001	1988	400mm	2adBEF	50hp			135,189
DRL50/400/407	1978	400mm	2adDHF	50hp Perkins D4.203	5¾T	135,190
DRL50/400/408	1978	400mm	2adDHF	50hp Perkins D4.203	5¾T	135,190
50/400/413	1978	400mm	2adDHF	50hp Perkins D4.203	5¾T	135,190
DRL50/400/414	1979	400mm	2adDHF	50hp Perkins D4.203	5¾T	135,186
DRL50/400/418	1980	400mm	2adDHF	50hp Perkins D4.203	5¾T	135,186
DRL50/400/422	1980	400mm	2adDHF	50hp Perkins D4.203	5¾T	135,190
DRL50/400/427	1980	400mm	2adDHF	50hp Perkins D4.203	5¾T	135,190
DRL50/400/428	1980	400mm	2adDHF	50hp Perkins D4.203	5¾T	135,190
DRL50/400/436	1980	400mm	2adDHF	50hp Perkins D4.203	5¾T	136,190
DRL50/400/437	1982	400mm	2adDHF	50hp Perkins D4.203	5¾T	136,190
DRL50/400/438	1983	400mm	2adDHF	50hp Perkins D4.203	5¾T	135,186
DRL50/400/439	1983	400mm	2adDHF	50hp Perkins D4.203	5¾T	135,186
DRL50/400/440	198x	400mm	2adDHF	50hp Perkins D4.203	5¾T	135,186
DRL50/400/441	1985	400mm	reb of DHF50/400/427			135,190
DRL50/400/442	1985	400mm	2adDHF	50hp Perkins D4.203	5¾T	135,186
DRL50/400/443	1985	400mm	2adDHF	50hp Perkins D4.203	5¾T	135,186
DRL50/400/444	1985	400mm	2adDHF	50hp Perkins D4.203	5¾T	189
50/400/445	1985	400mm	reb of DRL50/400/422			135,190
DRL50/400/446	1986	400mm	2adDHF	50hp Perkins D4.203	5¾T	135,186,190
DRL50/400/535	1978	400mm	2adDHF	50hp Perkins D4.203	5¾T	136,190
RL100/400/002	1981	400mm	2adDHF	100hp MWM D916/62	6¼T	136,190
RL100/400/003	1982	400mm	2adDHF	100hp MWM D916/62	6¼T	136,186
RL100/400/004	1983	400mm	2adDHF	100hp MWM D916/62	6¼T	136,190
RL100/400/005	1983	400mm	2adDHF	100hp MWM D916/62	6¼T	136,186,190
RL100/400/006	1984	400mm	2adDHF	100hp MWM D916/62	6¼T	136,190
RL100/400/008	1984	400mm	2adDHF	100hp MWM D916/62	6¼T	136,190
RL100/400/009	1985	400mm	2adDHF	100hp MWM D916/62	6¼T	136,190
RL100/400/010	1986	400mm	2adDHF	100hp MWM D916/62	6¼T	136,190
RL100/400/012	1986	400mm	2adDHF	100hp MWM D916/62	6¼T	136,190
RL100/400/013	1987	400mm	2adDHF	100hp MWM D916/62	6¼T	136,190

BLACK, HAWTHORN & CO LTD, Gateshead   BH

167	9.6.1873	4ft 8½in	0-6-0ST	OC	14 x 20	3ft6in	277
471	1881	4ft 8½in	0-6-0T	OC	13 x 19	3ft2in	252
899	1890	4ft 8½in	0-6-0ST	OC			251
1038	1893	4ft 8½in	0-4-0ST	OC	12 x 19	3ft3in	149

STANTON & STAVELEY LTD, BILSTHORPE BRICKWORKS   Bilsthorpe

	c1950	2ft 4in	4wBE	61
	c1966	2ft 4in	2w-2BE	61

BALDWIN LOCOMOTIVE WORKS, Philadelphia, USA   BLW

46489	1917	4ft 8½in	0-6-0T	OC	16 x 24	4ft0in	108

BEYER, PEACOCK & CO LTD, Gorton, Manchester — BP

20	1856	4ft 8½in	0-4-0WT	OC	15 x 24	4ft6in	21½T	107
774	13.8.1868	4ft 8½in	4-4-0T	OC	17 x 24	5ft9in	35½T	143
3809	6.12.1895	4ft 8½in	0-4-0ST	IC	14 x 18	3ft2in		94
4164	3.10.1899	4ft 8½in	0-4-0ST	IC	13 x 16	3ft0½in	16¾T	94
5623	18.5.1912	4ft 8½in	0-6-2T	IC	18 x 24	4ft3in	49T	215
6390	21.1.1927	4ft 8½in	0-4-0ST	OC	16 x 24	3ft10in	34T	215,241
6728	19.10.1931	4ft 8½in	0-6-2T	IC	18 x 24	4ft3in	49T	215

BRUSH TRACTION LTD, FALCON WORKS, Loughborough, Leics — BT

179	26.4.1960	4ft 8½in	0-6-0DE	400hp 51½T Natl E4AA6 [HC D1176]	218

BUTTERLEY CO LTD, Ripley, Derbys — Butterley

[B1C]	1887	4ft 8½in	0-4-0ST	OC	14 x 20	4ft0in	86,122,187
[B2C]	1889	4ft 8½in	0-4-0ST	OC	14 x 20	4ft0in	86
[B3C]	1892	4ft 8½in	0-6-0ST	OC	15 x 20	4ft0in	215
[B7C]	1904	4ft 8½in			14 x 18		86,87
[B9C]	1896	4ft 8½in	0-4-0ST	OC			86,205
[B13C]	1900	4ft 8½in	0-6-0ST	OC	15 x 20	4ft0in	87,222
[B14C]	1903	4ft 8½in	0-4-0ST	OC	12 x 18	3ft0in	215,225
[B20C]	1904	4ft 8½in	0-6-0ST	OC	15 x 20	4ft0in	86,205
[B21C]	1907	4ft 8½in	0-6-0ST	OC	15 x 20	4ft0in	87,222

CAFFERATA & CO LTD, Newark, Notts — Cafferata

	1934	3ft 0in	4wTG	71

NEI MINING EQUIPMENT LTD, CLAYTON EQUIPMENT, Hatton — CE

Originally **CLARKE CHAPMAN LTD**.
Note that, to save space, batches of locomotives are indexed as single entries. For example, 5792A-D refers to locomotives 5792A, 5792B, 5792C and 5792D.

5373/1	8.1967	1ft 6in	4wBE	7hp	2T		266
5792A-D	7.1970	2ft 0in	4wBE	7hp	1¾T		257
5882C	8.1971	1ft 6in	4wBE	7hp	1¾T		257
B0427	3.1975	2ft 4in	4wBEF	17½hp	4T	CRT 3½	
							135,163,185,236,245
B0949/1-3	7.1976	2ft 4in	4wBEF	17½hp	4T	CRT 3½	228
B0953.1-3	1979	2ft 6in	4wBEF	90hp	15T	CB15	214
B0970A-B	12.1976	2ft 3in	4wBEF	17½hp	4T	CRT 3½	223
B0985	1977	2ft 0in	4wBEF	17½hp	4T	CRT 3½	180,223
B1504A-C	6.1977	3ft 0in	4wBEF	17½hp	4T	CRT 3½	138,239
B1515	1977	2ft 3in	4wBEF	17½hp	4T	CRT 3½	223
B1530	1977	2ft 6in	4wDHF	35hp	Perkins 4.203		137,201
B1562	1977	2ft 0in	4wBEF	17½hp	4T	CRT 3½	243
B1574A	15.5.1978	2ft 0in	4wBEF	17½hp	4T	CRT 3½	232
B1574B	22.5.1978	2ft 0in	4wBEF	17½hp	4T	CRT 3½	232

Works No.	Date	Gauge	Type	Power	Trans	Brake	Pages
B1574D	15.5.1978	2ft 0in	4wBEF	17½hp	4T	CRT 3½	232
B1574E	1978	2ft 0in	4wBEF	17½hp	4T	CRT 3½	214
B1574G	1978	2ft 0in	4wBEF	17½hp	4T	CRT 3½	235
B1574H	1978	2ft 0in	4wBEF	17½hp	4T	CRT 3½	214,235
B1575A	3.1978	2ft 6in	4wBEF	17½hp	4T	CRT 3½	136,214
B1575D	1978	2ft 6in	4wBEF	17½hp	4T	CRT 3½	214
B1575F	1978	2ft 6in	4wBEF	17½hp	4T	CRT 3½	214
B1801	1978	2ft 3in	4wBEF	17½hp	4T	CRT 3½	223
B1804A	1979	1ft 7in	4wBEF	17½hp	4T	CRT 3½	177,231
B1804B	1978	1ft 7in	4wBEF	17½hp	4T	CRT 3½	231
B1829	1978	2ft 0in	4wBEF	17½hp	4T	CRT 3½	243
B1831A-B	2.1979	2ft 6in	4wBEF	17½hp	4T	CRT 3½	137,201
B1842A	11.4.1979	2ft 4in	4wBEF	17½hp	4T	CRT 3½	228
B1842B	1979	2ft 4in	4wBEF	17½hp	4T	CRT 3½	228
B1843A-B	1979	3ft 0in	4wBEF	17½hp	4T	CRT 3½	138,239
B1850A-B	1979	3ft 0in	4wBEF	17½hp	4T	CRT 3½	138,239
B1874A-E	1981	3ft 0in	4wWEF	150hp	12½T		196,200
B2205A-B	1980	2ft 4in	4wBEF	17½hp	4T	CRT 3½	139,246
B2239A	1980	2ft 0in	4wBEF	17½hp	4T	CRT 3½	135,185
B2273A	1981	3ft 0in	4wBEF	17½hp	4T	CRT 3½	138,239
B2273B	1981	3ft 0in	4wBEF	17½hp	4T	CRT 3½	138,240
B2274A-B	1981	3ft 0in	4wBEF	17½hp	4T	CRT 3½	138,240
B2278	1981	1ft 7in	4wBEF	17½hp	4T	CRT 3½	177
B2299	1982	2ft 4in	3-car BERF 64hp			CMR 24	#175,176
B2926	1982	1ft 10½in	Reb. of B0427				135,163,185,236
B2928	1981	2ft 3in	Reb. of B0985				180,223
B2933	1981	2ft 0in	4wBEF	17½hp	4T	CRT 3½	193,200
B2946A-D	1983	2ft 4in	4wDHF	140hp Caterpillar 3306	15T		175
B2959A-B	1982	2ft 6in	4wBEF	17½hp	4T	CRT 3½	214
B2970A-B	1982	2ft 0in	4wBEF	17½hp	4T	CRT 3½	232
B2972A-B	1982	2ft 3in	4wBEF	17½hp	4T	CRT 3½	136,223,224,230
B2974	1982	2ft 3in	Reb. of B1562				243
B2986A-B	1982	3ft 0in	4wBEF	17½hp	4T	CRT 3½	138,240
B3002	1982	2ft 3in	Reb. of B0970A				223
B3034A-B	23.1.1983	2ft 4in	4wBEF	17½hp	4T	CRT 3½	139,178,246
B3043A	2.1983	2ft 4in	4wBEF	17½hp	4T	CRT 3½	136,175
B3043B	2.1983	2ft 4in	4wBEF	17½hp	4T	CRT 3½	175
B3044	6.1983	2ft 4in	4wBEF	17½hp	4T	CRT 3½	136,176,191
B3045A-B	1982	3ft 0in	4wBEF	17½hp	4T	CRT 3½	138,240
B3056	1983	2ft 3in	Reb. of B0970B				223
B3092A-B	8.1984	2ft 4in	4wBEF	90hp	15T	CB15	134,178
B3093A-B	1984	2ft 4in	4wBEF	17½hp	4T	CRT 3½	134,178
B3100A	3.1984	2ft 0in	4wBEF	17½hp	4T	CRT 3½	134,185,197
B3100B	1984	2ft 0in	4wBEF	17½hp	4T	CRT 3½	134,169,185,197
B3101A-B	1984	2ft 0in	4wBEF	17½hp	4T	CRT 3½	233
B3102	1984	3ft 0in	Reb. of B1504B				138,239
B3111	1984	2ft 3in	4wBEF	17½hp	4T	CRT 3½	224,230
B3124	1984	2ft 3in	Reb. of B1515				223
B3133	9.1984		Reb. of B1575B				232

B3141A-B	8.1984	2ft 0in	4wBEF	17½hp	4T	CRT 3½	243
B3147	3.1985	3ft 0in	4wWEF	150hp	12½T		196,200
B3155A	11.1984	2ft 0in	4wBEF	17½hp	4T	CRT 3½	137,197,201
B3155B	11.1984	2ft 0in	4wBEF	17½hp	4T	CRT 3½	134,185,197
B3156	1984	3ft 0in	Reb. of B1504A				138,239
B3157A-B	1984	2ft 6in	4wBEF	17½hp	4T	CRT 3½	137,201
B3161	2.1985	2ft 4in	4wBEF	17½hp	4T	CRT 3½	139,246
B3187	3.1985	1ft 10in	4wBEF	17½hp	4T	CRT 3½	163,236
B3204A-B	1985	3ft 0in	4wBEF	17½hp	4T	CRT 3½	175,212
B3224A	11.1985	3ft 0in	4w-4wBEF 50hp		10T	BoBo	134,240
B3224B	1985	3ft 0in	4w-4wBEF 50hp		10T	BoBo	138,240
B3224C	1985	3ft 0in	4w-4wBEF 50hp		10T	BoBo	138,178,240
B3234	1985	2ft 4in	4wBEF				139,240
B3239	1985	3ft 0in	Reb. of B1504B			CRT 3½	138,239
B3246	5.1986	2ft 4in	4w-4wBEF 50hp		10T	BoBo	139,246
B3248	3.1986	2ft 0in	4w-4wBEF 50hp		10T	BoBo	243
B3250	1986	2ft 3in	4wBEF	17½hp	4T	CRT 3½	224,230
B3251	3.1986	2ft 3in	4wBEF	17½hp	4T	CRT 3½	223,230
B3252A-C	4.1986	2ft 3in	4w-4wBEF 50hp		10T	BoBo	223,230
B3270A-E	11.1986	2ft 4in	4wDHF 140hp Caterpillar 3306		15T		139,246
B3289A-B	3.12.1986	2ft 4in	4w-4wBEF 50hp		10T	BoBo	175
B3290	1986	2ft 6in	Reb. of B1831A				137,201
B3322A-C	3.1987	2ft 0in	4w-4wBEF 90hp		18T	CB18	137,197,201
B3328	2.1987	2ft 0in	4wBEF	17½hp	4.8T	CLH 5	134,178,197
B3335	27.3.1987	2ft 0in	4w-4wBEF 50hp		10T	BoBo	135,180,185
B3352A-B	4.1987	3ft 0in	4w-4wBEF 50hp		10T	BoBo	138,240
B3353A-B	.1987	3ft 0in	4w-4wBEF 50hp		10T	BoBo	212
B3362A	10.1987	2ft 4in	4w-4wBEF 50hp		10T	BoBo	228
B3362B	10.1987	2ft 4in	4w-4wBEF 50hp		10T	BoBo	139,228,246
B3363A-B	10.1987	2ft 4in	4w-4wBEF 90hp		18T	CB18	139,228,246
B3364A	1987	2ft 0in	4wBEF	17½hp	4.8T	CLH 5	134,178,197
B3369	6.1987	2ft 4in	Reb. of B1842A				228
B3383A-B	1987	2ft 3in	4wBEF	17½hp	4T	CRT 3½	193,223
B3393B	1987	2ft 6in	Reb. of B2933				193,200
B3410	1988	2ft 6in	4wBEF	17½hp	4T	CRT 3½	137,201
B3411	1988	2ft 6in	4wBEF	17½hp	4.8T	CLH 5	137,201
B3428	24.3.1988	2ft 3in	4wBEF			CEB 4	230
B3445	1989	2ft 4in	4w-4wBEF 50hp		10T	BoBo	139,228,246
B3468A	1988	3ft 0in	Reb. of B1843A or B1843B				240
B3468B	1988	3ft 0in	Reb. of B1850A or B1850B				240
B3477A-B	1988	3ft 0in	4w-4wBEF 150hp		21T	CB21	138,240
B3478	1988	3ft 0in	Reb. of B3352A				138,240
B3483	1988	2ft 1in	4wBEF	17½hp	4T	CRT 3½	163
B3490	1988	2ft 4in	Reb. of B0949B				228
B3494A	1988	1ft 7in	Reb. of B1804A or B1804B				231
B3494B	1988	1ft 7in	Reb. of B2278				177
B3501	1990	2ft 6in	4wBEF	17½hp	4T	CRT 3½	136,176,191
B3502A-B	1989	2ft 0in	4w-4wBEF 90hp		18T	CB18	137,197,201
B3507		2ft 3in	Reb. of B0970B				223
B3518	1988	2ft 6in	4wBEF				214
B3532	24.11.1988	2ft 6in	Reb. of B3151B				137,201
B3563B	1989	3ft 0in	4wBEF				136

Number	Date	Gauge	Description			Notes
B3565	1989		Reb. of B3353B			138,240
B3570	1989	2ft 6in	Reb. of B3157A			137,201
B3575	1989		Reb. of B1575A			136
B3591	1990	3ft 0in	4w-4wBEF 150hp	21T	CB21	138,240
B3605	1989	3ft 0in	Reb. of B3335			185
B3615	1990	2ft 6in	4wBEF			214
B3621	1989	2ft 0in	Reb. of B0427			185
B3634A-B	3.1990	2ft 6in	4wBEF 17½hp	4.8T	CLH 5	137,201
B3689A-C	1990	2ft 6in	4w-4wBEF 50hp	10T	CLH 10	137,201
B3699	1990	2ft 3in	Reb. of B3251			223,230
B3718	1990	2ft 4in	Reb. of B3235			139
B3723	1991	2ft 4in	Reb. of B3362B			228,246
B3732	1991	2ft 4in	4w-4wBEF 50hp	10T	BoBo	228
B3762	6.1991	2ft 3in	4w-4wBEF 50hp	10T	BoBo	223
B3763	4.10.1991	2ft 3in	4w-4wBEF 50hp	10T	BoBo	223
B3800A-C	12.1991	2ft 6in	4w-4wBEF	10T	CLH10	137,201
B3827	1991	3ft 0in	Reb. of B3224A			240
B3840	1992	2ft 6in	Reb. of B3322B			201
B3851	1992	3ft 0in	Reb. of B1574E			214
B3851A	1992		Reb. of B1574H			214
B3853	1992	2ft 6in	Reb. of B3322A			201
B3854	1992	2ft 4in	Reb. of B3364A			178
B3855	1992	2ft 4in	Reb. of B3252C			178
B3859	1992	2ft 6in	Reb. of B3322C			201
B3861	1992	2ft 6in	Reb. of B3502B			201
B3873A-B	1992	2ft 3in	Reb. of B3252A-B			223
B3882	26.10.1992	2ft 6in	4w-4wBEF 50hp	10T	BoBo	214
B3904	1993	2ft 6in	Reb. of B3155A			201
B3906/1	1993	2ft 3in	Reb. of B3250			136,223
B3906/2	1993	2ft 3in	Reb. of B2972B			136,224
B3906/3	1993	2ft 3in	Reb. of B3111			224
B3906/4	1993	2ft 3in	Reb. of B3251			224
B3906/5	1993	2ft 3in	Reb. of B3251			223
B4005	1993		Reb. of B3153B			214

\# Built by GMT using CE equipment.

ALEXANDER CHAPLIN & CO LTD, CRANSTONHILL WORKS,
Glasgow **Chaplin**

2368	22.12.1885	4ft 8½in	0-4-0VBTVCG	9 x 12	2ft 1½in	124,290

CROSSLEY BROS (MANCHESTER) LTD, ELSTOW WORKS,
Bedford **Crossley**

	.1925	4ft 8½in	4wPM	40hp	Crossley	12T	133

MACHINEFABRIEK DU CROO & BRAUNS NV, Weesp, Holland **D&B**

42	1925	3ft 0in	0-4-0WT	OC	$9^{5}/_{8}$ x 13½	12½T	51,165

DARLINGTON WORKS, LNER / BR **Dar**

[LNER 985]	9.1923	4ft 8½in	0-4-0T	IC	14 x 20 3ft6in 22¾T	168,288,293
[BR D3613]	6.1958	4ft 8½in	0-6-0DE	350hp	Blackstone ER6 48½T	171,207,218
[BR D3618]	8.1958	4ft 8½in	0-6-0DE	350hp	Blackstone ER6 48½T	163,171,192,218
[BR D3619]	8.1958	4ft 8½in	0-6-0DE	350hp	Blackstone ER6 48½T	171,195,207,218

DREWRY CAR CO LTD, London (see builders indicated) **DC**

2158	1941	4ft 8½in	0-4-0DM	153hp	[EE 1189]	154
2159	1941	4ft 8½in	0-4-0DM	153hp	[EE 1190]	154
2168	1942	4ft 8½in	0-4-0DM	153hp	[VF 4860]	112
2169	1942	4ft 8½in	0-4-0DM	153hp	[VF 4861]	108,110
2176	1945	4ft 8½in	0-4-0DM	153hp	[VF 5257]	154
2177	1945	4ft 8½in	0-4-0DM	153hp	[VF 5258]	112
2182	1945	4ft 8½in	0-4-0DM	153hp	[VF 5263]	108
2183	1945	4ft 8½in	0-4-0DM	153hp	[VF 5264]	112
2552	11.1955	4ft 8½in	0-6-0DM	204hp	[VF D278]	212
2573	4.7.1956	4ft 8½in	0-6-0DM	204hp	[RSHN 7859]	91
2574	16.7.1956	4ft 8½in	0-6-0DM	204hp	[RSHN 7860]	91
2602	10.1957	4ft 8½in	0-6-0DM	204hp	[RSHD 7879]	167
2680	9.1960	4ft 8½in	0-6-0DM	204hp	[RSHD 8158]	183,203
2681	10.1960	4ft 8½in	0-6-0DM	204hp	[RSHD 8159]	212,231,234
2708	5.1961	4ft 8½in	0-6-0DM	204hp	[RSHD 8186]	212
2709	5.1961	4ft 8½in	0-6-0DM	204hp	[RSHD 8187]	231,234
2713	6.1961	4ft 8½in	0-6-0DM	204hp	[RSHD 8191]	231

Note : 153hp locos had Gardner 6L3 engines; weight in w/o 21T approx
204hp locos had Gardner 8L3 engines; weight in w/o 29¾T.

DERBY WORKS, Midland Railway **Derby**

	10.1867	4ft 8½in	2-4-0	IC	16½ x 22 6ft2in	33T	115

DICK, KERR & CO LTD, Preston, Lancs   DK
             1915   4ft 8½in   0-6-0T   OC   14 x(20?)   3ft 2½in   107,146

GASMOTOREN FABRIK DEUTZ, Köln, Germany   Dtz
   709   .1909   2ft 0in   4wPM   69

E.B. WILSON & CO, RAILWAY FOUNDRY, Leeds   EBW
   522   .1856   4ft 8½in   0-6-0ST   IC   131

ENGLISH ELECTRIC CO LTD, Preston, Lancs   EE
   533   1922   4ft 8½in   4wBE   38hp   15T   108
   1189   1941   4ft 8½in   0-4-0DM   153hp   Gdr 6L3 21T [DC 2158]   154
   1190   1941   4ft 8½in   0-4-0DM   153hp   Gdr 6L3 21T [DC 2159]   108,154
   2083   1954   2ft 6in   4wBEF   64hp   EM2B1   13T [Bg 3435]
                                                                           137,193,202
   2086   1954   2ft 6in   4wBEF   64hp   EM2B1   13T [Bg 3434]   193,202
   2300   1956   2ft 6in   4wBEF   64hp   EM2B1   13T [Bg 3436]   193
   2301   1956   2ft 6in   4wBEF   64hp   EM2B1   13T [Bg 3437]
                                                                           137,193,202
   2521   6.12.1957 2ft 6in 4wBEF   64hp   EM2B1   13T [RSHN 7963]
                                                                           137,193,202
   2522   13.2.1958 2ft 6in 4wBEF   64hp   EM2B1   13T [RSHN 7964]
                                                                               193,202
   3000   10.1961 4ft 8½in   Bo-Bo.DE   1000hp EE8SVT   72T [RSHD 8252]   289
   3147   1963   2ft 6in   4wBEF   64hp   EM2B1   13T [RSHD 8289]   201
   3224   1962   2ft 6in   4wBEF   64hp   EM2B1   13T [RSHD 8345]   193
   3402   1963   2ft 6in   4wBEF   64hp   EM2B1   13T [EES 8421]   193
   3606   3.1966 4ft 8½in   Bo-Bo.DE   1000hp EE8SVT   72T [EEV D1005]   289

ENGLISH ELECTRIC CO LTD, STEPHENSON WORKS, Darlington   EES
   8421   1963   2ft 6in   4wBEF   64hp   EM2B1   13T [EE 3402]   193

ENGLISH ELECTRIC CO LTD, VULCAN WORKS, Newton-le-Willows   EEV
   D1005   3.1966 4ft 8½in   Bo-Bo.DE   1000hp EE8SVT   72T [EE 3606]   289
   3768   .1966   2ft 6in   4wBEF   64hp   EM2B1   13T   137,201

EASTLEIGH WORKS, LSWR   Elh
   [LSWR 101/147] 1910 4ft 8½in 0-4-0T OC 12 x 18 3ft 8in   45

FALCON ENGINE & CAR WORKS LTD, Loughborough, Leics   FE
   81   1885   4ft 8½   0-4-0ST   OC   77

F. C. HIBBERD & CO LTD, Park Royal, London — FH

2151	3.1940	4ft 8½in	0-4-0DM	135hp	Paxman 6RWT	24T	112
2163	12.1938	2ft 0in	4wDM	20hp	National 2D	2½T	287
2193	6.1939	2ft 0in	4wDM	20hp	National 2D	2½T	101
2194	6.1939	2ft 0in	4wDM	20hp	National 2D	2½T	101
2514	4.1941	2ft 0in	4wDM	20hp	National 2D	2¾T	90
2742	26.7.1943	2ft 0in	4wDM	20hp	National 2D	2½T	66
2747	20.8.1943	2ft 0in	4wDM	20hp	National 2D	2½T	66
2914	9.1944	4ft 8½in	4wDM	29hp	National 3DL	6T	282,291
3468	11.7.1950	3ft 0in	4wDM		Lister 27/3		227
3472	20.11.1950	3ft 0in	4wDM		Lister 27/3		227
3700	20.4.1955	4ft 8½in	4wDM		Dorman 3DL	11T	244,263

FLETCHER, JENNINGS & CO, LOWCA ENGINE WORKS, Whitehaven — FJ

188		1882	4ft 8½in	0-4-0T	OC	9 x 16	70,74

FOX, WALKER & CO, ATLAS ENGINE WORKS, Fishponds, Bristol — FW

385		1878	4ft 8½in	0-6-0ST	OC	14 x 20	B1	53

GREENWOOD & BATLEY LTD, ALBION IRONWORKS, Leeds — GB

1364	1.1.1935	4ft 8½in	0-4-0WE	80hp		17T		58
1960	*15.10.1943	2ft 0in	4wBEF	2 x 20hp		7T		48,172,184,196
1961	*15.10.1943	2ft 0in	4wBEF	2 x 20hp		7T		48,172,184,196
2862	11.12.1959	2ft 0in	4wBEF	2 x 20hp		8T	GB8	213,235
2863	14.12.1959	2ft 0in	4wBEF	2 x 20hp		8T	GB8	213,235

* quoted (may not be actual) delivery dates.

GEC TRACTION LTD, VULCAN FOUNDRY, Newton-le-Willows — GECT

5424	1976	3ft 0in	4wBEF	64hp	13T	EM2B1	193,202

GATESHEAD WORKS, NER — Ghd

[NER 71]	11.1877	4ft 8½in	0-6-0T	IC	17 x 22	4ft1in	244

GYRO MINING TRANSPORT LTD, Maltby, South Yorks. — GMT

[TRACEY]	7.1987	2ft 0in	4w-4wBEF	150hp	Type 285150	28T	169

JAMES & FREDK HOWARD LTD, BRITANNIA IRONWORKS, Bedford — H

950	28.3.1929	4ft 8½in	4wPM	45hp	Dorman 4JUL	7T	149

HUDSWELL, CLARKE & RODGERS, RAILWAY FOUNDRY, Leeds — HCR

No.	Date	Gauge	Type	Cyl.	Bore × Stroke	Wheels	Weight	Page
88	4.3.1870	4ft 8½in	0-6-0ST	IC	13 x 18	3ft0in	17T	147
97	5.11.1869	4ft 8½in	0-4-0ST	OC	9 x 15	2ft9in	10T	53
102	15.2.1871	4ft 8½in	0-6-0ST	IC	13 x 18	3ft0in	17T	147
136	8.7.1873	4ft 8½in	0-4-0ST	OC	13 x 20	3ft6in	17T	131
139	17.9.1874	4ft 8½in	0-4-0ST	OC	10 x 16	2ft9in	11T	151
171	5.11.1875	4ft 8½in	0-6-0ST	IC	13 x 18	3ft0in	18T	147
172	12.6.1877	4ft 8½in	0-4-0ST	OC	10 x 16	2ft9in	11T	45,131
215	29.12.1879	4ft 8½in	0-4-0ST	OC	11 x 16	2ft9in	11T	131

HUDSWELL, CLARKE & CO LTD, RAILWAY FOUNDRY, Leeds — HC

No.	Date	Gauge	Type	Cyl.	Bore × Stroke	Wheels	Weight	Page
220	16.6.1882	4ft 8½in	0-4-0ST	OC	10 x 16	2ft9in	12T	252
247	8.7.1883	4ft 8½in	0-6-0ST	OC	14 x 20	3ft6½in	22T	53
254	24.4.1885	4ft 8½in	0-4-0ST	OC	10 x 16	2ft9in	12T	131
308	4.4.1888	4ft 8½in	0-4-0ST	OC	11 x 16	2ft9in	13T	131
335	27.5.1889	4ft 8½in	0-4-0ST	OC	10 x 16	2ft9in	12T	115
347	30.1.1892	4ft 8½in	0-6-0ST	IC	13 x 20	3ft3in	18T	252
350	19.12.1889	4ft 8½in	0-4-0ST	OC	11 x 16	2ft9in	12½T	131
435	11.4.1895	4ft 8½in	0-4-0ST	OC	10 x 16	2ft9in	12¾T	276
441	20.5.1895	4ft 8½in	0-6-0ST	IC	12 x 18	3ft0in	17½T	276
471	20.10.1896	4ft 8½in	0-4-0ST	OC	11 x 16	2ft9in	12½T	131
472	20.10.1896	4ft 8½in	0-4-0ST	OC	11 x 16	2ft9in	12½T	106,131
476	9.3.1897	4ft 8½in	0-4-0ST	OC	10 x 16	2ft9in	12½T	57,199
531	11.9.1899	4ft 8½in	0-6-0ST	IC	12 x 18	3ft0in	17¾T	277,278
566	24.7.1900	4ft 8½in	0-6-0ST	IC	13 x 20	3ft3½in	20½T	146
576	14.12.1900	4ft 8½in	0-4-0ST	OC	14 x 20	3ft7in	21T	147,168, 235,237
591	17.5.1901	4ft 8½in	0-6-0ST	IC	16 x 22	3ft10in	29T	86,205
603	10.2.1902	4ft 8½in	0-4-0ST	OC	11 x 16	2ft9½in	12½T	131
604	10.2.1902	4ft 8½in	0-4-0ST	OC	11 x 16	2ft9½in	12½T	131
613	30.4.1902	4ft 8½in	0-6-0ST	IC	16 x 22	3ft10in	29T	86,205
638	11.2.1903	4ft 8½in	0-4-0ST	OC	10 x 16	2ft9½in	12¾T	277
727	28.7.1905	4ft 8½in	0-4-0ST	OC	14 x 20	3ft3½in	21½T	254
736	22.8.1905	4ft 8½in	0-6-0ST	OC	15 x 22	3ft7in	26T	182,220
765	30.8.1907	4ft 8½in	0-6-0ST	IC	12 x 18	3ft1in	17½T	84
796	27.3.1907	4ft 8½in	0-6-0ST	OC	15 x 22	3ft7in	25T	220
862	21.9.1909	4ft 8½in	0-4-0ST	OC	14 x 20	3ft3½in	21T	234
1142	13.5.1915	2ft 0in	0-4-0WT	OC	5 x 8	1ft8in	3¾T	152
1161	29.6.1915	2ft 0in	0-4-0WT	OC	5 x 8	1ft8in	3¾T	275,283
1208	19.6.1916	4ft 8½in	0-6-0ST	OC	14 x 20	3ft7in	23¼T	273
1305	30.11.1917	4ft 8½in	0-6-0ST	OC	14 x 20	3ft7in	24½T	116,117, 168,188,229,245
1317	31.10.1918	600mm	0-6-0WT	OC	6½ x 12	1ft11in	5¾T	257
1365	17.10.1919	4ft 8½in	0-6-0ST	OC	15 x 22	3ft4in	27½T	182
1397	5.9.1919	4ft 8½in	0-4-0ST	OC	10 x 16	2ft9½in	12¾T	57,199
1496	29.12.1924	4ft 8½in	0-6-0T	IC	15½x20	3ft4½in		182
1523	30.12.1925	4ft 8½in	0-6-0T	OC	16 x 24	3ft9in		271
1539	23.7.1924	4ft 8½in	0-6-0ST	IC	13 x 20	3ft3½in	20T	273
1611	25.1.1928	4ft 8½in	0-4-0ST	OC	11 x 16	2ft9½in	13½T	70,74
1639	26.8.1929	4ft 8½in	0-6-0ST	IC	12 x 18	3ft1½in	18¼T	198
1649	30.3.1931	4ft 8½in	0-6-0ST	OC	14 x 22	3ft3½in	24¾T	163,205, 235
1650	19.9.1932	4ft 8½in	0-6-0ST	IC	12 x 18	3ft1in	17¾T	

1654	29.10.1934	4ft 8½in	0-6-0ST	OC	15 x 22	3ft5in	29¾T	242
1667	31.7.1936	4ft 8½in	0-6-0ST	IC	13 x 20	3ft3½in	19¾T	270
1675	11.3.1937	4ft 8½in	0-6-0ST	IC	13 x 20	3ft3½in	19¾T	270
1682	29.5.1937	4ft 8½in	0-6-0ST	IC	13 x 20	3ft3½in	19¾T	84,288,290
1746	9.9.1943	4ft 8½in	0-6-0ST	IC	18 x 26	4ft3in	48T	108
1747	15.9.1943	4ft 8½in	0-6-0ST	IC	18 x 26	4ft3in	48T	237
1749	21.6.1946	4ft 8½in	0-6-0ST	IC	13 x 20	3ft3½in	19¾T	269
1759	18.2.1944	4ft 8½in	0-6-0ST	IC	18 x 26	4ft3in	48T	108
1764	1.6.1944	4ft 8½in	0-6-0ST	IC	18 x 26	4ft3in	48T	178
1770	22.9.1944	4ft 8½in	0-6-0ST	IC	18 x 26	4ft3in	48T	167,198,241
1771	29.9.1944	4ft 8½in	0-6-0ST	IC	18 x 26	4ft3in	48T	167
1775	9.11.1944	4ft 8½in	0-6-0ST	IC	18 x 26	4ft3in	48T	108,154
1797	1.4.1947	4ft 8½in	0-4-0ST	OC	14 x 22	3ft3½in	22¼T	203,207
1813	5.7.1948	4ft 8½in	0-4-0ST	OC	16 x 24	3ft9in	28½T	182
1876	4.10.1954	4ft 8½in	0-6-0T	OC	16 x 24	3ft9in	33½T	237
1877	25.10.1954	4ft 8½in	0-6-0T	OC	16 x 24	3ft9in	33½T	182
1878	24.11.1954	4ft 8½in	0-6-0T	OC	16 x 24	3ft9in	33½T	168
1879	30.12.1954	4ft 8½in	0-6-0T	OC	16 x 24	3ft9in	33½T	182,206

NOTE that HC allocated Class names as follows : 'Thornhill' 727, 765, 1654, 'Titus' 765, 'S.H.T.' 862, 'Queen Mary' 1161, 'Fords' 1208, 1305, 'Ganges' 1317, 'Dora' 1397, 'Countess of Warwick' 1650, 1667, 1675, 1682, 1749, 'Standard' 1611, 'New Standard' 1649, 'Austerity' (earlier described by HC as 'LMS Class 3' and 'LMS') 1747, 1759, 1764, 1770, 1771, 1775, 'Irlam' 1797, 'Leven' 1813, and 'PLA 68' 1876-1879.

E294	1929	2ft 0in	4wBE	9hp			270
D603	1936	4ft 8½in	0-4-0DM	88hp	Mirrlees-Ricardo	13T	85
D622	20.10.1942	4ft 8½in	0-4-0DM	110hp	McLaren MR4	22T	110
DM630	25.5.1948	2ft 0in	0-6-0DMF	100hp	Gardner 6LW	15T	232
DM634	21.10.1946	3ft 6in	0-6-0DMF	100hp	Gardner 6LW	15T	220
DM635	21.10.1946	3ft 6in	0-6-0DMF	100hp	Gardner 6LW	15T	57,220
DM645	30.7.1948	2ft 0in	0-6-0DMF	100hp	Gardner 6LW	15T	57,184
DM647	30.1.1954	2ft 1in	0-6-0DMF	100hp	Gardner 6LW	15T	180,208,246
DM648	2.2.1949	3ft 0in	0-6-0DMF	100hp	Gardner 6LW	15T	239
DM649	3.5.1949	3ft 0in	0-6-0DMF	100hp	Gardner 6LW	15T	239
DM650	20.5.1949	3ft 0in	0-6-0DMF	100hp	Gardner 6LW	15T	239
DM651	27.5.1949	3ft 0in	0-6-0DMF	100hp	Gardner 6LW	15T	239
DM652	19.7.1949	3ft 0in	0-6-0DMF	100hp	Gardner 6LW	15T	239
DM653	5.10.1949	3ft 0in	0-6-0DMF	100hp	Gardner 6LW	15T	239
DM654	24.10.1949	3ft 0in	0-6-0DMF	100hp	Gardner 6LW	15T	239
DM657	8.2.1954	2ft 1in	0-6-0DMF	100hp	Gardner 6LW	15T	208
DM663	21.6.1952	2ft 0in	0-4-0DMF	68hp	Gardner 4LW	10T	232
DM664	31.10.1952	2ft 0in	0-4-0DMF	68hp	Gardner 4LW	10T	213
DM671	31.8.1948	2ft 0in	0-6-0DMF	100hp	Gardner 6LW	15T	172,184
DM678	8.12.1952	2ft 0in	0-6-0DMF	100hp	Gardner 6LW	15T	172,209
DM679	8.12.1952	2ft 0in	0-6-0DMF	100hp	Gardner 6LW	15T	172,185
DM688	29.1.1948	2ft 0in	0-4-0DMF	68hp	Gardner 4LW	10T	184
DM693	28.9.1948	2ft 4in	0-4-0DMF	68hp	Gardner 4LW	10T	189,227
DM694	6.10.1948	2ft 4in	0-4-0DMF	68hp	Gardner 4LW	10T	189,227
DM695	29.9.1948	2ft 4in	0-4-0DMF	68hp	Gardner 4LW	10T	189
DM724	28.7.1949	2ft 6in	0-6-0DMF	100hp	Gardner 6LW	15T	137,200
DM725	3.8.1949	2ft 6in	0-6-0DMF	100hp	Gardner 6LW	15T	137,201
DM726	5.8.1949	2ft 6in	0-6-0DMF	100hp	Gardner 6LW	15T	137,201
DM727	30.11.1949	2ft 6in	0-6-0DMF	100hp	Gardner 6LW	15T	137,201

Loco	Date	Gauge	Type	Power	Engine	Weight	Pages
DM729	1.2.1950	2ft 6in	0-6-0DMF 100hp	Gardner 6LW	15T	137,201
DM732	20.6.1951	3ft 6in	0-6-0DMF 100hp	Gardner 6LW	15T	220
DM733	18.6.1951	3ft 6in	0-6-0DMF 100hp	Gardner 6LW	15T	220
DM769	6.10.1950	2ft 3in	0-4-0DMF 68hp	Gardner 4LW	10T	223
DM770	9.10.1950	2ft 3in	0-4-0DMF 68hp	Gardner 4LW	10T	223
DM771	11.1950	2ft 3in	0-4-0DMF 68hp	Gardner 4LW	10T	138,223,245
DM772	17.11.1950	2ft 3in	0-4-0DMF 68hp	Gardner 4LW	10T	138,189, 223,245
DM773	24.11.1950	2ft 3in	0-4-0DMF 68hp	Gardner 4LW	10T	139,223,245
DM791	28.7.1953	2ft 3in	0-4-0DMF 68hp	Gardner 4LW	10T	189,223,245
DM792	28.1.1953	2ft 0in	0-6-0DMF 100hp	Gardner 6LW	15T	184
DM793	31.7.1953	2ft 0in	0-6-0DMF 100hp	Gardner 6LW	15T	184
DM794	28.11.1954	2ft 0in	0-6-0DMF 100hp	Gardner 6LW	15T	172,184,196
DM811	30.6.1953	2ft 0in	0-6-0DMF 100hp	Gardner 6LW	15T	196
DM812	3.7.1953	2ft 0in	0-6-0DMF 100hp	Gardner 6LW	15T	169,173, 180,196,209,226
DM813	10.7.1953	2ft 0in	0-6-0DMF 100hp	Gardner 6LW	15T	196,226,232
DM836	12.7.1954	2ft 0in	0-6-0DMF 100hp	Gardner 6LW	15T	169,173,180, 196,209,226
DM837	30.11.1954	2ft 0in	0-6-0DMF 100hp	Gardner 6LW	15T	196
DM838	26.5.1955	2ft 0in	0-6-0DMF 100hp	Gardner 6LW	15T	196
DM863	15.5.1956	2ft 0in	0-4-0DMF 100hp	Gardner 6LW	15T	184,196
DM864	30.11.1953	2ft 4in	0-6-0DMF 100hp	Gardner 6LW	15T	227
DM865	31.1.1955	2ft 4in	0-6-0DMF 100hp	Gardner 6LW	15T	189,227
DM866	30.4.1955	2ft 4in	0-6-0DMF 100hp	Gardner 6LW	15T	175,189
DM867	30.9.1955	2ft 4in	0-6-0DMF 100hp	Gardner 6LW	15T	189
DM868	30.9.1955	2ft 4in	0-6-0DMF 100hp	Gardner 6LW	15T	175,189
DM869	7.12.1953	2ft 4in	0-6-0DMF 100hp	Gardner 6LW	15T	227
DM879	25.2.1954	2ft 0in	0-6-0DMF 100hp	Gardner 6LW	15T	172,185
DM949	27.2.1957	2ft 0in	0-6-0DMF 100hp	Gardner 6LW	15T	179
DM950	28.4.1958	2ft 0in	0-6-0DMF 100hp	Gardner 6LW	15T	179
DM951	28.5.1958	2ft 0in	0-6-0DMF 100hp	Gardner 6LW	15T	179
DM952	2.12.1955	2ft 1in	0-6-0DMF 100hp	Gardner 6LW	15T	208
DM953	30.4.1956	2ft 0in	0-6-0DMF 100hp	Gardner 6LW	15T	173,197
DM954	30.4.1956	2ft 0in	0-6-0DMF 100hp	Gardner 6LW	15T	173,196
D961	23.7.1956	4ft 8½in	0-6-0DM 260hp	National M4AA8	40T	222
DM969	30.4.1956	2ft 4in	0-6-0DMF 100hp	Gardner 6LW	15T	175,189,228
DM970	1.5.1957	2ft 4in	0-6-0DMF 100hp	Gardner 6LW	15T	139,177, 189,245
DM971	31.5.1957	2ft 4in	0-6-0DMF 100hp	Gardner 6LW	15T	139,189,245
DM975	1.12.1955	2ft 0in	0-6-0DMF 107hp	Gardner 6LW	15T	196
DM1011	29.4.1957	2ft 4in	0-6-0DMF 100hp	Gardner 6LW	15T	139,189, 228,245
DM1014	19.11.1956	3ft 0in	0-6-0DMF 100hp	Gardner 6LW	15T	239
D1016	24.4.1957	4ft 8½in	0-6-0DM 260hp	National M4AA8	40T	237
D1018	16.7.1957	4ft 8½in	0-6-0DM 260hp	National M4AA8	40T	163
DM1033	28.1.1957	2ft 0in	0-6-0DMF 100hp	Gardner 6LW	15T	196
DM1034	6.12.1957	2ft 0in	0-6-0DMF 100hp	Gardner 6LW	15T	196
DM1035	25.10.1956	3ft 0in	0-6-0DMF 100hp	Gardner 6LW	15T	239
D1085	28.3.1958	4ft 8½in	0-6-0DM 260hp	National M4AA8	40T	245
D1090	19.3.1958	4ft 8½in	0-4-0DM 204hp	Gardner 8L3	30T	212
D1111	12.9.1958	4ft 8½in	0-6-0DM 260hp	National M4AA8	35½T	245
D1114	29.10.1958	4ft 8½in	0-6-0DM 260hp	National M4AA8	40T	168,182
DM1116	1.3.1958	2ft 0in	0-6-0DMF 100hp	Gardner 6LW	15T	166

Works No.	Date	Gauge	Type	Power	Engine	Weight	Notes
DM1117	24.3.1958	2ft 0in	0-6-0DMF	100hp	Gardner 6LW	15T	166,185
D1121	30.4.1958	4ft 8½in	0-6-0DM	204hp	Gardner 8L3	35½T	212
DM1124	30.1.1958	2ft 1in	0-6-0DMF	100hp	Gardner 6LW	15T	185,207
DM1125	30.1.1958	2ft 1in	0-6-0DMF	100hp	Gardner 6LW	15T	175,180,208
D1133	27.1.1959	4ft 8½in	0-6-0DM	204hp	Gardner 8L3	35½T	194,212
D1152	25.6.1959	4ft 8½in	0-6-0DM	204hp	Gardner 8L3	35½T	212
DM1165	29.4.1959	2ft 0in	0-6-0DMF	100hp	Gardner 6LW	15T	173,209
DM1166	29.5.1959	2ft 0in	0-6-0DMF	100hp	Gardner 6LW	15T	184,196,209
D1176	26.4.1060	4ft 8½in	0-6-0DE	400hp	National E4-AA6	51½T	218
DM1277	9.5.1962	2ft 0in	0-6-0DMF	100hp	Gardner 6LW	15T	196
DM1278	28.5.1962	2ft 0in	0-6-0DMF	100hp	Gardner 6LW	15T	196
DM1280	27.6.1962	2ft 0in	0-6-0DMF	100hp	Gardner 6LW	15T	175,184
DM1286	17.7.1962	2ft 4in	0-6-0DMF	100hp	Gardner 6LW	15T	137,176,177, 202,228
DM1287	23.7.1962	2ft 4in	0-6-0DMF	100hp	Gardner 6LW	15T	139,228,245
DM1288	31.7.1962	2ft 4in	0-6-0DMF	100hp	Gardner 6LW	15T	228
DM1304	28.1.1963	2ft 6in	0-6-0DMF	100hp	Gardner 6LW	15T	192,204
DM1308	28.2.1963	2ft 1in	0-6-0DMF	100hp	Gardner 6LW	15T	208
DM1309	29.3.1963	2ft 6in	0-6-0DMF	100hp	Gardner 6LW	15T	137
DM1310	31.4.1963	2ft 0in	0-6-0DMF	100hp	Gardner 6LW	15T	134,166,185
DM1315	1.7.1963	2ft 6in	0-6-0DMF	100hp	Gardner 6LW	15T	192,204
DM1316	16.10.1963	2ft 1in	4wDMF	25hp	Gardner 2LW	4½T	208
DM1321	26.10.1963	2ft 0in	0-6-0DMF	100hp	Gardner 6LW	15T	185
DM1327	23.3.1964	2ft 6in	0-6-0DMF	100hp	Gardner 6LW	15T	192,204
DM1329	3.7.1964	2ft 6in	0-6-0DMF	100hp	Gardner 6LW	15T	192
DM1330	12.11.1964	2ft 6in	0-6-0DMF	100hp	Gardner 6LW	15T	192
DM1331	30.5.1964	2ft 1in	0-6-0DMF	100hp	Gardner 6LW	15T	185,208
DM1332	27.8.1964	2ft 4in	0-6-0DMF	100hp	Gardner 6LW	15T	139,228,245
DM1333	22.12.1964	2ft 4in	0-6-0DMF	100hp	Gardner 6LW	15T	228,246
DM1334	30.11.1964	2ft 1in	4wDMF	25hp	Gardner 2LW	4½T	208
DM1335	15.12.1964	2ft 1in	4wDMF	25hp	Gardner 2LW	4½T	208
D1343	2.3.1965	4ft 8½in	0-4-0DH	252hp	Cmns NH5-6-1P	34T	231
DM1348	1.11.1965	2ft 0in	0-6-0DMF	100hp	Gardner 6LW	15T	166
DM1360	3.5.1965	2ft 4in	0-4-0DMF	68hp	Gardner 4LW	10T	174,176
DM1361	31.5.1965	2ft 4in	0-4-0DMF	68hp	Gardner 4LW	10T	174
DM1362	1.6.1965	2ft 4in	0-4-0DMF	68hp	Gardner 4LW	10T	174
DM1367	30.8.1965	2ft 0in	4wDMF	25hp	Gardner 2LW	6½T	185
DM1368	9.12.1965	2ft 0in	4wDMF	25hp	Gardner 2LW	6½T	185
DM1380	31.1.1966	2ft 0in	0-6-0DMF	100hp	Gardner 6LW	15T	166,185
DM1383	24.3.1966	2ft 5in	0-4-0DMF	68hp	Gardner 4LW	10T	174,189
DM1384	14.6.1966	2ft 5in	0-4-0DMF	68hp	Gardner 4LW	10T	174
DM1393	7.2.1967	2ft 0in	0-6-0DMF	100hp	Gardner 6LW	15T	166,185
DM1394	9.1.1967	3ft 0in	0-6-0DMF	100hp	Gardner 6LW	15T	239
DM1395	3.11.1966	2ft 0in	0-6-0DMF	100hp	Gardner 6LW	15T	185
DM1397	26.6.1967	3ft 0in	0-6-0DMF	100hp	Gardner 6LW	15T	239
DM1404	25.4.1968	3ft 0in	0-6-0DMF	100hp	Gardner 6LW	15T	239
DM1408	2.10.1968	2ft 4in	0-6-0DMF	68hp	Gardner 4LW	10T	174
DM1448	4.12.1981	2ft 0in	0-6-0DMF	102hp	Gdr 6LW 15T [HE 8848]		137,201
DM1449	28.1.1982	2ft 0in	0-6-0DMF	102hp	Gdr 6LW 15T [HE 8849]		137,201
DM1450	25.3.1982	2ft 0in	0-6-0DMF	102hp	Gdr 6LW 15T [HE 8850]		137,201

HUDSWELL BADGER LTD, RAILWAY FOUNDRY, Leeds　　　　HB

Works No.	Date	Gauge	Type	Power	Engine	Weight	Notes
DM1420	13.3.1972	2ft 4in	0-4-0DMF	68hp	Gardner 6LW	10T	174,176,228

HUNSLET ENGINE CO LTD, Leeds — HE

No.	Date	Gauge	Type	Cyl			Weight	Works/Notes
1	18.7.1865	4ft 8½in	0-6-0ST	IC	12 x 18	3ft1in		259
3	23.10.1865	4ft 8½in	0-6-0ST	IC	12 x 18	3ft1in		250
11	13.9.1866	4ft 8½in	0-6-0ST	IC	13 x 18	3ft1in		115
15	11.3.1867	4ft 8½in	0-6-0ST	IC	12 x 18	3ft1in		77
31	19.10.1868	4ft 8½in	0-6-0ST	IC	13 x 18	3ft1in		115
67	18.12.1871	4ft 8½in	0-4-0ST	OC	13 x 18	3ft1in		51
151	22.1.1876	4ft 8½in	0-6-0ST	IC	13 x 18	3ft1in		104,207
152	10.2.1876	4ft 8½in	0-6-0ST	IC	12 x 18	3ft1in		91,269
159	4.4.1877	4ft 8½in	0-4-0ST	OC	12 x 18	3ft1in		126
162	13.4.1876	4ft 8½in	0-6-0ST	IC	12 x 18	3ft1in		108
169	19.9.1876	4ft 8½in	0-6-0ST	IC	13 x 18	3ft1in		115
172	12.1.1877	4ft 8½in	0-6-0ST	IC	13 x 18	3ft1in		274
187	31.5.1877	4ft 8½in	0-6-0ST	IC	13 x 18	3ft1in		187
190	29.4.1878	4ft 8½in	0-4-0ST	OC	12 x 18	3ft1in		59
191	17.10.1877	4ft 8½in	0-6-0ST	IC	13 x 18	3ft1in		104
196	9.7.1878	4ft 8½in	0-6-0ST	IC	13 x 18	3ft1in		59,259
223	1.5.1879	4ft 8½in	0-4-0ST	OC	12 x 18	3ft1in		126
264	2.1.1882	4ft 8½in	0-4-0ST	OC	12 x 18	3ft1in		59
266	29.11.1881	4ft 8½in	0-4-0ST	OC	12 x 18	3ft1in	18½T	274
313	16.5.1883	4ft 8½in	0-4-0ST	OC				253
457	8.6.1888	4ft 8½in	0-6-0ST	IC	13 x 18	3ft1in		155
469	21.12.1888	4ft 8½in	0-6-0ST	IC	13 x 18	3ft1in		155
529	31.1.1891	4ft 8½in	0-6-0ST	IC	13 x 18	3ft1in		251,277
577	22.12.1892	4ft 8½in	0-6-0ST	OC	14 x 18	3ft3in		51,164,187,207
619	20.12.1894	4ft 8½in	0-6-0ST	IC	13 x 18	3ft1in		277
637	13.12.1895	4ft 8½in	0-4-0ST	OC	12 x 18	3ft1in		127,215,225
876	8.6.1906	4ft 8½in	0-6-0ST	IC	12 x 18	3ft2½in		84,277
1450	15.4.1925	4ft 8½in	0-6-0ST	IC	15 x 20	3ft7in		215
1493	8.7.1925	4ft 8½in	0-4-0ST	OC	14 x 20	3ft2½in		127,215,225
1644	4.11.1929	4ft 8½in	0-6-0ST	OC	14 x 20	3ft4in	30¼T	198
1684	24.8.1931	4ft 8½in	0-4-0T	OC	12 x 18	3ft4in		289
1689	27.7.1931	4ft 8½in	0-6-0ST	OC	14 x 20	3ft4in	30¼T	167,241
1708	23.9.1935	4ft 8½in	0-6-0ST	IC	16 x 22	3ft9in	38T	215
1847	29.12.1936	4ft 8½in	0-4-0DM	40/44hp Fowler 4B			10T	110
1858	27.9.1937	4ft 8½in	0-4-0DM	40/44hp Fowler 4B			10T	108
1898	20.9.1939	4ft 8½in	0-4-0DM	40/44hp Fowler 4B			10T	110
2068	8.7.1940	4ft 8½in	0-4-0DM	153hp Gardner 6L3			21T	112
2078	8.7.1940	4ft 8½in	0-4-0DM	153hp Gardner 6L3			21T	154
2213	21.6.1941	2ft 6in	4wDM	20hp Ailsa Craig RF2			3¼T	112
2214	21.6.1941	2ft 6in	4wDM	20hp Ailsa Craig RF2			3¼T	112
2254	26.7.1941	2ft 6in	0-4-0DM	50hp Gardner 4L2			8½T	289
2407	20.10.1941	4ft 8½in	0-4-0ST	OC	15 x 20	3ft3in	28¼T Moss Bay	226,229
2408	24.4.1942	4ft 8½in	0-6-0ST	IC	15 x 20	3ft7in	34T	148,242
2409	20.5.1942	4ft 8½in	0-6-0ST	IC	15 x 20	3ft7in	34T	104,171,195,207
# 2515	13.11.1941	600mm	4wDM	20hp Ailsa Craig RF2			3¼T	110
# 2670	18.2.1942	600mm	4wDM	20hp Ailsa Craig RF2			3¼T	110
# 2695	19.5.1942	2ft 6in	4wDM	25hp McLaren LMRW2			3¼T	110
# 2722	25.8.1942	600mm	4wDM	20hp Ailsa Craig RF2			3¼T	110
2853	30.4.1943	4ft 8½in	0-6-0ST	IC	18 x 26	4ft3in	48T	164,170,171,187,207

	2854	14.5.1943	4ft 8½in	0-6-0ST	IC	18 x 26	4ft3in	48T 164,170,171, 187
	2864	27.7.1943	4ft 8½in	0-6-0ST	IC	18 x 26	4ft3in	48T 244
	2866	6.8.1943	4ft 8½in	0-6-0ST	IC	18 x 26	4ft3in	48T 218,225,244
	2871	21.9.1943	4ft 8½in	0-6-0ST	IC	18 x 26	4ft3in	48T 237
	2881	5.11.1943	4ft 8½in	0-6-0ST	IC	18 x 26	4ft3in	48T 198
	2882	12.11.1943	4ft 8½in	0-6-0ST	IC	18 x 26	4ft3in	48T 218
	2894	15.1.1944	4ft 8½in	0-6-0ST	IC	18 x 26	4ft3in	48T 217
	2897	27.1.1944	4ft 8½in	0-6-0ST	IC	18 x 26	4ft3in	48T 154
#	2937	8.5.1944	2ft 0in	4wDM	20hp	Ailsa Craig RF2	3¼T	110
	3157	22.3.1944	4ft 8½in	0-6-0ST	IC	18 x 26	4ft3in	48T 108
	3161	20.4.1944	4ft 8½in	0-6-0ST	IC	18 x 26	4ft3in	48T 108
	3170	31.5.1944	4ft 8½in	0-6-0ST	IC	18 x 26	4ft3in	48T 219
	3188	2.10.1944	4ft 8½in	0-6-0ST	IC	18 x 26	4ft3in	48T 167,215,241, 244
	3192	1.11.1944	4ft 8½in	0-6-0ST	IC	18 x 26	4ft3in	48T 108
	3193	10.11.1944	4ft 8½in	0-6-0ST	IC	18 x 26	4ft3in	48T 154
	3196	29.11.1944	4ft 8½in	0-6-0ST	IC	18 x 26	4ft3in	48T 215,219
	3197	2.12.1944	4ft 8½in	0-6-0ST	IC	18 x 26	4ft3in	48T 182,219
	3201	30.12.1944	4ft 8½in	0-6-0ST	IC	18 x 26	4ft3in	48T 108
	3204	1.2.1945	4ft 8½in	0-6-0ST	IC	18 x 26	4ft3in	48T 154
	3205	7.2.1945	4ft 8½in	0-6-0ST	IC	18 x 26	4ft3in	48T 154
	3208	14.3.1945	4ft 8½in	0-6-0ST	IC	18 x 26	4ft3in	48T 108
	3215	23.5.1945	4ft 8½in	0-6-0ST	IC	18 x 26	4ft3in	48T 108
	3299	31.10.1945	2ft 4in	0-4-0DMF	50hp	Gardner 4L2	6¾T	64,189,227
	3300	31.10.1945	2ft 4in	0-4-0DMF	50hp	Gardner 4L2	6¾T	64,189,227
	3328	9.11.1946	3ft 0in	0-6-0DMF	100hp	Gardner 6LW	10T	64,211
	3329	23.11.1946	3ft 0in	0-6-0DMF	100hp	Gardner 6LW	10T	64,211,239
	3332	29.10.1945	3ft 0in	0-4-0DMF	50hp	Gardner 4L2	8¾T	64,211
	3356	5.6.1946	2ft 0in	0-4-0DMF	50hp	Gardner 4L2	8¾T	179
	3388	9.4.1947	3ft 0in	0-6-0DMF	100hp	Gardner 6LW	15T	211
	3389	28.7.1947	3ft 0in	0-6-0DMF	100hp	Gardner 6LW	15T	211
	3390	29.7.1947	3ft 0in	0-6-0DMF	100hp	Gardner 6LW	15T	239
	3391	4.6.1948	3ft 0in	0-6-0DMF	100hp	Gardner 6LW	15T	211,239
	3392	7.6.1948	3ft 0in	0-6-0DMF	100hp	Gardner 6LW	15T	239
	3411	3.3.1947	2ft 6in	0-4-0DMF	50hp	Gardner 4L2	6¾T	284
	3429	16.1.1947	3ft 0in	0-4-0DMF	50hp	Gardner 4L2	8¾T	211
	3434	28.6.1948	3ft 0in	0-6-0DMF	100hp	Gardner 6LW	15T	211
	3435	9.6.1948	3ft 0in	0-4-0DMF	65hp	Gardner 4LW	15T	211
	3521	31.1.1948	3ft 0in	0-6-0DMF	100hp	Gardner 6LW	15T	211,230
	3522	29.1.1948	3ft 0in	0-6-0DMF	100hp	Gardner 6LW	15T	211,230,239
	3535	9.6.1948	3ft 0in	0-6-0DMF	100hp	Gardner 6LW	15T	211
	3557	11.6.1948	2ft 0½in	0-4-0DMF	65hp	Gardner 4LW	10T	232
	3558	11.6.1948	2ft 0½in	0-4-0DMF	65hp	Gardner 4LW	10T	232
	3591	31.8.1949	2ft 4in	0-4-0DMF	65hp	Gardner 4LW	10T	174,178,227
	3619	23.7.1948	2ft 0in	0-4-0DMF	65hp	Gardner 4LW	10T	195
	3620	1.10.1948	2ft 0in	0-4-0DMF	65hp	Gardner 4LW	10T	195
	3824	26.7.1954	4ft 8½in	0-6-0ST	IC	18 x 26	4ft3in	48T 215,217
	4123	31.8.1949	2ft 0in	0-4-0DMF	65hp	Gardner 4LW	10T	179
	4184	22.12.1950	2ft 0in	4wDMF	22hp	Ailsa Craig RFS2	? 3T	208
	4185	22.12.1950	2ft 0in	4wDMF	22hp	Ailsa Craig RFS2	? 3T	172
	4428	24.7.1953	2ft 0in	4wDMF	22hp	Ailsa Craig RFS2	? 3T	184
	4429	29.7.1953	2ft 0in	4wDMF	22hp	Ailsa Craig RFS2	? 3T	184
	4430	29.7.1953	2ft 0in	4wDMF	22hp	Ailsa Craig RFS2	? 3T	184

No.	Date	Gauge	Type	Power	Engine	Weight	Notes
4523	22.2.1954	2ft 0in	4wDMF	22hp	Ailsa Craig RFS2	? 3T	184
4612	29.1.1954	3ft 0in	0-4-0DMF	65hp	Gardner 4LW	10T	239
4687	2.1.1956	2ft 3in	0-4-0DMF	65hp	Gardner 4LW	10T	222
4755	9.8.1954	2ft 0in	4wDMF	22hp	Ailsa Craig RFS2	? 3T	173,209
4756	3.11.1954	2ft 0in	4wDMF	22hp	Ailsa Craig RFS2	? 3T	173,208
4757	3.11.1954	2ft 0in	4wDMF	22hp	Ailsa Craig RFS2	? 3T	173
4758	22.12.1954	2ft 0in	4wDMF	22hp	Ailsa Craig RFS2	? 3T	173,208
5597	12.5.1961	2ft 0in	0-4-0DMF	66hp	Gardner 4LW	11T	232
5623	# 1960	4ft 8½in	0-4-0DH	153hp	Gardner 6L3	24T	203,221
5629	23.12.1959	3ft 0in	0-6-0DMF	100hp	Gardner 6LW	16T	211
5630	23.12.1959	3ft 0in	0-6-0DMF	100hp	Gardner 6LW	16T	211
5656	18.10.1960	4ft 8½in	0-6-0DM	204hp	Gardner 8L3	32T	231,234
6042	9.6.1961	2ft 0in	4wDMF	23hp	Ailsa Craig RFS2	? 3T	173,208
6043	23.10.1961	2ft 0in	4wDMF	23hp	Ailsa Craig RFS2	? 3T	173,208
6044	23.10.1961	2ft 0in	4wDMF	23hp	Ailsa Craig RFS2	? 3T	184
6045	23.10.1961	2ft 0in	4wDMF	23hp	Ailsa Craig RFS2	? 3T	184,209
6046	18.3.1961	2ft 1in	4wDMF	23hp	Ailsa Craig RFS2	? 3T	208
6047	1.4.1961	2ft 1in	4wDMF	23hp	Ailsa Craig RFS2	? 3T	208
6051	29.12.1964	2ft 0in	0-4-0DMF	66hp	Gardner 4LW	10T	179
6060	30.3.1965	2ft 0in	0-4-0DMF	66hp	Gardner 4LW	10T	179
6079	6.2.1963	2ft 1in	4wDMF	23hp	Ailsa Craig RFS2	? 3T	208
6262	31.7.1964	4ft 8½in	0-4-0DH	195hp	Gardner	25T	235
6332	31.1.1967	2ft 0in	4wDMF	28hp	Perkins 3152	4T	185
6333	31.1.1967	2ft 1in	4wDMF	28hp	Perkins 3152	4T	208
6334	31.1.1967	2ft 1in	4wDMF	28hp	Perkins 3152	4T	208
6607	** 1966	2ft 1in	0-6-0DMF	100hp	Gardner 6LW	16T	163
6608	28.2.1966	2ft 1in	0-6-0DMF	100hp	Gardner 6LW	16T	163
6609	23.3.1966	2ft 1in	0-6-0DMF	100hp	Gardner 6LW	16T	163
6610	23.10.1966	2ft 3in	0-6-0DMF	100hp	Gardner 6LW	16T	222
6621	29.9.1972	2ft 0in	0-4-0DMF	66hp	Gardner 4LW	11T	179
6622	2.11.1972	2ft 0in	0-4-0DMF	66hp	Gardner 4LW	11T	179
6653	1.2.1966	2ft 3in	0-6-0DMF	100hp	Gardner 6LW	16T	222
6675	30.11.1966	4ft 8½in	0-4-0DH	233hp	R-R C6SFL	35T	168,183
6678	26.2.1969	4ft 8½in	0-4-0DH	233hp	R-R C6SFL	35T	167
6680	23.4.1970	2ft 0in	4wDM	51hp	Ford 592E	7T	100,102
6681	4.5.1970	2ft 0in	4wDM	51hp	Ford 592E	7T	100,102
6682	9.6.1970	2ft 0in	4wDM	51hp	Ford 592E	7T	100,102
7089	27.4.1973	2ft 1in	4wDHF	28hp	Perkins 3152	4T	209
7178	23.2.1973	2ft 0in	4wDM	45hp	Deutz F3L912	5T	100,102,151
7327	16.5.1973	2ft 6in	4wDHF	28hp	Perkins 3152	4T	192
7328	17.5.1973	2ft 6in	4wDHF	28hp	Perkins 3152	4T	191,192
7331	25.6.1974	2ft 1in	4wDHF	28hp	Perkins 3152	4T	209
7332	26.6.1974	2ft 0in	4wDHF	28hp	Perkins 3152	4T	185
7370	18.3.1974	2ft 3in	0-6-0DMF	100hp	Gardner 6LW	16T	222,239
7372	30.10.1974	2ft 6in	0-6-0DMF	100hp	Gardner 6LW	16T	192,204
7373	18.12.1974	3ft 0in	0-6-0DMF	100hp	Gardner 6LW	16T	239
7385	27.7.1976	2ft 6in	4wDHF	28hp	Perkins 3152	4T	177,201
7390	23.1.1978	2ft 0in	4wDHF	90hp	Perkins 6354	11.8T	179
7391	27.1.1978	2ft 0in	4wDHF	90hp	Perkins 6354	11.8T	179
7413	25.2.1975	3ft 0in	0-6-0DMF	100hp	Gardner 6LW	16T	239
7414	27.2.1975	3ft 0in	0-6-0DMF	100hp	Gardner 6LW	16T	239
7415	28.3.1975	3ft 0in	0-6-0DMF	100hp	Gardner 6LW	16T	239
7418	30.1.1976	2ft 1in	0-6-0DMF	100hp	Gardner 6LW	16T	163
7449	13.2.1976	2ft 6in	4wDHF	28hp	Perkins 3152	4T	176,201

7479	30.11.1976	2ft 6in	0-6-0DMF	100hp	Gardner 6LW	16T	179,204
7518	14.10.1977	2ft 0in	4wDHF	28hp	Perkins 3152	4T	179
7519	1.11.1977	2ft 0in	4wDHF	28hp	Perkins 3152	4T	135,179,185
8507	15.7.1980	2ft 6in	4wDHF	91hp	Perkins 6354	11.4T	214
8569	16.12.1977	2ft 0in	4wDHF	90hp	Perkins 6354	11.8T [AB 621]	179
8570	29.12.1977	2ft 0in	4wDHF	90hp	Perkins 6354	11.8T [AB 622]	180
8834	19.3.1979	2ft 1in	4wDHF	28hp	Perkins 3152	4T	209
8835	24.11.1978	2ft 6in	4wDHF	28hp	Perkins 3152	4T	174,204
8848	4.12.1981	2ft 6in	0-6-0DMF	102hp	Gdr 6LW 15T [HC DM1448]		137,201
8849	28.1.1982	2ft 6in	0-6-0DMF	102hp	Gdr 6LW 15T [HC DM1449]		137,201
8850	25.3.1982	2ft 6in	0-6-0DMF	102hp	Gdr 6LW 15T [HC DM1450]		137,201
8909	25.5.1979	2ft 0in	4wDHF	28hp	Perkins 3152	4T	134,166, 169,185
8910	31.10.1979	2ft 6in	4wDHF	28hp	Perkins 3152	4T	176,177,193
8911	31.1.1980	2ft 0in	4wDHF	28hp	Perkins 3152	4T	134,166, 169,185
8912	29.11.1978	2ft 6in	4wDHF	28hp	Perkins 3152	4T	176,193,204
8913	18.5.1979	2ft 6in	4wDHF	28hp	Perkins 3152	4T	193,204
8914	28.8.1979	2ft 6in	4wDHF	28hp	Perkins 3152	4T	193,204
8915	16.6.1980	2ft 1in	4wDHF	28hp	Perkins 3152	4T	209
8916	23.5.1980	2ft 1in	4wDHF	28hp	Perkins 3152	4T	209
8917	23.7.1980	2ft 1in	4wDHF	28hp	Perkins 3152	4T	209
8947	28.7.1980	2ft 6in	4wDHF	91hp	Perkins 6354	11.4T	214
8948	8.10.1980	2ft 6in	4wDHF	91hp	Perkins 6354	11.4T	214
8949	27.10.1980	2ft 6in	4wDHF	91hp	Perkins 6354	11.4T	214
8950	28.11.1980	2ft 6in	4wDHF	91hp	Perkins 6354	11.4T	214
8951	25.7.1981	2ft 6in	4wDHF	91hp	Perkins 6354	11.4T	214
8980	23.10.1980	2ft 0in	4wDHF	28hp	Perkins 3152	4T	134,185
8984	2.2.1981	2ft 0in	4wDHF	28hp	Perkins 3152	4T	185
8989	16.6.1981	2ft 4in	4wDHF	28hp	Perkins 3152	4T	175,176
9047	13.7.1981	2ft 0in	4wDHF	28hp	Perkins 3152	4T	180,185
9048	13.7.1981	2ft 0in	4wDHF	28hp	Perkins 3152	4T	135,180,185
9049	8.7.1981	2ft 6in	4wDHF	28hp	Perkins 3152	4T	176,193
9055	21.3.1982	2ft 0in	4wDHF	28hp	Perkins 3152	4T	134,185,197
9056	21.3.1982	2ft 0in	4wDHF	28hp	Perkins 3152	4T/134,185,197
9155	30.5.1991	2ft 0in	4wBEF	20hp		4½T	135,185
9156	30.5.1991	2ft 0in	4wBEF	20hp		4½T	135,185

\# 'Hudson-Hunslet' locos.

HOPKINS, GILKES & CO, TEESSIDE ENGINE WORKS, Middlesbrough   HG

253	.1868	4ft 8½in	0-4-0ST	OC		118

B. HOUSE, Devizes, Wiltshire   House

	c1974	2ft 0in	4wDM	287

R. & W. HAWTHORN, LESLIE & CO LTD, Newcastle-on-Tyne — HL

Works No	Date	Gauge	Type	Cyl	Dimensions		Notes
2081	25.1.1888	4ft 8½in	0-6-0ST	OC	14 x 20	3ft6in	53
2466	18.7.1900	4ft 8½in	0-4-0ST	OC	14 x 20	3ft6in	87
2657	21.6.1906	4ft 8½in	0-4-0ST	OC	14 x 22	3ft6in	168
2839	31.12.1910	4ft 8½in	0-4-0ST	OC	14 x 22	3ft6in	84
3052	27.2.1914	4ft 8½in	0-4-0ST	OC	14 x 22	3ft6in	64
3134	4.6.1915	4ft 8½in	0-4-0ST	OC	14 x 22	3ft6in	144,231,234
3137	18.8.1915	4ft 8½in	0-4-0ST	OC	14 x 22	3ft6in	64,188
3261	9.10.1917	4ft 8½in	0-4-0ST	OC	14 x 22	3ft6in	144,231,234
3319	27.4.1918	4ft 8½in	0-4-0ST	OC	14 x 22	3ft6in	198
3368	6.5.1919	4ft 8½in	0-4-0ST	OC	14 x 22	3ft6in	149
3389	9.10.1919	4ft 8½in	0-4-0ST	OC	14 x 22	3ft6in	65,188,226,238
3591	18.4.1925	4ft 8½in	0-4-0ST	OC	14 x 22	3ft6in	64,65,211
3606	29.11.1925	4ft 8½in	0-6-0ST	OC	13 x 22	3ft4½in	165,170,171,183, 207,263
3614	17.3.1925	4ft 8½in	0-6-0ST	OC	16 x 24	3ft10in	146,178
3630	5.5.1925	4ft 8½in	0-4-0ST	OC	14 x 22	3ft6in	64,188
3652	24.5.1927	4ft 8½in	0-4-0ST	OC	14 x 22	3ft6in	198
3684	12.4.1929	4ft 8½in	0-4-0ST	OC	12 x 18	3ft6in	45
3771	4.11.1930	4ft 8½in	0-4-0ST	OC	14 x 22	3ft6in	231
3912	4.3.1937	4ft 8½in	0-4-0ST	OC	14 x 22	3ft6in	64,65,211
3949	5.1.1938	4ft 8½in	0-4-0DM	150hp	Crossley		111

HOHENZOLLERN AG FUR LOKOMOTIVEBAU, Dusseldorf — Hohen

Works No	Date	Gauge	Type	Cyl	Notes
3283	.1914	4ft 8½in	0-6-0WT	OC	56,57,107,122,199

HORWICH WORKS, LYR/LMSR/BR — Hor

Works No	Date	Gauge	Type	Details				Notes
1111	1910	4ft 8½in	0-4-0ST	OC	13 x 18	3ft0in	21T	263
[BR 76084]	.1957	4ft 8½in	2-6-0	OC	17½x26	5ft3in	60T	291
[BR D4115]	1.1962	4ft 8½in	0-6-0DE	350hp	EE 6KT	48T		289

JOHN FOWLER & CO (LEEDS) LTD, Hunslet, Leeds — JF

Works No	Date	Gauge	Type	Details				Notes
4186	4.1882	3ft 0in	2-4-0T	OC	5½ x ?			75
4503	2.1883	3ft 0in	? T	OC	6 x 9			75
20684	3.1935	3ft 0in	2-4-0DM	106hp	RH engine		18T	63
20685	3.1935	3ft 0in	2-4-0DM	106hp	RH engine		18T	63
21048	14.12.1935	4ft 8½in	0-4-0DM	88hp	RH engine		21½T	82
22887	29.12.1939	4ft 8½in	0-4-0DM	150hp	Fowler 4C		26T	222
22916	29.7.1940	4ft 8½in	0-4-0DM	150hp	Fowler 4C		29T	110
22943	30.6.1941	4ft 8½in	0-4-0DM	150hp	Fowler 4C		29T	111
22979	30.6.1942	4ft 8½in	0-4-0DM	150hp	Fowler 4C		29T	112
22988	20.10.1942	4ft 8½in	0-4-0DM	150hp	Fowler 4C		29T	111
3900015	27.4.1948	3ft 0in	4wDM	40/44hp	Fowler 4B		6T	63
4200041	17.2.1949	4ft 8½in	0-4-0DM	150hp	Fowler 4C		29T	83
4200042	14.3.1949	4ft 8½in	0-4-0DM	150hp	Fowler 4C		29T	83
4200045	11.7.1949	4ft 8½in	0-4-0DM	150hp	Fowler 4C		29T	83
4200044	29.6.1949	4ft 8½in	0-4-0DM	150hp	Fowler 4C		29T	82
4210037	16.1.1951	4ft 8½in	0-4-0DM	150hp	McLaren M6		28T	66
4220021	27.11.1962	4ft 8½in	0-4-0DH	185hp	Leyland EN900		28T	282
4220022	11.12.1962	4ft 8½in	0-4-0DH	185hp	Leyland EN900		28T	282

H.W. JOHNSON & CO, Rainford, Lancs — Johnson

56	1913	4ft 8½in	0-4-0WT	OC	14½ x 20	3ft4in	118,182,225,235

KITSON & CO LTD, AIREDALE FOUNDRY, Leeds — K

1856	20.1.1873	4ft 8½in	0-6-0ST	IC	16 x 24	4ft0in	56,215,217
1996	23.10.1874	4ft 8½in	0-6-0ST	IC	16 x 24	4ft0in	56,217
3501	19.12.1891	4ft 8½in	0-6-0T	IC	16 x 24	4ft6in	56,215,217
3520	14.6.1893	4ft 8½in	0-6-0T	IC	16 x 24	4ft0in	56,217
3918	31.1.1900	4ft 8½in	0-6-0T	IC	16 x 24	4ft2in	56,217

KERR, STUART & CO LTD, CALIFORNIA WORKS, Stoke-on-Trent — KS

2489	23.6.1916	4ft 8½in	0-4-0WT	OC	14½ x 20	3ft4in	Priestley #	106,114
3111	1.8.1918	4ft 8½in	0-4-0ST	OC	15 x 20	3ft6in	Moss Bay #	87,222
4012	19.5.1919	4ft 8½in	0-4-0ST	OC	15 x 20	3ft3in	Moss Bay #	133
4248	31.1.1922	2ft 0in	0-4-0ST	OC	6 x 9	1ft8in	3½T Wren	261
4254	4.3.1922	2ft 0in	0-4-0ST	OC	6 x 9	1ft8in	3½T Wren	258
4270	31.7.1922	2ft 0in	0-4-0ST	OC	6 x 9	1ft8in	3½T Wren	258

\# weight in w.o. = 22½T

R. & A. LISTER & CO LTD, Dursley, Glos — L

3681	1931	2ft 0in	4wPM	6hp		JAP	R	58,66
4404	1932	2ft 0in	4wPM	6hp		JAP	R	125
7040	1935	2ft 0in	4wPM			JAP		150
10055	1938	2ft 0in	4wPM	9.8hp		JAP	RT	150
11435	1939	2ft 0in	4wPM			JAP		58
15613	1941	2ft 0in	4wPM			JAP		150
44052	1958	2ft 0in	4wDM	12¾hp		Lister	RM3	58

LOWCA ENGINEERING CO LTD, Lowca, Whitehaven, Cumbs — LE

246	1907	4ft 8½in	0-4-0ST	OC	12 x 20	131,182,205
247	1907	4ft 8½in	0-4-0ST	OC	12 x 20	131,182
248	1907	4ft 8½in	0-4-0ST	OC	12 x 20	131,182

MARKHAM & CO LTD, Chesterfield, Derbys — Mkm

104	1891	4ft 8½in	0-4-0ST	OC	13 x 20	3ft6in	47,171
110	1895	4ft 8½in	0-6-0ST	OC	13 x 20		245

MOTOR RAIL LTD, SIMPLEX WORKS, Bedford — MR

No.	Date	Gauge	Type	Power	Engine	Weight	Page
863	30.4.1918	2ft 0in	4wPM	20hp	Dorman 2JO	2½T	123
921	10.6.1918	2ft 0in	4wPM	20hp	Dorman 2JO	2½T	123
1347	21.10.1918	2ft 0in	4wPM	40hp	Dorman 4JO	6¾T	124,283
1379	17.12.1918	2ft 0in	4wPM	40hp	Dorman 4JO	6¾T	283
1386	18.2.1918	2ft 0in	4wPM	40hp	Dorman 4JO	6¾T	124
1790	24.9.1918	2ft 0in	4wPM	20hp	Dorman 2JO	2½T	262
1843	17.3.1919	2ft 0in	4wPM	20hp	Dorman 2JO	2½T	69
1902	5.11.1919	3ft 0in	4wPM	20hp	Dorman 2JO	4T	82
2026	26.10.1920	4ft 8½in	4wPM	40hp	Dorman 4JO	8T	288
2093	16.10.1922	2ft 0in	4wPM	20hp	Dorman 2JO	2½T	152
2260	25-3-1924	2ft 0in	4wPM	20hp	Dorman 2JO	2½t	257
3858	7.7.1928	600mm	4wPM	20hp	Dorman 2JO	2½T	152
3975	10.5.1937	2ft 0in	4wPM	20hp	Dorman 2JO	2½T	152
3981	5.6.1936	2ft 0in	4wPM	20hp	Dorman 2JO	2½T	152
3988	11.9.1935	2ft 0in	4wPM	20hp	Dorman 2JO	2½T	152
3992	12.2.1934	2ft 0in	4wPM	20hp	Dorman 2JO	2½T	152
3997	8.12.1933	2ft 0in	4wPM	20hp	Dorman 2JO	2½T	152
4713	11.1936	2ft 0in	4wPM	20hp	Dorman 2JO	2½T	152
4720	1.3.1937	2ft 0in	4wDM	20hp	Dorman 2JO	2½T	103
5007	16.5.1929	2ft 0in	4wPM	20hp	Dorman 2JO	2½T	79
5068	22.4.1930	2ft 0in	4wDM	20hp	Dorman 2JO	2½T	103
5208	2.9.1930	2ft 0in	4wPM	20/35hp	Dorman 4MRX	2½T	124
5209	2.9.1930	2ft 0in	4wPM	20/35hp	Dorman 4MRX	2½T	124,125
5234	13.11.1930	2ft 0in	4wPM	20/35hp	Dorman 4MRX	2½T	103
5303	15.3.1931	2ft 0in	4wPM	20/35hp	Dorman 4MRX	2½T	262
5339	5.8.1931	2ft 0in	4wPM	20/35hp	Dorman 4MRX	2½T	272
5605	15.1.1931	2ft 0in	4wPM	20hp	Dorman 2RB	2½T	69
5713	7.10.1936	2ft 0in	4wDM	25/36hp	Dorman 2RB	4T	97
5813	11.7.1934	2ft 0in	4wDM	12/16hp	Ailsa Craig RFS2	2½T	153
5819	7.6.1935	2ft 0in	4wDM	12/16hp	Ailsa Craig RFS2	2½T	153
5825	8.6.1936	2ft 0in	4wDM	16/24hp	Ailsa Craig RFS2	2½T	153
5826	8.10.1936	2ft 0in	4wDM	16/24hp	Ailsa Craig RFS2	2½T	153
5827	8.10.1936	2ft 0in	4wDM	16/24hp	Ailsa Craig RFS2	2½T	153
5828	27.10.1936	2ft 0in	4wDM	16/24hp	Ailsa Craig RFS2	2½T	153
5829	20.11.1936	2ft 0in	4wDM	16/24hp	Ailsa Craig RFS2	2½T	153
5830	20.1.1937	2ft 0in	4wDM	16/24hp	Ailsa Craig RFS2	2½T	153
5865	21.8.1934	2ft 0in	4wDM	20/28hp	Dorman 2HW	2½T	269
5889	.1935	2ft 0in	4wDM	20/28hp	Dorman 2HW	2½T	262
7034	.1936	2ft 0in	4wDM	20/28hp	Dorman 2HW	2½T	269
7038	.1936	2ft 0in	4wDM	20/28hp	Dorman 2HW	2½T	269
7181	27.5.1937	2ft 6in	4wDM	20/28hp	Dorman 2DWD	2½T	46
7218	5.9.1938	2ft 0in	4wDM	20/28hp	Dorman 2DWD	2½T	262
7356	23.12.1938	2ft 0in	4wDM	20/28hp	Dorman 2DWD	2½T	269
7358	c12.1938	2ft 0in	4wDM	20/28hp	Dorman 2DWD	2½T	103
7386	3.3.1939	2ft 0in	4wDM	20/28hp	Dorman 2DWD	2½T	275
7391	11.3.1939	2ft 0in	4wDM	20/28hp	Dorman 2DWD	2½T	275
7456	c12.1939	2ft 0in	4wDM	20/28hp	Dorman 2DWD	2½T	103
7467	c1.1940	2ft 0in	4wDM	20/28hp	Dorman 2DWD	2½T	103
8594	.1940	2ft 0in	4wDM	20/28hp	Dorman 2DWD	2½T	96
8621	28.4.1941	2ft 0in	4wDM	20/28hp	Dorman 2DWD	2½T	61
8715	24.3.1941	2ft 0in	4wDM	20/28hp	Dorman 2DWD	2½T	269
8716	24.3.1941	2ft 0in	4wDM	20/28hp	Dorman 2DWD	2½T	269
8719	21.3.1941	2ft 0in	4wDM	20/28hp	Dorman 2DWD	2½T	269

8725	4.4.1941	2ft 0in	4wDM	20/28hp	Dorman 2DWD	2½T		269
8762	26.4.1942	2ft 0in	4wDM	20/28hp	Dorman 2DWD	2½T		96
8998	3.4.1946	2ft 0in	4wDM	20/28hp	Dorman 2DWD	2½T		270
9381	15.12.1948	2ft 0in	4wDM	20/28hp	Dorman 2DWD	2½T		125,141
9416	18.5.1949	2ft 0in	4wDM	20/28hp	Dorman 2DWD	2½T		79
9417	24.5.1949	2ft 0in	4wDM	20/28hp	Dorman 2DWD	2½T		79
9778	18.2.1953	2ft 0in	4wDM	20/28hp	Dorman 2DWD	2½T		287
22128	12.9.1961	2ft 0in	4wDM	30hp	Dorman 2LB	2½T		141,153
22129	12.9.1961	2ft 0in	4wDM	30hp	Dorman 2LB	2½T		141,153
22258	20.10.1965	2ft 0in	4wDM	40hp	Dorman 2LB			292
102T007	21.2.1974	3ft 0in	4wDH	104hp	Deutz F6L912	14T		63
40S323	24.6.1968	3ft 0in	4wDM	40hp	Dorman 2LB	5½T		61

METROPOLITAN-VICKERS ELECTRICAL CO LTD, Manchester   MV

	1934	2ft 6in	4wBEF		10T		57
	1934	2ft 6in	4wBEF		10T		57
	1934	2ft 6in	4wBEF		10T		57
1175	1960	2ft 6in	4wBEF	90hp	DBF12	[Bg 3558]	214
1176	1960	2ft 6in	4wBEF	90hp	DBF12	[Bg 3559]	214
1177	1960	2ft 6in	4wBEF	90hp	DBF12	[Bg 3560]	214

MANNING WARDLE & CO LTD, BOYNE ENGINE WORKS, Leeds   MW

44	17.3.1862	4ft 8½in	0-6-0ST	IC	12 x 17	3ft1³/₈in			45
92	27.10.1863	4ft 8½in	0-6-0ST	IC	11 x 17	3ft1³/₈in		Old I alt	252
110	9.3.1864	4ft 8½in	0-6-0ST	IC	12 x 17	3ft1³/₈in	K		142
141	10.3.1866	4ft 8½in	0-6-0ST	IC	15 x 22	4ft2in		'West Yorkshire'	56
147	20.4.1865	4ft 8½in	0-6-0ST	IC	12 x 17	3ft1³/₈in	K		142,203
204	24.4.1866	4ft 8½in	0-6-0ST	IC	11 x 17	3ft1³/₈in		Old I	46
205	9.7.1866	4ft 8½in	0-6-0ST	IC	11 x 17	3ft1³/₈in		Old I	131,274
388	11.8.1873	4ft 8½in	0-6-0ST	IC	14 x 20	3ft9in	N		142
394	20.11.1872	4ft 8½in	0-6-0ST	IC	12 x 17	3ft1³/₈in	K		148
401	1.8.1872	4ft 8½in	0-4-0ST	OC	10 x 16	2ft9in	F		255
458	27.7.1874	4ft 8½in	0-6-0ST	IC	13 x 18	3ft0in	M		268
482	29.12.1873	1ft 6in	0-4-0ST	OC	6 x 8	1ft8in			93
488	3.8.1874	4ft 8½in	0-6-0ST	IC	12 x 17	3ft1³/₈in	K		264,267
513	2.11.1874	4ft 8½in	0-4-0ST	OC	12 x 18	3ft0in	H		142
528	16.12.1874	4ft 8½in	0-6-0ST	IC	12 x 17	3ft1³/₈in	K		144
538	29.7.1875	4ft 8½in	0-4-0ST	OC	12 x 18	3ft0in	H		144
557	8.11.1875	4ft 8½in	0-6-0ST	IC	12 x 17	3ft1³/₈in	K		264
559	27.5.1875	4ft 8½in	0-4-0ST	OC	8 x 14	2ft8in	D		250
561	29.11.1875	4ft 8½in	0-6-0ST	IC	13 x 18	3ft0in	M		47
562	24.1.1876	4ft 8½in	0-6-0ST	IC	13 x 18	3ft0in	M		255
563	25.1.1876	4ft 8½in	0-6-0ST	IC	12 x 17	3ft1³/₈in	K		255
584	21.2.1876	4ft 8½in	0-4-0ST	OC	10 x 16	3ft0in	F		45
589	3.4.1876	4ft 8½in	0-6-0ST	IC	12 x 17	3ft1³/₈in	K		250
596	20.4.1876	4ft 8½in	0-6-0ST	IC	12 x 17	3ft1³/₈in	K		84,277
598	1.5.1876	4ft 8½in	0-6-0ST	IC	12 x 17	3ft1³/₈in	K		266
610	10.8.1876	4ft 8½in	0-6-0ST	IC	12 x 17	3ft1³/₈in	K		266
626	23.10.1876	4ft 8½in	0-6-0ST	IC	12 x 17	3ft1³/₈in	K		255
653	29.8.1877	4ft 8½in	0-4-0ST	OC	10 x 16	2ft9in	F		256,264

656	25.5.1877	4ft 8½in	0-6-0ST	IC	12 x 17	3ft1³⁄₈in	K	250
715	9.10.1878	4ft 8½in	0-4-0ST	OC	10 x 16	2ft9in	F	259
793	9.12.1882	4ft 8½in	0-4-0ST	OC	12 x 18	3ft0in	H	277
849	23.6.1882	4ft 8½in	0-4-0ST	OC	14 x 18	3ft0in	P	144
871	26.3.1883	4ft 8½in	0-6-0ST	IC	13 x 18	3ft0in	M	143,267
882	30.3.1883	4ft 8½in	0-4-0ST	OC	10 x 16	2ft9in	F	252
899	31.5.1884	4ft 8½in	0-6-0ST	IC	13 x 18	3ft0in	M	277
902	8.9.1884	4ft 8½in	0-6-0ST	IC	12 x 17	3ft1³⁄₈in	K	148
915	26.11.1883	4ft 8½in	0-4-0ST	OC	8½ x 14	2ft8in		256,264
975	21.7.1886	4ft 8½in	0-6-0ST	IC	12 x 17	3ft1³⁄₈in	K	74
996	29.10.1886	4ft 8½in	0-6-0ST	IC	12 x 17	3ft1³⁄₈in	K	277
1017	2.11.1887	4ft 8½in	0-4-0ST	OC	9 x 14	2ft9in	E	133,276
1020	8.6.1887	4ft 8½in	0-4-0ST	OC	10 x 16	2ft9in	F	276
1025	4.1.1887	4ft 8½in	0-6-0T	IC	13 x 18	3ft0in	Spl M	276
1038	19.8.1888	3ft 0in	0-4-0ST	OC	9½ x 14	2ft9in	E	150,260
1048	6.2.1888	4ft 8½in	0-6-0ST	IC	12 x 17	3ft0in	K	75
1098	1.10.1888	4ft 8½in	0-6-0T	IC	13 x 18	3ft0in	Spl M	118
1100	2.11.1888	4ft 8½in	0-6-0T	IC	13 x 18	3ft0in	Spl M	260,276
1110	10.11.1888	3ft 0in	0-4-0ST	OC	9½ x 14	2ft9in	E	260
1123	8.5.1889	3ft 0in	0-6-0ST	OC	11½ x 17	2ft9in	Spl	260
1144	21.5.1890	4ft 8½in	0-6-0ST	IC	12 x 17	3ft0in	K	267
1153	7.4.1890	4ft 8½in	0-6-0ST	IC	12 x 18	3ft0in	L	267
1190	2.9.1890	4ft 8½in	0-6-0ST	IC	12 x 18	3ft0in	L	267
1191	18.9.1890	4ft 8½in	0-6-0ST	IC	12 x 18	3ft0in	L	267
1196	21.8.1890	4ft 8½in	0-6-0T	IC	14 x 22	3ft9in	Spl	267
1207	30.12.1890	4ft 8½in	0-6-0ST	IC	15 x 22	3ft6in	Spl	210
1210	22.12.1890	4ft 8½in	0-6-0ST	IC	12 x 18	3ft0in	L	267
1225	24.6.1891	4ft 8½in	0-6-0ST	IC	13 x 20	3ft4in	Spl	267
1231	29.6.1891	4ft 8½in	0-4-0ST	OC	14 x 18	3ft0in	P	145,231,234
1236	16.11.1891	4ft 8½in	0-6-0ST	IC	12 x 17	3ft1³⁄₈in	K	252
1255	27.3.1893	4ft 8½in	0-4-0ST	OC	9x 14	2ft9in	E	114,133
1280	27.2.1897	4ft 8½in	0-4-0ST	OC	9x 14	2ft9in	E	273
1284	4.6.1894	4ft 8½in	0-6-0ST	OC	15 x 20	3ft3in	Spl	142,203,207
1286	28.6.1894	4ft 8½in	0-6-0ST	OC	15 x 20	3ft1in	Spl	111
1290	29.3.1895	4ft 8½in	0-6-0ST	IC	13 x 18	3ft0in	M	256,264,270
1293	31.5.1895	4ft 8½in	0-6-0ST	IC	12 x 17	3ft0in	K	277
1303	3.8.1895	4ft 8½in	0-4-0ST	OC	10 x 16	2ft9in	F	256,264
1304	2.12.1895	4ft 8½in	0-4-0ST	OC	10 x 16	2ft9in	F	256,264
1327	19.3.1897	4ft 8½in	0-4-0ST	OC	12 x 18	3ft0in	H	284
1378	25.4.1898	4ft 8½in	0-6-0ST	IC	13 x 18	3ft0in	M	277
1393	10.11.1898	4ft 8½in	0-6-0ST	IC	13 x 18	3ft0in	M	276
1418	16.9.1898	4ft 8½in	0-6-0ST	IC	12 x 18	3ft0in	L	261
1423	18.11.1898	4ft 8½in	0-4-0ST	OC	14 x 18	3ft0in	P	144
1427	8.2.1899	4ft 8½in	0-4-0ST	OC	14 x 18	3ft0in	P	105,106
1440	27.11.1899	4ft 8½in	0-6-0ST	IC	12 x 17	3ft0in	K	143,171,203,207
1499	8.3.1901	4ft 8½in	0-6-0ST	IC	12 x 18	3ft0in	L	271
1519	25.3.1901	4ft 8½in	0-6-0ST	IC	12 x 17	3ft0in	K	271
1528	16.5.1901	3ft 0in	0-4-0ST	OC	8 x 14	2ft4in	Spl	75
1530	18.7.1901	4ft 8½in	0-6-0ST	IC	12 x 18	3ft0in	L	277
1544	10.3.1902	4ft 8½in	0-4-0ST	OC	12 x 18	3ft0in	H	144
1568	16.9.1902	4ft 8½in	0-6-0ST	IC	12 x 18	3ft0in	L	271
1569	22.9.1902	4ft 8½in	0-6-0ST	IC	12 x 18	3ft0in	L	271
1579	30.9.1902	4ft 8½in	0-6-0ST	IC	12 x 18	3ft0in	L	277

1580	24.9.1902	4ft 8½in	0-4-0ST	OC	12 x 18	3ft0in	H	144,231
1590	27.2.1903	4ft 8½in	0-6-0ST	IC	12 x 17	3ft0in	K	251
1595	4.3.1903	4ft 8½in	0-6-0ST	IC	12 x 18	3ft0in	L	82,108,268
1597	12.2.1903	4ft 8½in	0-6-0ST	IC	14 x 20	3ft6in	Q	143
1600	12.2.1904	4ft 8½in	0-6-0ST	IC	12 x 18	3ft0in	L	271
1668	13.11.1905	4ft 8½in	0-6-0ST	IC	12 x 18	3ft0in	L	277
1722	28.2.1908	4ft 8½in	0-6-0ST	IC	12 x 18	3ft0in	L	108
1774	2.8.1911	4ft 8½in	0-4-0ST	OC	14 x 20	3ft0in	Spl	65,226,238
1847	6.5.1914	4ft 8½in	0-4-0ST	OC	12 x 18	3ft0in	H alt	111,112
2004	4.6.1921	4ft 8½in	0-6-0ST	IC	13 x 18	3ft0in		198
2017	.1925	4ft 8½in	0-6-0ST	IC	15 x 22	3ft9in		271

NOTE that 'alt' = altered and 'Spl' = Special.

NORTH BRITISH LOCOMOTIVE CO LTD, Glasgow   NB
H HYDE PARK WORKS   NBH
Q QUEENS PARK WORK   NBQ

H 22600	1921	4ft 8½in	0-6-2T	IC	19 x 26	5ft8in		200
Q 27421	1955	4ft 8½in	0-4-0DH	275hp	National M4AAU5	32T		112
Q 27422	1955	4ft 8½in	0-4-0DH	275hp	National M4AAU5	32T		112
Q 27429	1955	4ft 8½in	0-4-0DH	275hp	National M4AAU5	32T		112
Q 27645	1959	4ft 8½in	0-4-0DH	275hp	National M4AAU5	32T		112
Q 27876	1959	4ft 8½in	0-4-0DH	330hp	MAN W6V		30T	282

NASMYTH, WILSON & CO LTD, BRIDGEWATER FOUNDRY,
Patricroft, Manchester   NW

656	1902	4ft 8½in	0-6-0ST	IC	16 x 20	4ft3½in	212

ORENSTEIN & KOPPEL AG, DREWITZ WORKS, Potsdam, near Berlin   OK

10903	5.1925	3ft 0in	0-4-0WT	OC	9½ x 14	51,165
4032	.1930	1ft 10in	4wDM			97
4156	c1930	1ft 10in	4wDM			97
4571	c1931	2ft 0in	4wDM			156
5672	.1934	2ft 0in	4wDM			106
5928	.1935	2ft 0in	4wPM			79

PECKETT & SONS LTD, ATLAS WORKS, Bristol   P

440	3.11.1885	4ft 8½in	0-4-0ST	OC	10 x 14	2ft6in	M3	256,264
442	1.9.1885	4ft 8½in	0-4-0ST	OC	10 x 14	2ft6in	M3	143
451	31.5.1886	4ft 8½in	0-4-0ST	OC	10 x 14	2ft6in	M3	53
455	18.4.1887	4ft 8½in	0-6-0ST	IC	12 x 18	3ft0½in	xL	256,264
468	19.3.1888	4ft 8½in	0-4-0ST	OC	14 x 20	3ft2in	W4	47,171
470	30.8.1888	4ft 8½in	0-4-0ST	OC	14 x 20	3ft2in	W4	59
528	14.6.1893	4ft 8½in	0-6-0ST	IC	13 x 18	3ft0½in	xL	253
547	11.7.1892	4ft 8½in	0-4-0ST	OC	14 x 20	3ft2in	W4	59

564	25.5.1897	4ft 8½in	0-6-0ST	OC	14 x 20	3ft7in	B1	277	
580	29.3.1894	4ft 8½in	0-4-0ST	OC	14 x 20	3ft2in	W4	59	
702	1.12.1898	4ft 8½in	0-4-0ST	OC	14 x 20	3ft2in	W4	215,225	
760	11.10.1899	4ft 8½in	0-4-0ST	OC	12 x 18	3ft0in	R1	45	
851	9.1.1901	4ft 8½in	0-4-0ST	OC	14 x 20	3ft2in	W4	198	
852	21.1.1901	4ft 8½in	0-4-0ST	OC	14 x 20	3ft2in	W4	127	
874	26.11.1900	4ft 8½in	0-6-0ST	OC	15 x 20	3ft6in	'Judith'	51,164	
959	30.5.1902	3ft 0in	0-4-0ST	OC	8 x 12	2ft3in	special	75	
981	15.1.1904	4ft 8½in	0-4-0ST	OC	12 x 18	3ft0in	R1	133	
1057	13.12.1905	4ft 8½in	0-4-0ST	OC	14 x 20	3ft2in	W4	84	
1080	24.1.1907	4ft 8½in	0-4-0ST	OC	10 x 15	2ft9in	M5	235	
1114	12.6.1907	4ft 8½in	0-4-0ST	OC	14 x 20	3ft2½in	W5	188	
1204	23.5.1910	4ft 8½in	0-6-0ST	OC	14 x 20	3ft7in	B2	108	
1208	12.8.1909	4ft 8½in	0-4-0ST	OC	12 x 18	3ft0in	R1	157	
1253	18.4.1911	4ft 8½in	0-6-0ST	OC	14 x 20	3ft7in	B2	53,195	
1265	17.6.1912	4ft 8½in	0-6-0ST	OC	14 x 20	3ft7in	B2	143,229, 242	
1273	11.12.1912	4ft 8½in	0-4-0ST	OC	12 x 18	3ft0in	R2	131,182	
1430	26.7.1916	4ft 8½in	0-4-0ST	OC	12 x 18	3ft0in	R2	108	
1439	31.7.1916	4ft 8½in	0-4-0ST	OC	14 x 20	3ft2½in	W5	84	
1454	3.1.1917	4ft 8½in	0-4-0ST	OC	14 x 20	3ft2½in	W5	231	
1469	27.7.1917	4ft 8½in	0-4-0ST	OC	14 x 20	3ft2½in	W5	122,187, 195	
1479	25.10.1917	4ft 8½in	0-4-0ST	OC	14 x 20	3ft2½in	W5	59	
1521	16.8.1918	4ft 8½in	0-4-0ST	OC	12 x 18	3ft0in	R2	45	
1555	8.3.1920	4ft 8½in	0-4-0ST	OC	10 x 15	2ft9in	M5	288	
1584	22.8.1921	4ft 8½in	0-4-0ST	OC	12 x 18	3ft0in	R2	143,164, 203	
1608	15.1.1923	4ft 8½in	0-4-0ST	OC	14 x 20	3ft2½in	W5	91	
1649	10.1.1924	4ft 8½in	0-4-0ST	OC	12 x 18	3ft0in	R2	84	
1678	18.5.1927	4ft 8½in	0-6-0ST	OC	14 x 20	3ft7in	B2	143	
1687	23.2.1926	4ft 8½in	0-4-0ST	OC	14 x 22	3ft2½in	W6	206,235	
1690	1.7.1926	4ft 8½in	0-4-0ST	OC	12 x 18	3ft0in	R2	77	
1691	10.6.1925	4ft 8½in	0-6-0ST	IC	12 x 18	3ft0½in	xL	112	
1703	25.10.1926	4ft 8½in	0-4-0ST	OC	12 x 18	3ft0in	R2	45	
1704	22.6.1927	4ft 8½in	0-4-0ST	OC	12 x 18	3ft0in	R2	74,76	
1725	20.4.1927	4ft 8½in	0-4-0ST	OC	14 x 22	3ft2½in	W6	84	
1749	3.12.1928	4ft 8½in	0-4-0ST	OC	14 x 22	3ft2½in	W6	167,291	
1791	11.7.1932	4ft 8½in	0-4-0ST	OC	14 x 22	3ft2½in	W6	65,238	
1879	24.10.1934	4ft 8½in	0-4-0ST	OC	12 x 20	3ft0½in	R4	94	
1902	24.2.1936	4ft 8½in	0-6-0ST	OC	16 x 24	3ft10in	OX1	205	
1906	10.8.1936	4ft 8½in	0-4-0ST	OC	14 x 20	3ft2½in	W5	91	
1924	26.4.1937	4ft 8½in	0-6-0ST	OC	14 x 22	3ft7in	B3	115,163 168,182	
1963	31.10.1938	4ft 8½in	0-4-0ST	OC	10 x 15	2ft9in	M5	70,74,76	
1972	29.6.1940	4ft 8½in	0-6-0ST	OC	16 x 24	3ft10in	OX1	220	
1975	10.7.1939	4ft 8½in	0-4-0ST	OC	12 x 18	3ft0in	R2	131,182	
1976	19.6.1939	4ft 8½in	0-4-0ST	OC	14 x 20	3ft2½in	W6	65,238	
2000	17.12.1942	4ft 8½in	0-6-0ST	OC	14 x 22	3ft7in	B3	84	
2018	2.12.1941	4ft 8½in	0-4-0ST	OC	14 x 22	3ft2½in	W7	144,231	
2022	16.2.1942	4ft 8½in	0-4-0ST	OC	14 x 22	3ft2½in	Spl W7	235	
2043	5.5.1943	4ft 8½in	0-4-0ST	OC	14 x 22	3ft2½in	W7	145,231, 234	
2044	13.7.1943	4ft 8½in	0-4-0ST	OC	14 x 22	3ft2½in	W7	149	

2045	14.9.1943	4ft 8½in	0-4-0ST	OC	14 x 22	3ft 2½in	W7	215
2056	28.2.1944	4ft 8½in	0-4-0ST	OC	16 x 24	3ft 10in	OX1	215
2085	23.2.1948	4ft 8½in	0-4-0ST	OC	16 x 24	3ft 10in	Spl OX1	291
2092	18.8.1947	4ft 8½in	0-4-0ST	OC	14 x 22	3ft 2½in	W7	211,226, 229
2109	23.1.1950	4ft 8½in	0-4-0ST	OC	14 x 22	3ft 2½in	W7	234,238
2110	20.2.1950	4ft 8½in	0-4-0ST	OC	14 x 22	3ft 2½in	W7	199,245
2112	11.4.1949	4ft 8½in	0-4-0ST	OC	12 x 20	3ft 0½in	R4	74
2129	5.2.1952	4ft 8½in	0-4-0ST	OC	12 x 20	3ft 0½in	R4	291

PEARSON & KNOWLES COAL & IRON CO LTD, Wigan   P&K

	1910	4ft 8½in	0-6-0ST	IC	16 x 22	4ft 0in	157

RANSOMES & RAPIER LTD, WATERSIDE WORKS, Ipswich   R&R

82	# 2.2.1938	2ft 0in	4wDM	20hp	2½T	139

Order date

RELIANCE   Reliance

	4ft 8½in	4wPM	95

RUSTON & HORNSBY LTD, Lincoln   RH

166027	4.7.1932	2ft 0in	4wDM	10HP	Lister 10/2	2½T	69
166045	23.9.1933	2ft 1½in	4wDM	10HP	Lister 10/2	2½T	72,81
168790	14.6.1933	2ft 2in	4wDM	16HP	Lister 18/2	2¾T	73,80
168792	26.6.1933	2ft 4in	4wDM	22/28HP	Lister 3JP	4T	79,140
168870	29.4.1932	2ft 0in	4wDM	16HP	Lister 18/2	2¾T	79,140
170205	1.6.1934	2ft 8½in	4wDM	22/28HP	Lister 3JP	4T	61
172335	30.4.1935	2ft 0in	4wDM	10HP	Lister 10/2	2½T	69,71,73
172888	1.8.1934	2ft 4in	4wDM	22/28HP	Lister 3JP	4T	150
174139	11.2.1935	2ft 0in	4wDM	27/32HP	Lister 3JP	4T	262
174140	13.2.1935	2ft 4in	4wDM	27/32HP	Lister 3JP	4T	61
174537	4.2.1935	3ft 0in	4wDM	18/21HP	Lister 18/2	2¾T	
175417	6.2.1936	2ft 3in	4wDM	18/21HP	Lister 18/2	2¾T	69,71-73
177607	12.1.1937	2ft 4in	4wDM	27/32HP	Lister 3JP	4T	60,283
177646	2.12.1936	2ft 0in	4wDM	10HP	Lister 10/2	2½T	97
182145	26.2.1937	2ft 1½in	4wDM	12HP	Lister 10/2	2½T	72
183060	27.1.1937	4ft 8½in	4wDM	44/48HP	Ruston 4VRO	7½T	76
183428	22.2.1937	2ft 0in	4wDM	20HP	Lister 18/2	2¾T	79
186340	11.10.1937	2ft 0in	4wDM	33/40HP	Ruston 3VRO	5¾T	61,150
187045	16.9.1937	2ft 0in	4wDM	16/20HP	Ruston 2VSO	2¾T	79
189947	18.1.1938	2ft 0in	4wDM	25/30HP	Ruston 3VSO	4T	258
189976	17.6.1938	2ft 0in	4wDM	11/13HP	Ruston 2VTO	2½T	106,127
191666	10.12.1938	2ft 0in	4wDM	16/20HP	Ruston 2VSO	3¼T	262
192864	3.9.1939	2ft 0in	4wDM	44/48HP	Ruston 4VRO	6½T	69
192868	5.9.1938	2ft 0in	4wDM	16/20HP	Ruston 2VSO	2¼T	72,79,81
192872	31.12.1938	2ft 0in	4wDM	16/20HP	Ruston 2VSO	2¾T	98,101
194783	17.5.1939	2ft 0in	4wDM	44/48HP	Ruston 4VRO	7½T	121
195843	9.5.1939	2ft 1½in	4wDM	16/20HP	Ruston 2VSO	2¾T	81

195848	2.6.1939	2ft 0in	4wDM	16/20HP Ruston 2VSO	2¾T	
198278	9.11.1939	2ft 0in	4wDM	44/48HP Ruston 4VRO	6½T	69,71,75
200069	16.2.1940	2ft 2in	4wDM	16/20HP Ruston 2VSO	3½T	73
200481	3.6.1940	2ft 0in	4wDM	25/30HP Ruston 3VSO	3¼T	103
200483	24.6.1940	3ft 0in	4wDM	25/30HP Ruston 3VSO	3¼T	157,213
200744	27.7.1940	2ft 0in	4wDM	33/40HP Ruston 3VSO	4½T	103
200766	6.3.1942	2ft 1½in	4wDM	11/13HP Ruston 2VTO	2½T	72,73
203006	10.3.1941	2ft 0in	4wDM	16/20HP Ruston 2VSO	2¾T	153
203016	22.5.1941	2ft 0in	4wDM	44/48HP Ruston 4VRO	7½T	44
203029	17.4.1942	2ft 0in	4wDM	44/48HP Ruston 4VRO	7½T	44
209430	22.6.1942	2ft 0in	4wDM	13DL Ruston 2VTO	2½T	77
210476	.1941	4ft 8½in	4wDM	80/88HP Ruston 4VPO	17T	95
210489	29.8.1941	3ft 0in	4wDM	33/40HP Ruston 3VRO	5T	157,213
210490	14.9.1941	3ft 0in	4wDM	33/40HP Ruston 3VRO	5T	157,213
210493	14.2.1941	2ft 0in	4wDM	33/40HP Ruston 3VRO	4½T	100,101
210494	9.3.1942	2ft 0in	4wDM	33/40HP Ruston 3VRO	4½T	98,99,101
210955	28.3.1941	2ft 0in	4wDM	16/20HP Ruston 2VSO	2¾T	153
211605	21.5.1941	2ft 0in	4wDM	16/20HP Ruston 2VSO	2¾T	153
211614	25.6.1941	2ft 0in	4wDM	16/20HP Ruston 2VSO	2¾T	153
211655	30.4.1942	2ft 0in	4wDM	16/20HP Ruston 2VSO	2¾T	153
211682	22.12.1941	2ft 5in	4wDM	30DL Ruston 3VRO	3¼T	150
215753	13.3.1942	4ft 8½in	4wDM	80/88HP Ruston 4VPB	20T	281
218045	23.12.1942	4ft 8½in	4wDM	48DS Ruston 4VRO	7½T	71
221593	13.11.1946	2ft 0in	4wDM	20DL Ruston 2VSO	2¾T	77,79
221602	28.9.1943	2ft 0in	4wDM	20DL Ruston 2VSO	2¾T	78
222068	28.8.1943	2ft 0in	4wDM	20DL Ruston 2VSO	2¾T	170
224308	19.3.1944	600mm	4wDM	13DL Ruston 2VTH	3½T	77
224337	29.8.1944	2ft 0in	4wDM	48DS Ruston 4VRO	7½T	292
224343	20.10.1944	4ft 8½in	4wDM	48DS Ruston 4VRO	7½T	110
224347	6.3.1945	4ft 8½in	4wDM	48DS Ruston 4VRO	7½T	110
224353	28.6.1945	4ft 8½in	4wDM	88DS Ruston 4VPH	17T	119
224354	8.10.1945	4ft 8½in	4wDM	88DS Ruston 4VPH	17T	281
224355	7.12.1945	4ft 8½in	4wDM	88DS Ruston 4VPH	17T	157
229633	2.11.1946	600mm	4wDM	20DL Ruston 2VSO	2¾T	110
235715	6.11.1945	2ft 0in	4wDM	20DL Ruston 2VSH	3½T	126
236364	12.7.1946	4ft 8½in	4wDM	88DS Ruston 4VPH	17T	71,74,78
237924	1.7.1946	4ft 8½in	4wDM	48DS Ruston 4VRO	7½T	286
243393	28.11.1946	2ft 0in	4wDM	13DL Ruston 2VTH	2½T	78,81
244559	22.8.1946	2ft 2in	4wDM	20DLU Ruston 2VSH	3½T	73
247178	3.7.1947	2ft 2in	4wDM	13DLU Ruston 2VTH	2¾T	72
247183	23.9.1947	2ft 0in	4wDM	13DL Ruston 2VTH	3½T	153
248484	10.3.1947	3ft 0in	4wDM	40DL Ruston 3VRH	5T	213
248486	24.1.1947	2ft 0in	4wDM	40DL Ruston 3VRH	4½T	
252684	1.11.1948	4ft 8½in	0-4-0DM	165DS Ruston 6VPH	28T	270
256268	14.11.1947	3ft 0in	4wDMF	48DLZ Ruston 4VRH	7T	233
259192	14.4.1948	2ft 0in	4wDM	40DL Ruston 3VRH	4½T	98,99,100
259770	25.10.1948	2ft 0in	4wDM	40DL Ruston 3VRH	4½T	98-101
263001	29.4.1949	4ft 8½in	4wDM	88DS Ruston 4VPH	17T	119
264252	5.3.1952	2ft 0in	4wDM	13DL Ruston 2VTH	2½T	262
268858	9.6.1949	2ft 6in	4wDMF	48DLZ Ruston 4VRH	7T	179,201,245
268859	9.6.1949	2ft 6in	4wDMF	48DLZ Ruston 4VRH	7T	179,201,227, 245
268863	30.6.1949	2ft 3in	4wDMF	48DLZ Ruston 4VRH	7T	179,201,230
268875	17.8.1953	2ft 0in	4wDMF	48DLZ Ruston 4VRH	7T	179,201

268880	10.6.1958	2ft 0in	4wDMF	48DLZ	Ruston 4VRH	7T	184,197
275881	27.6.1949	4ft 8½in	4wDM	88DS	Ruston 4VPH	17T	133
279620	23.6.1949	2ft 0in	4wDM	48DL	Ruston 2VRH	5½T	98-102
279627	1.7.1949	2ft 0in	4wDM	48DL	Ruston 2VRH	5½T	98-101
281290	17.11.1949	3ft 0in	0-6-0DM	100DL	Ruston 6VRH	14T	63
281291	20.12.1949	3ft 0in	0-6-0DM	100DL	Ruston 6VRH	14T	63
283507	21.7.1949	2ft 0in	4wDM	30DL	Ruston 3VSH	3¼T	141,153
283508	21.7.1949	2ft 0in	4wDM	30DL	Ruston 3VSH	3¼T	141,153
283512	22.8.1949	2ft 0in	4wDM	30DL	Ruston 3VSH	3¼T	141,153
283513	22.8.1949	2ft 0in	4wDM	30DL	Ruston 3VSH	3¼T	141,153
294265	23.6.1950	4ft 8½in	4wDM	48DS	Ruston 4VRH	7½T	133
299099	10.10.1950	4ft 8½in	4wDM	88DS	Ruston 4VPH	17T	95
299107	18.1.1951	4ft 8½in	4wDM	88DS	Ruston 4VPH	17½T	95,199
305302	13.8.1951	4ft 8½in	4wDM	48DS	Ruston 4VRH	7½T	133
305308	24.71952	4ft 8½in	4wDM	48DS	Ruston 4VRH	7½T	62,133
305313	16.2.1951	4ft 8½in	4wDM	88DS	Ruston 4VPH	20T	94
305314	9.4.1951	4ft 8½in	4wDM	88DS	Ruston 4VPH	20T	119
305316	16.3.1951	4ft 8½in	4wDM	88DS	Ruston 4VPH	20T	94
305318	30.3.1951	4ft 8½in	4wDM	88DS	Ruston 4VPH	20T	94
305327	28.10.1954	2ft 0in	0-4-0DM	LHT	Ruston 4YE	10T	101
312986	28.8.1952	4ft 8½in	0-4-0DE	165DE	Ruston 6VPH	28T	119
319292	30.5.1953	4ft 8½in	0-4-0DM	165DS	Ruston 6VPH	28T	85
319294	14.9.1953	4ft 8½in	0-6-0DM	165DS	Ruston 6VPH	28T	84
326671	16.7.1957	4ft 8½in	0-6-0DM	LWS	Ruston 6RPHX	44T	165
331263	24.10.1952	2ft 0in	4wDM	20DL	Ruston 2VSH	3¼T	184
338415	30.6.1953	4ft 8½in	4wDM	88DS	Ruston 4VPH	20T	281
339209	8.12.1952	2ft 0in	4wDM	30DLU	Ruston 3VSH	4½T	79
349080	10.8.1953	2ft 0in	4wDM	48DL	Ruston 2VRH	5½T	98-102
349081	1.9.1953	2ft 0in	4wDM	48DL	Ruston 2VRH	5½T	98,101
370554	30.7.1954	2ft 4in	0-4-0DMF	LHG	Ruston 4YE	10T	227
370555	8.9.1953	2ft 0in	4wDM	48DL	Ruston 2VRH	5½T	100,101
370566	13.10.1953	2ft 0in	4wDM	48DL	Ruston 2VRH	7T	100,101
371547	2.6.1954	2ft 2in	4wDM	LAU	Ruston 2VSH	3½T	73,81
374447	20.8.1954	2ft 4in	0-4-0DMF	LHG	Ruston 4YE	10T	228
374448	30.8.1954	2ft 4in	0-4-0DMF	LHG	Ruston 4YE	10T	228
374454	27.10.1954	2ft 4in	0-4-0DMF	LHG	Ruston 4YE	10T	228
374455	30.11.1954	2ft 4in	0-4-0DMF	LHG	Ruston 4YE	10T	228
374458	16.12.1954	2ft 4in	0-4-0DMF	LHG	Ruston 4YE	10T	228
375338	29.4.1954	2ft 0in	4wDM	48DL	Ruston 2VRH	7T	99-101
375347	22.7.1954	2ft 4in	4wDM	LAT	Ruston 2VSH	3½T	174,177, 210,227
375714	5.2.1955	4ft 8½in	0-4-0DM	165DS	Ruston 6VPH	28T	195,203
375718	16.6.1955	4ft 8½in	0-4-0DM	165DS	Ruston 6VPH	28T	85
384139	10.10.1955	4ft 8½in	0-4-0DE	165DE	Ruston 6VPH	28T	66
387878	6.5.1955	2ft 0in	4wDM	48DL	Ruston 2VRH	7T	100,101
387879	6.5.1955	2ft 0in	4wDM	48DL	Ruston 2VRH	7T	100
387889	7.6.1955	2ft 0in	4wDM	48DL	Ruston 2VRH	7T	99,101
387890	7.6.1955	2ft 0in	4wDM	48DL	Ruston 2VRH	7T	100,101
387891	17.8.1955	2ft 0in	4wDM	48DL	Ruston 2VRH	5½T	100,101
392147	28.5.1956	2ft 1in	4wDMF	40DLG	Ruston 3VRH	6T	205,208
395293	20.3.1956	4ft 8½in	0-4-0DE	165DE	Ruston 6VPH	28T	225
398616	1.10.1956	4ft 8½in	4wDM	88DS	Ruston 4VPH	17T	78
408427	4.4.1957	2ft 0in	4wDM	LAU	Ruston 2VSH	3½T	77
411322	28.2.1958	3ft 0in	4wDM	48DS	Ruston 4YC	7½T	82

412708	30.4.1957	4ft 8½in	0-4-0DE	165DE	Ruston 6VPH	28T		226
412716	2.11.1957	4ft 8½in	0-4-0DE	200DE	Ruston 6RPH	30T		195,205
417889	12.11.1958	4ft 8½in	4wDM	48DS	Ruston 4YC	7½T		279
418770	3.9.1957	3ft 0in	4wDM	LB	Ruston 3VSH	3¾T		287
418780	14.5.1958	2ft 0in	4wDM	LBT	Ruston 3VSH	3¾T		166
418781	14.5.1958	2ft 0in	4wDM	LBT	Ruston 3VSH	3¾T		166,171
418793	11.9.1957	4ft 8½in	0-4-0DH	165DSH	Ruston 6YEX	28T		74,77,119
420137	13.2.1958	4ft 8½in	0-4-0DE	165DE	Ruston 6VPH	28T		119
420140	28.2.1958	4ft 8½in	0-4-0DE	165DE	Ruston 6VPH	28T		91
420142	7.3.1958	4ft 8½in	0-4-0DE	165DE	Ruston 6VPH	28T		91
420143	9.5.1958	4ft 8½in	0-4-0DE	165DE	Ruston 6VPH	28T		211,226
421433	14.5.1959	2ft 0in	4wDM	LAT	Ruston 2VSH	3½T		287
421435	22.41958	4ft 8½in	0-4-0DE	165DE	Ruston 6VPH	28T		119
423657	26.9.1958	4ft 8½in	0-4-0DE	165DE	Ruston 6VPH	28T		85,199
425473	22.1.1958	4ft 8½in	0-6-0DE	165DE	Ruston 6VPH	30T		243
425479	21.8.1959	4ft 8½in	0-4-0DE	165DE	Ruston 6VPH	28T		226
425794	9.6.1958	2ft 0in	4wDMF	48DLZ	Ruston 4VRH	7T		196
425795	14.7.1958	2ft 0in	4wDMF	48DLZ	Ruston 4VRH	5½T		166,184
425796	5.9.1958	2ft 0in	4wDMF	48DLZ	Ruston 4VRH	7T		196
425797	5.9.1958	2ft 0in	4wDMF	48DLZ	Ruston 4VRH	7T		184
425798	4.11.1958	2ft 0in	4wDMF	48DLZ	Ruston 4VRH	7T		184,205
425799	27.11.1958	2ft 0in	4wDMF	48DLZ	Ruston 4VRH	7T		196
431762	14.9.1959	4ft 8½in	0-4-0DE	165DE	Ruston 6VPH	28T		174,226
441423	2.10.1959	2ft 0in	4wDMF	48DLZ	Ruston 4VRH	7T		205,208
441424	12.11.1959	2ft 0in	4wDMF	48DLZ	Ruston 4VRH	7T		196,210
441425	12.11.1959	2ft 0in	4wDMF	48DLZ	Ruston 4VRH	7T		196
441426	15.6.1960	2ft 0in	4wDMF	48DLZ	Ruston 4VRH	7T		166
441427	13.10.1961	2ft 6in	4wDMF	48DLZ	Ruston 4VRH	7T		173,192,205
441428	16.9.1961	2ft 6in	4wDMF	48DLZ	Ruston 4VRH	7T		173,192
441944	16.2.1960	600mm	4wDM	LBT	Ruston 2YDA	4½T		287
448157	2.11.1962	4ft 8½in	0-6-0DE	LVSE	Ruston 12YGA	44T		188,218
449754	15.3.1961	4ft 8½in	0-4-0DE	165DE	Ruston 6VPH	28T		119,288
458959	11.12.1961	4ft 8½in	4wDM	48DS	Ruston 4YC	7½T		95
466623	12.1.1962	4ft 8½in	0-6-0DH	LSSH	Ruston 6RPH	36T		108
468043	28.2.1963	4ft 8½in	0-6-0DH	LSSH	Ruston 6RPH	36T		108
468044	6.3.1963	4ft 8½in	0-6-0DH	LSSH	Ruston 6RPH	36T		108
468045	11.3.1963	4ft 8½in	0-6-0DH	LSSH	Ruston 6RPH	36T		108
480678	7.11.1961	2ft 6in	4wDMF	20DLG	Ruston 2VSH	3½T		204
480679	10.11.1961	2ft 6in	4wDMF	20DLG	Ruston 2VSH	3½T		204,210
480680	26.4.1963	2ft 6in	4wDMF	20DLG	Ruston 2VSH	3½T		204
480681	5.6.1963	2ft 6in	4wDMF	20DLG	Ruston 2VSH	3½T		204
512572	18.2.1965	4ft 8½in	4wDM	88DS	Ruston 4VPH	17T		288
513139	16.11.1967	4ft 8½in	0-4-0DH	LPSH	Ruston 6YE	28T		45
513141	7.7.1966	4ft 8½in	4wDM	LLSH	Ruston 6YDA	20T		95
7002/0567/6	28.10.1967	2ft 0in	4wDM	LBT	Ruston 2YDA	3½T		153,290
7002/0967/5	9.10.1967	2ft 0in	4wDM	LBT	Ruston 2YDA	3½T		141,153
7002/0967/6	9.10.1967	2ft 0in	4wDM	LBT	Ruston 2YDA	3½T		141,153

NOTE that the details in the 'Horse power' column are the Ruston Classes, which normally indicate the horse power. Details for the later 'lettered' classes are :

LAT/LAU - 20hp
LB/LBT - 31½hp
LHG - 75hp; LHT - 82½hp
LLSH - 104hp
LPSH - 192hp
LSSH - 287hp
LVSE - 400hp
LWS - 315hp

RUSTON & PROCTOR, Lincoln — RP

13003	.1888	4ft 8½in	0-4-0ST	OC			146
21232	7.1.1898	3ft 0in	0-4-0T	OC	9½x16	Type No.11	75

ROLLS ROYCE LTD, SENTINEL WORKS, Shrewsbury — RR

10178	2.7.1964	4ft 8½in	0-8-0DH	544hp	R-R C8NFL	55T	218
10190	20.8.1964	4ft 8½in	0-6-0DH	325hp	R-R C8SFL	48T	218
10193	13.10.1964	4ft 8½in	4wDH	229hp	R-R C6SFL	34T	222
10194	13.10.1964	4ft 8½in	4wDH	229hp	R-R C6SFL	34T	226,229,238
10195	13.10.1964	4ft 8½in	4wDH	229hp	R-R C6SFL	34T	237,238
10228	28.10.1965	4ft 8½in	4wDH	229hp	R-R C6SFL	34T	179
10231	6.4.1965	4ft 8½in	4wDH	256hp	R-R C6SFL	34T	178
10241	5.7.1966	4ft 8½in	4wDH	229hp	R-R C6SFL	34T	226,229,238
10257	23.2.1966	4ft 8½in	0-6-0DH	325hp	R-R C8SFL	48T	222
10262	23.2.1967	4ft 8½in	0-6-0DH	325hp	R-R C8SFL	48T	222
10270	26.9.1967	4ft 8½in	0-6-0DH	325hp	R-R C8SFL	48T	222

ROBERT STEPHENSON & CO, FORTH BANKS WORKS, Newcastle on Tyne — RS

? 634	1.1849	4ft 8½in	0-6-0	IC	18 x 24	5ft0in	56
1005	24.12.1855	4ft 8½in	4-4-0T	IC	15 x 22	5ft3in	122
4150	11.11.1937	4ft 8½in	0-6-0ST	OC	16 x 24	3ft8in	170,171
4156	25.11.1937	4ft 8½in	0-6-0ST	OC	16 x 24	3ft8in	170,182,207

ROBERT STEPHENSON & HAWTHORNS LTD — RSH

D DARLINGTON WORKS, Co. Durham — RSHD
N FORTH BANKS WORKS, Newcastle-upon-Tyne — RSHN

D	6947	24.5.1938	4ft 8½in	0-4-0ST	OC	16 X 24	3ft8in	35½T	195
N	7091	16.6.1943	4ft 8½in	0-6-0ST	IC	18 x 26	4ft3in	48T	219
N	7097	12.8.1943	4ft 8½in	0-6-0ST	IC	18 x 26	4ft3in	48T	241
N	7098	19.8.1943	4ft 8½in	0-6-0ST	IC	18 x 26	4ft3in	48T	167
N	7100	4.9.1943	4ft 8½in	0-6-0ST	IC	18 x 26	4ft3in	48T	241,244
N	7107	20.10.1943	4ft 8½in	0-6-0ST	IC	18 x 26	4ft3in	48T	241
N	7112	29.11.1943	4ft 8½in	0-6-0ST	IC	18 x 26	4ft3in	48T	108
N	7130	30.3.1944	4ft 8½in	0-6-0ST	IC	18 x 26	4ft3in	48T	108
N	7144	29.6.1944	4ft 8½in	0-6-0ST	IC	18 x 26	4ft3in	48T	51,164,167, 198,241
N	7161	19.9.1944	4ft 8½in	0-6-0ST	IC	18 x 26	4ft3in	48T	244
N	7164	4.10.1944	4ft 8½in	0-6-0ST	IC	18 x 26	4ft3in	48T	241
N	7172	16.11.1944	4ft 8½in	0-6-0ST	IC	18 x 26	4ft3in	48T	219
N	7204	13.3.1945	4ft 8½in	0-6-0ST	IC	18 x 26	4ft3in	48T	108
N	7206	14.3.1945	4ft 8½in	0-6-0ST	IC	18 x 26	4ft3in	48T	167,181
N	7285	6.11.1945	4ft 8½in	0-6-0ST	OC	14 x 22	3ft6in		51,164,170,187
N	7642	30.5.1950	4ft 8½in	0-4-0ST	OC	14 x 22	3ft6in	27½T	179,226,243
N	7643	27.6.1950	4ft 8½in	0-4-0ST	OC	14 x 22	3ft6in	27½T	188
N	7644	19.7.1950	4ft 8½in	0-4-0ST	OC	14 x 22	3ft6in	27½T	179
N	7667	29.8.1950	4ft 8½in	0-6-0ST	IC	18 x 26	4ft0½in		288
N	7675	8.1.1952	4ft 8½in	0-4-0ST	OC	16 x 24	3ft8in	27½T	188,222

N	7696	2.7.1953	4ft 8½in	0-6-0DM	330hp	Crossley RT6	40T		183,206
N	7697	25.1.1954	4ft 8½in	0-6-0DM	330hp	Crossley RT6	40T		183
N	7698	22.2.1954	4ft 8½in	0-6-0DM	330hp	Crossley RT6	40T		165,183
N	7761	22.6.1954	4ft 8½in	0-6-0ST	IC 18 x 26	4ft0½in			289
N	7794	25.3.1954	4ft 8½in	0-6-0ST	OC 16 x 24	3ft8in	43½T		222
N	7817	17.8.1954	4ft 8½in	0-4-0ST	OC 16 x 24	3ft8in	35½T		132
N	7818	23.8.1954	4ft 8½in	0-4-0ST	OC 16 x 24	3ft8in	35½T		91,288
N	7859	4.7.1956	4ft 8½in	0-6-0DM	204hp	Gardner 8L3	[DC 2573]		91
N	7860	16.7.1956	4ft 8½in	0-6-0DM	204hp	Gardner 8L3	[DC 2574]		91
D	7879	10.1957	4ft 8½in	0-6-0DM	204hp	Gardner 8L3	[DC 2602]		167
N	7963	6.12.1957	2ft 0in	4wBEF	64hp	EM2B1 13T	[EE 2521]		137, 193,202
N	7964	13.2.1958	2ft 0in	4wBEF	64hp	EM2B1 13T	[EE 2522]	193,202	
D	8158	9.1960	4ft 8½in	0-6-0DM	204hp	Gardner 8L3	[DC 2680]		171, 183,203
D	8159	10.1960	4ft 8½in	0-6-0DM	204hp	Gardner 8L3	[DC 2681]		212, 231,234
D	8186	5.1961	4ft 8½in	0-6-0DM	204hp	Gardner 8L3	[DC 2708]		212
D	8187	5.1961	4ft 8½in	0-6-0DM	204hp	Gardner 8L3	[DC 2709]	231,234	
D	8191	6.1961	4ft 8½in	0-6-0DM	204hp	Gardner 8L3	[DC 2713]		231
D	8252	10.1961	4ft 8½in	Bo-Bo.DE	1000hp	EE8SVT 72T	[EE 3000]		289
D	8289	1961	2ft 0in	4wBEF	64hp	EM2B1 13T	[EE 3147]		201
D	8345	1962	2ft 0in	4wBEF	64hp	EM2B1 13T	[EE 3224]		193

R. & W. HAWTHORN & CO, FORTH BANKS WORKS,
Newcastle on Tyne   **RWH**

1947	13.8.1883	4ft 8½in	0-6-0ST	IC 16 x 22	4ft0in		56,215,217

SENTINEL (SHREWSBURY) LTD, Battlefield, Shrewsbury   S

6516	1926	4ft 8½in	4wVBT	VCG	6¾ x 9	2ft6in	20T	106
6517	5.11.1926	4ft 8½in	4wVBT	VCG	6¾ x 9	2ft6in		83
6896	1927	3ft 0in	4wVBT	VCG	6¾ x 9	1ft8in	6T	63
6935	1928	4ft 8½in	4wVBT	VCG	6¾ x 9	2ft6in	16T	105,106
8207	1930	4ft 8½in	4wVBT	VCG	6¾ x 9	2ft6in	19T	74
8478	28.4.1931	4ft 8½in	4wVBT	VCG	6¾ x 9	2ft6in		83
R5/8749	1936	4ft 8½in	4wVBT	VCG	6¾ x 9	2ft6in		74,76
9373	1947	4ft 8½in	4wVBT	VCG	6¾ x 9	2ft6in	100hp 23T	74
9379	1947	4ft 8½in	4wVBT	VCG	6¾ x 9	2ft6in	100hp 24T	106
9395	30.8.1950	4ft 8½in	4wVBT	VCG	6¾ x 9	2ft6in	100hp 25T	212, 231,234
9397	14.9.1950	4ft 8½in	4wVBT	VCG	6¾ x 9	2ft6in	100hp 25T	205
9398	1.1.1950	4ft 8½in	4wVBT	VCG	6¾ x 9	2ft6in	100hp 25T	205
9399	14.9.1950	4ft 8½in	4wVBT	VCG	6¾ x 9	2ft6in	100hp 25T	235
9526	3.8.1951	4ft 8½in	4wVBT	VCG	6¾ x 9	2ft6in	100hp 25T	212, 231
9530	29.1.1952	4ft 8½in	4wVBT	VCG	6¾ x 9	2ft6in	100hp 25T	220
9531	28.4.1952	4ft 8½in	4wVBT	VCG	6¾ x 9	2ft6in	100hp 25T	221
9532	28.4.1952	4ft 8½in	4wVBT	VCG	6¾ x 9	2ft6in	100hp 25T	206, 221
9538	1952	4ft 8½in	4wVBT	VCG	6¾ x 9	3ft2in	200hp 34T	183,

									217
9548	7.11.1952	4ft 8½in	4wVBT	VCG	6¾ x 9	3ft 2in	200hp	34T	212, 234
9576	12.10.1954	4ft 8½in	4wVBT	VCG	6¾ x 9	3ft 2in	200hp	34T	164, 203
9578	10.11.1954	4ft 8½in	4wVBT	VCG	6¾ x 9	3ft 2in	200hp	34T	170, 171
10072	9.6.1961	4ft 8½in	0-6-0DH	310hp	R-R C8SFL		48T		183,207,218
10073	27.4.1961	4ft 8½in	4wDH	229hp	R-R C6SFL		34T		235,237
10086	4.10.1961	4ft 8½in	4wDH	229hp	R-R C6SFL		34T		220
10141	24.7.1963	4ft 8½in	4wDH	230hp	R-R C6SFL		34T		218
10157	28.3.1963	4ft 8½in	0-6-0DH	335hp	R-R C8SFL		48T		183,236
10160	17.12.1963	4ft 8½in	0-6-0DH	335hp	R-R C8SFL		48T		183,192,195 207,225
10161	9.1.1964	4ft 8½in	0-6-0DH	335hp	R-R C8SFL		48T		183,192,195
10163	24.7.1963	4ft 8½in	4wDH	229hp	R-R C6SFL		34T		218
10165	22.9.1964	4ft 8½in	0-4-0DH	311hp	R-R C8SFL		32T		192
10169	19.3.1964	4ft 8½in	0-8-0DH	544hp	R-R C8NFL		55T		218
10189	1.1.1964	4ft 8½in	0-4-0DH	311hp	R-R C8SFL		32T		178,245

SWINDON WORKS, BR   Sdn

[BR D2132]	2.1960	4ft 8½in	0-6-0DM	204hp	Gardner 8L3	30T	171,220,225
[BR D2138]	4.1960	4ft 8½in	0-6-0DM	204hp	Gardner 8L3	30T	171,225
[BR D2182]	3.1962	4ft 8½in	0-6-0DM	204hp	Gardner 8L3	30T	167,282
[BR D9520]	11.1964	4ft 8½in	0-6-0DH	650hp	Paxman 6YJX	50T	289

SEVERN LAMB LTD, Stratford-upon-Avon, Warwicks   SL

546.4.93	4.1993	1ft 6in	2-4-0RE		292

SIMPLEX MECHANICAL HANDLING LTD, Bedford   SMH

102T016	9.6.1976	3ft 0in	4wDH	104hp	Deutz F6L912	14T	63
40SD529	2.4.1984	2ft 0in	4wDM	40hp	Deutz F3L913	2½T	141

SHARP, STEWART & CO, ATLAS WORKS, Manchester   SS

1321	1862	4ft 8½in	0-6-0T	IC	14 x 20	3ft 6in	56

THOMAS HILL (ROTHERHAM) LTD, Kilnhurst, S Yorks   TH

113V	5.1.1962	4ft 8½in	4wDH	178hp	R-R C6NFL	30T	211
114V	6.2.1962	4ft 8½in	4wDH	166hp	R-R C6NFL	30T	243
137C	25.3.1964	4ft 8½in	4wDH	308hp	R-R C8SFL	36T	165,187,225
140V	15.6.1964	4ft 8½in	4wDH	179hp	R-R C6NFL	30T	203,237,245
141C	27.7.1964	4ft 8½in	0-6-0DH	325hp	R-R C8SFL	40T	163,165,207
147V	21.12.1964	4ft 8½in	4wDH	179hp	R-R C6NFL	30T	203
161V	31.12.1965	4ft 8½in	0-6-0DH	340hp	R-R C8SFL	42T	165,183,187
169V	31.8.1966	4ft 8½in	4wDH	173hp	R-R SF6SC	28T	188
170V	31.8.1966	4ft 8½in	4wDH	173hp	R-R SF6SC	28T	211,229

172V	24.10.1966	4ft 8½in	4wDH	173hp	R-R SF6SC	28T		188,211
174V	11.11.1966	4ft 8½in	4wDH	173hp	R-R SF6SC	28T		199,236,238
175V	24.11.1966	4ft 8½in	4wDH	173hp	R-R SF6SC	28T		179,188
176V	28.12.1966	4ft 8½in	4wDH	256hp	R-R C6SFL	34T		195
178V	25.1.1967	4ft 8½in	4wDH	173hp	R-R SF6SC	32T		188,199
181V	19.4.1967	4ft 8½in	6wDH	272hp	R-R C8NFL	48T		282
182V	29.3.1967	4ft 8½in	4wDH	256hp	R-R C6SFL	34T		195
190V	13.12.1967	4ft 8½in	4wDH	173hp	R-R SF6SC	32T		188,238
191V	14.2.1968	4ft 8½in	4wDH	173hp	R-R SF6SC	34T		235,237
192V	22.3.1968	4ft 8½in	4wDH	173hp	R-R SF6SC	34T		191,235,237
215V	8.1.1970	4ft 8½in	4wDH	173hp	R-R SF6SC	34T		188,229
247C	23.5.1973	4ft 8½in	4wDH	230hp	R-R C6SFL	34T		226,229,238
SE107	12.1979	3ft 0in	4wBERF			5T		138,239
SE108	24.3.1983	2ft 4in	4wBERF			5T		139,246
SE110	19.12.1980	2ft 6in	4wBERF			5T		214
SE117	25.3.1983	2ft 0in	4w-4wBERF			10T		138,240
SE118	27.2.1985	3ft 0in	4w-4wRF	(Unpowered trailer)				

THAKEHAM TILES LTD, Storrington, Sussex — Thakeham

	1950	2ft 0in	4wPM	292

THORNEWILL & WARHAM, Burton on Trent — TW

	1850	4ft 8½in	?	OC	52
	1850	4ft 8½in	0-6-0ST	OC	51
	1852	4ft 8½in	0-4-0tank		51
	1857	4ft 8½in	2-4-0tank		51
	1864	4ft 8½in	2-4-0tank		51

VULCAN FOUNDRY LTD, Newton le Willows, Lancs — VF

1236	1888	4ft 8½in	0-6-0ST	IC 12 x 17 3ft1in			111
4860	1942	4ft 8½in	0-4-0DM	153hp	Gardner 6L3	[DC 2168]	112
4861	1942	4ft 8½in	0-4-0DM	153hp	Gardner 6L3	[DC 2169]	108,110
5257	1945	4ft 8½in	0-4-0DM	153hp	Gardner 6L3	[DC 2176]	154
5258	1945	4ft 8½in	0-4-0DM	153hp	Gardner 6L3	[DC 2177]	112
5263	1945	4ft 8½in	0-4-0DM	153hp	Gardner 6L3	[DC 2182]	108
5264	1945	4ft 8½in	0-4-0DM	153hp	Gardner 6L3	[DC 2183]	112
5275	1.6.1945	4ft 8½in	0-6-0ST	IC 18 x 26 4ft3in		48T	108,154
5279	11.6.1945	4ft 8½in	0-6-0ST	IC 18 x 26 4ft3in		48T	215,217
5286	1945	4ft 8½in	0-6-0ST	IC 18 x 26 4ft3in		48T	215,217,220
D278	11.1955	4ft 8½in	0-6-0DM	204hp	Gardner 8L3	[DC 2552]	212
D1005	3.1966	4ft 8½in	Bo-Bo.DE	1000hp	EE8SVT 72T	[EE 3606]	289

NOTE that 153hp locos were 21T, 204hp loco was 29¾T

W. G. BAGNALL LTD, CASTLE ENGINE WORKS, Stafford — WB

1575	25.9.1899	4ft 8½in	0-4-0ST	OC	14 x 20	3ft6in	23T	77,78
1889	27.5.1911	3ft 0in	0-4-0ST	OC	6 x 9	1ft7in	6T	82
2167	24.12.1921	4ft 8½in	0-6-0ST	OC	13 x 18	2ft9¼in	25T	167

2168	13.2.1922	4ft 8½in	0-6-0ST	OC	13 x 18	2ft9¼in	25T	167,241
2197	12.1922	4ft 8½in	0-6-0ST	OC	13 x 18	2ft9¼in	25T	241
2233	26.7.1924	3ft 0in	0-4-0ST	OC	10 x 16	2ft9¼in	14¾T	82
2604	31.7.1939	4ft 8½in	0-6-0ST	OC	16 x 22	3ft6½in	42¼T	86,205
2605	28.8.1939	4ft 8½in	0-6-0ST	OC	16 x 22	3ft6½in	42¼T	87,222
2607	26.9.1939	4ft 8½in	0-4-0ST	OC	15 x 22	3ft6½in	33½T	215,222
2619	18.4.1940	4ft 8½in	0-4-0ST	OC	15 x 22	3ft6½in	33¼T	87,222
2650	9.1940	4ft 8½in	0-4-0ST	OC	14½x 22	3ft6½in	27T	112
2751	9.9.1944	4ft 8½in	0-6-0ST	IC	18 x 26	4ft3in	48T	206,241
2754	12.10.1944	4ft 8½in	0-6-0ST	IC	18 x 26	4ft3in	48T	167
2756	19.10.1944	4ft 8½in	0-6-0ST	IC	18 x 26	4ft3in	48T	206,241
2760	28.11.1944	4ft 8½in	0-6-0ST	IC	18 x 26	4ft3in	48T	205
2765	24.1.1945	4ft 8½in	0-6-0ST	IC	18 x 26	4ft3in	48T	219
2766	2.2.1945	4ft 8½in	0-6-0ST	IC	18 x 26	4ft3in	48T	219
2816	4.5.1946	4ft 8½in	0-6-0ST	OC	16 x 22	3ft6½in	42¾T	215
2817	12.6.1946	4ft 8½in	0-6-0ST	OC	16 x 22	3ft6½in	42¾T	215
3119	5.9.1957	4ft 8½in	0-6-0DM	208hp	National M4		29½T	282

WIGAN COAL & IRON CO LTD, Kirkless, Lancs — WCI

1874	4ft 8½in	0-6-0ST	IC			157
1887	4ft 8½in	0-6-0ST	IC	16 x 22	4ft3in	157
1908	4ft 8½in	0-6-0ST	IC	16 x 22	4ft3in	157
1912	4ft 8½in	0-6-0ST	IC	16 x 22	4ft3in	157

A. J. WILSON, Carlton, Nottingham — Wilson

c1969	2ft 0in	4wPM	292

D. WICKHAM & CO LTD, Ware, Herts — Wkm

4092	5.9.1946	3ft 0in	2w-2PMR	17A	JAP 1323	287
4164	19.2.1948	3ft 0in	2w-2PMR	8S	JAP 350cc	287
7441	30.5.1956	3ft 0in	2-2wPMR	27MkIII	Ford 10hp	287
9673	18.9.1964	3ft 0in	2-2wPMR	27A MkIII	Ford 10hp	287

WINGROVE & ROGERS LTD, Kirkby, Liverpool — WR

1298	29.11.1938	2ft 1in	0-4-0BE	4.8hp	1½T	W217	58
5537	26.1.1956	2ft 0in	4wBE	4.8hp	1½T	W417	262
5670	26.9.1957	2ft 0in	4wBE			W227	254
6308	27.2.1961	2ft 0in	0-4-0BE	4.8hp	1½T	W217	270
6309	27.2.1961	2ft 0in	0-4-0BE	4.8hp	1½T	W217	270
J7208	7.5.1969	2ft 0in	4wBE			W227	270
J7272	19.3.1969	2ft 0in	4wBE			W227	270
L3032F	1984	2ft 6in	4wBEF	18hp	5T		201
L5004F	1985	2ft 6in	4w-4wBEF	50hp	10T		177,201

YORKSHIRE ENGINE CO LTD, MEADOW HALL WORKS, Sheffield   YE

	No	Date	Gauge	Type	Cyl	Size	Wheels	Class/Engine	Extra	Works
	280	.1875	4ft 8½in	0-4-0ST	OC	12 x 16	3ft0in	Class Bx		255
	325	9.1878	4ft 8½in	0-6-0ST	OC	14 x 20	3ft3in	Class Cx		116,220
	948	1908	4ft 8½in	0-4-0ST	OC	14 x 20	3ft3in	Class Ex		64,65
	1021	# 8.11.1909	4ft 8½in	0-6-0ST	OC	14 x 20	3ft3in	Class G		212
	1300	28.3.1916	4ft 8½in	0-6-0ST	OC	14 x 20	3ft3in			243,245
	2197	5.6.1928	4ft 8½in	0-6-0ST	OC	15 x 20	3ft3in			116,168
	2241	20.6.1929	4ft 8½in	0-6-0ST	OC	15 x 22	3ft4in			212
	2307	1.6.1931	4ft 8½in	0-6-0ST	OC	15 x 20	3ft3in			116,168
	2407	26.11.1942	4ft 8½in	0-4-0ST	OC	14 x 20	3ft5in			149
	2521	6.5.1953	4ft 8½in	0-6-0ST	OC	16 x 24	3ft8in	Type 1		188,210
	2522	12.6.1953	4ft 8½in	0-6-0ST	OC	16 x 24	3ft8in	Type 1		199
	2605	16.9.1955	4ft 8½in	0-6-0DE	400hp	Paxman 12RPHII			51T	218
	2635	24.4.1957	4ft 8½in	0-6-0DE	400hp	2 x R-R C6SFL			Janus	218
	2652	29.7.1957	4ft 8½in	0-4-0DE	200hp	R-R C6SFL			30T	147,234
	2682	31.1.1958	4ft 8½in	0-4-0DE	200hp	R-R C6SFL				165,168,198
	2805	11.7.1960	4ft 8½in	0-4-0DH	220hp	R-R C6SFL				234
	2848	7.11.1961	4ft 8½in	0-4-0DH	170hp	R-R C6NFL			28T	62
	2895	19.1.1963	4ft 8½in	0-6-0DH	220hp	R-R C6SFL			34T	183
z	2940	1965	4ft 8½in	0-6-0DH	375hp	Cummins NT400			51T	183

\# alternative YE sources state 10.1909.
z completed at Kilnhurst by TH and ex-works TH on 28.3.1966.

INDEX OF LOCOMOTIVE NAMES

A
ADAM	108
ADMIRAL	51,163
AJAX	198
ALAN	183,206
ALBERT EDWARD	93
ALBERT	148
ALEXANDRA	144,231
ANDREW	165,183,187
ANNE	110
ANNESLEY COLLIERY No.1	115
ANNESLEY COLLIERY No.2	115
ANNESLEY No.1	115,163,205,235
ANNESLEY No.2	115,163,168,182
ANNESLEY No.3	235
ANNIE	53,286
ARTHUR	121
ASHBURY	60
ASTLEY	131
AUDREY	53,195
AYNHO	108

B
BALMORAL CASTLE	235
BARNSLEY	254
BARNSTONE	45
BATLEY	78
BEATRICE	143
BEAUMONT	215,225
BENNERLEY	59
BENTINCK No.1	168,235,237
BENTINCK No.2	116,168
BENTINCK No.3	116,168
BERYL	183
BESTWOOD	47,170,171,183
BILDWORTH No.1	121
BILL	93,194
BILLUM	121,179
BILLY	131
BILSTHORPE No.1	146,178
BILSTHORPE No.2	146,178
BIRKENHEAD	276,277
BIRKLANDS	242
BIRLEY No.5	231
BONNIE DUNDEE	205
BRADFORD	277
BRAMLEY No.6	198
BRIERLEY	183,236
BRUNEL	264
BUTTERLEY No.30	86,205
BUTTERLEY No.31	87,222
BUTTERLEY No.35	215
BUTTERLEY No.50	215
BUTTERLEY No.51	87,222

C
CARNARVON	146,147,220,235,237
CASTLE DONNINGTON No.2	91
CASTLE DONNINGTON POWER STATION	132,288
CATHERINE	53,195
CHARLES 1	196,232
CHARLES BUCHAN	163,183
CHARLES	183,203,279
CHATSWORTH HOUSE	208
CHELFORD No.1	112
CHORLEY No.7	112
CHURCHILL	147,237
CLARA	251
CLIFTON No.3	122
CLIFTON	122
CLIPSTONE No.1	188
CLIPSTONE No.xx	64
COCK O' THE NORTH	233
COCKER	259
COLDSTREAM	284
COLONEL	51,163,187,207
COLWICK HALL No.4	208
CORBY	289
COTES PARK No.xx	182
COXHOE No.1	149
CYPRUS	84,277

D
DAISY	93,108,110,157,168,194
DANBY LODGE	78,108,268
DARFIELD	108
DARLEY DALE	51,165
DAVID	148,171,207,218,222
DERBY	45
DEVONSHIRE	147,220,235,237
DEWSBURY	59,259
DIANA	64,65,203,211
DICK	131
DINNINGTON No.x	212,231,234
DO WELL (BRISTOL)	148
DON	277
DOWELL	245
DUDDON	144,231,234
DURBAR	215

Nottinghamshire Handbook. Page 369

E

EARL FERRERS	47
EASTNEY	276
ECCLES	146
EDALE	260
EDITH	144
EL 1	108
ELLEN	73
EMFOUR.1	237
EMFOUR.2	182
EMFOUR.3	168
EMFOUR.4	182,206
EMFOUR.5	237
EMFOUR.7	183
EMFOUR.9	168,182
EMLYN	146
EMPRESS	106
ENTERPRISE	215

F

FAITH	213
FANNY	131
FEARLESS	144,231,234
FELIX	165,171,187
FENELLA	183,192,195,207,225
FESTIVAL OF BRITAIN	220
FFIONA JANE	291
FIRBECK	194,212
FOLESHILL No.1	291
FORTESCUE	250
FOXHANGER	287
FRANCES	276
FRANCIS	74,76
FRANK	131,274
FRED	85,122
FRIAR TUCK	147
FULWOOD	251,277

G

GAVIN	252
GEDLING No.4	196
GENERAL	51
GEORGE EDWARD	215,225
GEORGE	215
GERT	110
GILLIAN	195
GLAMIS CASTLE	221
GRANBY	45

H

HADDON HALL	185,208
HARE	279
HARLAXTON	146
HAROLD	53
HARRY	131
HARWORTH No.1	199,237
HARWORTH No.2	199
HARWORTH	57
HASTINGS	155
HAYLE	273
HEATHER	173,184,205
HEBE	149
HEM HEATH 3D	282
HESKETH	252
HILDA	74
HORWICH	45
HUCKNALL COLLIERY No.xx	142
HUCKNALL TORKARD COLLIERIES	142,203,207
HUTHWAITE 7	116,117

I

I.C.L.36	198
I'LL TRY	225
IRENE NO.394	94
IRENE	94
ISABEL	131
IVOR	203

J

JACK	46
JACQUELINE	207
JAMES 1	291
JAYNE	165,187,225
JESSIE	145,231,234
JOE	255
JOHN	65,91,151,238
JUBILEE	116
JUDITH	183
JULIA	84
JULIAN	183,192,195
JUNE	149

K

KESTREL	208,246,282,291
KILINDINI	167
KINDER	51,165
KING GEORGE	84,104,171,195,207
KIRKBY	256,264

L

LADY ANGELA	77
LADY CORNWALL	259
LADY MARGARET	77
LANCASTER	47,171
LANDORE	112

LANGAR	45
LANGTON	131,182
LAUCHOPE	277
LESLEY	171,220,225
LIMERICK	155
LINBY COLLIERY No.xx	104
LINDSAY	157
LITTLE GEORGE	58
LITTLE JOHN	53,185
LIVERPOOL	277
LIZZIE	260
LLOYD	231
LOCO 28	244
LOD 758141	110
LONGWOOD	131,182
LOVATT	241
LUCERO	118

M

MAINDEE	264,267
MALTBY No.1	231
MANSFIELD No.2	64
MANTON	157,212
MANTON 521/71	212
MANTON No.2	212,231,234
MARELL	84,277
MARGARET	126,149
MARGUERITE	77
MARS	144
MARY	91,131,215
MICHAEL	51,163,170,187
MIDLAND	250
MOMBASA	167,241
MONITOR	267
MORECAMBE	276
MOW L 1	111
MURIEL	53

N

NANCY	119,151,292
NAPOLEON	51
NCB CLIPSTONE No.2	188
NELLIE	144
NEW HUCKNALL No.4	116,117,220
NORTH STAR	115
NOTTINGHAM	110,259

O

OLD BOB	185
OLLERTON No.xx	222
OLYMPIA	111,112
ORMISTON	278
OUGHTBRIDGE No.1	149

OUGHTBRIDGE No.2	234

P

PARKESTON	252
PARTINGTON	111
PATSY	131,151
PAUL	165
PECKETT No.2	131,182
PEGGY	264
PETER	163,170,171,187,207
PETERHEAD	277
PHILIP	163,170,187
PHILLIP	137,201
PHOENIX	45
PINXTON	131,182
PIONEER	57,220
PLEASLEY	256,264
POLLY	104,207
PORTLAND No.xx	117
PORTLAND	220
PRINCESS ROYAL	157
PROGRESS	115,235
PUCK	114,133

Q

QUEEN	53,195

R

RADCLIFFE	274
RAVEN	118,182,225,235
RIGLEY No.xx	133
RNCF No.3	235,237
ROBIN HOOD No.3	147
ROBIN	163,192,218
ROCKET	143,267,286
ROF 14 No.xx	112
ROF No.6 No.11	111
ROSEHALL	277
ROTHERVALE No.xx	212
ROYAL ENGINEER	108
RUFFORD No.1	65,226,238
RUFFORD No.2	65,188,226,238
RUFFORD No.3	229,226
RUNCORN	276
RUPERT	144
RUTH	170,171

S

SALAMANDER	112
SEA EAGLE	175,208
SENTINAL	105,106
SHAH	157
SHERWOOD No.1	

SHERWOOD No.1	143,229
SHERWOOD No.2	142,143,203,229,242
SHERWOOD No.3	143,171,203,207
SHERWOOD No.4	203,229
SHERWOOD No.6	142,143,229
SHIREBROOK No.4	243
SIEMENS	157,212
SILVER HILL	147
SILVERHILL	146
SIMON	171,195,207,218
SIR ALFRED WOOD	84
SIR HENRY	64,65
SKEGBY	256,264
SOLENT	252
SPEY	198
ST ALBANS	47,171
ST.MONANS	67,74,76
STANLOW	133,276
STANTON No.15	284
STANTON No.16	284
STANTON No.19	150
STANTON No.22	146
STANTON No.23	284
STEETLEY	145,231,234
STEPHEN / VANGUARD	163
STEPHEN	165,207
STIRLING CASTLE	220
SULTAN	212
SUSAN	195
SUTTON	256
SWANSEA	75
SWANWICK COLLIERIES No.4	205
SWANWICK COLLIERIES No.5	220
SWANWICK No.2	182
SWYNNERTON	273

T

TAME	198
TAWE	276
TEVERSALL	256,264
THE CITY OF NOTTINGHAM	108
THE CUB	63
THE HERBERT TURNER	45
THE TANK	282,291
THE WASP	292
THE WELSHMAN	210
THIKA	241
THORESBY No.1	64,65,211
TILTON	255
TIME	250
TISSINGTON	273
TOM	131
TOPHARD	65,238
TRAFFORD PARK	167,241
TRENT	255

U

UNION JACK	260

V

VALERIE	165,170,171,183
VANGUARD	57,207,217,220
VICTORIA	94,144
VICTORY	111,211,226,229,231
VIOLET	245
VIXEN	126

W

WARSOP	148,242
WAVERLEY	194
WD5 AVONSIDE	108
WELBECK No.5	118,245
WELBECK No.6	118,179,245
WELBECK No.7	229,245
WELBECK No.8	199,245
WEST BURTON No.1	91
WILLIE	279
WILLINGTON No.xx	91
WINDSOR CASTLE	206,221
WINNIE	144
WOODHALL	277
WOODSIDE	215,274

Y

Y.I.C.No.7	84

INDEX OF LOCATIONS AND OWNERS

A

Abbott & Co (Newark)	281
Adlington Geo.	320
Adlington Wm.	320
AEI	95
Air Ministry	44
Aird John & Sons	250
Andersons Gypsum Products	67,79
Angel Inn, Misson	286
Anglo Iranian Oil Co	300
Annesley - Staveley Contract	252
Annesley Colliery	107,115,163
APCM	45
Army Department	107
Arnold H. & Son	101,251
Associated British Maltsters	296
Associated Portland Cement Mfrs	45,62
Aveling-Barford	103
Awsworth Colliery Co	46
Awsworth Iron Co	46,59

B

B.A. Collieries	47,164,171183,195
Babbington & Cinderhill Colls & Rlys	48
Babbington and Cinderhill Collieries	164
Babbington Brick Co	50
Babbington Coal Co	47,48,51
Babbington Colliery Tramway	328
Babbington Colliery	48,164
Babbington Wharf	48
Baird Hugh & Sons	297
Balderton Gravel Pit	312
Balderton Quarry	98
Baldry & Yerburgh	252
Baldry, Yerburgh & Hutchinson	253
Baldwin H.J. & Co	297
Balfour Beatty Railway Engineering	254
Balfour, Beatty & Co	254
Barber, Walker & Co	54,180,198,199, 202,215,217,229,244,297,327,329
Barnstone Blue Lias Lime Co	45,78,305
Barnstone Cement Co	45
Barnstone Cement Works	45
Barton Gypsum Mines	69
Barton T.H.	286
Barton Transport	286
Basford Gasworks	94
Basford Scrap Yard	286
Bawtry Coke Ovens & By Products	58
Bayles & Wylie	298
Beacon Hill Plaster Works	70,322

Beacon Hill Works	281
Beardsley John	319
Beehive Works	308
Beeley Wm.	298
Beeston & Stapleford UDC	58
Beeston Boiler Co	58
Beeston Brewery Co	317
Beeston Cement Terminal	62
Beeston Creosoting Depot	82
Beeston Foundry Co	58
Beeston Sewage Works	58
Beeston Urban District Council	58
Beeston Works	58,66
Beggarlee Colliery & Workshops	54
Beggarlee Shops	215
Bell Rock Gypsum Industries	67
Bell Thos. & Son	298
Bellmoor Quarries	121
Bellrock Gypsum Industries	79
Belvoir & Newark Plaster Co	156
Bennerley Disposal Point	167
Bennerley Iron Co	59
Bennerley Ironworks	59,60
Bennerley Slag & Tarmac Co	60,167
Bentinck Colliery	107,116,163,168
Bentinck Training Centre	169
Benton & Woodiwiss	255
Berry Hill & Stapleford Sand Co	104
Berry Hill Sports Ground	170
Berry Hill Sand Co	104
Berry Hill Sand Quarries	104
Bestwood Central Workshops	170
Bestwood Coal & Iron Co	47,60
Bestwood Colliery & Ironworks	47
Bestwood Colliery	171
Bestwood Quarry	98
Bestwood Sand Co	47
Bestwood Sand Pits	60
Bestwood Training Centre	173
Bevercotes Colliery	174
Bevercotes Training Centre	176
Bilsthorpe Brick Co	61
Bilsthorpe Brickworks	61
Bilsthorpe Colliery	134,145,177
Bilsthorpe Contract	251
Bingham Contract	266
Bingham Wm. & Son	304
Binns Walter	256
Bishop R. & Son	315
Blackmires Brickworks	298
Blackwell Colliery Co	115,117

Bleasby Gravel Pits	98
Blidworth Colliery	120,179
Bloomsgrove Works	310
Blue Circle Industries	62
Bobbers Mill Colliery	48
Boleham Brick & Tile Works	298
Bolsover Col'y Co	63,188,211,226,238
Bone Mill Lane Brickworks	308
Bone Mill	298
Boot & Co	66
Boot, Sir Jesse	257
Booth Wm.	299
Boots Co, The	66
Boots Pure Drug Co	66
Bottesford Contract	255
Boughton Central Ordnance Depot	154
Bow Bridge Plaster Works	322
Bowley Silas	81
Bradshaw & Sansom	311
Bramcote Sand Co	304
Branston J.W. & H.	296,297
Branstons Malt Kilns	296
Brewery, Beeston	317
Brewery, Newark	323
Brick & Mineral Co The	299
Brick & Tile Works, Cropwell Bishop	299
Brickworks & Bramcote Sand Pits	304
Brickworks, Carlton	300,302
Brickworks, Cossall Marsh	302
Brickworks, East Kirkby	307
Brickworks, Misterton	302
Bridgford Brick Co	299
Bridgford Estates	299
Brierley Hill Colliery	117
Brinsley Colliery	54,180
Brinsley Disposal Point	180
British Coal	134
British Electricity Authority	90,119
British Glues & Chemicals	299
British Gypsum	67,69
British Petroleum Co	300
British Plaster & Boards	67,71,72,73,78,79,81
British Plaster Board Industries	67
British Railways	82
British Steel Corp, Stanton & Staveley Group	61
British Sugar Beet Growers Society	84
British Sugar Corporation	84
British Transport Commission	85
Brookhill Colliery & Railway	181
Brookhill Colliery	129,130,181
Brookhill Locoshed	181
Brooks Tom	286
Brothers Patent Plaster Co	78
Broughton W. & J.	300
Broxtowe Colliery	48
Buchan C.V.	257
Bulcote Sewage Works	313
Bulwell Brick Co	300
Bulwell Common Wagon Works	316
Bulwell Contract	274
Bulwell Colliery	50,51
Burgass William	314
Butcherwood Colliery	146
Butterley & Blaby Brick Cos	90,301
Butterley Co	86,90,205,222,301,330
Butterley Company, The	86
Buxton & Walker	300
Buxton J. & G.(or T?)	303
Buxton Mrs. Ruth	300

C

C & S Commercial Spares	281
Cabinet Works, Colwick	309
Cafferata & Co	67,69,70,74,76
Calverton Colliery	134,183
Calverton Contract	263
Calverton No 1 Shaft	47
Cammell Laird & Co	106,114
Canal Sand Pits	309
Canals at Langley Mill	329
Carlton Brickworks	305
Carlton Contract	272
Carlton Hill Brick Co	305
Carlton Road Brickworks	314
Carnfield Colliery	129
Carr Street Works	284
Carter, Barringer & Co	105
Carver Richard	73
Cauldwell Charles & Edward	320
Central Electricity Authority	90,119
Central Electricity Generating Board	90,93,119,132,315
Central Materials Depot	83
Charcon Tunnels	301
Chemical Manure & Glue Works	299
Chilwell Brickworks	320
Chilwell Central Ordnance Depot	107
Cinderhill Colliery	48,164
City Engineers Department	124
Clarke A.	281
Clarke J.R.	281
Clay Workings, Awsworth	325
Clayton Jas.	302,325
Cleaver Frederick	301

Cleveland Bridge & Engineering Co	257
Cliffnook Maltings	297
Clifton Colliery	122,187
Clifton Sir Robert	122
Clinton Colliery	319
Clipstone Colliery	63,135,188
Clipstone Contract	258
Clipstone Equipment Store	136,191
Clipstone Military Camp Railway	155
Clough C. & Co	322
Coal Investments	107
Cocking & Son	301
Cocking Thos.	301
Cockings (Walkeringham)	301
Coke John	129
Coking Plant	129
Colwick Contract	274,279
Colwick Estate	123
Colwick Estates Light Railway	123
Colwick Factory	84
Colwick Pits	99
Colwick Plant Depot	262
Colwick Riverside Wharf	85
Colwick Works	151
Coneygrey Colliery	54
Coolee	304
Cooper George	302
Cordy Lane Colliery	54
Cossall Colliery	92,192,302
Cotgrave Colliery	192
Cottam Power Station	132
Court L. & Co	258
Cow Lane Maltings	296,315
Cow Lane Wharf	307
Coxhead H. & Co	258
Crankley Point Pits	99
Craven J.	286
Cromford Canal	329,330
Crompton & Co	49
Cropwell Bishop Gypsum Mines	71,97
Cropwell Plaster Cement and Brick Co	71
Crown Farm Colliery	64
Crown Farm Junction Sand Pit	317
Cubitts & Pauling	258
Cuckney RAF	44
Cuckoo Bush Mine	72

D

Dalestorth Road Brickworks	319
Davis E.P.	59
Depot, Sutton in Ashfield	312
Derbyshire & Nottinghamshire Electric Power Company	119

Digby Coal Co	52
Digby Colliery Co	47,52,53
Docks & Inland Waterways Executive	85
Dodsley John	117,330
Doncaster Amalgamated Collieries	92,194
Dorket Head Brickworks	314
Duke of Newcastle	144
Dunn Bros	92
Dunn D. G. & Co	318

E

Eakring Road Oil Sidings	300
Earle G. & T.	45
East Bridgford Contract	275
East Leake Contract	268
East Midlands Gas Board	94,303
East Retford Quarry	98
Eastcroft Depot	124
Eastcroft Gasworks	94
Eastern Electricity	93
Eastern Group	93
Eastwood & Swingler	303
Eastwood (GNR) Goods Yard	284
Eastwood A. & Sons	316
Eastwood Brick & Tile Works	307,310
Eastwood Brickworks	310
Eastwood Collieries & Railways	54
Eastwood Colliery	54,297
Eastwood T.	316
Eckersley & Bayliss	259
Edward Eastwood	303
Edwards J.P.	259
Ellis & Co	142
Ellis John and William Richard Knight	311
Ellis John	311
Engineering Works, Nottingham	305
English Glass	95
Erewash & Nottingham Canals	328
Erewash Brickworks	311
Erewash Canal	329
Erewash Valley Brick Pipe & Pottery Co	303,311
Erewash Valley Brickworks	303
Erewash Valley Contract	265
Erewash Valley Wagon Works	303
Evans J.B.	319
Evans Richard	304
Explosives Magazine, Eastwood	310

F

Firbank J.	261
Firbeck Colliery	92,194
Firbeck, Harworth & Welbeck Contracts	271

Fisher Bros	304
Fletcher & Co (Contractors)	261
Flour Mill, Newark	315
Foraky	262
Forest Wagon Works	133

G

G.C.R. Northern Development Assn	288
Gamston Brickworks	298
Gas Light & Coke Co	94
Gedling Colliery	53,195
General Refractories	304
Gilstrap Earp & Co	296,297
Gilstrap J. & Sons	296
Giltbrook Colliery	52
Giltbrook Disposal Point	198
Girton Quarry	98
Glass Bulbs	95
Glass G. B.	95
Glebe Mine	73
Goddard & Massey	305
Goddard, Massey & Warner	305
Gotham Co	67,68,71,73,80,305
Grand Central Diner	288
Grange Colliery	315
Gravel Pit, Lound	313
Gravel Pit, Newark	305
Gravel Pit, Ranskill	324
Gravel Pits, Attenborough	321
Great Central Railway (Nottingham)	288
Great Northern Plaster Works	70
Great Northern Railway Co	305,309
Green & Baker	69
Green H & Co	69
Green Henry, Exors. of	69
Gregory & Robey	80
Gregory's Sandstone	306
Gringley Carr Pumping Station	140
Gripper Edward	125
Gunthorpe Gravel Pits	96
Gunthorpe Gravels (Trent)	96
Gyproc	67,70,74,76,77
Gypsum Mine, Gotham	326
Gypsum Mines	67,68,77
Gypsum Pit, Rushcliffe	325

H

H.M. Govt Explosives Magazine	305
Haigh Joseph	47
Hall William	96
Harlequin Brickworks	306
Harry Crofts Colliery	144
Harvey & Earp	297
Harvey & Quibell	299
Harworth Coking Plant	58,198
Harworth Colliery	57,122,137,199
Harworth Contract	278,279
Harworth Main Colliery Co	57
Harworth Works	95
Hathern Stn Brick & Terra Cotta Co	306
Hathern Station Brickworks	306
Hathern Ware	306
Hawton Gypsum Works	74
Hawton Tramway	74
Heaselden Samuel & Son	97
Hempshill Fan	50
Hermitage Brickworks	309
Heywood & Co	46
High Holborn Colliery	48
High Marnham Contract	269
High Marnham Power Station	93
High Park Colliery	54,202
Hill Bros	306
Hill Farm, Tollerton	291
Hill Top Colliery	54,307
Hill Top Colliery, Brick & Tile Co	307
Hill Wm.	306
Hole J & Co	297
Hollins Wm. & Co	307
Holloway Brothers (London)	244,263
Holly Hill Collieries	88
Holme Pierrepont Gravel Pits	100
Holmes Benjamin & Sons	307
Home Farm Wiseton	140
Home Grown Sugar	84
Hopkinson Charles	308
Hotchley Mills	78
Hoveringham Engineering Co	103
Hoveringham Gravel Co	98,307
Hoveringham Gravel Pits	101
Hoveringham Gravels (Midlands)	98
Hoveringham Works	103
Hoveringham Workshops	102,151
Howard C.A.E.C.	103
Hucknall Colliery	142,203
Hucknall No.1 Colliery	142,203
Hucknall No.2 Colliery	142,203
Hucknall Training Centre	205
Hutchinson W.H.	263
Huthwaite Colliery	117

I

Ilkeston Collieries	209,308
Innes Lee Industries	61
Inns & Co	103
Invicta Bridge & Engineering Co	103
Ipswich Malting Co	296,297

Iron Foundry, Mansfield	316
Isaacs Saul	122

J
Jackson J & A	308
Jacobs William	317
Jacobs	322
Jenkins W.J. & Co	308
Jericho Brickworks & Plaster Mill	76

K
Kelham Boreholes	127
Kelham Contract	277
Kelham Factory	84
Kett Street, Brickworks	300
Kettle A. B. & P. G.	289
Kier Construction	265
Kilton Road Sand Pit	321
Kilvington Gypsum Works	62
Kimberley Colliery	48
King J A & Co	308
Kings Meadow Works	106,110
Kings Mill	320
Kingsbury Concrete Co	104
Kingston Gypsum Co	77
Kingston on Soar Gypsum	77
Kirk Wm. James	308
Kirkby Colliery	86,205
Kirkby Disposal Point	206
Kirton Brickworks	301
Knighton & Smith	307

L
Lady Lee Quarry	311
Lancaster J. & Co	47
Lane Bros	309
Langley Mill Locoshed	54
Langton Colliery	129,207
Langton No.7, 8 & 9 Colliery	129
Larkfield Colliery	54
Lawrence Wm. & Co	309
Leather Works	322
Leen Valley Contract	256,268
Lilley F.J.	266
Lime Burners & Brickworks, Bulwell	310
Lime Works & Quarry, Cropwell Bishop	318
Limeworks & Quarry, Mansfield	304,309
Linby Colliery	104,207
Lindley Charles	306
Lindley R.	309
Lindley Robert	306
Lineker Robert	322

Lodge Colliery	96,209,308
Logan & Hemingway	266
Lomas A.	315
London & North Eastern Railway	309
London Midland & Scottish Rly	82,268
Lord Belper	77
Lord Middleton	92,327
Lound Hall Mining Museum	210
Lound Hall Training Centre	176
Lovatt Henry	268,305
Lovatt Wilson & Sons	269
Low Grounds Brickworks	304
Lowdham Plant Depot	270
Lowfield Brickworks	156
Lowfield Engineering Works	157
Lowfield Plaster Works	322
Lowmoor Shaft	86
Ludlow Hill Brickworks	299
Lynch & Cadogan	46,302

M
Manlove, Alliott & Co	310
Manners Brick Co	303,310
Manners Colliery Co	96,308
Mansfield and Pinxton Railway Co	330
Mansfield Brick & Stone Co	320
Mansfield Colliery	64,211
Mansfield Contract	253,259,261,265,274
Mansfield Sand Co	104,105
Mansfield Standard Sand Co	104,128
Mansfield Stone & Brickworks	320
Manson Dr	297
Manton Colliery	156,212
Mapperley Brickworks	125
Mapperley Plant Depot	284
Marblaegis	67,68,78,79
Marshall Brothers	311
Marshall J.T. & Co	311
McAlpine Sir Alfred & Son	269
McAlpine Sir Robert & Sons	269
McCarthy M. & Sons	310
McDonald & Co	310
Meadow Foundry Co	311
Meering or Besthorpe Gravel Pits	103
Meggitt Samuel & Sons	300
Metro-Cammell Carriage, Wagon & Finance Co	106,110
Mexboro' No.1 & 2 Collieries	88
Mexboro' No.3 (Lower) Colliery	88
Mexborough Collieries	88
Midland Mining	107
Midland Product Works	297
Midland Railway	82

Midland Works	323
Millgate Folk Museum	290
Millott & Mettham	320
Mine, Shireoaks	325
Ministry of Defence	107
Ministry of Munitions	107,114
Ministry of Supply	110,111,112,219
Ministry of Works	112
Misterton & West Stockwith Gas Co	120
Misterton Brickworks	306
Misterton Works	120
Mitchell Bros, Sons & Co	271
Molyneaux Colliery	303
Moor Green Central Workshops	215
Moor Green Colliery Railway	219
Moor Green Colliery	54,217
Morris, Little & Son	114
Morton Brickworks	323
Mosley J.& W.	311
Moss William & Sons	272
Mowlem John & Sons	273
Muschamp William	117

N

N.H. & B. Collieries	115,163,168,220,235,245
National Cold Stores (Management)	312
National Filling Factory No.6	107
National Mining Museum	210
National Ordnance Factory	114
National Power	90,119
National Projectile Factory	114
Naylor Bros	273
Needler Harold(Gravels)	98
Neep & Ward	72
New Beeston Brewery Co	317
New Brinsley Colliery	126
New David & Co	312
New Hucknall Colliery	115,116,117,118,220
New London Colliery	52
New Selston Colliery	127,221
New Skegby Colliery	117
New Watnall Colliery	54
Newark & Sherwood District Council	290
Newark Contracts	273
Newark Corporation Water Works	312
Newark Factory	84
Newark Gravel & Concrete Co	312
Newark Plaster Co	70
Newark Quarry	99
Newcastle Colliery	48
Newell Dunford Engineering	120
Newell Ernest & Co	120
Newstead Colliery	120,179,221,313
Newstead Contract	254
Newstead No.2 Colliery	120
Newstead	140
Newthorpe Colliery (1931)	313
Newthorpe Colliery	52,313
Newthorpe Lodge Colliery	304
Newthorpe Shops	215
Newton Peter	319
Nicholson & Hall	52
Nixon, Knowles & Co	313
Normanton Hills	305
North Maltings	296
North Notts Gravel Co	121,313
North Thos.	48,328
North Wilford Contract	251,269
North Wilford Power Station	90
Northern Union Mining Co	122
Nottingham - Melton Mowbray Contract	250
Nottingham & Clifton Colliery	122,187
Nottingham Builder's Brick Co	314
Nottingham Canal	327,328
Nottingham Colwick Estates Lt Rly	123
Nottingham Contract	255,257,259,266,275
Nottingham Corpn Electricity Dept	90
Nottingham Corpn Gas Dept	94,303
Nottingham Corpn Water Dept	140
Nottingham Corpn	124,313
Nottingham Factory	84
Nottingham Industrial Museum	290
Nottingham Patent Brick Co	125,314
Nottingham Plant Depot	263
Nottingham Power Station	90
Nottingham Quarry	100
Nottingham Royal Ordnance Factory	110
Nottingham Sewer Contract	257
Nottingham Sleeper Co	282
Nottinghamshire Gypsum Products	62
Notts & Derby Coke & By-Product Co Ltd	129,181
Nuthall Sandpits	150

O

Oakes James & Co.	126,221,224
Oakwood Grange Colliery	222,315
Oilfields of England	127
Old Hucknall Colliery	117
Old Watnall Colliery	54
Oldham Elisha Wright	273

Oliver Thomas	274
Ollerton Brickworks	90
Ollerton Colliery	87,222
Ollerton Contract	277
Orston Gypsum Mine, Brick & Plaster Works	322
Orston Road East	140
Orston Road,	152
Ossington Airfield Contract	269
Oughtibridge Silica Firebrick Co	149
Owston Ferry Plant Depot	140
Owston Ferry	152
Oxclose Limestone Quarry	316
Oxton Pits	128
Oxton Sand & Gravel Company	128

P

Papplewick Pumping Station Trust	290
Parker Vincent	299
Parker W.R. & Co	274
Parkinson Sir Lindsay & Co	275
Parnham Thos. & Sons	315
Peach R. & Co	315
Permanent Way Equipment Co The	282
Petrol Depot, No 17, Bottesford	153
Phoenix Works	318
Pickering & Mumford	319
Pickering Joseph	319
Piggin John	318
Pillatt & Co	283
Pinxton (No.2) Colliery	181
Pinxton & Brookhill Colliery Railway	129
Pinxton Coal Co	129
Pinxton Coking Co	130,181
Pinxton Coking Plant	181
Pinxton Collieries	129,181,207,224
Pinxton Contract	261,280
Pinxton Loco Workshops	181
Pinxton Locoshed	181,129
Pinxton No.1& 6 Colliery	129
Pinxton No.2 Colliery	129
Pinxton No.3 Colliery	129
Pinxton No.4 Colliery	129
Pinxton No.5 Colliery	129
Pinxton Old Colliery	129
Plainspot Colliery	54
Plaster Slab Works	308
Pleasley Junction Lime Works & Qy	317
Pleasley Vale Mills	307
Plumptre Colliery	88
Plumtre Colliery	88
Plumtree Colliery	88
Plymouth No 2 Colliery	129
Plymouth No 4 Colliery	129
Plymouth No 5 Colliery	129
Pollington Colliery	126
Portland & Mexboro' Collieries	88
Portland Limeworks	299
Portland No.1 Colliery	88
Portland No.2 Colliery	88
Portland No.3 Colliery	88
Portland No.4 Colliery	88
Portland No.5 Colliery	88
Portland No.6&7 Collieries	88
Portland Quarry	316
Potter & Burns	52
Potter Harold & Co	283
Potteries The	139
Powergen	90,93,132,315
Pre Cast Concrete Works	301
Price & Wills	276
Price A.H. & Co	275
Priory Farm	293
Pumping Station, Farnsfield	312
Pumping Station, Newark	312
Pye Hill Colliery	127,224
Pye Hill Colliery, Brick And Pipeworks	127

Q

Quarry and Mason's Yard, Mansfield	306
Quibell Bros	299

R

Radcliffe Brick Co	306
Radford Colliery	226,324
Radford Gas Works	303
Railway & General Engineering Co	323
Railway Siding, Mansfield	318
Rampton	292
Ranskill Royal Ordnance Factory	111
Ranskill Wagon Works	83
Ranskill Works	104
Ransome & Marles Bearing Co	132
Ransome A. & Co	132
Ransome Hoffman Pollard	132
Ratcliffe Power Station	315
Refuse Destructor, Nottingham	314
Retford Contract	258,280
Riddings Collieries	126,221,224
Rigley William & Sons (Nottingham)	133,316
Rigley William	133
River Trent Catchment Board	152
Riverside Malt Kilns	297
RJB Mining (UK)	134
Roberts Brian W. M.	291

Roberts Wm.	320
Robinson & Sykes	314
Rock Hill Quarries	105
Rolleston Contract	268
Rollin P.	291
Rotherham Sand & Gravel Co	139
Rouse Harry	316
Royal Ordnance Factory No.14	112
Royal Ordnance Factory No.38	111
Ruddington Contract	273
Ruddington Heritage Centre	288
Ruddington Ordnance Storage & Supply Depot	112
Rufford Colliery	65,226
Rufford Contract	273
Rushcliffe Halt Site	288
Rushcliffe Works	78

S

Sam Fay's Bar & Restaurant	288
Sand Pit, Sutton Forest	308
Sanderson & Robinson	316
Sandhole Sidings	321
Sandhurst Quarries	105
Sandpits, Worksop	321
Sands George & Son	317
Sankey Richard & Son	139
Sankey's Bulwell Brick & Tile Co	139
Savidge Bros	283
Scofton RAF	44
Scott Walter & Middleton	277
Scott William(or Stocker)	322
Second Anglo-Scottish Beet Sugar Corp	84
Seely Chas. & Co	48,51
Selston Colliery	54,127,229
Severn Trent Water	140
Sewage Disposal Department	124
Sewage Farm Siding, Netherfield	314
Shanks & McEwan	277
Shaw Brickworks	306
Sheepbridge Coal & Iron Co	120
Shelton Brick & Plaster Co	317
Shelton Brick, Tile, Pipe & Plaster Works	317
Sheppard J.W.	67,68,72,81
Sheppards No.1 Mine	72
Sherwood Colliery Co	142, 143,203,229
Sherwood Engineering Training Centre	231
Shipstone James & Sons	317
Shirebrook Contract	263
Shireoaks Colliery	144,231,234
Shireoaks Limeworks and Quarry	319
Shireoaks No.3 Colliery	144
Siding, New Basford	326
Sills Wm.	317
Silver Seal Mine	79
Silverhill Colliery	146,233
Simms W.J., Sons & Cooke	283
Simon Richard & Sons	318
Simpson James & Co	157
Skegby Colliery, Lime & Brick Co	117
Skegby Contracts	279
Skegby No.2 Colliery	117
Skegby Old Wharf	330
Sleights No 2 Colliery	129
Sleights No 3 Colliery	129
Sleights No 4 Colliery	129
Sleights No 5 Colliery	129
Smart T. & J.	299
Smith G	318
Snaith J.D.	71
Snaith Plaster & Cement Co	71
South Leverton	291
Southgate Colliery	144
Speedwell Colliery	52
Spital Maltings	297,315
Spring Close Works	283
Springfield Colliery	307
Standard Sand Co	105,318
Standhill Brickworks	300
Stanley Works	132
Stanton & Staveley	61
Stanton Ironworks Co	61,130,145,150,177,233,237
Stapleford Colliery and Brickworks	318
Stapleford Colliery Co	318
Stapleford Ironworks	283
Stapleford Lime Co	318
Stapleford Real Estate Co The	318
Star Brick Co	305
Star Gravels	100
Staunton-in-the-Vale Gypsum Quarry	79
Staveley Coal & Iron Co	120,148,242
Staveley Iron & Chemical Co	149
Staythorpe Contract	254
Staythorpe Power Station	119
Steer & Barnes	303
Steetley Co	149,319
Steetley Colliery	145,234
Steetley Dolomite (Quarries)	149
Steetley Lime & Basic Co	149,319
Steetley Lime & Building Stone Company	149
Steetley Lime Co	149,319
Steetley Limeworks	149

Steetley Refractories	149
Stewarts & Lloyds Minerals	150
Stirland C.F. & T.	292
Stocker and Odames	81
Stocker G. & Co	81
Stoke Bardolph Sewage Works	124
Stoke Bardolph Water Reclamation Works	140
Stoney Lane Brick	319
Structural Engineering Works, Colwick	317
Summit Colliery	86
Suncole (Nottingham)	50
Sundown Adventureland	292
Sutton Colliery	117,235
Sutton Forest Bone Mills	300
Sutton Gasworks	320
Sutton in Ashfield Brick Co	319
Sutton in Ashfield UDC	320
Sutton Sand Siding	301
Sutton-on-Trent Contract	258
Sydney Street Maltings	297
Sykes	317
Symington H. & Sons	278

T

Tarmac Roadstone (Eastern)	151
Taylor J.A.	320
Terry W.	314
Teversal Colliery	146,237
Teversal Contract	274
Thomlinson & Salkeld	73
Thompson Henry	320
Thompson Wm.	320
Thoresby Colliery	65,138,238
Thoresby Contract	267
Thorneywood Brickworks	314
Thorpe & Son	315
Thrumpton Mine	80
Timber Mills, Sutton-upon-Trent	323
Tomlinson Geo.	306
Tomlinson J & G	279
Tomlinson J.	320
Top End Mine	72
Top Quarries	139
Towlerton Leather John	265
Trackwork Associates	279
Traunter Wm.	304
Trent Concrete Co	307
Trent Concrete Pits	99
Trent Concrete	151
Trent Gravels	321
Trent Lane Wharf	85

Trent Mining Co	80
Trent Navigation Co	85
Trent River Authority	152
Trent River Board	140,152
Trowell Forge	312
Trowell Moor Colliery	92
Trowell Moor Disposal Point	92,241
Tunnel Colliery	127
Turkey Field Colliery	48
Turner James & Son	321
Turney Bros	322
Tuxford Contract	276
Tuxford P.	284

U

Underwood Colliery	54
Unknown Contract(s)	261
Upper Portland Disposal Point	241

V

Vale Of Belvoir and Newark Plaster Co	156,317,322
Victoria Mineral & Plaster Co	73
Victoria Steam Brickworks	320

W

Wagon Repairs	322
Wagon Works, Daybrook	298,324
Wagon Works, Foundry & Sawmill	301
Wagon Works, Lenton	311
Wagon Works, Mansfield	322
Wakefield and North	48
Walesby Light Railway	286
Walker Albert	297
Walker J. & T.	298
Walker Thomas	297
Walker, Hill & Co	284
Walkeringham Brickworks	301
Walton E. C. & Co	323
War Department	107,112,153
Ward James	72
Ward Thos. W.	156,280,284,323
Waring John & Sons	280
Warsop - Tuxford Contract	253
Warsop Colliery	242
Warsop Contract	276
Warsop Main Colliery	148
Warsop Sand Quarries	149
Warwick & Richardsons	323
Warwick Richard & Sons	323
Watnall Colliery Tramway	329
Watnall Colliery	54,244
Watnall Disposal Point	244

Welbeck Colliery	118,138,245
Weldon Mine	81
West Burton Power Station	91
West Leake Mine	77
Whisker Hill Sand Pit	309
Whitaker T.N.	304
Whitemoor Colliery	48
Widdowson H. & Sons	284
Wigan Coal & Iron Co	156,323
Wigan Coal Corporation	156,212
Wigsley Plant Depot	281
Wigsley Wood Scrap Yard	281
Wilford Brick Co	324
Wilford Brickworks	324
Wilkes Joseph	329
Willey Lane Colliery	54
Wilson & Robinson	74
Wilson A.J.	292
Winser & Co	323
Winser's Mines	323
Wollaton Brick Works	325
Wollaton Collieries	226,247,324
Wollaton Hall	290
Wood Bros	80
Works & Ways Department	124
Worksop Brick Co	304
Worksop RAF	44
Worksop Sand Co	321
Worswick W.	115
Worthington - Simpson	157
Wright & Co	48,51
Wright Francis T.	324

Y

Y7 Preservation Group	293
Yeomans	81

INDUSTRIAL RAILWAY SOCIETY

The Industrial Railway Society, which was formed in 1949 as the Industrial Locomotive Information Section of the Birmingham Locomotive Club, caters for enthusiasts interested in privately owned locomotives and railways. Members receive the INDUSTRIAL RAILWAY RECORD, a profusely illustrated magazine; a bi-monthly bulletin containing topical news and amendments to the Society's handbook series; access to a well-stocked library; visits to and rail tours of industrial railway systems; a book sales service, many Society publications being available at discounted prices; loco information service from the Society's team of records officers; photograph sales service; and access to archives held at the National Railway Museum, York. Further details are available by sending two first class stamps to:

Mr B. Mettam, 27 Glenfield Crescent, Newbold, Chesterfield S41 8SF

Subscriptions to the INDUSTRIAL RAILWAY RECORD are available to non-members of the Society. Enquiries regarding subscriptions and back numbers should be addressed to:

Mr R.V. Mulligan, Owls Barn, The Chestnuts, Aylsbeare, Exeter, Devon EX5 2BY

[Fig. 1] NCB Clifton Colliery from the nearby Nottingham Power Station.   [M. Castledine]
Locomotives visible are HE 2854, PHILIP and TH 137C, JAYNE. 8/4/1968   (see p.187)

[Fig. 2] HL 3684/1929 0-4-0ST OC   [J. Wallbank: copyright A Neale]
G. & T. Earle Ltd, Barnstone Cement Works. 23/5/1955   (see p.45)

[Fig. 3] RH 513139/1967 0-4-0DH THE HERBERT TURNER   [A.R. Etherington]
Associated Portland Cement Manufacturers Ltd, Barnstone Works. 28/9/1969   (see p.45)

[Fig. 4] TW 1850 0-6-0ST OC NAPOLEON [collection F Jones]
B.A. Collieries Ltd, Cinderhill Colliery. 5/1945 (see p.51)

[Fig. 5] OK 10903/1925 0-4-0WT OC KINDER [C.H.A. Townley: J.A. Peden collection]
       D&B 42/1925 0-4-0WT OC DARLEY DALE
B.A. Collieries Ltd, Cinderhill Colliery. 4/4/1946 (see p.51)

[Fig. 6] D&B 42/1925 0-4-0WT OC DARLEY DALE [P.D. Rowbotham]
NCB (ex B.A. Collieries Ltd), Cinderhill Colliery. 7/1947 (see p.165)

[Fig. 7] RH 170205/1934 4wDM 8418/18 [A.R. Etherington]
RH 174140/1935 4wDM 8418/19
Stanton & Staveley Ltd, Bilsthorpe Brickworks. 19/12/1964 (see p.61)

[Fig. 8] FJ 188/1882 0-4-0T OC [P.D. Rowbotham]
Cafferata & Co.Ltd, Hawton Works. 8/1953 (see p.74)

[Fig. 9] S 8207/1930 4wVBT G [A.R. Etherington]
Gyproc Ltd, Hawton Works. 13/7/1963 (see p.74)

[Fig. 10] S 9373/1947 4wVBT G ST MONANS [I.R. Bendall]
British Gypsum Ltd, Hawton Works. 12/12/1970 (see p.74)

[Fig. 11] WB 1575/1899 0-4-0ST OC [A.R. Etherington]
Gypsum Mines Ltd, Kingston on Soar Works. 10/9/1960 (see p.77)

[Fig. 12] WB 2233/1924 0-4-0ST OC 10 BATLEY [F. Jones]
British Railways, Beeston Creosoting Depot (see p.78)

[Fig. 13] WB 1889/1911 0-4-0ST OC No.1 [F. Jones]
British Railways, Beeston Creosoting Depot (see p.78)

[Fig. 14] P 1439/1916 0-4-0ST OC   No.1 [J. Wallbank: copyright A Neale]
British Sugar Corporation Ltd, Nottingham Works. 6/2/1955 (see p.84)

[Fig. 15] P 2000/1942 0-6-0ST OC [J. Wallbank: copyright A Neale]
British Sugar Corporation Ltd, Nottingham Works. 6/2/1955 (see p.84)

[Fig. 16] RH 319292/1953 0-4-0DM No.1   [J. Wallbank: copyright A Neale]
British Sugar Corporation Ltd, Nottingham Works. 26/2/1955   (see p.85)

[Fig. 17] HC 613/1902 0-6-0ST IC B19C   [F Jones collection]
Butterley Co Ltd. Kirkby Colliery.   (see p.87)

[Fig. 18] AB 1487 1916 0-6-0F OC [P.D. Rowbotham]
Central Electricity Authority, Nottingham Power Station. 1956 (see p.91)

[Fig. 19] Bg 3245/1949 4wWE No.4 [J. Wallbank: copyright A Neale]
Central Electricity Authority, Nottingham Power Station. 14/6/1955 (see p.91)

[Fig. 20] BP 3809/1895 0-4-0ST IC VICTORIA [IRS collection]
East Midlands Gas Board, Basford Works. (see p.94)

[Fig. 21] P 1879/1934 0-4-0ST OC (stationary boiler) [A.R. Etherington]
East Midlands Gas Board, Eastcroft Works. 7/3/1965 (see p.94)

[Fig. 22] RH 299099/1950 4wDM [A.J. Booth]
Glass Bulbs Ltd, Harworth Works. 14/2/1976 (see p.95)

[Fig. 23] RH 513141/1966 4wDH [A.J. Booth]
Glass Bulbs Ltd, Harworth Works. 14/2/1976 (see p.95)

[Fig. 24] RH 349080/1953 4wDM [J. Wallbank: copyright A Neale]
Hoveringham Gravels Ltd, Hoveringham Quarry. 20/4/1955 (see p.101)

[Fig. 25] HE 7178/1969 4wDM [A.J. Booth]
Hoveringham Gravels Ltd, stored at Hoveringham Workshops. 17/5/1980 (see p.102)

[Fig. 26] HC 472/1896 0-4-0ST OC EMPRESS [F. Jones]
Mansfield Standard Sand Co Ltd, Sandhurst Quarry, Mansfield. (see p.106)

[Fig. 27] MW 1017/1887 0-4-0ST OC STANLOW [P.D. Rowbotham]
William Rigley & Sons (Nottingham) Ltd, Bulwell Forest Wagon Works. 1952 (see p.133)

[Fig. 28] Crossley 4wPM [P.D.Rowbotham]
William Rigley & Sons(Nottingham) Ltd, Bulwell Forest Wagon Works. 1952 (see p.133)

[Fig. 29] MR 9381/1948 4wDM U196 [I.R. Bendall]
Severn Trent Water Authority, Stoke Bardolph Works. 7/7/1977 (see p.141)

[Fig. 30] RH 7002/0567/6 1967 4wDM   U84 [I.R. Bendall]
Severn Trent Water Authority, Stoke Bardolph Works. 5/7/1984 (see p.141)

[Fig. 31] SMH 40SD529/1984 4wDM   U168 [I.R. Bendall]
Severn Trent Water Authority, Stoke Bardolph Works. 5/7/1984 (see p.141)

[Fig. 32] MW 1038/1887 0-4-0ST OC STANTON No.19 [P.D. Rowbotham]
Stanton Ironworks Co Ltd, Nuthall Sandpits. 8/1948 (see p.150)

[Fig. 33] YE 2652/1957 0-4-0DE OUGHTIBRIDGE No.1 [A.J. Booth]
Steetley Refractories Ltd, Steetley Brickworks. 28/8/1977 (see p.149)

[Fig. 34] TH 141C/1964 0-6-0DH STEPHEN   [A.R. Etherington)
National Coal Board, Babbington Colliery. 19/12/1964   (see p.165)

[Fig. 35] HL 2657/1906 0-4-0ST OC DAISY   [A.R. Etherington)
National Coal Board, Bentinck Colliery. 27/6/1964   (see p.168)

[Fig. 36] Darlington / 1923 0-4-0T IC 985 [B. Mettam: IRS collection]
National Coal Board, Bentinck Colliery. 4/3/1956 (see p.168)

[Fig. 37] P 468/1888 0-4-0ST OC LANCASTER [B. Mettam: IRS collection]
National Coal Board, Bestwood Colliery. (see p.171)

[Fig. 38] Mkm 104/1891 0-4-0ST OC ST ALBANS
National Coal Board, Bestwood Colliery. 1/1955

[P.D. Rowbotham]
(see p.171)

[Fig. 39] AB 1517/1919 0-4-0ST OC BESTWOOD
National Coal Board, Bestwood Colliery. 7/3/1965

[A.R. Etherington]
(see p.171)

[Fig. 40] S 9578/1954 4wVBT G No.4 [P.D. Rowbotham]
National Coal Board, Bestwood Colliery. 1/1955 (see p.171)

[Fig. 41] RS 4150/1937 0-6-0ST OC RUTH [F. Jones]
National Coal Board, Bestwood Colliery. (see p.171)

[Fig. 42] LE 246/1907 0-4-0ST OC PINXTON [F Jones]
National Coal Board, Pinxton Colliery. 6/1954 (see p.182)

[Fig. 43] P 1975/1939 0-4-0ST OC PECKETT No.2 [B. Mettam: IRS collection]
National Coal Board, Brookhill Locoshed. 4/3/1956 (see p.182)

[Fig. 44] HC 1877/1954 0-6-0T OC EMFOUR.2. [B. Mettam: IRS collection]
National Coal Board, Brookhill Locoshed. 4/3/1956 (see p.182)

[Fig. 45] RSH 7698/1954 (reb 1965 as 0-6-0DH) 3 [A.J. Booth]
National Coal Board, Calverton Colliery. 22/6/1977 (see p.183)

[Fig. 46] YE 2940/1965 0-6-0DH [A.J. Booth]
National Coal Board, Calverton Colliery. 4/10/1980 (see p.183)

[Fig. 47] HE 8914/1979 4wDHF 8 [I.R. Bendall]
British Coal Corporation, Cotgrave Colliery. 22/2/1987 (see p.193)

[Fig. 48] AE 1895/1923 0-6-0ST OC DAISY
National Coal Board, Firbeck Colliery. 1/7/1957

[B. Mettam: IRS collection]
(see p.194)

[Fig. 49] TH 182V/1967 4wDH GILLIAN
National Coal Board, Gedling Colliery. 11/6/1985

[I. Bendall]
(see p.195)

[Fig. 50] Direct rope incline from Gedling Colliery. National Coal Board, Mapperley Landsale Depot. 29/4/1980 [A.R. Etherington] (see p.195)

[Fig. 51] Hohen 3283/1914 0-6-0WT OC No.1 National Coal Board, Harworth Colliery. 1/7/1957 [B. Mettam: IRS collection] (see p.199)

[Fig. 52] TH 174V/1966 4wDH NCB D12 70491
TH 178V/1967 4wDH NCB D14
National Coal Board, Harworth Colliery. 6/8/1977

[A.J. Booth]

(see p.199)

[Fig. 53] HC 1797/1947 0-4-0ST OC
National Coal Board, Hucknall Colliery. 7/3/1965

[A.R. Etherington]

(see p.203)

[Fig. 54] Butterley 1896 0-4-0ST OC B9C [P.D. Rowbotham]
National Coal Board, Kirkby Colliery. 1956 (see p.205)

[Fig. 55] WB 2604/1939 0-6-0ST OC 30 [B. Mettam: IRS collection]
National Coal Board, Kirkby Colliery. 2/4/1957 (see p.205)

[Fig. 56] MW 1284/1894 0-6-0ST OC HUCKNALL TORKARD COLLIERIES [P.D. Rowbotham]
National Coal Board, derelict at Linby Colliery. 3/1952 (see p.207)

[Fig. 57] RH 375347/1954 4wDM [A.R. Etherington]
National Coal Board, Lound Hall Mining Museum. 6/4/1981 (see p.210)

[Fig. 58] HL 3591/1925 0-4-0ST OC THORESBY No.1   [P.D. Rowbotham]
National Coal Board, Mansfield Colliery. 1956   (see p.211)

[Fig. 59] WCI 1908 0-6-0ST IC SIEMENS   [F. Jones]
National Coal Board, Manton Colliery.   (see p.212)

[Fig. 60] HC D1121/1958 0-6-0DM No.20 [A.J. Booth]
British Coal Corporation, Manton Colliery. 21/5/1987 (see p.212)

[Fig. 61] K 1856/1873 0-6-0ST IC 6 [P.D. Rowbotham]
National Coal Board, Langley Mill Wagon Works (Moor Green Railway). 1951 (see p.217)

[Fig. 62] K 1996/1874 0-6-0ST IC 5
National Coal Board, Moor Green Railway. 1947

[P.D. Rowbotham]
(see p.217)

[Fig. 63] RWH 1947/1883 0-6-0ST IC 8
National Coal Board, Moor Green Railway.

[F. Jones]
(see p.217)

[Fig. 64] K 3501/1891 0-6-0T IC 4   [P.D. Rowbotham]
National Coal Board, Moor Green Railway. 8/1949   (see p.217)

[Fig. 65] K 3918/1900 0-6-0T IC 7 (with ex Midland coach)   [P.D. Rowbotham]
National Coal Board, Watnall (Moor Green Railway). 1947   (see p.217)

[Fig. 66] S 10169/1964 0-8-0DH D11 [A.R. Etherington]
National Coal Board, Langley Mill Sidings (Moor Green Railway). 27/6/1964   (see p.218)

[Fig. 67] RR 10190/1964 0-6-0DH D13 [A.R. Etherington]
National Coal Board, Moor Green Colliery Tip. 29/4/1980   (see p.218)

[Fig. 68] YE 325/1878 0-6-0ST OC No.1 PORTLAND [P.D. Rowbotham]
National Coal Board, New Hucknall Colliery. 10/1955 (see p.220)

[Fig. 69] HE 637/1895 0-4-0ST OC 3 [P.D. Rowbotham]
National Coal Board, Pye Hill Colliery. 6/1955 (see p.225)

[Fig. 70] AB 2366/1955 0-4-0ST OC   No.19 [P.D. Rowbotham]
National Coal Board, Pye Hill Colliery. 17/10/1955 (see p.225)

[Fig. 71] CE B3252A/1986 4w-4wBEF [I.R. Bendall]
National Coal Board, Sherwood Colliery. 17/5/1986 (see p.230)

[Fig. 72] CE B3251/1986 4wBEF
National Coal Board, Sherwood Colliery. 17/5/1986
[I.R. Bendall]
(see p.230)

[Fig. 73] MW 1580/1902 0-4-0ST OC ALEXANDRA
National Coal Board, Shireoaks Colliery. 1948
[P.D. Rowbotham]
(see p.231)

[Fig. 74] HC D1343/1965 0-4-0DH No. 26 521/61 [A.J. Booth]
National Coal Board, Shireoaks Colliery. 11/7/1981 (see p.231)

[Fig. 75] HE 5656/1960 0-6-0DM D2607 [A.J. Booth]
National Coal Board, Steetley Colliery. 28/8/1979 (see p.234)

[Fig. 76] Johnson 1913 0-4-0WT OC RAVEN
National Coal Board, Sutton Colliery. 8/1947

[P.D. Rowbotham]
(see p.235)

[Fig. 77] AE 1360/1895 0-6-0ST OC No.5
National Coal Board, Sutton Colliery. 10/1954

[P.D. Rowbotham]
(see p.235)

[Fig. 78] P 2022/1942 0-4-0ST OC BC55 [P.D. Rowbotham]
National Coal Board, Sutton Colliery. 5/1955 (see p.235)

[Fig. 79] AE 1423/1901 0-6-0ST OC CARNARVON [F. Jones]
National Coal Board, Teversal Colliery, with well worn miners' coach. 6/1954 (see p.237)

[Fig. 80] AE 1976/1925 0-4-0ST OC R.N.C.F. No.3 [F. Jones]
National Coal Board, Silverhill Colliery. 4/1959 (see p.237)

[Fig. 81] HE 3188/1944 0-6-0ST IC 75137, in typical NCBOE shed [A.R. Etherington]
National Coal Board, Upper Portland Disposal Point. 27/6/1964 (see p.241)

[Fig. 82] Ghd 1877 0-6-0ST IC   NCB 8416   [P.D. Rowbotham]
In store at National Coal Board, Watnall Disposal Point. 28/11/1954   (see p.244)

[Fig. 83] RSH 7161/1944 0-6-0ST IC   71507   [P.D. Rowbotham]
In store at National Coal Board, Watnall Disposal Point. 28/11/1954   (see p.244)

[Fig. 84] S 10187/1964 0-4-0DH [I.R. Bendall]
National Coal Board, Welbeck Colliery. 13/8/1985 (see p.245)

[Fig. 85] Horwich 1111/1910 0-4-0ST OC 11257 [P.D. Rowbotham]
Holloway Brothers (London), Calverton Colliery Contract. 1/1951 (see p.263)

[Fig. 86] HL 3606/1924 0-6-0ST OC 6 [P.D. Rowbotham]
Holloway Brothers (London), Calverton Colliery Contract. 5/1952 (see p.263)

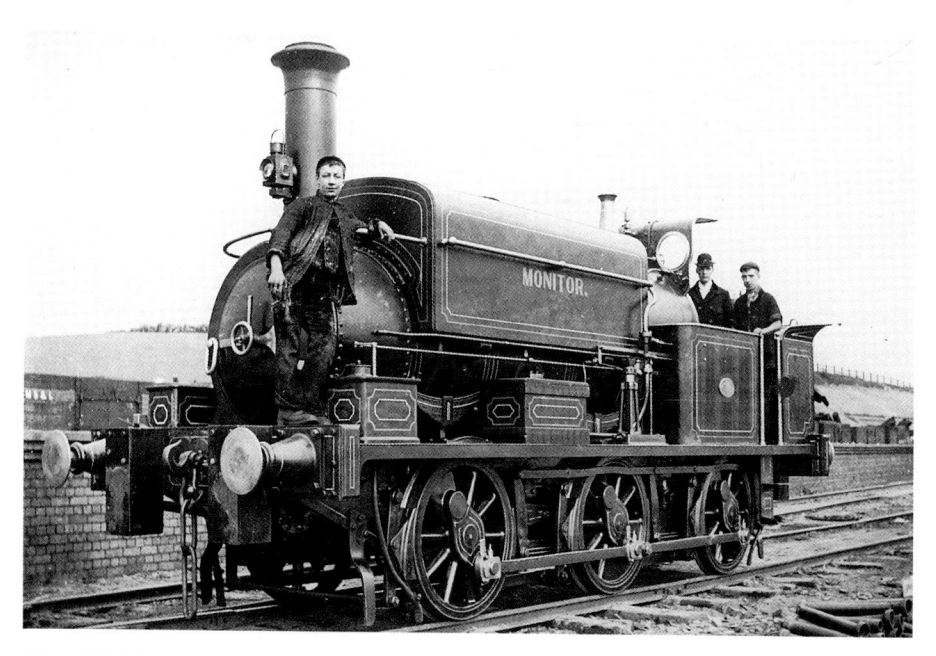

[Fig. 87] MW 1225/1891 0-6-0ST IC MONITOR [Newton; courtesy Leicester Museums]
Logan & Hemingway, Nottingham Contract. c1895. (see p.266)

Nottinghamshire Handbook. Page 428

[Fig. 88] HC 1749 1946 0-6-0ST IC [P.D. Rowbotham]
Sir Alfred McAlpine & Sons Ltd, High Marnham Power Station Contract. 6/1958.(see p.269)

[Fig. 89] AB 267/1884 0-4-0ST OC No.1 [F. Jones]
Shanks & McEwan Ltd, stored following a contract at Farnsfield. c1939. (see p.277)

[Fig. 90] MW 1530/1901 0-6-0ST IC BIRKENHEAD [F. Jones]
Shanks & McEwan Ltd, stored following a contract at Farnsfield. c1939. (see p.277)

[Fig. 91] HC 638/1903 0-4-0ST OC 82 [F. Jones]
Shanks & McEwan Ltd, stored following a contract at Farnsfield. c1939. (see p.277)

[Fig. 92] AB 973/1904 0-4-0ST OC   BURDALE   [B. Mettam: IRS collection]
Thos W Ward Ltd, stored at Pinxton Coking Plant contract. 4/3/1956   (see p.280)

[Fig. 93] P 1555/1920 0-4-0ST OC   [I.R. Bendall]
Preserved at the Grand Central Diner, Nottingham. 18/10/1986   (see p.288)

[Fig. 94] HE 2254/1940 0-4-0DMF P9261 [I.R. Bendall]
Preserved by A.B. & P.G. Kettle, Bilsthorpe. 5/3/1990 (see p.289)

[Fig. 95] BT 0-4-0DE BBT 3067/1954, 3098 & 3100/1956, 502,508 & 510 [I.R. Bendall]
Nottingham Sleeper Co Ltd, Elkesley. 7/10/1993 (see p.290)